SIT-DOWN: The General Motors Strike of 1936-1937

sit

down
The General Motors Strike of 1936-1937

by Sidney Fine

Ann Arbor   The University of Michigan Press

Copyright © by The University of Michigan 1969
All rights reserved
ISBN 0-472-32948-0
Library of Congress Catalog Card No. 73-83455
Published in the United States of America by
The University of Michigan Press
Manufactured in the United States of America

1991 1990 1989   9 8 7

*Published with the assistance of a grant
from the Horace H. Rackham School of Graduate Studies*

To Isadore, Rose, and Ruth

Preface

"Rarely," Jay Lovestone wrote of the General Motors sit-down strike just after its conclusion, "does a single event of and by itself mean so much." Historians of the American labor movement probably would be disinclined to challenge this judgment insofar as it applies to the growth of unionism in the automobile and other mass-production industries, and yet the strike has received surprisingly little scholarly attention and has not heretofore been the subject of a single, documented book-length study. Henry Kraus, to be sure, has written a vivid account of the strike in *The Many and the Few: A Chronicle of the Dynamic Auto Workers* (Los Angeles, 1947), but his narrative is undocumented, it does not concern itself in any depth with some of the most important aspects of the strike, and it is lacking in objectivity. The importance of the event, its relationship to subjects that have long been my concern, and the availability of important manuscript collections bearing on nearly all phases of the dispute explain my own interest in the strike and prompted my effort to write an account, based on the sources, of the origins, character, and consequences of this momentous labor conflict.

I first raised some of the questions considered in the book in an article on the strike that appeared in the *American Historical Review* in April, 1965. Since the positions defended by GM and the UAW in the strike reflected the prior experience of both organizations and the nature of the antecedent conflict between them, I have devoted a good deal of attention to the history of both the company and the union and especially to the confrontation between them that began in June, 1933, when Section 7 (a) of the National Industrial Recovery Act altered the rules governing industrial relations in the United States and adumbrated some of the principal issues over which the strike would eventually be fought. The key role of Frank Murphy in the ultimate resolution of the conflict and the central place occupied by Flint in the strike explain the consideration given in the pages that follow to Michigan's governor and GM's Michigan stronghold.

It is a pleasure to acknowledge here the assistance that I received in the writing of this book. My research and the publication of the book were facilitated by a Summer Faculty Fellowship and research and publication grants provided by the Horace H. Rackham School of Graduate Studies of the University of Michigan. Professor Maurice F. Neufeld of the New York State School of Industrial and Labor Relations of Cornell University read the entire manuscript and made many suggestions for its improvement. Professor Irving Bernstein of the University of California at Los Angeles kindly permitted me to examine his notes on a file of CIO materials that I was unable to locate. Dr. Philip P. Mason, Dr. Stanley D. Solvick, and Warner W. Pflug of the Labor History Archives of Wayne State University, and Dr. Robert M. Warner, J. Fraser Cocks, Charles Jones, Janice Earle, and Ida C. Brown of the Michigan Historical Collections all provided me with research services that went far beyond the call of duty. My manuscript research was also aided and made more pleasurable by Buford Rowland and Joseph D. Howerton of the National Archives and Records Service, Dr. Elizabeth B. Drewry, Dr. Edgar B. Nixon, and the staff of the Franklin D. Roosevelt Library, David C. Mearns and the staff of the Manuscripts Division of the Library of Congress, Josephine L. Harper and Margaret Hafstad of the State Historical Society of Wisconsin, James M. Babcock and the staff of the Burton Historical Collection, James J. Moylan of the Catholic University, and Catharine B. Williams of the Amalgamated Clothing Workers.

I am grateful to Winston Wessels for making it possible for me to examine Case File #5977 of the Michigan State Police Records and the Samuel D. Pepper Papers and for his enterprise in securing a microfilm copy of the relevant National Guard files for the Michigan Historical Collections. Dr. David L. Lewis aided me in gaining access to pertinent GM documents and made material in his own files available to me. W. D. Chase of the Flint *Journal* facilitated my use of the *Journal* library; Doris Hedde, Head of the General Reference Department of the Flint Public Library, kindly provided me with copies of sit-down items in the library's collection; Phyliss E. Janes of the General Motors Institute was similarly generous in supplying me with copies of GM executive training programs; and Elfrieda Lang of the Lilly Library made it possible for me to obtain copies of the relevant correspondence in the Powers Hapgood Papers. The persons who graciously permitted me to interview them and who responded to my letters requesting information about the strike are listed in the bibliography. I wish to thank Lee Pressman for permission to examine the transcript of his interview located in the Butler Library of Columbia University, and the late Norman Thomas for permission to use the Norman Thomas Papers. All of the photographs which are reproduced in the text were generously made available to me by the Labor History Archives of Wayne State University. My wife, Jean Fine, aided the preparation of this work in so many tangible and intangible ways that the mere expression of my gratitude seems grossly inadequate.

June, 1969 SIDNEY FINE

Contents

I. The Battle of the Running Bulls 1
II. The Corporation 14
III. The Workers 54
IV. Company Town 100
V. The Coming of the Strike 121
VI. The Sit-Down Community 156
VII. Strategy and Tactics: General Motors 178
VIII. Strategy and Tactics: The UAW 199
IX. Stalemate 231
X. Negotiated Peace 266
XI. Aftermath 313
Notes 343
Bibliographical Note 417
Index 427

ABBREVIATIONS

AAWA	Associated Automobile Workers of America
ACLU	American Civil Liberties Union
ACW	Amalgamated Clothing Workers
AFL	American Federation of Labor
AIWA	Automotive Industrial Workers' Association
ALB	Automobile Labor Board
AMA	Automobile Manufacturers Association
AWU	Auto Workers Union
CIO	Committee for Industrial Organization
CS	Conciliation Service
CWAW	Carriage, Wagon and Automobile Workers' International Union
CWW	Carriage and Wagon Workers' International Union
EWRC	Emergency Welfare Relief Commission
GEB	General Executive Board
GM	General Motors Corporation
FTC	Federal Trade Commission
MESA	Mechanics Educational Society of America
NIRA	National Industrial Recovery Act
NLB	National Labor Board
NLRA	National Labor Relations Act
NLRB	National Labor Relations Board
NRA	National Recovery Administration
TUUL	Trade Union Unity League
UAAVW	United Automobile, Aircraft and Vehicle Workers of America
UAW	United Automobile Workers
UMW	United Mine Workers
URW	United Rubber Workers

The Battle of the Running Bulls

I

The temperature in Flint, Michigan, fell to 16 degrees above zero on January 11, 1937. Strikers had been sitting in the massive Fisher Body Plant No. 1 and the smaller Fisher Body Plant No. 2 since December 30 of the old year. No effort had been made to dislodge them by the General Motors Corporation (GM), the police of the city of Flint, the sheriff of Genesee County, or the governor of the state of Michigan.

The more weakly held of the two plants was the Fisher Body No. 2 factory. Located in a valley about fifty yards north of the Flint River, the small No. 2 plant looked across Chevrolet Avenue to the sprawling Chevrolet complex on the western side of the street.* The plant employed about one thousand workers and had a daily capacity of 450 bodies, which were delivered to the Chevrolet No. 2 plant on the other side of the street across an overpass that connected the two plants.[1]

The strikers occupied only the second floor of the No. 2 factory while company police controlled the main gate. The food for the men inside the plant was prepared at a nearby restaurant and then delivered to the main gate, where it was inspected by the plant police—presumably to check against the presence of liquor—and then taken to the sit-downers.[2] Not more than one hundred strikers occupied the plant on January 11, and their morale was not high. Robert C. Travis, the director of organization for the United Automobile Workers of America (UAW) in Flint, wondered if the union could continue to hold the factory.[3]

Shortly after noon on January 11[4] the heat in Fisher Body No. 2, which the company, at the request of state authorities, had kept on since the beginning of the strike, was turned off without warning. During the course of the afternoon twenty-two plant policemen, armed with clubs and headed by Edgar T. Adams, the chief of the Fisher Body plant police in Flint, came through the main gate of the factory and joined the force of eight company guards already in the plant. The purpose of the visit was to remove the twenty-four foot ladder outside the plant that reached to the second floor and gave the

---

*See the sketch of the layout of the Flint Chevrolet plants and Fisher Body No. 2 on p. 2. This is a copy of the sketch included with Louis G. Seaton to Harry W. Anderson, Feb. 2, 1937, General Motors Labor Relations Diary, Appendix Documents to Accompany Section 1, Doc. 71-A, GM Building, Detroit, Mich.

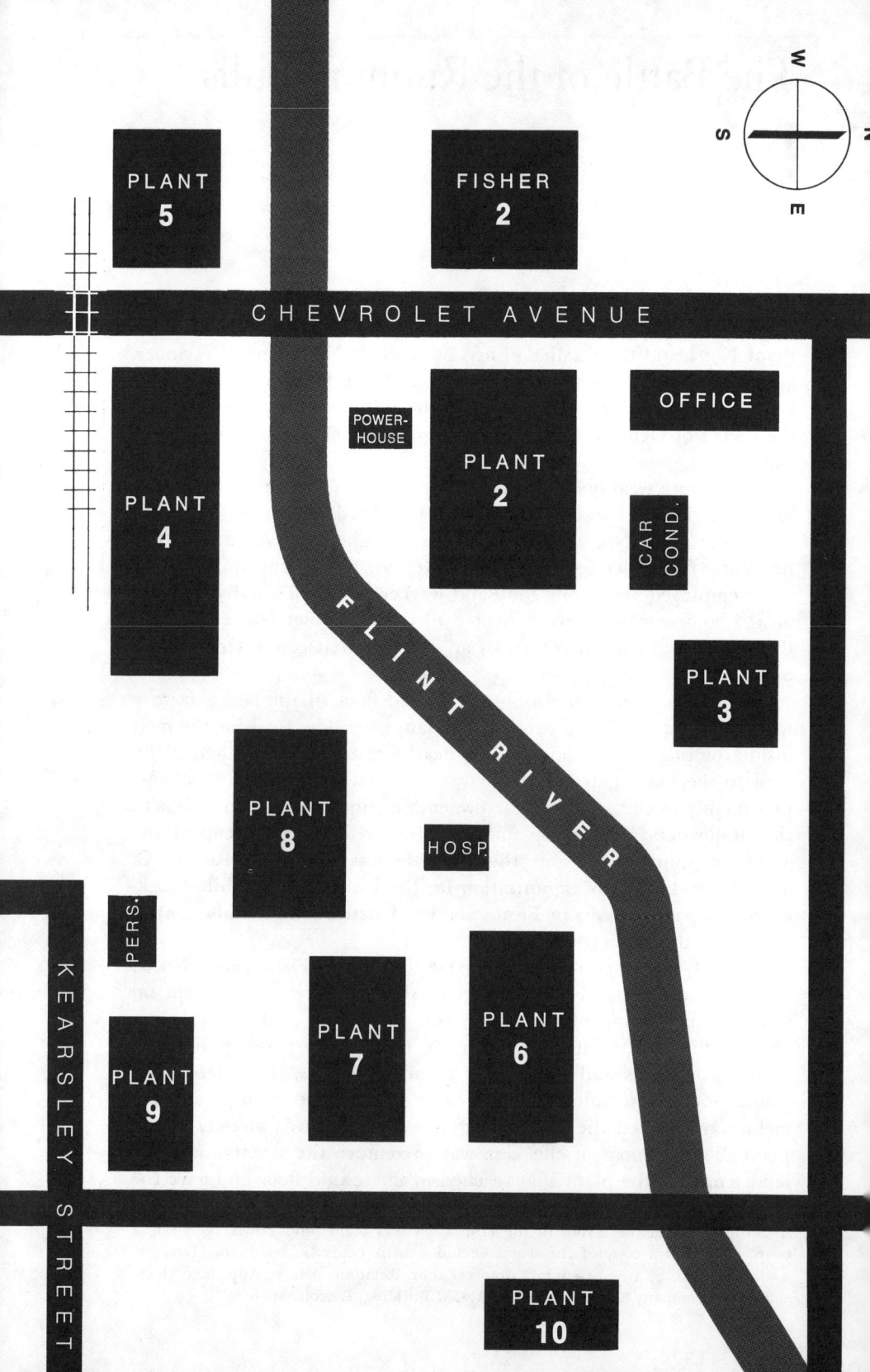

strikers access to the street. Their mission accomplished, the company police departed, leaving two or three of their number behind to supplement the regular force of company guards inside the plant.

Alarmed at the course of events, the sit-downers sent couriers to union headquarters in the Pengelly Building to request the dispatch of additional pickets to augment the union picket force outside the plant. At least two of the unionists who came to the plant that afternoon reported that they had observed city police about two blocks from the plant, diverting traffic from Chevrolet Avenue. The exact time when the Flint police arrived in the vicinity of Fisher Body No. 2 on January 11 remains a matter of uncertainty to this day, but it was the judgment of an investigator for the United States Senate's La Follette Civil Liberties Committee, and this was corroborated by an Associated Press reporter, that there was a police presence in the area in advance of the dramatic events that were soon to occur.[5]

About 6:00 P.M., as was customary, the union sought to take the evening meal for the strikers through the main gate, but entry to the plant was barred for the first time by the company police. The men inside then sought to hoist the food containers into the plant by rope, but it is not clear how successful they were, and there are conflicting accounts as to whether the company police attempted to interfere with this operation.[6]

At about 8:15 or 8:30 P.M. union organizer Victor Reuther, entering Chevrolet Avenue from a small side street, arrived in front of the plant in the union sound car, which was convoyed to the scene by a five-car escort. The strikers by this time, denied heat and their regular evening meal, were "in no pleasant mood."[7] Outside the plant Reuther found a group of about 150 pickets—not all of them strikers, not all of them Flint residents—and also a number of spectators. Seeking to cheer up the strikers, Reuther told them that the union would provide for them and asked if they wished to hear some music. No, replied the men. It was heat and food that they wanted, not music. Reuther then advised them to elect a committee to descend to the main gate and to request the company guards, of whom two shifts of eighteen to twenty men were by then present, to open the gate and to turn on the heat.

Roscoe Rich thereupon assembled a force of about thirty men, went down to the gate, and asked Captain Peterson, in charge of the No. 2 guards, for the key. When Peterson reported that he did not have the key, Rich or one of the others said that he would count to ten and, if the gate remained closed at that time, the men would have to force it open. The company police made no move either to open the gate or to deter the unionists, with the result that when the count ended the men broke the snap lock and forced the gate open. The pickets outside and the remainder of the sit-downers observing the scene from the inside cheered as some of the strikers rushed through the gate and mingled briefly with the people outside the plant. The captain of the company guards phoned the Flint police that he and his men had been "captured" and that the strikers were " 'crowding the door and were threatening,' " and then the guards ingloriously took refuge in the ladies' rest room, from where they did not emerge until the next morning, after the fighting had ended.[8]

Reuther, who had left the sound car to observe the proceedings at the main gate, instructed the sit-downers to return to the plant and to post a guard at the door. Peace prevailed for a few minutes as sit-downers and pickets began singing a chorus of "Solidarity Forever." Suddenly, someone outside yelled, "For God's sake, fellows, here's a tear gas squad." The "Battle of the Running Bulls," as the union was later to name it, had begun, and Chevrolet Avenue was soon to take on the character of a battlefield.

Squad cars carrying about thirty policemen had come across the bridge spanning the Flint River south of Fisher No. 2. The officers, perhaps fifteen of whom were equipped with gas masks and armed with tear-gas guns, left their cars and moved toward the plant. Captain Edwin H. Hughes, in command, approached the main gate and demanded that it be opened. There was no response from inside. The captain then broke the panels of glass above the double doors of the gate and twice fired his gas gun into the plant. The pickets pressed closer to the gate but were forced to retreat and disperse when the police exploded tear-gas bombs in their midst. The police also fired their gas into the plant as they advanced upon it, but the strikers, with Reuther giving the orders from the sound car, directed fire hoses, two-pound steel automobile door hinges, bottles, stones, and assorted missiles at the police and drove them back.[9]

The tide of battle ebbed and flowed outside the plant. After their initial repulse, the police regrouped on the bridge and drove down once again on the plant, firing their gas guns and hurling gas grenades toward the factory and into the pickets in front of the establishment. The sit-downers, many of whom had rushed to the roof of the plant, and the pickets, who had received a supply of "popular ammunition" from the men in the plant during the brief lull in the battle, responded with a water and missile barrage; and as the wind blew the gas back into their faces the police had to fall back. Hurling cans, frozen snow, milk bottles, door hinges, pieces of pavement, and assorted other weapons of this type, the pickets pressed at the heels of the

The Battle of the Running Bulls

retreating police. Undoubtedly enraged at the humiliation of defeat at the hands of so motley and amateur an army, the police drew pistols and riot guns and fired into the ranks of their pursuers. The strikers claimed that the police also fired into the pickets from the Chevrolet No. 2 plant directly across the street from Fisher No. 2, but this allegation appears to lack substantiation.[10]

Fourteen strikers and strike sympathizers, some of whom were from out of town, and two spectators were wounded in the attack on the plant, thirteen of them by gunshot. Nine policemen, Thomas Wolcott, sheriff of Genesee County, and a deputy sheriff were also injured in the affray. The deputy sheriff was shot in the knee, apparently by an errant police bullet, one policeman was gassed, and the remaining injured suffered mainly head wounds from flying missiles.[11]

Ambulances soon clanged up to the battlefield to remove the more seriously wounded to Hurley Hospital. The police in the meantime retreated to the bridge, continuing their shooting for a time, while their opponents outside the plant, according to one account, "limped away, vomiting, tears streaming down their faces, and with torn clothes."[12] The first phase of the Battle of the Running Bulls was over, and the strikers and their allies were in command of the battlefield.

The fury of the battle had, for a dangerous moment, engulfed Sheriff Wolcott, who had arrived on the scene with four deputies after the tear-gas assault had begun and who soon became a battle casualty. His car was turned over while he was still inside it, and as he emerged from the vehicle he was struck on the head by a flying door hinge. The gasoline spilled from his car, and one of the strikers or strike sympathizers, apparently overwrought from the excitement of combat, had to be prevented from setting the car on fire.[13] It was during this most violent phase of the battle that a Detroit *Times* reporter was slashed on the hand, and two reporters for the Flint *Journal*, which the strikers looked upon as a GM house organ, were beaten. One policeman during the melee was surrounded by strikers, knocked to the ground, and separated from his gas equipment.

Victor Reuther, from the sound car, directed the strikers' defense and a few days later was duly promoted to "General" by Bob Travis for his performance on the battlefield.[14] One observer of the scene thought that from the sound car, manned by Reuther and other organizers and alternating exhortation with martial music, emanated "one steady unswerving note" during the battle. "It dominated everything!" Reuther's voice, he said, was "like an inexhaustible, furious flood pouring courage into the men." Reuther berated the police and the company, and he urged the strikers to stand firm. It was to be charged that Reuther ordered the strikers and strike sympathizers outside the plant to "Go home and get your guns" and if they saw "any man in uniform" to "knock him off," but the evidence does not support this allegation. Apparently, however, Reuther at one point did threaten the destruction of the plant if the police did not desist in their attack.[15]

After the police had been driven up the hill to the bridge across the river, Reuther ordered the erection of a barricade of automobiles across both ends of Chevrolet Avenue in front of Fisher No. 2 to prevent the police from driving their squad cars in front of the plant and firing into the building. A large crowd of perhaps three thousand spectators had by this time gathered on the street at both ends of the plant to look down upon the extraordinary scene taking place in their city. As the police had retreated southward from the plant, they had driven the spectators before them. Some among the crowd threw rocks at the police, and they, in turn, fired gas into the midst of the onlookers.

After a period of comparative calm the police, now forty-five in number—the original force of officers had been reinforced by police moving south on Chevrolet Avenue toward the north end of the plant—opened fire once again, this time from both ends of Chevrolet Avenue. The police shot gas shells at long range toward the pickets in front of the plant and the strikers on the roof of the factory. There was to be no further direct assault on the plant, but the long-range firing was to continue for some time. It was at this stage of the battle or perhaps earlier—the accounts are unclear—that a restaurant on Chevrolet Avenue in which workers and reporters were congregated was hit by a gas bomb.

In the midst of this new phase of the battle, twenty-three-year-old Genora Johnson, the wife of a union man who worked in the Chevrolet No. 4 plant, asked permission to speak from the sound car to the spectators beyond the police lines at both ends of Chevrolet Avenue. Mrs. Johnson had been rehearsing a play at union headquarters that afternoon when she heard that trouble was brewing at Fisher No. 2. She drove to the plant but finding the scene peaceful did not remain. She returned, however, later in the day to take a turn on the picket line, and soon she found herself a combatant on the battlefield. "During this time," she later declared in an affidavit, "I did not know fear. I knew only surprise, anguish, and anger." Taking the microphone in the sound car, she addressed herself first to the police. "Cowards! Cowards!," she shouted. "Shooting unarmed and defenseless men." Then she spoke to the women in the crowd beyond the police lines, telling them that it was their fight also and urging them to join the picket line but warning them at the same time that if the police were cowardly enough to shoot unarmed men they would no doubt fire at women also.[16]

The firing from the bridge continued in the darkness until after midnight, as the strikers and their allies prepared for another direct assault on the plant that never came. The police ran out of tear gas and asked the Detroit police for an additional supply but were told that none could be spared. The atmosphere remained tense all through the night and into the morning, but the Battle of the Running Bulls was over.

The street in front of the plant by early morning was "littered with broken glass, bottles, rocks, hinges." A young Detroit *News* reporter who went into the plant at 3:00 A.M. was told by the strikers, who had crowded into the lobby in preparation for another attack, "We could hold this fort for a week." The reporter found the floor inside the main gate flooded with water and the windows of the plant full of bullet holes. Car bodies had been pulled across the lobby to serve as a barricade. The strikers were armed with iron bars, door hinges, and night sticks taken from the company guards, and door hinges had been placed in piles near the windows.[17]

The sit-downers in Fisher Body No. 1, who anticipated that their plant might also be brought under attack that day, were, if anything, even more determined than the strikers in the No. 2 factory to meet force with force. "An interested observer" who visited the plant on January 12 found every man inside armed with a blackjack made of rubber hose and with a lead heading. He saw fire hoses stretched everywhere and was told that water was the best means of combating tear gas and that a rag placed over the nose and eyes reduced the effect of the gas somewhat. He observed a hose attached to an air line and was informed that the purpose was to blow tear gas away. Near the windows were fire extinguishers filled with foamite and foamite tanks mounted on wheels. He also noticed large tanks of a colorless liquid which, he was told, the men were prepared to release and which, if ignited by burning tear gas, allegedly would have blown up the plant. He saw in the men "a determination that in this desperate struggle between capital and labor they should not lose nor retreat till every man was either dead or unable to fight anymore."[18]

Mrs. Johnson remained on the scene until 9:00 A.M. on January 12. She and others marched around a bonfire, sang the strikers' songs, and took turns going into the plant to sip coffee with the sit-downers. She went home for some sleep but returned once again to the plant at about 11:30 A.M. She saw that "the debris had been cleared away. The streets were swept and the broken windows patched. Many

Sit-Down

people were down there talking amongst themselves, but again, everything was peaceful and orderly."[19]

In celebration of their victory two of the strikers added to the repertory of songs sung by the strikers by providing new lyrics for "There'll Be a Hot Time in the Old Town To-nite":

I

Cheer boys cheer,
For we are full of fun,
Cheer boys cheer
Old Parker's[20] on the run;
We had a fight last nite
And I tell you boys we won,
We had a hot time in the old
   town last nite

II

Tear Gas Bombs
Were flying thick and fast
The lousy police
They knew they couldn't last
Because in all their lives they never
   ran so fast
As in that hot time in this old
   town last nite

III

The police are sick
Their bodies they are sore
I'll bet they'll never
   fight us anymore
Because they learned last nite
That they had quite a chore
We had a hot time in the old
   town last nite

IV

Now this scrap is o'er
The boys are sticking fast
We'll hold our Grounds [sic]
   and fight here to the last
And when this strike is o'er

The Battle of the Running Bulls

> We'll have our contract fast
> We'll have a hot time in the old
>   town to-nite[21]

The Battle of the Running Bulls had its repercussions outside Flint and especially in the Michigan capital city of Lansing. Here, Governor Frank Murphy from about 6:00 P.M. on January 11 was receiving word of the riotous events taking place in Flint. The information given him by union sources and City Manager John M. Barringer was inaccurate in detail, but the general picture was clear enough. At 10:20 and then again at 10:40 P.M. Barringer, who was also director of public safety in Flint, reported that the situation was "beyond him" and that his forces were "out of gas." It was apparent to Murphy that both the city government and the union leadership wished him to intervene in force.

At 11:00 P.M. the governor summoned the adjutant general of Michigan, John S. Bersey. After talking with Murphy, Bersey at 11:30 telephoned Colonel Thomas Colladay, the commanding officer of the 125th Infantry of the Michigan National Guard and a Flint resident, to mobilize an armory guard to protect the Flint armory and to assemble certain officers to meet with Murphy. At about midnight the governor left Lansing for Flint accompanied by Bersey, Oscar G. Olander, the commissioner of the Michigan State Police, and others. As he departed, Murphy declared: "It won't happen again. Peace and order will prevail. The people of Flint are not going to be terrorized. The State of Michigan will be supreme."[22]

Murphy reached Flint's Durant Hotel shortly after 1:00 A.M. on January 12 and began a series of conversations that continued for several hours. He conferred first, it would seem, with a group of city and county officials that included Barringer; the mayor of Flint, Harold Bradshaw; the chief of police, James V. Wills; and Sheriff Wolcott. He then talked with Frank Martel, the president of the Detroit and Wayne County Federation of Labor, and three federal conciliators who were seeking to settle the strike, the four of them having driven from Detroit to see the governor. Finally, at about 3:00 A.M., Murphy met with Bob Travis and Adolph Germer, the Committee for Industrial Organization representative in Detroit. The local officials wanted the National Guard and state police sent into Flint; and when Murphy asked that this be put in writing, Bradshaw and Wolcott provided him with a handwritten note stating that "a serious situation" had developed in Flint endangering life and property, that there had been "rioting and bloodshed" and that more of the same was anticipated, that because of the large numbers involved

Sit-Down

local law-enforcement agencies could not deal with the problem, and that therefore they were requesting him to order a sufficient number of National Guardsmen and state police to Flint to ensure the enforcement of law and order.

No less anxious than local officials to have the militia dispatched to Flint, union officials gave the governor their version of what had transpired in the preceding hours, and Travis, according to one account, warned Murphy that there would be "warfare" in the streets if one more worker were injured. The rioting was over by that time, but Murphy told Germer and Travis, " 'they [GM] have more up their sleeve.' "[23]

At 5:00 A.M. Murphy gave orders for the mobilization of the 126th Infantry. "Whatever else may happen," the governor declared in a public statement, "there is going to be law and order in Michigan. The public interest and public safety are paramount. The public authority in Michigan is stronger than either of the parties in the present controversy." Since he had been advised that the situation was beyond the control of local authorities and the two parties to the dispute, he was ordering the state police and units of the National Guard to be held in readiness to support local authorities and to take such action as was "needful."

Later that day, after receiving state police reports that strikers were being reinforced by "a lot of strong-arm boys" from outside the state, and on the recommendation of Bersey, who advised the governor that it was the unanimous opinion of the National Guard, the state police, and local law-enforcement officials that the situation in Flint that night would be "much worse" than it had been the previous night and that threats were being made "to burn the plant and to destroy machinery and cars," Murphy ordered the mobilization of the 125th Infantry, the 106th Cavalry, and the 119th Field Artillery. He also requested GM not to deny heat, water, or food to the strikers in the interest of public health and because "such moves would only befuddle the already complicated situation."[24]

Bersey and the military proved to be rather poor prophets, for January 12 in Flint was a day of peace, not war. The only dueling between the adversaries that took place that day and the next was verbal, as the union and management sought to fix the blame upon one another for the riotous events of January 11. The UAW, predictably, charged that "General Motors bears direct responsibility for the outrageous and premeditated violence employed against our peaceful pickets" and characterized the affair as a "well-planned attack to break the strike through terrorism" and as "the most disgraceful exhibition of irresponsible police leadership in recent years." The

UAW president, Homer Martin, asserted that the police had no "legal right" to aid GM by interfering with the occupancy of the plant and attempting to evict the sit-downers. They had, indeed, violated their oath of office "by engaging in a private enterprise with company-hired thugs." He accused GM of disregarding "positive verbal assurances" that it would not attempt to eject the men by force.[25]

GM, through Executive Vice-President William S. Knudsen, insisted that the battle had been between the city police and the strikers, not between GM and the strikers. "We were not involved in that riot. Our people were not in it," Knudsen told the press. The company, of course, was responsible for cutting off the heat and refusing to allow food through the main gate, but that had been done, Knudsen explained, because the plant office was closed and the plant was in a shut-down condition. At all events, there had been no trouble, he claimed, until the sound car arrived on the scene and incited the pickets to storm the gates and imprison the plant police. Knudsen stated that GM had no intention of denying heat, light, or water to the sit-downers, which was in compliance with the wishes of the governor, and that it would not encourage violence, "since we do not believe labor disputes can be helped by violence."[26]

The UAW to this day believes GM to have been the instigator of the Battle of the Running Bulls,[27] but a La Follette Committee investigator whose sympathies were clearly with the union was unable at the time to make a "definite connection" between the corporation and the Fisher Body No. 2 riot.[28] The available documentation still does not permit one to make that "definite connection," but GM's protestations of innocence simply do not appear to be the whole truth. The Fisher Body plant police had expected the sit-downers in the No. 2 plant to parade to the outside of the building on January 10 and had planned to offer mild resistance to this action so as to force the strikers to commit an act of violence, which presumably would have justified some counteraction against the occupants of the plant by either the plant or public police. The anticipated parade had not, however, been held.[29]

The next day it was GM that set the stage for the battle that was to follow by turning off the heat and having its plant guards shut off the entry of food into the plant through the main gate. Knudsen offered the shut-down condition of the plant as the explanation for what had occurred, but the factory had been in the same condition since December 30 without having produced the countermeasures taken on January 11. The actual physical combat, as GM accurately pointed out, was between the city police and the strikers, not the company guards and the strikers; but it is difficult to believe that, in a city in which corporation and law enforcement were so closely linked, the police would have undertaken an action that could conceivably have resulted in serious damage to the corporation's property without first consulting responsible GM officials. Although there was a substantial degree of sympathy in Flint for the GM position in the strike, "popular opinion," as *Business Week* pointed out, blamed the corporation for having permitted the violence to develop.[30]

Chief of Police Wills, although conceding that he himself had checked on the situation in front of the plant during the course of the afternoon of January 11, denied that police had been dispatched to the scene before the "capture" of the company guards had been reported. "No orders," he declared, "were issued to them [the police]. They went out to see what was going on and to act if there was anything illegal."[31] It is difficult, however, to view these remarks as anything more than self-serving. The evidence indicates that at least some police were in the area before the main gate was forced open from the inside, and the object of the police action seems to have been the ejection of the strikers rather than the rescue of the company guards. The Flint Police Department had added to its supply of tear and sickening gas only a few days earlier,[32] and when its men made their appearance before the No. 2 plant on January 11, they were prepared to use gas equipment in a major action and not just to ascertain the facts and to proceed against the sit-downers only if they were doing something "illegal."

It may be argued that if it had really been the intention of the police to seize the plant and thus to deal a shattering blow to the strikers' cause, a larger force would have been assigned to the task. It must be noted, however, that the forty-five men sent to the plant, which constituted about half of the city's entire "effective" police force, were the total number available to Wills and Barringer at that moment, that Fisher No. 2 was a small plant, that the company before the battle controlled the main gate while the sit-downers held only the second floor, and that the strikers did not possess firearms. The police were also more than likely aware that the number of strikers inside the plant probably did not exceed one hundred and that their morale was poor. Fisher No. 2, from the police and company point of view, must have looked like a far more inviting target than Fisher No. 1, a much larger factory that was held by a more numerous and more determined body of strikers who controlled access to the plant.

If the object of the police action of January 11 was, as seems likely, the seizure of Fisher Body No. 2, the effort ended in ignominious failure. The police, however, had succeeded in attaining what may have been a secondary objective of their plan: the dispatch of the National Guard and the state police to Flint. For several days prior to January 11 City Manager Barringer, no friend of the UAW, had been trying without success to involve the state police in the strike;[33] now the governor had found it necessary to order not only the state police but also the National Guard to be prepared to support local authorities. The intervention of the state militia in a labor dispute had all too often in the past weighted the scales of victory against the strikers. But this time matters were to be different. Barringer, the police, and GM officials must have been dismayed to learn that the strikers had "cheered lustily"[34] when they learned that the governor had ordered the Guard to Flint.

The principal actors in the drama of the Battle of the Running Bulls and its aftermath—GM, the UAW, the responsible officials of the city of Flint, and the governor of Michigan—were not driven by some ineluctable force to play the particular roles that they did play on January 11 and 12. They were, however, the products of their respective pasts, and their individual histories help to explain their part in the unfolding events that led to the great GM sit-down strike and to the clash of arms before the Fisher Body No. 2 plant that so fatefully shaped the subsequent course of the dispute.

The Corporation

I

When William Crapo Durant formed the General Motors Company on September 16, 1908, there was, we are told, no "undue excitement" in the world of industry and finance.[1] No one, indeed, could have anticipated that the first chapter was being written in the story of what was to become the largest privately owned manufacturing enterprise in the world.

Durant, whom *Fortune* characterized as perhaps "the most romantic hero in the whole melodrama of twentieth-century business," was born in Boston on December 8, 1861, and came to Flint when he was six years old. About a dozen years earlier his grandfather, Henry H. Crapo, had also journeyed from Massachusetts to Flint where he had invested in the lumber business part of a fortune made in whaling and had become one of Michigan's great lumber barons. Durant quit school at sixteen and entered the general store his grandfather had established in association with one of his lumberyards. He soon left this position and in the next few years worked as a drug clerk and sold real estate, insurance, bicycles, cigars, and patent medicines. In 1885 he purchased a patent for a two-wheel cart and teamed up with hardware-salesman J. Dallas Dort to form the Durant-Dort Carriage Company.

The new concern initially contracted with an established Flint carriage maker to build the Durant-Dort carts, but soon the firm was assembling its own vehicles and turning them out at the rate of two hundred per day. Before the end of the century, Durant, exhibiting the same imperial ambition he was later to evidence in his career in the automobile industry, had embarked on a vast expansion program, had absorbed a variety of vehicle firms, and was producing a full line of carriages. Dallas-Dort by 1900 was turning out fifty thousand vehicles a year, and it had become the largest carriage manufacturer in the world.[2]

It was the Buick car that provided Durant with his entree into the automobile business and that became "the rock on which General Motors was founded."[3] The Scots-born David Dunbar Buick had been brought to Detroit in 1852 as a child of two. After working for a time in a brass foundry, he went into the plumbing supply business and with William S. Sherwood purchased the concern that had employed him when it failed in 1882. More an inventor than a businessman, Buick developed a process of applying enamel to the surface of cast-iron bathtubs, the key to the modern bathroom. When his major attention turned to the internal-combustion engine in the 1890's, Buick sold his interest in the plumbing supply business and in 1899 organized the Auto Vim and Power Company to manufacture marine and stationary engines. The company failed three years later, and Buick then formed the Buick Manufacturing Company to produce the valve-in-head engine. Financial support for this venture came from two Detroit sheet-metal manufacturers, Benjamin and Frank Briscoe. The concern was reorganized in 1903 as the Buick Motor Car Company, with the Briscoes investing nearly the entire capital. The first Buick car, using a single cylinder engine, made its appearance that same year. Like Ransom E. Olds and Henry D. Leland, two of the other great pioneers of the automobile industry, Buick had turned from the manufacture of marine engines to the manufacture of automobiles.[4]

The Briscoes did not appreciate the potential of David Buick's vehicle and soon became anxious to unload their company. They found a purchaser in James H. Whiting, the owner of the Flint Wagon Works, who had concluded that the future probably lay with the horseless carriage rather than with the horse-drawn variety. The Buick machinery was brought to Flint from Detroit in 1903 and was lodged in a building adjoining the plant of the Flint Wagon Works. The two firms were then merged as the Buick Motor Company, with Buick serving as president and general manager.

At the outset the Buick gave little promise of its future greatness in the motor-vehicle industry: only twenty-three of the cars had been produced by the end of 1904. Discouraged by the company's prospects, Whiting turned to Durant, who had gone to New York to play the stock market, and asked him to take over the concern. Durant knew next to nothing about the automobile, but, after returning to Flint and personally testing the Buick for two months over all sorts of terrain, he decided to enter the automobile business. The deal between the Buick Motor Company and Durant was completed on November 1, 1904, the capital stock of the concern being increased from $75,000 to $300,000. Four years later, in 1908, the soundly engineered Buick, with sales of eighty-five hundred cars for the year, was the leader in the industry, and the Buick plant, which had been relocated in the northern part of Flint, was the largest automobile factory in the world.[5] David Buick, who seems to have been lacking in real business talent, had in the meantime left Flint and the company to which he had given his name only to suffer financial disaster first in a California oil venture and then in the collapse of the Florida land boom. He returned to Detroit in 1927 and taught for a

Sit-Down

16

time in a trade school. He died on March 5, 1929, at the age of seventy-nine.[6]

Prompted by a soaring ambition and believing that an automobile company that produced a variety of makes was in a stronger position than one which offered the consumer a single model, Durant, along with Benjamin Briscoe, sought early in 1908 to effect a merger of the companies producing the Buick, the Maxwell-Briscoe, the Ford, and the Reo but allegedly could not meet the cash terms insisted upon by Ford and Reo. Later in the year, on September 16, Durant launched the General Motors Company with a nominal capitalization of $2000. This figure was increased to $12,500,000 on September 28, and the next day the new concern purchased the Buick Motor Company. Durant, whose talents were primarily those of a salesman and a promoter rather than of an engineer or administrator—"Mr. Durant," Alfred P. Sloan, Jr., later observed, "was a great man with a great weakness—he could create but not administer"—embarked upon a program of breath-taking expansion and by the end of 1909 had acquired or gained substantial control of more than twenty auto, parts, and accessory firms and had narrowly missed annexing even Ford to his domain. The principal vehicle makes added to the Buick, the nucleus of the company, were the Oldsmobile, the Cadillac, and the Oakland.[7]

Billy Durant, a man whose "vision was always running far ahead of his treasury," overreached himself in putting together his first automobile empire and found it difficult to secure the funds to keep the venture afloat. The affairs of the company late in 1910 were in "chaos," and General Motors would have perished had not the investment banking houses of Lee, Higginson and Company of Boston and J. and W. Seligman of New York stepped in and, at a high cost, provided the funds needed to ensure the firm's survival. Durant was forced out of the presidency of the company, thus ending "the first phase of General Motors history," a period, as the historian of the company has written, marked by "the glamor of bold dreams and brave deeds."[8]

General Motors remained under banker control until 1915. The great accomplishment of the banker regime was to provide the firm with "a secure financial base for its future expansion." The water was squeezed out of the company, some of its properties were disposed of, the internal administration was improved, standardized accounting and reporting systems were put into effect, and General Motors began the changeover from holding company to operating company.[9]

Down but not out, Durant set about to fashion a second automobile empire. Within a little more than a year after his ouster from the

General Motors presidency he had become associated with two new automobile firms: the Little Motor Car Company, a Flint-based concern that produced a small, low-priced runabout, and, of greater importance, the Chevrolet Motor Car Company of Michigan. It was the Chevrolet that was to catapult Durant back into control of General Motors and was to provide "the most dramatic chapter" in the history of the corporation.

Durant, as early as 1909, had financed the Swiss-born Louis Chevrolet, a member of the Buick racing team, in experiments in Detroit with a six-cylinder car. In 1913 production of the Chevrolet was transferred from Detroit to Flint, and the vehicles produced by both the Chevrolet and Little Companies henceforth carried the name "Chevrolet." In 1915, by which time the Chevrolet had enjoyed at least a modest success, Durant organized the Chevrolet Motor Company of Delaware as a holding company for Chevrolet activities. He quickly increased the capital of the new firm and began exchanging Chevrolet shares for General Motors shares at a ratio of five to one. At the General Motors stockholders' meeting of September 16, 1915, Durant contested on just about equal terms with the existing management of the concern, and the next year he became its president.[10]

On October 31, 1916, General Motors Corporation (GM) was incorporated in Delaware and acquired all the stock of the General Motors Company. The individual companies making up the firm were dissolved the next year and became GM divisions. The General Motors Company was dissolved on August 3, 1917, and nine months later, on May 2, 1918, GM acquired the Chevrolet Motor Company.[11]

The restless and imperial-minded Durant had in the meantime been annexing new territories to the GM domain. In 1916 he had brought together in the United Motors Corporation a variety of parts and accessory makers—Hyatt Roller Bearing Company, Dayton Engineering Laboratories, New Departure Manufacturing Company, Remy Electric Company, and the Perlman Rim Corporation. In 1918 United Motors was purchased by GM, giving the corporation its own parts and accessories division and bringing into the GM family the president of United Motors, Alfred P. Sloan, Jr. Sloan had been born in New Haven on May 23, 1875, the son of a wholesale tea, coffee, and cigar merchant. After graduating from the Massachusetts Institute of Technology, the twenty-year-old Sloan secured a job as a draftsman in the Hyatt Roller Bearing Company. The concern began making enormous profits after Sloan convinced various automobile manufacturers to use Hyatt bearings rather than the heavily greased wagon axles they had been employing.

When GM purchased United Motors, Sloan became a GM vice-president and a member of its board of directors and its executive committee. In 1923 he became president of the corporation, a position he still held when the sit-down strike began. The tall, gaunt, impeccably dressed, and very abstemious Sloan was a no-nonsense type who worked at his tasks with single-minded devotion. Tending because of his slight deafness to be rather quiet in the presence of people he did not know, Sloan became known in the GM organization as "Silent Sloan." At the time of the sit-down strike he was the highest paid corporation executive in the United States.[12]

The years 1918–20 were a time of enormous expansion for GM. The corporation purchased the assets of United Motors, launched what later became the Frigidaire Division, created the General Motors Acceptance Corporation to aid in the financing of sales, formed General Motors of Canada, and began construction of the massive General Motors office building in Detroit. Of even greater importance for the future of the corporation and for the GM strike was the decision of the company on September 25, 1919, to purchase a three-fifths interest in the Fisher Body Corporation, possessor of the largest and best-equipped body-building plants in the world.[13]

The six Fisher brothers, Fred J., Charles T., William A., Lawrence P., Edward F., and Alfred J., were third-generation vehicle makers. The oldest brother, Fred J., came to Detroit in 1901 from Norwalk, Ohio, and went to work for the C. R. Wilson Body Company, then the largest firm in the automobile body business. The Fisher Body Company was incorporated in Michigan in 1908, the year all the brothers moved to Detroit. The business prospered from the start. In 1910 the company received an order from Cadillac for 150 closed bodies, the first large order for closed auto bodies placed in the United States. Later in the year the brothers organized the Fisher Closed Body Company and then six years later merged their two Michigan companies with a Canadian firm they had established in 1912 to form the Fisher Body Corporation. When GM acquired its majority interest in Fisher Body, it agreed to purchase all its bodies from Fisher for the next ten years. In 1926 GM gained complete control of Fisher Body, which became a division of the corporation although remaining under the management of the Fisher brothers.

Fisher bodies for Buick cars were at first produced in Detroit and then trucked to Flint, but in 1923 Fisher Body built the plant on Chevrolet Avenue in Flint that was to become Fisher Body No. 2 to supply bodies for Buick and Chevrolet. Three years later Fisher Body acquired from Durant Motors a large plant on Saginaw Street at the southern edge of Flint and transformed it into Fisher Body No. 1.

Buick bodies were thereafter made at this plant, which was expanded into the largest body-building plant in the world, and the No. 2 plant confined itself to Chevrolet bodies.[14]

When the post-World War I economic boom gave way in the fall of 1920 to recession, most automobile manufacturers, including GM, found themselves in an overextended position. The downturn in the economy was also to mark the end of Billy Durant's association with GM. Caught in an effort to arrest the decline in the market for GM securities, Durant was saved from ruin by the intervention of the du Pont Company, which in association with a Morgan syndicate bought his 2.5 million shares of GM stock for $23 million. As part of the arrangement Durant was forced once again to resign the presidency of the company, which was assumed by Pierre S. du Pont. Sloan, as executive vice-president, was now able to implement a plan for the reorganization of the chaotically administered and "physically unintegrated" company that Durant had appeared to favor but had failed to put into effect. Sloan's plan was guided by the concept of "decentralized operations with co-ordinated control." The GM divisions at the time enjoyed a substantial degree of autonomy, and they continued to do so under the Sloan plan, but in order to coordinate the functions of the corporation as a whole, Sloan organized a central office to formulate the general policies for the divisions and created a staff of specialists to serve the general officers and the divisions in an advisory capacity. The Sloan plan helped to produce "a wonderfully lithe organization" that at the time of the GM strike was rated by Wall Street as "the best managed big corporation in America."[15] As tends to be true of federal systems, however, the GM plan of organization did not entirely eliminate uncertainty regarding the precise distribution of powers as between the central corporation and its more or less autonomous divisions. This was to become a matter of considerable importance when union leaders, beginning in 1933, demanded that the corporation meet with them for purposes of collective bargaining.

The historian John B. Rae has pointed out that Sloan's "greatest achievement" as a GM executive was the quality of the men he selected to run the organization. The most important of these men, unquestionably, was William S. Knudsen. Signius Wilhelm Poul Knudsen—the name was later Americanized—was born in Copenhagen on March 25, 1879, the son of a customs inspector. He came to the United States in 1900 with only $30 in his pocket and with some experience as an apprentice mechanic in a bicycle shop. His first employment in the New World was as a reamer, at $1.75 a day, in a shipyard in the Bronx. He then took a job repairing locomotive bodies in the Erie Railroad shops in Salamanca, New York. In 1902

Knudsen went to work as a bench hand in the John R. Keim Mills of Buffalo, New York, and worked his way up during the next few years to the position of assistant superintendent.

The Keim Mills had originally manufactured bicycles, but with the development of the automobile industry in the first decade of the twentieth century it had become one of the principal producers of pressed steel parts for motor vehicles, particularly for the Ford Motor Company. Ford purchased the company in 1912 and acquired Knudsen's services in the process. Knudsen played a part in the refinement of mass-production techniques at Ford and directed the building of Ford assembly plants all over the United States. Ford, however, fired Knudsen in March, 1921, and the next year Sloan wisely brought him into GM. Knudsen was assigned the task of rehabilitating Chevrolet, which had been selling so poorly that a firm of consulting engineers engaged by Pierre du Pont had recommended the company's liquidation. Knudsen enjoyed phenomenal success in his new role, and by 1924, when he was made president and general manager of the division, Chevrolet sales were increasing more rapidly than those of any other American car. In 1927 Chevrolet, higher-priced but more stylish and comfortable than Ford's Model T, was the most widely purchased car in the United States, and GM, with 42.5 percent of the total new car registrations, had passed Ford as the leading producer of passenger vehicles for the first time since 1910.[16]

In 1933 Knudsen was promoted to executive vice-president of GM, the position he was occupying when the sit-down strike began. The six-foot, two-inch, heavy-set Knudsen was a frank, simple, down-to-earth type whose primary interest was in production rather than finance. He did not employ female secretaries lest he feel compelled to curb his expletives in their presence, and he liked to work with his hat on because he claimed that this helped him to think better.[17]

In 1928, the last full year of prosperity before the Great Depression and GM's "most successful year" to that time, the corporation's net sales were almost $1.5 billion, its net profit before income taxes was more than $330 million, and its net profit after income taxes was approximately $296 million. Its investment in just the motor-vehicle portion of its business (including Fisher Body) was, according to the Federal Trade Commission, more than $366 million, its profits on this portion of its business almost $216 million, and its rate of return on this group 58.89 percent.[18] The corporation's share of new car registrations was 41.3 percent, which placed it at the head of the industry. GM in that year employed 208,981 hourly and salaried workers, and its payroll exceeded $365 million.[19]

During the last half of 1929 GM, as it noted in its annual report for that year, had to reduce its manufacturing schedules "in a very material degree" because of "the declining trend in general business activity." But 1929 was a good year for the corporation compared to the lean years that were to follow. Between 1928 and 1932 sales of cars and trucks to dealers in the United States plummeted approximately 74 percent (from 1,810,806 to 472,859); net profits after taxes fell from more than $296 million to less than $8.5 million for the consolidated operations of the corporation as a whole and to a loss of almost $7 million for the motor-vehicle portion of the business; employment dropped almost 50 percent (from 208,981 to 116,152) and the corporation's payroll by about 60 percent (from $365,352,304 to $143,255,070). The Ford Motor Company, enjoying success with its new Model A, supplanted GM as the industry's leading producer in 1929 and 1930, but GM, with 43.26 percent of the new passenger-car registrations, forged to the front once again in 1931 and has remained there ever since.[20]

The New Deal, during Franklin D. Roosevelt's first term in office, was to introduce changes in the relationship of government to the economy and to the individual citizen that GM regarded as deplorable, but the more it protested the more its economic position improved. Net sales of the corporation for its consolidated operations more than tripled (from $440,899,312 to $1,439,289,940) between 1932 and 1936; net profits before income taxes increased more than thirty fold (from $8,824,212 to $283,696,144); and net profits after taxes increased approximately twenty-seven fold (from $8,359,930 to $239,550,075). For the motor-vehicle portion of its business the corporation converted its 1932 loss into a 1936 profit of approximately $163 million before income taxes, a rate of return of 37.93 percent. Sales of cars and trucks to dealers in the United States almost quadrupled between 1932 and 1936 (from 472,859 to 1,682,594), the company's total employment doubled (116,152 to 230,572), and its payroll jumped 168 percent (from $143,255,070 to $384,153,022).[21]

The corporation that the UAW struck at the end of 1936 was a concern of enormous economic strength. It was not simply "big," but, as *Fortune* remarked, it was "colossal." It had sixty-nine automotive plants in thirty-five cities and fourteen states, and its total assets exceeded $1.5 billion. It produced passenger cars "for every price and purpose" ("Chevrolet for *hoi polloi*, ... Pontiac ... for the poor but proud, Oldsmobile for the comfortable but discreet, Buick for the striving, Cadillac for the rich"), commercial vehicles, trucks and trailers, a great variety of parts and accessories, refrigeration, heating, and air-conditioning equipment, lighting equipment, household appliances, airplanes and aviation equipment, locomotives, and power plants, and it had very substantial interests in real estate, finance, and insurance. Its 342,384 shareholders at the end of 1936 received over $200 million in dividends for the year, a record for the corporation. It accounted for 43.12 percent of all new passenger-car registrations and 37.8 percent of new truck registrations in the United States that year, and the more than two million cars and trucks that it sold around the globe constituted 37 percent of the entire world's sales of such vehicles and was 7.3 percent above the corporation's 1929 sales. Its 171,711 hourly employees worked an average of 40.5 hours per week and received an average hourly wage of 75.6 cents, which compared very favorably with the average hourly rate of 55.6 cents for production workers in all manufacturing. Eighty-five percent (145,860) of these employees had been on the company payroll for the full year and had earned an average of $1541 for the year, which was 7 percent above the 1929 figure in current dollars and 29 percent above in real terms and which exceeded by 19.7 percent the average annual earnings for full-time employees in manufacturing as a whole.[22]

II

During the course of the sit-down strike GM explained to the supervisory personnel enrolled in the corporation's executive training program that the "recent serious problems in employee relations" indicated that GM had lagged behind in the development of policies, processes, and methods relating to the "human phase" of its activities and that this deficiency was threatening to offset the progress made in the areas of manufacturing, engineering, and distribution.[23] This was unquestionably an accurate judgment, although it is unlikely that the leaders of the corporation would have admitted the fact before the strike began.

GM, prior to the 1930's, had paid scant attention to the question of labor organization in its plants: the subject of labor relations, indeed, had yet to enter the "corporation consciousness." Some of the corporation's craftsmen, to be sure, were union members, and plant managers occasionally had conversations with them, but GM had no officially stated policy regarding labor unions and, as a matter of fact, given the unusually small number of unionists in its plants, had little need for such a policy. This did not mean, however, that GM was neutral on the question of unionism. It believed firmly in the virtues of the open shop, and it found it difficult to distinguish between bona fide efforts to organize and union "agitation" that allegedly posed a threat to efficiency and had to be dealt with summarily.[24]

To say that GM had not formulated a specific policy with regard to labor unions does not mean that it had failed to concern itself with the broader question of personnel administration. At the close of World War I GM, like so many other large American corporations, decided to introduce a program of welfare capitalism for its employees. Arthur Pound, the sympathetic historian of the corporation, contends that GM, in so acting, was responding to the "new spirit of brotherhood" of that era, but the corporation was also undoubtedly motivated by an understandable desire to link its employees more closely with their employer and thus, hopefully, to lessen the possible appeal of outside unionism to its workers at a time when labor organizing was on the upswing and to reduce labor turnover in its burgeoning work force and in such boom towns as Flint. At the same time that it embraced welfare capitalism, GM also joined with nine other major corporations in secretly establishing the Special Conference Committee, "an exclusive labor relations organization" that was clearly hostile to independent unionism. The Special Conference Committee was still functioning at the time of the sit-down strike.[25]

GM directed its executive committee in 1919 to investigate industrial conditions in communities where the corporation's plants were located. The committee appointed a research committee which made a study of working and living conditions as they affected GM employees and collected data on a variety of plans of welfare capitalism. The findings of the research committee formed the basis for the enlargement of the corporation's welfare program that had been initiated the previous year by the introduction of a bonus plan for GM employees. The bonus plan originally encompassed all corporation employees, but it was limited, beginning in 1922, to personnel earning at least $5000 per year (later reduced to $2400).[26]

Although blue-collar workers were eventually excluded from GM's bonus plan, they were permitted to take advantage of the housing program and the Employes Savings and Investment Plan initiated by the corporation in 1919. In communities where the rapid expansion of GM employment was making it impossible for the corporation's workers to find housing, GM itself began to make provision for the erection of homes that it occasionally rented to its employees but more commonly sold to them at cost on a deferred-payment basis. Houses were built in Flint and Pontiac, Michigan, Janesville, Wisconsin, and Walkerville and Oshawa, Canada. By the end of 1929 almost thirty-five thousand GM employees had availed themselves of corporation housing.[27]

The Employes Savings and Investment Plan provided for the establishment of two funds, a Savings Fund and an Investment Fund, with a new class beginning each year and maturing in five years. The individual employee could pay into the Savings Fund up to 10 percent of his annual earnings, but not more than $300, at a fixed rate of interest (originally 6 percent but reduced to 5 percent in 1935). The employee contribution was matched dollar for dollar (fifty cents beginning in 1922, twenty-five cents beginning in 1933, and thirty-five cents in 1935) by a GM contribution to the Investment Fund, the money being invested in GM common stock and the principal and earnings credited to the employees. The employee could withdraw his savings plus accrued interest in advance of maturity, but if he did so he forfeited the unmatured sum placed by the corporation in the Investment Fund. He could, however, apply his savings toward the purchase of a home without losing any of the benefits of the plan; and by the end of 1928 more than eighteen thousand employees had been aided in building or buying homes in this fashion. At the close of 1928, 89 percent of the eligible GM employees were participating in the savings plan; and by the time it was suspended on December 31, 1935, because of uncertainty caused by the Securities Act of 1933 and the Social Security Act of 1935, more than $242 million had been paid out by the corporation to its employees, of which GM had contributed slightly more than $100 million in the form of interest on employee savings, investment fund credits, accrued dividends, and the appreciation in the value of GM stock.[28]

In 1924 GM also adopted a preferred stock-subscription plan that permitted an employee to buy up to 10 shares of the company's preferred stock on the installment plan. As a special inducement, GM, in addition to its regular dividends, promised to pay $2 per share for five years to those employees who participated in the plan. Only 3342 employees took advantage of the new scheme in 1924, and at no time before the plan was discontinued in 1930 did an appreciable number of the company's workers participate.[29]

Of far greater impact in terms of the number of employees involved was the group-insurance plan inaugurated by GM on December 1, 1926. All employees of GM, its subsidiaries, and affiliated companies could be insured for $1000 under the plan, without a medical examination, provided they had worked for the corporation for three months. The cost was shared by GM and the insured worker, and the insurance was payable at death to the beneficiary of the insured or to the employee himself in twenty equal installments if he suffered total and permanent disability before the age of sixty. In 1928 the plan was expanded to include larger death benefits and health and non-occupational accident insurance. Ninety-eight percent of the eligible employees were participating in the plan at the end of

1936, and by that time a little more than $28 million had been paid out to employees.[30]

Still another feature of the GM program of welfare capitalism was the recreational and educational activities of the Industrial Mutual Association (IMA) of Flint, whose slogan for years was "Somewhere to go in Flint." The IMA was established in 1923 for recreational, educational, and welfare purposes as the result of the merger of the Flint Vehicle Factories Mutual Benefit Association, founded in 1901 for the workers of Flint's four major carriage producers, the Flint Vehicle Workers Club, formed in 1910 for social and recreational purposes as a subsidiary of the Flint Vehicle Factories Mutual Benefit Association, and the Industrial Fellowship League, created in 1921 to accommodate Flint workers not reached by the organizations for vehicle workers. The benefit and relief features of the IMA were of diminishing importance after the winter of 1930–31, but the organization during the depression increased its recreational activities as a response to the increased leisure time unfortunately available to so many Flint workers. Although the IMA was not specifically a GM enterprise, it had been established by Buick personnel, nearly all of its officers were GM officials, and it became GM's agent for the group-insurance program when the plan was introduced in 1926. It is not surprising, therefore, that the *I.M.A. News*, "The Factory Workers' Own Paper," was converted into a company propaganda sheet during the GM sit-down strike.[31]

At the beginning of 1937 some forty thousand Flint workers, a majority of them GM employees, were participating in one or another of the IMA's activities. The dues were ten cents a week, and they entitled a member to take advantage of a considerable variety of recreational activities. The IMA offered its members gymnasia, bowling alleys, billiard tables, card rooms, chess and checkers, facilities for dancing, an auditorium seating sixty-five hundred (the second largest facility of its type in Michigan), and a summer resort at Potters Lake. It carried on an elaborate intra- and inter-company sports program in cooperation with the personnel departments of the various plants— the editor of *Mill and Factory* described the IMA as "the largest amateur athletic association in the world"—and sponsored gardening, stamp, hiking, bridge, cribbage, youth, and similar clubs, a male glee club, a women's chorus, several bands, and classes in such things as handicrafts, sewing, and modern dance.[32]

Quite apart from the IMA, GM sponsored a variety of recreational programs in its plant cities. It supported orchestras, glee clubs, men and women's clubs, and a large number of sports programs. Management in the various divisions and plants was in "complete accord," one observer reported, regarding the value of the far-flung recreation program of the corporation.[33]

When GM at the end of 1931 surveyed the results of the depression for its workers, it pointed with pride to the part the Employes Savings and Investment Plan was playing in cushioning the impact of unemployment and reduced hours of labor. Through the operation of the plan, the corporation noted, GM workers had entered the year 1930 with a reserve of about $75 million to tide them over their time of troubles. They had withdrawn $35 million from the fund in 1930–31; and, in addition, by the end of 1931 they had applied about $23 million toward the purchase of homes. "So far as it is possible for any single institution to go in the way of discharging its responsibility to its workers," GM observed, "it is believed that this plan has, to a very great extent, been made to answer industry's social responsibilities to its workers."[34]

By the end of 1932 GM had abandoned the tone of self-congratulation with regard to its programs of welfare capitalism so evident in its annual report for the previous year. The inability of GM employees to maintain payments on their corporation-built housing and the increased cancellation of housing contracts caused great problems for the corporation's subsidiaries in the housing field and led GM on April 1, 1932, to reduce the interest rate on the homes it had built and to establish a relationship between employee earnings and their monthly mortgage payments. It began renting vacant houses that it was unable to sell and decided to build no new houses and to liquidate its housing investment. Of greater importance, heavy withdrawals forced the corporation to suspend the Savings and Investment Plan on April 30, 1932, despite the glowing remarks of a short time earlier concerning its value in times of economic adversity. The plan was resumed in August, 1933, but with a reduced corporation contribution. In addition to its Savings and Investment Plan, GM sought to counteract the ravages of the depression among its employees by such devices as sharing the work and the extension of loans to laid-off workers,[35] but the burden of unemployment was, perforce, increasingly carried by the public treasury rather than by the welfare schemes and the private treasury of the corporation.

The extent to which GM gained the loyalty and affection of its employees by its welfare program is necessarily difficult to gauge with any precision, but it would appear that if the plans won some friends for the corporation among its workers, they also made it some enemies. During the depression years in particular there were bitter complaints from workers who had lost their GM homes because they could not maintain their payments; some of them foolishly attributed their layoffs to the corporation's desire to repossess their homes. The Employes Savings and Investment Plan had many attractive features and was a boon to many employees, but some workers complained that it was a "big detriment" to them because they lost the principal benefit of the plan if they left the company or lost their jobs. There were charges that the payment of IMA dues and participation in the group-insurance plan were in effect compulsory since employees feared that they would suffer discrimination if they did not join in these programs. Some employees resented the fact that they did not participate in the management of any of the plans and that GM consequently could change the rules unilaterally or abandon a program altogether whenever it saw fit.[36] One may guess, however, despite these complaints, that the GM "cooperative plans," before 1929 anyhow, were a plus rather than a minus factor for the company in its relations with its employees; but welfare programs, at best, were of far less significance in determining the attitude of the GM worker toward his job than the wages he received, the hours that he toiled, the security of his position, and the conditions under which he labored.

Quite apart from its efforts to promote the idea of partnership among its employees by programs of welfare capitalism, GM hoped that its workers would remain loyal to the corporation because of the high hourly wages that it paid relative to other manufacturers. In the final weeks before the sit-down strike GM increased the wages of its hourly workers by five cents per hour and also began paying them time-and-a-half for hours worked above forty per week (rather than above forty-eight, as before) and on Sundays and six holidays. GM, on November 9, 1936, also decided to award its employees an Appreciation Fund bonus of about $10 million, with individual workers receiving between $35 and $60 depending on their rate of pay.[37]

It was a common complaint of automobile workers and of union spokesmen that the high hourly rates paid by the industry did not translate themselves into high annual wages because of the considerable irregularity of automobile employment. Prodded by the National Recovery Administration (NRA) and President Roosevelt and because of the obvious economic disadvantages of irregular production and employment, GM, along with the other automobile manufacturers, sought during the New Deal years to reduce the dimensions of the problem of seasonality. As a major step in this direction, the Automobile Manufacturers Association agreed at the end of 1934 to introduce new passenger-car models in the early fall rather than shortly after the first of the year, as the car makers had been doing, a practice that had accentuated the already heavy spring demand for new cars by "superimposing a new model urge on top of a normal seasonal urge."

The fall introduction of new models was designed to increase demand in the sluggish final quarter of the year and to lower the spring peak, thus providing a more level production curve for the year as a whole. The new plan was put into effect by GM and the other automobile manufacturers in the fall of 1935, and it had the stabilizing effect on automobile employment that had been predicted.[38]

It was to its foremen that GM looked to maintain discipline in its plants and to keep the individual worker reasonably satisfied with his job. They were "the first unit in the direction of production and the handling of employes." In the rather stilted foremanship training courses given in the General Motors Institute[39] in Flint, foremen were reminded that it was their role to represent management to the men and the men to management and that it was important to establish a "balanced relationship." It was the foremen before 1933 who had the primary responsibility for adjusting individual grievances in the plant and who were supposed to explain changes in company policy and in work standards to the employees. Had they performed their role properly, the foremen were told in one of their training courses in 1934, there would have been little need for any kind of employee representation in the company's plants.[40]

III

As Sloan later explained, GM was "largely unprepared for the change in the political climate and the growth of unionism" that followed the inauguration of Franklin D. Roosevelt in 1933. When it came to collective bargaining, GM, as *Fortune* wryly observed, was "a complete and rather skittish virgin." Despite GM's continuing membership in the Special Conference Committee, interest in industrial relations at the corporation level at the beginning of the New Deal was largely analytical and statistical; not until early 1934 when Merle C. Hale became director of the department of industrial relations did labor matters per se become the responsibility of an individual in the central office of the corporation. Hale was succeeded in the summer of 1935 by Harry W. Anderson, but not until 1937 were personnel programs centralized in a single department at GM.[41]

The "change in the political climate" that most concerned GM in the early months of the New Deal was that portended by Section 7(a) of the National Industrial Recovery Act (NIRA), which became law on June 16, 1933. Section 7(a) provided that every code, agreement, or license approved or issued under the statute had to stipulate that employees were to have "the right to organize and bargain collectively through representatives of their own choosing" and were to be free from employer "interference, restraint, or coercion" in designating such representatives, in self-organization, or in "other concerted activities for the purpose of collective bargaining or other mutual aid or protection"; and that no employee and no one seeking work was to be required as a condition of employment to join a company union or to refrain from joining, organizing, or assisting a labor organization of his own choice.

Firmly committed to the open shop, Sloan stated shortly before the recovery bill was approved by Congress that GM would "not subscribe to the Industrial Recovery Act as long as the possibility remains for the American Federation of Labor [AFL] to organize ... [its] plants." In the end Sloan and his fellow automobile manufacturers other than Henry Ford did subscribe to the NIRA but only after the NRA permitted the industry to include a merit clause in the automobile manufacturing code stipulating that employers in the industry could "exercise their right to select, retain, or advance employees on the basis of individual merit, without regard to their membership or nonmembership in any organization."[42]

The enactment of the NIRA did not in any way cause GM to modify its views concerning the open shop or the evils of outside unionism; it remained convinced that it was impossible to come to terms with the AFL short of surrendering basic management prerogatives and accepting the closed shop. The Federation, Sloan believed, was not interested in the real problems of the automobile industry but simply wished to force the automobile workers to pay tribute to a union in order to hold their jobs. "Under no circumstances," he declared in the spring of 1934, "will we recognize any union as that term is interpreted by the American Federation of Labor—that means the closed shop."[43]

Actually, GM, like the other automobile manufacturers, feared the growth of unionism in its plants less because organization was thought likely to raise the cost of automobile production than because it threatened to circumscribe the customary prerogatives of management. What Robert E. Lane has said of the reaction of businessmen in general to the labor legislation of the New Deal era applies to GM in its response to Section 7(a) and later to the National Labor Relations Act (NLRA): the danger posed was not one of economics but of "cost in status, in conceptions of the self, in freedom to make certain traditional decisions, in the [possible] disruption of once familiar and stable areas of managerial discretion." For GM as for so many other employers the union was "a disordering influence" which in seeking to share power with the corporation challenged its view of the proper manner in which the business should be conducted.[44]

In responding to the potential union threat to its prerogatives, GM, exhibiting the tendency of institutions and men to make as few changes as possible in their customary way of doing things when confronted with new conditions, evolved a set of principles with respect to its obligations under the NIRA to which it adhered with a high degree of consistency throughout the period that the statute remained in effect and to which it remained committed at the time the sit-down strikes were initiated in its plants. Of greatest significance was the corporation's rejection of the principle of majority rule in the selection of employee representatives for collective-bargaining purposes, which was championed by the United Automobile Workers (UAW) Federal Labor Unions (as the AFL plant unions in the automobile factories were known) and by the National Labor Board (NLB) and later the first National Labor Relations Board (NLRB), and its unswerving support of the concept of collective-bargaining pluralism. The phrase "representatives of their own choosing," GM, like the other automobile manufacturers, contended, meant precisely what the words said: any one purporting to represent a group of employees in bargaining with management must present "satisfactory evidence," as by an authenticated list, that he had been authorized to speak for these employees. An employer, it was alleged, would be violating the statute if, on the other hand, he accepted the principle of majority rule and agreed to bargain with union representatives on behalf of all the employees in a bargaining group, including employees who had not specifically authorized these representatives to speak for them. This interpretation of Section 7 (a) left the door open for each group in a plant to select its own representatives for bargaining purposes and for individuals who wished to do so to bargain for themselves. This made it unlikely that the employees in the foreseeable future would be able to present a united trade-union front to GM for collective-bargaining purposes even if the majority of workers in a particular plant or unit were able to agree on a bargaining representative.[45]

GM also insisted that just as Section 7 (a) protected employees against employer coercion so, "in fairness to the great majority of our employees who do not belong to unions," must any settlement with its employees or any new legislation seeking to define the nature of collective bargaining specify that employees were similarly to be protected against union coercion. Furthermore, despite the contrary decision of the NLB, GM stated that it would not recognize a labor organization *as such* nor would it enter into a contract with a union on behalf of the company's employees.[46]

GM and the other automobile manufacturers pitted their interpretation of Section 7 (a) against that of the UAW plant unions in a showdown battle between automobile unionism and automobile management in March, 1934, that ultimately had to be resolved by President Roosevelt himself. When the federal labor unions in the Buick, Fisher Body No. 1 and No. 2, and Hudson plants threatened a strike that might have spread to other automobile plants, President Roosevelt took charge of the dispute and on March 25, 1934, proclaimed a settlement that hewed more closely to the GM than the AFL concept of collective bargaining. The President, on the crucial question of the form that representation should take, rejected majority rule in favor of proportional representation. The employers, by the settlement, agreed to bargain with the "freely chosen representatives of groups," and if there was more than one group in a plant each bargaining committee was to have "total membership pro rata to the number of men each member represents."

The President made the victory of the automobile manufacturers complete on the issue of representation and collective bargaining by endorsing their view that automobile workers did not necessarily have to join a trade union to secure their rights under the NIRA. "The government," the settlement stated, "favors no particular union or particular form of employee organization or representation." The government's only duty is to secure absolute and uninfluenced freedom of choice without coercion, restraint or intimidation from any source." Thus the company union was, in effect, sanctioned as long as employees had not been coerced into joining it, and union coercion was put on a par with employer coercion.

Although victorious on the major issues, GM and the other automobile manufacturers did have to make some concessions to organized labor to achieve a settlement. The final terms agreed upon in Washington specifically barred discrimination against workers "because of their labor affiliation or for any other unfair or unjust reason" and provided that questions of discrimination would be passed on by a board—subsequently established as the Automobile Labor Board (ALB)—composed of a labor representative, an industry representative, and a neutral arbiter. The employers also surrendered a portion of their complete control over hiring, firing, and layoffs by agreeing that in reductions and increases of force "such human relationships as married men with families come first and then seniority, individual skill and efficient service." The ALB was later to devise a set of rules to implement these guiding generalizations with regard to the job tenure of automobile workers.[47]

"We all feel tremendously happy over the outcome in Washington," a GM vice-president understandably reported after the negotiations leading to the President's settlement had been completed. Although his prediction that the settlement would prove "tremendously constructive" in meeting problems of industrial relations in the automobile industry[48] was not to be borne out by events, GM continued to believe in the wisdom of the settlement's principles. GM thought poorly, on the whole, of the New Deal, and the corporation's leadership was among Roosevelt's most determined foes when he ran for reelection in 1936, but GM nevertheless was still proclaiming the virtues of the President's settlement and of proportional representation in collective bargaining when the sit-down strike paralyzed the company's operations early in 1937.

GM experienced a strike of some of its tool and die makers in Flint, Detroit, and Pontiac in September and October, 1933,[49] but the first work stoppage by GM production workers during the NRA era did not occur until April 21, 1934, when the key Cleveland Fisher Body factory was struck by the plant's federal labor union. The strike soon spread to Fisher Body and Chevrolet plants in St. Louis, Kansas City, and North Tarrytown, New York. In an effort to compose the dispute and to avert a further spread of the strike, the ALB arranged a summit conference between GM and Fisher Body management and representatives of the UAW and the plant locals involved. As a precondition of the meeting, however, GM successfully insisted that the Cleveland strike must be called off, and when the conference began on April 30 Knudsen would not agree to the admission of union representatives from the Kansas City and North Tarrytown plants, which were still on strike, because "we don't propose to deal with men on strike."[50] GM became committed to the idea of no negotiation with strikers, but it was a tenet from which the corporation would be compelled to recede before the NIRA had run its course.

At the Fisher Body-UAW conference, the first meeting in history between higher GM executives and union officials, Knudsen stood fast on the principle of which much was to be heard just before and during the GM sit-down strike, namely, that the corporation was willing to engage in top-level talks with employee representatives regarding labor matters that affected GM as a whole but specific issues like wage classifications and differentials would have to be negotiated at the plant level. "Collective bargaining is all right as long as it is confined to your own territory," Knudsen explained, "but when you begin to run around, I think we should step in there."[51] GM had its way on this question at the Fisher Body conference, and it was to continue to insist upon the principle, but the corporation did not define precisely which bargaining issues were general in scope and which local; and although it asserted that individual plant managers had the authority to come to terms with employee representatives on matters of local concern, the degree to which the factory heads were really autonomous in this area was less than GM indicated.

Union officials at the Fisher Body conference reluctantly accepted Knudsen's suggestion that, in Cleveland and Pontiac at least, representatives of all the organizations in the plants, including the company unions, should meet with the management in a single body. Since these meetings were barren of significant accomplishment and since the AFL was opposed to the procedure, the ALB did not insist on the holding of similar meetings in other Fisher Body plants. Pending the working out of its scheme of proportional representation, it simply stipulated, as it had from the beginning of its existence, that in accordance with the settlement's endorsement of collective-bargaining pluralism, employers must confer with all bona fide labor organizations in their plants.[52]

Having staved off the threat of majority rule in the choice of employee representatives, GM concluded that collective bargaining could contribute to the establishment and maintenance of "sound human relations" in its factories. Collective bargaining, GM foremen were told, "can be a logical means of communication and negotiation between management and worker and in most cases can be used for the purpose of adjusting differences. Through it, a better understanding can be had, and as a result the relationship between employer and employe can be improved and a better spirit of co-operation built up."[53]

With thoughts such as these influencing its action, GM decided to formulate a policy statement on collective bargaining that would apply uniformly to its various divisions. The statement was officially adopted on August 15, 1934, and was later mailed to all GM employees with an accompanying letter from Sloan in which he declared that the corporation recognized collective bargaining as a "constructive step forward" and that it was its intention "not only to continue the idea, but to develop it."[54] In the statement itself GM declared that the principles it embodied applied throughout the corporation and that uniform policies in industrial relations were not inconsistent with the GM system of decentralized operations. GM asserted its belief that there was "no real conflict of interests between employers and employees" and no reason why the problems as between them could not be settled *within the organization*. The company wished to make it clear, however, that its endorsement of collective bargaining did "not imply the assumption by the employee of a voice in those affairs of management which management, by its very nature, must ultimately decide upon its own responsibility."

Division managers were advised that they did not satisfy the requirements of collective bargaining merely by listening to employee proposals and that they must make every effort to arrive at a satisfactory agreement. They were reminded, however, that mere membership in a labor or employee organization did not in itself establish the right of an organization to represent its members in collective bargaining; representatives for this purpose would have to be specifically chosen by the employees, and the fact of this choice would have to be established. Although employees were to be given "entire freedom with respect to the selection and form and rules of their organization and their selection of representatives," management could aid or advise an employee organization in developing plans for the benefit of employees, provided that all employees could participate in the enjoyment of these benefits on a nondiscriminatory basis. If an outside union sought to coerce employees to become members, the divisional management was to investigate and to refer the matter to GM's industrial-relations department. The possibility that coercion might be used to enroll members in an inside union was ignored.

Each division was instructed to establish a definite plan providing for a conference with an employee or group five days after the receipt of a written notice setting forth the purpose of the meeting. The division was to report to the GM executive vice-president the grievances that could not be satisfactorily adjusted. Employees or their representatives were also permitted to take their grievances to the corporation's department of industrial relations. If the latter found that company policies had been violated or that the matter in contention was beyond the scope of divisional authority, it was to refer the facts through the group executive (the car-making and parts divisions were assigned either to the car, truck, and body group or the accessory group) to the executive vice-president, who was to report on the issue to the executive committee, the chief policy-making body of the corporation.

With regard to increases and reductions in force, employment departments were instructed to make every effort to hire local employees so as to avoid "the economic and social consequences" resulting from the importation of employees for limited periods of employment. Layoffs and rehiring, of course, were to be governed by the rules of the ALB, but the management retained the "just right" to discharge a worker for cause.[55]

The GM collective-bargaining statement, the first attempt by a large employer since the NIRA had been enacted to set down its labor policies in black and white, was hyperbolically described by the *Michigan Manufacturer and Financial Record* as "the most striking labor document which has been issued in the history of American industry," and even AFL secretary Frank Morrison hailed the statement as "a step forward beyond any position the motor companies have taken heretofore."[56] It is difficult, however, to understand why the GM statement was received with so much éclat. The corporation actually conceded nothing in the realm of collective bargaining not already required of it by Section 7 (a), the President's settlement, and the interpretations of that settlement by the ALB. GM did not deviate from its commitment to collective-bargaining pluralism, and it made no effort to disguise its preference for the company union over the outside union. It failed to indicate which "affairs of management" were not subject to collective bargaining, and it provided no guidelines that would have permitted interested parties to determine which issues could be taken up with the central management, which issues with the local management. The statement, moreover, as some of GM's friends appreciated, although addressed to the corporation's employees, lacked the clarity and specificity that might have given it some appeal to the average worker.[57]

That the collective-bargaining status quo had not been altered by the GM statement was quickly indicated when Francis Dillon, the AFL's national representative in the automobile industry, wrote Sloan on November 6 requesting him, in view of the statement, to meet with accredited representatives of the organized automobile workers to negotiate a joint agreement. Sloan advised Dillon to take up his request through "established channels," but the AFL representative found no ready reception when he pursued this course. Dillon thereupon denounced the statement as "unfair" and "unworkable" and as designed to thwart the development of "free and independent" unionism.[58] Whatever the AFL's views of the document, however, GM thought sufficiently well of it to preserve it intact until some of its workers, by sitting down in several of its plants, forced it to modify some of its collective-bargaining policies.

Whether or not Dillon was correct in his assumption that the GM collective-bargaining statement was intended to forestall the growth of outside unionism in GM plants, there is no doubt that the corporation from the very beginning of the NIRA experiment was determined to resist by whatever means necessary the development of independent unionism within its domain. In practice this meant not only the construction of the representation and bargaining rights of trade-union officials in as narrow terms as were possible, as already indicated, but also discrimination against union workers, refusal to abide by the decisions of labor boards that the company regarded as pro-union, the use of espionage, and the establishment of company unions in GM plants. The company's tactics met with a high degree of success; throughout the period from the enactment of the NIRA to the inauguration of the sit-down strike the UAW was never able to organize more than a small minority of GM's automotive workers.

Given the high rate of discharge, layoff, and rehiring in the automobile industry, it is not surprising that the UAW suspected that employers took advantage of the situation to discriminate against union members. GM was the principal target of the UAW's charges from the moment the federal labor unions were established in the automobile plants until the day the sit-down strike began. Discrimination, however, was more easily charged than proved, and there was certainly a tendency among unionists to assume that when union workers were laid off or discharged for cause, the real reason was their union affiliation. But if the AFL was inclined to exaggerate the extent of the practice, the record indicates that GM did sometimes discriminate against union members in its plants. In the period before the President's settlement of March 25, 1934, the NLB's regional labor boards ruled in a few instances that GM had been guilty of discrimination, and after the ALB was established the evidence is strong that the corporation discriminated in the reemployment of strikers in St. Louis and Kansas City following the walkouts at the Chevrolet and Fisher Body plants in those two cities in April, 1934.[59]

It is, as a matter of fact, extremely difficult to determine the extent to which GM may have practiced discrimination after the ALB was established. Leo Wolman, the chairman of the board, stated flatly soon after the ALB began to function that GM was unconcerned as to whether or not its employees were active unionists. Considering the number of workers in GM plants, relatively few cases of discrimination involving GM reached the ALB for decision, and in only a small minority of these cases did the board find for the plaintiff; but since the ALB relied primarily on voluntary procedures to dispose of the discrimination complaints brought to its attention, one can assume that GM allowed cases involving alleged discrimination to go to a board decision only when the company was fairly sure that its actions would be upheld. A majority of the 1129 workers who complained of discrimination to the ALB and then were voluntarily reinstated by their employers without a hearing or decision by the board were GM employees, and one has to assume that at least some of these workers were out of work for reasons other than the seasonality of employment in the industry and the depressed state of the economy.[60]

Appearances, at all events, were more important than reality where discrimination was at issue. It mattered little really how few were the cases of actual discrimination; the fear of discrimination was sufficient reason for a worker to eschew union membership. The UAW, as a matter of fact, may have done itself a disservice by its constant iteration of the discrimination theme. It hoped to convince the automobile worker that he could gain security against arbitrary employer action only by joining the union, but the majority of the insecure automobile workers may very well have concluded that if discrimination were so prevalent, the way to protect their jobs was to avoid any identification with an outside union.

Although GM did not have as perfect a record of compliance with ALB rules and orders as the chairman of the board was prone to assert, the corporation was on the whole satisfied with the personnel of the ALB and the principles under which it operated, and it generally made a conscientious effort to conform to the board's implementation of the President's settlement. The company, however, refused to submit to the rulings of the NLB and the first NLRB, both of which were more disposed to interpret the law in the union's favor than the ALB was and both of which, significantly, sought to implement the principle of majority rule rather than proportional representation in the choice of employee representatives for collective-bargaining purposes.[61]

"Espionage," the Senate's La Follette Committee concluded after extensive hearings on the subject, "is the most efficient method known to management to prevent unions from forming, to weaken them if they secure a foothold, and to wreck them when they try their strength." The best customer of the labor spy agencies before 1936 was GM, and its expenditures for espionage, according to the La Follette Committee, "strikingly reflected" the growth of union membership.[62]

Espionage was resorted to by some GM divisions even before 1933,[63] but the practice did not become widespread in the corporation until Section 7(a) sparked the formation of federal labor unions in GM plants. The relationship between espionage and unionism in GM was nicely described to the La Follette Committee by Alfred Marshall, Chevrolet's director of personnel relations. Detective services had originally been employed, he said, to ferret out "sabotage and theft and various other irregularities in the plants to more enlighten the management and the thinking of the people in the plant. . . . Now the service grew from that time on. N.R.A. came into the picture. The strike situations arose. Plant detection became quite a problem. Union activities became quite a problem. Collective bargaining came into the picture. We went into the collective bargaining ourselves, signed the N.R.A., ... it was a natural growth. There was a very natural growth for those services."[64]

The extent to which GM resorted to labor espionage was bewildering in its complexity and frightening in its implications. The corporation employed at least fourteen detective agencies for espionage services between 1933 and 1936, and it spent approximately $1 million for this purpose between January 1, 1934, and July 31, 1936. GM was Pinkerton's National Detective Agency's largest industrial client, and the La Follette Committee characterized the contract between the company and the agency as "an astonishing document" that "stands as a monument to the most colossal super-system of spies yet devised in any American corporation."

At times, as many as two hundred spies were reporting on union activities in GM plants. Every single GM plant manager used a private detective service, and, in addition, personnel directors of the Fisher Body and Chevrolet Divisions made independent contracts for their own espionage service. Similarly, the department of industrial relations of the central office of GM had a separate contract with Pinkerton, which it concealed from the corporation's plant managers. "A weird framework of spies among spies was created that bewildered even the Pinkerton officials." "The irresistible logic of espionage," according to the La Follette Committee, "reached its final stages" when GM, fearing that its spies might be betraying its trade secrets to a competitor, employed Pinkerton agents to spy on the operatives assigned to the company by the Corporations Auxiliary Company, another detective agency that serviced GM.[65]

It was the responsibility of espionage operatives "to furnish complete information to General Motors about anything which even remotely bore upon union organizing activity." Merle Hale told the La Follette Committee that he engaged Pinkerton in March, 1934, because he wanted to know "what the outside union was doing," how large its meetings were, the arguments organizers were using to enlist members, and their criticisms of the management. A survey summary of spy reports on employees in the Flint Chevrolet plant in 1936 names an employee who was prepared to rejoin the union "if there is any activity" and states that "it would be but a simple matter to get former members to reinstate ... if an organizer would work on them." There is much information in the report about employee efforts to restrict production, and one worker is quoted as saying that he intended to buy a Ford rather than a Chevrolet because "he knew how Chevrolets were built and he would not advise anyone to buy one."[66]

A spy on the basis of his day-to-day observation of workers in a plant could detect union members in the violation of plant rules and could then supply management with information that could serve as a safe basis for their dismissal. A spy who had worked his way into the union could help to create dissension in the ranks by bringing false charges against union leaders, and as a union leader himself he could sabotage the organization by the improper performance of his duties. Playing the role of *agent provocateur*, a spy could help to destroy a union by inciting it to violence or to the calling of a premature strike.[67]

The detective agencies employed by GM used their operatives to spy on high union officials in the AFL and the UAW, including William Green, the president of the AFL, Dillon, Homer Martin, and Walter Reuther. In an effort to keep track of UAW activities, Pinkerton on several occasions maintained an office next door, or at least as close as possible, to the Detroit headquarters of the automobile workers in the Hoffman Building. When the Toledo Chevrolet plant went on strike in April, 1935, GM "flooded" Toledo with labor spies, and Hale, as he told the La Follette Committee, "tried to keep track of the union activities very definitely." Two of the officials of the striking local were Pinkerton agents, and Pinkertons mingled with the strikers on the picket line. Not only were the AFL and the local leadership placed under surveillance, but when Edward F. McGrady, the assistant secretary of labor, was sent to Toledo to mediate the dispute, Pinkerton operatives took a hotel room next to his in a vain effort to listen in on his conversations. A Pinkerton official "found nothing impossible" in the suggestion that the company's agents might have undertaken to shadow Governor Frank Murphy of Michigan during the GM sit-down.[68]

Of the various labor spies who served GM, none received more publicity than Arthur G. ("Frenchy") Dubuc. Of French-Canadian origin, he was described by a La Follette Committee investigator late in 1936 as "a nervous, excitable, and overwrought man of about 40." Dubuc, who worked in the Chevrolet plant in Flint and had once been president of the Chevrolet federal labor union, revealed himself to union officials and the La Follette Committee in the fall of 1936 and for a time afterward served, in effect, as a double agent.

While still president of the Chevrolet local, Dubuc, on June 1, 1936, was visited in his home by the director of Pinkerton's Detroit office, Arthur Lawrence Pugmire, who identified himself as Arthur L. Palmer. He seemed to know everything there was to know about "Frenchy," except, as Mrs. Dubuc remarked, " 'when he went to the toilet.' " Dubuc, in his prolix, confused, and self-serving account of his activities to a La Follette Committee investigator and later to the committee itself, claimed that he had been suspicious of espionage in the plant and had concluded that Pugmire, who appeared to be so well informed of what was going on, might somehow be the cause of the trouble. Dubuc had recently seen and been much impressed with the movie *Bullets or Ballots*, in which Edward G. Robinson, playing the role of a police officer, had worked his way into a gang of thieves in order to expose them. Seeing himself in Robinson's role and heroically exposing espionage activities in the plant, Dubuc decided by the time of Pugmire's second visit to play along with him.

Pugmire, who on his first visit had offered to pay Dubuc $60 to $65 per month for daily reports on conditions in the plant, now told "Frenchy" that he wanted reports on "communistic activities and radical elements," shop conditions, safety and theft in the plant, and "public opinion." He said that the people he represented, who he implied were "big financiers" in New York, thought poorly of unions but were not in the union-busting business. Only after Dubuc had been "hooked," a point which Pugmire conceded,[69] was he asked to supply information about union activities as such.

Dubuc was originally told to mail his reports to Detroit, but then Pugmire began to collect them weekly in person. At the end of September, 1936, after Pinkerton had been served with a subpoena by the La Follette Committee, Dubuc was instructed to make his reports by long-distance telephone. He was to call from a pay phone and to use a different phone each time that he called. He was to "cover" his conversation by mentioning all kinds of harmless items and was always to refer to himself in the third person. After he had revealed himself to the union, Dubuc fed Pinkerton information supplied him by the union. When Dubuc, whose identity was unknown to his employer, was discharged on December 30, 1936, Pugmire took him to a Flint cemetery and paid him $125 for his month's work. Previously, Pugmire had told Dubuc that if he were called to Washington to testify he should reveal nothing—"we have a perfect system, they can't pick us up." When Dubuc subsequently appeared in Washington as a La Follette Committee witness, he was paid a sum of money by a Pinkerton official not for services rendered but so as " 'not to create any ill feeling between the two of us.' " He was invited to a hotel room by agency officials and plied with liquor in an effort to influence his testimony.

Pugmire, Dubuc reported, had an "intimate knowledge" of all the personalities in the Flint labor movement, and he also professed to know everything there was to know about the UAW in general. "I have so many contacts [in the UAW]," Dubuc remembered Pugmire's saying, "that it would be impossible to organize the union; I know everything that is going on inside, I know every move, I know what everyone is doing in that union."[70]

The effect upon the worker of the knowledge that his activities were possibly being observed by a labor spy was sharply etched for the La Follette Committee in an exchange between James H. Mangold, a unionist who worked in the Flint Chevrolet No. 10 plant, and Senator Elbert D. Thomas of Utah:

> *Mr. Mangold.* They are very quiet, they are skeptic [sic] about everything you have to say, they do not take part in activities at all. If you ask them to read anything that pertains to organization, or give them any pamphlets, stuff like that, they just glance over it and throw it aside because they figure someone is looking at them.
> *Senator Thomas.* Are they afraid to talk to their neighbors?
> *Mr. Mangold.* Yes. You don't know whom you are talking to.
> *Senator Thomas.* You never take a chance?
> *Mr. Mangold.* You never take a chance.
> *Senator Thomas.* You get suspicious of everybody?
> *Mr. Mangold.* You get suspicious of everybody.

"Fear," the La Follette Committee said of the spied-upon worker, "harries his every footstep, caution muffles his words. He is in no sense any longer a free American."[71]

The La Follette Committee concluded that GM's "network of espionage" had "destroyed" the federal labor unions in the corporation's Michigan plants and had driven UAW organizing efforts "underground." What had happened to the unions in GM's Flint plants constituted, in the committee's judgment, "an epitome of the process of union . . . busting." In Flint, the committee reported, union membership had fallen from twenty-six thousand in 1934 to 120 in 1936, and the cause had been espionage: three of the thirteen members of the executive board of the amalgamated Flint local were Corporations Auxiliary Company spies, and at least two others were Pinkerton agents. The La Follette Committee, however, grossly exaggerated the consequences of espionage in GM plants. Espionage undoubtedly was a factor in limiting union membership in GM, but it was only one factor, and it would be difficult to prove that it was the most important factor. As for Flint, the committee was guilty of accepting uncritically membership figures given to it by Robert C. Travis, the UAW's director of organization in the city. Membership in Flint may have dwindled to about 120 by the summer of 1936, but it had never even remotely approached the twenty-six thousand figure in 1934, which would have constituted a very substantial proportion of GM's production workers in the city; and the decline from the 1934 totals cannot be explained solely as a consequence of labor espionage, even conceding that union organizers who came to the city in the summer and fall of 1936 found the workers in a "state of terror" and had to operate underground "like a band of conspirators."[72]

GM used the one-month interval between the service of subpoenas on Pinkerton and on the corporation "successfully and completely to gut their files of all documents connected with their use of industrial espionage." About January 20, 1937, shortly before GM officials knew they would have to testify before the La Follette Committee and by which time Anderson knew that Fisher Body and Chevrolet plant managers had been "served a notice of discontinuance,"[73] he advised all other GM plant managers to discontinue all Pinkerton services. If it were "necessary to have people in our plants to tell about it," Anderson remarked, he preferred to use GM's own employees. This statement prompted Senator La Follette to ask Anderson whether the corporation simply wished to eliminate "the third party." "That is right," Anderson replied. GM had already hired three men "to go out in the various plant grounds and circulate among business people and employees and pick up whatever information they can as regarding the attitude of employees toward the plant, the attitude of the employees toward foremen, and the attitude of foremen toward the management, and the attitude of foremen toward employees."[74]

Unlike some other large corporations, GM had not thought it necessary in the 1920's to establish company unions in its plants. The threat of outside unions posed by Section 7(a), however, caused GM, like so many other employers, to view the company union as the safest means of satisfying the statutory requirement that employees be permitted to bargain through representatives of their own choosing. "The basic aim of the Employee Associations" in the GM plants, a GM source declared, "was to provide group organization through which employe sentiment and interest could find expression and thus indirectly render the militant outside union superfluous." Knudsen stated that the corporation advocated the establishment of employee associations because "no one seemed to have anything better to advocate," but the nature of the problem from GM's point of view was more accurately stated by the supervisor of maintenance in the Delco-Remy Division, who declared when the Delco-Remy company union was being formed: "Under this N.R.A., we are going to have to organize, and if we don't organize, someone will organize us."[75]

The question of company unionism was discussed at a GM divisional managers meeting in July, 1933, and the decision was reached to set up employee associations in GM plants on a corporation-wide basis. Articles of association were drafted under Hale's direction and supplied to the various divisions, but because of GM's policy of decentralized responsibility, the divisions could and did modify these articles as they saw fit. The various plans were inaugurated in GM's Michigan plants during August and September, 1933. Employees were notified that the management would suggest a plan to them providing a method for the consideration of their mutual problems. In the elections held in GM's Michigan plants to select employee representatives under the plans, an average of 77.9 percent of the eligible voters participated, the figures ranging from 46 percent in the Fisher Body No. 23 plant in Detroit to 98 percent in the Saginaw Steering Gear plant. In Flint the percentages ranged from 59 at Buick and Fisher Body No. 2 to 86 at Chevrolet.[76]

It would be a mistake to interpret the relatively large vote in company-union elections in GM plants as an indication of worker support for the employee-representation plans. Since the plans went into effect regardless of the number of workers who voted, employees must have concluded that they might as well cast their ballots for the candidates they favored. Many workers, undoubtedly, were afraid to abstain. The voting, after all, was done in the plant under the eyes of company officials, and the foremen generally let it be known that they expected a large vote. In the Fisher Body plant in Cleveland, for example, the machines were stopped to permit the employees to vote, the foremen led the men to the polling places, and supervisory personnel looked on as the workers cast their ballots.

The fear that workers who did not vote would be discriminated against was so pervasive that the AFL national representative in the industry found it necessary to advise union members to participate in the elections. The fact that one was a member of another labor organization did not, of course, prevent him from voting in a company-union election; and in some instances officers or members of UAW locals were elected to employee-association posts. Finally, the GM plans, at the outset, tied membership in the company union to various company welfare plans and thus provided workers with an additional incentive to participate. It is not difficult in view of these considerations to understand why the NLB specifically ruled that the election of employee representatives could not in itself be interpreted as constituting employee approval of a company-union plan.[77]

The employee-association plans put into effect in GM plants[78] provided for the division of the plants into voting districts and for primary and final elections leading to the designation of one employee representative for approximately every three hundred workers (at least two representatives for each major department in Fisher Body) to serve on the employee or works council. In the Fisher Body plants all employees who met certain qualifications were eligible to vote, whereas in the other GM plants only members of the employee association could vote. This distinction was not of particular significance, however, since voting qualifications and association membership qualifications were more or less the same: to qualify for either, one had to be twenty-one years of age, a citizen, and an employee of at least ninety days service. Eligibility for election to the employee or works council was limited to nonsupervisory workers who had been with the company for one year, were at least twenty-one years of age, and were citizens. Employee representatives had to be employed in the district they represented and had to vacate their position if they left the company or were promoted to a supervisory job.

Although Charles T. Fisher claimed that Fisher Body had tried to remove the company from the employee-association plans and Knudsen declared, "If anyone can find the company in them, they will find something I haven't been able to find," management was present to some degree in all the GM plants.[79] The employee-association constitutions thus generally specified that management was to bear the cost of the plan, to provide the meeting place for employee representatives, and to pay them for time spent on employee-association business. The Chevrolet plan provided that any dues paid by association members for welfare purposes were to be matched by the company. The Fisher Body scheme specified that minutes of the works council meetings were to be kept by a secretary who would be paid by the company and that the plant manager or someone designated by him was to attend meetings of the works council, although only in an advisory or consultative capacity. The plan, moreover, could not be amended without the approval of the plant manager.

All the GM plans established a grievance procedure permitting individual employees to carry their complaints by stages, either directly or through the works council, to the top management of the division. The Chevrolet plan called for the general management of the division to discuss with a committee consisting of the chairmen of all the Chevrolet works councils those grievances that affected all plants of the division, but this procedure never seems to have been invoked.

The GM employee-association plans, sponsored and paid for by the company, not submitted to the workers for approval, and containing restrictions both on the suffrage and on office-holding, were hardly consistent with the right of self-organization, free from employer interference, supposedly guaranteed to workers by Section 7 (a) and later the National Labor Relations Act (NLRA). The NLRB was later to find that Delco-Remy had "dominated, interfered with, and contributed support to" the administration of the Delco-Remy Employees' Association,[80] and the same can safely be asserted with regard to the company-union plans in other GM plants.

Following the criticism of its employee-association plans at the NLB automobile hearings in March, 1934, and the subsequent promulgation of the President's settlement, GM arranged for the revision of the employee-association constitutions in an effort to eliminate "any appearance of management domination."[81] Despite the changes made in the constitutions, however, employee associations continued to be identified with and favored by the division managements. GM officials were still inclined to make bulletin-board space available to the company unions but not to their rivals; they sometimes permitted the company unions, but not outside labor organizations, to solicit membership on company time and company property; and some of them supplied the names and addresses of employees to the employee associations but not to the UAW.[82]

The company unions were always suspect among GM workers as management instruments, and they failed, in the final analysis, to serve the purpose the corporation had intended for them. They were not the product of "a spontaneous or militant conviction" on the part of company employees; and, as a source friendly to GM conceded, they were "difficult to maintain as going organizations without constant stimulation on the part of management even to the point of actual domination in managing and keeping them alive." When the ALB late in 1934 and early in 1935 held its plant representation elections, which admittedly were more designed to yield a result reflecting the popularity of particular individuals than the comparative strength of competing employee organizations, only 14.4 percent of GM employees who voted selected candidates they identified with the employee associations. In the major plants later to be involved in the sit-down strike, the employee associations fared less well than in GM as a whole. The vote for company-union candidates in the Cleveland Fisher Body plant was 9.3 percent; in Fisher Body No. 1, 7.7 percent; in Fisher Body No. 2, 3.6 percent; and in Flint Chevrolet, 8.2 percent. The employee-association vote was greater than the 10.1 percent of the vote received by candidates identified with the AFL, but the Federation was boycotting the elections and the company unions were not, and the candidates identified with the employee associations were probably better known than those the voters associated with the AFL.[83]

Although the company unions fell considerably short of GM's hopes for them, they were not without significance in the evolution of labor-management relations in GM. Most important, they provided a mechanism by which management could be made aware of employee grievances and by which these grievances could be adjusted. The leadership of the employee associations understandably liked to point to improvements in working conditions for which the plans were responsible, and the specific items that they cited in the areas of welfare, safety, seniority, equalization of pay differentials, and adjustment of efficiency ratings were real enough. It is, indeed, entirely likely that many of the changes in working conditions that the company unions enumerated would not have occurred when they did had not the employee-association plans facilitated the airing of employee grievances. On the other hand, it must be noted that GM, in order to increase the appeal of the associations to the workers, liked to make it appear that improvements in working conditions that would have been introduced in any event had actually been secured by the company unions. The company union was thus, in a sense, assigned the role of conveyor of good news to the workers that in the pre-1933 era the company had generally accorded to the foreman.

Like the other automobile employers, GM saw the employee-association plans primarily as a means of dealing with the grievances of the individual worker rather than with the collective problems of the employees as a whole. The individual grievances most readily adjusted were not those concerned with the bread-and-butter issues of wages and hours but rather with housekeeping questions such as sanitation and ventilation and also with alleged favoritism in the plants. "The Works Council," declared a union official who had once been an employee at the Chevrolet Gear and Axle plant, "never got around to discuss anything but broken windows and safety hazards. When some unruly committeeman had the temerity to mention wages or seniority, the company representatives promptly sidetracked the discussions into less dangerous channels."

Just as the company union provided the individual worker who was not afraid to avail himself of its procedures with a means for seeking the adjustment of his grievances, so it provided at least a modicum of experience in the bargaining process for both employer and employee. This was of some importance in a company where no negotiation of any sort between labor and management had previously taken place. At least a few workers were now given some idea of managerial problems—in some plants works council members were even permitted to take the training courses designed for supervisors—

and GM, for the first time in its history, was forced to pay some attention to the subject of labor relations and to develop a technique for dealing with employee representatives.[84]

It is, of course, difficult to determine in any precise way how many workers were deterred from joining an outside union because of the obvious management support for the company union. It is not irrelevant to observe, however, that the AFL came to regard the company union as its "greatest menace" in the automobile industry and that it protested again and again that companies like GM were using the employee associations as a means of avoiding genuine collective bargaining.[85]

The company union in the GM scheme of things receded into the background once the ALB early in 1935 began to implement a complicated election plan designed to provide each of the plants under its jurisdiction with a bargaining agency whose membership reflected the proportionate voting strength in the plant of workers who designated company-union, outside-union, or unaffiliated persons to represent them.[86] That GM, however, viewed the new bargaining agencies as simply the company unions in a somewhat different guise was indicated by the nature of the rules that it issued to govern their operations in the period before the ALB devised its own set of instructions.

GM drew up its rules for bargaining agencies without consulting them and without indicating in any way that the rules were subject to negotiation. The instructions conceded that collective negotiation of the terms of employment was one of the purposes of the new plan but categorically stated that the determination of wages and hours was the exclusive prerogative of management, a nice indication of GM's constricted view of the bargaining process. The bargaining agencies, the GM rules provided, were to meet on the company premises twice a month, once without management representatives present and once in a joint meeting with management. The procedure for handling grievances was spelled out, with provision made for referring disputes within its jurisdiction to the ALB. Representatives not employed in the plant[87] were denied access to it but were permitted entry to the conference room for bargaining-agency meetings. Individual employees who so desired could bargain separately with the management. No dues or assessments were to be levied by the bargaining agency, nor was any representative to solicit membership for an organization on the premises. The company would compensate employed representatives at their usual rate for time spent during regular shift hours on bargaining-agency business. The GM rules were not dissimilar to the instructions for bargaining agencies later issued by the ALB, and they indicate clearly the framework within which the bargaining agencies functioned in the corporation's plants.[88]

The AFL, already differing with the ALB on a variety of other matters, decided to boycott the board's elections that preceded the establishment of plant bargaining agencies. The Federation not only vigorously opposed proportional representation in collective bargaining as a scheme that tended to pit a divided labor group against a single employer, but it was also undoubtedly evident to the AFL leadership that if the ALB bargaining agencies became the accepted medium through which bargaining took place in the auto plants, the auto workers would see little point in paying dues to a labor union.[89] It was, in the end, to head off a final election in the strongly organized Toledo Chevrolet plant and hopefully to gain exclusive rather than proportional representation and a signed contract that the AFL's powerful Toledo federal labor union initiated a strike on April 23, 1935, that developed into the most significant work stoppage in the history of GM to that date.[90]

Although the Toledo Chevrolet plant employed only about twenty-three hundred workers, it was one of the most important links in the GM chain of shops at that time since it was the corporation's sole producer of Chevrolet transmissions. The Toledo local sought to spread the strike to other GM plants, but it was primarily the lack of transmissions that resulted in the idling of thirty-two thousand of the corporation's workers before the strike was settled. The threat that the strike posed to the continued production of Chevrolets, combined with the rejection of the company's terms for settlement by a two-to-one margin in a poll of employees conducted by the Department of Labor, forced GM to abandon the policy that it had insisted on at the outset of the strike and at the time of the Fisher Body strike of April, 1934, and to agree to negotiate with the local strike committee while the strike continued.

In the agreement concluded on May 12 the strikers gained neither a signed contract nor exclusive representation, but GM, in substance although not on paper, retreated somewhat from the collective-bargaining position that it had defended since the enactment of the NIRA. The memorandum of negotiations that served as the agreement ending the strike indicated that the union *as such* had had something to do with working out the terms, a point that Knudsen, as the company's chief negotiator, had previously refused to concede.

The company did not grant the union exclusive bargaining rights and simply agreed, as it had from the outset of the strike, to meet with duly accredited employee representatives on all questions at issue, but there seems to have been an "informal understanding" that GM would not seek to form a company union in the plant, that no final ALB election would be held, and that no plan of proportional representation would be introduced. This left the Toledo local, de facto, as Knudsen privately conceded, the sole bargaining agency in the plant. Quite apart from the issue of representation, GM was compelled by the strike to improve its original offer to the union with regard to wages, seniority, and the timing of jobs. Also, Knudsen promised to confer at other GM plants with the AFL national representative in the industry and the local shop committees.

The Toledo strike demonstrated that GM could be compelled to modify its position with regard to collective bargaining by a show of union force at the right place and the right time and that, if pressed hard enough, the company might even concede exclusive bargaining rights de facto however strenuously it might oppose doing so de jure. If this was a lesson of the strike that impressed some of the UAW leaders, GM, for its part, thought that it too had learned something of importance for its future from the unpleasant Toledo experience. The corporation had been caught "napping" in Toledo, but Knudsen informed a federal conciliator that it was determined "never to be in such a position again."

Knudsen believed that to strengthen GM's hand in future union negotiations, the company should carry larger inventories of semi-finished and finished products than it customarily did and that it should also adopt a policy of "diversification of plants where local union strength is dangerous." In line with this kind of reasoning, GM in the fall of 1935 removed about 50 percent of the machinery from the Toledo plant to Saginaw, Michigan, and Muncie, Indiana, thus providing the company with alternative sources of transmissions for Chevrolets.[91] But GM did not implement a policy of diversification with adequate thoroughness, and as of the end of 1936 the corporation remained vulnerable to a shut-down in a few strategic plants, a fact of which union leaders were by no means unaware.

Less than two weeks after the Toledo strike had been concluded the United States Supreme Court declared the NIRA unconstitutional and thus relieved GM of the necessity of complying any longer with the requirements of Section 7 (a). GM had been compelled by the statute and the automobile code to pay far greater attention to the human aspects of production than it ever had before, but, although somewhat shaken by the Toledo strike, it had nevertheless kept the unionization of its plants to a manageable minimum. The flight of the Blue Eagle had now come to an end, but GM realized that it could not return to the pre-1933 pattern of employer-employee relations. It assured its employees that, despite the demise of the NIRA, GM would make no blanket changes in wages and hours, it would continue to observe the ALB seniority rules, it would not alter its policy of dealing with groups of its employees or with their representatives, and it would still handle labor cases in accordance with the corporation's official 1934 statement on collective bargaining. The corporation, however, advised its plant managers that they were to provide "no direct or indirect financial aid ... to employe groups organized for collective bargaining."[92]

To the consternation of GM, the end of the NIRA did not mean the abandonment of efforts by the federal government to prescribe rules for the conduct of labor relations in American industry: on June 27, 1935, the National Labor Relations Bill was approved by both houses of Congress, and the President, who had so often sided with the automobile manufacturers in the past and who had contributed so decisively to the sidetracking of similar legislation in 1934, signed the measure into law on July 5. The NLRA reasserted the right of employees to self-organization and to bargain collectively through representatives of their own choosing. It declared that it would be an "unfair labor practice" for an employer (1) to "interfere with, restrain, or coerce" employees in the exercise of this right; (2) to dominate or to interfere with a labor organization or to contribute to its support; (3) to discriminate against employees for the purpose of encouraging or discouraging membership in a labor organization; (4) to discriminate against an employee for filing charges or giving testimony under the measure; and (5) to refuse to bargain with employee representatives. The statute established a three-man nonpartisan National Labor Relations Board to carry out its terms and authorized the board to issue orders requiring the cessation by employers of unfair labor practices and to appeal to the federal circuit courts for the enforcement of these orders.

"Convinced" by the experience of the ALB that "pluralism provoked confusion and strife, defeating collective bargaining," the draftsmen of the NLRA included a provision that specifically endorsed the principle of majority rule in the designation of employee representatives. The act authorized the NLRB to hold elections when necessary to determine whom the employees wished to represent them and lodged in the board the power to determine the appropriate unit for collective-bargaining purposes.[93]

From the time in 1934 when Senator Robert F. Wagner of New York had first sought the enactment of a measure similar to the NLRA, GM had left no doubt of its unqualified opposition to legislation of this nature that departed so widely from the principles em-

Saginaw taxicab in which four union leaders were injured, Jan. 26, 1937.

Below:
Chevrolet No. 9, Feb. 1, 1937.

Outside Fisher Body No. 2, Jan. 12, 1937.

Strike leaders arraigned before Judge Edward D. Mallory (left to right—Victor Reuther, Robert Travis, Roy Reuther, Maurice Sugar, Henry Kraus).

Picketing in Flint.

National Guard blockades Chevrolet No. 4.

Sheriff Wolcott reads the Gadola injunction.

National Guard arriving in Flint.

Dancing in front of Fisher Body No. 1, Flint.

Robert Travis (in topcoat, with hand in pocket) in one of the Flint Fisher Body plants.

Strikers react to the Flint Alliance.

Flint Fisher Body sit-downers lean out the plant windows to chat with reporters.

Roy Reuther at the mike.

Bud Simons waving from Fisher Body No. 1.

Outside Fisher Body No. 1.

Women's Emergency Brigade.

Frank Murphy and John L. Lewis.

The strike is over. Fisher Body No. 1, Feb. 11, 1937.

bodied in the President's settlement of March 25, 1934. While Wagner's 1935 bill was before the Congress, Sloan denounced it as "most unfair and one-sided" and characteristically charged that its result would be "to promote the exploitation of the American worker for the benefit of a comparatively few professional labor leaders responsible only to themselves by making the worker pay them a price for his job through the instrumentality of the closed shop." Knudsen later animadverted that the measure was "thinly disguised class legislation." Like other automobile manufacturers, he complained that the bill prohibited coercion by employers but not by unions and that its validation of the contested principle of majority rule would place employee representatives in the "hands of professionals."[94]

GM was no more inclined than the other automobile manufacturers to comply with the terms of the NLRA unless and until the United States Supreme Court upheld its constitutionality. GM foremen were advised that the company would continue to adhere to the principles set forth in its statement on collective bargaining, even though these principles were at variance at some points with the NLRA. Specifically rejecting majority rule, GM told its foremen that collective bargaining suggests "a definite group of representatives properly authorized to represent definite groups of employees" and that management would continue to afford a hearing to "anyone presenting a reasonable claim to represent the employees, and desiring to discuss matters purporting to affect them." When an NLRB trial examiner began a hearing on June 30, 1936, on complaints that GM, in violation of the NLRA, had discharged numerous employees, employed industrial spies, and dominated employee organizations at its St. Louis Chevrolet-Fisher Body plant, the corporation secured an injunction from the Circuit Court of Appeals for the Eighth Circuit restraining the NLRB from proceeding any further with the matter. The injunction was still in effect when the sit-down strikes were staged in several of the corporation's plants.[95]

Refusing to accept the principles embodied in the NLRA and assuming that its employees were "not much interested in the subject," GM continued to cherish the hope that employer-employee differences could be settled within the GM family. Plant managers were therefore advised "to encourage supervisors to have a Management viewpoint," to ascertain whether their personnel officials were likely to contribute to the improvement of labor relations, and to adopt policies and procedures regarding hiring, wages, promotions, working conditions in hot weather, and plant safety that would reduce employee discontent. Also, although the employee associations had not lived up to management expectations and although the ALB bargaining agencies had not proved to be a workable alternative and, indeed, had come to be looked upon by many employees as simply "a continuation of the company union," GM, in many of its plants, sought to supplement the activities of its foremen in dealing with grievances by keeping alive either the company union or the bargaining agency or both. These organizations, however, were, if anything, even less effective from the employees' point of view in the year prior to the sit-down strike than they had been previously. One observer partial to GM thought that the corporation had defeated the AFL with " 'kindness' " in 1935 but that it had done a poor job of adjusting grievances in 1936, which indicated that the works councils and company unions were functioning ineffectively.[96]

In the Flint Chevrolet complex no new elections were held to replace bargaining-agency officials after the ALB ceased to function, and the bitterly anti-union plant manager, Arnold Lenz, forbade works-council representatives to meet with their constituents. When James Mangold, an elected member of the works council, sought in November, 1936, to secure a readjustment of wages and the speed of operations on the cab-top line, he was "thrown out" of the divisional superintendent's office. Mangold then took his complaint to Lenz, who, Mangold later testified, "jumped all over me, bawled me out, told me if I did not drop the matter I would never have the job, that it was agitated from the outside ... that he would not have anything to do with it, and he would not tolerate such agitation." Lenz, Mangold said, "wanted men that would not say anything ... about hours and wages, he did not want any of that." When the Chevrolet works council held a general discussion of its role on January 28, 1937, while the sit-down strike was underway, the members concluded that they had "never had any bargaining with [the] Chevrolet management. We was [sic] only beggars..., with no power to demand anything that we asked for. Although we have asked for plenty..., nothing was ever granted or even promised."[97] Other works councils and bargaining agencies may have had happier relations with their plant managers than the Chevrolet works council had with Lenz, but they were equally without power and equally unable to challenge a negative reply to their requests. They were regularly reminded of their infirmity as the UAW pressed its campaign to organize GM's automotive plants.

GM sought to counter the union campaign not only by providing alternative forms of organization within its plants and by schooling its foremen in the importance of grievance adjustment but also by striving to create "a favorable public opinion" in the cities where its plants were located. In the view of the corporation's executive committee, the development of good public relations in plant cities was "just as much a responsibility of the executives as the conduct of ordinary business." The value of good public relations, according to one GM source, had been demonstrated in Dayton, Ohio, in 1935, where strenuous corporation efforts to cultivate the press and to provide for the "direct education" of the city's influential citizens had won friends for the corporation and had resulted in the publication of favorable articles in Dayton's newspapers and "cooperation" in suppressing labor union "propaganda." "If," the same source declared, "we could have our own employes and the public of our plant cities think and say 'WHAT HAPPENS TO GENERAL MOTORS HAPPENS TO ME' this would be the most effective protection against efforts to undermine our corporate goodwill."[98] GM's public-relations campaign made headway in several GM towns, but the UAW sought by the strike route to challenge the concept that what was good for GM was necessarily good for its employees.

As 1936 drew to a close GM remained as opposed as ever to outside unionism, majority rule, and the signing of written agreements with employee representatives. It was still committed to the concept of collective-bargaining pluralism, the settlement of most issues between labor and management at the plant level, and the preservation of management prerogatives. The Cleveland Fisher Body strike of 1934 and the Toledo Chevrolet strike of 1935 had demonstrated, however, that the corporation's automotive production was vulnerable to shutdowns in a few strategic plants and that, when faced with the reality of union power, GM was willing to make substantial concessions to union demands. GM, for the most part, had been able to adhere to first principles between 1933 and 1936 because the UAW had enjoyed relatively little success in organizing the corporation's plants, but the use of the sit-down strike as a labor weapon was to bring a profound and historic alteration in power relationships in GM's automotive domain and was to compel the corporation to say "yes" or at least "maybe" where before it had said "never."

The Workers

III

I

The automobile workers who manned the motor-vehicle plants of GM and its competitors were drawn from Canada and Europe, from Michigan's declining lumber industry, from the coal fields of Pennsylvania, and from the border states and the upper South. Negroes and the foreign born, especially Poles and Italians, were conspicuous among the operatives and laborers in the Detroit automobile plants, but in the citadel of GM's power, in Flint, Michigan, native-born whites predominated.[1]

Although skilled workers were originally drawn to the automobile industry from the metal, machine, and woodworking trades, they were soon swamped by workers of lesser skill: the Automobile Manufacturers Association concluded on the basis of a 1935 United States Employment Service analysis of job specifications in the automobile industry that 26.9 percent of the workers in the industry required no training at all and that only 9.8 percent required more than one year of training. Contrary to popular belief, however, workers classified as semiskilled rather than unskilled predominated in the industry. Thus, according to a study by Michigan's State Emergency Welfare Relief Commission, 55 percent of GM's 28,455 employees in Flint at the beginning of 1935 were semiskilled (buffers and polishers, filers, grinders, operatives, guards and watchmen, truck and trailer drivers), 24 percent were skilled (blacksmiths, forge and hammer men, foremen, machinists and mechanics, metallurgists, molders, cranemen, upholsterers, tool makers, diesetters, etc.), and only 8.9 percent were unskilled (furnacemen, puddlers, heaters, janitors, and laborers). The remainder of Flint's automotive employees were classified as professional (1.8 percent), clerical (9 percent), and proprietors, managers, and officials (0.8 percent).[2]

The image of the automobile worker is of the man on the assembly line, but in the 1930's, as today, less than 20 percent of the workers in the industry were engaged in assembly-line operations. The work of the remainder, however, was "no less specialized or less carefully planned," and it was the line that determined "the rhythm of production" of the industry as a whole.[3]

To the observer of the work process in one of the great automobile plants, the workers looked more like robots than human beings. A New York *Times* reporter, describing a visit to one of Flint's GM plants at the time of the sit-down strike, saw "thousands of men working, but not moving back and forth." Each man stood at his place, tools and material in hand while the line moved past him with the part on which he labored. "He performs the same operation all day or night, five days a week, the year round." The final assembly line appeared to the reporter to be "the acme of efficiency. Here the men become animated as they turn out completed cars, sixty an hour, along a U-shaped line thousands of feet long, which works like a cogwheel railway. Some of these men move spasmodically. They walk or run along the line twenty feet or so, screwing something on, trimming a fender, spraying a side with paint, or performing their own special operation. They seem to work on strings as a monster jerks them back to begin on another car."[4]

The modern industrial sociologist views the automobile worker as the most alienated of America's factory employees. Because of the minute subdivision of labor in the industry, the automobile worker on the assembly line, Robert Blauner tells us, is more subject than other workers to the alienation of "meaninglessness." Because he cannot control the pace of his work but must conform to the centralized control of production standards, he is subject also to the alienation of "powerlessness." A survey by Elmo Roper in 1947 of three thousand factory workers in sixteen different industries revealed the automobile worker to be near or at the bottom of the group in nearly every indicator of job satisfaction.[5]

The GM workers of the 1930's were doubtlessly unfamiliar with the concept of alienation, and most of them were probably less concerned with the monotony of their tasks than scholars and outside observers were inclined to believe. They expressed their dissatisfaction with their jobs largely in terms of the "speed-up," and it was the speed-up in the view of the principal participants that was the major cause for the GM sit-down strike.[6]

The speed-up meant different things to different automobile workers. It was the inexorable speed and the "coerced rhythms" of the assembly line, an insufficient number of relief men on the line, the production standards set for individual machines, the foreman holding a stop watch over the worker or urging more speed, the pace set by the "lead man" or straw boss on a non-line operation, and incentive pay systems that encouraged the employee to increase his output.[7] However expressed, the complaints of the speed-up summed up the automobile worker's reaction to the fact that he was not free, as perhaps he had been on some previous job, to set the pace of his work and to determine the manner in which it was to be performed. Since the tempo of his work was determined for him and since he did not share in that determination, it was natural for him to complain that he was being driven, that he was being compelled to produce more and more without a commensurate, if any, increase in pay.

"The essence of Flint," a New York *Times* reporter who covered the GM sit-down found, was "speed." "Speed, speed, speed—that is Flint morning, noon and night." Charlie Chaplin's film *Modern Times*, a lampoon of the speed-up, played for two months in Flint and was shown to the sit-downers themselves with considerable success. After spending six days in Flint during the sit-down strike, James Myers, the industrial secretary of the Federal Council of the Churches of Christ, reported that union and nonunion men alike reported dissatisfaction with the pace of their work. Even "conservative citizens" of Flint who opposed the strike conceded that the speed in some of GM's Flint plants was "an unreasonable strain on the workers."[8]

When the Research and Planning Division of the NRA sent its investigators to Flint late in 1934 to hear testimony regarding conditions of labor in the automobile plants, GM workers talked feelingly of the speed-up and of how GM was "getting more production with less men." A Buick worker complained, "We didn't even have time to go to the toilet. ... You have to run to the toilet and run back. If you had to ... take a crap, if there wasn't anybody there to relieve you, you had to run away and tie the line up, and if you tied the line up you got hell for it." A Fisher Body No. 1 worker told of a fellow employee who did not have time to wring out the gasoline-soaked rag he was using to clean car bodies on the line with the result that gasoline spattered back on him and he was burned from the thighs to the knees. Some time later the man's nerves cracked—"He went crazy." A straw boss in the Chevrolet plant complained, "They keep rushing me to crowd the men more." A fifty-five-year-old worker testified that the only difference he could discern between a penitentiary and the GM plant in which he worked was that the GM worker could go home at night. "It is cruel; it is absolute cruelty." An employee of the Fisher Body No. 2 plant protested that the men were pushed "right down to their last nerve."[9]

The story as dissatisfied GM workers told it was much the same at the time of the sit-down strike. A UAW official reported in November, 1936, that one punch-press operator in GM's Guide Lamp plant in Anderson, Indiana, had lost three fingers and another a thumb because of the speed at which the machines were operated. "Lets [*sic*] not forget these tragedies," he wrote, "General Motors must pay for these happenings." At GM's Janesville Chevrolet plant workers complained of foremen and straw bosses yelling at the men to hurry, of an insufficient number of men on the line, and of too few relief men.

Flint workers told Myers during the strike that the work was "more than you can do." A worker who claimed that the men had been "speeded up more all the time" during the preceding two years said, "I can hardly stand it"; and another man, whose job required him to make 115 double motions per minute with his hands, complained of the "terrible nervous strain." A Flint Chevrolet worker later recalled that "The supervisors that they chose at that time were just people with a bullwhip, so to speak. All they were interested in was production. They treated us like a bunch of coolies. 'Get it out. Get it out. If you cannot get it out, there are people outside who will get it.' That was their whole theme." William "Red" Mundale, the leader of the sit-down strikers in the Fisher Body No. 2 plant, succinctly summed up the number one complaint of the strikers: "I ain't got no kick on wages, but I just don't like to be drove."[10]

The effect upon at least some of the automobile workers of the pace of their work and the nature of their jobs was graphically revealed at the time of the sit-down strike. A New York *Times* reporter discovered that when the men began to explain their jobs, "their bodies involuntarily begin to sway in the rhythmical motions they are accustomed to make on the line." Genora Johnson described her husband, Kermit, the leader of the sit-down strikers in the Chevrolet No. 4 plant, as "a young man grown old from the speed-up. He has come home at night, when the new models were starting, so tired he couldn't eat. He was wakened the next morning with his hands so swollen he couldn't hold a fork." The wife of another striker said that she would "like to shout from the housetops what the company's doing to our men. My husband, he's a torch solderer. . . . You should see him come home at night, him and the rest of the men in the buses. So tired like they was dead, and irritable. . . . And then at night in bed, he shakes, his whole body, he shakes." Her companion agreed. "Yes, they're not men any more if you know what I mean." Her husband was only thirty, she said, but he looked like fifty, "all played out."[11]

A Buick worker, Gene Richard, described work on the assembly line at his plant. "Men about me," he said, "are constantly cursing and talking filth. Something about the monotonous routine breaks down all restraint. . . . Suddenly a man breaks forth with a mighty howl. Others follow. We set up a howling all over the shop. It is a relief, this howling." When Richard left the plant one day after working overtime, he was "so dulled" he had forgotten how he had arrived there. "I stop—ponder. I can't think where I parked my car: the morning was so long ago." "When people glide along the smooth highway, enjoying the comforts of a modern automobile," Adolph Germer wrote a friend in 1936, "little are they mindful of the human price that has been paid to make this possible."[12]

In rebutting worker complaints of a speed-up, GM insisted that speed had to be kept at a " 'reasonable' rate" if only for efficiency sake and to maintain quality. Resentment about their jobs was generally greatest among the workers during the "grooving-in" period when new models were being introduced, but, industry engineers observed, the dissatisfaction expressed reflected primarily the shift of employees from accustomed tasks and familiar tools to new tasks and new tools. GM, however, could not explain away all the employee complaints about a speed-up. The industry worked on averages in the timing of jobs, but a tempo of work that was satisfactory for the mythical average worker was too fast for some workers. Foremen were also guilty of assigning men to jobs for which they were not fitted and which placed too great a strain on them. One reporter thus pointed out just after the sit-down strike that it was by no means GM policy "to grind the workers down and cast them aside as human wreckage" but that company engineers and supervisory personnel had not always succeeded in making the necessary adjustments between men and machines.[13]

Although the men unquestionably worked hard in the auto plants of GM and its competitors, there was nevertheless a tendency among them to confuse technological improvement with the speed-up: figures cited by the workers and union representatives as evidence of increased output sometimes indicated simply the introduction of new machines that might actually have lightened the burden of labor. It was true that output per man hour in automobile, body, and parts plants—conditions, of course, varied from plant to plant—increased much more sharply between 1934 and 1936 than in manufacturing as a whole, but this undoubtedly reflected the substantial increase in volume in the automobile industry and the abandonment of share-the-work policies of depression and NRA days. By contrast, during the period 1929–34, when automotive production declined drastically and there was a good deal of part-time employment in the industry, output per man hour in automobile, body, and parts plants had increased only 1.2 percent as compared to a 14.3 percent increase in manufacturing as a whole. During these years, as GM pointed out, there was actually an increase in the average number of hours required to produce a Chevrolet body and a Chevrolet car.[14]

The complaints of GM workers about the speed-up and the nature of their jobs were not, however, to be answered by the citing of statistics, however relevant, for the reaction to their work situation of the company's employees in Flint, Cleveland, Anderson, and elsewhere was as much psychological as it was physical. When they struck GM and joined the UAW, they were, in a sense, expressing the resentment of men who had become depersonalized, who were badge numbers in a great and impersonal corporation, cogs in a vast industrial machine. "Where you used to be a man, . . . now you are less than their cheapest tool," a Flint Chevrolet worker complained to Senator Robert La Follette during the strike. Had the corporation treated its workers "with a little respect," another GM worker later stated, it could have forestalled the union for years. "We were treated like a bunch of dogs in the shop and we resented it so much that the people with principle . . . were grabbing for anything to try to establish themselves as men with a little dignity. . . ." "The world is surprised to learn," a reporter declared shortly after the strike was over, "that these robots are human beings after all."[15]

Closely related to the commonly heard complaint of the speed-up was the charge emanating from some of the workers and the UAW that GM and the other automobile companies callously displaced their blue-collar employees when they reached the age of forty or so. "We draw our old age pension at the age of forty instead of sixty five," a Flint Chevrolet worker wrote the President during the sitdown strike. Earlier, a forty-five year old worker in Fisher Body No. 2 lamented, "It seems as though every year they try to see how quick they can kill you and get you out of there."[16]

It seems likely that the automobile manufacturing companies preferred to hire young men for their production lines, but the allegations of the deliberately premature superannuation of automobile workers do not seem to have been well founded, at least insofar as GM was concerned. The percentage of GM workers aged forty or over actually increased between 1930 and 1933 at a time when the corporation could easily have discriminated against older workers had it desired to do so. As of January, 1935, approximately 21 percent of GM's Flint employees were more than forty-four years of age, which did not differ too greatly from the 23 percent who were forty-five or older among the remainder of the city's gainful workers, most of whom were engaged in nonmanufacturing operations. GM reserved special jobs for men over forty, and it was the men in this age group who seem to have been the best paid and the most regularly employed among the corporation's hourly workers. It was, perhaps, the rural background of so many auto workers, which conditioned them to think of physical decline as a rather slow process, that caused them to exaggerate the extent to which workers were prematurely superannuated in the automobile industry.[17]

Second only to the speed-up among the grievances of the automobile workers was the irregularity of their employment, a result of the industry's reliance on new annual models as a means of stimulating demand for passenger vehicles. Irregular employment, an important source of job dissatisfaction, reduced the worker's loyalty to his employer and contributed materially to his profound sense of insecurity.

However serious the problem of irregular employment was in the automobile industry in the boom years of the 1920's, it became even more critical after 1929 when automobile employment contracted and automobile workers could no longer find other work during periods of layoff. For every year from 1930 to 1936 the layoff rates and total separation rates in the automobile and body industry and the automobile parts industry were substantially above the comparable figures for manufacturing industries as a whole. During the period September 4, 1933 — September 4, 1934, almost 40 percent of GM's 132,169 hourly employees worked fewer than twenty-nine weeks, and more than 56 percent worked fewer than forty weeks.

The fall introduction of models beginning in 1935 helped to make automobile employment somewhat more regular than it had been during the preceding several years, and GM, as we have seen, was able to report that 85 percent of its hourly rated employees had remained on the company's payroll throughout the year in 1936. This still meant, however, that twenty-four thousand of the company's hourly workers had been irregularly employed during the year, and it is likely that many of the remainder continued to view their future employment with some uncertainty. "The fear of being laid off," a church publication that was seeking to explain the GM sit-down strike declared, "hangs over the head of every worker. He does not know when the sword will fall."[18]

The GM worker was concerned not only about "when" the sword would fall but upon whom it would fall. GM continued to apply the ALB seniority rules even after the NIRA lapsed, but since seniority under these rules was determined not only on the basis of the length of service of the employee but also on his marital status, the number of his dependents, and the nature and degree of his skill, the workers tended to be uninformed or confused regarding their position on the seniority list; and, at all events, they knew that the corporation was under no obligation to pay any attention to such lists. The automobile workers were inclined to believe that it was the foreman who really determined the order of layoff and rehiring and that favoritism played a large part in his decision as to who worked and who did not. "If he happened to like you," a unionist who had worked at the Chevrolet Gear and Axle plant later declared, "or if you sucked around him and did him favors—or if you were one of the bastards who worked like hell and turned out more than production—you might be picked to work a few weeks longer than the next guy." Under the circumstances, the auto workers were disposed to look with favor on the idea of seniority based on length of service alone.[19]

The irregularity of employment in the automobile industry meant that the well-publicized high hourly wages of the auto workers did not necessarily become translated into equally high annual earnings, which persuaded the UAW federal labor unions to look favorably upon the idea of the guaranteed annual wage. As a Chevrolet worker told an NRA investigator late in 1934, "Of course, we make enough to live on while we are working, but we don't work enough time." Thus during the year beginning September 4, 1933, hourly employees on GM's payroll all year averaged $1197 for the year, but 61.7 percent of the company's hourly rated workers received less than $1000. During 1936 the steadily employed workers at GM averaged $1541, but 15 percent of the hourly rated employees earned less than $1150, and average earnings for hourly workers were probably between $1200 and $1300.[20]

How well one could live in 1936 on an income of between $1200 and $1300, which was above the $1184 average for full-time employees in all industries, is difficult to say, although it is relevant to note that a Works Progress Administration study estimated that a maintenance level budget for a family of four in Detroit as of March, 1937, was $1434.79. Hartley W. Barclay, the editor of *Mill and Factory*, thought that an income of $150 a month was quite adequate for a Flint auto worker, but most Flint auto workers received less than this in 1936. On the other hand, Barclay, who spent several days in Flint in January, 1937, did not detect any "starvation standards of living" and noted that the auto workers saved money, that some of them owned small businesses, that their income was supplemented by working wives, that retail sales in the city had reached record proportions in the last months of 1936, and that the auto workers and their children were well dressed. What he did not say was that some GM workers in the city lived in hovels and shacks without central heating or indoor plumbing.[21]

Although there was little complaint from GM workers about their hourly wages, there was a good deal of dissatisfaction among them with the methods of wage payment used in some of the corporation's plants. In 1934 and 1935 many automobile plants had abandoned the complicated systems of compensation that had come into vogue in the industry in the 1920's and had shifted to straight hourly rates. Incentive pay systems, however, continued to be used in many plants, including Fisher Body No. 1 and No. 2 in Flint, where individual and group piece rates determined the workers' pay above a guaranteed minimum. Barclay, an experienced industrial engineer, advised Harry W. Anderson after extended conversations with Fisher Body strikers that the workers in these plants objected to many features of their system of pay. They complained that they did not receive individual tickets specifying the going rate but were simply permitted to examine the sheet of time standards, which many of them did not understand and which left them uncertain as to their actual daily earnings. The rates, furthermore, were set in fractions (11.32 cents per hundred operations, for example), with the result that some of the men, who had problems with multiplication, found it difficult to determine the pay that was due them.

In so far as group piece rates were used, the abler Fisher Body workers complained that they had to "drive" the lazier workers or slow their own pace, neither of which alternative appealed to them. Experienced workers also thought that there should be a higher guaranteed minimum for them during the grooving-in period for operations similar to those on the previous model, and they objected to being placed on apprentice rates when the model changeover eliminated their previous jobs and they had to be broken in on new tasks. Finally, since perhaps 80 percent of the work on a Fisher body in Flint at that time was in the form of "hard manual labor," workers in the No. 1 and 2 plants could increase their earnings under the piece-rate system only at a considerable physical cost as compared to piece-rate workers—those at Flint Chevrolet for example—whose tasks involved the use primarily of machine power rather than human power.[22]

Barclay, who advised GM that there was "a great deal" to the workers' complaints regarding piece rates, not only thought that GM would have to revise its pay system in the Flint Fisher Body plants, but he also concluded after speaking to many of the workers that the nine-hour day in effect at these plants at the time of the strike was "too heavy a schedule to maintain without completely exhausting the workers." He thought that some of the men were suffering from "occupational psychosis" resulting from fatigue and that they even had encountered domestic difficulties because of their tiredness after work. The union at the time was pressing for a thirty-hour week, but Barclay concluded, and he was probably correct, that the men would have been satisfied with a forty-hour standard.[23]

The grievances expressed by automobile workers before the GM sit-down strike were of long standing and were not peculiar to the conditions of labor in 1936. The strike, however, as Professors George

W. Hartmann and Theodore W. Newcomb have indicated in their psychological interpretation of industrial conflict, is "a relatively brief and traumatic episode in the natural history of industrial conflict. What is really important psychologically is the long and continued process of thwarting and frustration to which human beings are subjected during the work processes of modern manufacturing. Accumulated tensions and suppressions mount until the threshold of restraint is reached and an explosion occurs."[24] By the end of 1936 that "threshold of restraint" had been reached by many GM workers.

II

With the exception of some former coal miners, the workers who were drawn to the automobile plants of Michigan and elsewhere during the first three decades of the twentieth century had at least one characteristic in common: they were almost entirely innocent of trade unionism in so far as their personal work experience was concerned. With wages high and jobs abundant, they appear to have been reasonably content with their lot before 1929, but depression and the opportunity provided by the New Deal for unionism and the airing of employee grievances revealed that working conditions were far from perfect in the automobile plants in the opinion of many automobile workers and that there were employee grievances upon which union organizers could seek to capitalize. Unionism, however, did not come easily to the automobile industry, and up to the eve of the GM sit-down strike the paid-up union membership in the plants of GM and its competitors constituted but a small minority of the production workers in the industry.

Organizational interest in the automobile workers was evidenced during the early years of the twentieth century by the Carriage and Wagon Workers' International Union (CWW), but like the UAW at a later date it was to discover that the AFL's craft unions would not permit the invasion of their claimed jurisdiction over some of the workers in the automobile plants even though they had made little if any effort to organize these workers themselves. Anxious to expand its small membership, the CWW petitioned the AFL in 1910 for a grant of jurisdiction over all workers in the automobile industry, and it was rechartered the next year as the Carriage, Wagon and Automobile Workers' International Union (CWAW). The AFL, however, prodded by the interested craft unions, ordered the CWAW in 1914 to abandon efforts to organize automobile workers falling within the jurisdiction of other national and international unions and to strike the word "automobile" from its name; but since the membership of the union by that time was made up largely of automobile workers, it refused to comply with this order and was consequently suspended from the Federation on April 1, 1918. It was then reorganized as the United Automobile, Aircraft and Vehicle Workers of America (UAAVW). Although primarily an organization of skilled craftsmen, particularly trimmers, painters, and woodworkers, it was "dedicated," it proclaimed, to "the principle of Industrial Unionism."

Prospering as the result of World War I, the UAAVW attained a claimed membership of forty-five thousand in 1920. The strongest unit in the organization was the Detroit local, which had succeeded in making some headway in Fisher Body, but the membership, for the most part, was concentrated in the small custom body shops in the East, where skill remained a factor. The recession of 1920–21, a disastrous strike against Fisher Body in Detroit in 1921, the introduction of lacquer in the automobile paint shops, and the resistance of the employers contributed to the disintegration of the union in the 1920's and made it an easy prey for Communist penetration.[25]

The Communists, who had initiated organizing work in the Detroit auto factories in the middle 1920's, gained control of the Detroit local of the virtually moribund UAAVW in the late 1920's, converted the national organization into the Auto Workers Union (AWU), and affiliated it in 1929 with the Trade Union Unity League (TUUL), which had just been established by the Communists as a center for dual unionism. Its membership probably not in excess of one hundred, the AWU was little more than a paper union when it joined the TUUL.[26]

The advent of the depression presented the AWU with an opportunity to spread its doctrine among the automobile workers, to urge them to organize, and to seek their support by leading their strikes, organizing hunger marches, and agitating for relief. At least one astute student of the automobile industry concluded in 1932, before the rules of the game were somewhat altered by the New Deal, that the Communists had made "a profound impression" on the auto workers by their "continuous and strenuous activity," and he predicted that if the industry were to be organized from the outside the Communists would be responsible.[27]

The AWU, however, was never able to enroll more than a handful of members. Despite its appeal that it was the only "militant union" in the industry and that, in contrast to the AFL, it was committed to industrial unionism and control by the rank and file, the automobile workers refused to enlist under its red banner. The result was that the Communists increasingly directed their main attention in the industry away from the AWU and toward the building up of opposition sentiment within the UAW and the Mechanics Educational Society of America (MESA), an independent organization of tool and die makers. In December, 1934, the Communists officially dissolved the AWU and instructed its members to join the UAW if they were production workers and the MESA if they were tool and die makers. At the time this decision was made there were only 450 members in the twenty-one locals of the AWU, and only a handful of even this small number were actually employed in automobile factories. Since the former AWU members, unlike most automobile workers, were, however, unionists of some experience and considerable dedication, their addition to the Communists and fellow travelers who had previously enrolled in the UAW gave the Communists a nucleus of adherents within that organization that was out of all proportion to the small numbers involved. Although they had failed to sustain an automobile workers union of their own, the Communists, by boring from within, were able to gain positions of power inside the UAW, and they were to play an important part in the GM sit-down strike.[28]

Insofar as strikes had occurred in the automobile industry after 1920 and before the NIRA was enacted they were largely spontaneous in character, although the AWU and the Communists were sometimes called in by the inexperienced workers after their walkouts to provide needed leadership. These strikes, almost without exception, were precipitated by suddenly announced changes in working conditions, particularly in piece rates. Nearly all the strikes occurred in body factories, with Fisher Body the principal target. Discontent had been building among the more skilled workers in the body plants as machinery downgraded their skills and reduced their pay, and yet their consciousness of skill, however slight, persuaded them that they were not without bargaining power.[29]

The most significant of the Fisher Body strikes in the pre-New Deal era, and one that was not without some relationship to the GM sit-down strike, occurred in July, 1930, among workers in the Flint Fisher Body No. 1 plant, the most important plant involved in the 1937 strike. The strike began on July 1 when two hundred metal finishers spontaneously quit work because of a reduction in piece rates. Advised by AWU and Communist representatives from Detroit, some of the strikers marched through the plant the next day and persuaded the rest of the seventy-six hundred workers to join the walkout. The prominent advisory role played by the Communists after the strike had begun enabled the police and the management to charge that the whole affair was the product of Communist and foreign agitation, which presumably justified the harshest repression. Reinforced on the third day of the strike by the Michigan State

Police, the city police dispersed the strikers' picket lines, used horses to ride down demonstrators, attempted to break up a mass parade of strikers to the Buick plant, arrested strike leaders and their AWU and Communist allies, seized the local AWU membership rolls, and interfered with the strikers' freedom of assembly by forcing them to meet outside the city and on one occasion chasing them beyond the Genesee County line. Defeated, the strikers returned to work on July 9. They were promised that there would be no discrimination against them, but their leaders were subsequently let go by the management for one reason or another.[30]

Several of the workers later involved in the GM sit-down received a demonstration in the 1930 Fisher Body strike of what a strike on the outside might mean in a city where company and municipal authorities were so closely allied. Jack Palmer, who participated in the strike and then subsequently transferred to the Chevrolet plant, recalled many years later how the police had raided a strikers' meeting held in an open field and how the men had fled "like a bunch of scared rabbits because we did not want to get run down by horses." He remembered that there was no talk of unionism among the workers following the collapse of the strike.[31]

Although the AFL had been able before the advent of the New Deal to enroll a few craftsmen in the automobile industry— principally pattern makers, metal polishers, and molders—it had failed altogether to organize the semiskilled and unskilled production workers who constituted the bulk of the labor force in the automobile and automobile parts plants. Following the expulsion of the CWAW in 1918 and prior to 1933 the Federation on two occasions projected organizing campaigns in the industry, but its efforts were more rhetorical than anything else and were singularly unsuccessful.[32]

When it became clear that the National Industrial Recovery Bill would become law, President William Green of the AFL called the presidents of the Federation's national and international unions to a conference in Washington on June 6 and 7, 1933, to formulate plans for the organization of the unorganized and to take advantage of the opportunity afforded by Section 7 (a). It was at this conference that the decision was reached to launch an organization campaign in the automobile industry. To head the drive, which was to center in Detroit, Green selected William Collins, an AFL organizer who had previously represented the Federation in the motor city. Collins served as the AFL's national representative in the automobile industry until the end of September, 1934, and was then succeeded the next month by Francis Dillon, who had been working as an organizer in the industry since February.[33]

The automobile workers who responded to the AFL's plea to join the union were placed in federal labor unions chartered directly by the Federation. One federal labor union was generally provided for each automobile plant, although a single local sometimes served Chevrolet and Fisher Body workers in the same city (Chevrolet and Fisher Body production was often carried on in the same plant); and in Toledo, for no logical reason, there was only one federal labor union for all of the city's automobile plants. Altogether, the AFL had chartered 183 federal labor unions in the industry by the time an international union of automobile workers was created in August, 1935.[34]

The AFL was never able to secure more than a beachhead of unionism within the automobile industry prior to the time that the UAW decided to cast its lot with the fledgling Committee for Industrial Organization (CIO). For this failure there were many reasons.[35] Some of the problems the AFL faced were the result of its use of the federal labor union as the means by which to enroll auto workers in the Federation. In contrast to the trade autonomy that normally prevailed in the AFL, federal labor unions were regarded as "wards" of the Federation, and the AFL, in theory at least and sometimes in practice, exercised direct control over most of their activities. This naturally raised the question of the rights of the rank and file, which plagued the AFL almost to the day the UAW joined the CIO.

Also, although federal labor union members paid dues of only $1 per month, thirty-five cents of this sum was sent to the AFL, whereas the national and international unions paid a per capita tax of only one cent per member per month. Moreover, when a federal labor union went on strike, it learned that it was not entitled to benefits from the AFL defense fund, despite its per capita tax, unless it had been in continuous good standing for one year. President Green might argue that the AFL performed "tremendous services" for its federal labor unions, but some auto workers felt that they had received much too little from the Federation in return for their per capita tax. "We have fought our fight alone," the president of the strong Bendix local complained to Green in the spring of 1934.

Since the federal labor unions had a direct relationship to the AFL but, at the outset, no relationship at all to one another, the AFL was faced with the problem of coordinating their efforts. Collins tried to create some sense of unity in Detroit by establishing a Detroit District Council to represent the city's automobile federal labor unions, but not until June, 1934, was a National Council set up for the automobile unionists and not until August, 1935, was an international union of automobile workers created. The result was that many of the federal labor unions developed as virtually autonomous organizations and were disinclined to consult interests other than their own in determining strategy and tactics in the struggle to unionize the automobile workers. The consequences of this lack of centralized control were to become evident as the UAW organizing drive gathered force in the closing months of 1936.

Since the UAW federal labor unions were free to accept any plant worker not already in an AFL union, they were temporarily at least of an industrial-union character. Inasmuch as the federal labor unions were regarded as a recruiting device for the trade unions, however, the likelihood was that the skilled workers in these locals would at some future date be parceled out among the craft unions. The craft unions gave little indication that they had any real desire to organize the bulk of the automobile workers—the Metal Polishers, one of their members recalled, "wanted to build a fence around themselves even in the big plants"—but they insisted that their jurisdictional rights be respected.

Green was aware that the relentless technological progress in the automobile industry had "practically wiped out" craft lines, but as president of the AFL he had no choice but to advise AFL organizers that the jurisdictional rights of the International Association of Machinists and other internationals would have to be observed. He knew, however, that this was easier said than done. "It is impossible for us," he told the AFL Executive Council, "to attempt to organize along our old lines in the automobile industry. . . . I must confess to you that I am come, you will come, and all of us will always come face to face with the fact, not a theory but a situation actually existing, that if organization is to be established in the automobile industry it will be upon a basis that workers employed in this mass production industry must join an organization en masse. We cannot separate them." But Green's views were not the views of the majority of the Executive Council, and the AFL president, in the end, had neither the strength nor the influence to make his ideas prevail over those of his craft-minded colleagues.

To the members of the federal labor unions, there was always the possibility that the craftsmen in their midst would be transferred to one of the national or international unions. "We face our work here [Detroit]," Collins reported to Green, "with more temerity so far as the Machinists are concerned than we do in facing the united hostility of the Employers' Association." One UAW leader protested to the AFL president that craft-union jurisdictional claims constituted "one of the greatest hindrances of organization" and warned that if the attempt were made to place auto workers in the craft unions, it would "kill" auto unionism. The attempt was made, and although it did not "kill" auto unionism, it reduced substantially the AFL's chances of keeping the auto workers within its ranks.

The failure of the AFL to make an all-out effort in its campaign to organize the auto workers also helps to explain the meagerness of its accomplishment. The Federation, a member of the National Council of United Automobile Workers later declared, "could have organized all the automobile workers by the middle of 1935 if they had sent the right number of people in to do it. And the people with the right kind of orders to do it." "It was not easy, believe me," the leader of the sit-down strike in the Cleveland Fisher Body plant declared, to secure AFL help in the early days. "They did very little. . . ." Green claimed in 1936 that the AFL had expended almost $250,000 on its federal labor unions in the industry between July 1, 1933, and October 1, 1935, but this sum exceeded the per capita tax paid by the automobile locals by only $67,000, and, however large it may have appeared at the time, it was insufficient considering the magnitude of the job confronting the Federation and the opportunity that the New Deal presented.

The AFL was particularly defective in the leadership that it supplied to the auto industry. Although the handful of organizers the Detroit office engaged were drawn from the automobile plants, the organizers the AFL assigned to the industry, including Collins and Dillon, knew precious little about shop conditions even though they were familiar with the "technique of joint relations." "We had Organizers that came into our plant," one federal labor union president declared, "who did not know what the hell the automobile industry was, they didn't know one thing about it."

Neither Collins nor Dillon had the force or the imagination necessary to lead a campaign so fraught with difficulties as the AFL's organizing drive in the automobile industry. Both men reflected in their attitude the discouraging experience of the AFL in the 1920's, when the Federation had thought it necessary to shift "from militancy to respectability."[36] They believed that the labor movement, "above all else, must move cautiously," and both of them sought to further union ends by enlisting government support and seeking to convince the employers that the UAW was a "good" union rather than by encouraging militant action on the part of the workers themselves. This cautious, almost timid approach to automobile unionism limited the effectiveness of the AFL in the automobile industry and lessened its appeal to the auto workers.

Both Collins, who told the auto manufacturers, "I never voted for a strike in my life," and Dillon, who was afraid of "making a mistake which would bring to our people disaster," backed away from the use of the strike weapon. Such strikes as were called in the industry during the NRA era were called by the federal labor unions themselves, often without the knowledge and generally without the advance approval of the AFL. Conscious of its limited membership in the industry and of the generally depressed state of the economy, the AFL hesitated to risk a showdown with the automobile manufacturers in the economic field and was reluctant to support or to expand strikes initiated by its federal labor unions. One can well understand the caution of the AFL, even though the demand for automobiles was on the upswing, but the Federation was too timid for its own good. Neither Collins nor Dillon seemed to realize that the auto workers, like workers in general, were more likely to join a union under strike conditions than otherwise, that "Once they were released from the plant," to quote a UAW member, "they felt their own freedom." The AFL was unquestionably wise to recognize, at long last, the crucial role that government could play in the organization of the unorganized, but as the auto workers were to demonstrate when they broke away from the Federation, bold action in the economic field was a necessary supplement to government assistance in winning the day for unionism against the giants of the industry.

The nature of the labor force in the automobile industry was a further deterrent to organization. The overwhelming majority of the automobile workers were not only without the personal experience or the family background in trade unionism that might have made them susceptible to the appeal of organizers, but all too many of them were easily replaceable because of their lack of any significant degree of skill. The presence of a considerable number of Negroes and foreign born in the automobile plants, particularly in the Detroit area, also posed a problem for the AFL, which for a variety of reasons found it difficult to enlist their interest in the UAW.

Finally, and probably of greatest importance, the AFL had to contend with the fear engendered among the automobile workers by their awareness of the implacable opposition of their employers to independent unionism in the industry. Recognizing that they were expected by management to join the company union in their plant rather than the UAW, suspicious that there were spies everywhere in the industry, worried at a time when there was much less than full employment that, if identified with an outside union, they might be discriminated against in layoffs and rehiring or dismissed altogether, the automobile workers understandably hesitated to commit themselves to a cause so fraught with danger for their livelihood. Collins, from the start, recognized that the fear that possessed the workers was a major obstacle in his path, and three years later organizers in the industry were still being told that fear was "the one great deterrent to organization."[37]

Insofar as AFL organizing efforts met with success prior to the establishment of the international union in the industry, it was largely in the plants of the independent automobile manufacturers and the automobile parts plants. Independents like Nash, Studebaker, and White were in a far more precarious financial and market position than GM, Ford, and Chrysler were and hence were less able to resist union pressure. The parts companies were also vulnerable since many of them felt that they could not afford prolonged labor strife lest their inability to deliver their products on schedule would cause them to lose business to their numerous competitors or to the main plants themselves.

The AFL fared better in its organizing efforts outside Michigan than inside the state. This was in good measure because the power of the Big Three was concentrated in Michigan, but it also reflected the fact that several of the non-Michigan locals, removed from the restraining influence of the AFL's national representative in the industry, were considerably more militant than their Michigan counterparts. This greater daring not only brought them occasional success in their struggles with management but also won them adherents among the automobile workers in the plants that they were seeking to organize.[38]

As the AFL at the end of June, 1935, prepared for the forthcoming constitutional convention of the automobile workers, the total paid-up membership of the UAW federal labor unions was 22,687, which was approximately 5.4 percent of the 421,000 wage earners employed in the automobile industry at that time. The paid-up membership figures were, to be sure, a rock-bottom indication of UAW strength, but they reveal nevertheless how inadequate were the results of the AFL's organizing efforts in the industry. Of the UAW's paid-up members, only 4481 were GM workers, which meant that less than 3 percent of GM's hourly workers had embraced the organization. The bulk of the GM membership, moreover, was located outside Michigan: the five Flint locals had only 757 paid-up members, the four GM Detroit locals only 423 members, and the remaining GM locals in Michigan only sixty-five members. The UAW as a whole had only 2197 paid-up members in all of Detroit and a mere 1493 additional members in the rest of Michigan.[39]

Insofar as automobile workers were organized in Detroit, they belonged principally to unions not affiliated with the AFL: the Associated Automobile Workers of America (AAWA), the Automotive

Industrial Workers' Association (AIWA), and the MESA. The AAWA, which had been formed by several UAW federal labor unions that had seceded from the AFL in the late summer of 1934, had achieved a position of power in the plants of the Hudson Motor Car Company; the AIWA, which developed out of the ALB bargaining agency in the Dodge plant, was building its strength primarily in the Chrysler plants in Detroit; and the MESA, formed early in 1933, had the core of its membership in Detroit's numerous job shops and parts plants. The combined membership of the three independents was probably somewhat greater in the summer of 1935 than the total membership of the UAW was.[40]

In their efforts to provide organization for the automobile workers between 1933 and 1936, the conservative leaders of the Federation in the industry came increasingly into conflict with militant and sometimes radical local leaders and members who disagreed with the AFL on strike policy, the proper time to establish an international union of automobile workers, and the jurisdiction that should be assigned to this international. The character of this conflict lessened the appeal of the AFL to the automobile workers, gave the "progressives," as they liked to call themselves, the leadership of the UAW once it gained full control of its own affairs, led the UAW to affiliate with the CIO, and set the tone for the organization campaign in the automobile industry that culminated in the GM sit-down strike at the end of 1936.

The first major difference between the AFL and the UAW militants over the use of the strike weapon occurred in March, 1934, when the Flint Fisher Body No. 1 and No. 2, Buick, and Hudson locals were threatening a strike that might have spread throughout the industry. Collins, however, who was convinced that the auto workers lacked the necessary funds and leadership to stage a successful walkout against the giants of the industry, had no intention of allowing the strike to develop and simply used the threatened dispute to secure the government intervention that led to the formulation of the President's settlement of March 25, 1934.[41]

Collins' view was not, however, shared by the officers and rank and file of the federal labor unions involved, who were deadly serious about striking. The possibility of a large-scale strike, as a matter of fact, had served as a decided fillip to union membership, which reached its high point for the entire NRA period in that month. The most spectacular gains were recorded in Flint. A federal conciliator reported that he had been "reliably informed" by union officials, who were probably confusing enthusiasm for the union with actual membership, that a substantial majority of the workers in the Chevrolet,

Buick, and Fisher Body plants in Flint had joined the union, and he had concluded that "if this situation breaks it will involve a tremendous number of people."[42]

Assuming that they would have been victorious in a showdown battle with GM and the other auto companies, which is problematical, the inexperienced automobile unionists were dissatisfied with the character of the President's settlement and then with its failure to bring any immediate improvement in employer-employee relations in the industry. UAW vice-president Leonard Woodcock, who was in Flint the night the men heard of the settlement, recalls that they felt "a deep sense of betrayal" and began to tear up their membership cards. As the paid-up membership of the UAW dwindled after March—the Flint membership had fallen to 528 by October—many automobile unionists concluded that they had made a fatal mistake in failing to strike and in agreeing to the settlement. "That day," Delmar Minzey, the president of the AC Spark Plug local and later the president of the amalgamated Flint local, privately informed Dillon late in November, "was the turning point of our Unions. . . . Where last March we had a splendid union . . . we [now] have only a handful of the faithful. . . . The morale of our people is broken and where there was hope there is now only fear and despair."[43]

Less than a month after the promulgation of the President's settlement, on April 22, 1934, the Cleveland Fisher Body local went out on strike. Before taking this action, the local leadership had written to other GM locals urging a united strike. This plea was answered, in a sense, by Fisher Body and Chevrolet unions in St. Louis, Kansas City, and North Tarrytown, all of them at that time outside the AFL, but the Federation discouraged a favorable response by its own automobile federal labor unions, thinking that they were not ready for combat. Since the Cleveland Fisher Body plant made all the stampings for two-door Chevrolet models and some parts for all Chevrolet bodies and the Fisher Body No. 1 plant in Flint made all the bodies for Buick and vital parts for Pontiac and Oldsmobile bodies as well, the Federation might conceivably have allowed the latter plant at least to join Cleveland on strike and thus, hopefully, to force GM to terms. Rather than follow this strategy, however, the AFL leadership decided to use the Cleveland strike to secure a conference with the top GM and Fisher Body management.

When GM insisted on the termination of the Cleveland strike as a precondition of the conference, Collins and Green did not demur. Regarding a conference with GM and a demonstration of the Federation's conservatism as of greater long-range significance for the cause of automobile unionism than a continuation of the Cleveland strike, of whose ultimate success they were dubious in any event, they persuaded the Cleveland federal labor union to call off its walkout. "As rank and file," one of the local leaders declared shortly thereafter, "we built up the membership of the local, we pulled the strike and closed the plant. That was our part of the job, and we did it. After that it was the job of the higher officers of the union to use the situation we had brought about to the best advantage to get concessions from the company. If they bungled their part of the job, that was our hard luck."[44]

When the GM-Fisher Body summit conference of April 30–May 2, 1934, and the subsequent local conferences at individual Fisher Body plants did not materially alter the industrial-relations status quo in GM,[45] UAW progressives concluded that the Federation leaders had indeed "bungled their part of the job." The militants, as it turned out, were eventually able to put into effect themselves the strike strategy that the AFL leadership had rejected in April, 1934.

When the automobile manufacturing code was renewed on January 31, 1935, in a manner that angered the AFL,[46] there was talk that the Federation would resort to the strike weapon to indicate its displeasure with the administration and to wrest from the automobile manufacturers the improvements in the terms of employment that it had failed to incorporate in the code. Late in February, 1935, the National Council of the UAW instructed the auto locals to designate Green as their representative in bargaining with the auto companies and to take strike votes authorizing the AFL president to call a strike if the automobile manufacturers refused to accede to demands to bargain collectively. Green's efforts to negotiate with GM and the other auto concerns proved unproductive, and since nearly all the UAW locals had voted in favor of a strike, the stage seemed set for the much talked about auto work stoppage.

Among the UAW federal labor unions none was more insistent than the Cleveland locals upon the calling of a "united general strike" in the automobile industry. After the management of Cleveland Fisher Body had rejected the demands of the UAW local in its plant, President Louis Spisak wired Green late in February, "We are depending on you for immediate action with General Motors. We are ready." The Fisher Body local somewhat later not only urged the National Council to set a strike date but, ignoring the AFL leadership, sent delegates to the GM locals in Flint to promote joint strike action.[47]

It seems likely that Green never had any intention of permitting an automobile strike to develop. The auto workers "wanted to engage in a general strike," he later told the Executive Council, "but I stopped that. I said, you are in no position to engage in a general strike." Green's caution is understandable in view of the UAW's limited membership at that time—the paid-up membership at the end of January was only 18,412—and the weakened condition of the federal labor unions in the Detroit main plants and in GM's Flint stronghold. The AFL leadership, however, once again underestimated the potentiality of the strike as an organizational device. Some of the UAW leaders, indeed, were advocating a strike precisely because their organizations were in a virtually somnolent state and because they thought "the first constructive militant step" taken by the AFL would be "the spark that is now so badly needed." One National Council member thought that "the only means we have now is to strike.... One thing is certain," he wrote, "and that is, we must prove to the Automobile workers that we can help them...."[48]

When a strike did develop, at GM's Toledo Chevrolet plant beginning on April 23, 1935,[49] it was without AFL authorization, although the Federation quickly came to its support. It was this strike that brought the sharpest conflict during the NRA era between the AFL leadership and the militant elements within the UAW and that was of fateful significance for the future of the Federation in the automobile industry.

The nine-man Toledo strike committee was tinged with radicalism: its chairman, the twenty-three year old James Roland, and at least one or two others on the committee were under the influence of A. J. Muste and his Workers party, which had been formed by a merger of Muste's leftish American Workers party and the Trotskyite Communist League of America.[50] Dillon, who moved in to take charge of the strike, quickly found himself at odds with the strike committee on the most vital matters of strike policy.

The strike committee sought to convert the Toledo walkout into a general strike against GM that would not be settled until all the GM federal labor unions had won signed contracts. The Norwood Chevrolet and Fisher Body local went out on strike, and the Cleveland Fisher Body and Atlanta Chevrolet and Fisher Body locals converted plant shutdowns caused by the lack of Chevrolet transmissions into strikes; but Dillon maneuvered successfully to localize the dispute since he, like other AFL officials, did not believe that other GM locals were strong enough for a contest with the corporation. Dillon prevented the establishment of a general strike committee representing the various GM plants to conduct strike negotiations, and in a crucial test of strength with the Toledo strike committee, he prevented the Buick local from going on strike. Had the great Buick plant been successfully shut down, GM's position would have been weakened, but Dillon, who did not think that the Buick local was strong enough to win a strike, exerted pressure on the union's executive board to defer a walkout even though the president of the local thought that the very "survival" of the union was at stake and that "further delay would be fatal."

Although the "Memorandum of negotiations" agreed on by the company and union negotiators on May 12 included some gains for the union, the strike committee was miffed that the local had failed to win a signed contract and, officially anyhow, exclusive bargaining rights. Dillon, however, decided to recommend the acceptance of the agreement to the strikers, partly because Knudsen had made it clear to him that this was the company's final offer and that the Toledo plant would be dismantled if the terms were rejected.

The strike committee, aided and abetted by Communists and Musteites, advised the strikers to reject the terms of settlement, but in a wild meeting on the evening of May 13 Dillon secured the strikers' acceptance of the agreement by a two-to-one margin. The *American Federationist* contended that "for the first time in history one of the major automobile manufacturing concerns . . . has agreed to recognize and meet with a spokesman for its employees," but the militants in the Toledo local thought that Dillon had "sold out" the automobile workers and that the AFL, because of its basic fear of the strike weapon, had capitulated when it would have been possible to tie up GM as a whole and to win a national agreement and the original union demands. The Toledo Chevrolet strike not only marked "the beginning of Dillon's downfall" in the UAW but also made the prospects of the AFL in the automobile industry even bleaker than they already were. When the UAW was to clash with GM again at the end of the next year, its leadership, remembering the Toledo strike, was to pursue a strategy of spreading rather than localizing the strike and of insisting on a national rather than a local settlement.

The Toledo settlement was followed by further negotiations in May and June between Dillon and GM executives in Cleveland, Norwood, Atlanta, Janesville, and Kansas City. As a result of these meetings agreements were concluded by which the company, as in Toledo, recognized the UAW shop committees as the spokesmen for UAW members. Dillon was elated with this turn of events and was now "confident" that the union was "upon the way to the achievement of great things."[51] Dillon, however, undoubtedly as a reaction to charges that he had settled for half a loaf in the Toledo strike, was indulging in flights of fancy. As the future was to demonstrate, he was too optimistic about GM's good will with regard to the establishment of independent unionism in its plants.

The AFL leadership clashed with the UAW militants not only over strike policy but also regarding the establishment and the jurisdiction of an international union of automobile workers. Stimulated to take action by the unauthorized activities of some of the federal labor unions that pointed toward the creation at an early date of an international union or, at least, the closer coordination of the efforts of the UAW federal labor unions, Collins convoked a conference of automobile locals in Detroit on June 23-24, 1934, which resulted in the establishment of the National Council of United Automobile Workers Federal Labor Unions. The Council consisted of eleven members elected by the delegates and apportioned among the locals on a geographical basis, was to meet only at the call of the AFL national representative, and was to help him in organizing work and in gathering information to assist the auto workers in collective bargaining.

William Green made it clear at the June conference that it was premature to talk of establishing an international union. From the start he had indicated that this step should not be taken until the automobile workers had gained additional trade-union experience, developed effective leadership, and, above all, been able to assure the AFL that the organization would be self-sustaining. He was understandably annoyed by the naiveté of those auto workers who thought that the mere establishment of an international would solve the difficult organizational problems in the industry.[52]

From the AFL point of view the National Council provided a convenient mechanism for coordinating the activities of the federal labor unions while at the same time permitting a deferral of the difficult jurisdictional question. As it turned out, the Council did not play a particularly important role in the development of organization in the automobile industry.[53] It did, however, help to give a certain importance to three of its members who were eventually to achieve prominence in the UAW, Fred C. Pieper, Ed Hall, and, most notably, Homer Martin.

Pieper, who had been born in Germany and brought to the United States at the age of three, was only twenty-five years old when he was placed on the Council to represent the workers of the South. He had worked in the Atlanta Fisher Body plant and had become an officeholder and the dominant figure in its federal labor union. He was one of the most vociferous advocates of a GM strike before the outbreak of the Toledo Chevrolet dispute, and he was to advocate a similar policy in the weeks preceding the sit-down strike.[54] Hall, who had been born on July 25, 1887, had worked as a welder in the Seaman Body plant in Milwaukee. He was a heavy-set, loud-mouthed, and often profane person who, it was said, "carried the colorful language of the factory into his union work."[55]

Born in Marion, Illinois, on August 16, 1902, Homer Martin was a graduate of William Jewell College and did postgraduate work at a seminary in Kansas City. Since he had been the AAU hop, skip, and jump champion in 1924 and 1925 and had done some preaching since 1919, he came to be known as "The Leaping Parson." He assumed the pastorate of the Baptist church in Leeds, Missouri, a Kansas City suburb, in 1931, but when his pro-labor utterances antagonized some of his parishioners, he left the pulpit and took a job in 1932 in the Kansas City Chevrolet plant. When the federal labor union was formed in the plant, Martin became active in it and eventually became its president. He lost his job in 1934—it is not clear whether he was fired or simply laid off—and allegedly said that the company would regret the decision since he would eventually organize every GM plant in the country.

A man of medium height, blue eyes, and a pleasant face, Martin looked far more like a minister or a school teacher than like the public's stereotype of the labor leader. What primarily thrust him forward in the labor movement was his talent as an orator, an important leadership asset in the eyes of inarticulate workingmen and particularly so in a union like the UAW that was without experienced leadership. Martin, to quote Irving Howe and B. J. Widick, "spoke with other worldly fervor; his language was colored by Biblical phrases; no other man could pierce the hearts of Southern-born workers [so conspicuous in GM's Flint plants] as he could. . . . he made men feel that in organizing a union they were going forth to battle for righteousness and the word of God."

But as Martin rose to the top leadership position of the UAW, it became evident that he lacked the administrative abilities to match his oratorical gifts. He was impulsive, unpredictable, inattentive to detail, difficult to work with, and temperamentally unsuited to deal steadily with day-to-day union affairs. In the months before the GM strike Martin's defects as a union leader were to become painfully apparent to many of his associates.[56]

Quite a few of the delegates who attended the UAW conference of June, 1934, opposed the idea of a National Council and argued rather for the immediate establishment of an international, industrial union, controlled by the rank and file. The most important spokesman for this position was the president of the powerful White Motor local and one of the few experienced unionists in the UAW's ranks, Wyndham Mortimer. Older than most of the UAW leaders at that time, Mortimer had been born on March 11, 1884, in a small Pennsylvania coal-mining community. His father was a Knights of Labor member, and Mortimer "grew up in that atmosphere of unionization and strikes and things of that sort." His first memory, he was later to recall, was "walking behind the parades of the striking miners." Mortimer entered the mines himself at the age of twelve and joined the United Mine Workers four years later. Apparently fired for his union activities, he was subsequently to work for the National Tube Company in Lorain, Ohio, as a brakeman on the Pennsylvania Railroad, and as a street-car conductor in Cleveland. He took a job at the White Motor plant in Cleveland in 1916, helped to organize its federal labor union in 1933, and became the local's president.

Colorless and on the quiet side but industrious, tenacious, and well informed about shop problems, Mortimer was one of the UAW's most effective organizers. He was to become the leader of the progressive wing of the UAW and would play a decisive part in the GM sit-down. A follower of the Communist line, Mortimer was later alleged by Benjamin Stolberg to have been "a Stalinist from the very beginning," and Joseph Zack testified before the Dies Committee in 1939 that, when he had been secretary of the Communist party in Ohio in 1933, he had approved Mortimer's application for party membership.[57]

The more militant, progressive members of the UAW, who had favored the early establishment of an international union, were dissatisfied with the lack of progress made by the National Council after the June, 1934, conference. The principal center of disaffection was the nine UAW locals in Cleveland, which shortly after the June conference set up their own city Auto Council, with Mortimer as president, to push the progressive program for an international union. It was the Cleveland locals that were mainly responsible for the convocation of unauthorized, rump conferences of auto unionists in Cleveland on September 16, 1934, Flint on November 10, 1934, Detroit on January 26, 1935, and Toledo on June 8–9, 1935, that condemned the AFL's allegedly timid strike policy and its commitment to craft unionism and ritualistically resolved in favor of the early establishment by the AFL of an international, industrial union of auto workers controlled by the rank and file.[58]

The AFL denounced the rump movement for an international as Communist-inspired and sought to discourage the attendance of AFL members at its meetings. The AFL did not err in its assumption that the movement was in part at least the result of Communist machinations, but it might well have paid heed to the fact that, whether Communist-influenced or not, the demand for a complete industrial jurisdiction for the international union and for rank-and-file control struck a responsive chord among the auto workers, the vast majority of whom knew little about Communism and who, in any event, were not then as concerned about the presence of Communists in their midst as they were later to become.[59]

The AFL was in the meantime proceeding in its own fashion toward the establishment of an international union of automobile workers. At the San Francisco convention of the Federation in October, 1934, the delegates unanimously adopted a resolution directing the AFL Executive Council to issue charters for internationals in several mass-production industries, including the automotive, with the Federation, for a "provisional period," to direct their policies, administer their affairs, and designate their officers.[60]

At the winter session of the Executive Council in January–February, 1935, John L. Lewis remarked that the Federation's failure to set up "a comprehensive and outstanding organization" in the automobile industry was "operating to discredit" the AFL in the eyes of the country, and he urged his colleagues to "throw money, men and a charter" into the industry. The Council was willing to give the UAW a charter, but it was unwilling to surrender to it the jurisdiction over some of the auto workers claimed by the craft unions. Green explained to the Council that the auto workers, because of the nature of their jobs, were "mass-minded," and Lewis, whose interest was less industrial unionism as an end in itself than it was the organization of the unorganized,[61] urged that the jurisdictional issue be postponed until organization had been achieved. "Contention over the fruits of victory," he sensibly advised, should "be deferred until we have some of the fruits in our possession." He chided his associates that they had been "too long straining at a gnat and swallowing the camel."

The Council was, however, unpersuaded by what Green and Lewis had to say and by a vote of eleven to three decided that the jurisdiction of the new union should be defined as embracing "all employees directly engaged in the manufacture of parts (not including tools, dies and machinery) and assembling of those parts into completed automobiles but not including job or contract shops manufacturing parts or any other employee engaged in said automobile production plants."[62] This left the projected union with only a semi-industrial jurisdiction and made a reality of the fear of many unionists that, in the end, they would not be permitted to include in their jurisdiction all the workers in and around the automobile plants regardless of their craft. Like Lewis, they wanted to bring organization to the mass of the auto workers, and their experience since 1933 had convinced them that craft unionism was a deterrent to large-scale organization in the industry and that an industrial-type union was more likely to appeal to the auto workers and had a greater chance of success.

The Executive Council authorized the Federation's officers to form the union when in their judgment it was "appropriate and convenient" to do so and provided that the officers of the new union were to be designated by the president of the AFL for a temporary period to be determined by the Executive Council. Green and Dillon discussed the subject on June 17, following which Dillon announced that preparations would be made for a convention beginning on August 26 to launch the new international.[63]

The impending UAW constitutional convention prompted the convocation of a national conference of UAW progressives in Cleveland at the end of June, 1935. The principal document presented to the conference bitterly attacked the AFL for relying primarily on government agencies and boards rather than "taking the one sure path to winning the demand of the auto workers—the path of organization and militant strike action." What was required, the progressives thought, was preparation in the next production season on *"a national scale for a national strike to win a national agreement."* They expressed their disapproval of the jurisdictional limits imposed by the proposed charter for the new international and urged that the auto workers be permitted to elect their own officers. The progressives reiterated these views in a statement to the delegates who came to Detroit for the UAW's constitutional convention and declared that their purpose was not to advocate Communism but to build a strong union. "Take your stand with us, the progressives," they urged the delegates, "for an Industrial Union, for a union controlled by the membership and led by auto workers, for a union pledged to a policy of militant action in defense of the workers in our industry."[64]

The sentiments of the majority of the delegates who attended the UAW constitutional convention in Detroit at the end of August, 1935, were clearly with the progressives, but it was the AFL that controlled the convention machinery, and it was the AFL that prevailed on the two principal issues debated on the convention floor: the jurisdiction of the new union and the right of the delegates to choose their own officers. The delegates reluctantly accepted the jurisdictional limitations imposed by the charter, but in a show of independence they defeated by a vote of 164.2 to 112.8 a resolution calling upon Green to appoint Dillon the president of the new international. After surveying the situation for two days, Green, however, concluded that to allow the convention to select the union's officers would create "serious internal dissension," and he therefore decided to follow the instructions of the Executive Council and to appoint all the officers himself. He selected Dillon to serve as president during the probationary period, Martin as vice-president, Hall as secretary-treasurer, and the remaining members of the National Council, none of whom represented the power centers in the union, as members, along with the three officers, of the union's General Executive Board (GEB).

Clearly displeased at what had transpired, the indignant delegates resolved to select a committee of seven to protest to the AFL Executive Council and, if necessary, to the next AFL convention Green's designation of the union's officers and also, although the proceedings of the convention do not reveal it, the jurisdictional limitations of the charter. The delegates left no doubt regarding their preferences with respect to the issues in contention by selecting a committee dominated by progressives.[65]

After being rebuffed by the Executive Council—Mortimer later claimed that David Dubinsky and William Hutcheson wanted to know how many Communists there were in the group—the committee of seven carried its protest to the floor of the AFL's October convention in Atlantic City, a convention whose defeat of a proposal calling for "the organization of workers in mass production industries upon industrial and plant lines, regardless of claims based on jurisdiction," led the following month to the formation of the CIO. The decision of the convention on the industrial-union question presaged the defeat of the proposals of the committee of seven. The delegates voted down the committee's resolution requesting that the UAW be granted "complete jurisdiction ... over all employes in or around plants engaged in the manufacture of automobile parts and the assembly of such parts into completed automobiles" and referred to the Executive Council a second resolution that provided for the calling of a special convention of the UAW not later than March 1, 1936, to permit the auto workers to elect their own officers. The Executive Council left the question of the termination of the probationary period up to Green, with the proviso that no final decision on the subject was to be made before the Council's January meeting. The decisions taken by the Atlantic City convention not only led to the formation of the CIO but made it virtually certain that the UAW would eventually cast its lot with the new organization. The committee of seven, as a matter of fact, met with Lewis at the convention, and he assured them that he was "in back" of them.[66]

The fall of 1935 and the winter of 1935–36 were a time of troubles for the UAW—its average paid-up membership for the last four months of the year was an incredibly low 5135—and particularly for the AFL leadership in the union. Disgruntled at the reluctance of the majority of the delegates at the Detroit convention to accept him as their leader, Dillon pursued a course of action during the months after the convention that lost him whatever support he still enjoyed among the automobile workers. He largely ignored the GEB members and unwisely held up the reimbursement of the members of the committee of seven for the expenses they had incurred in carrying the protests of the Detroit delegates to the Executive Council and the Atlantic City convention.[67] Of greater importance in serving to widen the breach between the UAW's first president and an increasing number of its members were the tactics Dillon employed with regard to the granting of a charter to the Toledo federal labor union and the participation of the UAW in a strike at the Motor Products plant in Detroit that began on November 15, 1935.

The composite Toledo federal labor union had sought Dillon's ouster as the AFL's national representative in the automobile industry following the Toledo Chevrolet strike and had spearheaded the opposition to him at the Detroit convention. When Dillon after the convention rejected the powerful local's request for a charter from the new international and adamantly insisted that charters could be assigned only to individual plant unions, it looked as though he was seeking to gain revenge on an old enemy rather than being concerned with the best interests of the international.[68]

The "bloody, violent, vicious" Motor Products strike was less important in the long run as a conflict between labor and management than as a dispute affecting the relationship of the independent auto unions to the UAW. The strike was called by the AIWA and quickly supported by the MESA, which had organized the plant's tool and die makers. Some of the Motor Products workers belonged to the UAW and a lesser number to other AFL unions, and they too were forced from the plant on November 16, when the management decided to cease production temporarily. Denouncing dual unionism, Dillon rejected a MESA invitation to the UAW to join the strike that gave the AFL unions more substantial representation on the strike committee than their numbers warranted and injudiciously characterized the walkout as "the most ill-advised and unpopular strike ever called in Detroit." He insisted that the Motor Products management was willing to negotiate with its workers but did not know which of the several unions in the plant should be treated as their spokesman, and he therefore proposed a return to work pending an NLRB election. The UAW members voted to accept this suggestion and accordingly marched into the plant on November 25 behind their shop committee and with a police escort.

When it became apparent after the UAW returned to work that

the Motor Products management, despite Dillon's previous assurances to the contrary, was anxious to "avoid" all unions rather than to recognize and deal with one, the UAW local on December 8 voted to strike but left the timing of the walkout to the president of the local. A brief sit-down appears to have been staged in the plant on December 18, but Dillon, after conferring with the management, announced the UAW withdrawal from the strike because, he said, it had "no possible chance of success." The MESA and the AIWA, however, continued the strike—the MESA did not admit defeat until May 27, 1936—and denounced Dillon as a "Judas" and a strikebreaker.[69]

Dillon's tactics threatened further to weaken the already weak AFL position in Detroit and to make it impossible for the independents to merge with the UAW once its probationary period had come to an end, which was a prime UAW objective. Claiming a membership of thirty thousand, which was almost certainly an exaggeration, the three independents had begun to talk about a merger of their forces shortly before the start of the Motor Products strike. This had caused the newly formed CIO to dispatch John Brophy to Detroit to undertake his "first field job" as the committee's "director." Brophy met with Matthew Smith of the MESA on November 11 and concluded that the proposed merger was "a bona-fide attempt on the part of the workers to set up an industrial union in the automobile industry." Late in November the leaders of the AIWA and the MESA wrote to Lewis indicating their willingness to affiliate with the AFL should the UAW receive an industrial-union charter and attain "internal democracy." The CIO took the matter under advisement, but in the meantime the independents went ahead with their merger plans. Seeking to capitalize on Dillon's bewildering policy in the Motor Products strike, they appealed to UAW members to choose "between a delapidated [sic], reactionary group asking you to scab on your co-workers and ... a new mobile industrial organization, democratically controlled." The independents, primarily because of differences among their leaders, were to find it easier to talk about merger than to achieve it, but, largely because of the Motor Products strike they continued to look askance at affiliation with a UAW controlled by Francis Dillon.[70]

The coolness between the UAW and the regular AFL leadership toward the end of 1935 was reflected in the growing antagonism between Vice-President Martin and President Dillon and the enthusiasm expressed in UAW circles for Lewis and the CIO. In the middle of November, 1935, Martin journeyed to Cleveland to present the charter of the White Motor local and there talked with such opponents of Dillon as Mortimer. Martin "made a great hit" with the

Cleveland unionists and apparently agreed with their leadership on the need for "militant progressive unionism." He was becoming increasingly aware of the desire of the auto workers for a full-fledged industrial union and of their interest in Lewis and the CIO. "I find," he wrote, "that every where the Auto Workers are of the same opinion, they all want Lewis. . . ." The Cleveland Auto Council had decided to launch an organizing campaign in the industry, and Martin joined the delegation that visited CIO headquarters in Washington on November 26 to request that Lewis be the speaker at a mass meeting that would initiate the campaign. The Cleveland group explained that "a gigantic mass organizational drive" was required "to overcome . . . apathy and suspicion" among the workers and that only Lewis could draw a large crowd at the meeting. Brophy informed the delegation that the CIO wanted to "encourage and keep alive [the] feeling for organization" in the automotive and other mass-production industries but that its "procedure and policy" were not yet "fully developed." The appropriate action at the moment, he advised, was for Adolph Germer to visit the automotive centers to canvass the situation.[71]

Germer, the first field representative of the CIO and soon to become director of its Detroit regional office and, in effect, its man in the automobile industry, was a large hulk of a man, six-feet two inches in height and weighing 240 pounds. Born in Germany in 1880, he had joined the United Mine Workers at age eleven, when he quit school to enter the mines, and eventually became an organizer for the union and vice-president of one of its sub-districts. He had become a member of the Socialist party in 1900, and from 1916 to 1920 had been its national secretary. He had long been an opponent of John L. Lewis, but Lewis now put him to work for the CIO. He was to serve the CIO as an organizer for twenty years until his retirement in 1955.[72]

Germer visited Cleveland and Detroit early in December and also met with delegations of auto workers from Toledo and Flint. He discovered that there was "a quite general organization sentiment" but that it was "wholly" for the industrial form of organization. He reported that the UAW had five thousand members in Cleveland among the city's twenty-five to thirty thousand auto workers, which was undoubtedly an exaggeration, but that there were only three to four thousand members in Detroit out of a potential of 200,000 and a bare five hundred members in Flint out of a possible forty thousand.

While in Detroit, Germer had two conferences with Dillon and concluded, as the CIO representative advised Lewis, that he was "with us," that he believed the auto workers could be organized only along industrial lines, and that he would go along "passively" with the CIO drive although he could not "openly cooperate" since he had to implement AFL policy in the industry. Germer was later to offer Dillon CIO organizers and funds, but he rejected the offer. When Germer then asked him what his reaction would be if individual UAW locals sought and received CIO aid, he replied, " 'Well, I wouldn't know anything about that.' " At the same time, Dillon, who told Germer one thing and his AFL superiors something quite different, reported to the AFL Executive Council that he had rejected CIO support since it was a dual organization; and Ed Hall told Germer that Dillon had said that the CIO " 'can shove their organizers up their a– –.' "[73]

On the basis of information supplied by Germer that union sentiment was increasing among auto workers but that the AFL's craft-union policies were a deterrent to organization, Sidney Hillman recommended at a CIO meeting of December 9, 1935, that the new committee should "centralize its efforts on the automobile industry." Believing that "real results" could be achieved in two to three months, Hillman argued that the CIO should advise the UAW "to take in all the workers" and that the industrial-union committee should "stand by" the auto workers should a strike develop in the automotive industry. This led to "an extended discussion" of the problems of organizing the unorganized, after which the CIO decided to support organizational efforts in the automobile industry and to press both for the amalgamation of the independents and the UAW and an "unrestricted industrial union charter." "Sound the unity note for auto workers on basis of industrial unionism in affiliation with AF of L," Brophy wired Germer on December 20, 1935.[74]

Seeking to implement his instructions, Germer conferred in early January, 1936, with Dillon and the leadership of the independents in an effort to effect a merger of their organizations. Dillon proved conciliatory for the moment and suggested that Matthew Smith of the MESA and Richard Frankensteen of the AIWA prepare a unity statement that he would submit to the AFL Executive Council meeting later in the month. Dillon, however, was pursuing his usual policy of being all things to all men, and in the end he made no effort to promote amalgamation at the Executive Council meeting. The CIO's initial efforts to achieve unity among the union forces in the automobile industry thus ended in failure, as did the simultaneous attempt of the independents to effect a merger of their own.[75]

The CIO was in the meantime moving to implement its promise to assist in the organizing efforts of the UAW. To dramatize CIO support for the auto unionists, Lewis accepted the invitation of the

Cleveland Auto Council and appeared in Cleveland on January 19, 1936, to make his first public address in the interests of industrial unionism since the formation of the CIO. Speaking to a huge crowd that had braved a blizzard to attend, Lewis delivered a "fiery attack" on the automobile companies and called for the "complete unionization" of the industry. He pledged the UAW the aid of the CIO and expressed the hope that the AFL Executive Council, then meeting in Miami, would see the light, "like the Apostle Paul on the Damascus Road," and grant the UAW a thoroughgoing industrial-union charter.[76]

The AFL Executive Council was, however, quite unlike the Apostle Paul. At its Miami meeting it reaffirmed the jurisdiction of the UAW as previously defined by the Council and the Atlantic City convention and ordered the union to withdraw the charters it had already granted to forty-three job and contract shops not owned by automobile manufacturing companies. This decision was received with consternation by the independent unions in the industry and the UAW. Matthew Smith told Germer that his " 'people' " refused " 'to be parceled out like fish on the market,' " and Frankensteen remarked, " 'that is awful; that is not union that is disunion.' " " 'Let them go to hell,' " a UAW official angrily declared, and even Frank Martel, the president of the Detroit and Wayne County Federation of Labor, thought that the Executive Council members were " 'crazy.' " There was no likelihood, as a matter of fact, that the UAW locals would abide by the decision. As the recording secretary of one of the strongest locals had previously advised the AFL when informed that some of the members of his union were being claimed by the Pattern Makers' League: "Definately [sic] and with out [sic] any hesitancy let us inform you that every employee in the industry we claim as within our jurisdiction. For thirty years no craft Union has been able to organize these workers. Today, we have performed that merical [sic] which was said to be impossible. What we have, we hold, relinquishing no one. . . ."[77]

Although angered by the AFL decision on the jurisdiction question, the UAW did feel that it had won "a distinct victory" when the Executive Council, urged on by Martin, Mortimer, and Hall, decided at its January meeting to bring the probationary period of the UAW to an end and to hold a convention not later than April 30 to permit the auto workers to select their own officers and thus to secure the internal democracy for which they and their friends were clamoring. Seemingly emboldened by this decision, Martin and Hall, who had also become disillusioned with Dillon, attempted to oust the UAW president from office even before the convention to end the probationary period was held. Without consulting other GEB members, they impetuously "assumed complete charge of the [Detroit] office," and three days later Martin informed a UAW friend, "Dillon is out! ... We are in charge and propose to stay in complete charge until the convention." The rival UAW leaders refused to talk to one another, bolted the door between their offices, spied on one another, and Martin and Hall charged that Dillon had gone so far as to place a dictograph in their office. Germer reported to CIO headquarters that UAW affairs in Detroit were now "a badly mixed up mess" and that organization work in the city was "virtually at a standstill."[78]

Proceeding as though the executive authority were vested in them, Martin and Hall quickly dispatched a charter to the Toledo local (Dillon by this time had already granted a charter to the Toledo Chevrolet workers as Local 12, and so the charter presented by Martin and Hall applied only to the remainder of the old federal labor union, now reconstituted as Local 14) and, in an attempt to win the support of the independents, decided to put "everything we have got" into the barely surviving Motor Products strike. Martin thought that the UAW could "make a lasting impression" on the city if it came to the aid of the strikers, and Germer concluded that the fact that at least part of the UAW "official family" was now cooperating with the independents had "eased" the "sting" resulting from Dillon's strike behavior.[79]

Despite Martin's statement that Dillon was "out," he was able to hang on to his presidency until the April convention of the UAW. Green called the disputants to Washington and told them that the fight would have to cease or he would be compelled to take appropriate action, and Germer, Mortimer, and others were arguing that the best strategy for the UAW to pursue was "to lay quiet until after [the] convention" when the unionists could "show their teeth a little more." "Now that the Convention is assured," Mortimer advised Martin, "I think our best plan would be not to rock the boat, as the Craft organizations are capitalizing on our difficulties, and the reaction may damage us." Martin was seemingly content to accept this judgment, but the abortive coup d'état had not been without considerable gain for him: he had succeeded in establishing his independence of the unfortunate Dillon and had increased his popularity among the auto workers.[80]

The progressives were in the meantime making their preparations for the second UAW convention, scheduled for South Bend in April. They held an informal meeting in Toledo early in February and elected a committee of twelve, headed by Mortimer, to draft a program that was to be presented to a caucus of progressive unionists scheduled for the next month in South Bend. More than 140 delegates, representing most of the big UAW locals, met in the Indiana city on March 14 and 15 and adopted resolutions prepared by the committee that allegedly embodied "the best thought and experience" of the UAW. The resolutions called for a major organizing drive, particularly in Michigan, following the convention, industrial unionism in the mass-production industries and the expansion of the UAW's jurisdiction, the extension of an invitation to the independents to affiliate with the UAW, the revision of the UAW constitution to reduce the power of the officers and to permit locals to strike on their own initiative as long as they notified the international in advance, and, in consonance with the Communist line, AFL support for the formation of a labor party.[81]

The progressives had begun work on the preparation of a slate of officers to be presented to the April convention as early as January 19, 1936, and apparently had agreed at their Toledo conference to support Martin for president and Mortimer for vice-president. They clearly, however, preferred Mortimer to Martin, whom some of them characterized as "injudicious," and they would try for a time to gain the top spot in the organization for the former; but in the end they would go along with the choice of Martin because he was the more popular figure of the two and because they assumed, in any event, that he was in their camp. The progressives had come to the 1935 UAW convention without an agreed-upon slate of candidates, and this, they believed, had handicapped them in their conflict with Green over the selection of the union's officers, but they now declared, "we do not intend to be caught napping again." Martin reported after the March caucus that "our lines still hold," and they were to "hold" throughout the South Bend convention despite a belated effort by Mortimer just before the meeting to gain CIO support for his candidacy. The long struggle between the AFL leadership and the progressives for control of the UAW was now to be decided in favor of the progressives.[82]

The second convention of the UAW opened in South Bend on April 27, 1936. Dillon claimed a membership for the organization of forty thousand, but the paid-up membership at the time was less than twenty-four thousand. Most of the membership, moreover, as had been true from the start, was concentrated in auto companies and parts plants outside Michigan. None of Flint's five locals, judging from their representation at the convention, had much more than one hundred members, and the total Detroit membership was probably less than two thousand. More than half the paid-up members were concentrated in five locals: Studebaker, Toledo parts, White Motor, Kenosha Nash, and Seaman Body.[83]

"The prime purpose" of the delegates, to quote the managing editor of the Federated Press, "was to run Frank Dillon out of the convention and keep him out, and all others like him—and this was done with great relish." Dillon stepped down from his position, and the progressives, who were in control of the convention and enjoyed the support of most of the big locals, put through their slate of candidates. Martin was elected president; Mortimer, first vice-president; Hall, second vice-president; Walter N. Wells, whose Detroit Gear local had the largest paid-up membership of any of the Detroit locals, third vice-president; and George Addes, of Toledo's Local 12, secretary-treasurer. Of the eleven GEB members, five were definitely linked with the left wing, and three others leaned that way. Only three GEB members could be classified as "Dillonites." Most of the officers and board members were under thirty-five—Pieper and Walter Reuther, the latter one of the least known of the group at that time, were under thirty—and every one of them had worked in an automobile plant, which reflected the long-standing antagonism of the auto workers to organizers and union officials without experience in the industry.[84]

One place on the GEB was held open for a representative of one of the independent unions, all of which had spokesmen at the convention who expressed a desire for unity with the UAW. Following the convention the AIWA and the AAWA affiliated with the UAW, giving the union a measure of strength in the plants of Chrysler and Hudson. The MESA National Administrative Committee, however, declined a merger invitation, but following the convention three of MESA's Detroit locals, which contained a large segment of the organization's membership in the city and the bulk of its Communists, seceded and joined the UAW. The addition of the MESA members further "radicalized" the UAW, bringing into its ranks such men as John Anderson, who had been the Communist party's candidate for governor of Michigan in 1934 and who now became the president of Local 155.[85]

The power of the radical elements in the UAW was very much in evidence at the South Bend convention. The delegates refused to approve a resolution to expel known Communists from the union's membership or, as amended, to deny officeholding in the international or the locals to "proven" Communists, approved a Communist party-line resolution calling for the establishment of a farmer-labor party, and refused to endorse Roosevelt for a second term. The latter action prompted Germer to charge that Socialists and Communists had "taken over the convention" and were "voting not as auto workers but according to their political views." Germer, whom the CIO had assigned to the convention to "take care of whatever steps are necessary to keep the situation in hand," took Martin aside and told him that the UAW's failure to support Roosevelt would be a boon to the Liberty League. Martin thereupon raised the question on the convention floor a second time, and the resolution endorsing the President was approved. "The Communists," a veteran observer of the auto labor scene declared shortly after the convention, "are riding high, wide and handsome in the United [Automobile Workers]."[86]

The diminished prestige of the AFL and the rising influence of the CIO among the auto workers were quite apparent at the convention. There was "no great demonstration" for Green when he was ushered into the convention hall, and he did not help matters when he told the delegates in reviewing the efforts of the Federation in the industry, "I do not see where a mistake was made." CIO organizers had already come to the assistance of the UAW in its organizing efforts in Cleveland and Detroit, and CIO representatives Rose Pesotta of the International Ladies' Garment Workers' Union and Leo Krzycki of the Amalgamated Clothing Workers had apparently helped to round up delegates for the South Bend convention. Pesotta, Krzycki, Germer, and Charles Howard were present at the convention and played an important role in its deliberations. Martin and "all other CIO supported" candidates had been elected and "our entire program adopted," Krzycki wired Hillman from South Bend. Green concluded when the convention was over that the CIO "completely dominated and controlled" the UAW, but this was certainly an exaggeration.[87]

The South Bend delegates approved a resolution calling for the launching of a nation-wide organization drive and the raising for this purpose of a minimum of $250,000, at least $75,000 of which was to be contributed by UAW locals and the remainder by the AFL and "all sympathetic organizations." Mortimer accurately predicted that the "fight" with GM would come before the next convention was held, and Hall similarly stated that "General Motors will know damn well we are not running away from them."[88]

The planning of some sort of action against GM was very much on the mind of the youthful president of the Toledo Chevrolet local, Robert C. Travis. Born in Flint on February 7, 1906, Travis had been active in organizing the Toledo Chevrolet plant, had served on the strike committee during the 1935 strike, and had eventually become president of the local. He had attended the UAW's constitutional convention and there had met Wyndham Mortimer; the two men soon came to symbolize the Cleveland-Toledo axis formed as the result of the Toledo Chevrolet strike and the pursuit of common goals at the 1935 convention. Mortimer would stop in Toledo on his way to Detroit or South Bend, and Travis would visit in Cleveland. Travis many years later was to say that Mortimer had been "the main influence in my life, in raising things that I'd never heard about before in a way that seemed logical to me."

Travis had a winning smile and a tremendously attractive personality. He was energetic and ebullient, knew the problems of the shop, and was able to inspire confidence in insecure workers. He had learned during the Toledo Chevrolet strike, and he was not to forget the lesson, how vulnerable GM was to a strike in one of its key plants and how a small, strategically placed group of workers could successfully challenge even a corporation as powerful as GM.

Travis recommended just before the South Bend convention that delegates from the GM plants should caucus and consider the establishment of a GM council, made up of representatives of the various GM locals, to present a united front to the corporation. Travis, who sometimes thought in military terms, saw the conflict between the UAW and GM as a battle between armies of grossly unequal power.

> The situation as it stands now [he wrote] is comparable to a vast army on one side with all the hideous advantages of modern warfare—airplanes—poison gas—machine guns—long range guns, and hand grenades, and last but not least, their secret service. This vast army is a well oiled, well disciplined outfit, having a perfectly designed program which when worked out step by step, their final objection [objective] is practically assured.
> On the other side, we see scattered battalions, unskilled ... in this modern warfare, armed with bows and arrows, spears, and swords. They have no secret service working ... in the enemy lines. They have no airplanes, poison gas, machine guns or hand grenades. They have not the advantages of a specifically concentrated method of attack. Each battalion is fighting its own battles, without the aid of the other, in its puny way against this vast army. Regardless how well founded their cause, these men are doomed to defeat, unless they concentrate their armies to enter upon the field equipped to fight fire with fire, the odds are greatly against them.[89]

On Germer's advice, the GM delegates at South Bend took no action on a resolution calling for the formation of a GM council.[90]

The events of the convention, however, made it appear that there would be a confrontation with GM before many months had passed, and when that occurred Travis would be given a chance to demonstrate how a small army could defeat a much larger one if it had the right strategy and tactics and the proper sort of external support.

Two months after the close of the South Bend convention, on July 2, Martin met with the CIO leadership and, as was predictable, aligned the UAW with the new organization, a decision that was ratified by the GEB on August 3. The CIO promised its full support in the UAW drive to organize the automobile workers, and by the end of August it was paying for three full-time organizers in the motor-vehicle industry quite apart from the aid being rendered the UAW by Germer and Krzycki. Although the automobile industry was the first in which the CIO provided "concrete organizational aid," it did not make its formal entry into the auto organizing campaign until after the November elections, and at no time prior to the GM sit-down did it make the same kind of organizational commitment to the automobile industry that it was making in the steel industry.[91]

The UAW was beset throughout the organizational drive preceding the GM strike by discord and factionalism within its high command, a problem that was to afflict the auto workers for many years to come. Communism, the persistence of "Dillonism" on the GEB, and a certain ambivalence of Martin toward the CIO all contributed to disharmony among the UAW leadership. Martin, who on occasion attacked red-baiting within the UAW, complained on other occasions that the Communists were "busy trying to control the International" and that there were Communist party "undercover agents" within the UAW family. In March he had told Mortimer that he (Martin) had "never had anything to do with raising a red scare against anyone, let alone you" and that he considered Mortimer to be "a special friend," but some months later he concluded that Mortimer and some Communists in the organization were opposed to him and were seeking to "capture" the UAW. No real effort was made by Martin before the GM strike, however, to rid the UAW of the Communist presence, and, indeed, there would have been relatively little support within the union for any such move. The prevailing view of the organization at that time was undoubtedly that expressed by a rubber worker who was aiding the UAW organization drive: "It doesn't make any difference if a man is a Communist, Socialist, Republican, or Democrat, as long as he is loyal to the union."[92]

Perhaps to offset the power of the progressives on the GEB, Martin seems to have forged an alliance with the former Dillon supporters on the board, Pieper, F. J. Michel of the Nash Racine local, and Russell Merrill of Studebaker, who had been Martin's opponent for the presidency at the South Bend convention. When other GEB members learned of secret meetings of this group, they complained to Germer that Martin was seeking to build a "machine" and that the men involved were red-baiters who wanted to oust such people as Mortimer and Anderson from the UAW.[93]

Martin pursued a perplexing policy with regard to the CIO. Publicly, he sought CIO aid in the form of money and organizers, but privately he attempted on occasion to exclude the CIO representative in Detroit from GEB deliberations. Martin's motives can only be surmised. Perhaps he thought that the CIO was too closely linked with the progressives in the UAW and on the GEB; perhaps, as Germer thought, he was " 'feeling his oats' " and was disinclined to take advice from anyone; perhaps he did not like the particular kind of advice that Germer was giving him, namely, that the UAW must proceed with caution in challenging the giants in the automobile industry.[94] In any event, the lack of complete rapport between Martin and the CIO, like the conflict between Dillonites and left-wing elements on the GEB, in part explains the confused beginnings of the GM sit-down.

Quite apart from the division among UAW leaders in ideology and on policy matters, members of the GEB and Germer as well were disturbed by Martin's lack of administrative ability, his erratic behavior, and his indecisiveness. Germer complained that Martin was spending "too much [time] running around" and was not giving enough attention to "getting his organization machinery in shape," that he was unable "to organize himself and assert himself." Germer found it so difficult to get along with Martin that he asked Lewis in November for a different assignment. Secretary-Treasurer Addes, whose talents were administrative and bureaucratic, was troubled because "Martin does not direct affairs but leaves everybody go at will." Several UAW board members complained similarly in November that "things are not 'clicking,' that there is no real system." The lack of "system" and the strong prejudice of UAW members against centralizing tendencies in the organization, a product of the UAW's history, created a condition of near anarchy in the union that made it possible for each local to go its own way and make its own decisions on the most important of union matters.[95]

The UAW ostensibly launched an organization campaign on June 22, and it was soon claiming substantial increases in its membership, but little if any progress seems to have been made by the auto workers prior to the national elections of November. Some important organizational steps were, however, taken in the months between the

South Bend convention and the Democratic sweep in the fall. An educational director (Merlin D. Bishop, who had been on the extension staff of Brookwood Labor College) was added to the UAW staff on June 19, and a research director (William L. Munger, a former president of the Olds local) was appointed in October. When the GEB met early in August, it appointed a field staff of fifteen paid organizers and provided for an increase in this number to twenty during the next few weeks. UAW officers and GEB members were themselves assigned some of the key organizational responsibilities: Richard Frankensteen, who had been given the seat left vacant on the GEB for a representative of one of the independent unions, was placed in charge of organizational work in Detroit; Delmond Garst, the general executive secretary of the St. Louis Chevrolet and Fisher Body local and a GEB member, was assigned to St. Louis and Kansas City; Mortimer, who was already at work in Flint, was confirmed as organizational director in that city; and Ed Hall was placed in charge in Anderson, Muncie, and Newcastle, Indiana.[96]

Following the GEB's August session, representatives of the GM locals met to discuss their common problems. The union representatives of the various GM divisions met again on September 14 and finally approved Bob Travis' plan to establish a GM Advisory Council. Travis, Munger, and Garst were designated as a steering committee to plan a GM organizing campaign.[97]

The UAW did score one "significant material and psychological victory" before the November elections in a struggle with the Chrysler Corporation over the question of seniority in the Dodge plant. During the summer layoffs the Dodge management told thousands of workers that they would not be rehired because their jobs had been obliterated by machines. When production resumed, the Dodge local complained that the company had violated the principle of seniority in its rehiring policy and had discriminated against union men. Confronted by a strike threat as the negotiations dragged on, the company capitulated on October 16 and accepted the union demands regarding the procedures to be followed in the reemployment of Dodge workers. Since the UAW record in Detroit had largely been one of defeat, the "sweet smell of success" resulting from the Dodge victory was not only important for the morale of union members, but it also strengthened the UAW appeal to the unorganized. Soon the word was out that "things are cracking open in Detroit and they are signing them up by [the] hundreds."[98]

Far more important than the Dodge victory was the stimulus to organization provided by Roosevelt's smashing victory over Alfred M. Landon and the American Liberty League in the presidential election of November 3, 1936. In a thinly veiled appeal for Republican votes about three weeks before the election, Alfred P. Sloan, Jr., who was prominently associated with the Liberty League and was a heavy contributor to the Republican party, told GM workers that the company was not in politics but that the workers should assure themselves of the economic soundness of the various proposals being spewed forth during the campaign and should understand who would pay for them if they were implemented. Under the circumstances, the election results were understandably viewed by the workers as representing a victory not only over the unfortunate Landon but over GM and the other automobile manufacturers as well. "You voted New Deal at the polls, and defeated the Auto Barons—Now get a New Deal in the shop," the UAW told the auto workers. With the election of Roosevelt and so many liberal governors, the most important of whom from the UAW point of view was Governor-elect Frank Murphy of Michigan, "our opportunity for a great organization," Martin reported to the UAW, "should be realized in the next few months. The government is obviously with us." Perhaps now, the former mine worker John L. Lewis thought, the President "would hold the light" for the union forces while they "went out and organized." The election, said a CIO leader in Detroit, is "a mandate to labor to organize."[99]

Adolph Germer had observed before the election that the auto workers were "still gripped with a feeling of fear," but he was "sure the election of Roosevelt will inject *some* stiffening in their backbone." Roosevelt's victory seems to have had precisely the effect that Germer had anticipated. It helped to make the idea of joining the union somewhat more attractive to the auto worker, somewhat less of a hazard than it had previously appeared to be. He had become more conscious of his power, and perhaps, after all, President Roosevelt did want him to join the union and would protect his right to do so. There were signs in the auto industry during the next few weeks of that great upsurge of unionism, of labor on the march, that was to make the year 1937 the *annus mirabilis* of the American labor movement, but it would take a victory over a foe as formidable as GM before the flow of workers into the UAW would reach flood tide.

When the CIO leadership met in Pittsburgh on November 7–8, with Martin present, it was decided to step up the organizing campaign in the automobile industry so as to capitalize on "the favorable climate for the union" resulting from the Roosevelt and Murphy victories and the rise in the "fighting spirit" of the auto workers stemming from the Dodge success. Brophy and Philip Murray, the chairman of the Steel Workers' Organizing Committee, visited Detroit on November 12 and 13 to counsel with the UAW and by their presence to mark the formal opening of the new organization campaign. They met with the officers of the UAW and with union organizers, who had been brought in from the field for the occasion, and also spoke at three UAW meetings.[100]

The UAW and CIO leadership announced that the goals of the automobile organizing campaign were an annual wage "to assure security during periods of idleness" and "to provide a standard of health, decency and comfort" for the worker, the elimination of the speed-up, seniority based on length of service alone, an eight-hour day and a forty-hour week, time-and-one-half pay for overtime, the progressive reduction of hours until all the unemployed auto workers and those displaced by machines had been reemployed, improved safety measures, and the establishment of "true collective bargaining through the representatives of the bona fide labor organization." The UAW asserted that these demands reflected the desires of the auto workers themselves and also the excellent financial condition of the industry.[101] It is noteworthy and somewhat puzzling in view of events to come that the UAW did not demand acceptance as the exclusive representative of the auto workers for collective-bargaining purposes and that it called for the forty-hour rather than the thirty-hour week that it had been officially seeking.

The organization drive, pushed by mass meetings, solicitation at factory gates, and even home visits, was aided by victories in sit-down or "quickie" strikes in November and December against Bendix Products Corporation, Midland Steel, Kelsey-Hayes Wheel Company, and Flint Fisher Body No. 1, the increase in automobile production and the usual worker complaints associated with the grooving-in period, the support of the CIO,[102] and the assistance rendered by the United States Senate Subcommittee on Education and Labor (the La Follette Committee), which had been cooperating with the union since the beginning of the fall and which announced on December 19 that it would soon conduct an inquiry into GM labor practices and would examine charges of strikebreaking, espionage, and illegal anti-union activities. On December 8 the UAW and the Federation of Flat Glass Workers set up a council for joint action and authorized it to take such common action as it deemed necessary to cope with any labor situation confronting either of the two unions. The Flat Glass Workers had struck the Pittsburgh Plate Glass Company, which supplied Chrysler, on October 24, and it was to strike the Ottawa, Illinois, plant of Libby-Owens-Ford, which supplied GM, on December 2 and its remaining plants on December 15. The prolongation of these two strikes posed a major threat to the continued operation of two of the three major automobile producers.[103]

As its organization campaign continued, the UAW claimed that thousands were "clamoring for organization," and it appealed for more funds and placed additional organizers in the field. Gains were being reported everywhere. Cleveland told of "the greatest upsurge in union activity" since the strike of April, 1934; from Anderson came word of "a tidal wave of organization"; the auto union in Flint was said to be "sweeping everything before it"; and Frankensteen reported major membership gains in Detroit.[104]

Although the UAW exaggerated its membership gains, undoubtedly to create the impression of an irresistible union force about to conquer all opposition in the industry, the organization, at least in comparison with its past record, did add appreciably to its membership strength during the closing weeks of 1936. It enrolled approximately 15,500 members in December alone, more than ten thousand of these, significantly, in Michigan; and its total paid-up membership in that month, judging from per capita tax figures and initiation fees, was close to sixty-three thousand, as compared to an average monthly membership of about twenty-seven thousand between April 1 and December 31, 1936.[105]

The paid-up membership figures, which constituted about 13.7 percent of the average employment in the industry (460,000) in 1936, almost certainly understate the actual membership of the UAW since they do not include workers who, although loyal to the union, were delinquent in their dues because they had been laid off or for some other reason. Also, as one union official later pointed out, it was possible in those turbulent days when the organization was still relatively new and procedures had not been completely regularized to have "a good union atmosphere" in an automotive plant without the union's having very many dues-paying members. It must also be recognized that it is difficult for a new union to organize a majority of the workers within its jurisdiction until it proves its ability to secure recognition and tangible gains for its members.[106] The majority of the automobile workers were not necessarily opposed to the UAW so much as they were waiting to see what its fate would be in a struggle with the giant employers in the industry.

Despite the gains registered by the UAW and other unions in the closing weeks of 1936, the labor movement as a whole had failed to realize the hopes that had been entertained by union leaders when Section 7(a) was included in the NIRA. The limited economic recovery that attended the beginning of the New Deal, coupled with the stimulating effect of Section 7(a), had caused union membership to rise from just under three million in 1933 to approximately 3.6 million in 1934 (from 5.8 percent of the civilian labor force to 6.9

percent), with most of the gains coming among the coal miners and the needle trades; but the number of unionists increased hardly at all in 1935. The tempo of organization picked up somewhat the next year, but the slightly more than four million union members in 1936 constituted only 7.6 percent of the civilian labor force, which was below the corresponding figure for 1925.[107]

The AFL as 1936 came to an end was still slumbering, and the CIO, infinitely more daring and energetic than its foe, had yet to prove that it could successfully organize the largely unorganized mass-production industries. The NLRA, to be sure, was the law of the land, and it went well beyond Section 7 (a) in the legal protection that it afforded to unionization and collective bargaining, but employers like GM had effectively blocked its operation, and there were widespread doubts about its constitutionality. It seemed evident that if there was to be a surge forward in unionization, the impetus would have to come from the ranks of the workers themselves. It was the UAW, as events were to show, that would provide that impetus.

The progressives in the UAW, almost from the time the federal labor unions had been formed in the various automobile plants, had been complaining about the lack of militancy of the AFL leadership in the organization. The progressives were now themselves in control of the UAW, and the time seemed ripe for a test of their theory that major success would come to the union only if it had the daring to challenge one or more of the three major producers in the industry. As it turned out, the issue was joined with GM, the principal battlefield was the city of Flint, and the weapon employed was the sit-down strike. The fate of the UAW and of industrial unionism in general rested upon the outcome.

Company Town
IV

I

Although the GM strike of 1936-37 involved GM plants and workers across the land, the vital center of the conflict was Flint, Michigan, the principal seat of GM's power. Flint was to the nation's leading automobile producer what Pittsburgh was to steel, Akron to rubber, and Minneapolis to milling. There was a city of Flint, however, before there was a General Motors Corporation, and it was known as a vehicle center before it became identified with the automobile.

What is now the city of Flint—the name is derived from the river which runs through the town and which allegedly supplied the Indians in the area with flints for their arrows—was founded in 1819 by Jacob Smith as a fur-trading post along the Indian trail between Saginaw and Detroit. The fact that the Flint River could be forded at this point encouraged growth of a permanent settlement; and after a sawmill had been erected along the river some years later, settlers began to come to the area, particularly from northern New York and New England. In 1855 the river settlement was incorporated as the city of Flint. Its population at the time was less than two thousand.[1]

From the time of its incorporation, Flint has been primarily a one-industry town, as first the lumber industry, then the carriage industry, and finally the automobile industry followed one another in a more or less logical progression to dominate the economic life of the community. The lumber industry began to develop in the Flint area in the 1850's to exploit the magnificent white pine forests that surrounded the Flint River. Within a decade the industry had reached boom proportions, and Flint became the lumbering center of Michigan. In 1870 its sawmills processed ninety million board feet of lumber, and lumbering and associated woodworking industries were the city's most conspicuous form of economic endeavor. The industry went into decline at the end of the 1870's, however, as the natural resource upon which it was based approached exhaustion; but, fortunately for the future of Flint, the great entrepreneurs and firms of the industry—H. H. Crapo, J. B. Atwood and Company, Begole, Fox and Company—kept their capital and profits in the city and provided investment funds for the development there of first the carriage industry and then the automobile industry.[2]

The carriage industry in Flint traces its beginnings to 1869, when W. A. Paterson set up shop in the city as a carriage blacksmith. As the profits from the lumber industry began to dwindle, lumber capital and personnel began to be diverted to the carriage business. In 1882, for example, Begole, Fox and Company established the Flint Wagon Works on the site of the company's sawmill and at the future location of Chevrolet, graphically demonstrating the historical continuity of the three industries that explain Flint's economic growth. The large-scale expansion of the carriage business in Flint began in 1885 when William Crapo Durant, as we have seen, joined with J. Dallas Dort to form the Durant-Dort Carriage Company and contracted with W. A. Paterson to build the firm's two-wheel carts. By the end of the century Flint's various carriage firms, of which Durant-Dort was the most prominent, were turning out 150,000 vehicles a year, twice the number being produced in South Bend, the other great center of the industry, and Flint was "The Vehicle City" of the United States. More than half the community's 13,103 inhabitants were associated with the carriage business in one way or another.[3]

Some of Flint's vehicle producers became interested toward the end of the century in the new-fangled horseless carriage and began installing equipment to manufacture automobile parts. In 1901 A. B. C. Hardy, one of the Durant-Dort lieutenants, organized the Flint Automobile Company, the city's first automobile manufacturing concern, to assemble the Flint Roadster, "a dashing model all red paint, red leather and brass." The firm enjoyed a modest success but was forced out of business by the owners of the Selden patent. Another Flint carriage maker, James H. Whiting, brought the Buick to Flint in 1903, as already noted, and Durant and Flint capital were soon to make the vehicle an outstanding success. Flint's growth was henceforth to be associated with the automobile industry and with components of the GM complex.[4]

On July 4, 1905, Durant invited Charles Stewart Mott to bring his Weston-Mott Company from Utica, New York, to Flint. "Flint," Durant wrote, "is in the center of the automobile industry, a progressive city, good people, with conditions for manufacturing ideal." Mott moved his axle firm to Flint the next year and was to be joined there in 1908, the year GM was formed, by Albert Champion, whose ignition company eventually became the AC Spark Plug Division of GM. Chevrolet moved to Flint from Detroit in 1913, and Fisher Body established its No. 1 and No. 2 plants there in the 1920's, giving Flint the basic structure of GM plants that it had at the time of the sit-down strike.[5]

When Buick was moved to Flint in 1903, the city had a population of only about fourteen thousand, but as the automobile industry grew, Flint grew with it. The expansion of Buick toward the end of the first decade of the century, the great increase in automobile production during the boom years of World War I, and the growth of Chevrolet and Fisher Body in the 1920's created an enormous demand for labor in Flint, caused agents of GM to search the land for workers, and brought migrants to Flint from elsewhere in Michigan, from the Middle West and the South, and to a more limited extent from abroad. Flint's population increased to 38,550 in 1910, 91,599 in 1920, and 156,492 in 1930.

Flint grew like a mining camp, without design, without planning. As the workers came in, "the city stretched itself and strained itself to absorb them so that it was as uncomfortable as an adolescent in knickerbockers." The incoming thousands overtaxed Flint's limited housing supply, and some workers were compelled to live for a time in tar-paper shacks, tents, and even railroad cars. The same lodging rooms were rented to night-shift workers for the day and to day-shift workers for the night. GM itself felt constrained to enter the home construction business in 1919, and through the Modern Housing Corporation it had built thirty-two hundred homes for its Flint workers by 1933.[6]

Like housing, public services in Flint failed to keep pace with a rapidly expanding population. Recreational facilities were woefully inadequate until the federal government after 1933 intervened to redress the balance, and the city "never provided" enough personnel, funds, or services to meet its health problems. Among twenty-two cities of from 100,000 to 250,000 population in 1934 Flint ranked nineteenth in the infant death rate and the death of children from diarrhea and enteritis, seventeenth in maternal deaths, in a tie for thirteenth and fourteenth place in the typhoid-fever death rate, thirteenth in the diptheria death rate, and tenth in the tuberculosis death rate.[7]

Flint's relative lack of concern for its citizens was matched by the lack of concern for Flint on the part of many of its inhabitants. A large proportion of the workers who were lured to the city by automobile jobs and the high wages that GM paid were from rural backgrounds, and many of them reacted unfavorably to the industrial discipline imposed by the factory. Instability of employment, a characteristic of the automobile industry as a whole in the 1920's, was especially marked in Flint, where labor turnover rates in some plants sometimes reached 200 or 300 percent. Many workers did not identify with Flint as a community and tended to see the city as "a place to camp, rather than a place to settle."[8]

Flint's population in 1930 was composed principally of native-born white Americans: only 3.6 percent (5725) of the city's inhabitants were Negroes, and only 14.2 percent (21,365) of the whites were foreign born. In Detroit, by contrast, 7.6 percent of the population as of 1930 were Negroes, and 27.9 percent of the whites were foreign born. About 55 percent of the operatives and laborers in Detroit's automobile plants were foreign born or Negroes, but the corresponding figure in Flint was 28 percent. Negroes were especially inconspicuous among GM's Flin workers, their employment being limited to the most menial of occupations.

Among the foreign born in Flint, old immigrants and English-speaking immigrants were more conspicuous than the new immigrants from southern and eastern Europe who were so important an element in Detroit's population. About half of Flint's foreign born came from British Canada (28.3 percent), England (15 percent), and Scotland (6.2 percent), and an additional 5.2 percent were German in origin. In Detroit about 32 percent of the foreign born were from Poland, Russia, Italy, Rumania, and Greece, but less than 16 percent of Flint's foreign born came from these countries. The ethnic composition of the native-born whites in Flint of foreign-born and mixed parentage, who constituted about 29 percent of the native-born whites, corresponded closely to the composition of the foreign-born population itself.[9]

Of Flint's 128,617 native-born whites in 1930, 64.8 percent (83,290) had been born in Michigan and only about 30 percent in Flint itself. Of the remaining native-born whites in Flint in 1930, about 12 percent (15,383) had migrated to the city from Ohio, Indiana, Illinois, and Wisconsin, and about 12.2 percent (15,689) from the states of the South. The overwhelming proportion of Flint's Southerners were drawn from the Central South, from Arkansas, Kentucky, Missouri, and Tennessee: about 10 percent (12,818) of Flint's native-born white population in 1930 derived from these four states, and sections of the city had come to be known as "Little Missouri."

More than three-quarters of the Southern whites in Flint in the middle 1930's had first come to the city during the prosperity decade of the 1920's. Because of their "group consciousness" and the persistence of regional attitudes, they were less readily assimilated than Northern whites who journeyed to Flint. They were more attached to their Southern homes than to the city where they were employed, and they returned regularly to the South when they were laid off or during vacation time. In Flint most of them worked in the GM plants as unskilled or semiskilled workers. They tended to be young people, in the twenty to thirty-four age group, and were less affluent and less skilled than the city's population as a whole. They were entirely without union experience, but they were to play their part in the sit-down strike, and they would in the end react to the CIO with something akin to the fervor they displayed at the religious revivals that were so much a part of their cultural heritage.[10]

Flint, like Detroit, lost population when the great depression that followed the stock-market crash of 1929 began to ravage the city. The estimated population of the city had risen to 165,000 in 1931, but a Civil Works Administration survey in 1934 revealed a decline to 144,429. Much of the population loss was attributable to the sharp falling off of GM employment, which dwindled from a high of fifty-six thousand in June, 1929, to a depression low of just under seventeen thousand in August, 1932, and which was only about twenty-one thousand early in 1934. The drop in GM employment was reflected in the decline of the number of whites from the Central South in Flint, their number having fallen by almost thirty-seven hundred between 1930 and 1934.[11]

Welfare facilities in Flint were quite inadequate to cope with the serious decline in employment. Until 1931 private agencies sought to deal with the problem, caring for an average of 907 families (about thirty-five hundred people) during this period. A public relief agency was created for the city in 1931, the year the full force of the depression hit Flint, but it was privately financed, and its budget was inadequately responsive to public needs. It was nevertheless providing some assistance for 5229 families (almost twenty thousand people) toward the end of November, 1932. More generous financing and assistance came with the fall of 1933, when the federal government through the Federal Emergency Relief Administration and the state through its Emergency Welfare Relief Commission began channeling funds into Flint for relief. It was undoubtedly becoming apparent to GM workers that the corporation alone could not provide for all their needs and that government could serve as the provender of good things.[12] Perhaps, some may have thought, the union could also be of some assistance to them, even in a company town, in improving the conditions under which they labored and lived.

When the State Emergency Welfare Relief Commission made a study of employment and unemployment in Flint as of January 14, 1935, it found that 42,435 of the city's 53,929 workers were employed and 11,494 (21.3 percent) were unemployed. More than half of the city's labor force (28,455 persons) was made up of automobile workers, nearly all of them employed by GM. Among those classified as automobile workers, 23,216 were employed at that time and 5239 (18.4 percent) were unemployed.[13] Of the unemployed automobile workers remaining in the city, six hundred (11.4 percent) had been without work at least twelve months, and 4777 (91.1 percent) at least three months. Among the employed workers in the auto industry,

9641 (41.5 percent) had received an income of less than $1000 in 1934; 9227 (39.7 percent) had earned between $1000 and $1499; and 4329 (18.7 percent) had earned $1500 or more. Among those who were unemployed in January, 1935, more than 61 percent (3234) had earned less than $500 in 1934, and more than 95 percent (4996) had earned less than $1000.[14] The plight of many of Flint's automobile workers in the depression years is suggested by the figures cited.

The improving economic conditions in Flint during the eighteen months before the GM strike began are reflected in the rise of GM employment, the decline in the relief cases of Genesee County, whose population was made up chiefly of Flint residents, and the increase in the city's population. GM employment, which stood at about twenty-one thousand early in 1934, rose to 47,247 in December, 1936. Whereas the average number of persons receiving general relief in Genesee County was 18,504 (8.8 percent of the 1930 population) during the fiscal year July 1, 1933–June 30, 1934, and 24,514 (11.6 percent of the 1930 population) during the fiscal year 1934–35, only 13,148 persons (6.2 percent of the 1930 population) received general relief during the fiscal year 1935–36; and from July, 1936, through December, 1936, the number receiving relief *from all programs* did not reach 8800 (4.1 percent of the 1930 population) in any month. Only about 35 percent of the relief cases in 1936 were directly attributable to unemployment in the automobile industry. As for the city's population, it rose to an estimated 160,000 in 1936, which was somewhat above the 1930 figure.[15]

When it issued its report for the period May 1, 1934–June 30, 1935, the Flint Public Welfare Board commented that the "great need" in the city was better housing for its wage earners and dependent families. The report noted that the board had been unable to find satisfactory housing at reasonable rentals for families on relief and that the poor of the city lived in "shacks, huts, and hovels."[16] Of Flint's 35,248 housing units as of 1934, only thirteen had been built in 1932 and fourteen in 1933 as contrasted to 3538 units in 1927, 2504 in 1928, and 2214 in 1929, and there was to be little new construction in the next few years.[17] Among the existing housing units, 14.34 percent required structural repairs, meaning that there had been "serious deterioration" in one of the essential elements of the dwelling, and 1.94 percent of the units were altogether unfit for occupation. More than 20 percent of the homes were without a bath, and 12.7 percent had no toilet. About one-fourth of the homes were without hot water, and about 6 percent had no running water at all. About 18 percent of the homes had no central heating. A local housing expert reported at the time of the sit-down strike that approximately one-fifth of Flint's inhabitants lived in homes that he did not consider adequate in terms of the American standard of living. In some working-class districts half of the homes were reported to have been without baths, indoor toilets, and running water. When the UAW stepped up its organizing activities in Flint in the summer of 1936, it reminded workers of the "poor houses" in which they lived.[18]

Flint's houses helped to give the city the dingy look and the appearance of "drab uniformity" that impressed so many Flint visitors. One of the characters in Catherine Brody's Flint-based depression novel, *Nobody Starves,* described the workingmen's homes in the city as "Shacks—neat packing-boxes upended, unpainted many of them, row after row of them, divided by dirt roads ... each with a leaner, taller box of privy behind it." " 'Who would *live* in such a place?' " the chief female character in the novel asks. Twenty years later a visitor to the city was struck by the lack of variety in the houses that GM had built in the 1920's, which stood "row on row and mile on mile as ugly reminders of two hectic decades." The neighborhoods adjacent to the great GM plants were particularly depressing, with their cheap housing, unattractive workingmen's restaurants, beer halls, and cheap stores.[19]

Prior to 1932 Flint and Genesee County had been solidly Republican in their politics, although Flint had elected a Socialist mayor in 1911. This had shocked the power structure of the city, with the result that the Republicans and Democrats had joined forces the next year to form an Independent Citizens' party and to elect Charles Stewart Mott as the city's mayor. The election of November, 1932, marked the "unprecedented elevation to power" in Genesee County of the Democratic party, which swept every county office being contested. The Democrats, whose votes were drawn from Flint's low-income districts just as the Republican strength was concentrated in the high-income areas, repeated their triumph in 1934 and 1936, but in the spring elections of 1935 the three Republican Circuit Court judges, Edward D. Black, James S. Parker, and Paul V. Gadola, were retained in office.[20] Two of these judges were to play prominent roles in the GM sit-down strike.

At the time of the GM strike Flint had a nonpartisan, commission-city manager type of government. Voters in each of the city's nine wards biennially elected a commissioner, and they in turn selected one of their number to serve as mayor and also designated the city manager, by far the more important of the two officials. The city manager when the sit-down strike began was John M. Barringer, who had come to Flint in 1917 and had been prominent in the foundry business. Although totally without experience in politics and public life, Barringer became the president of Flint's Civic League when it was organized in 1928; and when the League bloc gained control of the city commission in 1932, he was appointed city manager. Barringer was an excitable person who was difficult to approach, lacked political awareness and the common touch, and was inclined to see the problem of industrial relations essentially as Flint's GM executives did.[21]

"Flint is decidedly a Company Town," the superintendent of the Flint District of the Methodist Episcopal church declared shortly after the GM sit-down strike had been concluded. He observed that one of the leading social-gospel advocates who had been in the city during the strike had remarked that the only difference between Flint and the usual company town was that in Flint the workers did not have to buy at a company store. The company " 'owns this town,' " the bus driver declares in Catherine Brody's novel. "It was hardly possible," the author noted, "to find a person" in the city "who was not conversant or did not appear to be conversant with its [the company's] affairs."[22]

GM's factories, "long, squat, and seemingly all windows," were dispersed throughout Flint: Buick, which took up nine million square feet of floor space, in the north, Chevrolet and Fisher Body No. 2 in the west, Fisher Body No. 1, the largest plant of its kind in the world, in the south, and AC Spark Plug in the east. GM's 47,247 employees as of December, 1936, constituted more than two-thirds of all the gainfully employed in the city and more than one-quarter of the city's entire population. It was estimated that 80 percent of Flint's families were dependent on GM's payroll. The goal of GM public relations in the corporation's plant cities, it will be recalled, was to have GM employees and the public at large "think and say 'WHAT HAPPENS TO GENERAL MOTORS HAPPENS TO ME.' "[23] In Flint, this message must have appeared self-evident.

The establishment in Flint was dominated by GM. Its top executives and their wives, along with members of some of the old pre-automobile era families, formed the upper crust of Flint society, and the company's influence radiated throughout the community. When the UAW in the summer and fall of 1936 pushed its organizing drive in Flint, it found itself unable to secure a permit to pass out handbills, to purchase radio time, or to secure publicity in the Flint *Journal*, the city's only daily newspaper. "Both outfits," Bob Travis informed Adolph Germer with regard to the local radio station and newspaper, "shiver in their boots when an attempt is made to obtain publicity for the automobile workers." The Flint *Journal* was not inclined to print anything that might offend the most powerful business in the city and the newspaper's principal advertiser. There was no doubt where the *Journal's* sympathy would lie in any conflict between the union and the corporation.[24]

The political leaders of Flint at the time of the sit-down were closely allied with the city's principal employer. At least three of the city commissioners worked for GM. Barringer had been invited to come to Flint by Walter Chrysler when he had headed GM's Buick Division in order to establish a foundry that would provide Buick with castings. The chief of police, James V. Wills, had once been a Buick detective. One of the Genesee County Circuit Court judges held a sizable bloc of GM stock, and the county prosecutor was a minor GM stockholder. The mayor of Flint, Harold Bradshaw, had been employed by Buick since 1919. He had edited the *Buick News*, served as the division's recreation director, worked in its payroll department, and at the time of the strike was employed in its sales and distribution department. He represented one of Flint's "better" residential districts and had the political support of the minor GM executives, merchants, professional men, and better-paid workers who resided in the district.[25]

In times of crisis GM could count on the loyal support of the Flint police department. During the Fisher Body No. 1 strike in July, 1930, the city police had in effect served as an arm of the company in the suppression of the walkout. In September, 1933, the city of Flint, which was, among public agencies, the eleventh largest purchaser of gas in the United States during the period 1933–37, bought $400.73 worth of tear gas. The order was billed to the Manufacturers' Association of Flint, but the salesman who forwarded the order thought that the gas was really being purchased for Chevrolet. When the Toledo Chevrolet strike threatened to spread to the Buick plant in May, 1935, city and county law officers agreed to cooperate to "the fullest possible degree" in the implementation of the Buick "Plan of Action for Emergency." The city police arranged to have thirty to fifty police officers report for assignment to the plant at the expected zero hour, and police headquarters were linked to the plant by direct wire.[26] In seeking to organize Flint's automobile workers the UAW had to contend not only with the most powerful manufacturing concern in the world but also with local law officers who were prepared to support the corporation at every turn.

II

Flint in 1936 was a laboring man's town, but it was not a union town. The UAW, it will be recalled, had registered impressive membership gains in the city immediately preceding the President's settlement of March 25, 1934, but disillusionment and despair had set in after that date; and as of June, 1936, the total membership in good standing in the five GM locals in the city was a paltry 150. It was apparent to the UAW leadership, however, and to no one more than Wyndham Mortimer, that if the automobile workers were to be organized the UAW would have to penetrate GM's Flint stronghold. In early June, 1936, Mortimer was sent to Flint to take charge of the UAW's organizing work in the city. It is possible, as has been alleged, that Homer Martin, who distrusted his first vice-president, hoped that Mortimer would discredit himself in a vain effort to stir Flint's hitherto apathetic auto workers into action, but it is more likely that Mortimer asked for the assignment because he saw Flint as "the most important point in the whole organization Campaign."[27]

When Mortimer arrived in Flint, the prospects for the UAW in the city could not have appeared more somber. The membership of the five locals was miniscule, and their treasury was depleted—the cash assets of the locals totaled $24.41, and they had debts for rent alone of $700. Mortimer reported that his steps were "dogged by stool pigeons," that the workers were enveloped in "a pall of fear," and that "a wall of hate and dissention [sic] had been erected between various factions." His initial action was to consolidate the five locals into a single organization (Local 156) to promote a feeling of unity among union members and to discourage parochialism. Elections were then held by the members to select a thirteen-man executive board for the consolidated local.

Mortimer, however, soon found himself at odds with the members of the union's board, and he was to claim that two of them were allegedly members of the Black Legion, a Ku Klux Klan-type organization that was centered in the industrial cities of southern Michigan and that the UAW charged was intimidating unionists, two were suspected of espionage, and five were not employed in the industry or were inactive in union affairs. Mortimer insisted further that the executive board deliberately kept the union small so that it could be "more readily controlled." The instrument to achieve this result, he contended, was the so-called investigating committee which reported on the eligibility of applicants for union membership following a two-week probationary period. Although Mortimer was rarely inclined to attribute noble motives to the opposition in the UAW's factional fights, there was some substance to his allegations. But he did not tell the whole story. Partly, the opposition to him in Flint simply reflected continuing, conservative Dillonite sentiment within the board, partly it bespoke an anti-Communist reaction to his left-leaning proclivities and his refusal to exclude Communists from the local.[28] The tension between the local's executive board and the UAW vice-president remained unresolved throughout Mortimer's stay in Flint.

Mistrusting a majority of the Local 156 executive board, Mortimer took personal charge of the union's records, had the combination changed on its safe, assured new unionists that their identity would not be revealed, and established an organizational apparatus that was "entirely independent" of the local leadership. Since the union's meetings were poorly attended, either because the workers were afraid to appear or were simply disinclined to identify themselves with so impotent an organization as the UAW, Mortimer decided to take the union message directly to the rank and file in their homes. He visited dozens of former members and attempted to ascertain why they had quit the organization and what would induce them to rejoin. When he enlisted a member, Mortimer might designate the recruit as a voluntary organizer, thus giving him a sense of self-importance. Key workers were encouraged to hold house parties for their "trustworthy friends" at which Mortimer would spread the union gospel and for which the UAW provided the refreshments.

Mortimer directed special appeals at the ethnic groups, particularly the Poles and the few Negroes in the Flint plants. He later recalled addressing a small Negro meeting in a Spiritualist church and stating that the UAW would not be a Jim Crow union, whereupon the preacher rose and said that Mortimer was "'an emissary of God'" and that the members must therefore join the union, which they all did. The initiation fee for new members and the reinstatement fee for delinquent members were reduced for the time being to lighten the financial burden of membership.[29]

Since the UAW did not have a journal of its own, Mortimer decided to send out a weekly letter to more than one thousand Flint auto workers to acquaint them with the union cause.[30] In these letters, the first of which was dated July 10, Mortimer, realizing that there was no hope for the union in Flint as long as it remained identified with the old AFL leadership and policies, contrasted the UAW of the time of Collins and Dillon with the UAW that had now decided "to sink or swim with the Lewis Committee." The UAW, he wrote, was now "completely autonomous," it was committed to industrial unionism, it had "a really 'Progressive' leadership" that was drawn from the shops, and it was controlled by the rank and file. He reminded the workers of the "mere shacks or shanties" in which they lived, told them that GM was interested in profits, not humanity, and explained that the solution to their problems lay in their own hands. It was not the union that they should fear but the loss of their jobs because of the speed-up, machinery, and old age, and it was to the union that they should look for job security.

As might have been anticipated, Mortimer's letters were not without their ideological overtones. The workers, he wrote again and again, must be class conscious just as the employers were class conscious; they must be aware that the struggle was between "the robber and the robbed," that the union was "a class weapon." He criticized the individualistic attitudes of laborers who were "capitalists from their ears up, and slaves from their ears down." As for the allegations of Communism within the union, Mortimer insisted that such charges were advanced by either stool pigeons or fools, but he declared at the same time that it was "now possible for a member to hold an opinion originating since the Civil War, without being called a 'Red' or a Communist."[31]

Despite Mortimer's zealous efforts in Flint, despite the importance attached to his efforts in the literature of the sit-down strike,[32] his organizational work in the GM stronghold did not result in any noteworthy increase in union membership. He persuaded a few former UAW members to rejoin the organization, but, if the report of the financial secretary of Local 156 is accurate, he was singularly unsuccessful in getting workers not previously identified with the union to become UAW members.[33] The overwhelming majority of Flint auto workers remained uncommitted, and it would require some dramatic display of union strength before they would be willing to embrace the UAW.

Mortimer himself did not claim impressive membership gains for the UAW. "These were by no means days of spectacular growth...," he later reported, "but rather days of slow plodding and painful preparation which only much later bore its fruit." Mortimer not only failed to increase the Flint local's membership to any appreciable extent, but he was also unable to win over his opponents within the union, who were convinced that he was fashioning a " 'Red Empire' " in Flint and was "taking everything politically." A union delegation from Flint visited Germer in Detroit on September 27 to complain that Mortimer was working with Communists and persons who leaned that way and to request that he be removed. They asked that Fred Pieper be brought in to replace Mortimer, but if they could not have Pieper they were willing to accept Bob Travis.

Germer was apparently persuaded by what he had heard and, probably unaware of the close ties between Mortimer and Travis, suggested to Homer Martin that he place Travis in charge of organizational work in Flint. Martin, who had also received complaints from Flint and had discussed Mortimer's ouster with some GEB members, had himself decided by this time that the UAW's first vice-president must leave Flint, and so he indicated his agreement with Germer's suggestion.[34]

In a letter to the UAW's officers, Mortimer struck back at his opponents and defended himself against charges of "lack of cooperation," but he was not unwilling to have Travis, who was very much under his influence, become the organizational director in Flint. Mortimer agreed to remain in the city for three weeks to break in his successor, and he thereafter made frequent trips to Flint to keep in touch with developments there. Mortimer never lost sight of the strategic importance of Flint for the conquest of union power in the automobile industry.[35]

When Travis drove to Flint and discovered how many workers were employed at the mammoth Buick and Chevrolet plants, he decided that the job assigned to him was beyond his capacity, but UAW officials persuaded him to remain at the post. Pieper was also assigned to Flint to aid Travis and to "investigate" Mortimer, but he appears to have stayed in the city only briefly and then to have returned to his home base in Atlanta.[36] The job of aiding Travis was then given to Roy Reuther, who, along with his older brother Walter and younger brother Victor, was to be one of the significant figures in the great sit-down strike.

The Reuthers were sons of a German immigrant to the United States who had become an organizer for the United Brewery Workers and then president of the Ohio Valley Trades and Labor Assembly. As Victor said of himself, all three brothers, in a sense, had been "born into the labor movement." In the late 1920's Walter left the family home in Wheeling for Detroit, where he worked as a tool and die maker, and he was later joined there by Victor and then Roy. The three Reuthers, all of whom had been attending Wayne State University (the present name) on a part-time basis and had taken part in Socialist activities there, came to the aid of the Briggs strikers in Detroit in early 1933, and Roy retained an ankle scar resulting from an encounter with the police as a memento of that event.

During the course of the Briggs strike, Victor and Walter, who had lost his Ford job because he was considered an "agitator," began a three-year tour of the world, bicycling their way through Europe, working for sixteen months as tool and die makers in an automobile plant near Gorki that had been built for the Soviet Union by Ford, and then returning to the United States via Manchuria, North China, Japan, and the Pacific. Walter took a job at the Ternstedt plant in Detroit, began to play a part in the small West Side UAW locals that were eventually amalgamated into a single local, and was elected to the GEB at the South Bend convention. Victor, after his return to the United States, toured the country as a speaker for the Emergency Peace Campaign but was summoned to Detroit by Walter and Roy at the end of November, 1936, to join in the campaign to organize the auto workers.

After his brothers left for Europe, Roy attended Brookwood Labor College, a resident school for workers in Katonah, New York, that championed the "progressive" line in the trade-union debate and was critical of the conservatism of the AFL, and then enrolled in an FERA teacher-training program in workers' education at the University of Wisconsin. He taught in the FERA's workers' education program in Detroit and was then assigned to Flint in 1934 in a similar capacity. His knowledge of the city and of working conditions in the automobile plants persuaded the UAW leadership to send him back to Flint as an organizer in November, 1936. A fine speaker, as were his brothers, Roy nicely supplemented the talents of Travis, who was extremely effective in face-to-face relationships and in small groups but lacked the oratorical power to sway an audience.[37]

Travis, in the main, followed Mortimer's tactics of organization. He tended to ignore the executive board of Local 156 in the making of policy and, convinced, as Mortimer had been, that the local was "shot full" of stool pigeons, kept the names of new members secret insofar as it was possible to do so. Travis did, however, use executive board members to aid in the job of organization. Each member of the board was assigned a ward in Flint and was in turn to set up precinct committees to reach every auto worker in the city. Travis also used new members as voluntary organizers and, like Mortimer, made special efforts to attract the city's ethnic groups. Following his predecessor, Travis concentrated on enrolling such strategically located workers as those employed in the "body-in-white" department in Fisher Body No. 1, where the principal soldering and welding took place. He sought further to prepare the ground for future action by appointing a number of shop stewards in the various plants, but for the moment their identity was kept secret. Since he found that the men in the plants "will not attend meetings in the Labor Hall," Travis continued the practice of home meetings; but to capture the imagination of the workers and to make them feel both secure and important, Travis, who had a sense of the histrionic, sometimes staged these meetings in basements, with the windows covered by black rags and the only light being supplied by candles.[38]

Unable to secure a license to pass out handbills or to obtain publicity through the local press and radio, Travis decided to supplement Mortimer's weekly letter by putting out a local UAW paper, the Flint *Auto Worker*. To edit the paper, he undoubtedly followed Mortimer's advice and turned to Henry Kraus, who had been the editor of the *United Auto Worker*, the organ of the Cleveland Auto Council. The Flint *Auto Worker*, the first issue of which appeared at the end of October, amplified some of the themes that Mortimer had been developing in his letters, highlighted the grievances of the automobile workers, and sought to convince them of the power that lay in organization. Mortimer was later to report that the journal had been "a major factor" in the UAW's Flint campaign.[39]

Travis found an ally in his organizing work in the Senate's La Follette Civil Liberties Committee, which had sent investigators to the Detroit area shortly after it had served GM with a subpoena on September 10. No sooner did Travis arrive in Flint than he wrote to committee staff member Ben Allen to obtain "all information that is possible on the General Motors Corporation in Flint"; and since he thought that the city was "lousy with these people," he specifically asked about labor spies in the GM auto plants. He also sought and secured the aid of the committee in attempting to discover whether the Flint police department was cooperating with GM in establishing a "spy system" in the company's plants. Travis was hoping that the "publicity value" of such information could be capitalized upon by the UAW to the union's advantage. He sought to persuade the insecure automobile workers that the government was on their side by informing them that La Follette Committee staff members would investigate persons, including foremen, who spread false reports about the union.[40]

Some of the committee staff members saw themselves more as allies of the UAW in its struggle with GM than as impartial investigators seeking to develop information for the committee's use. This was especially true of the committee's chief investigator in Detroit, Charles Kramer, who was later identified by Whittaker Chambers, Lee Pressman, and Nathaniel Weyl as having been a member of a Communist cell (the Harold Ware group) in the Agricultural Adjustment Administration.[41]

Kramer and Allen visited Flint on November 6 and 7 to secure information on labor espionage activities within the UAW. Kramer reported to the committee that the visit had been "quite fruitful" and that there was a spy "practically ready to be torn apart" by the UAW on the local's executive board but that he had advised the union to hold off for the time being lest uncovering the individual might cause the detective agency for which he was working "to shut down shop on us." Kramer also reported that he was planning to write an article for the UAW newspaper regarding the committee but that he would not sign it and would "have it appear as something done by the union itself." It appears that on this or perhaps an earlier visit to Flint Kramer had discussed with Travis the possibility of the latter's gaining the confidence of a female employee in the employment office of one of the GM plants. Travis, at all events, reported to Kramer in a few days that he had met with "utter failure" since he was not a " 'ladies' man' " and suggested that since Kramer was "young and good-looking" he might himself undertake "this extremely cautious business."[42]

At a public meeting of Flint Chevrolet unionists on December 26, Travis and Roy Reuther, acting on information supplied by La Follette Committee investigators, dramatically exposed a Corporations Auxiliary Company spy who was then serving as the chairman of the union's welfare committee. The Flint *Auto Worker* revealed at the same time that another Corporations Auxiliary Company operative, the one that had been "ready to be torn apart" in November, was a member of the local's executive board and that the La Follette Committee was on the trail of still other spies. Travis was undoubtedly trying to instill courage in the auto workers by demonstrating that an agency of the federal government was aiding the union in rooting out the labor spies in its midst, and Kramer, at least, was not at all reluctant to cast the committee in this role. The committee, Kraus concluded, was "an enormous boon to the union campaign."[43]

From the time that he arrived in Flint Travis had been thinking in terms of a strike against GM. On October 21, a few weeks after he had assumed his new duties, he advised his own Toledo Chevrolet local that "Things are popping so fast here that by the time you receive this letter we may be in one of the biggest strikes yet. At least I hope so." Organization had proceeded most rapidly in Fisher Body No. 1, which Travis reported as "just about boiling over." Anticipating the nature of the GM strike when it would come, Travis advised the Toledo local to be prepared "to come out on the street" at any time and to "organize every man possible that is willing to come to Flint on an hour's notice." The day after this letter was written, the first issue of the Flint *Auto Worker*, a special Fisher Body No. 1 edition that Kraus and Travis had worked through the night to complete, made its appearance. "The iron is hot out there," Travis wrote to Mortimer, "and so we are striking."[44]

The national elections of November 3, 1936, had the same exhilarating effect on auto workers in Flint as elsewhere, but Mortimer advised the Flint unionists that they should remember their experience under the NRA and should not expect anything more from the

Sit-Down

President than the protection of their constitutional rights; they must fight their own battles rather than look to someone else to do the fighting for them.[45] This advice was, in a sense, applied in Fisher Body No. 1 on November 13 when a dramatic, quickie sit-down was staged under the direction of Travis' principal lieutenant in the plant, Berdine Arlington (Bud) Simons.

The lanky, dark-eyed, and dark-complected Simons had been born on April 16, 1905, in southern Indiana, the son of a tenant farmer. A very proud youngster, he quit school after a junior high teacher had told him when he was unable to pay $5 for a school dance, " 'You've always been a disgrace to this school, Berdine!' " After working in a number of towns and at a variety of jobs, Simons journeyed to South Bend, where in 1924 he became a torch solderer in the Studebaker plant. He moved on to Hayes Body in Grand Rapids in 1928 and there joined the Communist-dominated Auto Workers Union and participated in a 1930 strike that was led by AWU representatives. It was at Hayes Body that Simons formed an enduring friendship with Joe Devitt and Walter Moore, and the three men were later to work closely together during the GM sit-down.

Like so many other automobile workers, Simons lost his job as the result of the depression and had to go on relief. Early in 1934 he joined Devitt and Moore in a move to Flint, where the three men went to work in the No. 1 plant and joined its federal labor union. Simons identified with the "progressive opposition" to the AFL within the UAW and attended the rump convention of the progressives in Cleveland in September, 1934, even though his local had voted against sending a delegation. The three friends were later to become part of the "secret union nucleus" that Mortimer and Travis fashioned in Fisher Body No. 1.[46]

Following a string of brief sit-downs in the No. 1 plant late in October and early in November that had brought concessions from the management, Simons urged Travis to permit him to call a strike " 'before one pops somewhere that we won't be able to control!' " When Travis asked if the men were ready for a strike, Simons reportedly replied, " 'They're like a pregnant woman in her tenth month!' "[47] Simons was thus prepared for action when the opportunity presented itself on the evening of Friday, November 13. Three welders who had participated in a quickie sit-down the previous night discovered when they arrived for work on the thirteenth that they were to be dismissed for their behavior. The news of this decision, coupled with the apparent intention of the plant superintendent to dismiss a unionist who protested the firing of his fellow workers, led Simons to order a shutdown of the key body-in-white department, of which he was the steward. This resulted in the idling of seven hundred men.

Hoping to secure a quick resumption of work, the plant manager, Evan J. Parker, agreed to meet a committee headed by Simons. Simons informed Parker that it was a committee of the union to which he was speaking and that there would be no resumption of work until the men who had been fired had been returned to their jobs. Parker said that the three men would be reemployed on Monday, but Simons, supported by the sit-downers, insisted upon their immediate reinstatement as the condition for the resumption of work. Anxious for the line to be started, Parker agreed to this and also to paying the sit-downers their regular rate for the period of their inactivity. It proved difficult to find one of the discharged men, who was out on a date, and so the company enlisted the aid of the police for this purpose. When the three men returned to the plant, Simons had each of them state to the workers that it was the union that had been responsible for his reinstatement.[48]

The news of what had transpired in Fisher Body No. 1 on November 13, this minor but clear-cut victory over a powerful employer, had an electrifying effect on Flint's auto workers. "We have cracked her open at last," Mortimer told the *Daily Worker*. The *United Automobile Worker* reported that five hundred No. 1 workers had joined the UAW on November 14 and that Mortimer and Travis had signed up fifty No. 2 members on the same day. By the end of the month the Flint UAW, whose paid-up membership was probably not in excess of 150 at the end of October, had a membership of fifteen hundred, most of it concentrated in the two Fisher Body plants.[49] The steward system, "the vital heart of the union in the shop" that had functioned so effectively in the November 13 sit-down, was now spread to the No. 2 plant as well, and the stewards in both plants were able during the next few weeks to settle some of the minor grievances of their men.[50]

The UAW in Flint was once again injected into the city spotlight on December 18, when 110 bus drivers of the Flint Trolley Coach Company went on strike in an effort to raise their wages from fifty-five cents to seventy-five cents an hour. The strikers were members of a local of the Amalgamated Association of Street Electric Railway and Motor Coach Employees of America, but since they had struck in violation of the union's contract with the management, they were repudiated by the Detroit leadership of the local and were eventually suspended from the union. UAW Local 156, however, quickly came to the support of the strikers, and Roy Reuther became their spokesman.

Sit-Down

With the city deprived of its public transportation, the city commission approved a resolution calling on the strikers to return to work pending arbitration of the dispute and threatening the inauguration of city jitney service should the strikers reject the proposal. Reuther warned the city not to sponsor a jitney service and said that the union would meet pressing needs by operating its own system of courtesy cars, which it quickly proceeded to do. Shortly thereafter the company, supported by Detroit officials of the Amalgamated, announced that it would operate its coaches with newly engaged workers and thus attempt to break the strike. When the UAW, however, let it be known that it would oppose this tactic, the company deferred action. Flint was still without public transportation when the auto workers joined the trolley workers on strike.[51]

The UAW, displeased when Barringer, in November, had sought to have the city commission pass an anti-noise ordinance to drive the union's sound car from the streets, thought that the trolley strike provided additional evidence of the anti-labor tendencies of Flint's city manager and the city commission. Reuther clashed frequently with Barringer and Bradshaw during the strike, and the UAW denounced the commission as "a tool of the moneyed interests and an enemy of the working people." The Flint local also included GM among the opponents of the trolley strike, insisting that the auto firm had put pressure on the trolley company not to meet the wage demands of the bus drivers lest this influence the auto workers to demand higher wages for themselves.[52]

The UAW's support of the bus drivers undoubtedly enhanced its reputation among the auto workers as a defender of the underdog and a militant champion of the laborer's aspirations for a better life. Throughout December the UAW and its friends reported impressive membership gains in Flint. "The trickle that became a stream" after the November 13 sit-down, the *United Automobile Worker* declared, "has now become a veritable tidal wave." The metaphor employed by the union journal creates an impression of UAW membership gains that is not altogether supported by the facts, but it is nevertheless evident that the union enrolled more new members in Flint in December, 1936, than in any month since the President's settlement of March, 1934. According to the UAW's records, slightly more than three thousand Flint workers joined the organization in December, which brought the total membership of Local 156 at the end of 1936 to about 4500, approximately 10 percent of Flint's GM workers. Organization had proceeded most rapidly in the No. 1 and No. 2 plants, partly the result of the November 13 strike, partly the result of dissatisfaction stemming from a particularly trying grooving-in period, always a time of discomfort for such body workers as bumpers, finishers, and sanders whose labor was primarily manual. Some of the workers in the No. 1 plant, their fear apparently abated, began to wear their union buttons in the plant, and on December 20 the plant became the first of the GM units in Flint to elect its own shop committee. As the chairman of the committee, the No. 1 unionists, appropriately enough, turned to the hero of the November 13 work stoppage, Bud Simons.[53]

The UAW's organizing efforts in Flint met with least success in the great Buick plant. Buick workers, employed in the oldest GM division in Flint, were, on the average, older than Fisher Body and Chevrolet workers, had lived longer in the city, and were far more inclined to identify with Flint and with the company than were their counterparts in the other GM plants, who were newer to the city and more hard-boiled in their attitude toward the company and toward their jobs. Working conditions were also better at Buick than in the other GM plants, and the question of production standards was less of a problem.[54] When the sit-down strike came, it was the men of Fisher Body and the workers of roughly similar background in Chevrolet who formed the spearhead of the UAW's thrust, whereas the Buick workers and the largely unorganized employees of AC Spark Plug, about half of whom were women, were not called on by the UAW to strike their plants.

GM in November, 1936, increased the wages of its workers, began to pay them time-and-a-half for hours worked above forty per week, and announced that it would grant them a year-end bonus,[55] but it gave no sign that it would soften its opposition to the UAW. On the contrary, it is possible that GM had decided to improve the terms of employment in part at least to frustrate the union drive. The hard line of GM with regard to the UAW and its ambitions was best exemplified in Flint by Arnold Lenz, assistant manufacturing manager of Chevrolet and the manager of the Flint Chevrolet plant. Early in December Travis, Roy Reuther, and Mortimer visited Lenz to complain about alleged company discrimination against union members. Lenz rejected this charge and informed the union leaders that he would fire any worker wearing a union button in the plant since this was a form of intimidation. He berated Reuther and Travis, telling them that they had "a lot of piss and vinegar" in their blood and that they were "trying to cause a lot of trouble." Lenz made no effort to conceal his opposition to unionism, informing the union delegation that in his native Germany union workers in the foundry in which he had been employed had burned his legs with hot metal because of his refusal to join their organization.[56]

Lenz's attitude could hardly have surprised Mortimer and Travis. They had assumed from the start that GM would grant the UAW the kind of recognition that it desired only if compelled to do so by a strike. When the two men began their assignment in Flint, they were undoubtedly thinking in terms of a conventional strike as the culmination of their organizational efforts; but by the end of 1936 the sit-down strike had captured the fancy of many automobile workers and of some of their leaders as well, and when the issue between the UAW and GM was finally and fully joined at the end of 1936, it was the sit-down tactic to which the union resorted.

The Coming of the Strike
V

I

The term "sit-down strike" has generally been used to embrace a variety of work stoppages ranging from the brief strike or "quickie," in which a group of workers cease their labors for a few minute. r hours or for a single shift until their grievances are settled, to the "stay-in strike," in which a portion or all of the workers remain in the plant overnight and perhaps for an extended period of time. Most commonly when the term is used the reference is to the extended sit-down strike, the so-called stay-in strike.[1]

Assuming that its legality could be sustained or its illegality ignored, the sit-down strike had numerous advantages over the conventional strike from the point of view of the strikers. The fear that his job would be taken by a strikebreaker or that production would somehow be maintained without him, a fear that deterred the potential striker or impaired the worker's morale when he was on strike, was removed when the employee sat by his idle machine inside the plant. As a picket outside the plant, moreover, the striker might be attacked by the police or even arrested and sent to jail. The employer, however, would hesitate to employ force to dislodge strikers inside his plant because this cast him in the role of aggressor, because violence might damage his machinery, and because the strikers were capable of putting up a more formidable defense inside the plant than on an exposed picket line. The strike on the inside thus offset the advantages which access to the forces of law and order normally gave the employer.

It was in some ways easier to maintain the morale of participants in a sit-down than in a conventional strike. The strikers were removed from outside pressures and the hostility of the community that their action might have induced. Bad weather did not constitute a problem for sit-downers as it did for the pickets in an outside strike. The strikers inside the plant might even find the experience an enjoyable one in many ways. They became better acquainted with fellow workers and might develop a group feeling, a " 'consciousness of kind,' " that they had not heretofore experienced on the job. If the strikers controlled the gates, they could be provided with necessities from the outside without difficulty, they could keep in touch with family and friends, and they could come and go subject to such regulations as governed the conduct of the strike. Provided that the sit-down did not continue for too long a time, the strikers might find the experience of striking considerably more exciting than the routine of the job.

It is not surprising that the sit-down strike became, for a season, the favored tactic of the automobile worker. Because of the closely interrelated processes of automobile production, a small group of automobile workers could tie up a large factory by closing down a few key departments, and they could paralyze even one of the major producers by stopping production in a few strategic plants that fabricated the parts upon which its other plants depended for their uninterrupted operation. All this could be accomplished by a minority of workers in any given plant or in any given company, which meant that the sit-down was marvelously effective as an organizing device for a union like the UAW that had succeeded in enrolling only a relatively small percentage of the automobile workers.

The sit-down strike, moreover, satisfied the urge for recognition of the depersonalized and alienated automobile worker. Looking at the idle machine beside which he sat, he could believe, for the first time perhaps, that he was its master rather than its slave and that without him the line could not move nor the machine perform its tasks. He was, after all, a human being not just a badge number, an indispensable rather than a dispensable man.[2]

The origins of the sit-down, using the term in the broadest possible sense, have in all probability gone unrecorded. Governor Frank Murphy, who had every reason to stress the antiquity of the tactic, traced its beginnings to ancient Egypt and a group of masons who sat down near the chapel in which they were working in order to compel the Pharaoh to listen to their grievances. Murphy also pointed to sit-down strikes of workers building the Rouen Cathedral in fifteenth-century France, of textile workers in Lille in 1715, and of English textile workers in 1817.[3] The first stay-in strike in the United States is said to have occurred in 1884 in Cincinnati, where brewery workers sat down in the establishment of the Jackson Brewery Company and, using barrels of beer as a barricade, successfully defended themselves against state troopers whose efforts to pierce the strikers' fortifications resulted in the flow of beer into the streets. The Industrial Workers of the World staged a sit-in strike in some of the departments of General Electric's Schenectady plant late in 1906; and apparently for the first time in a strike of this sort in the United States food had to be brought into the plant for the strikers, who remained inside the factory for sixty-five hours.

In 1907 there was a sit-down strike of fifteen hundred workers in an engineering works in Coventry, England; and in 1919 and to a far greater extent in 1920 Italian workers, with metallurgical operatives

The Coming of the Strike

in the van, occupied and continued production in a large number of factories, but the objective, as strike leaders saw it, was less the simple improvement of working conditions than it was the achievement of worker control of the factories or, as a minority of Communists desired, the outright sovietization of Italian industry. Sit-down strikes were staged in 1934 by coal miners in Jugoslavia, Hungary, and Poland, copper miners in Spain, and rubber workers in Salonika. Seventy-one Welsh miners remained in their colliery for a little more than a week in 1935, and there were "stay-down" strikes the next year in mines in England, Wales, Poland, and France.

There was a three-day sit-down at the Hormel Packing Company plant in Austin, Minnesota, in 1933, some brief sit-downs in the rubber factories of Akron in 1933, and quite a few sit-downs of the quickie variety in the automobile industry, especially in body plants, in 1933, 1934, and 1935; but it was not until the next year, 1936, that the sit-down strike began to receive widespread attention and to become a matter of some public concern.[4] There were forty-eight strikes in 1936 in which the strikers remained at their jobs for at least one day; in twenty-two of these work stoppages, involving 34,565 workers, the strikers stayed inside the plants for more than twenty-four hours. Most of these strikes were over organizational issues rather than over wages, hours, and working conditions. Thirty-five of the stoppages involved CIO unions, but the strikes were generally called without advance union authorization.[5]

Although its sit-down phase was very brief, the Goodyear rubber strike of February 14–March 21, 1936, was the first American work stoppage really to focus public attention on the sit-down tactic. It was the "'first CIO strike,'" and it was in some ways a rehearsal for the automobile sit-downs that came at the end of the year.[6] The strike, which was immediately preceded by a three-day sit-down at the Firestone Tire and Rubber Company and very brief sit-downs at Goodyear and Goodrich plants,[7] began spontaneously on Friday, February 14, when workers on three of the four shifts in Goodyear's Plant 2 sat down for various lengths of time to protest the layoff of seventy workers on the fourth shift without the customary three-day notice that might have permitted work sharing. Goodyear closed for the weekend and was not scheduled to reopen until February 18, but on the evening of the seventeenth the Plant 2 unionists voted to strike because the company had refused to guarantee 180 tire builders on the fourth shift that they would receive the usual notice before their threatened layoff.

The United Rubber Workers (URW), a weak union whose history since 1933 had in many ways paralleled that of the UAW, agreed to support the Goodyear strike although it had had nothing to do with the February 14 sit-downs. Late at night on February 17 the URW established an "endless human chain" of pickets around Plant 2; and the next day five hundred tire builders sat down in Plant 1, and pickets appeared before Plant 3. The sit-downers remained inside Plant 1 for twenty hours, and when they emerged, pickets effectively closed this unit also. By February 19 production at Goodyear had been paralyzed and fifteen thousand workers idled. The CIO sent in organizers and funds to aid the strikers, and Adolph Germer in particular helped to direct their efforts.

The company was able to secure an injunction limiting the number of pickets at each entrance to the plant, but it failed to persuade Governor Martin L. Davey of Ohio to send in militia to police the strike. Efforts by an official of the Goodyear Industrial Assembly, a company union, to stimulate a back-to-work movement were unsuccessful, and the same fate befell the provocative action of C. Nelson Sparks, a former mayor of Akron, who created a "Law and Order League" and invited the good citizens of Akron to " 'gang up upon the out-of-town radicals and communist leaders who have brought to our city the threat of a reign of terror.' " The strikers obeyed the injunction in the main, but when the police threatened to tear down the sixty-eight shanties that served what has been characterized as the longest picket line in the history of the strike in the United States to that time, the strikers congregated on the line in numbers that exceeded the limits imposed by the court order.

The strikers failed to gain some of their principal demands, such as the elimination of the company union in the plant and the designation of the URW as the exclusive bargaining agency for Goodyear workers, but the union and the CIO chose to characterize the settlement as a victory, and the strike at the very least enhanced the URW's prestige and helped to attract members to its ranks. This fact was not lost on the UAW leadership, which from the start of the strike had displayed a keen interest in what was going on in an industry so closely allied with the automobile industry.

"Your fight is our fight," the Detroit District Council of the UAW wired the striking rubber workers. The Cleveland Auto Council sent an official delegation headed by Mortimer to Akron to offer all possible aid to the URW; and the organ of the Council, the *United Auto Worker*, observed that the auto workers "feel very close to the rubber workers and can almost see themselves in their shoes, going to bat with their own oppressors, with General Motors and Ford, who are no whit better than the rubber magnates when it comes to crushing down their employees!" The relationship between their own fate and that of the Goodyear strikers was impressed upon the auto workers when one of the company conferees "let it slip" that the auto and steel manufacturers had warned Goodyear that they "could go into the rubber business" if the company yielded to the strikers. The auto and steel industries know, Germer informed Brophy on March 12, that if the Goodyear strike succeeds, "they are next in line for a battle."[8]

Homer Martin, Walter Reuther, and other UAW leaders traveled to Akron for the URW's "victory" celebration, and Martin told CIO representatives, " 'We'll be next.' " The UAW progressives in particular saw the "victory" as a triumph for industrial unionism, and they gave much of the credit for this success to the assistance rendered the strikers by the CIO and to the rubber workers' defiance of the injunction. Whether the progressives' assessment of what had occurred was accurate or not is less important than that they were prepared to apply what they regarded as the lessons of the strike to their own industry. The strikes against the major rubber producer and the major auto producer were to be linked not only in terms of tactics but in terms of personnel: CIO and URW organizers who had participated in the Goodyear strike were later to play a part in the GM sit-down, and Merlin D. Bishop, who was to direct the UAW's educational program during the GM strike and to be active in Flint, had spent a few days in Akron during the Goodyear strike aiding the efforts to maintain striker morale.[9]

About two months after the settlement of the Goodyear strike, the first mass sit-down strikes in history took place in France.[10] The strikes were preceded by the reunification of the sundered French labor movement, which was consummated in March, 1936, and by the Chamber of Deputies elections of April 26–May 3, which resulted in victory for the Popular Front, strengthened the "self-confidence" of the workers, and persuaded many of them that they no longer had to submit to existing conditions of labor.

When reunification was accomplished, the Confédération Générale du Travail (CGT) had a membership that included only 6.3 percent of the workers employed by the private sector of the French economy, and only 1.4 percent of the workers in the metal industries were covered by collective agreements. The CGT was not responsible for the sit-down strikes, which were entirely spontaneous in origin, but it counseled the strikers and coordinated their action once the strike movement was underway. The intransigent attitude of management with regard to collective bargaining, which was especially true of employers in the metal industries, contributed importantly to the development of strike sentiment among the workers; the strikes were less designed to improve working conditions as such than to enhance the bargaining power of the workers and to raise their status vis-à-vis management.

The strike movement began almost without notice in northern France on May 8, spread from there to the provinces and to Paris and its industrial suburbs, and by May 26 had taken on mass proportions. In June approximately 1.9 million workers, almost one-fourth of all the wage earners in industry and commerce, were on strike, and nearly three-fourths of the strikes, involving 8941 establishments, were of the sit-down type. Among the factories occupied by the strikers were the automobile plants of Citroen and Renault, including the latter's factory at Boulogne Billancourt, the largest in France. The employers insisted upon the evacuation of their plants as a precondition of negotiations, and their press attributed the entire strike movement to Communist influence.

Léon Blum took office on June 5 as France's first Socialist premier and was immediately importuned by the Confédération Générale de la Production Française, which spoke for management, to intervene to end the strikes, although employers apparently did not press for the forcible eviction of the strikers lest this lead to bloodshed and the worsening of the industrial-relations outlook. Despite criticism from the center and right that he was sacrificing legality and property rights in the interests of public order, Blum, although conceding that the sit-down violated French civil law, refused to use force to evacuate the plants and stated that it was his responsibility not to provoke violence but to conciliate the dispute.

Taking advantage of the fact that the employers were willing to make concessions to the workers in return for the evacuation of their plants, Blum brought both sides together for the negotiations that led to the Matignon Agreement of June 7 and the gradual decline of the strike movement. "Matignon," a historian of the French labor movement has written, "blazed the path to a definite recognition of the trade-union movement and to full recognition of the freedom to organize."[11] The agreement was quickly followed by the enactment by the Chamber of Deputies of a group of laws that in effect constituted the " 'French New Deal,' " including a statute dealing with collective bargaining that provided for agreements between the "most representative organizations" of employers and employees.[12] This legislation, coupled with the Matignon Agreement, led to an enormous expansion of the French labor movement, with the membership gains coming chiefly among the mass-production workers, such as the semiskilled and unskilled operatives in the metal industries.

The French sit-down strikes of May–June, 1936, were similar in many respects to the GM sit-down that began at the end of the year. Like the GM strike, they were initiated without official union authorization at a time when the labor movement was weak. National elections in the two countries had the same exhilarating effect upon the mood of the workers, and the goal of the strikes was primarily recognition, strongly opposed by French employers and by GM. French employers, like GM, originally insisted on evacuation as a precondition for negotiations, but the political leadership in France and Michigan refused to use force to evacuate the plants. Frank Murphy, who like the French premier, took office after the strike movement was underway, was the Léon Blum of the GM strike, and both men took pride in the fact that their efforts had led to the peaceful composition of the disputes with which they were faced and that bloodshed had been avoided at a time of profound social upheaval. Both men indicated that they would have resigned their office rather than use force to drive the strikers from the plants.

Like the GM strike, the French strikes were without revolutionary intent, and the workers in both countries took great pains to protect the property of the plants in which they were sitting. In both France and the United States the successful outcome of the sit-down strikes proved to be a decisive factor in the organization of the unorganized and the unionization of the mass-production industries. After the strikes, employers in both countries were to complain about a rash of sit-down and quickie strikes in their plants resulting from a lack of discipline among the newly organized and inexperienced labor unionists and also, allegedly, from Communist agitation.

But there were differences between the two strike movements as well as similarities. In France the reunification of the labor movement preceded the strikes and strengthened worker morale, whereas in the United States a split in the labor movement buoyed the auto workers and was an important precursor of the GM strike. Union leaders, as distinguished from the UAW as an organization, and individual Communists were directly involved in the origins of the GM strike, but the trade unions did not begin to play a part in the French strikes until some time after they had begun, and the Communists apparently sought to stave off the strikes lest they endanger the Popular Front. In France, labor legislation providing for collective bargaining and employee representation was enacted after the strikes, whereas the NLRA, the corresponding American law, was placed on the statute books several months before the beginning of the GM strike. The American statute, however, did not become effective until its constitutionality was upheld by the United States Supreme Court in April, 1937, after the GM strike; and then, like the French law, it helped materially to stimulate the expansion of the labor movement.

The French sit-down strikes did not go unnoticed by elements of the UAW leadership.[13] They were aware of what the unorganized workers in the automobile and other mass-production industries in France had wrought, and they had undoubtedly concluded that what could be accomplished in France could also be accomplished in the United States. Knudsen, however, did not believe that the experience could be repeated in his own country. He had visited France in September, 1936, and had been warned by one of the French auto manufacturers whose plant had been closed by a sit-down that the same might happen to GM if it did not take care, but Knudsen thought otherwise. " 'No,' " he told the Frenchman. " 'That could not happen in the United States. The American people would not stand for them [sit-down strikes].' " Several weeks later the first sit-in strike (to use the UAW's terminology) in the history of the American automobile industry occurred in the South Bend plant of the Bendix Products Corporation, 24 percent of whose stock was owned by GM.[14]

The Bendix strike originated in the desire of the fairly strong UAW local in the plant to secure the closed shop or at least to be designated as the exclusive bargaining agency for the company's forty-three hundred workers.[15] The immediate cause of the dispute was the favored status allegedly accorded by the management to the Bendix Employees Association. The strike began on November 17 when some of the workers sat down by their machines. The works manager thereupon ordered all the employees to evacuate the plant, but more than a thousand of them refused to do so.[16]

The importance that the UAW and the CIO attached to the strike was indicated by the fact that Homer Martin, Adolph Germer, and Leo Krzycki all came to South Bend to lend a hand in the negotiations. The Bendix management, after first meeting with the union negotiators, refused to continue bargaining unless the plant was evacuated. On instructions from their leadership, the strikers therefore left the factory on November 23; and two days later an agreement was concluded whereby the company recognized the UAW local as the bargaining agency for its members and such other employees as chose to avail themselves of its services, pledged itself not to conclude an agreement regarding working conditions with any group other than the UAW without previously coming to terms with the union on the same questions, and agreed to the establishment of a union-management board of review to which any union member or any other employee who had secured the consent of the local's executive board could protest the decisions of the plant personnel director.[17] The union had failed to win exclusive bargaining rights and the elimination of the company union, but it had achieved a position of power and prestige within the plant, and its membership was to grow rapidly after the strike.[18]

The Bendix sit-in was the longest strike of its kind in American history to that date, and it is understandable that the UAW should have been impressed with what had transpired. A minority of the Bendix workers had quickly and successfully tied up the South Bend plant, and despite what one source described as "the very unique and rarely seen situation as this strike was," the management had not sought an injunction against the strikers, the police had made no effort to eject them, and no violence had occurred. If, as was suggested at the time, the Bendix strike was "a major testing ground" for the CIO's program of organization, the test had proved successful.[19]

There was one disturbing note for the UAW and CIO high command to consider however: Homer Martin had revealed himself in the Bendix bargaining to be an erratic, inept, and undependable negotiator. He twice left South Bend in the midst of negotiations, despite pleas from Germer to remain in the city, and after agreeing on November 20 to request the strikers to evacuate the plant, he delayed taking the action for three days. When the negotiations reached a climax on November 24, he prepared once again to leave town, and only Germer's warning that he would be "discredited" if he followed this course caused Martin to reconsider.[20] Martin's shortcomings as a negotiator were to plague the UAW throughout the sit-down era.

Two days after the settlement of the Bendix strike the UAW brought the sit-down tactic to the Detroit heart of the automobile industry by a strike at the plant of the Midland Steel Products Company, which made steel body frames for Chrysler and Ford. The union had been negotiating with the management for a wage increase, reduction of hours, and the abolition of piece work, but it decided to seek its objectives via the strike route rather than at the bargaining table when the management refused to extend a proferred wage increase to all the departments in the plant. About twelve hundred of the company's day-shift workers sat down in the plant on November 27, and the resulting halt in the production of steel frames caused the layoff within the next few days of at least fifty-three thousand workers at the Plymouth, Dodge, Chrysler, Lincoln-Zephyr, and Briggs plants. The strike was settled on December 4 and resulted in what the UAW described as "the most significant union victory in the history of the automobile industry in Detroit." The company increased its original wage offer, agreed to abolish piece rates as soon as was "practicable," reconfirmed the offer it had made just before the strike to pay time-and-a-half for hours worked above forty-five per week and on Sundays and holidays, and promised "free access for discussion" to its employees and to union representatives. The UAW might have obtained even better terms from Midland had not Ford threatened to remove its business from the company if it made any further concessions to the union.[21]

The Midland sit-down demonstrated graphically how a strike in one key automobile plant could paralyze the operation of other motor-vehicle factories that depended on its product. The strike also gave evidence of that sense of solidarity, that bond among the automobile workers and between the automobile workers and the rubber workers that was to characterize the sit-down era in the automobile industry. Chrysler and Dodge unionists informed their employers during the strike that they would not work on frames supplied by companies other than Midland, and at a crucial juncture in the strike Dodge unionists in three hundred cars paraded in front of the Midland plant. William Carney, a veteran of the Goodyear strike and a URW organizer, rendered "invaluable assistance" to the UAW throughout the strike. The strike also demonstrated how women could support a sit-down by activities on the outside: the female Midland workers and the wives of the strikers prepared the food for the strikers throughout the dispute. The head of the women's buying and cooking committee was Dorothy Kraus, the wife of the editor of the Flint *Auto Worker*, and she was to play an approximately similar role in the GM strike.[22]

Just as Communists, fellow travelers, and sympathizers with Communism were to be conspicuously involved in the GM strike so the far left was at the center of things in the Midland strike. John Anderson was the UAW organizer in charge of the strike; Nat Ganley, who had served as an organizer for the Communist-dominated National Textile Workers Union and as general organizer for the Communists' Trade Union Unity League and had been a *Daily Worker* correspondent, was an official of the UAW local involved and edited the *Midland Flash*; and Wyndham Mortimer was in on the negotiations to settle the strike. William Weinstone, the secretary of the Communist party of Michigan, called on Communists to support the strike, and the *Daily Worker*, delighted with the whole affair, predicted that the sit-down would "take the automobile industry by storm." A handbill "exposing" the Communist role in the dispute was distributed in the strike area, but it had no visible effect on the course of events.[23]

December, 1936, as it turned out, was a month of sit-down strikes in Detroit. In addition to the Midland workers, employees of the Gordon Baking Company, the fabricating and extrusion plant of the

Aluminum Company of America (Alcoa), Kelsey-Hayes Wheel Company, National Automotive Fibres, Incorporated, and Bohn Aluminum and Brass Corporation all sat down at their posts for varying periods. The UAW must have noted with keen interest that only in the Gordon Baking strike was a warrant charging trespass issued against the strikers, and only here was an effort made by police, constables, and some company employees to eject the sit-downers.[24] The UAW must also have been heartened by the opinion of the Wayne County prosecutor, Duncan McCrea, that, although employers might seek redress in the civil courts, the police could not interfere with a peacefully conducted sit-down since no statute forbade such a strike and since the applicable common law did not authorize police intervention. The sit-downers, the prosecutor declared, were inside the plant by the invitation of their employers, "so there can be no trespass."[25]

In addition to the Midland strike, several of the Detroit sit-downs of December affected the automobile industry: National Automotive Fibres made upholstery and floor mats for automobiles, Bohn Aluminum and Alcoa made a variety of automobile parts, and Kelsey-Hayes produced wheels and brakes. Of the auto-related sit-downs other than Midland, the most important was the Kelsey-Hayes strike. There were brief sit-downs in the two Kelsey-Hayes plants on December 11 and 12, but both were called off on the promise that the company would meet with union representatives. Dissatisfied with the progress of negotiations, however, the union broke off the talks, and a third sit-down was initiated on December 14 that continued to December 23. Before the third sit-down the UAW—the unit involved was Walter Reuther's West Side local—had secured the virtual dismantling of the Kelsey-Hayes company union and company agreement to a seventy-five cent minimum wage;[26] but it wanted additional increases in the higher brackets, time-and-a-half for hours worked above eight per day and forty per week, adjustment of complaints involving an alleged speed-up, and exclusive bargaining rights.

Since the Ford Motor Company received most of its brake shoes and brake drums from Kelsey-Hayes, production at the giant Rouge plant was crippled by the strike. Ford, consequently, put pressure on the company to settle and, at the same time, persuaded the union to be reasonable by threatening to seek a court order authorizing the Wayne County sheriff to seize Ford brake dies in the possession of Kelsey-Hayes. The union won the overtime rate it was seeking and the promise of adjustment of rates above the minimum, but it did not secure exclusive bargaining rights.[27] The union defeat on this point, however, was more apparent than real since the strike had an almost miraculous effect on union membership. Before the sit-down began the local had enrolled at most two hundred of Kelsey-Hayes' forty-five hundred employees, but after the strike the membership "just swelled like a great tidal wave," and before long the union had a majority of the firm's production workers in its ranks.[28]

The Kelsey-Hayes sit-down brought into prominence three UAW officials who were later to apply in the GM strike what they had learned in the Kelsey-Hayes affair: Walter and Victor Reuther and Merlin D. Bishop. Little known in the UAW at the time of the South Bend convention, Walter Reuther enhanced his reputation among the auto workers by his leadership role in the Kelsey-Hayes strike. Victor, who had just joined his brothers in the UAW campaign, and Bishop, who had once lived with the Reuthers in Detroit and had been at Brookwood with Roy, hired in at Kelsey-Hayes shortly before the strike, and Bishop in particular helped to organize the strike on the inside. After the strike began Victor left the plant to lend a hand outside the factory, and he became the union's voice in the sound car. Both Victor and Bishop were soon to be sent by the UAW to Flint to help with organization work in that city.[29]

Like the Bendix and Midland strikes, the Kelsey-Hayes strike had once again demonstrated the effectiveness of the sit-in technique, and like the Midland strike it had revealed the vulnerability of the automobile industry to a work stoppage in a key parts plant. The CIO had sent in organizers to aid the Kelsey-Hayes strikers just as it had aided the Bendix and Midland sit-downers, and public authorities had not interfered in the Kelsey-Hayes sit-down just as they had avoided involving themselves in the other two strikes. This latter fact caused *Iron Age* to remark with foreboding that "the whole political aspect of employer-employee relations has taken an abrupt turn toward organized labor in the last few months." The UAW undoubtedly reached the same conclusion, although without any foreboding.[30]

The sit-downs at Bendix, Midland, and Kelsey-Hayes provided the UAW with the necessary know how to conduct a strike of the same type against one of the major auto producers. The union had learned how to organize the sit-downers inside the plant and how to coordinate their efforts with pickets on the outside. It had experimented with workers' education inside the plant and with the sound car as a strike weapon, and it had acquired some knowledge of the logistics involved in supplying sit-downers with food and other necessities. It had discovered that worker morale might be less a problem in a sit-down than in a conventional strike, that "it became a sort of festivity for these guys."[31] Above all, the UAW had learned that a minority of auto workers could tie up a large plant by a sit-down and by so doing could bring a recalcitrant employer to terms.

It has been said that it required "a brilliant meteor flaming across the dark sky" to capture the attention of the auto workers, who, in the main, had hitherto resisted the appeals of union organizers. If so, the sit-down strikes became that "meteor." Not only did they bring the union a good deal of publicity, but they provided it with something it badly needed—the aura of victory. Before the UAW would be able to gather the majority of the auto workers within its ranks, however, it would have to win the kind of victory over one of the major producers that it had achieved in strikes against the far more vulnerable and far less powerful independent parts makers. There was an awareness among observers of the auto scene as 1936 drew to a close that the struggle with the Big Three was near at hand and that the first union target among them would be GM. "The successful sit-down strikes in the 'feeder'... [plants]," observed the *Daily Worker*, which had excellent contacts within the UAW, "have been a prelude to the march forward upon the General Motors Corporation."[32]

Of the Big Three, GM was the logical UAW target. Chrysler, which had once been Germer's first choice, seemed to be ruled out because the union enjoyed somewhat better relations with it than it did with Ford and GM, and a victory over Chrysler, in any event, was not likely to have the same impact on the auto workers as a victory over Ford or GM. Ford was more bitterly anti-union than even GM, but the UAW had almost no membership among Ford workers, and the mammoth Rouge plant seemed impregnable to union attack. GM had the advantage from the UAW point of view of not only being the leading producer in the industry but also, because of its size and the fact that du Pont was its principal shareholder, as personifying "Big Business" in the United States to a far greater extent than its rivals did.[33] If the UAW could somehow widen the narrow salient that it had thrust into the GM lines and could effect an actual breakthrough on this front, its forces would be in a strong position to conquer the auto industry as a whole.

Speaking on September 11, 1936, to representatives from the various GM locals, Homer Martin declared that the right of GM workers to organize would have to be established during the existing production season even if this required a "general strike" against the corporation. At least one GM local leader, GEB member Fred Pieper of Atlanta, who had been one of the leading protagonists of a GM strike in the spring of 1935, construed these remarks as seriously intended rather than as mere rhetoric and was soon to involve the Atlanta local in a strike against GM that would spread to the farthest reaches of the corporation.[34]

With Pieper in the lead, Atlanta Fisher Body workers staged a brief sit-down on October 30 to protest a short delay on the part of management in meeting with union representatives to discuss the piece rates announced by the company for the 1937 models, which the union alleged would result in a reduction of earnings as compared to the previous model year. An agreement was quickly reached between the local and the plant manager regarding the points in dispute, but the union was soon complaining that the agreement had not been posted, as it claimed the management had promised, that the rate adjustments made were unsatisfactory, and that plant police had passed out company-union literature inside the factory but that the union had been prevented from distributing its handbills on company property.

The local decided on November 6 to present demands to the company dealing primarily with piece rates, but since Pieper assumed that these proposals would be rejected by the management, he began to think in terms of another strike. Publicly, the local warned that, as "a last resort," the "demonstration" of October 30 would "not only be repeated on a local basis but it will develop [sic] into a National sit-down"; privately, Pieper wrote to members of the GM Advisory Council informing them that he was writing with Martin's knowledge and asking them to what extent they were prepared to support the Atlanta Fisher Body workers should they go on strike. Declaring that it would be necessary to close all Fisher Body plants to defeat GM, Pieper promised to avoid strike action until he was assured of "your support 100%."[35]

The Fisher Body and Chevrolet locals of Norwood, Kansas City, and St. Louis and the Toledo and Janesville Chevrolet locals all more or less expressed support for Atlanta. Travis advised Pieper that he would do whatever he could to persuade the executive board of the amalgamated Flint local to back the Atlanta workers, and when Atlanta did go out on strike, the Flint union declared its readiness to aid this effort.[36] Before the GM strike had been concluded, every one of the UAW locals that had pledged Atlanta support had itself joined the strike.

On November 18 some of the Atlanta Fisher Body workers sat down in the plant allegedly to prevent the layoff of a few workers for wearing union buttons inside the factory. The strikers remained in the plant overnight but evacuated it the next morning when the management agreed not to operate the factory until the dispute had been settled. When the strikers left the plant, they met jointly with the Chevrolet employees, and those present voted to declare a strike affecting both companies. The strike was spread to the parts and service division on November 24 after Pieper had told the employees of this unit that other GM locals would give them "active support" when and if their assistance was required.[37]

Why Pieper should have called the Atlanta workers out on a strike that he himself admitted they were not prepared to fight[38] remains something of a mystery to this day. The shutting down of a single assembly plant was of no great consequence to a concern like GM, which could simply transfer the work of the struck plant to other units of the corporation. This fact persuaded UAW progressives and some others in the organization as well to suspect that Pieper was playing GM's game and had deliberately provoked a premature strike at an unimportant plant so as to tip off the corporation regarding the UAW's intentions and to enable it to throttle the strike movement in its infancy.[39] There is, however, no evidence to support this thesis, and GM, at all events, made no direct effort to break the Atlanta strike, nor did it seem to view the events in Atlanta as a prelude of things to come in more important units of the corporation.

The Atlanta Fisher Body plant manager was convinced that Pieper had called the strike "purely for revenge": he recalled—and what he said was confirmed by the president of the local—that when Pieper had been dismissed two years previously, he had stated that he would make GM "pay" for this action. Revenge, thus, may very well have been one of the factors that motivated Pieper, but he insisted that he had acted from the start with the full knowledge of Martin, who, he claimed, had led him to believe that the UAW would strike all GM in support of Atlanta. Pieper so advised the Atlanta workers and then, if one accepts his version of what had occurred, used the buttons episode as a pretext to initiate the Fisher Body sit-down in the expectation that the Atlanta tail would wag the UAW dog. Martin, however, denied Pieper's allegations and charged that the Atlanta leader had blundered his way into a foolish strike and then had tried to "unload" onto others responsibility for his rash action.[40]

The Pieper version of the origins of the Atlanta strike seems closer to the actuality than the Martin version does. The Atlanta UAW leader was one of Martin's cohorts on the GEB, and it is not unlikely that, unbeknownst to other board members and certainly to the progressive faction, they had discussed GM strike tactics prior to the Atlanta sit-down. Since Martin, as events would show, was dissatisfied with the official UAW-CIO position of restraint in initiating a GM strike, he undoubtedly made remarks that led Pieper to believe that the UAW president would persuade other GM locals to support an Atlanta strike by strikes of their own. Three days after the Atlanta strike began, Martin, probably in conformity with promises made to Pieper, sent a wire to various GM locals instructing them to advise their members to "stand by for notification from the international union concerning action to be taken." This wire had been sent without the knowledge of other UAW officers, and Henry Kraus tells us that they were stunned when it came to their attention. Germer, who was also caught unawares by the UAW president's wire, let Martin know that the UAW was not prepared for the all-encompassing GM strike that he apparently had in mind.[41]

Called without the authorization of the GEB that the UAW constitution required,[42] the Atlanta strike pointed up the lack of discipline that characterized the fledgling UAW and the virtual autonomy of its locals even with regard to so crucial a matter as the initiation of a strike. The veteran unionist Germer complained to John Brophy, "It seems to be a custome [sic] for anybody or any group to call a strike at will. . . ."[43] The anarchy prevailing in the UAW helps to explain the rather anomalous manner in which the GM strike spread after its Atlanta beginnings.

The strike in Atlanta compelled the UAW officers, the GM Advisory Council, and the GEB to devise a GM strategy. Three different plans seem to have been advanced at the time. Martin, apparently, was thinking of calling out as many GM locals as could be persuaded to strike. If he had a carefully thought out strike strategy that involved any meaningful assessment of the advantages and disadvantages of alternative lines of action or of the plants that had to be struck were victory to be won, it was not apparent to his UAW confreres. Pieper and Hall favored a strike at the GM assembly plants across the land. If all or virtually all of the numerous GM assembly plants could have been closed by strikes, this strategy would have made some sense, but since the UAW simply did not have the membership needed to execute so difficult a plan, it is hard to understand why Pieper and Hall pushed it so vigorously.[44]

More experienced than the UAW leadership, Germer advised union officials to adopt a strategy of striking only the key GM plants in Cleveland, Flint, and Detroit whose shutdown would paralyze the corporation's production of automobiles. Germer, however, counselled the UAW to proceed with caution. He was aware that the union at that time had only about nine thousand members among GM's production workers, that its Flint membership was only fifteen hundred, and that the GM plants in Pontiac, Saginaw, Lansing, and Muncie were virtually without organization. He was concerned about the enormous power that GM wielded in Flint affairs and what this portended should a strike occur in that city. He realized, moreover, that it would be unwise to strike before the GM workers received the bonus that the company was scheduled to pay them beginning December 18 and before New Dealish Frank Murphy replaced conservative Republican Frank Fitzgerald as governor of Michigan.

Germer repeatedly told Martin that he must consult the CIO leadership before taking any strike action since it was the CIO that would have to finance the strike. He cautioned Martin not to build up strike hopes among the automobile workers that could not be realized lest this adversely affect UAW membership. The UAW could win, Germer wrote John L. Lewis, if it could "pull the key plants," but he feared that the union lacked the strength for this undertaking. The immediate action to be taken, he advised, was to ask GM for a conference to discuss basic demands and to defer strike talk until the corporation's response became evident.[45]

Martin and Dillonites like Pieper, undoubtedly because they were opposed to Germer's "go slow" policy, sought to exclude the CIO field representative from at least some of the meetings of the GM Advisory Council and the GEB, but wiser heads among the union's leadership, despite the "general strike talk," realized that Germer's advice was sound. By a vote of 7-6, with Hall, who was chairing the meeting in Martin's absence, casting the deciding vote, the GEB on December 4 apparently voted against an immediate strike and in favor of delay until Cleveland and Flint were ready to act, presumably after January 1, 1937. In effect repudiating Martin, the board voted to take the CIO into its "full confidence" regarding GM strategy. The general officers, Germer and Allan Haywood of the CIO, and the three-man GM steering committee then secured GEB approval for a recommendation that the general officers should seek to negotiate an agreement with the GM high command and should be given the authority, should efforts to secure the conference fail or should its results prove unsatisfactory, "to take any further action necessary to protect the best interests of the members" employed in GM. The GEB had previously decided that each GM local should begin negotiations with GM plant managers on the basis of a contract that was being drawn up by the GM steering committee and the general officers.[46]

The GEB also officially decided on November 30 to give UAW support to the Atlanta strike. Ed Hall contacted Harry Anderson about the strike, but Anderson informed him that it was GM policy for plant managers to settle disputes locally. The GEB therefore dispatched Hall to Atlanta, but he reported back in a few days that "the only word the Company knew was 'No' " and that it had proved impossible to establish a basis for collective bargaining. The UAW then sent Germer to Atlanta to see if he could arrange a settlement. Germer, who regarded the Atlanta strike as "senseless" and thought that Pieper had run "amuck," wanted to close out the affair, but he saw the need for a face-saving settlement that would not cause the UAW to lose its momentum. The local management, however, would agree to nothing but a return to work on a status quo ante basis. Despite what GM said in Detroit, the Atlanta negotiations revealed that the corporation's plant managers were without power to make concessions to the union that involved any real change in its status. They apparently could not even agree on their own to permit union members to wear union buttons on the job. Unable thus to win a local victory, the strikers were reconciled to remaining away from their jobs until the UAW spread the strike to more important units of the GM domain.[47]

The Libby-Owens-Ford glass strike that began on December 15 became an additional factor in the UAW's GM strategy since the continuation of GM automotive production was now threatened by a potential shortage of plate glass. How much plate glass GM had on hand was not publicly known, but Glenn McCabe, the president of the Federation of Flat Glass Workers, contended on December 24 that the glass strike would tie up the auto industry within fifteen to thirty days and that his organization would help the UAW to "force" its demands on GM.[48]

The day after the Libby-Owens-Ford strike began the GM strike spread to Kansas City. The alleged cause of the dispute was the decision of the local Chevrolet management on December 15 to dismiss a union employee who, despite two warnings, had violated a frequently violated company rule by jumping over the line on his way to the lavatory. When the union leadership the next day failed to persuade the company to reconsider its decision, the Fisher Body workers, who belonged to the same local as the Chevrolet unionists and worked in the same plant, sat down at their jobs, which forced the closing of Chevrolet as well and the idling of about twenty-four hundred workers. The sit-down continued until December 23, when the union moved the strike to the outside primarily because of the difficulties it was encountering in feeding the sit-downers. Martin soon stated that the Kansas City strike, which involved his home local, would have to be settled on a national basis, and he allegedly told the strikers that there would be a general auto strike if the GM strikes then underway were not settled.[49]

The strikes in Atlanta and Kansas City prompted Knudsen to state in a speech of December 18 that collective bargaining was "here to stay" but that it should occur "before a shutdown rather than after."[50] The same day that Knudsen made this speech, Lewis, Brophy, Mortimer, Hall, Martin, and McCabe held a conference of crucial importance in Washington. Rejecting the idea of waiting until the production season of the fall of 1937 to mount an "intensified effort" against GM, they agreed to implement at once the GEB decision to seek a general conference with GM to discuss outstanding grievances and decided that if the company should refuse to negotiate "on a broad scale" the union objective should be "to move towards a climax in January."[51] Undoubtedly the considerations Germer had previously advanced regarding the GM bonus and the date of Murphy's assumption of office, plus the fact that the Christmas season was psychologically a poor time to ask workers to go on strike, prompted the decision to delay a possible work stoppage until after the beginning of the New Year.

It is unlikely that the Washington conferees set any specific date after January 1 for a strike should the GM negotiations fail as expected. The CIO must have been aware, however, that UAW leaders were impressed with the "influx" of workers into the organization in the previous few weeks, that Martin believed the membership was "enough to do business with," that the UAW was committed to a confrontation with GM, and that a strike could not be delayed for very much longer. Lewis told the press that GM's policy, unlike Chrysler's, was "antagonistic," called on the company to "do a little collective bargaining," and said, "That will be up to General Motors" when asked if there would be a strike.[52]

When John Brophy arrived in Detroit on December 20 to aid Martin in preparing the necessary communications to GM requesting a conference, he sought to bring further pressure on the corporation by declaring that the CIO would back the UAW if there were a strike and that his presence testified to this fact. He had previously sent a statement for publication to the writer Louis Adamic in which he noted that the CIO did not "condemn sit-down strikes *per se*. In the formative stage of unionism in a certain type of industry," he observed, "the sitdown strike has real value.... Sitdown strikes ... occur when the employer fails to meet in full the requirements of collective bargaining." Brophy made it clear shortly after his arrival in Detroit that these remarks were relevant to the UAW's relations with GM.[53]

In consonance with the strategy agreed upon in Washington, Martin on December 21 sent a wire and a letter to Knudsen requesting an "immediate general conference" between GM and the UAW. The international and local officers of the union, Martin stated, had made every effort to negotiate at the local level, as the corporation had advised, but the plant managers had taken an "unyielding position." He blamed the Atlanta and Kansas City strikes on "flagrant" discrimination against union workers and asserted that there was "widespread dissatisfaction" among GM workers because of the speed-up, the lack of job security resulting from the absence of proper seniority rules, piece-work methods of pay, and other matters affecting wages and working conditions. "Bona fide collective bargaining," Martin concluded, "is the only workable instrument for the establishment of [a] satisfactory relationship between the employers and employes. . . ."[54]

The next day Knudsen met with Martin and Addes in the GM Building, and the union officers formally presented the discrimination cases and grievances noted in the UAW communications of December 21. Knudsen, however, advised the UAW to take up these grievances with the appropriate plant managers or, if necessary, the general managers having authority in the particular locality. Just after the meeting Martin said that it was satisfactory "as far as it went" and that he would comply with Knudsen's suggestion; but on December 24, after Lewis had attacked the GM position on local bargaining as "impractical and an evasion of General Motors' responsibility to bargain collectively," Martin renewed his request to GM for a general conference. He stated that, although the UAW would try to settle minor grievances locally, the principal issues that it wished to discuss with the corporation—collective bargaining, seniority, speed of work, rates and methods of pay—were "national in scope" and would have to be considered at the summit.[55] In view of what had occurred in local bargaining in Atlanta and elsewhere[56] and the limited authority of plant managers to alter GM policy in matters of substance, the UAW position on this question was altogether realistic. By the time Knudsen replied to Martin's letter, the sit-down strike had spread to the vital center of the GM domain.

Although it was the Christmas season, late December, 1936, was by no means an inauspicious time for a GM strike from the UAW point of view. It was the rush season for automotive production as well as a time of record or near-record output for Chevrolet, Buick, and Fisher Body, factors that might conceivably have weakened GM's determination to take a prolonged strike; and also, since the grooving-in process had not been altogether completed in the various auto plants, the automobile workers, who, like most workers, tend to be upset by changes in their work routine, were grumbling about working conditions.

It is not surprising, moreover, that the major phase of the strike was initiated in some of the body plants of the corporation in view of what has already been said about the discontent of the more skilled body workers as machinery undermined their skills and reduced the pay differentials between themselves and the less skilled, the surviving consciousness of skill and of bargaining power on the part of such body workers as metal finishers, and the hard manual labor required in body plants like Fisher Body No. 2. The Fisher Body plant managers, also, had a relatively poor record from the UAW point of view in dealing with individual grievances as compared to the plant managers of other GM divisions. Finally, bodies were extremely difficult to store so that the UAW could be certain that the company had no bank of bodies to draw on should the flow of bodies suddenly be halted by a strike.[57]

It is a matter of no wonder that when the GM strike spread to the key plants of the corporation it took the form of the sit-down. The sit-down strike had been receiving a good deal of publicity, and it had proved itself a formidable weapon and one ideally suited to the automobile industry. It seemed more sensible, moreover, to sit down inside the plant in the cold of winter than to march in a picket line on the outside. In Flint, in addition, union leaders thought that the police might attempt to break up an outside picket line as they had done in the 1930 Fisher Body strike but were less likely to storm a large plant to dislodge strikers sitting on the inside.[58]

The GM strike took a far more serious turn for the corporation when a small number of workers sat down in the Cleveland Fisher Body plant on December 28. Whereas the Atlanta and Kansas City assembly plants were of minor consequence to the continued operation of the corporation, the Cleveland plant, which made all the body stampings for two-door Chevrolet models and some parts for all Chevrolet bodies, was one of the most important of all GM plants. It employed about seventy-two hundred workers and at the time of the strike was turning out stampings for about twenty-seven thousand bodies a week.[59]

The UAW local involved in the Cleveland Fisher Body strike had been one of the most militant in the organization in the NRA era, but it had since fallen on hard times, and its membership had dwindled into insignificance. The closing of the plant's wood mill in the summer of 1936 and a belief that the speed of work had been increased and piece rates cut at the beginning of the 1937 production season caused concern among the plant workers upon which UAW organizers sought to capitalize. The local held its largest meeting since the 1934 strike on November 8, 1936, and at the end of the month the UAW representative in the city, Elmer Davis, reported that "things are really getting hot."[60] Although union membership was thus on the upswing toward the end of the year, the local had enrolled probably no more than 10 percent of the plant's work force as of late December,[61] which perhaps explains why the strike began as a sit-down.

Shortly before Christmas the local arranged to meet with the plant manager, Lincoln R. Scafe, on December 28 at 11:00 A.M. to discuss union allegations of discrimination by the company in the layoff of tool and die makers and the possibility of having the employees work shorter hours to avoid additional layoffs. At 10:40 A.M. on the twenty-eighth the company asked the president of the local, Louis F. Spisak, to postpone the meeting until 2:30 P.M., and Spisak agreed to the delay.

Spisak, however, did not control the union situation within the plant, where the key figure was Paul Miley, the chief steward of the union and the chairman of its bargaining committee. Miley, who had once played freshman football at Western Reserve University and had been the president of the local at the time of the 1934 strike, worked in the quarter-panel department of the plant, which was a center of union strength. After checking with Travis to make sure that a Cleveland strike would not upset Flint's plans, Miley decided that the time had come to act. Following his instructions, the workers in his department sat down at about noon to protest the alleged "runaround" the company was giving the local by delaying the conference; and Miley then went to other departments of the plant and persuaded the union stewards to ask their men to cease working. The plant supervision, after failing to secure a resumption of operations, ordered the workers to leave the plant. Most of them complied, but 259 employees, according to the company, remained inside the idle plant.[62]

It has been customary to view the Cleveland sit-down as having been entirely spontaneous in its origin,[63] but the available evidence raises serious doubts about this presumption. Elmer Davis, according to Miley, had been "begging" the local to join Atlanta and Kansas City on strike, and Martin[64] had been encouraging similar action. A few days after the strike began Martin told Germer that he (Martin) had ordered the Cleveland strike, and Hall provided the CIO representative with a similar account of what had occurred. The conservative officers of the local—Miley thought them "reactionary" or worse—opposed a strike because of the local's limited membership, but more militant unionists like Miley were receptive to the idea. "We knew," Miley recalled, "that we were going out the first opportunity. This was going back and forth like wildfire."[65] The men held back until their Christmas bonus had been paid, and then the militants saw their "opportunity" when the management asked for a brief postponement of the scheduled December 28 conference.

Mayor Harold Burton of Cleveland proposed to the union and the company that work be resumed pending negotiations, but when Spisak presented this suggestion to Miley and other union leaders inside the plant, they objected and urged him to call Mortimer, the former head of the Cleveland Auto Council, who was then in Flint. Mortimer, long a proponent of a confrontation with GM, had assumed that the major challenge to the corporation by the UAW would not come until after January 1, but he was shrewd enough to realize that the moment of truth had now arrived. Like Germer, he had long favored the key-plants approach to a GM strike, and he knew that Cleveland Fisher Body and Fisher Body No. 1 of Flint, which was the source of Buick bodies and of parts for Pontiac and Olds bodies as well, were indispensable to this strategy—perhaps three-fourths of GM's production was dependent on these two plants. He therefore advised Spisak to keep the Cleveland strike going and decided to leave for Cleveland himself to provide direction for the strike.[66] At the same time Mortimer told his friend Travis to strike Fisher Body No. 1 at the earliest possible moment.[67] There is no reason to think that Mortimer consulted with other UAW officers before advising this course of action.

At an outside meeting of Fisher Body workers on December 28 Spisak, who had announced his support of the strike, declared, "I'll bet that within forty-eight hours you hear that the whole General Motors is shut down." It is not entirely clear whether Spisak was simply trying to bolster the spirits of the strikers or was making a prediction on the basis of information that he had received from Martin, with whom he had spoken, but the latter seems more likely. Spisak said that the international knew precisely what was going on and that "they're back of us," which may mean that Martin had told him that additional shutdowns were impending.[68]

When Mortimer arrived in Cleveland on December 29, he rejected the Burton peace plan and then went out to the Fisher Body plant to address the strikers. Undoubtedly thinking back to the Toledo Chevrolet strike of 1935, Mortimer, as Martin had asserted with regard to the Kansas City strike, said that the strike was "no longer a local issue" and would therefore have to be settled on "a national scale," a judgment with which the local agreed. He reported that Flint stood behind the Cleveland workers and that the international would support them "to the limit of its resources." The next morning he correctly predicted that a Flint strike was only hours away.[69]

On December 31 Homer Martin, who had come to Cleveland,

asked the strikers to evacuate the plant. The decision was made, apparently, because the layout of the factory made the feeding of the sit-downers a formidable undertaking whereas the plant could be picketed without special difficulty. When the workers paraded from the plant on the afternoon of the last day of 1936, they wore colored paper caps and tooted festooned horns, and, as the Cleveland *Plain Dealer* observed, "looked more like New Year greeters than men in an industrial struggle."[70] The Cleveland Fisher Body strikers were thus to celebrate New Year's eve outside the plant, but in Flint, to which the focus of strike attention had by that time shifted, the strikers welcomed 1937 while sitting inside the city's two Fisher Body plants.

Although the Cleveland Fisher Body strike led to predictions of an imminent Flint strike,[71] the precise timing of that strike may have surprised even most of the UAW high command. On December 29 the UAW announced that, in view of the "growing seriousness" of the situation stemming from the strikes in Atlanta, Kansas City, and Cleveland, there would be a conference of GM union representatives in Flint on January 3 to which the general officers of the UAW would submit a proposed contract as a basis for collective bargaining. Mortimer, possibly with tongue in cheek, stated that the UAW by proceeding in this manner was conforming to Knudsen's admonition to bargain before striking. That same day the Flint local presented a proposed contract to Evan J. Parker, the manager of Fisher No. 1 and No. 2, and arranged to confer with him about the document on January 4.[72] It appeared from these two actions that there would not be a Flint strike before January 4, but on December 30 sit-down strikes occurred in both the Fisher Body plants.

At 7:00 A.M. on December 30 not more than fifty workers on the body line in Fisher Body No. 2 sat down in the plant and tied up production. The plant at the time employed about one thousand workers and was turning out 450 Chevrolet bodies a day. The ostensible cause of the strike was the decision of the employer to transfer three inspectors, who had refused to quit the union when the management, which regarded them as part of supervision, had instructed them to do so. The strike appears to have been entirely spontaneous. At 10:00 P.M. on the same day, following the night-shift lunch hour, the vastly more important Fisher Body No. 1 plant was also closed by a sit-in strike. The massive three-storied plant employed about seventy-three hundred workers and was turning out fourteen hundred Buick bodies daily.[73]

The initiative in calling the No. 1 strike was taken by Bob Travis in consonance with instructions given him by Mortimer. Ostensibly, the cause of the strike was the report that the company was loading

The Coming of the Strike

dies on freight cars outside the plant for shipment to weakly unionized Grand Rapids and Pontiac in an effort to circumvent a possible No. 1 strike. Travis, upon hearing this, flashed the red light in front of the union office across the street from the plant, which was the signal for the shop stewards to gather at the first available moment. When they came together during the evening lunch hour, Travis, according to Kraus, reminded them how GM had removed machinery from the Toledo Chevrolet plant following the 1935 strike, thus causing several hundred Toledo workers to lose their jobs; and so to protect the jobs of No. 1 workers, it has been said, Travis and the stewards, without waiting for the vote of the membership required by the UAW constitution, decided to shut down the plant at once. The men returned to the factory, and then in a few minutes one of them opened the third-floor window and hollered, " 'Hooray, Bob! She's ours!' " The strikers celebrated what had apparently happened in the verses of "The Fisher Strike," sung to the tune of "The Martins and the Coys":

> Gather round me and I'll tell you all a story,
> Of the Fisher Body Factory Number One.
> When the dies they started moving,
> The Union Men they had a meeting,
> To decide right then and there what must be done.
>
> Chorus:
>
> These 4000 Union Boys
> Oh, they sure made lots of noise,
> They decided then and there to shut down tight.
> In the office they got snooty,
> So we started picket duty,
> Now the Fisher Body shop is on strike.[74]

The above is the usual account of what happened, and it is largely substantiated by Roy Reuther,[75] but Bud Simons, the chairman of the No. 1 shop committee, tells another story. As he remembers it, the plant was running out of glass because of the Libby-Owens-Ford strike, and Travis, anxious for the union to seize the initiative rather than be the passive victim of a plant shutdown, therefore came to Simons and said, " 'We have got to find something to start a strike about around here.' " The story of the dies was then fabricated—GM insisted that only part of one die had been shipped to Pontiac, because of a machinery failure, and that the transfer of dies was a routine action—and the decision was then made to strike the plant.[76] There is no real corroboration of this version of the strike's origin, but it is clear that Travis was concerned about the implications of the glass shortage for Fisher Body No. 1, and he was not inclined, many years later, to dismiss the Simons account as entirely fictional.[77]

Whether GM really intended to remove large numbers of dies from the No. 1 plant remains a moot point, but, whatever the truth of this matter may be, it is perfectly apparent that the dies story was at most the *occasion* for rather than the cause of the strike. Travis was determined because of the Cleveland strike to shut down No. 1 as soon as it was possible to do so; and, as he concedes, he would have found one pretext or another to initiate the strike. For the Flint local's leadership and the rank and file, also, the dies story was probably less important as a reason to strike than were their basic complaints about working conditions and their desire for recognition and an improved status in the plant. It is not clear whether Travis and the stewards weighed the pros and cons of the sit-down as compared to an outside strike, but given the popularity of the new strike technique, the time of the year, the minority status of the union, and the nature of the city, it is hardly surprising that the strike when it came was of the sit-down variety.[78]

After December 30 attention in the GM strike centered on Flint, but in the days and weeks that followed, the strike spread to additional GM plants and to other cities and states. On December 31, on orders from Martin, Fisher Body and Chevrolet workers in Norwood, Ohio, went out on strike, and the Guide Lamp plant in Anderson, Indiana, was closed by a sit-down.[79] Toledo Chevrolet workers sat down on January 4, Janesville Chevrolet and Fisher Body workers on January 5, Cadillac workers on January 8, and Fleetwood workers, who made bodies for Cadillac, on January 12. On January 13 a conventional strike closed the St. Louis Fisher Body and Chevrolet plant, and on January 25 Oakland's Fisher Body and Chevrolet workers joined the strike, according to the union, but GM contended that the shutdown was the result of a shortage of materials.[80] The last plant to be struck was the important Chevrolet No. 4 plant in Flint, which the UAW seized in a dramatic maneuver on February 1.

It was assumed at the time and has been accepted ever since that the CIO was caught unawares by the sit-downs in Cleveland and Flint, which changed the GM strike from a peripheral dispute between the corporation and some weak, outlying UAW locals into a direct confrontation between the international union and GM at the center of the corporation's power. Lewis, according to the usual view, was preoccupied with the steel organizing drive and was secondarily

The Coming of the Strike

147

concerned with the United Mine Workers campaign in soft coal and the struggle between the CIO and the AFL and was simply unprepared for an automobile strike.[81] "The fight," one observer declared, "is not taking place in the scarred field of well-planned industrial civil war: steel, but in a flank maneuver neither at this moment expected nor adequately prepared for: autos."[82]

There is a degree of truth in the conventional version of the CIO and the beginnings of the GM strike, but it is not the whole truth. The CIO was surprised only that the "climax" of the UAW drive came at the end of December rather than after January 1, as had been agreed upon at the UAW-CIO conference of December 18. It is thus not altogether accurate to argue that Lewis' hand was "forced" by the strike but that, foreseeing the shape of things to come and aware that all would be lost for the UAW and perhaps for the CIO as well if the CIO did not involve itself in the strike and if the strike did not succeed, he shrewdly stepped in, gave the strike support and direction, and led the auto workers to a brilliant victory. Lewis, as a matter of fact, had realized from the time the CIO was formed that its fate and that of the auto workers were intertwined, and he had declared at the CIO meeting of December 9, 1935, that support of organizational efforts in the auto and rubber industries was "the only practical thing as our first thrust."[83] As it turned out, the "first thrust" of the CIO did come in these two areas of the economy, and it is unlikely that CIO leaders were "left blinking," as *Time* suggested,[84] by the one-two punch the UAW directed at GM in late December.

There was less certainty at the time, as there has been since, regarding the role that the UAW leadership played in the calling of the major sit-downs of late December. The most common view of what occurred is that the UAW certainly intended a GM strike eventually but that "a few live wires" took matters out of the hands of the leadership and initiated the strikes prematurely. "The people," said Merlin Bishop, himself a participant in the sit-downs, "felt that this was a chance to throw off the yoke and get their freedom, and they just did not wait for leadership."[85] If this interpretation of events is understood to mean that the GEB did not specifically authorize the Cleveland and Flint sit-downs, as the UAW constitution required, it is true enough, but if it is construed to imply that militants in the plants involved simply took affairs into their own hands without instruction from high UAW officials, the statement is inaccurate. Homer Martin, who on the one hand wanted CIO aid and support but on the other hand wanted to keep control of matters himself, did not choose to be bound by the December 18 CIO-UAW decision and, acting on his own responsibility, ordered the strike in Cleveland and in Norwood and Anderson as well, even though he later stated that the UAW had never instructed anyone to sit down. First Vice-President Mortimer, once Cleveland was shut down, realized that there was no longer any point in waiting for a January showdown, and so he instructed Travis to strike Fisher Body No. 1 forthwith. It was possible in the loosely organized UAW, which had no tradition of local obedience to or dependence on an international organization, for events to unfold in this seemingly anarchic manner. As Allan Haywood complained to Germer, there was in the UAW "a lack of policy—no head no tail."[86]

11

One of the reasons that the CIO and the UAW had thought it wise to delay a GM strike in Michigan until after January 1, 1937, was the fact that Frank Murphy would become governor of the state on that date. "We felt," said Mortimer, "that while he may or may not have been on our side, he at least would not be against us."[87] If that is all the UAW and the CIO expected of Murphy, and Mortimer was certainly guilty of an understatement, they had no reason whatsoever to be disappointed in their expectation.

Frank Murphy was born in Harbor Beach (then Sand Beach), Michigan, on April 13, 1890. After completing high school in his home town, he enrolled at the University of Michigan, where he received his law degree in 1914. He then worked for a Detroit law firm until he joined the Army shortly after the United States entered World War I. He served with the American Expeditionary Force in France and Germany, studied briefly in England and Ireland while on detached service, and then returned to the United States in the summer of 1919 to become first assistant United States attorney for the Eastern District of Michigan. He served in that capacity until March 1, 1922, when he entered private law practice with his close friend, Edward G. Kemp. He was elected to the Detroit Recorder's Court in 1923 and served as a Recorder's Court judge until August 19, 1930, when he resigned to run for mayor. He won the mayoralty election in September and was reelected in November, 1931.

Murphy was a supporter of Franklin D. Roosevelt in the 1932 presidential election and was rewarded for his efforts by being designated governor-general of the Philippines, a post that he officially assumed in May, 1933. When the Philippines became a commonwealth in November, 1935, Murphy became high commissioner. He announced his candidacy for the governorship of Michigan in July,

1936, and defeated his Republican opponent, Frank Fitzgerald, in November.[88]

Murphy was a very ambitious person who aspired from an early date to the highest elective office in the land. He believed that the best way to realize his lofty ambition was through dedicated public service rather than through partisan maneuverings. "His creed," a Detroit newspaper accurately observed just after he was elected governor, "is that the politician who gives the best government is the politician who travels the furthest." Murphy's abstemious personal habits—he neither drank nor smoked—were very decidedly related to his ambitions for himself. As he told a reporter early in his public career, "I cherished definite aims in life. I figured I'd need a lot of independence and self reliance and they depend upon self control and firm will. In short I figured I'd go further in attaining my aims if I steered clear of the stimulating influences of alcohol and tobacco." Keeping in trim through boxing, riding, and other exercise was another means by which Murphy sought to fulfill his ambition to be "the best possible public servant my limitations will permit."[89] The gruelling, around-the-clock negotiations during the GM sit-down strike were precisely the sort of endurance contest for which Murphy had been preparing himself from the time of his youth.

Murphy's vaulting ambition for high office did not mean that he was inclined to sacrifice principle to win public favor nor that he feared to challenge accepted views. "I like public office," Murphy wrote to his brother George, "but I am no slave to it and from the first I have practiced and preached the doctrine that I would rather be out than in office if to be in meant surrendering a worthy principle." Indeed, Murphy liked to think of himself as a fighter for unpopular causes who would triumph despite the formidable character of the opposition. "I don't want the odds my way in any race," he wrote his mother from overseas at the end of World War I. "I want the odds to be against me if the race isn't even and I shall expect to win, too. I find that the real zip in life is not in winning but in fighting [,] not in going easily with the current but beating back the breakers."[90] In the sit-down strike Murphy was to be given the opportunity to "beat back the breakers."

As a public servant, Murphy acquired a deserved reputation as a civil libertarian, as a zealous advocate of the freedoms embodied in the Bill of Rights. From the point of view of the leadership of the American Civil Liberties Union, Murphy was just about the ideal government official.[91] Americans, Murphy thought, were "often a little slothful and drowsy about this precious right we call liberty" and were indifferent about "the chains forged for our fellows," but they would do well to remember that "a wrong to the liberty of one citizen is a blow at the liberty of all citizens."[92] As Recorder's Court judge, mayor, and colonial official, Murphy tried to live by this creed. As governor dealing with the sit-down strikes, he was undoubtedly influenced by his belief that the civil liberties of the automobile workers had been violated by their employer.

Murphy had "a deep reverence for human life" that made it impossible for him to accept the idea of capital punishment. The admonition "Thou shalt not kill," he declaimed in a debate on the subject of capital punishment in 1927, came from Mr. Sinai and has been "the cornerstone of civilization" ever since. Because he loathed crimes of violence, he did not wish the state to become "an example of violence and ferocity." For Murphy, the problem of crime was "interwoven with social and economic conditions," and he advised those who wished to solve the problem "to seek its causes at their source, and strive to apply the remedy at the beginning, rather than at the end, of a sordid life-story."[93] It is thus not surprising that when Murphy was confronted with the GM sit-down, he refused to order the forcible evacuation of the strikers and that he thought it necessary to consider the social and economic conditions that had led the workers to sit down and not merely to deal with the problem by labeling their action a crime for which they were to be punished.

As a criminal-court judge in Michigan, which forbade capital punishment, Murphy was spared the necessity of ordering the execution of persons convicted of capital crimes, but even the sentencing of the unfortunate to prison caused him some pain. When he was a United States Supreme Court justice many years later, he wrote feelingly to his brother about "expiring a little each time you have to take part of another man's life from him." When he assumed his seat on Recorder's Court, he characteristically stated that he knew that he would frequently "drop into error" as a judge, but "I trust and pray that when this occurs it shall be on the side of mercy."[94] In the sit-down strike the governor of Michigan was influenced by similar considerations.

Murphy had great compassion for the weak, the afflicted, the down-trodden, the flotsam and jetsam of humankind. "To me," he wrote his mother in 1918, "there is deep satisfaction in giving help and relief to the trouble[d] and depressed. I would rather do that than any task I know." Speaking to the Women's Club of Manila in the summer of 1933, Murphy declared, "We are not here for ourselves alone; we are here to do things for those around us...." It was the common responsibility to aid the sick and the aged and to heal "broken spirits."

As Recorder's Court judge, Murphy sought to salvage "fragments" of the human wreckage that passed before him by "granting a parole, exercising judicial clemency or handing out advice," and he was a prominent figure in efforts to persuade the Michigan legislature to enact old-age pension and unemployment-insurance legislation. When he was mayor of Detroit during the depression, he did more to feed the hungry than any other municipal official in the nation, and he was, in the pre-New Deal era, one of the most conspicuous and influential advocates of federal relief for the unemployed. In the Philippines, Murphy's "most distinctive accomplishments . . . were the awakening of a new social consciousness . . . and the improvement and extension of government services for the amelioration of the lot of the common people."[95]

Murphy concluded at an early age that the workingman was among the disadvantaged in American society. He worked as a high school and college student in the starch factory in Harbor Beach, and he was later to recall that "it was a slave's life, those long hours and the living by whistles." When asked to write a paper for a sociology course he was taking at the University of Michigan, Murphy chose the subject "Politics and the Laborer." "It is because I lived and worked with the common, ordinary, day, laborer and have listened to his complaints and his joys, and feel that I know his wants and needs," the young college student wrote, "that I have ventured upon this difficult problem. I love the subject. I want to make it my life's work. If I can only feel, when my day is done, that I have accomplished something towards uplifting the poor, uneducated, unfortunate, ten hour a day, laborer from the political chaos he now exists in, I will be satisfied that I have been worth while."[96] By this criterion, Frank Murphy at the end of his illustrious career had every reason to be "satisfied" that he had indeed been "worth while."

In addition to his personal experience as a day laborer, Murphy was heavily influenced in his stance with regard to labor by his Catholic religion and particularly by the labor encyclicals of Leo XIII and Pius XI. As mayor of depression-ridden Detroit, Murphy, in an interpretation of *Rerum Novarum*, declared that he had been guided by "the signpost set up by the beneficent Leo" to put the welfare of his fellow man above balanced budgets. Leo, Murphy thought, had shown the way to those concerned with "safeguarding the worker" in the contemporary world. The encyclical told them that it was their responsibility, as rulers who must protect the "safety of the commonwealth," to put the idle to work, to remove the causes of poverty and unemployment, to stabilize the worker's income, to care for the destitute and the aged, and to secure appropriate labor legislation. No Christian, Murphy declared shortly thereafter, could be indifferent to depressed labor conditions or to the differences between employer and employee that resulted in strikes. Interestingly enough, he joined the Third Order of St. Francis, whose Rule required its members to cultivate charity, love peace, and heal discord and misunderstanding.[97] As governor during the GM strike, Murphy was provided with an unparalleled opportunity to practice the Order's Rule of Peace.

Quite apart from personal experience and religion, Murphy was undoubtedly influenced to take a pro-labor position by his conviction that labor and the Catholic church were emerging as the "two strongest forces" in the United States.[98] Few public officials in the entire nation in the 1920's and 1930's were as closely allied with organized labor as Murphy was, and few were willing to accord it the status and recognition that he was.

Murphy first ran for the position of Recorder's Court judge in part out of a desire to break up a court ring allegedly unfair to labor. He received the endorsement of the Detroit Federation of Labor (DFL) in this election as in every subsequent election in which he was a candidate. As a criminal court judge, Murphy conducted himself in a manner that pleased the forces of organized labor in Detroit. He did not assume that labor was always responsible for violence in industrial disputes, and in one case he criticized the prosecutor's office for showing an interest in misdemeanor charges only when they stemmed from a strike, thus creating the dangerous impression that the state was on the side of the employers.[99]

Murphy, in the 1920's, saw organized labor as "the natural nucleus" of a movement to aid the downtrodden and to solve the problem of the "industrial frontier." He advised organized labor in Detroit to work for the five-day week, a living family wage, the right to engage in collective bargaining, the right to strike, unemployment insurance, and limitations on the use of injunctions in labor disputes.[100]

In view of Murphy's record on the Recorder's Court, it is quite understandable that the DFL was the first organization to ask him to run for mayor in the late summer of 1930 following the recall of Mayor Charles Bowles. As mayor, Murphy worked closely with the DFL in evolving his policy to deal with unemployment, and, believing that "labor must have its share in a well-balanced government," he made a large number of labor appointments. When Detroit celebrated Labor Day in 1931, Murphy invited Vice-President Matthew Woll of the AFL to deliver the main address, which Woll declared was the first time that any city government, to his knowledge, had invited the Federation to share in the observance of the occasion. The Detroit *News* unhappily remarked that "Mayor Murphy is a labor union mayor in open shop Detroit. . . ."[101]

"The existence of a strike" Murphy declared shortly after he gave up the Detroit mayoralty, "shows that things are not in their natural order, that something is wrong. The government, therefore, should intervene in such conflicts ... to protect, first of all, the interest of the public." The only major strike that confronted Murphy as mayor was initiated on January 23-24, 1933, by unorganized workers at the four Briggs plants in Detroit, but since the company would not agree to the city's mediation of the dispute, the Mayor was limited in what he could do to compose the strike. He did, however, appoint a Mayor's Fact-Finding Committee of distinguished citizens to investigate the strike, which deplored the company's refusal to meet with strikers and called for collective bargaining between organized workers and their employers to resolve labor disputes in the future.[102]

The active picketing of the Briggs plant by the strikers and the company's determination to operate despite the walkout brought the Detroit police into the strike and led to striker complaints of misuse of their power by the law officers. Murphy, in this difficult situation, told department heads that it was the city's policy "to maintain the peace" but not "to take sides." Since he did not believe that he could order the company to close its factories, he thought that workers going to and from their jobs were entitled to "a certain amount of protection," but at the same time he ordered the police to protect the strikers from attack and not to interfere with the conduct of the strike. He made it clear that there were to be no "illegal arrests," that no strikers were to be held incommunicado, and that no one was to be deprived of his rights simply because he protested industrial conditions or went on strike. The mayor had to concede, however, that despite his best efforts the police sometimes went "too far." It was far easier for the mayor to outline a strike policy than to ensure that it would be observed by the police.[103]

Privately, Murphy thought that the Briggs management was, to some extent at least, responsible for the strike because of the labor conditions that prevailed in its plants. The city of Detroit refused to use its Free Employment Bureau to provide strikebreakers for Briggs, and it rejected a company request for transportation equipment to move employees into and out of one of the plants. The city, also, as Murphy was to do in the GM strike, made relief available on the basis of need regardless of whether or not the recipient was a striker.[104]

In the Philippines, Murphy manifested the same interest in the condition of the workingman and in organized labor that he had demonstrated in Detroit. His administration was responsible for an eight-hour day law for workers in hazardous occupations or engaged in employments requiring great physical effort, the creation of a department of labor, efforts to control usury, the relief of unemployment, slum clearance, and the provision of public defenders for the indigent; and the governor-general vetoed a bill requiring compulsory arbitration. Murphy also made "the first appreciable effort" in the history of the Philippines "to bring the labor movement into its full dignity . . . [as a] co-operative element in the social and economic life of the people."[105]

When a strike of cigar workers occurred in Manila beginning on August 16, 1934, Murphy, as he had done in the Briggs strike, appointed a Fact-Finding Board to investigate the dispute. He called for the settlement of the strike by arbitration rather than by force; but the policing of the walkout took a violent turn, and in a clash between strikers and the constabulary on September 17, three strikers lost their lives. "This regrettable and unnecessary incident," to use Murphy's phrasing, led to an inquiry about the strike from the American Civil Liberties Union. "At such times of excitement," Roger Baldwin wrote the governor-general, "you know fully as well as we, it is possible for wise policing to avoid the kind of tragic conflict which here took place."[106] Murphy learned in Detroit and the Philippines that police forces tend to have a life of their own and that it was sometimes difficult for the chief executive of a governmental unit to control their operations. In the GM strike he was determined to keep firm control of major policing activities so as to provide the "wise policing" that would prevent the sort of tragedy that had occurred during the Manila cigar strike and that must have weighed heavily on his conscience.

When he campaigned for the governorship of Michigan in 1936, Murphy, who was endorsed by labor organizations throughout the state, emphasized his close ties with organized labor. "I am heart and soul in the Labor Movement," he told the Detroit *Labor News*. "I have yet to go contrary to the expressed wish of Organized Labor in matters that affect it, and as expressed by its official chosen representatives, and you all know that I shall never do so." Speaking to an audience in Muskegon, he declared that it was the "duty" of a public official to avoid strikes, but it was not his "duty or prerogative . . . to permit the use of the police power except to protect the public," nor should he deny welfare aid to strikers. When he won the election, he wrote William Green, "I am certain that you will find that my administration ... will mark a new day for labor in Michigan"; and he told the Detroit and Wayne County Federation of Labor at a victory celebration, "If I worked for a wage, I'd join my Union."[107]

Although Murphy identified strongly with the unfortunate and with organized labor, he delighted at the same time in the company of the well-to-do, and some of his closest friends were among the social and economic elite of Detroit and Michigan. Murphy was on especially good terms with several of the automobile magnates, including Walter Chrysler, B. E. Hutchinson, and Byron C. Foy of Chrysler Corporation and Lawrence Fisher of Fisher Body and GM. Murphy was also a heavy investor in automobile stock. When he became governor at the beginning of 1937, he held 1650 shares of GM stock, 550 of Chrysler, and five hundred of Packard. The GM stock alone at the end of the year was worth $104,875. On January 18, 1937, during the course of the GM strike, Murphy sold his GM stock at a minimum profit of $52,800.[108] How the parties to the GM dispute would have reacted to this information had it been known to them is an interesting speculation.

Murphy was of medium height and build and had what Russell B. Porter of the New York *Times* described as a "distinctly Celtic countenance." Although not handsome in a conventional sense, he was exceedingly attractive to the opposite sex. He had blue eyes, receding red hair, and very bushy red eyebrows—a cameraman remarked after the strike, "I expected a couple of sit downers to jump out of those eyebrows any minute." The eyebrow-to-eyebrow confrontation of Murphy and John L. Lewis during the strike negotiations must surely have been something to behold. Murphy was gentle in manner, very soft-spoken, and had more than his share of charm, but behind the exterior of charm and affability, there was a reserve that few if any penetrated.[109] It was this man who played so decisive a role in the GM strike.

The Sit-Down Community
VI

From the end of December, 1936, attention in the GM strike was centered on Flint, where the UAW strikers occupied the Fisher Body No. 1 and No. 2 plants. The ability of the sit-downers to retain their hold on these two plants, particularly the larger and more important No. 1 plant, and such other factories as they had occupied and would occupy was essential to victory in the strike. Whether this could be accomplished depended not only on what transpired outside the occupied plants but, also, on whether the strikers on the inside, who had never before engaged in such a venture, could organize their activities with sufficient effectiveness to be able to live within the walls of a factory until a settlement of the strike could be reached. The pattern of organization of the GM sit-down did not differ greatly from factory to factory, but since the records are most abundant for the sit-down in the Fisher Body No. 1 plant, the focus in the pages that follow will be primarily, but not exclusively, on that establishment.[1]

Since no advance preparations had been made for the Fisher No. 1 sit-down, all was confusion within the plant for the first day or so of the strike. It was "the biggest nightmare I ever went through," Bud Simons, the chairman of the strike committee, later recalled. The plant was too large to occupy as a whole, and so the leadership decided to confine the sit-down to the so-called North Unit, which contained the cafeteria and where there were finished bodies that the men could use for sleeping purposes. It was also decided at the outset, for rather obvious reasons, that the organization of life within the plant would be less difficult if the sit-in were confined to male workers, and so the three hundred female employees inside the plant when the strike began were sent home during the first night of the sit-down.[2]

Nearly all observers were impressed with the high degree of organization achieved by the sit-in strikers. "The most astonishing feeling you get in the sit-down plants is that of ORDER," one of the strikers' bulletins accurately reported. "Every action is systematized."[3] Analogies to the military most readily came to mind to many of those who had the opportunity to witness life within the struck plants. The editor of *Mill and Factory*, Hartley W. Barclay, after spending many hours with the No. 2 sit-downers, thus described the "system of organization" in the plant as "a completely military type."[4]

In a real sense, the strikers formed a "new and special kind of community"[5] within the plants in which they sat. As Charles R. Walker has noted, the nature of the technology employed in a particular plant "not only affects the individual on the job in his daily work experience but also molds in good measure what might be called in-plant society." In the automobile industry, the assembly line and the work methods severely limited the size of the work groups and the "team relationships" possible and tended to keep group morale at a low level. The noise and strain of the line also restricted the degree of social intercourse within the plant.[6] In the sit-down, by contrast, the strikers, almost for the first time, became acquainted with one another and began to develop a sense of fellowship and coherence. There was, during the strike, "a greater sociability," a recognition of a " 'consciousness of kind,' " a feeling of solidarity produced by the common struggle in which the strikers were engaged. "It was like we were soldiers holding the fort," one of the Chevrolet No. 4 sit-downers declared. "It was like war. The guys with me became my buddies."

Enthralled by the sit-down, a psychologist writing in the *New Masses* contended that "the atmosphere of cooperativeness" in the sit-down reoriented the thought of the sit-downers and created "a veritable revolution of personality" so that the pronoun " 'We' " came to replace the pronoun " 'I.' "[7] One need not go this far, however, to recognize that a feeling of kinship did develop among the strikers who remained inside the plants for any length of time that was unique in the experience of automobile workers and that gave a special quality to the social organization developed in the plants that they occupied.

The chief administrative body of the "little government" created within the No. 1 plant was the strike committee of fourteen members selected to represent the various departments of the plant. The chairman of the committee was Bud Simons, and he and four other members of the committee also served as the executive board or council. The decisions of the strike committee and the executive board were subject to the approval of the strikers, although in an emergency the executive board was empowered to act on its own initiative. The available records indicate that the strike committee recognized the strikers themselves as the final authority in the plant and that it sought their consent for virtually all of its decisions. Although Simons recalls that his leadership within the strike committee was occasionally challenged, the minutes of the strikers' meetings give no evidence of friction within the community of strikers. As with all organizations, however, decisions reached were not always implemented. "Recommendations of strike committee ignored," Simons wrote in his notebook probably during the first week of the strike.[8]

There were daily meetings of the strike committee and the strikers as a whole and frequent meetings of the executive board, and on occasion the stewards held their own meetings or met with the strike committee.[9] Life in the struck plants must have seemed to some like a round of meetings, but since idle time was a commodity in abundant supply in the plants, the meetings were probably a welcome break in the daily routine for most strikers. The mass meetings were also an occasion for song: it was agreed on January 13 that all such meetings should be opened and closed with a verse of "Solidarity," the strikers' favorite.

> Solidarity forever
> Solidarity forever
> Solidarity forever
> For the Union makes us strong.[10]

The sit-down strikers had their daily duties to perform, and these chores were apparently assigned on a shift basis that comported with the work schedules familiar to the strikers.[11] One of the first acts taken by the leadership in the No. 1 plant was to organize a special patrol or police force to make regular tours of the entire plant to ensure that the company was making no effort to resume production in the unoccupied portion of the factory, to see that the gates of the plant were secured, to detect any possible sabotage of the company's property by individual strikers, and to make sure that no one was inside the plant who was not supposed to be there. Joe Devitt of the strike committee recalled that the patrol on one occasion apprehended two supervisors who were attempting to listen in on one of the strikers' meetings and that the sit-downers released the two men after they had been given an appropriate warning. The patrol committee was "the hardest working group" in the plant, and its head, Pete Kennedy, selected because he had had National Guard training, had to be deterred from performing his duties around the clock to the detriment of his health.[12]

Committees were organized for every conceivable purpose in the No. 1 and the other occupied plants: food, recreation, information, education, postal services, sanitation, and contact with the outside. In Fisher Body No. 1 a complaints committee was formed to listen to the grievances of the workers; and Simons tells us that it received "a continuous string of complaints," some of them, he insists, instigated by company men. The No. 1 strike body also had its committee on rumors, which sought to track down the numerous rumors that not surprisingly circulated in the plant. The strikers discovered that one of the members of this committee was reporting on their activities to the Flint Police Department.[13]

The No. 1 sit-downers were very much concerned about maintaining systematic contact with the union and strike organization outside the plant. Travis and other strike leaders came into the plant regularly to report on the progress of the strike, but this did not seem to satisfy the strike committee, which decided on January 21 to send delegates to the daily meeting of the UAW in the Pengelly Building, the union's Flint headquarters. In addition, some of the sit-downers were designated as "runners" to carry messages from inside the plant to union headquarters when this seemed necessary. The No. 1 strikers cooperated in the city-wide recruiting drive of the UAW in Flint, they held regular meetings with the union's welfare committee, and they created their own "outside defense squad." They even had their own two-man espionage team, which was to "get around everywhere [on the outside] and pick up info."[14] The sit-downers expected the support of the outside strike apparatus when circumstances required this. ". . . when I see I'm losing the fight and ask for action from the out side," Red Mundale, the strike leader in the weakly held No. 2 plant, wrote Travis on one occasion, "see to it that I get it."[15]

The sit-downers in several of the occupied plants instituted their own judicial system in the form of kangaroo courts. In the Cadillac plant the oldest worker was made the judge, and a striker who had studied law was designated the prosecuting attorney.[16] In the No. 1 plant the decision to establish a court was not made until January 27. Prior to that date the executive board had apparently assigned the penalties for infraction of the rules.[17]

The list of punishable offenses in the No. 1 plant and the rules of behavior adopted there and in other plants provide an insight into the nature of the institutional life that developed in the occupied plants and what was regarded as good citizenship on the part of the sit-downers. Workers were to be sentenced for failing to report for the performance of any of their assigned duties, leaving their duty post before the scheduled time or sleeping while on duty, failing to return their dirty dishes to the kitchen, throwing paper or rubbish on the floor or throwing foreign matter into the urinals or toilets, using toilet stools designated as out of order, failing to assist in the daily clean up, using the plant loud-speaker system for an improper purpose, carrying matches up the stairs or smoking in places other than the plant cafeteria, failing to search everyone entering or leaving the building, and contempt of court. They were not to bring liquor into the plant, they were to be quiet in areas set aside for sleeping and were not to "yell" anywhere in the plant, and they were to shower only at specified hours. The most serious "crime" in the eyes of the sit-down strikers was failure to perform assigned duties since derelictions of this sort weakened the strike community.

The punishments meted out by the kangaroo courts were designed to fit the crime. Strikers who did not perform their assigned duties were sentenced to perform extra duties, and if they did not observe the sanitation rules they were assigned to the clean-up detail. The ultimate punishment for the serious offender was expulsion from the plant. As in any community, there were law breakers in the strike communities, but the citizenship rules of the various plants appear, for the most part, to have been rather faithfully observed.[18]

Sometimes, the sessions of the kangaroo courts served as a form of theater for the sit-downers, and entertainment rather than the dispensing of justice became the court objective. On one occasion, for example, a striker who entered the No. 1 plant without the proper credentials was sentenced to make a speech, which no doubt provided a great deal of merriment for the strike body. Edward Levinson, a reporter close to the auto workers, observed at the time that "there was more substantial and original humor in a single session of the Fisher strikers' Kangaroo courts than in a season of Broadway musical comedies."[19]

The strikers were willing to admit visitors to the plants when they believed that it would serve the purposes of the strike to do so. Everyone authorized to enter the No. 1 plant, including clergymen, was searched for concealed weapons and liquor, and his credentials were carefully checked. Once he came into the plant through the high window that served as the gate of entry, the visitor was never out of sight of his guides, and he traveled only along designated routes. Information was given visitors inside the plant only by the strike committee; individual sit-downers were not normally permitted to grant interviews lest they reveal information damaging to the common cause.

Aware of the publicity value of the right kind of pictures and news stories, the No. 1 strike committee on January 5 agreed to admit Pathé News men into the plant and on January 10 to allow cameramen and newsmen to enter to take pictures and to conduct interviews "where directed." The leadership in the No. 1 plant understandably preferred to admit newspaper and magazine writers who were likely to be sympathetic to the UAW cause and for a time, therefore, excluded reporters who were not members of the American Newspaper Guild. "We don't interview no un-union [sic] men," one

The Sit-Down Community

161

of the guards at the plant's Information Window announced. The nonunion reporter in Paul Gallico's novelette based on the Flint sit-down, which Gallico had covered, is told by a union official, " 'It's war. We don't recognize any neutrals.' "[20]

Although the No. 1 sit-downers controlled the plant cafeteria and were able to prepare sandwiches and coffee on the inside, the bulk of their food, and all the food of the strikers in the No. 2 and later the Chevrolet No. 4 plants, was prepared on the outside. Ray Cook, the owner of a restaurant across the street from the No. 1 plant that was normally patronized by Fisher Body workers, placed his establishment at the disposal of the strikers a few days after the sit-down began; and shortly thereafter Max Gazan, who had been a chef at the posh Detroit Athletic Club for fourteen years and had cooked for the sit-down strikers in Detroit in December, came to Flint to take charge of the strike kitchen. The chairman of the UAW food committee in Flint was Dorothy Kraus, who, like Gazan, had gained experience along these lines during the Detroit sit-downs, and she was aided by the wives of some of the strikers.[21]

Since, on occasion, as many as two thousand strikers had to be fed three meals a day in the occupied Flint plants, it was necessary for the UAW to purchase a good deal of additional kitchen equipment for its restaurant. On a typical day the kitchen provided the strikers with five hundred pounds of meat, one hundred pounds of potatoes, three hundred loaves of bread, two hundred pounds of sugar, and thirty gallons of fresh milk. The food was taken to the plants, under guard, in large kettles; insofar as vehicle transportation was required, the responsibility was assumed by Flint Trolley Coach employees, whose strike the UAW was directing. Henry Kraus reports that two hundred persons in all were involved in the preparation and distribution of food for the Flint strikers.[22]

On a typical day the strikers received eggs, fruit, cereal, fried cakes, and coffee for breakfast, pot roast, boiled potatoes, green beans, and coffee for lunch, and chili, sandwiches, cookies, and coffee for supper. There seems little doubt that the food was ample and that many strikers ate better-balanced meals inside the plants than they had consumed in their own homes. So many strikers and unionists outside the occupied plants began appearing at the strike kitchen for their meals that it became necessary to limit the food available to them. Inside the No. 1 plant the strikers stored a reserve supply of food to tide them over for about a week should the introduction of supplies into the plant be shut off for any reason.[23]

In a body plant like Fisher No. 1 sleeping arrangements presented no special problem for the sit-downers, who, as one observer discovered, had "managed to create a home out of a factory." Strikers slept on the floor of the cars in the plant or, more commonly, improvised bedding by arranging car seats between the conveyor lines or placing the wadding for the seats on back-seat springs. When the Chevrolet No. 4 plant was seized, the No. 1 plant supplied the new group of strikers with pads from the cushion room in addition to the cots and blankets that the UAW was able to send into the plant.[24]

After the hectic first few days in an occupied plant, life became routinized, and the strikers had to combat the monotony of idleness that replaced the monotony of the assembly line. They entertained themselves by playing cards, checkers, chess, dominoes, ping pong, and volleyball and, at least in the Chevrolet No. 4 plant, by roller skating. On the second day of the strike in the No. 1 plant the strike officials decided that the men should exercise in the open air. It is not clear how faithfully this decision was implemented, but apparently the strikers did engage in some form of daily exercise. Reading, particularly of newspapers and magazines, was another means of passing the time for the sit-downers. In the No. 1 plant a special area was set aside as a "reading room," with the rear seats of auto bodies serving as chairs. When someone raised the question as to whether the *Daily Worker* should be allowed into the plant along with the more than a dozen other newspapers that were brought in through the Information Window, the strike committee designated Bud Simons to explain the issue to the strikers. He told the men that their constitutional rights would be violated if any one were allowed to censor what they read. "We are only here to better our conditions at home," he said, "and men who can make a decision as to this are able to make their own decision as to reading material."[25]

The strikers were provided with some entertainment from outside the plants. Maxie Gealer, the operator of the Rialto Theater in Flint, sent a variety of entertainers into the No. 1 plant, and the sons and daughters of the strikers also entered the factory to entertain their fathers with song and dance. On one occasion the still cameramen engaged the movie cameramen in a baseball game on Chevrolet Avenue outside the Chevrolet No. 4 plant, with the strikers serving as the umpires. At one point in the game, one of the teams protested a decision of the umpires by sitting down and singing "Solidarity Forever" and promptly won a reversal. The Contemporary Theater of Detroit, a workers' group, put on the two-act play *Virtue Rewarded* in both the No. 1 and No. 2 plants. The play had been especially adapted for the sit-downers from a Brookwood Labor College play and was presented in a burlesque, melodramatic style.[26]

Strike Marches On, the most ambitious dramatic production

prepared for the Flint strikers, was not seen by the sit-downers until just after the strike came to an end. Written by Josephine Herbst, Mary Heaton Vorse, and Dorothy Kraus and directed by Morris Watson, the managing producer of the Living Newspaper of the Federal Theater Project and the vice-president of the American Newspaper Guild, the play was of the living-newspaper type. It was a dramatic version of various strike events, which were interpreted for the audience by a "radio announcer." The actors, themselves strike participants, took the sketchy script given them and filled it out with their own interpretations.[27]

The strikers provided most of their own musical entertainment. Nearly every occupied plant had its orchestra, and the Kansas City strikers, at least, had a glee club as well. The strikers' orchestra in the No. 1 plant, consisting of two mandolins, one guitar, one banjo, and three mouth organs, had a fifteen-song repertory and gave nightly concerts that were piped outside for the benefit of pickets and sympathizers. The orchestra on at least one occasion even went "up town" to give a concert.[28]

Singing was an important form of striker recreation and also a means of maintaining morale. It was encouraged by the UAW's educational director, Merlin D. Bishop, for he had learned at Brookwood Labor College that music could play an important part in building a union.[29] The strikers themselves composed crude verses which they set to popular tunes. The following verses, sung to the tune of "Gallagher and Shean," emanated from the Chevrolet No. 4 group:

I

Oh! Mr. Sloan! Oh Mr. Sloan!
We have known for a long time you would atone,
For the wrongs that you have done
We all know, yes, everyone.
Absolutely, Mr. Travis!
Positively, Mr. Sloan!

II

Oh! Mr. Sloan! Oh! Mr. Sloan!
Everyone knows your heart was made of stone,
But the Union is so strong
That we'll always carry on.
Absolutely, Mr. Travis!
Positively, Mr. Sloan!

Another striker favorite was sung to the tune of "Goody, Goody":

> We Union men are out to win today,
>   Goody, Goody
> General Motors hasn't even got a chance,
>   Goody, Goody
> Old Sloan is feeling blue,
> and so is Knudsen too,
> They didn't like the little sit-downs,
> Now what could they do?
> So they lie awake just singing the blues all night,
>   Goody, Goody.[30]

The verses most frequently associated with the sit-down strikes, "Sit Down!" were written by Maurice Sugar, one of the UAW's attorneys, probably shortly after the close of the GM strike:

> When they tie the can to a Union man
>   Sit down! Sit down!
> When they give 'im the sack, they'll take him back
>   Sit down! Sit down!

Chorus:

> Sit down, just take a seat
> Sit down, and rest your feet
> Sit down, you've got 'em beat
> Sit down! Sit down!

> When they smile and say, no raise in pay
>   Sit down! Sit down!
> When you want the boss to come across
>   Sit down! Sit down!

> When the speed up comes, just twiddle your thumbs
>   Sit down! Sit down!
> When you want 'em to know they'd better go slow
>   Sit down! Sit down!

> When the boss won't talk, don't take a walk
>   Sit down! Sit down!
> When the boss sees that, he'll want a little chat
>   Sit down! Sit down![31]

The Sit-Down Community

165

Programs of education were introduced into many of the occupied plants to supplement the recreational activities. In Flint, Eugene Faye, who directed the UAW's education program in the city, and later Merlin Bishop conducted classes in the plants in parliamentary procedure, public speaking, collective bargaining, the duties of shop stewards, and the history of the labor movement. Classes in journalism and creative writing were also provided for the strikers by University of Michigan graduate students.[32]

Since there was always the possibility that the company or public authorities might seek to eject the sit-downers from the plants they occupied, the problem of defense could not be ignored by the strikers. In Fisher Body No. 1 the men at an early stage of the sit-down set up "a regular production line" to make blackjacks out of rubber hoses, braided leather, and lead, and the blackjack became a sort of symbol of the strikers' readiness to defend themselves. Some of the left-wing observers of the strike were impressed with the communal aspects of life within the plants,[33] but private enterprise reared its head inside the strike community in the No. 1 plant as the strikers began selling blackjacks to the souvenir hunters. The "No. 3A" blackjack plaited in leather sold for $1.25, and the "Model 9F skull crusher" for $2.00 or $2.50 if autographed.[34]

In the No. 1 plant the strikers covered the windows with metal sheets containing openings through which fire hoses could be placed, and there were regular drills in the use of the hoses. Door hinges, bolts, and nuts were stockpiled at strategic points, and security groups were assigned to the doorways and stairwells. The strikers were prepared to carry their resistance to the roof of the plant, where they would have made their final stand had they come under attack.[35]

There were persistent rumors that the strikers had firearms in the Flint plants in addition to their blackjacks and clubs. Occasionally, a worker would, indeed, bring a gun into one of the plants, but this was strictly against the rules, and when such weapons were discovered they were removed from the plants. Observers who went into the factories reported that they saw no firearms,[36] but had there been any guns in the plants the sit-downers would surely have kept them out of sight when visitors were present.

Because of its obvious relationship to morale, the strike leadership took every care to maintain sanitary conditions within the occupied plants. Also, aware of the danger to their cause that would result from damage to the expensive machinery inside the plants, the sit-downers were, on the whole, equally solicitous for the company's property that they now physically controlled. Without exception, persons who had visited the Flint plants remarked on their tidiness and the lack of significant damage to company property.

The sanitation committee in Fisher Body No. 1 made a daily inspection of the living and sleeping areas in the plant. During the clean-up period beginning at 3:00 P.M. every day, the windows were opened, and refuse was removed by the plant maintenance men, who, Henry Kraus says, remained at their jobs throughout the strike. The management, again according to Kraus, supplied the brooms for the clean-up and the paper towels and toilet tissue for the lavatory. After visiting the Chevrolet No. 4 plant, George A. Krogstad, a state labor commissioner, remarked on the cleanliness of the commissary and reported that its floor was cleaned every hour. Hartley Barclay observed in the middle of January that men were detailed in shifts to sweep the floors in Fisher No. 2 and noted that State Department of Health officials had visited the Fisher plants three times and had complimented the strikers on the condition of the factories.[37]

Barclay discovered that fire protection groups in the No. 2 plant were always prepared for action and that the men had been instructed by the state fire marshall on the use of the sprinkler system. The *Mill and Factory* editor saw no evidence of sabotage of production materials. Krogstad observed that machinery parts were oiled and greased in Chevrolet No. 4 and learned that crews had been assigned to protect the machinery. A La Follette Committee investigator, on February 3, found the property of the company undamaged in the No. 1 plant. In the Fleetwood plant in Detroit the rules called for the ejection of a striker who damaged company property or created a fire hazard.[38]

It was impossible, however, to avoid some damage to property in plants occupied by large numbers of men for as many as forty-four days. The most extensive property damage occurred in the No. 1 plant. There was damage to body seats used for sleeping purposes, and some of the men cut up expensive leather hides to make their blackjacks, a practice that the strike committee anxiously sought to halt by providing the strikers with such scrap leather as was available in the plant. At the strike committee meeting of January 15 it was reported that someone was deliberately "mutilating" car bodies, which the leadership angrily interpreted as an effort to "discredit" the strike community. Simons conceded at a later time that, despite determined efforts to prevent sabotage, "a few things" happened in the plant that "we were not proud of."[39]

When company officials, insurance investigators, and newsmen inspected the Flint plants after the strike was over, they found the No. 1 plant, to quote the Flint *Journal*, to be "a scene of wanton destruction, filth and disruption." Most of the damage, the New York *Times* reported, had resulted from striker efforts to barricade doors and windows by welding and from the attempt to devise living and sleeping quarters in the plant. Stocks of wrenches, door hinges, wood, leather, and other articles had been depleted by the strikers to make weapons. Some expensive material in the sewing room and in upholstery stores had been cut up for bedding, and many sewing machines required servicing. Heavy steel fire doors had been rammed out of commission and their opening mechanisms wrecked; and the fire protection system itself had been disrupted. Telephones, plumbing fixtures, and cafeteria equipment had been ruined. There had been some petty vandalism in the form of scratched car bodies and broken car roofs. The floor was littered with refuse, and some of the toilets had been stopped up and had overflown. Despite all this, however, the dies, the expensive machines, and the production lines of the occupied plants were unscathed at the end of the strike, and, considering the duration and character of the dispute, the damage in monetary terms was not great.[40]

It is difficult to explain the lack of cleanliness and the disorder in Fisher Body No. 1 at the end of the strike in view of reports during the strike of the neat and tidy appearance of the plant. Perhaps, with victory won, the strikers during their last day in the factory ceased to pay any further attention to the rules that they seem faithfully to have observed up to that time. Perhaps, as Powers Hapgood declared, the plant was not left in good order because the strikers marched out on the same day that the settlement was reached and did not have time for the final clean-up effort that had been planned. There is no reason to accept Travis' explanation that the condition of the plant could be attributed to Pinkertons among the stay-in strikers.[41]

The population of the communities of sit-down strikers fluctuated widely during the period of occupancy of the various plants. As long as strikers controlled the gates or windows of a particular plant, it was possible for individual sit-downers to leave the plants and then return, if they so desired, and it was also possible for the union to reinforce the group within the plant from the outside. Where the company or public authorities controlled entry and exit, as in Fisher No. 2 before the Battle of the Running Bulls or in Chevrolet No. 4, strikers were permitted to leave the plant, but their return and the ingress of new recruits were barred.

Concern for the well-being of their families or the desire to spend more time with them than was possible at a plant window, the customary meeting place, caused even some dedicated unionists to quit the sit-down in their plant either temporarily or for the duration of the strike. Just as many wives assured their husbands that they understood the necessity of their remaining inside until victory was achieved, so other wives made it clear to their men folk that they expected them to come home. "Honey I miss you dreadfully but I know you are fighting for a good cause," one wife wrote her husband in Chevrolet No. 4, but another wife informed her husband in the same plant, "I have felt so sad all the week would thought you would have known better than to stay in this long."[42] Relations between husbands and wives were not eased any by rumors that there were prostitutes inside the plants. Simons recalls that irate wives would come to the Information Window and tell their husbands to "get the hell out of there" and that it was difficult to convince some of the women that "there was not the biggest brothel in there that ever happened any place." Well-dressed, attractive prostitutes, as a matter of fact, did begin to appear outside the No. 1 plant, and since they did not charge for their services, the UAW concluded that this was probably "a G.M. stunt." The strike leadership instructed the union's pickets to keep the women away from the plant and urged the strikers, several of whom had already contracted gonorrhea, to "cut it out."[43]

Counteracting the pull of family ties was the commitment of most of the sit-downers to their cause and also the fear on the part of some, like the fear of the soldier in battle, that they would look cowardly or weak to their associates if they did not remain at their posts. "I don't know how long we will be here but we will never give up," one Chevrolet sit-downer wrote to his wife. Another wrote, "I could of come out wend they went on strike. But hunny I just thought I join the union and I look pretty yellow if I dident stick with thim."[44]

The number of sit-downers inside the No. 1 plant, which exceeded one thousand on some days, fell to a low of ninety on one occasion, according to Simons, hardly enough for the strikers to have been able to hold that large plant against attack from the outside.[45] The population in the No. 2 plant, according to the Michigan National Guard, fell to seventeen on January 26, whereas the total on January 5 had been about 450.[46] To be sure, the problem of feeding the sit-downers made it desirable to limit the population on the inside to a number adequate to hold the plants. Also, the union could not allow all its members and sympathizers to sit in since it had to deploy some of its forces outside the plant to collect funds, provide food, picket, and enlist sympathy for the cause. As it worked out, however, the problem faced by the sit-down organizations in Flint was not that of persuading strikers to leave the plants because it was difficult to feed them or because their talents were required on the outside but rather of keeping enough men inside to be able to hold the factories.[47]

The need to maintain an adequate force of sit-downers was a continuing concern of the strike organization in Fisher No. 1. On January 5 the strike committee decided that the stewards were to permit only 10 percent of the men to leave the plant at any one time. It was proposed at the executive board meeting a few days later that an article be printed in the Flint *Auto Worker* addressed to the wives and sweethearts of the sit-downers and stressing how important it was that the men remain in the plant. The police patrol was instructed by the strike committee on January 12, the day after the Fisher No. 2 riot, to prevent the membership from leaving the plant that day. On January 23 the executive board considered the "Question of getting more men in [the] shop."

The strike committee in Fisher Body No. 2 decided to restrict leaves from the plant to twenty-four hours and to grant such requests only when there was a replacement for the individual concerned. When the number of men in the plant on one occasion fell to twenty, Mundale requested assistance from the outside: "God Damn lets have some action out there. I haven't enough men in here to hold." Under the circumstances, it is not difficult to believe the assertions that some men were kept in the occupied plants against their will.[48]

Not all of the men sitting in the Flint plants were employees of those plants. UAW members in Flint whose plants were not on strike, like Norman Bully of Buick, climbed into and out of the occupied factories to relieve fellow unionists and to augment their numbers. In addition, UAW members from Toledo, Detroit, and elsewhere came to Flint on their own initiative or, more commonly, at the request of the union to participate in the sit-in. As one of the Kelsey-Hayes unionists who sat in for a time in Flint declared, "we loaded those plants so that they would not chase us out." Simons recalls that on one occasion when the number of sit-downers in the No. 1 factory had declined to a dangerously low level, Travis requested his home Toledo Chevrolet local to dispatch reinforcements. Believing that trouble was imminent in Flint, the Toledo group sent forty or fifty of the "toughest guys" that they could find. "I have never seen a bunch of guys that were so ready for blood in my life," Simons declared.[49]

Morale among the sit-downers was a compound of many factors: the marital status of the men, the quality of their leadership, physical conditions within the plant, the commitment of the strikers to their cause and their view of their role in the dispute, and the progress of the strike. UAW and CIO leaders and organizers regularly visited the

Fisher Body plants to bolster the spirits of the sit-downers. Powers Hapgood thus told the men in the No. 1 plant on January 13 that, whereas the auto workers had stood alone in previous strikes, they now enjoyed the support of Lewis and the CIO unions. He urged the men to "stick together" since they had GM "on [the] run." Hapgood was followed by Stanley Edward of the URW, who described to the strikers what the Goodyear workers had achieved by their strike, advised them of the support the URW was giving the strike, and told them that the "safest place" to be was inside the plants. The sit-downers on other occasions were informed by visitors like the Reuther brothers that the UAW was rapidly increasing its membership and was winning local settlements and that auto unionists in other plants were providing moral and material support for the strike.[50]

The strikers were also persuaded to see themselves as heroes who were selflessly putting up with hardship and discomfort not only in their own interests and that of the other auto workers but in the interests of American workingmen in general. Thus John L. Lewis, in an astute effort to bolster striker morale, wired the men in the two Fisher Body plants that they were "undoubtedly carrying through one of the most heroic battles that has ever been undertaken by strikers in an industrial dispute. The attention of the entire American public," he wrote, "is focussed upon you, watching the severe hardships you are suffering in order to demonstrate the strength of labor in the present struggle to organize for the purpose of obtaining a decent standard of living. For every working man in America, every worker and representative of labor in this country owes a debt of gratitude to each of you and I trust that this knowledge will cheer you through your long weary hours of waiting for the honorable settlement which in the nature of things must inevitably come." Pickets and union sympathizers outside the plants were similarly telling the sit-downers that "the eyes of the whole world" were on them.[51] It must have enormously boosted the self-esteem of the sit-downers suddenly to be transformed from badge numbers and easily replaceable cogs in an impersonal industrial machine into heroes of American labor.

No longer drawing any pay and many of them without savings to tide their families over, the strikers were understandably concerned about the plight of their dependents so long as the strike continued.[52] Aware of the importance of this matter for the morale of the sit-downers, the UAW assured them that it would aid their families in obtaining welfare and would provide them with necessities until public aid was forthcoming. "Dady dont be worried about us," one wife wrote to her striker husband, "everything is allright we got some help from the penengelly [Pengelly Building] they give us coal in some money to bye groceries with."[53]

Although some men found life inside the plants irksome and withdrew from the sit-down community at the first opportunity and others who remained in the plants grumbled about conditions, for many of the strikers the sit-down was a truly enjoyable experience, a glorious moment in their otherwise drab lives. Sitting down and participating in the life of the new plant community were more pleasurable than the tedium of work on the assembly line and were, additionally, a means of " 'getting even' " with management for accumulated grievances. For some of the men, although they were concerned about their families, it must have been a relief, at least for a time, to be away from nagging wives and bawling children and to be free of the concerns and frustrations of their normal, everyday life. "We like it so well here," a Guide Lamp sit-downer declared, "that we'll hate to leave when the strike is settled." "I like it here," a Chevrolet No. 4 sit-downer wrote his girl friend. "All we have to do is Sit! Eat! Sleep! Wash dishes! and Guard!" Another No. 4 sit-downer wrote, "I am having a great time something new, some thing different, lots of grub and music." The reporter in Paul Gallico's sit-down novelette sensed "a gaiety and excitement" about the sit-downers when he entered one of the Flint plants. "They were children playing at a new and fascinating game. They had made a palace out of what had been their prison."[54]

Morale, it would seem, was higher in the No. 1 than in the No. 2 plant. There was a far greater percentage of married men with families—possibly 90 percent according to Barclay—among the No. 2 than among the No. 1 strikers and fewer of the young, "hard, reckless type" who Russell B. Porter of the New York *Times* reported as predominating among the strikers both inside and outside the factories. It was the married men in the No. 2 plant, according to the National Guard, who were "decidedly worried" and among whom there was a morale problem.[55]

The stronger leadership in Fisher Body No. 1 than in No. 2 may also account for the superior morale in the former. Red Mundale, the strike leader in No. 2, was, unlike Bud Simons, a "retiring kind of person" and lacked the force and dynamism of his counterpart in the No. 1 plant. Simons, moreover, was supported by a small group of left-wingers who worked zealously for the success of the strike. "There were some in there that were called left-wingers," strike committeeman Joe Devitt later declared, "but those that were called left-wingers, I believe, probably played a most active part in the organizing and conduct of the sit-down strike. They played a major role."[56] Some of the members of the No. 1 strike community, not necessarily among the radical element however, worked so diligently at their tasks that the strike committee had to order them to rest or to provide relief for them.[57]

The strikers in No. 1 displayed a fierce independence in their relationship with the UAW leadership on the outside. When Travis asked the strike committee's permission for one of his men to go through the plant to gather information for the strike bulletins and the press, the committee agreed but assigned one of the sit-downers to the Travis emissary and specified that the notes he took must be approved by the executive board. When newsmen protested the refusal of the No. 1 sit-downers to admit non-American Newspaper Guild reporters to the plant, a member of the executive board replied that the No. 1 strikers made their own decisions and did not necessarily pay heed to Travis' instructions. A No. 1 sit-downer told a New York *Times* reporter that his colleagues and he would not evacuate the plant even if Martin or Lewis ordered it "unless 'we get what we want.' "[58]

The temper of the men, or at least of the leadership, in Fisher Body No. 1 was illustrated a few days after the Battle of the Running Bulls when Captain Lawrence A. Lyon of the state police came into the plant. The discussion between the captain and the strike committee apparently turned to the possible use of the state police to evict the sit-downers, whereupon Lyon was told that if the troopers wanted to repeat the "experience" of Flint's "yellow bellied coppers" they were welcome to try. Later, Travis and Roy Reuther visited the plant, and Simons invited them "to come and live with us" to avoid arrest for their part in the Fisher No. 2 riot. The offer was declined. Reuther, with the recent battle in mind, told the men that he did not counsel violence but that "every thing hinges on the hinges."[59]

All in touch with the situation agreed that morale was at its lowest in Flint among the sit-downers in the Chevrolet No. 4 plant, which the UAW seized on February 1. Since the plant was, from the start, surrounded by the National Guard,[60] the sit-downers were cut off from the regular visits of family and friends, the plaudits of pickets and sympathizers, and even news of the outside world, and this was part of the problem. The plant itself was also physically the least comfortable of the three occupied in Flint. Known by the workers as "The Hell-Hole," it was located in a valley bordering on the Flint River. It was damp and poorly ventilated, and its equipment and facilities were obsolete. From the start, moreover, the company, which still held the powerhouse, put pressure on the men by frequently turning off the heat and lights.[61] Since the sit-downers did not have enough warm clothing to cope with the cold, they had to write to their families to send them the proper garments. After visiting the plant and seeing the plight of the men, Rose Pesotta, acting for the UAW, bought out the stock of winter underwear and pajamas, woolen socks, mufflers, and similar items of one of Flint's general stores and had the apparel sent into the factory.[62]

The dampness of the plant and the drastic alterations in the in-plant temperature, coupled with the normal hazards of life in a northern climate during the winter, contributed to a certain amount of illness in Chevrolet No. 4; and there were widespread rumors that the men were suffering from amoebic dysentery and intestinal flu. A National Guard source claimed that fifty men had to be evacuated from the plant because of dysentery, but the UAW actually had to remove only twelve of the strikers. Although a pro-UAW doctor who entered the factory on February 7 alleged that he had found no cases of influenza or dysentery, one of the strike officials privately conceded that there had been an "epidemic of intestinal flu" in the plant and that there were some cases of dysentery. The strikers blamed the illness in the plant not only on the company's manipulation of the heat but also on the water they were drinking, and so they began to drink only water sent into them by the union.[63]

Quite apart from the problems that they faced inside the plant, the men in Chevrolet No. 4 were distressed by letters that they received from their families complaining of sickness and urging the strikers to return to their homes. The UAW charged that company representatives had induced these letters, and the strikers' "special investigating committee" allegedly ascertained that several of the letters were spurious. Wives also reported that foremen were visiting their homes in an effort to influence them to bring pressure on their husbands to quit the plant. One sit-downer advised his wife that "if anyone gos to the house ask him their name and we will do the rest. if they don't want to leave shot the basterd."[64]

It is hardly surprising in view of the pressures to which they were subjected that many of the men in Chevrolet No. 4 did not appear as "cheerful" to visitors as the sit-downers in No. 1 did.[65] At one point, Kermit Johnson, the youthful strike leader in the plant, wrote Travis that he had not slept for more than three hours a night since the strike began because of "the growing dissention [sic] among the boys in here. These boys don't need democracy they need a king," Johnson observed. Despite the reports of low morale and dissension, however, many of the strikers appeared to be enjoying life in Chevrolet No. 4 or, at least, so they advised their families. "We are one happy family now," one of them wrote. "We all feel fine and have plenty to eat. We have several good banjo players and singers. We sing and cheer the Fischer [sic] boys & they return it. . . . Do not worry at all for we are peaceful Chevrolet workers and are bound to win."[66]

It was possible, of course, to see the sit-down strikes as a revolutionary challenge to the rights of private property in the United States, and a few radicals inside and outside the plants undoubtedly did so; but the mass of the sit-down strikers were utterly without revolutionary intent, and, unlike the Italian automobile workers who occupied the great Fiat plant in Turin in September, 1920, they evinced no desire to operate the factories that they were temporarily occupying or to achieve labor control of industry. They were sitting in to secure meaningful collective bargaining with their employer and better working conditions, not to transform property relationships.[67]

The sit-downers did not see themselves as law breakers, nor did they, indeed, give much thought to the legal implications of their action. "All that's up to the union and the lawyers," a spokesman for the Fisher No. 2 strikers told a reporter. "We're not up on those things. We're just here protecting our jobs. We don't aim to keep the plants or try to run them, but we want to see that nobody takes our jobs. . . . We don't think we're breaking the law, or at least we don't think we're doing anything really bad, any more than people who violated the prohibition laws a few years ago."[68]

It may be, as Seymour Martin Lipset has suggested, that in a society in which so much stress is placed on success, workers are persuaded to believe that "the most important thing is to win the game, regardless of the methods employed in doing so." Those who believe themselves "handicapped" in our society may feel constrained "to 'innovate,' that is, to use whatever means they can find to gain recognition."[69] In the automobile industry in 1936 and 1937 the sit-down tactic became the "means" to achieve the desired end of recognition.

The UAW adopted the sit-down tactic against GM rather than resorting to the conventional strike not for ideological reasons but because the technique had proved itself effective. It was, of course, aware that the automotive sit-downs in the preceding weeks had gone unchallenged in the courts and that, with the exception of the Gordon Baking Company sit-in, public authorities in Michigan had made no effort to evict sit-down strikers; but, aside from this, it is doubtful that the UAW leadership or organizers had given much thought to the question of the legality of the device. Once the strike was underway, however, and its legality came under attack, the UAW felt it necessary to adopt some rationale for its behavior.

In defending the sit-down, the UAW took the position that the new strike tactic was just another means by which workers protected their jobs against strikebreakers and was not essentially different from the conventional picket line, which also entrenched upon the employer's property rights. The union, as a matter of fact, contended that it would have struck in the conventional manner had it had any confidence that GM would not attempt to break the strike by introducing scabs into the struck plants, removing equipment from plants on strike to strike-free plants, and seeking by itself or through public authorities that it controlled to smash the UAW picket lines, secure injunctions against the strikers, and do whatever else was necessary to break the strike. A strike on the inside, according to the UAW, neutralized the "arsenal of weapons" available to GM and gave the union a chance to win.[70]

On a loftier ideological plane, the UAW contended that the strike was legal since the worker enjoyed a property right in his job and, in striking, was therefore "protecting his private property—his right to a job." The property right of the worker in his job, it was alleged, was superior to the right of the company to use its property as it saw fit since the workers had invested their lives in the plant whereas the stockholders of the company had invested only their dollars. As one Fisher Body sit-downer graphically phrased it, "Our hides are wrapped around those machines." The property, the Flint *Auto Worker* declared, belonged to GM, but "there is something else inside these plants that the workers have earned by years of sweat and toil—and that is THEIR JOBS!"[71]

The concept of the worker's right to his job was without basis in law, and no court accepted the doctrine, but the idea did have a few adherents outside the UAW ranks, including, most notably, the dean of the Northwestern School of Law, Leon Green.[72] Other union sympathizers, aware that the concept lacked a legal basis, argued for the recognition of the idea as a moral right or took the position that the sit-down would eventually receive legal recognition just as other union tactics once considered illegal, like the strike itself, had gained the sanction of law.[73] The weakness of the right-to-a-job thesis, however it was expressed, was that it ignored the numerous workers who wished to continue working but were denied their right to a job by the sit-downers, and it could not logically be applied to sit-downers who were not employees of the plants in which they were sitting and were thus clearly trespassers.

If the sit-down tactic were indeed illegal, resort to it was nevertheless justified, the UAW claimed, because GM was itself violating the law of the land, the NLRA, by refusing to engage in meaningful collective bargaining and by employing a variety of unfair labor practices designed to thwart organization.[74] This argument, even though its essence was that two wrongs make a right, did help to weaken the force of GM's attack on the illegality of the sit-down for at least some of those concerned about the strike. The columnist Dorothy Thompson thus wrote during the strike that she was unable to work up very much "moral indignation" regarding the illegality of the sit-down since the strikers were fighting for a status recognized by law but being sabotaged by employers who had "the bigger guns and the stronger strategical positions." The Department of Research and Education of the Federal Council of the Churches of Christ pointed out that the GM sit-down was opposed to all the Council's "accepted principles of law and equity" but that workers could be expected to adopt "extreme measures" when the owners denied them their legal right to organize and to engage in collective bargaining.[75]

Sympathizers with the UAW cause differed as to whether the sit-down was legally to be construed as a trespass in Michigan and elsewhere; not until 1939, when the United States Supreme Court declared a sit-down in the Fansteel Metallurgical Corporation to be "a high-handed proceeding without shadow of legal right,"[76] was this question definitively resolved. The *New Republic* contended that trespass statutes were not relevant since they were designed to apply to persons who forcibly entered upon the property of another and caused damage to it whereas the sit-downer had entered the plant where he was sitting with the consent of the owner and had not damaged the property. The leadership of the American Civil Liberties Union, on the other hand, concluded that the sit-down was obviously a trespass and was "clearly illegal."[77]

Actually, the legal status of the sit-down in Michigan was somewhat clouded, at least insofar as the criminal law was concerned. Forcible entry and detainer was not a statutory offense for which a penalty had been expressly provided, but it was to be argued later that since it was an indictable offense under the common law, sit-downers were guilty of a felony according to the terms of a Michigan statute that made it felonious to commit an offense indictable under the common law for which no statute had specified a punishment. An assistant to Wayne County Prosecutor Duncan McRea contended, however, that employees who "passively" participated in a sit-down strike were not committing a criminal act but were subject to eviction by civil action through the institution of summary proceedings before a Circuit Court commissioner. According to the assistant prosecutor, these proceedings, provided for in a statute of 1915, superseded the applicable common law. Law enforcement officers, he pointed out, could institute criminal proceedings only if the strikers disturbed the peace, were guilty of kidnapping, or maliciously destroyed the employer's property.[78]

McRea, it will be recalled, had stated in December, 1936, that sit-downers were not trespassing since they had entered the plants in which they worked at the invitation of their employers, but this view was later challenged by a writer in the *Michigan Law Review*, who, assuming that the sit-downers were no longer employees, a questionable conclusion at best, contended that, on the basis of Michigan cases, the sit-down was a trespass and the civil liability of the strikers was clear. The sit-down, he thought, might also be regarded as a tort of civil conspiracy against non-strikers and the employer since the strikers were denying them their right to work. The writer was less certain about the applicability of the criminal law to the sit-down.[79]

Quite apart from the legality of the sit-down strike in Michigan, there was a real question as to whether even peaceful picketing was legal in the state. The Supreme Court of Michigan had last pronounced on the question in 1922 and, following a long line of precedents, had ruled against picketing in any form. It could be argued, however, that the Dunckel-Baldwin Act of 1935 assumed peaceful picketing to be legal in the state, but this was far from certain. Given the doubts about the legality of both the sit-down and peaceful picketing, the UAW can hardly be blamed for pragmatically adopting what appeared to be the more effective strike technique. "You have fought a great fight," Martin told the Flint Fisher Body workers at the conclusion of the strike, "and the ends justified the means."[80]

As GM and other employers saw it, there was no question about the illegality of the sit-down. "Sit-downs are strikes. Such strikers are clearly trespassers and violators of the law of the land," Knudsen declared on the last day of 1936.[81] Regarding the strike as clearly illegal, GM had to decide which of several legal remedies it would be most appropriate and expedient for it to employ in an effort to regain control over its property. The company made its decision early in the new year, but, as it turned out, it was unable to secure the evacuation of its plants until it had agreed to terms that brought the strike to an end.

Strategy and Tactics: General Motors
VII

As the major phase of the sit-down strike began at the end of 1936 GM's Stephen M. DuBrul, then on special assignment to Vice-President Donaldson Brown, reminded the corporation's leadership that Franklin D. Roosevelt, after his sensational victory in November, was likely to be a " 'Popular' leader" who would support any group championing " 'the cause of the workingman.' " Under the circumstances, DuBrul warned, GM was "peculiarly vulnerable" since it was successful, big, and making large profits and since most of its executives had opposed the administration in the election. It would consequently have to be *"so fair in every position"* that it took with regard to the UAW that it placed the union *"on the defensive both with the public and the Administration"* and made Lewis, whom DuBrul characterized as "probably the keenest labor strategist" in the nation, appear to be an "obstructionist."

For the public to accept its position as fair, DuBrul contended, GM would have to engage in collective bargaining with the representatives of its workers on " 'bargainable' " issues. It would have to be "very cautious," however, with regard to matters of principle that might be in dispute. On the crucial question of majority rule, it should make the President's settlement of March, 1934, which endorsed collective-bargaining pluralism, the "keynote" of its position. DuBrul assumed that GM would be unyielding should the union seek an election under the NLRA, which embodied the principle of exclusive representation.

DuBrul thought that GM would expose itself to public and political criticism were it adamantly to refuse to sign an agreement with the UAW. It was his opinion that the corporation should be willing to consider the signing of a contract with a union that was a responsible organization, was not coercing the company's employees, and was able to furnish evidence of its good faith, and if the agreement stipulated that the union could represent only those workers who had designated it as their bargaining agency, recognized the open shop, and did not compromise management prerogatives. "In short," DuBrul concluded, "our position at all times must be that of a reasonable employer who is unfortunately being victimized by irresponsible professional agitators whose demands exceed all reasonable limits. Any other attitude at this time would place our whole case in jeopardy, regardless of the basic merits of our side, and would be politically about as stupid a blunder as we can commit. We must not forget that there has been an election."[1]

Whether the GM leadership studied DuBrul's document, which so astutely appraised the strike issues from the corporation's point of view, is not known, but GM was in the end to follow rather closely the policy guidelines DuBrul had drawn. GM appreciated the fact that the world had changed and that in the year 1937 it was no longer possible, or at least was unwise, for a great corporation to respond to a union challenge by the application of ruthless force; but, although aware that there had been "an election," it was not prepared to surrender meekly the principles of collective bargaining to which it had been committed since 1933.

Responding to the UAW's request of December 24 for a general conference, Knudsen, on the last day of 1936, attacked the sit-down strike as an illegal tactic and defined the collective-bargaining policy that the corporation would observe in the face of the strike. GM, he declared, accepted the principle of collective bargaining and had specified a procedure for implementing this principle in its statement of August 15, 1934. It believed that the proper manner of bargaining was for its employees to take up their grievances with the local plant managers, who were familiar not only with the "basic general policies" of the corporation but with the varying local conditions that the terms of employment must reflect.

The union itself, however, Knudsen contended, had made "real" collective bargaining impossible by shutting down the plants then on strike against the wishes of the great majority of the workers in these plants and without making any prior attempt to bargain with the local managements. The strikers, moreover, were illegally trespassing upon the company's property, and it would not, therefore, bargain with them or their representatives until its plants had been evacuated. "We cannot have bona fide collective bargaining with sit-down strikers in illegal possession of plants." Insofar as the UAW represented the strikers, Knudsen therefore suggested that it order them to vacate the company's premises as a precondition for collective bargaining. He was willing to meet with the union at any time for "general discussion," but the issues raised in its December 24 letter—collective bargaining, seniority, the speed-up, rates and methods of pay, and "other conditions of employment"—would have to be discussed with the local plant managers, who were authorized to bargain with the union for its members.[2]

Knudsen's December 31 letter, although correct to a degree in its assertion that the sit-down strikes in the GM plants had been initiated by UAW locals before they had exhausted the process of collective bargaining, was a confused document. It was not entirely clear from the letter whether GM was opposed to any conversations with the UAW prior to the evacuation of the company's plants or whether the ban on collective bargaining applied only to discussions at the local level where sit-downs had occurred but not to discussions at other plants nor to the undefined "general discussion" with the UAW that Knudsen declared himself willing to undertake. The GM executive vice-president insisted that all the issues about which the UAW wished to talk were local in nature and must therefore be discussed locally; but what the union was most concerned about was the nature of collective bargaining and employee representation in the corporation, and local plant managers certainly had no independent authority to deviate from the national policy of the corporation regarding these matters nor even regarding the standard work week, which was uniform throughout the corporation.

Since operating responsibilities in GM, unlike the formulation of policy, were decentralized, local GM executives theoretically had the power of decision with respect to such matters as the methods of pay and the speed of the line; but the experience of the UAW before the sit-down did not suggest that plant managers could function altogether as independent sovereignties in resolving even these questions without reference to the "basic general policies" of the corporation that they were powerless to alter. In an interview on January 2, however, Knudsen reiterated that it would be "impracticable" for him to try to settle problems arising in the corporation's far-flung plant cities, and he stated flatly that GM would not sign an agreement with the UAW for the corporation as a whole.[3]

Homer Martin replied to GM for the UAW on January 4, submitting to Sloan and Knudsen the official demands of the union agreed upon at a UAW strategy conference in Flint the preceding day. The UAW president stated that GM's proposal for local bargaining was unacceptable to the union. For one thing, GM, in contravention of the NLRA, appeared to be pursuing a nation-wide policy to forestall the organization of a union among its employees, and there could be no meaningful discussion of grievances with local plant managers until this policy was discontinued. Second, although there were "diverse factors" among the plants of the corporation, there were certain "fundamental issues" that could be determined only by its national officers, and it was to arrive at a national agreement concerning eight such issues that the UAW was seeking a conference: a national collective-bargaining conference; the abolition of all piecework systems of pay; the thirty-hour week, the six-hour day, and time-and-a-half compensation for overtime; establishment of a minimum rate of pay "commensurate with an American standard of living"; reinstatement of employees who had been "unjustly" dismissed; seniority based upon length of service; recognition of the UAW as the "sole bargaining agency" for GM workers; and the mutual determination by management and union committees of the speed of production in all GM plants.[4]

It is perfectly apparent that the eight issues Martin set forth in his January 4 letter were properly subjects of national discussion, and Martin was on the whole correct in charging that it was "absurd" to contend that basic questions of this sort should or could be determined entirely by local plant managers. The UAW was aware that there were differences from plant to plant regarding such matters as rates and methods of pay, but it believed that these subjects could be more meaningfully discussed at the local level within the context of general guidelines developed at the summit and after a national policy for collective bargaining had been agreed to by company and union. Martin, as a matter of fact, had stated on January 2 that the union was not seeking to define all the terms of employment in a national agreement. "We don't ask a national agreement binding all the plants [on all working conditions]. What we are asking is a code of rules for collective bargaining. We are willing to bargain with plant managers."[5]

Among its eight demands the UAW attached the greatest significance to that calling for the recognition of the union as the sole bargaining agency for GM employees. Its "long and sad experience" with membership lists as a basis for representation, the ALB's scheme of proportional representation, and management efforts to checkmate outside unionism with company unions had convinced the UAW that collective-bargaining pluralism was productive of "confusion, disruption and industrial strife." "Unified representation," the UAW was to contend, was the only proper method of collective bargaining, the indispensable prelude to the orderly determination of the conditions of employment by employers and employees, and those who opposed the idea were really opposed to collective bargaining itself.[6]

The proper legal procedure for the UAW to have pursued in seeking to validate its claim to speak for GM workers as a whole was to have requested an NLRB election among the company's employees to determine whether or not a majority of those voting wished the union to be their representative for collective bargaining. The UAW, however, with good reason considering the size of its membership, doubted that it enjoyed sufficient worker support to win such an election. It was certain, moreover, that GM, which refused to recognize the NLRA as the law of the land, would contest an NLRB election order in the courts; and the UAW, like GM and most everyone else, assumed that the law would be declared unconstitutional. The union, therefore, did not hesitate to charge GM with engaging in unfair labor practices in violation of the NLRA, but it did not attempt to put its own claim to speak for the company's workers to the statute's electoral test. Its response at the outset of the strike to questions regarding the size of its membership was that it was sufficient to close GM's plants and that, in a company as hostile to unionism as GM, actual membership, in any event, was not a just criterion of union strength. As its membership grew during the strike, the UAW began to assert its majority status among GM workers, but it offered no proof of this other than its own word.[7]

To the plant workers who supported the UAW, exclusive representation was the means by which the conditions under which they labored could be improved. Of the demands listed by the union in its January 4 letter, the auto workers were most concerned, as has already been indicated, with the speed-up, seniority determined by length of service alone rather than in accordance with the ALB's complicated rules, and, in some plants, with the abolition of incentive methods of pay. It is doubtful, as Hartley Barclay pointed out,[8] that they really favored the thirty-hour week, and they were, for the most part, less concerned about their hourly rates of pay, which were certainly more than "commensurate with an American standard of living," than about steady employment, regarding which the January 4 letter, surprisingly, had nothing to say.

Sloan, in effect, sought to rebut the union's January 4 communication and to clarify GM's position in the strike in an open letter to the corporation's employees that was published on January 5. Asserting that the UAW was seeking the closed shop and a labor dictatorship, Sloan declared that the "real issue" in the strike was: "Will a labor organization run the plants of General Motors . . . or will the Management continue to do so?" He asserted that the sit-down strikes, "widespread intimidation," and shortages of materials were forcing the corporation's employees from their jobs at a time when the earnings of GM workers were the highest in GM's history and when significant progress had been made in the regularization of their employment.

Despite what the union might say, Sloan asserted, GM employees did not have to join a labor organization to keep their jobs. Work in GM's plants would continue to depend on merit alone, which meant that the corporation's employees did not have "to pay tribute to anyone for the right to work." GM would not accept any union as the sole bargaining agency for its employees, but in accordance with its statement of August, 1934, the corporation would recognize all representatives of its employees, whether union or nonunion. The corporation would continue to observe the ALB's seniority rules, forty hours would remain its standard work week, and, as always, it would pay "the highest justifiable wages."[9]

Sloan's January 5 letter, an overreaction to the demands of labor that was characteristic of employers in the 1930's, raised questions as to whether the "basic general policies" of GM regarding representation, hours, and so forth were subject to negotiation even at the summit. Replying to the letter, which Frances Perkins criticized as "one of expediency rather than one of philosophy," Martin quite rightly pointed out that the UAW had not requested the closed shop and that it was not labor dictatorship for it to seek to alter working conditions in the automobile industry. The NLRB, in a case involving Delco-Remy, was later to declare that the statement "clearly interfered with and restrained the rights of the employees" guaranteed by the Wagner Act; but, for the moment anyhow, Sloan's letter had the intended effect at least in some quarters: the chairman of the publicity committee of the Cleveland Fisher Body strikers thus reported to the UAW that the letter "created a worse situation as far as public opinion is concerned than we bargained for."[10]

The GM and UAW statements of early January sharply defined the differences between the two antagonists regarding the vital issues of collective bargaining and representation. During the ensuing weeks of the strike the corporation and the union continued to trade verbal blows, but they added relatively little to the substance of the debate. The combatants would have to move out from their entrenched positions if a negotiated peace were to be attained.

In opposing the UAW's demand for recognition as the exclusive bargaining agency for GM workers, the corporation was soon to find an ally in the craft unions of the AFL. The Metal Trades and Building Trades Departments of the Federation and six international unions affiliated with them, led by John P. Frey, the president of the Metal Trades Department and an implacable foe of industrial unionism, wired GM on January 7 and 8 protesting any grant of exclusive bargaining rights to the UAW and requesting the corporation to make no agreement that would give some other organization the authority to represent workers over whom the craft unions claimed jurisdiction. The craft unionists were primarily concerned about the strike in Cleveland, where their membership was apparently greater than in Flint; and here, on January 7, the machinists, electrical workers, plumbers and steamfitters, and bricklayers unions, acting on the advice of Frey and J. W. Williams, the president of the Building

Trades Department, complained to the Fisher Body plant manager that the UAW local, which was not authorized to speak for them, had called the strike without consulting them and without their approval and asked him to reopen the plant so that they could return to work.

Despite this seeming effort to break the strike, Frey, who thought that the "strike movement" was aimed at driving the craft unions in the automobile industry "out of existence," declared that AFL unionists would not work with scabs and did not intend to violate the picket line of the strikers. In an ambiguous joint statement of January 19, the Metal Trades and Building Trades Departments asserted that they would do nothing detrimental to the efforts of the auto workers to secure improved terms of employment but, at the same time, that they would not surrender their rights nor would they remain "inactive" in protecting the welfare of their members.[11]

Seizing an apparent opportunity to drive a wedge among the company's workers and to deflate the UAW's pretensions to speak for all the corporation's workers, GM made public the telegrams from the AFL craft unions, and Harry Anderson wired Frey on January 9 that he could "rest assured that General Motors has no intention of entering into any agreement with any other organization interferring [sic] with [the] legitimate jurisdiction" of unions affiliated with the Metal Trades Department. A few days later Frey, at GM's request, met secretly with Knudsen, Anderson, and GM attorney John T. Smith and was asked what the policy of his department was regarding agreements with corporations. Frey provided the information requested and indicated that the Metal Trades and Building Trades Departments were prepared to confer with GM at any time regarding their affiliated groups.[12]

About February 1 Frey was invited to Detroit for another unpublicized conference with Knudsen and Anderson. Knudsen asked the Metal Trades president what he wished GM to do regarding Cleveland, and Frey replied that the AFL wanted him to meet with union representatives there and to instruct the plant manager to inform the superintendents and foremen that there was to be "a new deal" and that they were not to interfere with the right to organize. Frey had a two-hour conference on February 3 with Lincoln R. Scafe, the Cleveland plant manager, in which the AFL official talked "very plainly" and told Scafe that he would have to meet with a committee representing the metal trades and building trades councils of the city. Scafe agreed to meet this demand and also promised to tell plant supervisory officials that "there is a new deal here in so far as the crafts are concerned." He stated that foremen who did not comply with these instructions would have to obtain jobs elsewhere.[13]

The AFL not only sought to persuade GM to resist the UAW demand for exclusive jurisdiction but also, as we shall see, interceded with President Roosevelt and Governor Murphy to the same end.[14] Not all of the Federation's local organizations, however, subscribed to the hard-line policy of Frey and some of the craft unions. Although the AFL itself did not endorse the strike and, as a matter of fact, was never requested to do so, the local federations in the three cities most directly involved in the strike, Flint, Detroit, and Cleveland, all officially approved the strike; and only the Cleveland Federation, undoubtedly as the result of pressure from the Metal Trades and Building Trades Departments, rescinded its action.

Frey contended that several of the metal trades unions were strongly organized in GM and that some of the craft unions had verbal understandings with the corporation to which it faithfully adhered, but the total craft-union membership in GM plants appears to have been miniscule. The UAW mocked the pretensions of the AFL in the controversy, declaring that the craft locals in the Cleveland Fisher Body plant did not have enough members " 'to fill a thimble.' "[15]

Frey was to claim a few days after the GM strike ended that the CIO had failed "to drive us out of the industry" because he had secured an agreement with GM that it would not grant the UAW exclusive bargaining rights.[16] Frey, however, magnified his importance in the strike. GM was determined from the start to resist the UAW's representation demand, and it simply used the AFL to buttress a position that it would have maintained with equal determination had the Federation not involved itself in the dispute. GM undoubtedly looked upon the conservative AFL craft unions as a lesser evil than the UAW, and it may be that corporation executives wondered whether events might have taken a different turn had GM at an earlier date welcomed the AFL into its plants, but the corporation was to learn that it was now too late to resist the UAW tide by announcing a new deal "in so far as the crafts are concerned."

In challenging the UAW's demand for exclusive bargaining rights, GM could point not only to the statements of AFL leaders that the UAW did not speak for the craft unionists in the corporation's plants but, more important, to the apparent protestations of an overwhelming majority of GM workers that they were satisfied with existing conditions of labor and wished to return to or remain at work. Beginning about January 5 GM employees were given the opportunity by a variety of means to express their loyalty to the company, their satisfaction with working conditions, their opposition to the strike and to having the UAW pretend to speak for them, and their desire to go back to work or, if still working, to remain at their jobs. GM declared at the end of the month that 83 percent (123,724) of the 149,249 workers affected by the strike had by way of petitions, mass meetings, ballots, and other means protested the strike and that this total included 82 percent of the company's Flint workers, 69 percent of its Cleveland workers, and 90 percent of its Anderson workers.[17]

In addition to the loyalty pledges signed by GM workers, thousands of the company's employees sent wires, letters, and petitions to President Roosevelt and Governor Murphy complaining about the strike and about being "forced to submit to labor dictators of a minority group" and affirming their desire to return to or remain at work. "Please end Chevrolet strike. I want to work," one GM employee wired Roosevelt. "Why should we, the ready to work for our money citizens of Flint, Michigan," one woman asked Murphy after the Battle of the Running Bulls, "have to sit idle in our homes while the few union men of this city and the other men who have come from other cities to keep us from working and earning an honest living go their merry way—breaking all laws and making [a] laughing stock of all our police officers?" Messages of a similar sort were also sent to John L. Lewis. "We the employees [of] Chevrolet Gear and Axle," one such communication declared, "defy you and your malicious un-American tactics. As law abiding citizens we will fight shoulder to shoulder with General Motors until your defeat is definitely determined."[18]

The UAW protested at the time and before the La Follette Committee later that GM had gathered its loyalty pledges through a process of "coercion, intimidation, and the threat of loss of jobs" for non-signers. It claimed that the company had financed the employee committees that had gathered the signatures and had provided them with the addresses of its workers, that foremen had in some cases distributed the petitions, that employees were threatened with the loss of their jobs and company benefits and even with violence if they did not sign, and that the union itself in some plants had found it necessary to advise the workers to sign petitions and postcards to protect their jobs.

Although one could have anticipated this sort of union reaction to GM's claims of employee antagonism to the strike, the UAW charges were by no means without some substance. Scafe admitted that GM had helped to finance the employee committee gathering signatures in Cleveland, and he conceded that "a small portion" of the Cleveland Fisher Body workers who asserted their loyalty did so at the "solicitation" of foremen. Insofar as employee committees sought signatures by mail, one can be certain that the mailing addresses of employees were provided by the company, and, of course, loyalty petitions could have been circulated within the plants only by permission of the management.[19] James Myers, the Industrial Secretary of the Federal Council of the Churches of Christ, after talking to a large number of strikers and non-strikers in Flint, concluded that the loyalty pledges in that city had not been given voluntarily. "We all felt we had better sign," he quoted one Flint resident as saying, "since we thought it was a method to spot union sympathizers." Another Flint signer wrote the President that GM was "all powerful" in the city and "Most of us would sign anything to keep our jobs."[20]

It would be a mistake, however, to assume that employee support for GM and opposition to the strike were entirely synthetic. There was, as Representative Fred L. Crawford of Michigan informed the President, a "third side" of the strike, employees ready and willing to work but unable to do so. GM over the years had succeeded in convincing many of its employees that it was a good employer, that their jobs and well-being depended on the open shop and the absence of labor trouble in the corporation's plants, and that what was good for GM was good for them. A clinical psychologist who practiced in Detroit during the sit-down reveals that he often heard even unemployed GM workers remark, "Why can't the union let General Motors alone? If they make trouble, there won't be jobs for any of us." Robert and Helen Lynd have written that the mood of GM's Muncie workers in 1937 was reportedly, " 'Why pick on General Motors, which treats its men better than any other outfit in town.' " A Buick worker similarly wrote Governor Murphy during the strike that "General Motors should not have to join a union. It is their Company and they are O.K. as is." Russell B. Porter, who covered the strike for the New York *Times*, concluded on the basis of his observations that the "overwhelming majority" of GM workers in Flint, Pontiac, Detroit, and Lansing were opposed to the strike and wanted to return to work and that only "a small minority" were strikers. Although certainly correct about the limited number of actual strikers, Porter probably exaggerated the extent of opposition to the strike and overlooked a large middle group of workers who, although preferring work to idleness, were uncommitted to either side in the dispute and were awaiting its outcome to determine where their best interests lay.[21]

The loyalty, back-to-work movement in Flint was given organizational status with the appearance on January 7 of "The Flint Alliance for the Security of Our Jobs, Our Homes, and Our Community." The Alliance was headed by George E. Boysen, a forty-seven year old vice-president of the C V S Manufacturing Company who had been a Buick paymaster from 1917 to 1932 and had later served as a city commissioner and as Flint's mayor for one term. Boysen, who talked too much and came to be regarded by reporters as "something of a crackpot," was a poor choice for the assignment, but, as Roy Reuther later remarked, "it wasn't a particularly good assignment."[22]

The official Flint *Journal*-GM view of the origins of the Flint Alliance was that workers who were anxious to bring the strike to an end had "induced" Boysen to head the organization because of "his well-known interest in the men in the shops." The Alliance, Boysen asserted, was not directed against anyone but was intended as a "rallying point" for those who desired to work and wanted "industrial peace" in Flint. In addition to showing where the overwhelming majority of the good people of Flint stood with regard to the strike and giving them " 'an outlet for their vent,' " to use Boysen's phrasing, the Alliance was allegedly designed to prevent the claimed popular resentment in Flint against the strike leaders and outside "agitators" from erupting into violence. Although the movement to establish the Alliance, according to the official version, had originated among factory men, membership was open to all citizens, and a large enrollment was desired, Boysen said, for "its moral effect toward smothering the strike movement."[23]

While Alliance membership cards were circulating among GM workers in Flint, the organization began to take on the character of a "citizens' alliance." On the morning of January 11, some hours before the Battle of the Running Bulls, two hundred of the city's business and professional men met in a downtown hotel, endorsed Alliance objectives, and established a "cooperating committee" to assist in its activities. Boysen, at first, had indicated that he was financing the organization himself, but he was soon declaring that the downtown business and professional leaders had made substantial contributions to the Alliance. It was presumably with funds so obtained that the organization was able to hire Floyd Williamson of the Lawrence Witt agency of New York to handle its publicity.[24]

Although a Michigan State Police investigator who made frequent visits to the Alliance office reported that the organization appeared "to be doing little business," Boysen advised Governor Murphy on January 14 that 25,887 persons in Flint had joined the Alliance or signed loyalty pledges. Boysen contrasted this massive display of anti-strike sentiment with an alleged UAW membership in the city of only two thousand.[25]

The UAW viewed the Flint Alliance as a serious threat to its strike ambitions, as the spearhead for the possible use of violence against the strikers or even, despite the fact that its membership was not limited to auto workers, as the nucleus for a rival organization. The union ridiculed the notion that the Alliance had been "inspired" by GM workers to articulate their opposition to the strike and contended that it was, on the contrary, a "Strike-Breaking Agency," "an illegitimate organization ... financed, controlled and dominated" by GM. Its membership cards, the UAW said, had been distributed by foremen, supervisors, and company-union representatives, and the signatures on these cards had been obtained by coercion and intimidation. Two of the Alliance press agents, the UAW charged, worked for the Arthur Cudner firm, which handled Buick's public relations, and GM public-relations men were Boysen's constant companions. The UAW scored a minor victory when it forced the withdrawal of the treasurer of the Alliance by revealing that he had been convicted of embezzlement when he had previously served as the treasurer of the city of Flint.[26]

According to Bob Travis, one of the UAW's undercover men in the Alliance discovered that Harlow Curtice, then president of the Buick Division, was GM's "man" behind the Alliance,[27] but the UAW was unable to offer convincing proof of a GM link to the organization. A state police investigator did, however, report two days after the Alliance was launched that it was "a product of General Motors brains,"[28] and the organization was such an obvious concomitant of GM's loyalty campaign and was such a convenient anti-strike weapon that it does not strain one's credulity to believe that there may have been some connection between the Alliance and the company. The year after the strike, it is probably relevant to note, Boysen once again became a GM executive, and he worked for the company until his retirement in 1953.[29]

On the other hand, given the nature of the Flint community and its close ties with GM, the corporation could confidently have expected its friends to launch an organization like the Alliance without itself taking the initiative.[30] It may be that Michael Gorman, the editor of the pro-GM Flint *Journal*, was involved in the birth of the Alliance. Cyril Player, who was a Flint *Journal* reporter at the time of the strike, recalled the next year that he had asked Gorman, probably on January 5, why, if the vast majority of Flint GM workers opposed the strike, as Gorman alleged, they were not " 'vocal' " about their discontent and had no spokesman. Gorman told him the next day with regard to this conversation, " 'I think something is going to be done. I may have news for you tonight.' " The following day the *Journal* announced the formation of the Alliance in an extra edition under the headline, "Flint Workers Start Revolt against Strike." Two weeks later a state police agent investigating the Alliance reported that Gorman was "connected" with the organization.[31]

The UAW's charges of coercion in the enrollment of Alliance members, like its allegations concerning the gathering of loyalty pledges, were not without basis in fact. A state police investigator reported that union men were obliged to sign membership cards under the eyes of foremen and that when the employees were paid at Buick on January 8 they first received Alliance cards to sign. Myers found that membership cards had been distributed by company employees on company property during working hours and that the distributors had been compensated for the time involved. "Spontaneous sentiment solicited under the eyes of the boss," one worker wrote the President, "is quite obviously a synthetic brand of spontaneity." Another worker complained to Senator La Follette that the names of non-signers were sent to Sloan as a prelude to their dismissal, and so one had to sign "or Else." "I think this is legalized Blackmail," he wrote, and "it is time that High Jacking of Personal libertys [sic] be stopped."[32]

Despite union charges of coercion, the widely publicized allegations that large numbers of GM workers had signed loyalty pledges or Flint Alliance membership cards constituted, at the very least, "a huge paper success" for GM, as Kraus has observed,[33] and helped to strengthen the impression that the company wished to convey, namely, that an overwhelming majority of contented GM workers were being kept from their jobs by a small band of strikers. The minority character of the strike was the principal theme stressed by GM in its effort to win public opinion to its side, a matter of no small concern to a company that sold its product directly to the consumer. In Flint, the *I.M.A. News*, which became a GM mouthpiece during the strike, thus charged repeatedly that 5 percent of the city's GM workers were forcibly keeping the remaining 95 percent from their jobs. GM also insisted that it was "outside agitators" who dominated and exploited even this "small handful of workers," who alone stood to benefit from Flint's suffering, and who sought to array class against class in a thoroughly un-American fashion. The *I.M.A. News* asserted that a still more sinister force was manipulating the strikers: Russian Communism. The seizure and occupation of private property, it pointed out, was, after all, the same Communist tactic as had been employed in Italy and Russia. Lewis and Martin were dupes of the Communists and were being used by them to spread Communist influence in the United States. "The strikers think that they are acting for their own best interests; in reality they are acting for the best interests of a vast conspiracy to destroy all for which life is worth living."[34]

To demonstrate that the issue in the strike was union power rather than working conditions, GM stressed the high hourly and annual wages that it paid its workers as compared to workers in other industries and pictured its employees as members of "One Happy Family."[35] As further evidence of its solicitude for its workers and as a reminder of the benefits associated with GM employment, the corporation announced on January 26 that since so many of its employees were then without work through no fault of their own, it would distribute one month in advance the proceeds under its Employes Savings and Investment Plan for the class of 1931. Of the $10.7 million to be disbursed to 12,229 employees, 4250 of them in Flint, GM declared that it had contributed $6.5 million. The next day the corporation announced that it would pay the necessary monthly charges to maintain group-insurance coverage for all of its idled employees and that they could reimburse the company when they returned to work.[36]

GM also sought to show its concern for its employees by announcing on January 23 that it would provide at least a day or two of work per week for as many as possible of its workers who up to that time had been idled by shortages caused by the strike but who were not themselves on strike. The primary purpose of this act, GM insisted, was the well-being of its workers since there was no immediate need for the parts that they would produce. GM reinforced its re-employment drive with a nation-wide broadcast in which it was argued that the right to work had from the beginning of the nation's history been "the acknowledged right of each one of us to decide for himself, with no man's interference." Homer Martin bitterly complained that GM had first closed many of its factories prematurely in order to turn public opinion against the UAW and that it was now reopening them as "a further development of that scheme of exploitation."[37]

In resisting the sit-down strike, GM saw itself as fighting for interests beyond its own. If it surrendered on the issue of the occupation of its plants, the company alleged, it would set a precedent dangerous to the security of every automobile manufacturer, every businessman, and even every homeowner since the CIO was "striking at the very heart of the right of the possession of private property." If GM, however, thought that the automobile industry as a whole would support its defense of property rights by a common shutdown, it was disappointed in its expectations. Walter Chrysler was "in close consultation with General Motors people" throughout the strike, but there is no evidence that this influenced Chrysler Corporation policy in any way. *Steel* reported that a plan for an industry-wide shutdown beginning on January 15 had been presented at a "secret meeting" of automobile manufacturers in Detroit but had been rejected because Ford contended that it would put the industry "in a bad light" and might even induce a panic.[38] It was unnecessary for Ford to point out, assuming the accuracy of the *Steel* report, that what was good for GM in this instance was not, at least in the short run, necessarily good for its competitors, which were now presented with the opportunity to fill automobile orders that would otherwise have been filled by the industry's leading producer.

GM, on the whole, did not handle its public relations with the finesse and skill that one might have expected of the nation's largest manufacturing corporation. Its public-relations department was relatively small and inexperienced; it did not keep its press representatives sufficiently well informed of strike developments; it was slow in getting strike news cleared and made available to the public; it was not prepared "statistically and factually" to combat union arguments; and it was less skillful than the union in cultivating the hordes of newsmen who flocked to Flint to report on one of the great dramatic events of the era. The fledgling UAW, capitalizing on a fleeting moment in American history when a large segment of the American public sympathized with the workingman's efforts to attain recognition and a higher status, bested GM in capturing the headlines and getting its message across. "The union," one source declared, "made news happen and was articulate, whereas the Corporation was suspicious, slow and inarticulate."[39]

GM's most vital immediate concern upon the outbreak of the strike was less to influence public opinion in its favor, important as that objective was, than to secure the evacuation of its property. There were several conceivable methods that the corporation might have employed to attain that objective. It might have resorted to "self-help," that is the use of "reasonable force" (tear gas, shutting off utility service) to dislodge the strikers, since a property owner could employ such force as was necessary short of inflicting " 'death or serious bodily harm' " to expel a trespasser; but it could not be sure that this method would achieve its objective nor that violence could be avoided that would be damaging to the corporation's image. It might also have called on the Flint police for assistance, but, as already noted, there was some uncertainty as to whether trespass was a criminal offense in Michigan and, consequently, whether sit-down strikers were subject to eviction by other than civil process. GM might also have resorted to civil suits against the union to recover the monetary damage caused by the trespass, but this tactic did not promise an early evacuation of the company's property, nor did the size of the UAW treasury indicate that such a procedure would be particularly effective in the long run.[40]

Rejecting alternative approaches to the subject, GM decided that the mandatory injunction was the remedy most suitable for the sit-down offense. On January 2 the company petitioned the Genesee County Circuit Court for a "temporary restraining injunction" to prevent the union defendants from interfering with entry into or exit from the two Flint Fisher Body plants, interfering with the delivery of merchandise to and from the plants, picketing the factories or loitering near their approaches, "continuing to remain in said plants in idleness in a so-called 'sit-down' strike and ... remaining in said plants at any time outside of their regular specified working hours," damaging or trespassing upon the plaintiff's property, intimidating employees who wished to work, using physical force upon them, or addressing "insulting or abusive language" to them, protecting or aiding anyone in committing the specified acts, and unlawfully conspiring or combining with anyone for these purposes. GM stated in its petition for the injunction that the defendants were damaging its property, that unsanitary conditions in the plant were likely to endanger the public health, and that the plaintiff was suffering "irreparable injury and loss" for which it had no adequate remedy at law.[41]

The injunction was promptly granted on January 2 by the eighty-three year old Judge Edward D. Black, a life-long Flint resident who had served on the bench for twenty years. Evan J. Parker stated that the company was seeking the injunction solely to recover its property and that its action was not to be construed as an attempt to resume operations, but had the full terms of the injunction been enforced—"The only thing" the writ permitted the union to do, Travis said, "was to take a deep breath"—the UAW would have found it difficult to continue the strike.[42] GM was undoubtedly on sound legal ground in seeking an injunction to undo what it regarded as a trespass upon its property, a fact which such friends of organized labor as the American Civil Liberties Union recognized,[43] but, in asking the court to restrain all picketing and to limit other striker activities, the corporation unwisely raised a civil-liberties question when it was unnecessary for its purposes to do so.

Sheriff Thomas Wolcott read the injunction at the No. 1 and No. 2 plants on the evening of January 2, giving the sit-downers thirty minutes to leave the two factories; and in the next few days he served the injunction on the national and local officers of the UAW to whom it also applied. The sheriff deputized one hundred city policemen and sixty company guards to aid him in enforcing the writ; but since no writ of attachment had been issued requiring the apprehension of the offenders, Wolcott, who later claimed that he had been under some pressure to enforce the injunction, presumably from persons in high places, made no move against the sit-downers.[44]

Homer Martin criticized the injunction as "part of the general procedure of corporations which don't want to bargain collectively." He stated, however, that the UAW would not "fight the law," although he reserved a final decision on the matter until he could consult with union counsel. On the evening of January 3 John Brophy, Adolph Germer, Martin, Ed Hall, George Addes, Larry Davidow, the UAW's chief lawyer, and Lee Pressman, the chief counsel for the CIO, gathered in Davidow's Detroit home to discuss the Black injunction. Germer suggested that Black might be the owner of GM stock, and so Pressman called his law partner in New York to ask him to check out the matter.[45]

On January 5 the UAW called a press conference and "exploded" the news that Black held 3665 shares of GM stock worth $219,900 at the market price. Black, Martin charged, had been guilty of "unethical conduct" and had dealt a "cruel blow" to the integrity of the judicial system. Since Michigan law, moreover, forbade a judge to "sit as such in any cause or proceeding in which he is a party, or in which he is interested," the UAW contended that Black had violated his oath of office and the law and demanded both his impeachment and his disbarment.[46]

"It sounds like Communist talk to me," Judge Black remonstrated, and the Genesee County Bar Association rushed to the venerable judge's defense. The president of the association declared that Black was "one of the ablest jurists" in Michigan and that Flint's lawyers resented the attack upon him by the UAW president, who was not even a resident of the state. When the Committee on Professional Ethics and Grievances of the House of Delegates of the American Bar Association quietly undertook a probe of the affair, Black informed the secretary of the committee that he had held GM stock for twenty-five years but that he also held stock in two Flint banks and paid taxes in Flint and no one had questioned the propriety of his sitting in cases involving the banks or the city. One of the GM attorneys who had prepared the company's injunction petition insisted that the statute cited by the UAW applied only when judges presided over trials and not when they issued preliminary orders, as in the instant case. For the American Bar Association to conduct a hearing because of such charges, he wrote, would be "to directly lend aid and encouragement to a group of men who are avowed communists and enemies of the American form of government."[47]

GM, it is clear, had been unaware of Black's large stock-holdings in the company. Its attorneys, as a matter of fact, had sought the injunction in Black's court only because the presiding judge of the Circuit Court could not be found at the time the application for the writ was made. Understandably embarrassed by the whole affair, GM quickly had further proceedings in the case transferred to the court of Judge Paul V. Gadola; but, for the time being, it made no effort to press for action. There is no gainsaying Kraus's conclusion that the UAW had scored a "brilliant victory." The revelations concerning Black, as Lee Pressman later remarked, "lent color to the accusation that General Motors controlled the community, that people [in Flint] were peons and slaves of General Motors."[48]

In addition to seeking an injunction to secure the evacuation of its Flint plants, GM took measures to strengthen its offensive power and to keep itself informed on the plans of its union opponent. The corporation augmented its force of plant police in Flint and elsewhere and laid in a supply of tear and sickening gas. GM, until the end of January, also continued to avail itself of the labor espionage services provided by such detective agencies as Pinkerton. Although the testimony of Pinkerton officials on the point was utterly confusing, it appears that there were at least two Pinkerton agents among the sit-downers in the Fisher Body No. 1 and No. 2 plants. Travis and Simons charged that espionage agents inside the plants supplied anti-union reporters with information that reflected adversely on the sit-downers and that they also were a source of rumors inside the plant that were damaging to morale, but there is little hard evidence concerning the disruptive role of labor spies inside the plants during the sit-down.[49]

In addition to the Pinkerton operatives inside the plants, the detective agency continued to employ labor spies on the outside in Flint and other towns. Dubuc remained on the company's payroll until the end of January, receiving his last payment from Pinkerton just after February 1. The night that the sit-down began in Flint two Pinkerton officials took Dubuc to Fenton, a small town near Flint, and sought to ascertain the UAW's intentions regarding Chevrolet and particularly the key Chevrolet No. 4 plant. Pinkerton similarly sought to learn from one of its Lansing agents who was serving as a vice-president of the Lansing Fisher Body local and who, like Dubuc, was also cooperating with the UAW whether the union intended to strike the Fisher Body plant in that city.[50]

A La Follette Committee investigator reported from Flint at the end of January that he had learned that a Flint police lieutenant had placed spies among the sit-downers and that he might be giving fuller reports to GM than to Chief Wills. The same investigator also wrote the committee's secretary that he was becoming "firmer" in the opinion that there was "a definite company espionage system" in the city and that GM was planning to replace detective-agency spies with its "own set-up," a development that was later confirmed in a general way by Harry W. Anderson.[51] Whether served by Pinkerton or its own agents, however, GM seems to have learned relatively little of union strategy as devised by the strike organization in Flint; and, in the end, the strike leaders in the city took advantage of the probable presence of labor spies in their midst to help mask the most daring union maneuver in the entire strike.[52]

Following the Battle of the Running Bulls, Knudsen, describing himself as "a peaceful party," stated for GM, "We are not going to encourage violence because we do not believe that labor disputes can be helped by violence."[53] Whatever its role may have been in the Fisher No. 2 riot of January 11, GM did not attempt to use its own guards to eject the strikers occupying its plants, nor does it appear to have requested state or local authorities, at least after the Battle of the Running Bulls, to employ such forces as were available to them to secure this objective. GM supervisory personnel, however, on a few occasions both before and after January 11, were involved in acts of violence against strikers, although they presumably acted on their own initiative rather than on instructions from the corporation. They may have been seeking by a show of force to forestall the spread of the strike to their own plants or, if their plants were already on strike, were perhaps giving vent to their frustration at having failed in their assigned role as intermediaries between the company and the men to maintain harmonious employer-employee relations. The most conspicuous involvement of GM supervisory personnel in acts of violence against UAW unionists occurred in Anderson, Indiana, as will be described later,[54] but in Michigan also, in Flint on January 7 and in the Saginaw area three weeks later, GM foremen were implicated in the use of force against UAW members.

The first "open hostilities" in the Flint strike occurred on January 7. The UAW had set up a loudspeaker system across the street from the Chevrolet No. 9 plant on the outside of a tavern that it was using as a branch office, and as a shift of workers emerged from the plant in the afternoon Roy Reuther spoke to them over the loudspeaker. A group from Chevrolet that included foremen and supervisors thereupon rushed the crowd being addressed by Reuther, smashed the sound equipment, and engaged in fisticuffs with some of the listeners. One unionist who worked in Chevrolet No. 9, Ted LaDuke, received a one and one-half inch gash on his scalp. A state police trooper reporting on the violence declared that he had reliable information from neutral sources that what had occurred was premeditated," and he stated that foremen and straw bosses at all the plants still working were prepared to "deal with" union assemblages outside their factories in the belief that their jobs depended on halting the spread of the strike.[55]

In Saginaw, Michigan, the home of several GM plants, intense hostility had developed by the second week of the strike against the "outside" organizers who were seeking to enroll workers in the area in the UAW. At a public meeting on January 13 of a newly organized Loyalty Committee, the chairman announced, " 'These organizers will find that Saginaw is a hot town; in fact, we will make it so hot they won't be able to stay.... We might send them home in a pine box with a bunch of Saginaw Forget-me-nots on top.' " In the days that followed UAW organizers and workers learned that Saginaw was indeed "a hot town" for them, and this persuaded the strike leaders to call on the assistance of the United Mine Workers (UMW), which was well-established in the city. The local UMW agreed to sponsor a meeting for the auto workers, to be held on January 31, and it was able to arrange for the use of the municipal auditorium for this purpose, something that the UAW could not have done on its own.[56]

On January 27 Joseph B. Ditzel, the secretary of the Toledo Chevrolet local, and three United Mine Workers organizers, Anthony Federoff, John Mayo, and William J. Hynes, arrived in Saginaw to mobilize support for the January 31 meeting. The four men contacted Francis O'Rourke, a UAW organizer in the city, and the group then went to nearby Bay City to purchase radio time for spot announcements of the meeting. They conferred in the lobby of the Hotel Wenonah with John Mundy, a UMW board member and a long-time Bay City resident, and then Ditzel, Hynes, and O'Rourke left to put an ad in the local paper. After their departure a "gang" of about twenty men whom the three unionists had noticed as they left the hotel went into the lobby, instructed Mundy to leave, and then drove Federoff and Mayo to the Saginaw police station and advised them to leave town.

When Hynes, Ditzel, and O'Rourke returned to the hotel, they were set upon by the vigilantes, who were armed with blackjacks, and were chased around the lobby. Ditzel recognized a former Toledo Chevrolet foreman among the group, one of several Toledo foremen who had been transferred to Saginaw when part of the machinery for making transmission gears had been moved to that city following the

Toledo Chevrolet strike of 1935. The police arrived after about thirty minutes and escorted the three organizers to the Saginaw police station.

When Powers Hapgood, in Flint, heard about the events in Bay City and Saginaw, he called the Saginaw police station and advised the unionists to remain there until he could arrive with a posse of rescuers. The organizers, however, decided not to follow this counsel when the police promised them a safe escort to the Genesee County line, where they would be met by state police troopers. The men were first taken to the Hotel Bancroft, where the out-of-towners were registered, but they were attacked in the lobby by a "big gang" (the estimates of the number involved range from thirty-five to three hundred!) that included at least six former Toledo foremen, and O'Rourke was "beaten severely." Mayo was knocked through an open doorway that led into a drugstore and was able to escape. The other four were put in a cab and were driven toward Flint over icy roads at a speed of sixty-five to seventy miles per hour, with one police car ahead of the cab and one behind it and perhaps thirty-five to forty cars filled with vigilantes trailing the procession.

When the motorcade reached the county line, there was no sign of the troopers who were supposed to have been there to escort the cab to Flint; but as the cab and its police escort proceeded into Genesee County they encountered a large grey sedan, parked alongside the road. The sedan sideswiped the cab and caused it to skid off the road into a telephone pole. Federoff had "most of his scalp taken off," O'Rourke sustained a broken hip and a piece of bone penetrated his bladder, and Hynes was badly cut. The cab, La Follette Committee investigator H. D. Cullen wired the committee's secretary from Flint, had been "crashed ... deliberately according to police records," a judgment agreed in by the cab driver and the organizers.[57]

In describing the events of January 27, the Flint *Auto Worker* charged that GM was now "unleashing a wave of terrorism" against the UAW.[58] The occupants of the grey sedan were never identified, but GM foremen were involved in the antecedent vigilantism in Bay City and Saginaw. The UAW surely magnified GM's role in such violence as occurred in the strike, but some GM subordinates, on occasion at least, did appear anxious to settle the dispute by force rather than by negotiation. Their behavior not only embittered GM-UAW relations but, coupled with the embarrassing Black affair, revelations of espionage, and allegations of coercion that GM could not completely refute, handicapped the corporation in presenting its case to the public. GM, *Fortune* later observed, "was in no spiritual shape to fight an honest holy war."[59]

Strategy and Tactics: The UAW
VIII

I

On January 3 two hundred delegates from fifty GM locals in sixteen cities, the UAW international officers, and several CIO representatives gathered in Flint to draft a collective-bargaining agreement that would be submitted to GM and to establish the necessary organizational machinery to conduct the strike. The collective-bargaining terms agreed upon took the form of the aforementioned eight demands that Martin forwarded to GM on January 4. The responsibility of planning for the strike and the power to call additional strikes at GM plants were placed in the hands of a board of strategy consisting of the general officers of the UAW, national representatives of the CIO, and the president of the Flat Glass Workers Union. The delegates also created a variety of other committees, none of which seems to have played a particularly conspicuous role in the strike.[1]

Flint, after December 30, was the center of the strike, and here the local leadership, and particularly Bob Travis and Roy Reuther, made the day-to-day decisions regarding the conduct of the strike. They consulted with UAW and CIO representatives, who drifted into and out of Flint, but, as Reuther later said, the decisions were "pretty much ours."[2] The headquarters of strike activity in Flint and, to a degree, the social center during the sit-down for the unionists and their families was the rickety, decaying Pengelly Building, smelling of mold and age and altogether unsafe in the event of fire. It was "a regular beehive of activity," "a teeming place," and, as one observer noted, "All of striking Flint was there: the strikers, their wives, fathers, daughters." The strikers outside the plants met daily in the Pengelly, and the numerous strike committees operated out of its rooms. Strikers and their friends dropped in to do some typing, help put out bulletins, attend meetings, arrange for relief, or just for the sake of companionship.[3]

A network of committees was created in Flint to support the strike in all its aspects: defense (protection), sound cars, picketing, transportation, welfare, kitchen (food), publicity, organization, entertainment, information, education, distribution, car repairs and gas, finances, hall sanitation, speakers bureau, women's auxiliary, and war veterans. In addition, organizers and staff members were assigned specific responsibilities for each of GM's plants. As in the inside so on the outside, life for the strike activists became a round of meetings: committee heads met together every morning, the strategy committee met twice daily, and organizers met every night and were to report hourly to the main office.[4]

To check on disloyalty in its own ranks and also to engage in undercover work in the camp of the enemy, the Flint UAW created an "investigation department," "a slick idea" in the view of a La Follette Committee investigator. The strike organization infiltrated the Flint Alliance, placing one of its agents in the Alliance leadership group and receiving daily reports of its activities; it tapped the telephone lines of the National Guard in Flint; and, until the "leak" was discovered, it kept itself informed of opposition activities centering in the Durant Hotel, the city's best, from information supplied by the chief switchboard operator at the hotel, who was the wife of one of the trolley strikers.[5]

The women participated in the strike through two organizations, the Women's Auxiliary and the much publicized Women's Emergency Brigade. Following a street dance in front of Fisher Body No. 2 on New Year's eve, about fifty women met in the Pengelly Building and decided to form a Women's Auxiliary to support their men inside and outside the plants. The Auxiliary set up its own speakers bureau and publicity department, engaged in picketing on a regular basis, staffed a first-aid department in the Pengelly Building, maintained a nursery where wives could leave their youngsters while they themselves engaged in strike duty, collected food and money for the strike, and contacted sit-down "widows" who complained about the absence of their husbands to explain the strike and to enlist their support.[6] In the second verse of their theme song, sung to the tune of "Marching through Georgia," the women referred proudly to their role in the strike:

> The women got together and they formed a
> mighty throng,
> Every worker's wife and mom and sister will
> belong,
> They will fight beside the men to help the cause
> along,
> Shouting the Union forever![7]

The initiative in forming the Women's Emergency Brigade as a unit of the Auxiliary was taken by the twenty-three year old Genora Johnson, a tall, curly-haired, and brown-eyed mother of two and the wife of the Chevrolet No. 4 strike leader, Kermit Johnson. Her participation in the Battle of the Running Bulls convinced her of the need for the "courageous women" to band together to fight beside their men should similar crises develop. Fifty volunteers answered her call to join the emergency unit, and their number eventually swelled to 350. The Brigade, and how characteristic this was of the strike organizations both inside and outside the plants, was structured along semi-military lines, with Genora serving as commander-in-chief and captains in charge of the various squads. The insignia of the Brigade was a red arm band with white lettering and a red tam. The Brigade was ready for action by January 20, and Genora defiantly declared, "We will form a line around the men, and if the police want to fire then they'll just have to fire into us." The Brigade members, who were to prove that they had the courage of their convictions when the Flint strikers on February 1 seized the Chevrolet No. 4 plant, were not "flaming Joan of Arcs of the labor movement," to use Mary Heaton Vorse's phrasing. "It is just a case," she observed, "of 'Ma' and the girls protecting their husbands and sons."[8]

The Auxiliary and the Emergency Brigade—similar organizations were formed in Detroit, Cleveland, Toledo, and elsewhere—had a "rallying effect" upon the men in the plants. When the women appeared before the occupied plants, the men rushed to the windows and roofs to give them a cheer. But the participation of the women in the strike was probably more important for them than for the men. "I found a common understanding and unselfishness I'd never known in my life," the wife of a Cadillac striker wrote. "I'm living for the first time with a definite goal. . . . Just being a woman isn't enough anymore. I want to be a human being with the right to think for myself."

The union, almost certainly for the first time, became an important element in the lives of many of the female activists. "The union is entering into every aspect of life," declared one strike observer, "the home and the union are being fused." Seeing the relationship between union success and the improvement of the material conditions under which they and their families lived, some of the women concluded that they must henceforth involve themselves actively in union affairs. "A new type of woman was born in the strike," one of the "new women" exulted some weeks after the strike had ended. "Women who only yesterday were horrified at unionism, who felt inferior to the task of organizing, speaking, leading, have, as if overnight, become the spearhead in the battle of unionism."[9]

Another ancillary organization of the Flint strikers was the Union War Veterans of Flint, Post No. 1, made up of union veterans in Local 156. The idea for the group seems to have originated with Henry Kraus and was inspired by the formation of a similar organization during the Goodyear strike. Since some members of the American Legion were openly hostile to the sit-down and were even rumored to be preparing to march on the plants, the organization of a post of union veterans was at least in part designed to remind the uncommitted that patriotism was not the monopoly of strike opponents. New members of the post swore that they would help to protect the rights of organized labor, be loyal to the UAW, protect the women and children of the community, and "not become a stool pigeon of the Capitalists and give them any information of our order." The organization, which began to function about the middle of January, provided bodyguards for strike leaders, helped to defend the union sound cars, and sent delegations to the governor in the interests of the union cause.[10]

Building up Local 156's small membership was an important concern of the Flint strike leadership, and this became the responsibility of a special organization committee. The committee dispatched its volunteer workers to the city's wards and precincts to canvass on a house-to-house basis, and the initial reports were that the campaign was "going good."[11]

It was the job of the kitchen or food committee to secure the supplies needed to feed the men sitting down in the Flint plants. Some of the food was purchased, some donated by strike sympathizers, and some "donated" by merchants who were bluntly reminded by union solicitors that they made their living selling to GM workers or who were simply coerced into contributing. The minutes of the Cleveland Fisher Body strike committee of January 25 reported Travis as having said, "Merchants will be run out of Business if they don't donate." Norman Bully, on the other hand, remembers going out into the farm areas surrounding Flint and receiving truckloads of potatoes and beef carcasses from sympathetic farmers.[12]

The welfare committee of the Flint UAW was charged with the important task of looking after the relief needs not only of strikers and their families but also of other Flint UAW members made jobless by the spreading effects of the dispute. Had the strike been conducted in an era when public relief assistance was less readily available or in a state whose governor was less committed to the principle of feeding the hungry regardless of the cause of their distress, the UAW might have been hard put to secure the funds required to sustain the strike, but in the year 1937 and in a state where Frank Murphy was governor public authorities could be expected to shoulder a large part of the burden of strike relief.

If the decision whether to extend relief to strikers had been left entirely to the Genesee County Emergency Relief Commission, it is likely that public assistance would not have been provided for Flint's strikers. The commission was scheduled to resolve this question at a

January 12 meeting, but well in advance of that date a spokesman for the group talked in terms of disaster if the existing welfare burden were increased since the commission was already running a $43,000 deficit and the city of Flint was without funds to advance for welfare purposes. The compassionate and pro-labor Governor Murphy, however, who as mayor of Detroit had made city welfare funds available to Briggs strikers and who had promised in the 1936 gubernatorial campaign that as governor he would not deny relief to strikers, stated on January 10 that he had advised the State Emergency Relief Administrator, William Haber, that relief was to be provided strictly on the basis of need. "I won't permit the women, children, sick and the old folk to go hungry because of this situation."[13]

Under the circumstances, the union welfare committee saw its major responsibility as assisting the needy Flint UAW members in obtaining public relief, but until a union applicant was placed on the welfare rolls and began to receive public assistance, the UAW stood ready to grant him temporary relief provided that he was engaged in strike duty. UAW relief took the form of a small amount of cash, groceries, and one-quarter ton of coal; by January 25 the union was dispensing an average of $300 a day in this fashion.[14]

Since the Flint UAW had for some time regarded the county relief administrator, Victor S. Woodward, as anti-union[15] and since it complained, as the relief load increased, that the welfare intake staff in Flint was inadequate in numbers and was processing requests too slowly, the governor sent Haber to the city to survey the welfare situation. After a "very satisfactory meeting" on January 16 with the UAW's welfare committee, Woodward, and the county relief commission, Haber advised the governor that matters were "well in hand," that the intake staff was being increased,[16] that complaints were being "amicably adjusted," and that there was, consequently, "no cause for concern." Three days later the State Emergency Welfare Relief Commission specifically ruled that "relief shall be granted to workers striking in industry on the basis of individual need."[17]

There continued to be "much grumbling" in the UAW, however, about welfare and particularly about the slowness with which applicants for relief were processed. Ella Lee Cogwill, the field representative of the State Emergency Welfare Relief Commission, quite properly rejected a UAW request that strikers' families be given a preferential position in relief lines, but despite this a "fine rapport" developed between the Flint UAW welfare committee and the relief organization, and certainly the Flint strikers had no reason to complain as the Cleveland strikers did that "someone is using the relief agency [Cuyahoga County Relief Administration] to break the strike."[18]

During December, 1936, 8448 persons in Genesee County received relief under all public programs, but this figure mounted to 28,025 in January and 42,459 in February. Nearly all these persons were Flint residents, which meant that by the close of the strike about one-quarter of the city's population were receiving relief, an all-time record for Flint to that date. The case load, as distinguished from the number of persons receiving relief, stood at 2360 in December, 1936, and rose to 7161 in January (as compared to 2776 in January, 1936) and 11,168 in February (as compared to 2894 in February, 1936). Of the 8376 persons, mostly heads of families, who applied for relief between January 1 and February 8, 1937, 6032 were GM workers. Haber estimated in March that the strike had increased relief costs in Flint by about $400,000, the main burden of which had been carried by the state.[19] Miss Cogwill reported that the attitude of the Flint community was cooperative in the matter of relief, but she did note that one out-of-town welfare worker who unwittingly made some house calls while wearing a red tam, the head covering of the Emergency Brigade, had doors slammed in her face.[20]

Henry Kraus, who was in a position to know, has stated that the "immediate cost" to the union of the strike in Flint was "considerably under" $50,000, which does not seem unreasonable, although the records are unavailable to corroborate this estimate. Between January 1 and February 9, 1937, two days before the strike was settled, the UAW received $29,106.53 in contributions for its strike fund. Of this sum, locals of the United Rubber Workers, more than reciprocating the UAW support in the Goodyear strike, contributed more than $6300, and most of the remainder came from UAW locals, notably the Studebaker local, which contributed $6000. The Amalgamated Clothing Workers (ACW) voted on February 5 to contribute $25,000 to the UAW, but Martin, fearing that UAW funds might be attached at any moment, asked Sidney Hillman to forward "only a small sum" initially. The ACW dispatched $5000 to the UAW on February 10, but the money was probably not received by the UAW until the strike was over. That same day, Martin, declaring that "the hour of need is upon us," wired Hillman for as much of the $25,000 as the ACW could spare. It was reported at the close of the strike that the International Ladies' Garment Workers' Union had donated $50,000 to the UAW, but, like the ACW contribution, this sum was probably not received before the conclusion of the strike.[21]

The UAW and the strike organization on the outside in Flint were as conscious of the value of publicity as the strike leaders inside the plants were. At the outset of the sit-down the only news organ of the strikers was the Flint *Auto Worker*, but Kraus's efforts were soon to be supplemented in a variety of ways. Early in January Len DeCaux, the editor of the CIO's *Union News Service*, arrived in Michigan to handle strike publicity for the CIO. At the end of the month Carl Haessler, the managing editor of the Federated Press, a labor news service, came to Flint to take charge of press relations for the UAW. He was soon issuing Local 156 releases to supplement the releases issued by the UAW's publicity director in Detroit, Frank Winn, another Brookwood Labor College product serving the UAW. Haessler tried to influence the large number of reporters covering the strike in Flint by dispensing news favors to pro-labor reporters and also to newsmen he considered "honest" but not pro-union, like Russell B. Porter of the New York *Times*.[22]

About January 20 the *Punch Press*, a mimeographed strike bulletin addressed particularly to the men inside the plants, made its appearance in Flint. The bulletin, which appeared irregularly thereafter until the end of the strike, was edited by a small group of University of Michigan students, the union's " 'Baby Brain-trust,' " who had been caught up in the fervor that surrounded the strike and the CIO's effort to unionize the mass-production industries. The editor of the *Punch Press*, Ralph Segalman, and his student associates in the venture were concerned about Fascism abroad and injustice at home and, like many college students of the yeasty New Deal years, felt an obligation to become personally involved in the effort to fashion a better social order. They had helped Ann Arbor pinboys in a strike to raise their pitifully low wages, and when the GM strike began they went to Flint to observe the sit-down and possibly to lend a hand. They were persuaded by strike officials of the need for a strike bulletin, and the homely and rather crudely constructed but nevertheless effective *Punch Press*, which they put together whenever they could get away from Ann Arbor, was the result.[23]

The UAW made relatively little use of radio in seeking to publicize its cause, although it did arrange for a series of broadcasts on a Windsor, Canada, station. Martin, who had confidently advised the CIO in July that the UAW, "by the use of radio alone, could whip any auto co.," delivered the first of these addresses on January 19, but Mortimer was prevented from going on the air the next night because his speech, a rather routine presentation of the UAW case, was deemed "too controversial" by the station management, and this episode apparently brought the scheduled series to a premature end.[24]

The Flint UAW, in an effort to influence middle-class opinion in the city, seems to have played a behind-the-scenes role in instituting a free-speech forum to consider strike issues. The first meeting of the forum, on January 29, was ostensibly arranged by two Ann Arbor strike sympathizers and was attended, according to the Flint *Auto Worker*, by some two hundred business and professional men. The principal speaker was Bob Travis, and most of the evening was taken up with a question-and-answer session that followed his talk. A Citizens Committee elected at the meeting to conduct the forum included Eugene Faye, the UAW's Flint education director, and a Flint public-school teacher sympathetic to the union cause.[25] The UAW also sought to capitalize on the visits to Flint by such well-known personages as Mrs. Gifford Pinchot and Ellen Wilkinson, a Labor party member of Parliament, both of whom spoke in support of the strike and lambasted GM.[26]

The UAW attempted in its strike publicity both to parry the verbal thrusts of GM and to counterthrust by setting forth the reasons why the union had felt itself compelled to go on strike. It responded to GM's statements that it was paying the highest wages possible by claiming that company profits per employee had increased from $1.42 in 1932 to $1080 in 1936, about a 760-fold increase, whereas average annual wages in the same period had increased only 15 percent. The high hourly wages at GM, the UAW insisted, were offset by the irregular employment of the company's workers, but the union tended to rely on out-of-date 1934 figures in making this point. The UAW also liked to contrast the high, $100,000 plus salaries paid some GM officials with the wages received by the company's blue-collar workers. In the happy GM family, Martin said, "father eats the bacon and mother the gravy, and the kids lick the skillet."[27]

To GM's charges of labor dictatorship, the UAW responded that the CIO unions were democratic and that it was the du Pont-Morgan-GM combine that was dictatorial. Where GM complained that outside union agitators were invading its plant cities, the UAW called attention to GM executives and stockholders in far-off places who made decisions affecting the destiny of GM workers in their local communities and who dominated local authorities and institutions. Sloan and Knudsen asserted that the sit-downers were law breakers, but the UAW replied that they were simply exercising "their right as human beings to remain with their jobs" and that it was GM that had "trampled the law of the land under its feet." GM pointed to the loyalty pledges of its employees to demonstrate the opposition of the majority to the strike, and so the UAW began flooding Governor Murphy with postcards from its supporters that they favored a return to work "only under Union conditions, and under the protection of the United Automobile Workers as our bargaining agency."[28]

The UAW in its publicity sought to depict GM as the blackguard among the automobile companies by pointing to the favorable relations that the automobile workers allegedly enjoyed with the other motor-vehicle firms. Martin declared that the UAW had a "fine relationship" with Nash, Studebaker, Graham-Paige, and Willys, all of which, the union claimed, were 100 percent organized; and Chrysler, according to the UAW, was engaging in meaningful collective bargaining with its workers and treating the unionists in its plants fairly. Even Ford, the UAW observed, with some disregard for the truth insofar as Midland was concerned, had been helpful in settling the Midland and Kelsey-Hayes strikes in December, 1936, and the brief Briggs strike that occurred in January.[29]

The UAW sought to raise the morale of its troops and to create the impression of an army marching to victory by stressing in its publicity the gains in its membership in GM plants and throughout the automobile industry. Martin thus commented on January 16 on the "extraordinary influx" of new members and the long queues of workers at union headquarters waiting to join the UAW, and soon the union was claiming a majority of GM's workers as its members. The UAW was, indeed, making a major effort to increase its membership—by January 21 it had placed one hundred organizers in the field, triple the number of a month earlier—but it was obviously inflating the results for both tactical and public-relations purposes. Initiation fees collected outside of Flint suggest a probable membership increase during January of about fourteen thousand, most of this in Michigan, and per capita tax figures plus initiation fees indicate a probable membership by the end of the month of over seventy thousand for the industry as a whole, which means that the UAW could not possibly have enrolled a majority of the GM employees.[30]

The UAW did not expect to win the GM strike by the use of words but rather by the mobilization and deployment of such power as was available to it so as to put maximum pressure on the corporation. In conducting the strike in Flint, the strike organization in the city not only utilized the services of Flint auto unionists whose plants were not on strike but who "wanted to be a part of it,"[31] but it also was able to augment the strength of the local union forces by drawing on reserves from other cities. Outsiders moved into and out of Flint throughout the strike, but they came to the city especially at moments of great crisis, like after the Battle of the Running Bulls, or when the UAW wished to stage a mass demonstration as a show of force, as in the early days of February.

Auto workers from Detroit and Toledo in particular were frequent visitors in Flint during the strike. After their own plants were evacuated, Cadillac and Fleetwood workers, when needed, left for Flint in every available car; and workers on the night shift at Kelsey-

Hayes would go to Flint in the daytime, and daytime workers would then replace them on the strike front in the evening. The two Toledo locals dispatched members to Michigan whenever called upon to aid. Travis' Local 12 organized a squad of "Minute Men" to be on call for Flint duty, and after the strike Travis referred to "the hundreds upon hundreds" of Local 12 unionists who had seen strike action in Flint. The rubber workers in Akron, sensitive to their close ties to the auto workers, not only supported the strike with funds but also with manpower. "If them Flint Alliance men rush you," a Goodyear unionist wrote Martin, "don't be bashful in asking for rubber workers. We are with you to a man. . . . Don't back one inch, this is our fight same as yours."[32] Nothing approaching this demonstration of the solidarity of the auto unionists one with the other and of auto workers with rubber workers had ever been seen before in an automobile strike.

Just as motor vehicles brought outsiders to the Flint strike front to reinforce the local troops so the automobile, appropriately enough in this most important of all automobile strikes, became a weapon of war on the battlefield itself. The sound car, "that feared and hated symbol" of the strike for its opponents, had been used in previous automobile strikes, but never before had it played so conspicuous a part in a labor conflict. It was employed in Flint to communicate with workers inside the plants, providing them with news of the strike and even personal messages and thus helping to keep up their morale, and it served as "a mobile field unit" in directing the movement of the strikers and their allies when the occasion demanded. When it appeared at the scene of action, the sound car, like a command post in battle, was guarded by six passenger cars occupied by trusted unionists.[33]

The Flint strike organization also used the automobile to supplement the conventional picket line, a sensible tactic considering both the nature of the strike and the time of the year. Cars patrolled the plants around the clock to detect any surprise move against the strikers. Strike headquarters also had cars at its disposal so as to be able to move "flying squadrons" to one or another of the plants at a moment's notice.[34]

CIO and UAW strategy called for the placing of maximum pressure on GM both by arranging for the settlement of strikes that would otherwise have interfered with the production of GM's competitors and by the extension of the GM strike to additional company plants. The UAW thus brought the Bohn Aluminum strike to a close on January 20 partly to ensure the uninterrupted flow of pistons to the Ford Motor Company; and in a more important move John L.

Lewis intervened to arrange a settlement of the Pittsburgh Plate Glass strike on January 20 and the Libby-Owens-Ford strike on January 27[35] so as to forestall any possible curtailment of Chrysler production. Lewis reportedly arranged the glass settlements with Walter Chrysler, who could not resist "the temporary lure of rather unrestricted profits" at the expense of his GM competitor even though it meant playing the CIO's game. At the end of January the UAW triumphantly called attention to the fact that GM automobile production for the week ending January 30 had totaled 6100 units as compared to 25,350 units for Chrysler and 28,325 for Ford and that for the month as a whole GM had produced less than 60,000 units as compared to a predicted 224,000.[36]

The most important GM plant to which the UAW extended the strike after January 1, 1937, was Chevrolet No. 4, but before the dramatic seizure of that establishment had occurred, the strike had spread to the Toledo Chevrolet plant, the Janesville, St. Louis, and Oakland Fisher Body and Chevrolet plants, and to Cadillac and Fleetwood in Detroit. The Toledo strike began on January 4 when, on order from "higher authorities," about forty workers stopped production by a sit-down that idled about 860 employees.[37]

The day after the Toledo strike was initiated the GM strike spread to Janesville, Wisconsin, about twenty-six hundred of whose twenty-five thousand inhabitants worked for Fisher Body and Chevrolet. When the sit-down began in the Fisher Body unit—it was quickly extended to Chevrolet—the plant manager implored the local's president to "thrash it out in the office" but was told to "Go to H - - -." The plant manager reportedly exclaimed, "My God, My God, They Are All Union." After securing Detroit's approval, the sit-downers, on the first day of the strike, accepted an agreement worked out by the Janesville city manager, Henry Traxler, whereby they consented to the evacuation of the plant that night and GM promised not to resume operations for the duration. On January 14 a nonunion group of workers calling themselves the Alliance opened an office where the "loyal" employees could register their opposition to the strike. The union forced the closing of the office, but the Alliance nevertheless gathered the signatures of about eighteen hundred allegedly satisfied workers. In contrast to what transpired in Flint, both the city manager and the Janesville newspaper preserved an admirable neutrality throughout the strike.[38]

The GM sit-down moved into Detroit on the morning of January 8 when Walter Reuther, president of the West Side local, called a Cadillac sit-down that affected thirty-eight hundred workers. Four days later about ninety of the more than thirteen hundred workers at

Fleetwood, which made the bodies for Cadillac, sat down at their jobs and forced the plant's closing. Reuther, in whose West Side domain this plant was also located, announced that the strike had been called to protest GM's "brutality" at the Battle of the Running Bulls the preceding day. The two plants were evacuated on January 15, but they continued to be picketed. The only incident to mar the otherwise peaceful remainder of the GM strike in Detroit occurred at the Cadillac plant on January 26 when police tangled with pickets who were attempting to prevent company executives and clerical workers from entering the factory because the pickets believed the company was trying to smuggle strikebreakers into the plant in automobiles. The next morning a picket line of at least one thousand persons that included Dodge, Kelsey-Hayes, and other Detroit unionists shut off entry into the plant's administration building. The union removed the picket line from the building two days later but was prepared "to clamp down completely" should the company attempt to bring strikebreakers into the plant.[39]

On January 13, after the UAW had failed two days previously to stage a sit-down in the Pontiac Motor Company plant,[40] the St. Louis Fisher Body and Chevrolet plant was closed by a conventional strike that idled about thirty-seven hundred workers. Delmond Garst, the executive secretary of the small St. Louis local, reported that the response of the workers had been "wonderful" and that the Kansas City local and the CIO had given "fine support." "We feel jubilant about the whole matter," he wrote.[41] Two weeks later the Oakland, California, Fisher Body and Chevrolet plant, employing about two thousand workers, also became a strike victim, according to the UAW, but GM was to insist otherwise and was able to have the factory excluded from the list of struck plants to which the settlement that ended the strike applied.[42] The strike itself, coupled with the shortage of key parts as the result of the dispute, had, by the time of the Oakland shutdown, forced the closing of fifty GM plants and the idling of more than 125,000 GM workers. The Chevrolet No. 4 plant was the only GM unit to be struck after the closing of the Oakland plant, but in a symbolic gesture directed against GM as a whole, UAW unionists from Tarrytown, New York, joined by workers from the needle trades, picketed the GM Building in New York on February 1; and one hundred Detroit UAW members, supported by fifty women and a dozen children and urged on by a sound truck, demonstrated in front of the GM Building in Detroit on February 6.[43]

Of the strikes initiated against GM plants outside Michigan before January 1 only the Guide Lamp dispute attracted much national attention once Flint became the center of strike concern. The first of the strike fronts, Atlanta, reported to Travis on January 12 that "we are still holding down the fort. everything is running smooth down here. the main trouble is no money and no new's [sic]."[44] In Kansas City, where snow and cold became a problem for the strikers, the UAW maintained a heavy picket line in front of the struck plant in the morning but only a small patrol the remainder of the day. The local forced the shutdown of the parts plant on January 18 because it was allegedly supplying GM units that were still open, and two days later pickets stopped superintendents, foremen, and office help from entering the main plant. "At present," the executive board of the local reported on February 1, "everything is under control and the moral [sic] is exceptionally high considering the length of time we have been out and the severe weather, also the distance that separates us from the real strike center."[45]

In Cleveland, the UAW, after ending its sit-down, undertook the systematic picketing of the Fisher Body plant. On the whole, the Cleveland strikers conducted themselves "nicely," to quote the city's chief of police, but on January 4 police scuffled with pickets when they refused to allow the plant manager to enter the factory. The union attributed the action of the pickets to error and voted to allow the plant manager, the maintenance crew, watchmen, doctors, and nurses to enter the plant without molestation. The minutes of the strikers' meetings reveal a concern about the "acute" relief problem, but they attest at the same time to a growing union membership.[46]

In Norwood, the "loyal" Employee's Bargaining Committee called for a return to work and alleged that the local workers were on strike not because of any grievances but simply because the international had ordered the action. The "ring leader" of the anti-union forces was William H. Black, the first president of the UAW local and the brother of the distinguished agricultural economist, John D. Black. Black charged that "outside elements" had gained control of the local, and he protested to Senator La Follette that Norwood unionists were beating up their opponents, picketing and damaging their homes, and coercing them to join the union and that they had instituted a "near reign of terror" in the city.[47]

Of the strikes outside Flint none led to more turmoil than the Guide Lamp dispute in Anderson, Indiana. A city of about forty thousand population, almost all of whom were native-born whites,[48] Anderson was strictly a GM town. Of its approximately fourteen thousand wage earners in 1937, about three thousand were employed in the Guide Lamp Division, which manufactured headlights and other automotive lighting equipment, and about eight thousand worked in the Delco-Remy Division, whose five Anderson plants produced distributors, generators, and other electrical equipment.[49] As a GM public-relations report indicated, the corporation enjoyed "high public standing" in Anderson: nearly everyone knew the extent to which GM contributed to the city's employment, and the corporation's relations with the city's newspapers, public authorities, and civic leaders were "intimately friendly." ". . . this gigantic corporation," Charles B. Salyer, a local attorney aiding the UAW declared, "is the government, is the voice of the people, and the voice of the people is the voice desired to be spoken by the General Motors."[50] A strike affecting the employer upon whom the city was so dependent for its well-being was bound to have serious local repercussions.

The alarm caused in Anderson by the strike at Guide Lamp beginning on December 31 was heightened when Delco-Remy did not reopen following the New Year holiday because of a cancellation of orders, although it was widely believed in Anderson that fear of a strike was the real cause. With "industrial paralysis" spreading in Anderson, back-to-work movements were soon initiated by nonunionists in both plants. The UAW charged that foremen and group leaders were visiting workers in their homes to secure signatures for loyalty petitions, while the Anderson police chief, Joseph Carney, accused the union of coercing nonunion workers. Although press accounts of what had transpired were exaggerated, a few Guide Lamp strikers, until ordered to desist by the Indiana State Police, halted and impounded several trucks carrying GM products to and from Anderson.[51]

On January 8 three hundred Anderson businessmen assembled to form the Citizens League for Industrial Security and elected Homer Lambert, a local real-estate operator, as its chairman. The stated objectives of the League were to encourage industry by promoting harmony between labor and management, to foster obedience to the law and to oppose mob violence, and to promote "steady and uninterrupted employment" in the city at fair wages. The League urged Anderson's GM workers to reject "alien leadership" and the advice of "strangers from far away places" and asked townspeople to indicate their support for the majority who wished to work by joining the new organization, which more than seventeen thousand of them did. The union saw the League as a "thinly disguised strike-breaking organization," and Salyer charged that all sorts of pressure had been applied by local businessmen and officials to secure members. The kind of fervor being whipped up against outsiders was manifested in a letter sent to Hugh Thompson, the veteran UAW organizer in charge of the union campaign in the city, advising him and his "organization" "to get out of Anderson, and do it now, while getting is safe. We don't need your trash in Anderson."[52]

The abandonment of the sit-down strike at Guide Lamp on January 16 was followed two days later by the reopening of Delco-Remy. The management now augmented the normal force of fifty-seven uniformed plant police in Delco-Remy by one hundred "special duty guards" armed with blackjacks. The new guards, some of whom were leaders of the back-to-work movement, patrolled the plant for the next three weeks.[53] Tension mounted in the city and finally erupted into violence on the night of January 25, described by the regional director of the NLRB as "the most violent night ever experienced in Anderson."[54] The UAW was scheduled to hold a public meeting in the local courthouse that night, but preceding the meeting loyal employees assembled at a local theater, some of them having been urged to attend by Delco-Remy foremen. Amidst "much disorder and drinking," to quote an NLRB source, the men armed themselves with clubs by breaking up the furniture and then divided into two groups, one proceeding to the courthouse and the other to the UAW's headquarters. Warned of impending trouble, the union had cancelled its meeting, but some unionists were still in the vicinity of the courthouse, and three of them were badly beaten by a group that included GM foremen and group leaders.

The attackers then moved on to the union headquarters to join the rest of the mob, and the combined force of about one thousand, which included Delco-Remy and Guide Lamp supervisory personnel, laid siege to the building. An outside staircase led to the union office where Thompson, seven other men, six women, and a four-year-old child awaited an expected attack. The unionists stood off their besiegers with a 22-caliber pistol and some billiard balls while Thompson sought frantically to summon the National Guard, the state police, and city police. During the course of the next three hours eleven policemen and deputy sheriffs arrived and escorted the union group to the county jail, from where Thompson left for Detroit.

The mob in the meantime had completely ransacked the union office and destroyed the local's records and had then moved on to the Guide Lamp plant, where it drove off the union pickets and demolished a picket shack that had been placed on private property. F. L. Burke, the Guide Lamp plant manager, then emerged from the factory and, according to several affidavits, thanked the loyal employees for their good deeds that night, told them that they had destroyed the union, and stated that work would be resumed at Guide Lamp in two or three days.[55]

GM officials made no effort at any point to restrain the mob, nor were any of the special guards who had served as leaders of the vigilantes relieved of their duties. The chief of police, who was accused by the NLRB regional director of having permitted the mob "to run wild," explained that he had not made any arrests because this would have precipitated still greater violence. The notation on the police blotter for this night of violence was " 'nothing to report.' " Salyer thought that the events of January 25 provided proof of GM's control over Anderson's public officials. "The police and officials," he wrote, "have done everything within their power to break the Union, drive it out of Anderson and play ball with General Motors."[56]

Victor Reuther arrived in Anderson at about 4:00 A.M. on January 26 to replace Thompson. He found, as he later recalled, that many of the union officials had gone into hiding; and because of the fear that prevailed it was necessary for him to hold his first meeting in Alexandria, twelve miles north of Anderson. Reuther was unable at the outset to rent a hotel room since hotel operators were afraid that his presence would lead to an attack on their property. He lived with friends in Anderson, moving night after night to conceal his whereabouts.[57]

Following the events of January 25 unionists in Delco-Remy were subjected to "wholesale intimidation" by the loyal employees and the special guards. Union members were approached in the plant by loyal employees, ordered to leave the factory, and told that they could not return to work unless they first destroyed their union cards and presented affidavits of resignation from the union; ninety-one employees were actually ejected from the plant. The NLRB, which held Delco-Remy "to a large degree responsible for the formation and growth of this allegedly overpowering employee revolt," found that company officials had urged loyal workers to evict unionists and had personally evicted some of them, had not penalized the assailants in any way, and had not made deductions from their pay for time spent away from their jobs intimidating unionists. They had, by contrast, shown hostility to those who had been driven from their jobs and had not compensated them for the time that they had been forcibly kept from the plant. The NLRB rejected as "incredible" the company's contention that it had not known that weapons were being carried in the plant and dismissed as contrary to fact its statements that it had attempted to calm the situation.[58]

On January 27, after Thompson had brought news to Detroit about events in Anderson, Ed Hall, attorney Maurice Sugar, three additional unionists, and two armed bodyguards left by train for Anderson to reestablish the union's headquarters there. Hall stated,

Strategy and Tactics: The UAW

ironically in view of GM's protestations about union trespass upon its property, that his purpose in going to Anderson was "to get back the property that belongs to the union." He was awakened on the train between Union City and Winchester, and an Anderson unionist was brought to him to advise him not to go on to Anderson since "gangsters and vigilantes" were waiting for the train there and were guarding all roads leading to the city. Hall was told to get off the train at Muncie, where four unionists would meet him and drive him to Alexandria.

Heeding the advice given them, the union party left the train at Muncie, where they found "many shady looking characters" loitering about the station. One of the loiterers told Hall that the four unionists who were to meet him had been arrested and that he was not to go to Anderson. Hall called Governor M. Clifford Townsend and the sheriff of the county to request protection but was promised none, and the local police refused to escort the union group to Alexandria, where Hall allegedly intended to mobilize twelve hundred unionized steel rock workers for a march on Anderson. After breakfasting in the train station, Hall again called the governor and arranged to meet him in Indianapolis. The police then escorted the union party to Newcastle, from where they left by interurban for the state capital, thus avoiding Anderson. Hall and Sugar asked Townsend the next day to deputize one hundred Anderson unionists to offset the force previously deputized by city officials.[59]

In Anderson, in the meantime, hundreds of Delco-Remy employees, armed with clubs and iron bars, had been permitted to leave their jobs on the morning of January 28 to meet the Hall party at the Anderson railroad station. There were no police in sight at the terminal, but GM supervisory personnel, some of whom had apparently helped to organize the group, were present. None of the employees had his pay docked for the hour or so spent away from the plant, nor were any of them disciplined.[60] The mayor of Anderson, Harry Baldwin, announced the next day that if Hall did reach Anderson, he would be arrested and returned to Detroit—UAW organizer James Roland had been arrested the day before only a few hours after his arrival in the city and forced to leave Anderson—and that he was having Reuther watched and had prevented him from making a radio address the previous night. Reuther had intended to say that Anderson was being "ruled by mob action" and that hundreds of armed men were roaming the streets, destroying property, and endangering human life but that the police were "unwilling or unable" to stop them. He had planned to urge that Anderson be "re-annex[ed]" to the United States.[61]

On January 30, by which time the Department of Labor, the Federal Bureau of Investigation, the La Follette Committee, and the Indiana attorney general all had investigators in Anderson, the UAW was permitted to reopen its headquarters and, according to the mayor, was promised police protection provided that no out-of-town organizers were brought into the city and no attempt was made to inflame local anti-union sentiment. The UAW wanted the National Guard sent into the city, but since the entire Indiana Guard was at that time deployed in seventeen Indiana counties that had been ravaged by floods, Governor Townsend could not comply with this request. He did, however, arrange for the appointment of seventy-five additional deputies, and Mayor Baldwin agreed to select the men from a list acceptable to the union and to drop some of the anti-union men already deputized. Picketing was then resumed at the Guide Lamp plant. The unionists returned to the factory in a caravan of old jalopies, the lead car flying the Stars and Stripes, circled the plant, and then parked their cars and reestablished the line. Victor Reuther recalls that some of the deputies on the scene, "big burly plug-uglies," sought in vain to provoke violence as picketing was resumed. All was not to be peaceful on the line, however. On February 3 police congregated at the plant, and a police captain struck Reuther on the face. Carney some time later confiscated the local's sound truck, and he ignored a court order to release the vehicle. The union obtained another truck in Alexandria, but the Anderson city council then forbade the use of sound equipment on the city's streets.[62]

On February 6 the Anderson unionists evidenced their "grim determination" by staging a parade with six hundred men in line.[63] Anderson was thereafter to be relatively peaceful until the end of the strike brought a new outburst of violence and persuaded Governor Townsend to send the National Guard into the city and to declare martial law. What happened in Anderson pointed up the dangers inherent in a community where public officials and a single employer were so closely linked, where so many citizens understandably related their own well-being to the well-being of that employer and the continued operation of his business, and where the only opposition force was a small union that enjoyed very little public support. The Anderson story also reveals that however sincere Knudsen was in saying that GM wanted the strike settled without violence, corporation plant managers and supervisory personnel, under circumstances favorable to the company, were willing to sanction the use of force and the tactics of intimidation to break the strike and to defeat the union.

In the strategy and tactics that it pursued in the GM strike, the

UAW, to a degree, modeled itself after GM, although it was not always simply reacting to the initiatives of the corporation. GM engaged in labor practices proscribed by the NLRA, but the UAW defied the law of trespass. Both GM and the union were guilty of spying on one another. GM attempts to stimulate back-to-work movements were countered by UAW efforts to spread the strike. GM asked its employees to sign petitions indicating their desire to return to or remain at work under existing conditions, and so the UAW had its members advise Murphy that they wished to return to work only under union conditions. Some GM employees were coerced into signing loyalty pledges and Flint Alliance membership cards, but the union also resorted to coercion both inside and outside the plants. What happens in so many social conflicts happened to some extent in the GM sit-down strike: "One defeats the enemy," David Riesman has written, "by becoming more like him."[64]

The UAW did not wage its struggle against GM without important allies. The CIO, liberal-reform groups, radicals of various hues and shadings, and government officials came to the union's assistance, sometimes in a crucial way. Recognizing the importance of the battle to the entire campaign of the CIO in the mass-production industries, Lewis made it clear from the very beginning of the strike that the new organization was "squarely behind" the UAW. When CIO and UAW leaders met in an emergency session in Detroit in the middle of January, one CIO leader remarked, "The C.I.O. is in this thing up to its neck," and its unions "will not stop to count their nickels and dimes." Before the strike began there was ambivalence in the GEB and particularly on the part of Martin regarding CIO aid, but once the strike was underway the UAW wanted "more, not less" CIO assistance.[65] The CIO provided the UAW with money, experienced organizers like Adolph Germer, John Brophy, Powers Hapgood, Rose Pesotta, and Leo Krzycki, and, in the final negotiations that led to the conclusion of the strike, the formidable presence and skill as a bargainer of John L. Lewis himself.

It is easy, however, to overestimate the contribution made by the CIO to the UAW triumph, important as that contribution was. It is not true, for example, as alleged, that Lewis directed "every important step" of the strike, although his assistance toward the end of the dispute was crucial. The extent of the CIO financial aid can also be exaggerated. Powers Hapgood told a Flint mass meeting on January 24 that the United Mine Workers was assessing its 625,000 members $1 per month to aid the UAW, but the assessment was actually designed to build up the financial reserves of the mine union, and it is not clear how much, if any, of this money reached the UAW. The contributions of the Amalgamated Clothing Workers and the International Ladies' Garment Workers' Union do not seem to have reached the UAW until the strike was over, whereas the earlier contributions by UAW locals and the United Rubber Workers presumably would have been made had there been no CIO. Brophy and Germer were the CIO officials charged with the greatest responsibilities in the strike until Lewis entered the final negotiations, and they certainly brought far greater experience to the affair than the youthful UAW strike leaders did, but Travis thought both men too cautious and actually worked more closely with UAW officials on the scene and the militant Powers Hapgood than with the two senior CIO representatives.[66]

In a decade when the right of workers to organize free from employer interference came to be recognized as an important civil liberty,[67] it is not surprising that civil-liberties groups came to the UAW's support. The American Civil Liberties Union (ACLU) did not accept the right to engage in a sit-down strike as a civil liberty,[68] nor did it deny the propriety of the injunction process as a means of dealing with the GM sit-down, but it nevertheless protested the sweeping terms of the Black and later the Gadola injunction and the restrictions that they imposed on peaceful picketing and other union activities, and it supported Murphy's refusal to eject the strikers by force. At the request of a UAW attorney, the ACLU protested to Governor Townsend the "lawless rule" in Anderson and urged him to deputize men "capable of fair police administration"; and in response to the appeal of Victor Reuther and UAW international officers the affiliated Chicago Civil Liberties Committee sent its executive secretary to Anderson at the end of the strike to investigate alleged violations of civil liberties in that community. The committee eventually issued a report that was severely critical of GM's behavior in Anderson. The ACLU also secured the consent of such prominent citizens as Archibald MacLeish, Reinhold Niebuhr, and Alexander Meiklejohn to serve on a National Citizens Committee 'for Civil Rights in the Automobile Industry, which aligned itself with the UAW in its struggle against GM.[69]

The ACLU efforts were supplemented and complemented by the left-leaning Conference for the Protection of Civil Rights, a Michigan organization established in 1935 that claimed the affiliation of 311 labor, farm, cultural, and civic groups. The Conference offered its aid to the UAW the day after the Black injunction was issued, and from that time forward, often in collaboration with the National Citizens Committee, which it had helped to establish, it attempted "to focus almost immediate attention on menaced liberties" and to sway public

Strategy and Tactics: The UAW

opinion in the strikers' favor. It sent groups of ministers to Flint as observers and bombarded public officials in Michigan and elsewhere with telegrams and resolutions demanding the impeachment of Judge Black, calling for the investigation of the relationship between GM and the governments of Flint and Genesee County, and, above all, protesting the use of violence and the threat of vigilante action in Flint, Saginaw, and Anderson.[70] The Fisher Body No. 1 strike committee, on January 22, duly noted the assistance being rendered the strikers by the Conference, and after the strike Local 156 expressed its appreciation to the organization for its "vigilant support" of civil rights in Flint.[71]

Clergymen of a liberal-reformist point of view also spoke out for the UAW. Early in the strike Monsignor John A. Ryan, the director of the Social Action Department of the National Catholic Welfare Conference, the Reverend James Myers of the Federal Council of the Churches of Christ, and Rabbi Barnett Brickner, the chairman of the Social Justice Commission of the Central Conference of American Rabbis, jointly urged the settlement of the strike in accordance with the principle of exclusive representation, which GM staunchly opposed and the UAW supported. Myers, a Presbyterian minister who had joined the council staff in the 1920's and had "carried the social gospel to factory towns, coal fields, textile villages, and cotton plantations," visited Flint for several days in January and then issued a report on the strike, contained in the Council's *Information Service* that was distinctly partial to the union cause. Travis expressed his "admiration" of the report and requested several hundred copies for distribution in Flint, "especially among citizens who have an open mind."[72]

In Michigan, the *Michigan Christian Advocate*, the journal of the Methodist Episcopal church, dealt with the dispute in terms sympathetic to the strikers. John E. Marvin, the associate editor, visited the No. 1 plant in January with two other clergymen and then reported in the *Advocate* that the strikers were men of an "unusually high type" and that he was impressed by their loyalty to a cause that they believed just. Of the dinner he was served in the plant, he wrote, "we ate as though we were at a church pot-luck."[73]

A group of students from the University of Michigan, identifying with the movement to organize the unorganized much as college students thirty years later would identify with the civil-rights movement, came to Flint to aid the strikers. Not only did they edit the *Punch Press*, as already noted, but they took their turn in the welfare office, performed leg work for the strike organization, and aided in the union's educational effort in the occupied plants.[74]

Socialists, Communists, and far-left sympathizers, although generally aware that the strikers were without revolutionary intent, saw the strike nevertheless as a somewhat sharper challenge to property rights than the ordinary strike was and, in any event, as of critical importance to the entire struggle to organize the mass-production industries and consequently deserving of their whole-hearted support. Norman Thomas thus wrote Martin shortly after the strike began wishing him "all possible success in a great cause" and indicating that the Socialist party "will do what it can" to aid; and the party's Labor and Organization Secretary reported that Socialists and other "working class and progressive forces" were supporting the strike directly and through the Conference for the Protection of Civil Rights. The Central Committee of the Communist party called on its members "to rally wholeheartedly and at once to the aid of the strikers." Communist-controlled organizations responded by contributing to the UAW's strike fund and by aiding in the collection of food and money for the strike, and the *Daily Worker* gave the dispute extensive coverage and featured several special auto strike sections.[75]

More important than the role in the strike of the Socialist and Communist parties *qua* parties was the part played by individual radicals within the UAW and the CIO. That there was a sprinkling of left wingers within the UAW at the time of the strike is not at all surprising. In the difficult early days of auto unionism, the substantial risks involved in organizational work were apt to discourage those who did not bring to their task some ideological commitment and a conviction that trade unionism was a means by which large social objectives might be attained. It was frequently also these same radicals who alone had the experience and organizational skills required to build and sustain the new unions, and in the absence of an established leadership group in the UAW some of them were able to gain positions of influence. It did not, of course, harm the cause of the radicals and particularly of the Communists, who had been so vocal about the matter, that the UAW as an organization had decided that they had been "right" on the vital issues of industrial unionism, the early establishment of an international union, and the need for greater democracy in the union and that Dillon and the AFL leadership had been "wrong." Finally, the fact that the strike and the beginnings of the UAW as an international union coincided with the Popular Front period discouraged the kind of critical thinking about Communist goals in the labor movement that was later to come. In the era of the Popular Front liberals looked upon Communists as good trade unionists and were disposed to attack "red-baiting" as playing the employer's game.[76]

Strategy and Tactics: The UAW

221

The attention given to Communist participation in the sit-down has tended to obscure the very substantial part played in the dispute by Socialists in both the CIO and the UAW. When Homer Martin's secretary, Julia Loewe, wrote Norman Thomas during the strike about the "good work" being accomplished by "our comrades," she was not indulging in flights of fancy. Germer and Hapgood of the CIO; William Carney and B. J. Widick of the Rubber Workers, both of whom helped out in Flint during the strike; Victor, Walter, and Roy Reuther; Genora and Kermit Johnson; Joe Ditzel; Larry Davidow, the UAW's principal attorney at the beginning of the strike; Merlin Bishop; and Phil Wise, who became Pete Kennedy's aide in the No. 1 plant, were all Socialists, and their contribution to the final victory was large.[77]

Because of the clandestine nature of American Communism, the different levels upon which the Communist party has operated, and the problem of distinguishing among bona fide Communists, fellow travelers, and non-Communists who supported Communist policies, it is no easy task to determine the precise role played in the strike by the Communists and their allies and friends. That the role was important has been steadily asserted by both the left and the right. William Weinstone declared shortly after the strike had ended that there was *"no doubt that where the Communists were active and took an outstanding part, . . . there the strike was strongest, and this made for the success of the whole battle."* During the Dies Committee hearings in the fall of 1938 witness after witness asserted that the Communists were behind the entire sit-down strike movement, and Martin Dies himself stated that "well-known Communists instigated and engineered the sit-down strike."

More recently two of the participants in the strike have made similar evaluations. Larry Davidow, who moved considerably to the right following the sit-down era, stated in an interview in 1960 that "the major fact to keep in mind is that the whole strategy of the sit-down strike was communist inspired, communist directed and communist controlled." And Wyndham Mortimer, who was certainly in a position to know, declared in 1964 that, although quite a number of the people who were prominent in the strike were not Communists, "the main strategy of the sitdown strike itself was conducted by the Communists. . . . I think the Communists had a lot to do with running the strike."[78]

Mortimer himself, of course, had begun the reorganization of the union in Flint in 1936 and had been involved in the decision to strike the No. 1 plant. As a UAW vice-president he was a member of the strike strategy committee, and he was one of the three principal

Sit-Down

negotiators for the union with the company. Bob Travis, accurately described as "the leading personality . . . in the strike" in Flint, later became associated with several front organizations and was active in the Farm Equipment Workers Union, described by Max Kampelman as having been "completely within the Communist orbit." It is difficult, however, to know precisely what Travis' commitments were in January, 1937, but Roy Reuther, who was closely associated with him during the strike, believed that Travis at that time was "a good dedicated trade union guy" and was not "political" and that only after the strike did he gravitate to the left. Travis, by his own admission however, was very much influenced by Mortimer—Carl Haessler has characterized Travis as "Mortimer's man in the union at the time"—and it has been reported that he received advice from Weinstone, among others, during the strike.[79] At the level of the strike leadership in the plants, Bud Simons and some of his cohorts in Fisher No. 1 had been members of what Earl Browder called "the Red Auto Workers Union," and Simons, as we have seen, had participated in the Communist-infiltrated rump movement to promote the formation of an auto international.[80]

Lee Pressman, the CIO's general counsel, a close associate of Lewis throughout the strike, and one of the signers of the final settlement, admitted in 1950 that he had been a member of the Communist Ware group in the Agricultural Adjustment Administration. He testified that he had broken organizationally with the Communist party in 1936, but he did not sever his ideological connections with Communism until more than a decade later.[81] Maurice Sugar, one of the UAW's attorneys during the strike, had been identified with such front groups as the International Labor Defense, the Friends of the Soviet Union, and the John Reed Clubs. In 1939 he had criminal libel charges brought in the Detroit Recorder's Court against an auto worker who had distributed a leaflet that accused Sugar, among other things, of being a Communist, but the worker was acquitted by the jury.[82]

Like Pressman, Charles Kramer, the La Follette Committee's chief investigator in Detroit at the beginning of the sit-down and a Travis and UAW ally, was, as we have seen, identified as a member of the Ware group, and he later refused to answer questions of a Congressional committee concerning his alleged Communist affiliations. It was undoubtedly because of his suspicions concerning Kramer's politics that Germer asked La Follette on January 11 to send in a replacement for Kramer, a request with which the Senator complied.[83]

Although Communists, fellow travelers, and non-Communists

who sympathized with Communism were prominently involved in the sit-down, it would be a mistake to interpret the strike as a Communist plot or to assume that the Communists and their friends pursued policies that conflicted importantly with the organizational interests of the UAW. The workers struck because of their grievances against management—the strike "emanated from the conditions," to quote Roy Reuther—rather than from any desire to promote Communist objectives, and the Communists do not appear to have made any serious effort to politicize the dispute. Arthur M. Ross has distinguished between the "agitational" and "organizational" motives of the Communists in a strike, between the use of the strike as a weapon of propaganda to sharpen class lines and its use in building a strong union. The GM strike undoubtedly strengthened the position of the Communists and their allies within the UAW, but their principal contribution was in helping to develop a powerful union that would eventually drive the Stalinists from its ranks rather than in imbuing the strikers with revolutionary fervor or converting them to Communism.[84]

Finally, and enormously important in determining the outcome of the strike, was the assistance rendered the UAW during the sit-down by federal and state officials. The UAW failed to persuade the Michigan legislature to investigate a long list of union complaints about the behavior of GM, and it did not seek to invoke the assistance of the NLRB to buttress its demand for exclusive representation,[85] but it did receive significant support from the La Follette Committee and from the governor of Michigan.

Throughout the strike the La Follette Committee investigators who had been instructed to observe strike developments were, like the committee's staff men who had been investigating GM before the strike, allies in effect of the UAW rather than neutral observers seeking objectively to ascertain the facts. Kramer, Harold Cranefield, and H. D. Cullen were all sympathetic to the union cause and worked closely with strike officials in Flint. "The explosion is coming sure as God made little green apples," Cullen wrote from Flint on January 21, "unless those damn fools of GM get busy and give up! ! ! !" He thought that "the biggest thing" the committee could do during the year "would be to drive this GM thing out into the open and thus create a public sentiment that would FORCE the right action. A complete back-down by GM would not only be best, from our standpoint, but for the whole damn country as well—." Kramer, when he learned that the Flint strikers had seized the Chevrolet No. 4 plant, wrote Travis, "You guys seem to be the only ones who are really doing a job."[86]

La Follette Committee investigators in Flint gathered affidavits from workers who claimed that they had been coerced into signing loyalty pledges or Flint Alliance membership cards; they collaborated with the union in seeking to uncover anti-union espionage (Cullen thought that the discovery of "a few more spies" in Flint would be "a lot of help"), in the development of its own "intelligence" network and in checking out stories whose revelation might prove harmful to GM; and they "prepared" union witnesses to testify before the committee in Washington. On January 25 Cullen served subpoenas on Boysen, Wills, Wolcott, and Genesee County prosecutor Joseph R. Joseph to appear before the committee with records relating to the purchase of gas and gas bombs and other matters pertinent to the January 11 Fisher Body No. 2 riot. Cullen thought that the public revelation of the subpoenaing of Boysen had helped to deflate the importance of the Flint Alliance. Cranefield gathered fifty strikers together for a mass interview on the No. 2 riot, and Cullen tried to establish "a definite connection" between GM and the battle.

In Washington La Follette Committee hearings in late January revealed GM to have been the second best customer of the Corporations Auxiliary Company, and hearings that began on February 8 exposed the more important links between GM and Pinkerton and further embarrassed the corporation. Cullen had advised the earliest possible GM hearings because he thought that the introduction of "evidence of duplicity" on the corporation's part regarding its assertions concerning the loyalty of its employees would "carry more than ordinary weight and swing sentiment."[87]

During one of the strikers' demonstrations in Flint a union spokesman told his audience that Governor Murphy would "take care" of them,[88] and in a sense the governor did just that. His decision regarding relief for strikers and their families was a boon to the union, and his position with respect to the use of force in the strike and the necessity of settling the dispute by negotiation was the single most important factor in bringing the strike to a conclusion that was not unfavorable to the union.

11

The company and the union, appreciating the influence that public opinion might have in determining the outcome of the strike, sought to communicate their version of events and of the issues at stake to the Flint community and to the larger community outside of that city. Flint, so heavily dependent on GM employment, was dealt a severe economic blow by the strike; a "dark cloud of economic fear" hovered over the city throughout the dispute. By January 20 thirty-eight thousand of GM's forty-three thousand hourly workers in Flint were on strike or laid off because of the strike. As compared to January, 1936, new car registrations in Flint dropped 62.6 percent in January, 1937, retail sales 23.6 percent, outbound car loadings 75.1 percent, and water consumption 11.4 percent. Sears Roebuck reported a 75 percent decline in sales as compared to December, and even the sales of foodstuffs and milk were reported to have dropped. On the other hand, building permits increased 3.5 percent, bank clearings 19.4 percent, and postal receipts 23.6 percent, workers paid their bills promptly, and the hotel business boomed as newsmen, photographers, newsreel personnel, and radio crews flocked to the city. Economic conditions in Flint almost certainly would have been worse than they actually were had not $6 million in additional funds been distributed in the city in December as the result of bonus payments by GM and other companies, payments to the depositors of three banks that had closed during the bank holiday, and Christmas fund checks.[89]

The strike, as one Flint citizen noted, "came very close and was very real to us in Flint." Observers sensed the tension in the air, and as the strike continued there was apprehension that the antagonism engendered by the conflict would at any moment erupt into violence. In his strike novelette Paul Gallico described Flint as "all tightened up with nerves—jumpy, jittery, waiting for something." A La Follette Committee investigator wrote from Flint on January 21 that "this place is a powderkeg—and these birds are throwing lit matches all around. I mean both sides." Early in the next month another La Follette staff member reported the town "aflame," and on February 9 a National Guard intelligence estimate referred to "an increased tenseness about the city." Roy Reuther recalled having been threatened so many times that he stationed an armed man outside his room and kept a bodyguard inside the room when he slept. In view of the prevailing atmosphere in Flint, Reuther thought it was "miraculous" that no one had been killed.[90]

Automotive Industries reported that correspondents in Flint found it to be "an anti-strike community," but one of the union participants later insisted, "There wasn't one reaction. There wasn't a united community. There were many communities." Flint, indeed, did not express a single reaction to the strike, but it is evident that the company enjoyed more influential and, almost certainly, far more numerous support than the union did. As the strike dragged on, it appears that there was "a trend of sympathy *away* from the sit-downers" even among some of their former supporters. "The people of Flint," a National Guard source reported late in the strike, "are coming to feel that the majority are suffering economic and social distress at the hands of the minority."[91]

The power structure of the community, its officials, the board of education, the city newspaper, and the more influential business and professional people were pro-GM. Of the city's officeholders, Barringer was the most opposed to the UAW and its goals. He had tangled with the union during the early days of the trolley strike and had sought to drive the sound car from the streets, and the UAW now suspected him of plotting its very destruction.[92] Barringer later blamed the strike on the Communists, and he bitterly resented the role played in the dispute by Murphy, the National Guard, and the La Follette Committee. "Jittery" about the sit-down, which he later characterized as "something new to us, and ... something that we were confused to know how to handle," he sought to involve the State Police in the dispute as early as January 5, and at a critical moment in the strike he began raising a force of vigilantes to combat the union in a provocative action that could have led to widespread violence. Mayor Bradshaw was nominally Barringer's superior, but the city manager had the greater influence in the city's government, and as safety director he controlled the city's police.[93] He did, however, have his enemies on the city commission, some of whose members were not as hostile to the UAW as he was, and in the end he lost the backing of the commission's majority.[94]

The city's police force, headed by James V. Wills, who was no friend of the strikers, became involved on at least two occasions in provocative acts that raise questions about the quality of its leadership and its neutrality in the strike: a show of force on the evening of January 7 following the destruction of the union's sound equipment across the street from the Chevrolet complex and the attack on Fisher No. 2 on January 11. The police arrested two unionists as the result of the January 7 fighting and held them incommunicado during the remainder of the day. At a union meeting at the Pengelly Building that evening Roy Reuther, in a fiery address, advised his audience to proceed to the police station and to demand the release of their two comrades. A crowd of about 150 strikers and sympathizers, "shouting loudly for justice," gathered at the police station, but when Reuther and a few others entered the building to request the release of the two unionists, they were denied an audience. There were shouts from the strikers to free the men by force, but Reuther, seeking to avoid trouble, urged rather that Michael Evanoff, a local attorney representing the union, be summoned. Evanoff arrived after about twenty minutes and described the legal steps he would follow in the case, whereupon union speakers advised the crowd to return to union headquarters.

The unionists had begun to disperse when the doors of the police station opened, and about ten officers wearing gas masks and aprons filled with gas bombs filed out onto the steps and, in a ridiculous action reminiscent of the Haymarket Affair, called to the retreating unionists to return and then warned them that they would be subjected to a gas attack if they did not disperse. The police followed the crowd to the next corner, keeping the throng covered with gas guns. There were some "ugly murmurs" from the unionists and some threats of reprisals for this totally unnecessary show of force, which can only be described as deliberately provocative, but the evening passed without further incident. Barringer thought that the demonstration outside the police station warranted the intervention of the state police in Flint, but his efforts to secure such assistance were unavailing.[95] In view of what had occurred, it is no wonder that the union interpreted the police behavior on January 11 outside the Fisher Body No. 2 plant as being part of a premeditated action to eject the sit-downers from the factory.

In the UAW view, among the city and county officials with whom the union dealt in Flint only Sheriff Wolcott, described by Kraus as "a cartoonist's image of the typical sheriff: enormously paunchy, battered slouch hat, unlit cigar stub in mouth-corner," was "inclined to be fair." Travis, who thought of the city police as "tools" of GM, considered Wolcott to be "a decent guy," and Kraus characterized him as a Democrat who "thoroughly hated" his assignment and who was the closest among the local officials to Murphy's point of view.[96]

The Flint Board of Education and many of the city's school teachers evidenced a marked animus toward the strikers and the union. Merlin Bishop reported at a meeting of the strike council in the No. 1 plant on January 28 that Flint teachers were attempting to start an anti-strike movement among the school children. Teachers were reported to have asked their students to write essays on the "wrongs" of the sit-down and to have made adverse comments to children who wore their fathers' union buttons to class. One school teacher complained after the strike that the "spirit of lawlessness" of the strikers had affected their children and that teachers had had to deal with "this defiance of authority."[97]

The Board of Education turned down a request from the UAW to use a school auditorium for a meeting on the ground that school buildings should not be used at a time of crisis for a purpose that would "tend to cause dissention [sic]." When a small group of teachers who were members of the Flint Federation of Teachers issued a statement supporting the UAW and criticizing the Flint Alliance and GM, they were denounced by school authorities as "a group of a dozen parlor pinks, representing less than one per cent of the teaching staff" and were reportedly subjected to "open intimidation" by their superiors. Contracts of five of the teachers involved were not renewed in the spring.[98]

The Flint *Journal* was denounced by one La Follette Committee investigator as being "purely a General Motors Company organ" and by another as being partly responsible for "the definite cleavage" in the community.[99] It treated strike leaders as "agitators," emphasized the loyalty to the company of its workers, and insisted that the sit-downers were armed. The UAW began distributing form letters addressed to the *Journal* cancelling the sender's subscription because of the newspaper's "flagrant one-sidedness" and its alleged distortion of strike news.[100]

The leading business and professional people in Flint, concerned about the threat to property rights posed by the strike and interlocked in so many ways with GM and GM executives, identified themselves with the Flint Alliance and were hostile to the strike. The Flint Chamber of Commerce thus blamed "a small minority" for the "almost complete stagnation" of the city's business and for injuring its reputation as a peaceful community where there had always been a "fine relationship" between employer and employee, and it objected to the "unjust and violent methods" used by the strikers.[101] Some of the smaller Flint businessmen, however, and particularly some of the merchants who catered to GM workers were sympathetic to the union cause and supported it with contributions in cash or in kind and by a generous extension of credit to strikers who were pressed for funds.[102]

The strike probably had its most divisive effect among the working class in Flint and particularly among the largest segment of that group, the GM workers. What has already been said of GM workers in general was true of Flint's GM workers in particular: a small minority belonged to the union, a far larger number opposed the strike, and a very substantial group were "just sort of watching" to see what the outcome of the conflict would be. Nonstrikers in Flint as in other GM towns complained about being deprived of work by a minority and about the city's being "overrun" by outsiders who were allegedly "terrorizing" the populace, and there was talk, but no more than that, that loyal workers would march on the plants to reclaim their jobs. On the other hand, the union appears to have increased its membership steadily throughout the strike, and the wife of one sit-downer wrote her husband early in February, "Every place you go in Flint you see Union buttons flashing. Every body wears them. . . ."

The intensity of the union feeling and the divisions that the strike created in Flint were revealed in the letter of another wife who informed her husband sitting in the Chevrolet No. 4 plant that she would make no more purchases from her cheese man since he was "scabby" and that she guessed that she would quit the Ladies Aid since "Those old hens make me sick."[103]

The segment of the Flint community whose reaction to the strike can be most fully documented is the membership of the Methodist Episcopal church, Flint's largest Protestant denomination.[104] The sympathetic treatment of the strike in the denomination's organ, the *Michigan Christian Advocate*, was met with a barrage of criticism from church communicants. Shortly after the strike, in an effort to aid the editors of the *Advocate* in determining "where our people stand," the Reverend Gernsley F. Gorton, the minister of the Flint Oak Park Methodist Episcopal church, polled his membership about the sit-down. Among those who replied to the questionnaires, thirty indicated that they had opposed the strike, and only six that they had favored it; thirty-one disapproved of the methods of the strikers, four approved; and thirty blamed the strikers for such rioting as had occurred, three the nonstrikers.[105]

The superintendent of the Flint district of the Methodist Episcopal church, the Reverend R. M. Atkins, was a social-gospel advocate and was one of the few Flint clergymen who was partial to the strikers, but the Gorton poll and the numerous letters sent to the editors of the *Michigan Christian Advocate* and to Gorton suggest that most of the Flint communicants of the Methodist Episcopal church, including members of the working class, did not agree with Atkins. These letters and the comments on the Gorton poll reflect the standard themes expressed by strike opponents throughout the land: GM the good employer ("We do not claim ... [that GM] has reached perfection in their relationship with their employees, nevertheless, I believe they have come as close to it as any other large corporation and a lot closer than many of them"); the illegality of the sit-down ("I cannot reconcile myself to endorse a condition in which a group of men have seized property which is not their own"); the criticism of outsiders ("a clever, unscrupulous, highly organized crew of outsiders"); the fear of labor domination ("The fight is not for the right to organize, but against the dread dictatorship of John L. Lewis"); and the Communistic character of the sit-down ("We can see in the strike leaders' strategy, more implications of Communism and Anarchism than desire for betterment of the automobile workers").[106]

Although there are no separate figures for Flint, it would appear, judging from the Gallup poll, that there was somewhat more support for the UAW and the strikers outside of Flint than at the center of the conflict. The first Gallup poll on the strike, released on January 31, 1937, revealed that 53 percent of those who had an opinion favored "the employers" as compared to 47 percent who favored "the John L. Lewis group of striking employees." In the East Central area (Michigan, Ohio, Indiana, and Illinois), where the strike centered, the percentage of company supporters rose to 57, and the percentage of union supporters fell to 43. Persons on relief (69 percent) and Roosevelt voters (59 percent) favored the strikers, but farmers (60 percent) and Landon voters (79 percent) favored GM.[107]

Considering the challenge that the sit-down strike seemed to pose to property rights and the poor phrasing of the Gallup question from the UAW point of view—Travis suggested that "John L. Lewis group of striking employees" be changed to "union" or, if the original phrasing for the UAW were retained, that "company" be altered to "Dupont-Morgan group of Employers"[108]—the GM strike enjoyed a surprisingly large degree of public support at the end of January, a reflection, no doubt, of widespread popular approval of the right of workers to organize free from employer interference.

A second Gallup poll on the strike, published on February 7, revealed a slight ebbing of support for the strikers: the percentage favoring the Lewis group had now dropped to 44. Only 38 percent of those responding thought that Lewis represented the majority of GM workers, and only 34 percent thought that GM was wrong in refusing to negotiate while sit-down strikers occupied its plants. *Business Week*, however, was probably correct in its judgment that although a majority of the people opposed the strike, they nevertheless believed that the "worst thing" GM could do would be to use force against strikers who were behaving in an exemplary fashion and were not physically damaging the company's property. The prevailing view, as *Business Week* saw it, was that "it's 'not right' for the strikers to stay in or for the company to throw them out." GM, it would seem, agreed with this judgment.[109]

Some of the opponents of the strike believed that Lewis was seeking to establish "a labor dictatorship" and that he must be stopped before it was too late.[110] Power, although not necessarily dictatorial power, was, of course, what the dispute was all about, the desire of one side to maintain its power, the desire of the other to circumscribe that power and to augment its own, and it would be the task of the negotiators and the public officials who involved themselves in the dispute to register in the language of a settlement the degree, if any, to which the power relationships prevailing in the GM domain before 1937 had been altered by the strike.

Stalemate
IX

Federal and state authorities sought from the very beginning of the sit-down strike to assist in the resolution of the dispute, but they succeeded in bringing the two parties together for meaningful discussion of their differences only after the violence of January 11 and the union's seizure of the Chevrolet No. 4 plant on February 1 made it difficult for GM to resist the appeal to come to the bargaining table without waiting for the prior evacuation of its plants. From January 1 to January 11 both Secretary of Labor Perkins and Governor Murphy involved themselves in efforts to compose the strike but without at any time bringing the disputants together. Following the Battle of the Running Bulls Murphy summoned the UAW and GM to Lansing and secured their agreement to an armistice that provided for the evacuation of the occupied plants and then for bilateral negotiations between the union and the company. The truce broke down, however, before its terms could be fully implemented, and Washington and Lansing had to resume their roles as peacemakers. Frances Perkins sought to initiate strike talks in the nation's capital during the final two weeks of January, but her attempts at mediation were completely unsuccessful. Governor Murphy once again assumed direction of peace efforts after the UAW broke the strike stalemate by capturing the Chevrolet No. 4 plant. Supported by the White House, he was able to bring the two sides together in Detroit, where he directed the prolonged negotiations that led to the settlement of the strike.

Strike negotiations for GM were conducted by William Knudsen, Donaldson Brown, and John T. Smith. Knudsen was far less interested in stubbornly defending the principles regarding representation and collective bargaining to which GM was committed than in resuming production in the company's idle plants. "It was just hurting him," Lee Pressman later recalled, "that his machinery was idle." Unlike Knudsen, who spoke "'the language of the workingman,'" Brown, who had perfected GM's statistical and financial controls, spoke "'the language of finance'"—one is reminded of Thorstein Veblen's celebrated distinction between industry (technology) and business (pecuniary institutions). The son-in-law of T. Coleman du Pont, Brown had come from du Pont to GM in 1921 as vice-president in charge of finance, and there he began "a long and congenial relationship" with Sloan, whose views on the management of the corporation Brown shared. By no means an expert in the field of industrial relations and unfamiliar with working conditions in the automobile plants, Brown, as Sloan's representative in the negotiations, was primarily concerned with the defense of GM's basic policies with regard to collective bargaining and representation. Pressman, who had no love for Brown, described him as "about as cold a human being as I've ever met in all my life. He gave you an impression of dollars and cents."

Smith, a very competent attorney, was the draftsman for the GM negotiating team and, like Brown, sought to prevent the inclusion in the settlement terms of any language that might compromise GM principles. Fearful that Knudsen might yield too much to the union position, Brown and Smith kept a wary eye on him during the negotiations and increasingly pushed him into the background. Knudsen, Adolph Germer concluded at an early point in the negotiations, "has his hands tied and receives orders from New York—the DuPonts."[1]

The burden of the negotiations for the UAW was initially carried by Homer Martin, Wyndham Mortimer, and John Brophy. Whatever Martin's talents as a union leader may have been, they did not lie in the realm of negotiation, as had already been amply demonstrated by the beginning of the GM strike. He was impatient and unpredictable, and he did not always grasp the relationship between the specific language to be embodied in an agreement and union objectives. Brophy tried to give him "some sense of trade union order and direction," but it was a hopeless task, and in the end Martin had to be removed from the negotiations. Mortimer was an experienced trade unionist and was intimately familiar with shop conditions, but he lacked the personality and the flair for the dramatic to play a leadership role in the negotiations. Brophy in the strike talks spoke for John L. Lewis, with whom he was in frequent contact, and he conveyed to union negotiators Lewis' advice to stand firm and to take a "hard line" on the representation issue.[2]

Following the UAW's capture of the Chevrolet No. 4 plant, Lewis himself came to Detroit to take charge of negotiations for the union, and in the final talks it was Lewis, Pressman, and Mortimer who represented the UAW. It was the presence of Lewis, Pressman, Brown, and Smith in the negotiations that prompted Knudsen to complain to Mortimer, not altogether jocularly one suspects, "This is a hell of a committee. It's all lawyers and coal miners, no auto workers." Lewis, bringing his immense bargaining talents and histrionic skills to the negotiations, never lost sight of the significance of a UAW breakthrough in the auto industry to the future of the CIO.

Pressman was at the time "the prime agent and leg man" for Lewis and his "closest advisor in general CIO and related matters."[3]

Frances Perkins directed such efforts as were made by the federal government to resolve the dispute, but Franklin D. Roosevelt played a larger role behind the scenes than was evident at the time. The secretary of labor reported in her memoir of the New Deal that both the President and she thought that GM was being rather "stuffy" in refusing to negotiate before its plants were evacuated. The President did not regard the sit-down as legal, but he did not believe in the use of "marching troops" against workers who had violated only the law of trespass.[4] His reluctance to involve himself directly in the dispute stemmed from his unwillingness to commit his prestige to the resolution of the strike when the intransigence of the parties made the chances for success appear problematical at best, his awareness that his intervention in the automobile labor dispute of March, 1934, had in the end antagonized organized labor, and his disinclination to become entangled in the fratricidal conflict between the AFL and the CIO. William Green was to charge publicly late in the strike that the President had done everything for the strikers "except call out the Marines," but the AFL president told his Executive Council the next day that Roosevelt had assured him on several occasions that he would not side with "the group," meaning the CIO, and that the President's word would have to be accepted in the absence of evidence to the contrary.[5]

The sit-down strike in the end was to be settled not in Washington but in Detroit, and here the role of mediator was successfully undertaken by Frank Murphy. Michigan's governor was well suited for the part. He enjoyed the confidence of both organized labor and many of the automobile magnates, and he possessed the patience, the persistence, and the ability to restrain his temper required of the skilled mediator. He had prepared himself by the austere habits of a lifetime for the marathon bargaining that the settlement of the strike was to require, and he kept the talks going day and night until the weary negotiators resolved their differences. "He has the most excellent capacity for work of any negotiator I have ever known," Knudsen commented when the strike was concluded.[6] As happened in other crises of his life, however, the physical and mental strain of the sit-down negotiations took its toll of the inwardly tense Murphy, and he would soon feel the need to seek repose in a warmer climate.

Murphy impressed upon the union and the management that there was "a third party" in the dispute, the people of Michigan, to whom consideration must be given and that it was the governor of the state who spoke for this party. The outbreak of a strike in a highly industrialized society, he had long believed, was a symptom of trouble in the body politic that required the intervention of government. "These difficulties in the days of mass production," he declared during the GM sit-down, "are no longer private affairs. The government must play a helpful part." His concern was less the right or wrong of the sit-down than it was the settlement of the dispute by the "method of reason" and without the use of force. His strategy was to keep the talks going in the hope that somehow a solution would be found. "It must and will be settled peaceably, around the conference table," he declared as the negotiations got underway. The question at issue, he stated later, was "whether supposedly intelligent and reasonable men could settle a dispute peacefully or whether they must revert to the stupid, thoroughly futile method of violence."[7]

Murphy, it is evident, regarded the sit-down as an illegal trespass. He so advised union representatives privately throughout the strike negotiations and indicated as much publicly in his statements following the Battle of the Running Bulls.[8] Murphy, however, was not inclined to "rely on strict legalism or a conformist attitude toward the law, but tried to go deeply into questions of justice." To be sure, he had stated when he was assistant district attorney that public officials had "no possible excuse for deviation from their duty to strictly enforce all laws," but while lecturing in the 1920's on the criminal law, he had made it clear that he did not view an action as evil simply because it was forbidden by law. He came to see the law not as "a set of rigid rules" but as a flexible code by which men lived, and he thought that it was "justice ... rather than its form" that men "must love."

Murphy believed that if the strikers had sinned they had also been sinned against and that GM in refusing to abide by the NLRA was itself violating the law of the land and had, to a degree, provoked the employee reaction about which it was complaining. He saw the strike as the symptom of "a vast social readjustment" taking place in American life and therefore sought to persuade GM that the occupation of its factories went "deeper into social and economic questions than the ordinary violation of legal rights to protection of use and enjoyment of private property."

Like some others at the time, Murphy seems to have believed that although the sit-down was illegal under existing law, it might at some later date receive legal sanction. He thus remarked to union negotiators at one point during the strike, "It is realized that what today may be a mere claim of equity, tomorrow may obtain recognition of law." The idea that a worker has a right to his job undoubtedly had a certain appeal for Murphy, and he was probably interested to learn in this regard that the sit-down, according to the *Catholic Worker*, had "eminent defenders" in the Catholic church and that his favorite philosopher, Jacques Maritain, regarded the tactic as "morally" just.[9]

The exact status of the sit-down under Michigan's criminal law, as has been noted, was by no means clear, and Murphy was content to have the matter resolved at a later time in a "more judicial atmosphere." Murphy's close friend and legal advisor, Edward G. Kemp, who had more conventional views of law and order than the governor did, definitely regarded the tactic as a criminal trespass and believed that public authority must be employed to protect the legal rights involved, but he advised Murphy late in January that both he and the attorney general of Michigan, Raymond W. Starr, agreed that the initiative in dealing with the sit-down must come from local authorities, to whom the parties involved could turn for aid. Local officials, on the "proper showing of fact and complaint," could not only provide relief by injunction but could also arrest persons guilty of criminal trespass, "the State standing by to enforce peace and order." GM, to be sure, had secured an injunction from Judge Black, but the writ had been thoroughly discredited, and neither the corporation nor local authorities had sought its enforcement. Thus, although Murphy was being criticized in some circles for failure to enforce the law and to secure obedience to a court order, neither GM nor Flint officials, as the end of January neared, were pressing the point, and the company had not sought a writ of attachment calling for the arrest of sit-downers who had violated the Black injunction.[10]

Although Murphy regarded the sit-down as illegal, he was disinclined to apply a remedy that would result in bloodshed or the loss of life. The assertion that the liberal places human rights above property rights has become an almost meaningless cliché, but it is nonetheless an accurate characterization of Murphy's position with regard to the enforcement of the law in the sit-down strike: he was not prepared to take the kind of forcible action to protect property rights that might have resulted in the death of some of the strikers. "I abhor violence," he wrote to the Reverend R. M. Atkins on January 9, "and you may be sure that the State of Michigan will do everything honorably within its power to prevent it." "I would have relinquished my post as governor to prevent a fatality during the strike," Murphy declared when the dispute came to a close.[11]

Murphy was reinforced in his reluctance to use troops against trespassers who were "peacefully occupying their place of employment" by the knowledge that GM shared his views and feared that the loss of life in the strike might adversely affect the well-being of the corporation and the sale of its cars for years to come. Knudsen publicly stated that GM wanted the strike settled by negotiation rather than by violence, and GM officials told Murphy privately that they did not want the strikers "evicted by force." As Murphy's executive secretary later remembered the governor's account of the conversation, Lawrence Fisher remarked to Murphy at one point during the strike, "Frank, for God's sake if the Fisher ... brothers never make another nickel, don't have bloodshed in that plant. We don't want to have blood on our hands. . . . just keep things going . . . it'll work out." Bloodshed in the occupied plants, the Fisher brothers felt, would "besmirch their entire record for managing plants."[12]

In serving as a mediator during the sit-down strike Murphy was influenced not only by his view of the law and his abhorrence of violence but also by his long-standing sympathy for organized labor, his commitment to civil liberties, and his political ambition. As he wrote to a friend just after the strike, "I am not entirely in sympathy with sit-down strikers as such, but I am in sympathy and deeply so with the worker and feel that he is justified in using the means at his disposal to safeguard his rights." Murphy was willing to overlook at least some transgressions by labor since it was not accustomed to the exercise of power, but he was concerned about the infiltration of outsiders into the occupied plants, regarding this as "morally repulsive."[13]

Like most civil libertarians in the 1930's, Murphy probably viewed the right of employees to organize and to bargain collectively through representatives of their own choosing as a civil liberty, and he was sensitive to GM's invasion of that right. He was no doubt disturbed by the sweeping terms of the Black and later the Gadola injunction, and he was properly impressed by the complaints of the Conference for the Protection of Civil Rights and the American Civil Liberties Union concerning the strike tactics of GM and Genesee County officials. He thus sent troops into Flint not simply to preserve law and order but also to protect the civil liberties of the strikers, and his action was consequently applauded by the American Civil Liberties Union, which normally opposed the intervention of militia in labor disputes.[14]

As a political leader ambitious for still higher office, Murphy, who had great respect for the potential of the labor vote, did not wish to take any action in the strike that might cost him labor support in future elections. He appreciated that the manner in which he played his role as mediator in the strike might "make or break him politically," and he undoubtedly shared the view of one of his close friends that his use of force in the dispute would have been "contrary to the public interest" had it impaired his future as "a national leader."[15]

Before the Battle of the Running Bulls peace efforts were initiated by Frances Perkins in Washington and Murphy, aided by three Department of Labor conciliators, in Michigan. The secretary of labor conferred separately with John L. Lewis and GM officials on January 2, but she reported after these talks that she had not "seen a way to settlement." Mediation efforts by Perkins and Assistant Secretary of Labor Edward McGrady in the next several days were no more productive of results. Governor Murphy first became involved in the dispute on January 4, when Brophy, Germer, Martin, Hall, Mortimer, Pressman, and Davidow rode with him on the train between Detroit and Lansing "to explain the strike situation." After arriving in the state's capital city, the governor indicated that his administration would always be "available" to preserve the public peace and that he was giving thought as to how he might be helpful in the dispute without "intruding."[16]

During the next several days Murphy, assisted by Conciliator James F. Dewey, conferred separately and at length with GM officials and the UAW board of strategy in an effort to devise a formula that would lead to the beginning of negotiations. GM during the course of these talks, undoubtedly prodded by Murphy, who seems to have sided with the UAW on this issue, and perhaps realizing that its position was untenable, retreated from its previous insistence that bargaining on the UAW's January 4 proposals must be at the local level and agreed to meet with the union at the summit to discuss such of its proposals as involved general corporate policy; but this was to occur only after the sit-down strikers had evacuated the corporation's plants. This met the substance of the UAW's demand for a national conference with GM, but, lacking confidence in the good faith of the corporation, the union would agree to abandon the sit-down only if it received certain guarantees regarding GM's behavior during the course of the negotiations that would follow the surrender of the occupied plants. GM would have to promise that it would not operate these plants until an agreement was reached with the union, that it would not remove any machinery from the plants, that it would cease all hostile activity directed against the union, such as the circulation of loyalty petitions, the organization of vigilantes, and the intimidation of union workers, that it would withdraw the injunction, and that it would accept the UAW as the exclusive bargaining agency for the corporation's employees. The UAW wanted GM to sign an agreement embodying these commitments or to accept the union's conditions in the presence of Murphy and Dewey, thus making them, in effect, parties to the agreement.[17]

GM was willing to keep the struck plants closed while negotiations were underway, but it was not about to agree to all of the union's preconditions for ending the sit-down. Knudsen appeared ready to yield on the crucial issue of exclusive representation, but he did not speak for GM on this question. The AFL's intervention in the dispute on January 7 in opposition to the grant by the corporation of exclusive bargaining rights to the UAW and the appearance on the same day of the Flint Alliance doubtlessly served to harden the GM position, and the UAW, aware that the corporation would not retreat on this issue, capitulated and decided not to press its demand for exclusive bargaining rights until the formal peace talks were initiated.[18]

Neither side was inclined to permit the injunction or discrimination issues to stand in the way of an armistice, but they could not reconcile their differences regarding the far more important question of the removal of materials from the struck plants. GM refused to promise the union that it would not withdraw needed tools and dies since to commit itself in this way, the company averred, would compromise its right to dispose of its property as it saw fit; but GM was willing to state to Governor Murphy that it had no intention of taking this action. GM's position on this matter is difficult to understand since the agreement not to operate certain of its plants, which it was seemingly willing to make, was as much a restraint on its property rights as an agreement not to remove materials from these plants would have been.

What GM was willing to state concerning the withdrawal of materials from the struck plants was not good enough for the UAW, which attached great importance to this matter because of what had happened at the Toledo Chevrolet plant following the 1935 strike and because of the union's contention that a threatened removal of dies had precipitated the Fisher Body No. 1 sit-down. Murphy sought a way out of the impasse on January 8, but a conference with the union that extended into the early hours of the next day failed to break the stalemate, and the talks collapsed. This, apparently, did not displease Lewis, who claimed to be "running the show" and who had advised the UAW not to leave the plants since GM would bring in strikebreakers if the discussions after the evacuation did not lead to a settlement.[19]

The failure of the initial negotiations to settle the strike intensified the animosity of the strike leadership toward GM. Adolph

Germer, far more cautious on the strike issue than UAW officials were, was now convinced that GM was "determined to break the union," and Brophy and he agreed that the union had no alternative but to "take a firm and bold stand and show no signs of surrender."[20]

Believing that it had proved its reasonableness by agreeing to bargain with the union on the basis of the January 4 demands if the occupied plants were evacuated, GM may have concluded that the public at large and public authorities would now support the corporation in its use of self-help and the Flint police to regain its illegally held property.[21] If GM were implicated in any way in the series of events in Flint on January 11 that culminated in the Fisher No. 2 riot, its assumption that the nature of the talks that had collapsed on January 9 had placed it in a favorable light as compared to the union could very well explain its behavior.

The Battle of the Running Bulls led Murphy to send the National Guard and the state police into Flint. In a statement on the morning of January 12 the governor explained that neither party to the dispute would be permitted "by recourse to force and violence ... to add public terror to the existing economic demonstration." The state, he indicated, had not wished to "countenance *the unlawful seizure of private property*" but had refrained from taking "strong measures" heretofore because it had hoped that there would be an amicable settlement of the dispute. Since, however, he had now been advised that the situation was beyond the control of local authorities and the two parties to the dispute, he had ordered state police and National Guard units to hold themselves in readiness to support local authorities and to take such actions as were "needful." Murphy declared that the troops would be used "only to protect the public interest and preserve peace and order" and that "[u]nder no circumstances" would they "take sides."[22]

The next day, when additional Guard units were mobilized, Murphy, in another public statement, asserted that the dispute involved "an important question of law observance and interference with the rights of private property." He emphasized that "the public peace and safety are paramount, and the public authority must prevail at all costs." He pleaded for a "return to the rule of reason" and urged both parties to attempt to resolve the dispute and to bring an end to "the present anomalous situation, which is incompatible with American principles of law and order and ought not to be countenanced."[23]

Murphy's statements of January 12 and 13 leave no doubt that he regarded the sit-down strike tactic as illegal. They also reveal his determination to use the power of the state to preserve peace and order in the strike, but only for that purpose. If the state had to deploy its armed forces in the strike, it must do so, the governor believed, in a neutral manner. Opponents of the governor's course of action would charge, however, that his policy of neutrality was really a pro-strike policy, that it was his obligation to "take sides" in the dispute by employing the power of the state to restore private property to its rightful owners, and that despite his claim of preserving peace and order he was, in effect, using the National Guard to protect "an outrageous manifestation of disorder."[24]

In line with his efforts to quiet the turmoil in Flint and to prevent a recurrence of the events of January 11, Murphy, as we have seen, requested GM not to deny heat, water, light, and food to the strikers, a request that the company declared it would honor. At the same time he urged strike leaders to obey the law and to refrain from "inflammatory acts and utterances," and he informed them that he would not tolerate "hordes of outside agitators and strong-arm men coming into Michigan to cause violence."[25]

Murphy also sought to deal with a potentially dangerous problem created when Flint municipal court judges, with the approval of Genesee County's prosecuting attorney, Joseph R. Joseph, issued three hundred John Doe warrants authorizing the arrest of Fisher Body No. 2 strikers on the charges of kidnapping GM plant guards, malicious destruction of property while rioting, felonious assault, and criminal syndicalism. Since John Doe warrants authorized the police, as Germer put it, to "pick up and arrest anybody and everybody," the strike leaders were understandably concerned when they learned on the morning of January 12 that the warrants had been issued. A delegation of UAW and CIO officials visited Joseph that day to discuss the matter and also to urge him to secure warrants against Chief of Police Wills, Boysen, the publisher of the Flint *Journal*, and GM officials for their alleged complicity in the riot. During the course of the ensuing conversation Joseph let it slip that he owned GM stock—sixty-one shares as it turned out—which convinced Germer that the prosecutor was a "pliant tool" of the corporation and led the UAW to decide to seek his ouster just as it had sought the impeachment of Black.[26] Although Joseph held only a small block of GM stock, the UAW was able once again to point to the ties that bound local officials to GM and allegedly prevented them from acting in a disinterested manner in dealing with strike affairs.

Knowing from his experience as a criminal court judge that John Doe warrants were subject to abuse and concerned lest their use "provoke the sort of condition we are attempting to prevent," Murphy asked Joseph on January 12 to hold the warrants in abeyance and let it be known that neither the National Guard nor the state police, whose aid Joseph had requested, would be permitted to assist in serving the warrants without the governor's consent. Joseph, who would have needed the aid of the state to make large-scale arrests in Flint, reluctantly complied with Murphy's request.[27] Once again the governor had given evidence that he would seek to forestall violence in the strike and that he would use his influence to prevent public force from being used against the strikers.

The police did, however, arrest and jail the fourteen strikers injured on January 11. Wolcott, characterizing the prisoners as "dangerous men," deputized special guards to protect the jail, trained floodlights on the building at night, laid in machine guns and tear gas in preparation for a possible attempt by the strikers to free their comrades, and held the prisoners virtually incommunicado. Warrants were also out for the arrest of seven strike leaders, Victor and Roy Reuther, Travis, Kraus, and three out-of-towners, B. J. Widick and William Carney from Akron and Leslie Towner from South Bend.

UAW attorney Maurice Sugar discussed with Murphy on January 15 the issues raised by the actual and potential arrests of strikers and strike leaders, and the two men reached an understanding that Murphy would persuade Joseph to drop charges against the fourteen injured strikers but that the four strike leaders still in Flint—the three out-of-towners had by then left the city—would appear in court voluntarily without warrants being served on them and would then be released on bail. The explosive situation was defused on January 16 when the Reuthers, Travis, and Kraus came to court and were released on $500 bail each; and Joseph and Wolcott acceded to the governor's request to release the fourteen others so as not to endanger the truce just concluded between the union and the company. The examination of the four strike leaders was later deferred until February 18, by which time the strike was over.[28]

Although Murphy did not authorize the state police to be prepared to support local authorities in Flint until January 12, at an early date in the strike State Police Commissioner Oscar G. Olander, with the knowledge of the governor, had assigned two men to Flint, one of them an undercover investigator, to gather information on striker attitudes and other matters and to report to him nightly. After the Fisher No. 2 riot, a state police detail was organized in Flint which, consistent with the governor's objectives, was to keep "a watchful eye on the general conditions during the strike, to maintain a neutral position, to watch all factories, and to collect infomation that would aid in the prevention of bloodshed, and for the preservation of law and order." By January 16 the state police had thirteen men engaged in strike duty in Flint: ten troopers in five unmarked cars patrolled the city's industrial district; one detective sergeant was engaged in undercover work; and two detective sergeants served as contact men and were available for investigations.

As it turned out, the principal role of the state police in fulfilling its basic strike mission of keeping itself in a state of readiness to help preserve law and order was the gathering of information on such matters as the numbers of workers in the plants, the number of outsiders in Flint, and the attitude of strikers and nonstrikers in the city. The state police worked closely with the National Guard in Flint and also maintained contact with the city police, the sheriff's office, and the GM plant protection departments.[29] Whatever the personal preferences of the troopers assigned to Flint may have been, the state police, as the governor had instructed, maintained a neutral stance throughout the strike.

The National Guard began arriving in force in Flint on January 13. "Equipped with all the panoply of war," the Flint *Journal* reported on that date, "armed forces of the state of Michigan took command of the tense situation in Flint today." By the end of the day 1289 officers and men had reached the city, and by January 30 their number had risen to 2375. Most of the Guardsmen were youngsters in their late teens or early twenties, and they appeared to at least one observer to be taking their assignment as "a lark." Flint, understandably apprehensive after the riotous events of January 11, seemed relieved that the Guard had arrived.[30]

The strikers, despite at least one report to the contrary, were delighted when they learned that the Guard was being sent to Flint because they saw the troops as "the arm of the governor," whom they trusted. At a UAW meeting in Detroit on January 13 Travis secured the defeat of a motion calling for the withdrawal of the Guard by telling the unionists that Murphy had informed him that the troops would protect the strikers inside and outside the plants and would prevent the ejection of the sit-downers by local authorities. Similar information had been conveyed to Lewis by representatives of the governor.[31]

Some of the Guardsmen were themselves unionists, and a few of them had been participating in the strike. When one of the Cadillac sit-downers was ordered to join his Guard unit in Flint, the shop committee approved his leaving the plant because of its "great respect for law and order and the Michigan National Guard." In Flint the UAW sought to propagandize the Guardsmen by directing speeches at them from a sound car, distributing copies among them of the Flint *Auto Worker*, and having UAW veterans explain the union's objectives to them. The commanding officer of the Guard in Flint not surprisingly disapproved of these tactics, and at his request Travis had them discontinued.[32]

Anxious that the Guard remain neutral in the strike, Murphy did not entrust the command of the troops sent to Flint to the ranking officer of the Guard, General Heinrich Pickert, the police commissioner of Detroit. Murphy passed Pickert over not only because the Detroit official had other duties to perform and because Adjutant General John S. Bersey doubted his competence but because his "militaristic policies" as police commissioner and his alleged "brutality" against strikers had antagonized labor and civil-rights groups and had led them to demand his ouster, and Murphy was afraid to rely on his discretion in an emergency.[33] Murphy's choice for commanding officer was Colonel Joseph H. Lewis, commander of the 119th Field Artillery, a seasoned, unaggressive soldier who had once been a tool maker in an automobile plant. Born in 1888, Lewis had joined the Guard in 1908, had served with the militia in the Michigan copper strike in 1913, on the Mexican border in 1916, and in World War I, and had attended the Army War College and the Command and General Staff School for National Guard officers. In Flint, Lewis benefited from the advice of Samuel D. Pepper, a calm, deliberate man who had been judge advocate general of the state since 1908 and who was an authority on military law and the use of the Guard on riot duty.[34]

As Lewis assumed command in Flint, Bersey advised him that the governor had instructed that "no unnecessary force be used" by the Guard and was most anxious that "everything be done by the troops to avoid bringing on a conflict. He does not desire that anyone be shot or seriously injured." Murphy, Bersey informed Lewis, wanted the troops held in readiness for any eventuality, but he did not wish them to make "an unnecessary display" and hoped that they would provide an opportunity for an amicable settlement by preserving a "calm and peaceful attitude."[35]

In line with these instructions, Colonel Lewis sought to impress upon his men that the controversy between the strikers and GM was "a private fight" and that the Guardsmen must, "above all," remain neutral.

> Our mission here in Flint [he informed the Guard in the first bulletin issued to the men] is to protect life and property should the situation develop to a point where civil law enforcement agencies cannot do so. Unless and until such a situation develops, our task is that of mere watchful waiting. . . . We must not take

sides. We must lean backwards so as to avoid the semblance of seeming to take sides. Our troops include men of all walks of life and many of us are naturally sympathetic to one side or other. However, as long as we are in uniform, our personal leanings must be made secondary.[36]

In an effort to avoid involvement in the strike, the Guard leadership sought to discourage any contact between Guardsmen and civilians unless this was required in the performance of assigned duties. The troops were warned to ignore heckling by civilians and to express no opinions on the strike, and except for short-term passes given a few men at a time, they were confined to their quarters when not on duty. The men were "kept very strictly in the background," and as a La Follette Committee investigator observed, "one could stay in Flint for days and not realize that the National Guard was there." Despite the restrictions imposed upon them, however, some Guardsmen obviously did establish contact with civilians: at least four of the soldiers were exposed to venereal disease during their stay in Flint.[37]

The Guardsmen arriving in Flint a few days after the Battle of the Running Bulls were housed in publicly owned structures—school buildings, the Berston Field House, Haskell Community House, and Lakeside Coliseum. One thousand of them spent two nights in an old junior high school building whose lavatory facilities were so inadequate that a straddle trench latrine had to be dug outside the property, which was near the central business district of Flint. When additional troops were ordered to Flint after February 1, they were quartered in the county jail, three privately owned buildings, and the IMA Auditorium.[38]

The closely restricted Guardsmen were entertained by movies and plays put on for them by Flint school children; and reading material was made available to them by the Flint *Journal*, Flint citizens, and by the Guard itself, which published its own bulletin. At the start of their service in Flint, the morale of the men suffered because they were concerned, in view of the inadequacy of the state's legislation on the subject, about the possible loss of their jobs, the forfeiture of property on which they could no longer make payments, and the distress that their families would suffer. To meet this problem the Guard had the men fill out questionnaires detailing their individual conditions, and the Flint Chamber of Commerce then cooperated with Guard and state officials in requesting employers to assure the men that their jobs would be waiting for them when their tour of duty was completed and to make up the difference between civilian and military pay, asking credit agencies to suspend collections on time and loan payments, alerting welfare agencies to the needs of the families of the soldiers, and contacting educational institutions to secure consideration for soldiers who were missing their classes. The agencies and individuals contacted responded sympathetically to these requests with the result that the problem of morale was "greatly alleviated."[39]

In an effort to prepare for action should it become necessary to quell a civil disturbance, the area commander marked out three major areas of possible trouble in the city, each designated as an "Importance": Importance #1 included the Chevrolet complex and Fisher Body No. 2; Importance #2, Fisher Body No. 1; and Importance #3, the Buick plant and the downtown factory of AC Spark Plug. Lewis then directed Colonel Thomas Colladay, the commanding officer of the 63rd Brigade, which included the 125th and 126th Infantry, to prepare a plan for the tactical employment of the troops should trouble develop in any of the Importances. The plan Colladay devised called for the use of assault, support, and reserve battalions in each of the Importances to deal with an emergency. The troops, without experience in this type of assignment, received intensive training in the methods of riot control, and tests were conducted to determine the speed with which they could be moved to particular plants should their services be required.[40]

A good deal of the work of the Guard in Flint, like the activity of the state police, consisted in the gathering of intelligence. G-2 of the Guard sought to collect information on individuals, groups, and organizations whose activities might jeopardize peace and order in the city. It used plain-clothes operatives and undercover agents, intercepted strikers' radio messages, developed a number of "civilian contacts," and exchanged information with the state and local police. The Guard also sought by means of aerial reconnaissance to keep itself informed of any unusual activity in the Flint industrial area.[41]

When the Guard first arrived in Flint, Colonel Lewis was apparently under the impression that his force, in accordance with the traditional interpretation of the relevant statutes, was at the disposal of the responsible local authorities. His first field order specified that "upon official request of competent civil authorities to these headquarters for aid in quelling Major civil disturbances, this command will advance upon affected area or areas and restore peace and order." Lewis and his staff conferred with Olander, Wolcott, and Wills two days later, and they agreed that in the event of rioting the Guard would be responsible for the restoration of order in the affected areas whereas the city police, aided by the state police and the sheriff's office, would control traffic and guard strategic points. This agreement assigned the Guard a more active role in the dispute than Murphy had intended, and so he advised Bersey on January 19 that the troops were to be used in Flint "only after development of trouble and inability of local authorities to handle [it]."[42]

Murphy's instructions of January 19 made it clear that the Guard was not to act immediately in the event of civil disturbance in Flint, but the governor left unanswered the question as to whether the troops could be ordered into action by local authorities. Pepper and Lewis conferred with Murphy in Detroit on this matter on January 26, and the governor told them that the Guard was under his jurisdiction, had not been turned over to local authorities, and was not to "move" without first advising him and securing additional instructions. The state law on the subject, members of the attorney general's staff stated in a memorandum the next day, provided that the Guard was subject to the direction of the sheriff or other civil officials requiring aid but the means employed to accomplish the purpose for which the troops had been called out were to be determined by the governor.[43] The law was thus more than a little ambiguous on the subject of where jurisdiction over the Guard lay, but Murphy, anxious to avoid any precipitate action by the Guard, undoubtedly mistrustful of Flint officials, and recalling his experience as governor-general of the Philippines, was determined that the finger on the trigger should be his alone.

Although Murphy had sent the Guard into Flint, he never wavered in his determination that the strike must be settled by negotiation, not by force. Agreeing with Murphy, Knudsen stated that there was nothing in the UAW's demands that could not be "straightened out" by discussion locally and in Detroit. Like Murphy, he did not want the Guard to evict the strikers. "I don't want that now," he said. "No, I don't like that."

The UAW, for its part, was not averse to talking with GM, but it did not want the events of January 11 to be forgotten. Lewis stated that GM, through the Liberty League, had tried to drive Roosevelt from office, and it was now seeking to drive organized labor from its plants, and he demanded, but failed to secure, a Congressional investigation of the strikebreaking activities and financial structure of the corporation. Travis and Delmar Minzey wired GM strikers outside of Flint that injunctions and tear gas had failed to "crush" the spirit of the Flint unionists and that they were "all the more determined to carry on our fight to complete victory." The successful defense put up by the strikers actually proved to be a spur to the UAW's membership in Flint. "They just flocked down to the union hall and joined," one unionist remembered.[44]

Murphy on January 12 formally invited GM and the UAW to confer with him on January 14 "without condition or prejudice, in an effort to find a basis of agreement, tentative or otherwise, that will avoid the possibility of further disorders and permit early resumption of work." Both sides accepted the governor's offer, with GM advising Murphy that it did not wish to participate in joint conferences with the union but only in separate conferences with him and reiterating that it would not negotiate with the strikers until its plants had been evacuated. The corporation was attempting to draw a distinction between talks that would lead to the evacuation of its plants, in which it was willing to engage, and negotiations regarding the UAW's January 4 demands, which it would consent to undertake only after its property had been restored.[45]

When Knudsen, Smith, Brown, Martin, Mortimer, and Brophy sat down together at a table in Murphy's office in Lansing on January 14 at 11:00 A.M., it was the first time that the union and management high commands had met face to face since the sit-down in the Cleveland Fisher Body plant. Murphy declared in an opening statement that the dispute must be settled "in accordance with the principles of law and order" and, referring obliquely to his belief that the sit-down was illegal, stated that no one should seek to place him "in the position of suspending the law of the land." He wanted the parties to settle their differences by "peaceful negotiation" and collective bargaining, "without prejudice to legal rights as established by law," rather than by "rioting, threats, and intimidation," and he thought that they could more readily reach an understanding if they first conferred together "frankly and directly." If, however, either one or both of them wished to proceed through an intermediary, he had no objection.

In the discussions that ensued, GM and UAW representatives conferred directly with one another for part of the time, GM thus receding from its objections to face-to-face negotiations with the union; and for the remainder of the time the two groups met in separate offices, with Murphy "taking the proposals and concessions of one to the other and then returning with compromises or suggestions." The union negotiators conferred once or twice with members of the board of strategy, who were waiting in an anteroom of the governor's office, and Brophy kept in touch with Lewis by phone. Murphy described the tenor of the talks as "perfect—no bitterness—only a spirit of cooperation."[46]

The position of the UAW in the Lansing talks was that it was willing to negotiate with GM on the basis of the status quo or to evacuate the plants it occupied subject to the conditions it had previously set forth. If Murphy followed the notes that he took with him to the conference, which had undoubtedly been prepared by Kemp, he advised that the strikers should voluntarily withdraw, without conditions, from the plants that they occupied, since they were in "unlawful possession" of the company's property, but that GM should simultaneously agree to the union's conditions or should at least state its intentions with regard to these matters. As before, the most difficult question to resolve was the right of GM to withdraw tools and dies from the struck plants after their evacuation and while negotiations for a settlement were underway. GM remained unwilling to commit itself on this point, and so Murphy apparently recommended that the corporation simply state its intentions regarding this question and that the union accept this in good faith. Murphy's proposal broke the deadlock on this issue.[47]

With respect to the negotiations that would take place once evacuation of its plants had occurred, GM declared itself ready to bargain at the summit on the thirty-hour week, seniority, and the nature of representation, and it seems to have recognized the possibility that the union's other demands, which the corporation insisted involved the policies of local plants, might also raise some questions concerning general corporation policy that could then become the subject of top-level consideration. The UAW, however, wanted GM simply to state that it would bargain with the union on the January 4 demands without any distinction being made in the agreement between general and local demands, and the union view on the subject prevailed.[48]

Brophy, abetted by Lewis, who talked to Martin by phone, thought that the UAW should not agree to evacuate the plants it held until negotiations on the January 4 demands had been completed since it would be surrendering its strongest weapon in advance of the talks with management. Brophy later wrote that the UAW negotiators did not follow CIO advice on this point because they were "wobbly," had been "worn out" by the lengthy talks, and were "unsure of their ability to hold the line";[49] but the UAW from early January had expressed its willingness to abandon the sit-down under certain conditions, and when GM met most of these conditions, the union could not very well have refused to pull its men from the plants until a contract with the management had been negotiated.

Shortly after 3:00 A.M. on January 15 Murphy emerged from the conference, his face showing the strain of the prolonged discussions that had begun thirteen hours earlier, his voice hoarse, to announce that the negotiators had "arrived at a peace"; and the terms of the agreement, which took the form of a letter from Knudsen, Smith, and

Brown to Murphy, were formally announced at 4:30 A.M. Since the UAW had agreed to evacuate the Fisher Body plants in Flint, Guide Lamp in Anderson, and Cadillac and Fleetwood in Detroit[50] "as soon as practicable" and before January 18, GM, the letter stated, would meet with the union on January 18 to bargain on the proposals contained in its January 4 letter. The corporation stated that it would continue its policy of non-discrimination against workers because of their union affiliation and that during the period of negotiations it had no intention to, and would not, remove "any dies, tools, machinery, material (except for export trade[51]) or equipment" from any of the struck plants, and it would not resume operations in these plants during that time. The negotiations were to continue until an agreement could be reached, if possible, but the talks could be broken off after fifteen days if no settlement had been effected by then.[52] Just what would happen under these circumstances the letter did not state, but presumably the corporation would then seek to resume operations in the struck plants, which is probably why Brophy thought that the union had surrendered too much in the talks. The UAW may have assumed, however, that public opinion would definitely swing to its side if it were GM that broke off the talks.[53] The other terms of the agreement were presumably to remain in effect should the negotiations continue for more than fifteen days.

Having yielded on the subject of a general conference with the UAW and on meeting with the union prior to the evacuation of its plants, GM emphasized publicly that it had not retreated on the question of representation, which was not referred to in the agreement because of the inability of the negotiators to reconcile their differences on this issue.[54] "No rights of any worker not represented by the union," the corporation declared, "will be prejudiced in any of the proposed negotiations." Knudsen explained that the fifteen-day proviso had been included in the agreement so that negotiations would be "on a sensible basis" and the employees in the struck plants would not be kept from their jobs for too long a period. With this same reemployment objective in view, GM announced in releasing the terms of the January 15 agreement that in order to "alleviate distress" it would resume operations in plants that had not been struck but had been closed because of the shortage of materials created by the strike.[55]

In explaining the agreement to UAW officials and organizers, Martin contended that GM had recognized the union and that the basis had been laid for collective bargaining on a national basis. He cautioned, however, that the UAW had won only "the first skirmishes and that the real battle is ahead, for the strike is still on." Martin,

Addes, and Hall wired the sit-down strikers in Flint that the agreement was "a tremendous step in the right direction" and that the world was aware of the part that they had played in achieving this "most dramatic and important victory." UAW sound trucks in the city went through the streets proclaiming a union victory and urging GM workers to join the union so as "to share in the benefits of collective bargaining."[56]

The Flint strike leadership and some of the sit-in strikers as well did not accept Martin's interpretation of the agreement and did not understand why the union should be required to give up the occupied plants before a contract had been successfully negotiated with the company. " 'I don't see no sense in the boys moving out if that's all we got,' " a discouraged No. 2 picket declared, and Travis bluntly told Addes and Germer, "You don't win by quitting." After Powers Hapgood, Sugar, and Germer came into the No. 1 plant and characterized the agreement as a "Partial Victory" upon which the union could capitalize, the strikers, however, voted to leave the plant as a "body" on January 17 and then, as their minutes state, to "start organizing every employee of all Plants into [the] Union." The strikers wished to delay their exit from the plant until January 17 so as to demonstrate to GM that they were not "too anxious to get out."

The members of the by then closely knit strike community, proud of what they had accomplished and reluctant to share their "glory" with non-participants, were perturbed by fellow workers now coming into the factory for the first time since the sit-down began so as to be included among the strike heroes who would march out of the plant. One strike committee member thought that the new arrivals should be "set down," and it was also suggested that they be registered and named, but wiser heads pointed out that the UAW, as a "young organization," could not afford to "antagonize" members or potential members. It was therefore agreed that the stewards should pass on the new arrivals and should bring before the strike council any entrants deemed to be unsatisfactory.[57]

Observers publicly and privately accorded the chief credit for the January 15 truce to Governor Murphy. The Flint *Journal*, which reluctantly editorialized that Murphy had "done the state a great service," remarked that he had received the "greatest flow of congratulatory messages" ever received by a Michigan governor in a comparable period of time. Chrysler's B. E. Hutchinson thought that Murphy had done "an extraordinarily good job in a most difficult situation," and the Detroit *News,* not normally one of the governor's admirers, congratulated him for his "dogged insistence on the priority of the public interest." "However the play ends," the Republican

Battle Creek *Enquirer and Evening News* remarked, "Governor Murphy has displayed qualities of leadership and statesmanship during the first act."[58]

In accordance with the terms of the Lansing agreement, the sit-down strikers evacuated the Cadillac, Fleetwood, and Guide Lamp plants on January 16. The 208 Cadillac and forty-nine Fleetwood sit-downers, looking none the worse for their experience, were led in a parade outside the two plants by UAW officials and a twelve-piece Detroit Federation of Musicians band, and Walter Reuther directed them in song from a sound car:

> The boss is shaking at the knees,
> Parlez-vous.
> The boss is shaking at the knees,
> Parlez-vous.
> The boss is shaking at the knees,
> He's shaking in his B.V.D.'s.
> Hinky dinky parlez-vous.

The UAW was to charge the next day that Cadillac workers were receiving telegrams from GM to report to work on January 18 despite the company's agreement to keep the plant closed, but GM replied that it had informed the union negotiators that it would recall 135 men working on distribution and records and that Mortimer had agreed to this on the phone. The UAW insisted, however, that no UAW representative had made a commitment regarding the entry of the 135 workers and that Mortimer had agreed to the admission into the plant of only a few office workers.[59]

When the ninety-six sit-downers paraded from the Guide Lamp plant, they were led by a police motorcycle escort, their own band, and a visiting band from the Cleveland White Motor Company local. Fifteen minutes later, according to the UAW, 150 police and special deputies, including plant supervisory personnel, tore down the union's picket shacks and declared that no more picketing would be permitted. GM, however, secured a telegram from Mayor Baldwin stating that only fourteen police had been assigned to the plant and that peaceful picketing was being permitted but that the pickets had been warned not to restrain anyone wishing to enter the plant. The UAW's allegations were, as a matter of fact, "completely erroneous. Nothing of the sort happened . . . ," a Guide Lamp sit-down striker later wrote.[60]

Cadillac, Fleetwood, and Guide Lamp were, however, of only minor importance in the UAW's strike strategy as compared to the

Fisher Body plants in Flint, which were scheduled to be evacuated at 1:30 P.M. on January 17. As the hour of departure approached, the sit-downers cleaned the two plants and packed their belongings—they had been warned to keep their blackjacks out of sight—while outside the factories thousands gathered for the ceremonies that were to follow evacuation.[61] There was, however, to be no evacuation on January 17, and before the day was out the armistice that Murphy had arranged was to be repudiated by the UAW, allegedly because its terms had been violated by GM.

In accusing GM of "a double-cross" the UAW pointed to the events that had followed the evacuation of the Cadillac and Guide Lamp plants, but it was mainly concerned about GM's dalliance with the Flint Alliance. Following the announcement of the armistice terms, Boysen on the evening of January 15 wired Knudsen that he had been instructed by Flint Alliance representatives to advise GM that the "greatest majority" of the corporation's Flint employees would not be represented at the projected conference with the UAW, that they did not wish the UAW to speak for them, and that they wanted assurances that their position would not be overlooked in GM's dealings with "this small group." GM had already announced that it had made no concession to the UAW on the issue of exclusive representation, and so Knudsen wired Boysen on January 16 that he could assure his people that "no man's right to be represented by whomsoever he chooses will be denied. General Motors will never tolerate domination of its employes by a small minority."[62]

The Flint Alliance, whose membership was not limited to GM workers, had never before asked to meet with GM for collective-bargaining purposes nor to be represented in conferences that the corporation might hold with the UAW,[63] but after receiving Knudsen's January 16 wire, Boysen immediately asked for a GM-Flint Alliance meeting on January 19 to discuss collective bargaining as it affected the "vast majority" of GM's employees. To this request, Knudsen prepared a telegraphic reply stating: "We stand ready always to discuss with your group or any group of our employes any question without prejudice to anyone. We shall notify you as soon as possible as to time and place for a meeting."[64]

It is not clear at what time on January 17 GM had intended to release Knudsen's second wire to Boysen, but the UAW contended that the information was not to have been made public until after the two Fisher Body plants had been evacuated and that the union had become aware of the wire before the evacuation only because a reporter had inadvertently stumbled on it and passed the information on to the UAW. The newsman was William H. Lawrence, then working for the United Press, who had stopped "entirely by chance" in the Durant Hotel office of the Flint Alliance on the morning of January 17 and had there seen a copy of the press release announcing the Knudsen wire to Boysen. After contacting Floyd Williamson, the Alliance's publicity agent, who confirmed the information contained in the release, Lawrence proceeded to union headquarters to gain permission for a visit to Fisher Body No. 1 and "almost casually" told Travis of the release that he had seen. Travis, Lawrence recalls, simply "scoffed" at Boysen and advised Lawrence to hurry out to Fisher No. 1.[65]

Once John Brophy, in Detroit, learned of the Knudsen wire to Boysen—Travis presumably had passed on the information—he perceived that the UAW had been presented with a golden opportunity "to get rid of the absurd preliminary agreement." It is entirely likely that John L. Lewis, who had publicly stated that the agreement was "eminently satisfactory" but who privately shared Brophy's view of the terms, had urged his representatives in Detroit to find some pretext that would permit the agreement to be "kicked over." Brophy got in touch with Martin and urged him to call off the scheduled evacuation, but Martin was at first "non-commital" because, according to Brophy, he did not appreciate the significance of Knudsen's wire. Brophy finally persuaded Martin, however, and the UAW president then called Travis with instructions to suspend the evacuation.

Brophy and Martin then went to visit Governor Murphy. The governor, who had already indicated his displeasure at the intervention of "loyal" employees and organizations in the dispute, was, according to Brophy, "deeply distressed" by what he now learned. He called Knudsen and suggested that GM should cancel the arrangements with the Flint Alliance since they endangered the full implementation of the Lansing truce. Knudsen would not, however, yield to the governor's wishes.[66] The union strategy committee then met and decided against the evacuation of the Flint plants primarily, as Germer wrote in his diary, because the "slimey Boysen had messed things up."[67] Word was relayed to Flint, where Mortimer and others went into the No. 1 and 2 plants to explain what had occurred and to request the workers to remain at their posts, which they agreed to do. The UAW expressed its willingness to begin negotiations with GM on January 18, as scheduled, but since the corporation refused to bargain with the union until all its plants had been evacuated, the union decision not to surrender the Flint factories brought the Lansing truce to an end.[68]

The UAW insisted that GM, in agreeing to meet with the Flint

Alliance, had violated the January 15 terms since it had, in effect, eliminated as a subject for negotiation the chief of the union's January 4 proposals, namely, that the UAW be recognized as the exclusive bargaining agency for GM employees. The UAW had good historical reasons to distrust collective-bargaining pluralism, and its fears that the Flint Alliance might become a counter-organization seemed about to be realized, but the union was on shaky ground in accusing GM of bad faith on this issue. GM representatives had been emphatic before, during, and just after the promulgation of the January 15 agreement that the corporation had no intention of abandoning collective-bargaining pluralism and of speaking only to the UAW. In the ill-fated wire to Boysen, Knudsen had simply translated a general corporation policy into a specific commitment to meet for collective bargaining at some future time with an organization claiming to represent the overwhelming majority of GM's Flint employees. This was assuredly a blunder on GM's part since wisdom should have dictated the postponement of any decision to converse with organizations other than the UAW until the talks that were to begin on January 18 had run their course and since the Alliance was not, strictly speaking, a bona fide labor organization, but what GM had done was perfectly consistent with its oft-expressed policy regarding representation. Despite protestations of betrayal and of "a stupendous and dastardly double-cross,"[69] the UAW and the CIO could hardly have been surprised at the turn of events, and one suspects that they used Knudsen's offer to meet with Boysen as a convenient pretext to kill a truce arrangement whose terms at least some of the leadership were no longer willing to implement.

"It would be helpful," an indignant Murphy declared, "if civic bodies and all other organizations hold themselves in the background," and Boysen, understanding the governor's reference, stated that he would follow Murphy's advice insofar as it pertained to the Flint Alliance and would not press for an immediate conference with GM even though he would continue to represent the loyal workers of Flint.[70] It was too late, however, to resurrect the Lansing armistice. Some new formula would have to be found to resolve the dispute, and it was Frances Perkins who would now direct the search.

Perkins' efforts in Washington, initiated on January 19, were designed to bring Lewis and Sloan together on the assumption that they were "the real principals" in the dispute. On January 19 the secretary of labor, Dewey, McGrady, and Murphy conferred at length with Lewis, and Murphy offered to surround the Fisher Body plants with the National Guard while negotiations were underway if the UAW would evacuate the strikers.[71] Murphy's plan was intended, in effect, to reinstitute the January 15 truce and to use state troops to ensure its enforcement, but Lewis, who would accept a similar proposal during the Chrysler sit-down strike in March, 1937, was now determined not to surrender his strongest bargaining weapon until the company had yielded something of substance to the union. As long as the workers remained in the plants, GM could not resume production or defeat the strikers, but once the workers left the plants, the advantage, Lewis sensed, would rest with the company, which could marshal the necessary force to defeat an outside strike. Murphy was apparently angered by Lewis' intransigence, but he was careful to avoid criticism of the miners' chief in public.[72]

Frances Perkins told reporters after the long conference on January 19 that the "chief obstruction" in the path of a settlement was "[i]ntellectual trouble," by which she meant the refusal of Sloan to meet face-to-face with Lewis. The secretary of labor had phoned Sloan that afternoon to request that he confer with Lewis and her the next day, but the GM president, after considering the matter for four hours, agreed to a meeting with Perkins and Murphy but not directly with Lewis. Since Sloan had insisted that there be "absolute silence" on the subject, Perkins had a chauffeur meet the GM delegation of Sloan, Knudsen, Brown, and Smith when they arrived in Washington in a private railroad car; but the reporters discovered their presence in the city, and Sloan's hopes for a secret meeting were dashed. Murphy and Perkins conferred with the GM representatives throughout the afternoon of January 20—Perkins left the inauguration stand to participate in the conference, and Murphy was unable even to attend the inaugural ceremonies—and the discussions continued the next day. Sloan proposed that the struck plants be reopened and that any benefits the workers secured in the ensuing negotiations be made retroactive, and it is possible that he agreed not to bargain with any other group of GM employees until the bargaining with the UAW had been completed, but he was unyielding in his refusal to meet with Lewis until GM's plants had been evacuated.[73]

It appears that Murphy and Perkins in their talks with Lewis and Sloan asked them to consider some kind of an election plan as the means of ending the strike, but both the company and the union objected to a solution along these lines. Murphy favored a representation election under the NLRA, but for reasons already noted neither side was willing to submit to this test. Murphy then seems to have raised the possibility of an election conducted under the auspices of the state of Michigan, but Lewis, who was obviously unwilling to run the risks of any kind of election in view of the size of the UAW's membership, contended that GM would have an advantage in such an election because of its "intimidation machine." "The important thing," he later declared, "is we have enough men to close the plants and we have closed them."[74]

According to Brophy, Sloan, in the Washington conversations, was less interested in settling the strike than in having the administration condemn the sit-down as illegal. He seems to have been anxious to break off the talks, and it was John L. Lewis who provided him with the pretext to do so. Lewis and Martin had conferred with Perkins and Murphy during the morning of January 21, and then in the afternoon Lewis held a press conference in which he stated that the UAW would not surrender its "arms" and agree to a "half-baked compromise" that would permit GM to "double-cross" the strikers again. Lewis also indicated that he expected the administration to side with its supporters and not with its opponents. "We have advised the administration ...," he declared in his inimitable prose style, "that for six months the economic royalists represented by General Motors contributed their money and used their energy to drive this administration out of power. The administration asked labor for help to repel this attack, and labor gave its help. The same economic royalists now have their fangs in labor. The workers of this country expect the administration to help the workers in every legal way, and to support the auto workers in General Motors plants." When Perkins called Sloan later that night, he told her that the GM representatives were quitting Washington and that any further meetings were futile in view of what Lewis had said at his press conference.[75]

Secretary of the Interior Harold L. Ickes confided to his diary that the Lewis statement "sounded pretty raw," and the President apparently agreed with this judgment. When he was questioned about Lewis' remarks at his press conference the next day, Roosevelt replied, "Of course, I think that, in the interests of peace, there come moments when statements, conversations and headlines are not in order." Since the President permitted himself to be quoted, the press interpreted his remarks as a sharp rebuke to Lewis and concluded that the CIO head had blundered in a manner that belied his reputation as "a supreme labor tactician."

William Green told his Executive Council that "inside sources" had advised him that Lewis "resented" the President's remarks and was saying things about Roosevelt that were "not fit for publication," but actually the President's criticism was quite mild in tone, and Lewis, whose words may have been intended for the "troops in the field" as much as for the administration, was too shrewd to overreact to the President's words.[76] "Of course," he insouciantly declared the next day, "I do not believe the President intended to rebuke the working people of America who are his friends and who are only attempting to obtain rights guaranteed to them by Congress. . . ." This time it was GM that Lewis attempted to needle. Its "high command," he said, had again "run away" from a conference with the union. Sloan, Brown, and Knudsen had returned to New York "to consult their allies to determine how far they can go in their organized defiance of labor and the law." But Sloan would have to meet with him sooner or later. "Perhaps," Lewis observed, "he feels his intellectual inferiority to me."[77] Whatever Sloan's reaction to these remarks may have been, it was not for publication.

Annoyed at the failure of her informal efforts to bring GM and the UAW together and urged on by Sidney Hillman, who was seeking "to pick up the pieces" after the verbal exchange between Roosevelt and Lewis, Perkins on January 23 issued a formal invitation to the chief officers of GM and the UAW and to Lewis as the union's "principal advisor" to attend a conference in Washington on January 27, "without condition or prejudice," to consider a renewal of the negotiations agreed upon at Lansing. Lewis had no desire to reinstitute the Lansing agreement, but he accepted the secretary of labor's invitation to confer. Sloan, however, could not be budged: GM would not negotiate until its plants had been evacuated; and since the UAW was saying that there would be no evacuation until the company recognized it as the exclusive bargaining agency for GM workers, a conference would produce "no beneficial result." Sloan indicated in his reply to Perkins that GM's patience in the face of the illegal occupation of its property was running out and that if public authorities did not do something about the matter, GM might feel obliged to act on its own. "In the interest of peace" and at Murphy's request, he wrote, GM had made no effort to reopen its struck plants, but the corporation was gravely concerned about its many employees who had been thrown out of work through no fault of their own. "You can appreciate," he ominously wrote, "we have no intention to permit either technical considerations or personal feelings to interfere with anything that may lead to a solution of the problem of such grave consequences, actual or potential, in which the public interest and innocent sufferers are so importantly involved."[78]

It was now Sloan's turn to be rebuked by the administration, and both the President and the secretary of labor left no doubt about their disapproval of his behavior. Sloan, the President told his press conference on January 26, and for quotation, had made "a very unfortunate decision." When informed that Sloan had indicated that he would respond affirmatively to an invitation from the President himself, Roosevelt, who seems to have regarded the GM president's obstinacy as a "personal affront," retorted "with some emphasis" that a representative of the President had extended the invitation.

Less guarded than the President, Perkins, her face "flushed" and making no effort to conceal her anger, accused Sloan of shirking his moral responsibility and ignoring the public interest. She could understand, she said, in view of the Flint Alliance imbroglio that had upset the Lansing truce why the UAW did not "trust the word" of GM. The corporation and its officials were "high-handed," and they had "made the mistake of their lives in failing to see the moral issues here and proceeding on them, rather than basing their position on a legal technicality and sulking in their tents." Characterizing the illegality of the sit-down as "unexplored," she read to the reporters an excerpt from a letter she had written but not sent to Sloan: "do unto others as you would have done unto you; agree with thine adversary quickly; forgive us our trespasses."[79]

Sloan, in effect, replied to Perkins the next day in a message to GM employees in which he made it explicit that he did not intend to "forgive" the union trespassers and, indeed, was likely to renew court action against them. "We propose to demonstrate," he wrote, "that these trespassers who have seized our plants and who have taken from you the privilege of working, have not the right to do so." GM was being falsely accused of responsibility for the breakdown of negotiations simply because it had refused to confer with "a group that holds our plants for ransom without regard to law or justice."[80] Perkins' response to the collapse of her efforts to bring the parties in the dispute together and also to news of the violence in Anderson on January 25 was to request Congress on January 27 to grant the Department of Labor the power to deal with strikes by subpoenaing the principal parties and forcing them to attend a negotiating conference.[81] That GM was the immediate target of the requested legislation was all too obvious.

In the next two days the secretary of labor made a final effort to persuade Sloan to meet with Lewis and the UAW. The GM president, undoubtedly at Perkins' request, made a secret visit to Washington on January 29 and had a two-hour talk with her. According to Perkins, he agreed to participate in a conference in Michigan that Murphy would arrange but then reneged on his promise. "In other words," she angrily declared, "he ran out on me." Sloan, however, gave a different version of what had occurred. The secretary of labor, he reported, had asked him if he were willing to return to the status of affairs that had obtained before Murphy had intervened in the dispute and attempt "to negotiate the men out of the plants." Sloan, according to his account, said that he would consider the proposal and give the secretary his answer the next morning, but he had called her from New York that night to tell her that he could not accept her proposal since GM desired a prompt return to work of its employees and had reinstituted court proceedings that day to regain its property.[82]

Whichever version of the Sloan-Perkins conversations of January 29 is correct, the GM president's rejection of the secretary of labor's proposal signaled the end of Washington's efforts to mediate the dispute and returned the initiative in peacemaking to Michigan's governor. The secretary of labor appeared to be "on the verge of tears" when reached by reporters in the early hours of January 30. "It seems," she unhappily but accurately declared, "that all of my work has gone to waste."[83]

The unproductive strike talks in Washington during the second half of January were damaging to GM from a public-relations point of view and in terms of its standing with the administration. Whatever advantage the company might have derived from the President's rebuke to Lewis, it more than lost by its stubborn refusal to meet the CIO leader. Whereas the President had dealt Lewis only a glancing blow, his criticism of Sloan had been "specific and personal," and the secretary of labor had been even blunter in her remarks about the GM president. "Sloan," the January 27 minutes of the Cleveland Fisher Body strikers read, "has been critisized [sic] by Roosevelt and Perkins. We are in a better position now."[84] Sloan not only succeeded in antagonizing the President and the secretary of labor, but he also made "an awfully poor impression" on the press by his clumsy efforts to conceal his presence in Washington and by the evasive answers he gave in the one press conference that he held.[85]

Sloan was primarily influenced in his intransigence by his view of unionism in general and the illegality of the sit-down strike in particular, but he may also have been persuaded to act as he did by the animosity that he felt for Roosevelt and the New Deal.[86] GM, despite the sage advice offered by Stephen M. DuBrul at the end of 1936, had not yet successfully adjusted to the change in the political climate that had occurred in Washington since 1933. The corporation, as Walter Lippmann wrote, was lacking in "industrial politicians."[87]

While efforts were underway in Washington to bring union and management representatives to the bargaining table, Flint was threatening to erupt once again into violence. The city had been "plunged in gloom" by the collapse of the January 15 armistice, and when Buick, which had been operating at about 65 percent of capacity, was forced to shut down completely on January 20, thus leaving only AC Spark Plug employees still at work among the city's GM workers,

Flint appeared to be on the verge of "economic breakdown." Under the circumstances, tension between the strikers and the loyal employees mounted, and a La Follette Committee investigator concluded that "civil war" was "not beyond the possibilities."[88]

GM did nothing to lessen the tension in Flint when it announced on January 22 that, insofar as it was able to carry inventory, it would implement its pledge of January 15 and seek to provide employment on a reduced basis for employees in strike-free plants who had been idled by the dispute. Knudsen insisted that GM's only motive in taking this action was the welfare of its employees; "Don't get the idea," he told reporters, "that this is a big strategic move of some sort." The UAW, fearful of the impact of a back-to-work movement, thought otherwise however, and strike leaders in Flint on January 24 threatened additional strikes if Buick and Chevrolet reopened.[89]

GM's plan called for a return to work at Chevrolet, except for employees on the final assembly line, on January 27. Seizing on this news, the Flint Alliance called a mass meeting on January 25 for the afternoon of the next day so that Flint's GM workers could vote on whether they favored "direct and forceful action" to secure the rights to which they were legally entitled. The UAW interpreted the Alliance bulletin announcing this meeting as an incitement to riot and violence, and there was grave concern in the city as to what would occur when pickets outside the No. 2 plant saw workers going into Chevrolet across the street.

Since "every one close to the situation" thought that Flint was a "powder keg," city officials sought to ascertain if the National Guard could be used to aid in keeping order in front of the Chevrolet plant, but Murphy urged that the threatened conflict should be avoided by agreement rather than by a show of force. Murphy's efforts to maintain the peace in Flint were, in effect, supplemented by La Follette Committee investigator H. D. Cullen, who sought to restrain the Flint Alliance by serving a subpoena on Boysen on January 25 and summoning him to his room, where Boysen gave assurances that he would not permit a "flare up" between the strikers and nonstrikers.[90]

Although there was fear in Flint that January 27 would be a day of war in the city, appropriate action taken on the preceding day insured that it would be a day of peace. In an effort to forestall possible violence, Prosecutor Joseph R. Joseph, at Murphy's telephoned request, summoned the strike leaders and Boysen to a conference with Bradshaw, Wills, Wolcott, and the prosecutor preceding the scheduled public meeting of the Flint Alliance. The rumors of impending violence caused many of the worried inhabitants of the city to remain in their homes that day, and Roy Reuther recalled that the streets were strangely deserted when Travis, some others, and he walked to the county courthouse for the meeting.

Joseph's attitude at the meeting, Cullen, who was present, reported, was "impartial and fair." He told the strikers' representatives and Boysen that he expected them to keep the peace. The union provided assurances that it would not interfere with the workers returning to Chevrolet and would not picket the plant, although Travis said that the UAW would not "tolerate" discrimination against any of the returning workers. Actually, the union was too weak to have prevented the return to work, and since it knew that GM could not produce Buicks or very many Chevrolets as long as the strikers could prevent the reopening of the Cleveland and Flint Fisher Body plants, there was little point in the UAW's challenging an action that might have compelled the National Guard to array the force of the state against the union.

Boysen, although stating that the "main objective" of the Alliance was to forestall violence, was quite belligerent at the meeting, but Joseph warned him that he would be arrested, just as union leaders would be, if he disturbed the peace. Reuther and Boysen engaged in what Cullen described as a "heated discussion" about the strike, and then the Flint Alliance leader, nettled by Reuther's taunts, stalked from the room and told the inquiring reporters waiting outside that they could " 'go to hell.' "[91] With a subpoena hanging over his head and Joseph's warning fresh in mind, Boysen, however, was not likely to engage in any provocative action.

The threat of a major disturbance in Flint on January 27 led to a second meeting on January 26, this one in Detroit, with Murphy, Colonel Lewis, Pepper, Olander, Germer, and Frank Martel in attendance. Murphy on this occasion not only advised Lewis that the Guard was not subject to the control of local authorities but made it perfectly clear that he would not use the militia to break the strike nor would he permit the kind of attack on unionists pursuing their legal rights as had occurred in Anderson. He called Bradshaw in Flint while the conference was in session to warn that he would not tolerate any disorder and to ask the mayor to urge loyal employees to avoid any action that might lead to violence.[92]

An "immense crowd" of more than eight thousand[93] attended the meeting of the Flint Alliance on January 26 that followed the Joseph conference in Flint and the Murphy conference in Detroit. The Alliance itself, its motives having been brought into question by public authorities, remained in the background, and when a somewhat subdued Boysen spoke, he pleaded with the audience, "Please don't fight anybody. We'll do it in a legal way. . . ." There were some incendiary remarks made by other speakers, most of them members of the bargaining agencies surviving from the days of the ALB. One speaker, the oldest retired Buick employee in Flint, advised the crowd to "get all that riff raff that came from Toledo and Detroit out of here" and to "go to the plants . . . and get those boys out of the plants." Sanford Rasbach, a Buick worker, attacked Murphy for condoning the illegal occupation of private property and secured the approval of the audience by a voice vote for the dispatch of a committee to the governor to pose the question, "Will you guarantee all workers full protection in going to and coming from work?" The *I.M.A. News*, with its penchant for extreme statements, interpreted the "yes" response when the audience was asked if it favored the resumption of work as "the voice of America and not the voice of Moscow," and Russell Porter thought that the size of meeting proved that the "overwhelming majority" of the idle Flint workers wanted to return to their jobs.[94]

The UAW claimed that the Alliance meeting was rigged, that the chairman had arbitrarily ruled that the ayes were in the majority when the voice votes were taken even though this appeared uncertain, that union members had been denied the floor, and that the attacks on Murphy and John L. Lewis by various speakers had been poorly received. Cullen, who saw Flint events through the union's eyes, thought that the Flint Alliance had had "all the wind taken out of its sails" by the announcement that Boysen had been subpoenaed and the fact that the UAW did not intend to interfere with the return to work and that the meeting itself had been "a flop."[95] It is reasonable to assume, however, that a large majority of the nonunionists among Flint's GM workers were ready to return to work under conditions obtaining before the sit-down began even though this meant the defeat of the strike. Russell Porter was probably closer to the truth regarding the significance of the meeting than the UAW and Cullen were.

About forty thousand Chevrolet workers across the land returned to their jobs on January 27, almost eleven thousand of them in Flint. A UAW sound car and a few union pickets were on hand in the bitter cold in front of the Flint Chevrolet complex, and the National Guard, which had devised plans for a possible disturbance, was on the alert, but there was no disorder of any sort.[96] Murphy had demonstrated once again that Flint was not Anderson, but he was himself coming under increasing pressure to take some action that would bring the sit-down in Michigan to an end. On January 27 a resolution was introduced in the Michigan Senate asking the governor to explain why he had not used his power to uphold a court order and "the dignity of this state."⁹⁷ What the legislature and the friends of law and order ignored, however, was that GM itself regarded the Black injunction as a dead letter, and neither it nor Flint officials up to that time had asked the governor for assistance in enforcing the writ. GM, however, taking the offensive in an effort to defeat the strike, supplemented its back-to-work movement by going into Judge Paul V. Gadola's court in Flint on January 28 in quest of a new injunction. Judge Gadola ordered a hearing on the GM petition for February 1 and directed Martin and the other UAW officials named to show cause at that time why the injunction should not be issued.⁹⁸

On the same day that GM renewed its plea for an injunction a committee headed by Sanford Rasbach visited Murphy to pose the question agreed upon at the Flint Alliance meeting of January 26. The governor, who had already stated that if the resolution applied to struck plants he was definitely opposed to it, refused to give a yes or no answer to the query and told the committee that the Alliance had been at least partly responsible for the breakdown of negotiations and that it should not attempt to "embarrass or compromise" his efforts to find a peaceful solution for the strike. When Rasbach complained, "That's an awfully poor answer to take back when our streets are not safe," Murphy retorted, "I might say that yours was not a very good question." The governor wanted to make sure that there was no misunderstanding regarding his position. "Nothing in the world," he said, "is going to get the Governor of Michigan off the position of working it out peacefully. All the power of General Motors or the Flint Alliance or Mr. Lewis's organization is insufficient to get the Governor of Michigan off that path."⁹⁹

That same day Murphy received a resolution allegedly bespeaking the opinion of fifty thousand GM employees in Michigan that called upon him to order a plebiscite among GM workers to ascertain if they desired to return to work while negotiations were underway and if they wished the UAW to be their representative and warned that continued delay in the enforcement of the law would lead to "the destruction of the right to private property" and the "further invasion of Communism." On January 29 two delegations of loyal workers, one of them from the Chevrolet Gear and Axle plant in Detroit, one of them representing the same group that had petitioned him the previous day, visited the governor in Lansing to urge him to remove the sit-downers and threatening to sit in his office until he complied with this request. One of their spokesmen told Murphy that when "constituted government" failed to function properly, it might become necessary for those whose rights were denied "to return to the methods used in the Old West. . . ."

Murphy, his patience wearing thin as the result of pressure from loyal forces, said to one of the groups that visited him on January 29 that the Flint Alliance had tried to "embarrass" him the previous day and that he knew of plans to turn "sham mobs" loose in Flint to force him to use the militia. He thought that he detected a pattern of provocation in the events of the preceding few days, and he threatened an investigation to ascertain whether GM was "behind a sinister, vicious, skillful attempt to force me to use violence in this strike." He would not, however, resort to bullets and bayonets to drive the strikers from the plants "even if 10,000 men marched up here and asked me to do it." After conferring with the two groups, Murphy left for Detroit for the week-end; the two committees remained in a corridor of the state capitol for several hours and then departed.[100]

Consistent with his policy of seeking to avoid confrontations that might lead to violence, Murphy on January 29 asked the UAW to call off a mass meeting scheduled for Saginaw on January 31 to protest the roughing up a few days earlier of Joseph Ditzel and other organizers seeking to promote the UAW cause in that city. Since the UAW was planning to bring thousands of its supporters to the meeting from Detroit and Toledo and the "loyal" workers were preparing to disrupt the affair, the mayor of Saginaw, contending that the city would be unable to guarantee the safety of the participants if the meeting were held, had requested the governor to send in the National Guard. Murphy was reportedly "sore as hell" at the Saginaw police and regarded the loyalists as "the aggressors," but he did not wish to dispatch Guardsmen from Flint to prevent the "bloody battle" that appeared to be developing. The UAW was reluctant to cancel the meeting, but, believing it wise to "play ball" with the governor, the union leadership acceded to his request.[101]

Concerned that the strike was soon likely to take a violent turn, Murphy in the closing days of January quietly sought to bring the company and the union to the bargaining table. His principal proposal was for the UAW to evacuate the occupied plants, still GM's precondition for collective bargaining, in return for his promise to use state troops to keep the plants closed for two weeks or more while the negotiations were underway. Germer relayed the proposal to Lewis, but the CIO chieftain, who had already rejected an identical Murphy proposal in Washington, did not think that the idea was "so hot."

On January 31, with the injunction hearing imminent, Powers Hapgood telling the strikers that injunctions were "mere slips of paper," and the sit-downers in Fisher Body Nos. 1 and 2 preparing to defend themselves against attack from the outside, the governor, doubtful that the injunction method would settle the strike although declaring himself in accord with GM's proceeding in this manner, engaged in "whirlwind conferences" with the strike antagonists in an effort to arrange an armistice. Martin was becoming pessimistic about the outcome of the strike and appears to have been inclined to accept Murphy's proposals, but Lewis was counseling the union to hold firm for the time being, and his wishes prevailed. Murphy had as little success with GM as he did with the UAW; he told Martin and Germer that he "couldn't get anywhere" in his conversations with Knudsen, and he expressed a fear that GM intended "to get rough" with the strikers. The exhausted governor continued his peacemaking efforts until 3:00 A.M. on February 1, but he was unable to break the stalemate.[102] A few hours later, however, the union made a daring move in Flint that altered the status quo in the strike and led directly to the negotiations that brought the strike to an end.

Negotiated Peace
X

As January, 1937, drew to a close, the prospects for union success in the GM strike seemed to be lessening. Although the UAW continued to hold vital plants that prevented GM from resuming full-scale production, the company's reinstitution of its injunction suit in the Genesee County Circuit Court posed a major threat to the continuation of the sit-down in the Flint Fisher Body plants, and the successful implementation of the back-to-work movment in other GM plants made it appear that the strike everywhere was on the wane. The violence employed against strikers and organizers in Anderson and Saginaw had gone unpunished, and there were rumors aplenty that the company or its agents would now resort to "direct action" in Flint as well. Morale, the strike leaders sensed, was beginning to sag, and the strike as a whole seemed to be "bogging down." The strike leadership in Flint realized, to quote Paul Gallico, "If we stand still, we're through," that the moment had come for "some dramatic action" that would revive the flagging spirit of the strikers and that would demonstrate to the company that the union was still on the offensive and had not yet committed all its reserves to the battle.[1]

It was almost inevitable that in seeking to enlarge the strike the union leadership in Flint should have focused its attention on the Chevrolet No. 4 plant. The sole producer of engines for Chevrolet cars, this plant was one of the two or three most important units in the entire GM complex. It was located at the base of the hill on Chevrolet Avenue, just south of the Flint River and across the street from Fisher Body No. 2 and Chevrolet No. 5.* Working conditions in the plant were far from ideal, and there was much grumbling among the approximately thirty-eight hundred workers who manned the two shifts in the factory.[2]

From the point of view of strategists planning a sit-down strike, Chevrolet No. 4 had the advantage of access to the street and of having only two principal entrances to defend, but it had the more than counterbalancing disadvantage of being located just one hundred feet or so from the Chevrolet personnel building, the headquarters for the Chevrolet plant police and "a virtual arsenal."[3] This factor, plus the limited union membership in the plant, had probably discouraged the union from attempting to seize Chevrolet No. 4 at an earlier stage of the strike and made a frontal assault on the plant

*See the sketch on p. 2.

appear foolhardy. If, however, the Chevrolet plant police could be drawn off to another plant by a diversionary strike, the nucleus of unionists in Chevrolet No. 4, reinforced by unionists from the outside, might be able to capture the factory before the Chevrolet management realized that it had concentrated its defensive forces at the wrong point. That the strike leadership should have devised an essentially military strategy of this sort to capture the vital Chevrolet No. 4 plant is entirely understandable since the strike from the start had resembled a military conflict in which leaders like Travis and Roy Reuther, to use Murray Kempton's phrasing, had played the part of "battalion commander[s]."[4]

Participants in the strike and those who have written about it have generally given either Bob Travis or Roy Reuther the principal credit for having devised the strategy that resulted in the UAW's seizure of Chevrolet No. 4.[5] Travis himself has declared that Mortimer, Kraus, and he worked out the details of the maneuver; but he has said that his own thinking had been influenced by Kermit Johnson, who was to be designated the chairman of the strike committee in Chevrolet No. 4 and who had advised Travis that if the UAW planned to capture the plant it should try to create a diversion somewhere else. Travis insists that Reuther took no part in the planning of the strategy, but he is certainly in error on this point.[6]

Reuther's own recollection, and it seems correct, is that it was "a kind of joint thing in which four or five people sort of refined and developed the idea." Travis and Reuther would appear to have been the principal originators of the stratagem, but they then perfected the plan in conversations with Powers Hapgood, Johnson, and five or six others. Germer and Brophy of the CIO and some of the UAW high command with whom the plan was discussed thought that it would not work, but its proponents believed that the union was "losing the strike" and that the "big gamble" was therefore necessary.[7] It was, at all events, the local Flint leadership rather than the UAW international officers or CIO officials who were primarily responsible for initiating and implementing the "gamble" that in the end played such a large part in determining the outcome of the strike.

The plan to seize Chevrolet No. 4 called for the unionists in Chevrolet No. 9, one of several sources of bearings for Chevrolet cars, to initiate what appeared to be a sit-down on February 1 at about 3:20 P.M. (near the time when the shifts changed and when there would consequently be a maximum number of unionists in the plant) in the expectation that the company police, who would presumably be concentrated in the personnel building immediately east of Chevrolet No. 9, would be enticed into the plant. While the anticipated battle was being waged for control of the No. 9 plant, unionists in Chevrolet No. 4, reinforced by comrades coming from Chevrolet No. 6, about three hundred yards northwest of No. 4, and by other unionists from the outside would seek to gain control of the No. 4 plant.[8]

The strike leadership planned to implement its daring strategy behind a smokescreen of charges that the Chevrolet management in Flint was discriminating against unionists who had returned to work beginning on January 27.[9] There was a large meeting of Chevrolet workers at the Pengelly Building on January 30 to protest the alleged discrimination, and it was decided that although "the time had come for action" a last effort should be made to settle the matter amicably. At a meeting of shop stewards held after the general meeting, a committee of fifteen was designated to negotiate with the Chevrolet management, and arrangements were subsequently made for a conference with Arnold Lenz on February 1. On Sunday evening, January 31, there was a large and enthusiastic mass meeting at the Pengelly. About 150 Chevrolet stewards and volunteer organizers were asked to remain behind after the meeting, and Travis, who delighted in the mysterious and the dramatic, had them pass one by one through a darkened room, where Kraus, Roy Reuther, and he gave about thirty of the men, including some who were believed to be "stool pigeons," written notices to appear in Fisher Body No. 1 at midnight.

When the designated group gathered in the Fisher plant, Travis informed them that plans called for a sit-down in Chevrolet No. 9 the next day. This news was received with something less than enthusiasm since the plant was not vital to GM's operations, but Travis assured the men that the seizure of No. 9 was essential to the success of the strike. Following the meeting he called aside two of the union leaders in Chevrolet No. 9 and instructed them to begin a strike at 3:20 and to try to hold the plant until about 4:10 P.M.; and he informed Ed Cronk, the corpulent UAW leader in Chevrolet No. 6, that he was to lead the unionists in that establishment to the No. 9 plant just after 3:30 P.M.[10]

When Travis called Lenz on the morning of February 1 to arrange the time for the meeting that had been scheduled for that day, the Chevrolet plant manager, without offering an explanation, advised the Flint strike leader that he could not meet with the union group until the next day. This convinced Travis that the company, as the strike leadership had hoped, had been informed by its spies that the union planned to take the No. 9 plant. The word, to be sure, was out in Flint that there was likely to be a sit-down in the Chevrolet plant that afternoon, and the Chevrolet plant police and law-enforcement officials in Flint were ready for action.[11]

The UAW had scheduled a meeting at the Pengelly for 2:30 P.M. on February 1 ostensibly to organize a march on the Genesee County Courthouse, where the hearings on GM's injunction suit were to be held that afternoon. Shortly after 3:00 P.M. two union sound cars left union headquarters, one manned by Merlin Bishop and John Monarch, a Socialist party organizer, proceeding to Bluff Street, overlooking Chevrolet No. 6, the other, manned by Roy Reuther and Powers Hapgood, moving to Kearsley Street, alongside Chevrolet No. 9. At about 3:20 P.M. Travis, who was speaking to unionists in the Pengelly, informed them that there was trouble in the No. 9 plant and that they should proceed to the scene at once. About three to four hundred strike sympathizers and about fifty members of the Emergency Brigade, armed with clubs, quickly left by auto for Chrevolet No. 9, arriving there just about the time fighting began in the plant. State police troopers, reporters, and newsreel crews were already on hand.

At about 3:20 P.M., ten minutes before the end of the day shift, night-shift unionists who had entered the No. 9 plant began to call for a strike. Day-shift unionists started to close down the machines and to join in the strike, but they came into conflict with loyal employees and plant guards inside the building. About two hundred Chevrolet plant police, mobilized for the occasion in the personnel building, quickly filed into Chevrolet No. 9 and joined the loyal workers in an effort to eject the strikers. Using clubs and tear gas, the company forces drove the unionists toward the rear of the plant, and there was "just a hand-to-hand battle there for a good little bit." Outside, the Emergency Brigade and some of the men, receiving their orders from the sound car, rushed up to the plant and began smashing the windows so that air could get into the factory. Some of the unionists wanted to rush the gates to join the fighting inside, but Hapgood and Reuther, knowing that this would have led to "a slaughter," discouraged such action. The disturbance outside was quickly quelled by city police and sheriff's deputies, while on the inside the fighting stopped shortly after 4:00 P.M., and the unionists, getting the worst of it, soon emerged from the plant, nearly all of them assuming that they had been defeated and unaware that they had performed their assigned role to perfection.[12]

The battle of Chevrolet No. 9 having come to an end, the sound car and most of the union crowd outside the plant departed for the principal battlefield, Chevrolet No. 4. At 3:35 P.M. the horn was sounded on the overhead crane at Chevrolet No. 6, whereupon Ed

Cronk took out a small American flag from his pocket, picked up a piece of lead pipe, and called for the workers to follow him. About thirty-five men, armed with hammers and pieces of sheet metal and pipe, followed Cronk from the plant. When they emerged, ready to go to Chevrolet No. 9, they were directed by Bishop and Monarch to proceed to the No. 4 plant. Cronk burst into the No. 4 plant, "his hairy chest bare to his belly" and leading "the most ferocious band" of men Kermit Johnson had ever seen but not the army of three hundred he had expected. Johnson realized that Cronk's small force, the No. 4 unionists who had remained over from the day shift and had hid in the toilets, and the activists on the afternoon shift were too few in number to capture the plant, and so Cronk and he returned to the No. 6 plant and gathered another hundred or so men.

The new force surged into No. 4 and aided by perhaps two hundred unionists on the inside sought to take over the plant. The unionists marched up and down the aisles, pleading for support and "threatening" workers who would not join the strike. The strikers turned off the machines only to have supervisory personnel turn them on again. Many workers left the plant while the battle raged, some of them climbing over the fence since the strikers were guarding the gates. Some company police tried to enter the plant but were driven off by strikers armed with pistons, connecting rods, rocker arm rods, and fire hoses. As the strikers gained the upper hand, the small number of plant police inside the factory barricaded themselves on the second floor. The supervisory personnel were rounded up by the strikers, instructed to leave the plant, and told, in the words so familiar to the frequently laid-off auto workers, "We'll let you know when to come back." The strikers won complete control of the plant shortly after 5:30 P.M. and during the next few hours, aided by hundreds of outsiders from Detroit and Toledo—Walter Reuther led a contingent from the West Side local—barricaded the entrances with a variety of heavy objects moved into place by cranes and electric trucks.[13]

Outside the plant, city police sought to enter one of the gates shortly after 4:00 P.M., but a few Emergency Brigade members stood in front of the building with locked arms and ignored police orders to disperse. One of them defiantly told the police, "Nobody can get in except our men." Other Brigade members soon came marching down Chevrolet Avenue, a flag bearer at the head of the procession. On instructions from Genora Johnson, who was issuing commands from a sound car, they formed a revolving picket line in front of the plant. They picketed to the rhythm of such songs as "We Shall Not be Moved" while the police looked on rather sheepishly.[14]

At a cost of a score of injured on both sides and no fatalities, the UAW had brilliantly executed its imaginative strike strategy. The union had regained the initiative, and the turning point of the strike had been reached. "We have the key plant of the G.M. and the eyes of the world are looking at us," one of the proud Chevrolet No. 4 strikers wrote his wife. "We shure [sic] done a thing that G.M. said never could be done. . . ."[15]

The UAW's capture of the Chevrolet No. 4 plant compelled Governor Murphy once again to consider how the armed force of the state of Michigan should be deployed to preserve the public order in Flint. He had arranged a conference in Detroit for February 1 with Colonel Lewis, Pepper, Olander, Bersey, and Kemp, probably to consider the role of the state should GM be successful in its injunction suit.[16] The Flint strikers put their plan into operation while the conference was on, and in his temporary headquarters in the Book-Cadillac Hotel, Murphy received an almost blow-by-blow account of the unfolding developments.[17] Both Wolcott and Bradshaw had asked the governor for assistance by 3:50 P.M., but Murphy delayed taking any action pending the receipt of further information from Flint. The National Guard in the city was alerted in the next few minutes to move to the area of the Chevrolet complex "to disperse the mob," and Lewis, supported by Bersey, thought the Guard "ought to go down there [Chevrolet No. 9] and scatter the crowd in a quiet manner"; but the governor, not yet persuaded that local authorities were incapable of dealing with the situation, forestalled the move.

The responsible officials on the scene in Flint reacted differently to the ebb and flow of the battle in the two Chevrolet plants during the next two-and-a-half hours, and the governor, who interpreted the union's action as a "counter action" to the injunction hearing, hesitated to act on the basis of their conflicting appraisals of the situation. Sheriff Wolcott reported at 4:30 P.M. that if the troops were not sent to his aid, he would have "to gather men and see what he could do," and shortly before 6:00 P.M. the turmoil outside Chevrolet No. 4 and his belief that the strikers would pay no attention to the police convinced him that martial law should be declared; but Mayor Bradshaw had been reporting that matters were under control, and Colonel Colladay had suggested delay. The governor had asked Larry Fisher shortly after 4:30 P.M. if he thought it "necessary to put the militia in there," and Fisher too had advised that "we should wait a while longer."

Not until 6:40 P.M., by which time the strikers had gained control of Chevrolet No. 4, did both the mayor and the sheriff agree that local authorities could no longer cope with the situation. When they advised Murphy of this fact, he issued an executive order directing Bersey "through the use of the military forces and the employment of such means as may be necessary or advisable to take immediate and effective steps to bring the situation under the control of the public authorities, suppress and prevent any breach of the peace, and ensure that the laws of the state are faithfully executed."[18]

"The immediate and effective steps" taken by the Guard, on the instructions of the governor, were to establish a cordon guard around Importance #1 (Chevrolet and Fisher Body No. 2), to prevent anyone from entering this area, and to deny supplies of any kind, including food, to the occupants of the two plants. At 7:33 P.M. Colonel Lewis telephoned instructions to the Guard in Flint to establish the blockade, and by 11:45 P.M. the 126th Infantry was in complete control of all streets in the area and was "occupying all points of advantage with rifle patrols and machine guns." Soldiers with fixed bayonets stood in front of Chevrolet No. 4 and Fisher Body No. 2, and about twelve hundred Guardsmen in all surrounded the eight-acre area with "a bayoneted ring of steel." Their orders were to "peaceably disperse" all people in the streets adjoining the cordoned zone, to block all approaches to the area, and to permit persons to leave the zone but not to enter it. They were not to evict the strikers in the two occupied plants, and they were to attempt to accomplish their mission "peaceably," but they were authorized to use "drastic means . . . wherever necessary to protect the members of this Command." An additional eleven hundred Guardsmen were sent to Flint to reinforce the troops already there, the total number of soldiers reaching 3454 by February 7, which was about two-thirds of the entire complement of the Guard.[19]

On the morning of February 2 the Guard escorted outside its lines the thirty or so pickets who had remained overnight in front of Chevrolet No. 4, destroyed the picket shack that had been erected there, impounded the sound car in the area, arrested Bishop, who was manning the car, and five others who were protecting it on the charge of inciting to riot, and marched them to the county jail as "military prisoners." The sit-downers inside the No. 4 plant were now completely cut off from their confederates outside the plant. During the night they had feared an attempt by the Guardsmen to drive them from the plant, and when GM at about 1:30 A.M. turned off the lights in the plant and reduced the heat, some of the sit-downers erroneously thought an attack upon them was impending.[20]

The major problem faced by the strikers inside Chevrolet No. 4 was not the lack of heat and light but rather the lack of food. The governor had decided to shut off the food supply to the plant because he had been advised by the Guard that outsiders had assisted materially in the capture of the plant and that a sizable number of them had remained in the factory. If the state allowed food to pass through Guard lines to these men, Murphy felt that it would, in effect, be condoning a practice of which he strongly disapproved and which could not be justified even by the UAW's right-to-a-job thesis. The hungry strikers were free, of course, to leave the plant, as Colonel Lewis pointed out, but reentry into the factory would then have been denied them.[21]

Lewis called the governor on the morning of February 2 to tell him that of the 850 men then in the plant, only 150 actually worked there, whereas four hundred worked in other Chevrolet units, and about three hundred were not even Chevrolet employees. This was not the sort of information that was likely to persuade Murphy to alter his decision, and so the food blockade continued. Roy Reuther sought to meet the problem by contracting with the owner of a small plane to drop food on the roof of the plant, but as the plane was being loaded at the airport, the pilot was informed that he would lose his license if he made the flight, evidence, Reuther thought, of GM's pervasive influence in Flint.[22]

Sometime during the morning of February 2 John Brophy called the governor and "berated" him for his action. " 'What do you want to do,' " Brophy asked, " 'starve to death poor workers who are only seeking their lawful rights?' " When Murphy explained the reason for the food blockade, Brophy offered to enter the plant to check on the presence of outsiders, and Murphy agreed to lift the food blockade once all the non-employees were out of the factory. Lewis made the arrangements for the admission into the plant of an investigating team that included Brophy, Roy Reuther, Kraus, and Travis, but the Guard commander refused to join the group himself. A check of badges inside the plant revealed that only Walter Reuther and Powers Hapgood of the non-Flint Chevrolet employees still remained in the plant, the others having previously been asked to leave, and the two of them departed with the investigating committee.

A member of Lewis' staff made an independent inspection of the plant later in the day, after which Lewis phoned the governor that he was "confident" that "practically all" the men inside the plant were "regular employees," by which he presumably meant Flint Chevrolet employees but not necessarily No. 4 workers. The governor then lifted the food blockade, and food cars sped from union headquarters to the plant, receiving a military escort through National Guard lines. The arrested unionists and the union sound car were returned to "civilian life" the same day.[23]

When Brophy called Murphy that night, the governor told him that it was the union itself that had been responsible for the cordoning of Importance #1 and that Fisher Body No. 2 had been included in the blockade because of its location in the area. Murphy asserted, erroneously to be sure, that GM was seeking his impeachment for not driving the workers from its property,[24] but he unwisely assured Brophy, "The military will never be used against you. I'd leave my office first."[25] Brophy must have been aware that almost any governor but Murphy would have reacted to the union offensive of February 1 by ordering the ejection of the strikers from the No. 4 plant and that, in deciding to order a cordon guard thrown around the Fisher Body No. 2-Chevrolet zone, Murphy had taken the least harmful action from the union's point of view that could have been expected of him in view of the riotous events of that day.

The Guard continued to maintain its blockade of Importance #1 until the end of the strike, but it made no attempt to eject the strikers or to deny them access to food. The militia, in effect, protected the sit-downers from any outside attack—the strikers referred to the Guardsmen as "pickets"[26]—but at the same time deprived them of regular contact with their families and the union and the moral support of admiring pickets and sympathizers.[27] There was always the possibility that Murphy would use the blockade as the means of starving the strikers out of the two plants, but the governor does not appear to have had this purpose in mind when he ordered the establishment of the cordon guard even though he briefly denied food to the sit-downers. His objective, it would seem, was simply to prevent further disorder in the area and to forestall any clash of arms between the strikers and their opponents. It may be, also, that he was warning the UAW that he would not tolerate any further extension of the strike in Flint, at least by the means employed by the strike leadership in seizing Chevrolet No. 4.

February 1, 1937, was a day of great tension in Flint not only because of the expansion of the strike but because it was the day that Judge Paul V. Gadola held hearings to determine if he should grant the GM petition for an injunction against the strikers. Although Michigan courts could issue temporary injunctions ex parte on the basis of statements in a bill of complaint, Gadola had decided to hold a hearing in this case, allegedly as "a matter of courtesy" but also, almost certainly, because of the significance of the suit. Just before the hearing Murphy, in response to an inquiry from Maurice Sugar, had advised the UAW attorney in a display of optimism that was unwarranted by the facts that he was hopeful of a strike settlement within a few days. Sugar, who like the other union attorneys desired somehow to stave off the issuance of the injunction because of the adverse effect that it might have on the strike, had thereupon asked for permission to advise Gadola that the governor wanted a "short delay." Murphy had refused to go this far, but he did authorize Sugar to inform the judge that the governor thought a settlement was imminent. When Sugar conveyed this information to Gadola and possibly implied that Murphy desired an adjournment, the judge, no friend of organized labor and a staunch Republican, responded sulphurically, " 'The hell with the Governor.' "[28]

During the course of the hearing that afternoon the UAW attorneys continued their efforts to delay the court proceedings. After the fighting broke out in the Chevrolet complex, Pressman, at 4:20 P.M., called Murphy to enlist his aid in securing a postponement, and the governor told him "to get it." Gadola, however, was unmoved by this information. About forty minutes later Pressman interrupted to say that an adjournment was necessary because he had just received word, inaccurate to be sure, that seven men had been killed in the Chevrolet fighting, but Gadola refused to order a delay. One hour later, however, the judge adjourned the hearing until the next day to permit the UAW attorneys to file briefs setting forth their legal arguments.[29]

The GM attorneys at the injunction hearing stressed the illegality of the sit-down, but Gadola on several occasions animadverted that the issue was not the legality or illegality of the strike but the "right to hold property." UAW counsel skirted the question of legality, arguing rather that GM was not entitled to an injunction since, as an alleged violator of the NLRA, it had not come into court with clean hands. "Do you claim," Gadola asked, "that one wrong justifies another?" Pressman replied that he was not saying this but simply that the appellant had to be "free from any blame for illegality." "The issue," he asserted, "is whether the company can make use of a court of equity to deny [defy?] National and State laws and Government officials."[30]

In a lengthy opinion issued the next day Gadola granted GM the preliminary mandatory injunction that it had requested. The sole question involved, he argued, was the right of strikers to occupy the premises involved in the litigation, namely Fisher Body Nos. 1 and 2. This matter, he contended, had been "clearly settled" in a 1914 Michigan case (*Lane* v. *Au Sable*) in which the state's highest court had ruled that a striker could not legally remain in possession of a company-provided residence once he severed his employment relationship by going on strike. It was proper to grant equitable relief in such a case of trespass "not merely because the injury is essentially destructive, but because, being continuous or repeated, the full compensation for the entire wrong cannot be obtained in one action at law for damages." As for the right of the defendants to engage in picketing, Gadola cited several Michigan cases to support the conclusion that all picketing was illegal in the state.

Having established the legal basis for granting the injunction, Gadola ordered the UAW national and local officers, the sit-downers, "all other persons to whom knowledge of said injunction shall come, and ... their counselors, attorneys and agents" to evacuate Fisher Body Nos. 1 and 2, to refrain from picketing or loitering near the plant, not to interfere with nonstrikers by "threats, personal violence, intimidation or any other unlawful means" designed to prevent them from working or from enjoying free access to the premises, and to refrain from aiding anyone in the commission of the prohibited acts or from "unlawfully conspiring, confederating or combining directly or indirectly" for these purposes.

Whereas the Black injunction had set no time limit, had made no provision for its enforcement, and imposed no specific penalty for disobedience, the Gadola injunction specified that the occupation of the plants was to cease by 3:00 P.M. on February 3, that the sheriff was to read the injunction to the occupants of the two plants and was to cause the factories to be evacuated, and that a penalty of $15 million was to be levied upon the "lands, goods and chattels" of the defendants if they failed to comply with the terms of the injunction. Gadola also informed UAW counsel that the court would amend the injunction to cover the Chevrolet No. 4 plant if GM requested this and the strikers continued to occupy the building.[31]

The Gadola injunction is subject to criticism at many points. In relying on *Lane* v. *Au Sable*, Gadola assumed that a striker was no longer to be considered an employee and was therefore automatically trespassing when he remained on company property, but this assumption was at variance with the rulings of the NLRB and predecessor government labor boards and federal court decisions.[32] Gadola would have been on stronger ground had he separated the issue of trespass in the strike from the question of whether a striker automatically severed his employment relationship.

Both GM and Gadola would have been less vulnerable to attack had the injunction been confined to the evacuation of the occupied plants rather than encompassing picketing and other strike activities. In Cleveland, where GM on February 1 filed a petition in Common Pleas Court for an injunction against the city's Fisher Body strikers, the company did not ask that all picketing be restrained, even though picketing was by then the principal strike activity, but only that there be no more than two pickets at each plant entrance and that their activities be confined to "observation and peaceful persuasion."[33]

Gadola was quite right in arguing that Michigan court decisions were antagonistic to picketing per se, but he should have considered the question of whether the Dunckel-Baldwin Act of 1935 had altered this situation.[34] As it was, the terms of his injunction, like Black's injunction, went far beyond the legal issues raised by the sit-down strike and caused civil libertarians who did not necessarily oppose the restraint imposed on the sit-down itself to criticize the remainder of the writ. The Citizens Committee for Civil Rights in the Automobile Industry thus professed itself to be "shocked" by the sweeping terms of the injunction and denounced the writ as the "most drastic labor injunction in recent history and wholly unwarranted by considerations of law or facts."[35] Frank Murphy, a dedicated civil libertarian, had to bear in mind that in enforcing the Gadola injunction he would not only be compelling the strikers to abandon the illegal sit-down but would also be imposing crippling and questionable restraints on the conduct of an outside strike as well.

In fixing in advance the penalty that would apply if the injunction were violated, Gadola was departing from the accepted practice in such cases. Nathan Greene, an authority on injunctions, contended that Gadola's purpose was to "terrorize" the defendants, but, as Greene and others pointed out, the Flint judge had made the penalty so enormous in terms of the financial resources of the union and the strikers that it was unenforceable and became, actually, "a laughing matter." A smaller figure would have worried the union, Pressman recalled, but not $15 million. "If the judge can get fifteen million bucks from us," a Fisher No. 1 sit-downer reportedly remarked, "he's welcome to it."[36]

It has been alleged that there was "no adequate discussion" in Gadola's opinion of two principles of equity that on the basis of precedent conceivably could have served as grounds for the denial of the injunction, namely, that "equity will not decree a vain thing" and "the clean hands maxim."[37] Gadola did not consider in his opinion the enormous difficulty of enforcing the injunction against so many strikers lodged in factories that favored the defense but simply left the matter to the sheriff. Gadola, however, unaware of Murphy's contrary opinion on the subject, did state publicly when the writ was issued that either the sheriff or he, without petitioning the governor, could order the National Guard to assist in enforcing the writ, and he was later to claim that Colonel Lewis had led him to believe that he would aid in enforcing the injunction if that proved necessary. As for the clean-hands doctrine, Gadola said nothing more on this point than he had in the hearing that preceded the issuance of the injunction. The principle, as a matter of fact, had been only infrequently applied in labor cases before 1937, and, although the Norris-La Guardia Act had incorporated the doctrine in statutory form, there was no applicable Michigan law on the subject. It is quite unlikely, moreover, that Gadola thought GM guilty of any law violation.[38]

Sheriff Wolcott read the injunction to the sit-downers in the two Fisher Body plants in the early evening of February 2 and posted a copy of the writ in both plants. He was greeted with some derision by the sit-downers, but Russell Porter thought that the men looked "rather glum and disconcerted."[39] That night the Flint strike leadership met with members of the board of strategy who happened to be in the city to decide what course to follow with regard to the injunction. There is conflicting evidence concerning the advice given the leadership by the three UAW and CIO attorneys,[40] but the decision, in any event, was not made in terms of what the law required but rather in terms of the course of action that was most likely to contribute to victory. Martin, who had publicly stated, "We will not fight the government," probably advised compliance, but the strike leadership decided to hold firm and to look to Murphy to forestall the enforcement of the injunction. Telegrams to Murphy were prepared, ostensibly drafted by the strikers in the two plants, indicating the intention of the sit-downers to ignore the injunction. The wire of the No. 1 strikers asked the governor whether GM was "to be permitted in spite of its unfair, illegal, and murderous tactics to force the workers out of the plants through the use of military force." The strikers declared themselves to be "completely unarmed" and warned that the use of force against them would result in a "bloody massacre" of workers for which Murphy would be personally responsible.

The wire from the No. 2 strikers recalled Murphy's assurances that he would not use force to drive the sit-downers from the plants. The police, the sheriff, and the county judges, it was alleged, were subservient to GM, and it would now be determined whether the governor of Michigan was also beholden to the corporation. "Governor," the wire of the No. 2 strikers concluded, "we have decided to stay in the plant. We have no illusions about the sacrifices which this decision will entail. We fully expect that if a violent effort is made to oust us many of us will be killed and we take this means of making it known to our wives, to our children, to the people of the state of Michigan and of the country that if this result follows from the attempt to eject us you are the one who must be held responsible for our deaths."[41]

It is most unlikely that the dramatic wires from "those who are about to die," to quote John Brophy's diary entry of February 2,[42] were drafted by the sit-downers themselves or that they were even consulted in the preparation of the wires. The messages were probably composed by men like Pressman, Sugar, and Kraus, who were aware of Murphy's abhorrence of bloodshed and who thought that the bravado tone of the wires was precisely what was required to dissuade the governor from using force to implement the injunction.[43] A member of Murphy's staff, almost certainly Ed Kemp, prepared a press release for the governor declaring that it was the duty of the state's chief executive to enforce the law and that the effort to deter him from performing his duty by "threats or intimidation or suggestion of unhappy personal consequences" was "hostile to the public interest and a threat to the public authority." If the men who were in illegal occupation of GM's plants decided to remain in those plants despite the injunction, the responsibility for the "unfortunate consequences" that might ensue rested upon them and their leaders, not on the governor. Murphy, uncertain as yet regarding the course that he would pursue, decided that the press release should not be issued.[44]

Wednesday, February 3, 1937, was, in the opinion of one Detroit newsman, "the wildest day in Flint's history," and it unquestionably was the day when the Flint strike came the closest to erupting into something akin to civil war. After the injunction was issued, Mortimer and Travis got in touch with automobile locals "all over the United States practically" to urge them to dispatch as many men as possible to Flint by 3:00 P.M. the next day when the twenty-four hour time limit set by the injunction would elapse, and "shock troops" were soon on their way to the city.[45]

The temperature was near zero in Flint as February 3 dawned. In the early morning the roads leading to the city were filled with vehicles carrying UAW members and sympathizers to the scene of the strike. Walter Reuther brought in several hundred men from his West Side local, and the Toledo UAW dispatched every available man. Some of the outsiders went into Fisher Body No. 1 to augment the force of sit-downers in preparation for a possible attack, but most of the out-of-towners congregated outside the plant. The outsiders included a substantial number of women since the strike leaders had designated February 3 as Woman's Day, and Auxiliary members had come to Flint from Detroit, Saginaw, Bay City, Pontiac, and elsewhere to join in the scheduled parade. Six or seven hundred women marched through the business district of Flint, some of them wearing the red berets of the Emergency Brigade, others the green tams of the Women's Auxiliary. They sang as they marched and shouted imprecations at the Flint Alliance and Sheriff Wolcott.[46]

Sit-Down

The women proceeded from their parade to Fisher Body No. 1, where an enormous crowd of three thousand pickets and seven thousand spectators gathered as the 3:00 P.M. zero hour approached.[47] In "one of the most amazing labor demonstrations ever seen in America," singing pickets, six abreast, circled the plant for an hour while the sit-downers leaned out of the factory windows to join in the singing and cheering. The pickets carried "clubs, pieces of pipe, claw hammers, iron bars, sod cutters, spades," clothes trees, and body parts. The most common weapon was a thirty-inch long, one-and-one-half inch square wooden brace thrown to the pickets from inside the plant. As the pickets marched, sound cars "bombarded all ears" and exhorted the unionists to keep up their courage. A La Follette Committee investigator thought the crowd "fairly good humored but determined," but two state police observers described the throng's mood as "ugly."

The strikers and strike sympathizers spilled over onto Saginaw Street, the city's major artery on which the plant fronted. There was not a policeman in sight, and such traffic as could get through the crowd was directed by the strikers themselves. Chief of Police Wills drove up to the plant at one point but was chased out of the area—"running for his life," one observer thought—by thirty to forty strikers. Had he stopped his car and fired, Wills said, "The war would have been on," and he may have been correct. One citizen reported that he had been stopped by strikers as he attempted to drive past the plant, was ordered to take some men to union headquarters, and was clubbed when he refused. There were reports of drinking and of additional beatings, but it was the kind of day that is likely to produce the wildest of rumors.[48]

When word came at about 3:00 P.M. that neither the sheriff nor the National Guard would seek to eject the strikers—Wolcott and Gadola explained that no action could be taken against the sit-downers until GM sought a writ of attachment against them for failure to comply with the injunction—about one thousand of the demonstrators broke away from the crowd in front of Fisher No. 1 and staged an auto parade through downtown Flint, honking their horns, shouting as they drove, and ignoring traffic regulations.[49]

To worried middle-class citizens of Flint the wild confusion of February 3 signalized the complete breakdown of law and order in the city and the arrival of mob rule. A Flint clergyman who had observed the demonstration at the No. 1 plant was to write shortly thereafter, "I have witnesse[d] the abdication of the law and the rule of the pugugly [sic] by the law of the jungle; the law of club and fang." But the day had nothing of that quality for the strikers and their friends. Brophy thought it was "a gala day," and one female strike sympathizer summarized what must have been the feeling of exultation experienced by many of the participants: "To see and hear TEN THOUSAND union men and women on guard and picket duty—to be a part and feel the spirit of many thousands, all battling together for a better life, is an exciting, overwhelming feeling that probably comes to each person but once. In plain words, I was just thrilled, through and through!"[50]

No public official in Flint reacted with more alarm to the events of February 3 than City Manager John Barringer. He asked the National Guard during the course of the afternoon to break up the demonstration in front of the Fisher plant but was turned down by Lewis, possibly on instructions of the governor, who wanted nothing to interfere with the negotiations to end the strike then underway in Detroit. Efforts were made by Wolcott and Bradshaw to have state police disperse the crowd or at least direct traffic in front of the plant, but their calls for help were also turned aside. It was under these circumstances that Barringer, in the late afternoon or early evening of February 3, after meeting with Bradshaw and Wills and informally with some of the city's commissioners, ordered all the city's police to duty and decided to organize a five-hundred man " 'army of our own' " in the form of a special police reserve. Barringer's original intention, "without question" according to the head of the state police detail assigned to the strike, was not simply to augment the forces of law and order in a city that he believed to be succumbing to anarchy but to use his vigilantes to eject the sit-downers from Fisher No. 1. " ... we are going down there shooting," he declared. "The strikers have taken over this town and we are going to take it back."[51]

The enrollment of the special police began some time after 7:30 P.M. on February 3 in the City Hall and at three other locations in the city. Somewhat subdued by this time—Wolcott had warned that vigilantes sent to evict the strikers would be killed—Barringer told the City Hall registrants that they were not being organized to drive the sit-downers out of Fisher No. 1 (the National Guard, of course, blocked access to the other two occupied plants) but rather as a special police reserve that would come to the aid of the regular police force in an emergency.

The UAW was to charge that members of the Flint Alliance, foremen, "disreputable underworld characters," and Pinkerton types had been assembled by Barringer, and it saw as more than a coincidence the presence of a Pinkerton official in the city while the force was being enrolled; but the union presented no real evidence to support its allegations, and most of the men who joined the police reserve appear to have been Legionnaires and veterans aroused by what they regarded as the crumbling of law and order in Flint. George Boysen disassociated himself from the mobilization, declaring the action to be "very foolish and very unfortunate," but Paul Loisel of the Flint Alliance "bustled about" while the force was being enrolled and threatened to shoot any photographer who took pictures of the registrants. Two La Follette Committee investigators sought to learn from Barringer that night the purpose of his action and the identity of his troops, but the city manager, as he himself put it, told them "in effect, to go to hell."[52]

When word spread in Flint that the municipal government was mobilizing a force of vigilantes that might eject the strikers, there was "near panic" in the city and considerable apprehension that the dreaded confrontation of striker and nonstriker was at hand. Strikers and strike sympathizers streamed back to Fisher Body No. 1 by the hundreds and once again took "complete possession" of the area. It was later to be alleged that the UAW had even stationed men armed with rifles in a room above the restaurant across the street from the plant.[53] In the end though, the forces of reason were to prevail over the forces of violence and unreason, and Flint was to be spared the kind of clash that might have left scars in the community for years to come. Mayor Bradshaw, less emotional than the city manager, advised Barringer to enlist the assistance of the National Guard in drawing up peace terms, and Colonel Lewis, who was appealing for the demobilization of the reserve, was more than willing to lend his good offices to the cause of peace. Murphy quietly urged restraint upon Barringer, but more important was the intercession of GM. Mike Gorman of the Flint *Journal* informed Knudsen of what was going on in Flint, and then, presumably at Knudsen's request, a company official asked Barringer to demobilize, saying, "The last thing we want is rioting in the streets."[54]

About midnight Roy Reuther and Travis, representing the UAW, and Bradshaw and Barringer, representing the city, gathered in Lewis' office in the Genesee County Courthouse, and a treaty of peace was quickly arranged. The city, for its part, agreed to "demobilize" the reserve police force and promised to notify all concerned before it would again be called into service so that the necessity for its mobilization could be removed. The UAW agreed to keep its men from congregating in such numbers as to create a traffic hazard or as would be "detrimental" to the enforcement of law and order, and it promised to notify city officials in advance whenever it wished to hold a parade or an outdoor meeting. Since men and women were appearing in the street carrying "sundry pieces of wood and missiles," it was agreed that "such practices" should cease. Roy Reuther brought the news of the treaty to the throng in front of Fisher Body No. 1, and those present began to leave. The police called to special duty were sent home, and the demobilization of the reserve began. The "wild night of terror," as the state police described it, had come to an end.[55]

The enrollment of a citizen police reserve had not, however, come to an end. Interpreting the truce as requiring the demobilization but not the disbandment of the reserve, Bradshaw and Barringer authorized the city police to proceed with the enrollment. Chief of Police Wills, shaken and angered by his own experience of the previous day, did nothing to calm the situation when he warned John L. Lewis to "call off his union men" unless he wished to see a repetition of the Herrin massacre.[56] "The good citizens of Flint," Wills declared, "are getting pretty nearly out of hand." About seven hundred of "the good citizens" signed application blanks for the police reserve and became subject to call should the police require their services.

The UAW, capitalizing on the opportunity to portray itself as the intended victim of aggression and the defender of law and order, accused the city administration of "vicious and illegal efforts to deliberately perpetrate violence" and declared that the responsibility would be Bradshaw's and Barringer's if bloodshed resulted. At the same time Travis requested the city to deputize union members equal in number to the vigilantes Barringer had enrolled.[57] The strike leadership realized, however, that the treaty of the previous night had mitigated the threat of a vigilante effort to drive the sit-downers from Fisher No. 1. On the night of February 4, in the falling snow, several hundred men and women of the UAW, minus their clubs of the day before, danced on the lawn in front of the plant to music played by the strikers' orchestra from inside the factory. Coffee and sandwiches were served to the crowd, and the dancing continued into the night. A Detroit *News* reporter thought that the scene in front of the plant resembled a street carnival, and it was, to say the least, in bizarre contrast to the demonstration of the preceding day.[58]

The mobilization of the police reserve had its repercussions not just on the sit-down strike but on Flint's city government as well. Commissioner Joseph Shears, a member of the works council in the Chevrolet plant and not regarded as a union supporter, responded to Barringer's action by securing a special meeting of the city commission on February 6 to investigate the mobilization of the reserve. Shears explained that he had been disturbed by Barringer's alleged violation of the truce agreement and that he did not intend to "allow innocent citizens to be mowed down by a group of prejudiced and irresponsible people." It is more likely that Shears' attack on Barringer was another maneuver in the long struggle in Flint between the Civic League, the "good-government," pro city-manager forces of which Barringer was a leader, and the so-called "Green Slate" group, which had been led by former mayor and machine politician William H. McKeighan and which had opposed the introduction of the city-manager plan in Flint.

The "whereases" of a resolution calling for an investigation of the mobilization of the special police that Shears and another commissioner introduced at a packed meeting of the commission on February 6 characterized the formation of the reserve as "highly provocative of trouble and disorder" and made reference to the "wild and irresponsible utterance" of public officials. In response to questions, Bradshaw and Barringer explained that the special police had been mobilized at a time when the city police force had only ninety "effectives," that the deputies had volunteered for service and would not be paid, that they did not know if Flint Alliance members had been included, that the reserve was open to UAW members who could take the oath and obey orders, and that no attempt had been made to ascertain if enrollees were prejudiced against the union. Bradshaw conceded that some "unwise statements" had been made and reported that he had imposed a ban on statements by city officials. The resolution was tabled, and it was agreed that Barringer should submit a report on the reserve at the February 8 meeting of the commission.[59]

That Barringer's position in the city government was weakening was indicated at the February 8 meeting when the commission authorized Mayor Bradshaw to take command of the police department and such other departments and "subordinates" of the city government as might prove necessary to maintain law and order. This decision not only reflected greater confidence on the part of the city fathers in the mayor than in the city manager, who as director of public safety was normally in control of the city's police force, but it may also have indicated a certain dissatisfaction with the police force itself, which had been humiliated at the Battle of the Running Bulls and had done nothing in the face of the tumultuous events of February 1 and 3 to repair its diminished prestige. Bradshaw two days later resigned his Buick position so that he would be "freer" to deal with any emergency that might arise. As for the special police force, it received an assignment only once during the strike, on February 9, when thirty to forty of the civilians were assigned to guard the city's water works, which Barringer convinced himself Communists intended to sabotage so as to "cripple" Flint. The UAW, expecting the worst, feared that the force had been assembled to strike at Fisher

Body No. 1, and so the unionists made appropriate defensive deployments, but no clash of arms occurred.[60]

Events in Flint beginning with the seizure of Chevrolet No. 4 formed the backdrop for the negotiations to settle the strike that were resumed in Detroit on February 3. In the early morning of February 2 Travis and Pressman telephoned Lewis from Flint and asked him to come to the strike front in Michigan. The CIO leader, who had perhaps been asked by Roosevelt the previous day to involve himself more directly in the strike, no doubt sensed that the UAW's bold maneuver of February 1 had improved the chances for a settlement favorable to the union and, realizing the advantages that would flow to the CIO if its leader were one of the principal authors of that settlement, agreed at last to go to Detroit. As he boarded the train that morning in Washington, he remarked enigmatically to reporters, "Let there be no moaning at the bar when I put out to sea."[61]

Shortly before Lewis left Washington Frances Perkins called Murphy to request him to arrange a conference between Knudsen and the United Mine Workers president for the next day. Murphy spoke with Knudsen and Larry Fisher that evening and learned that GM would agree to confer with Lewis only if this were specifically requested by the President. Only then, apparently, did GM believe that it could justify the abandonment of its oft-stated principle of no negotiation without evacuation. Murphy very much opposed Presidential intervention in this form since he believed that the intent was to "embarrass" Roosevelt. He so informed the secretary of labor and advised her that he was prepared to surround the occupied plants with troops if she could persuade Sidney Hillman to secure the evacuation of the sit-downers. "Then," he said, "we will begin negotiations with Mr. Lewis and be able to terminate this matter without embarrassment." After conferring with the President, however, Perkins advised the governor that Roosevelt, who was obviously anxious not to become directly involved in the negotiations, wanted Murphy to say to GM that it was the President's wish that the company confer with union representatives. "The President wants you to do it," the secretary of labor declared. "He doesn't want a conference in Washington and isn't going to have one."[62]

Murphy conveyed this information to Knudsen by phone and then sent him an official letter asking that, "In view of the condition of serious unrest and public disorder" in Flint and threatened elsewhere, he meet with Lewis, and the governor the next day. "This request," the letter stated, "is made in accordance with the wish of the President of the United States." In his reply to Murphy, Knudsen, rejecting the governor's advice that he make no reference to the matter in his letter, stated specifically and for the record that the corporation was acceding to a conference because "[t]he wish of the President of the United States leaves no alternative except compliance."[63]

The next morning negotiations between UAW and GM were initiated in cramped quarters in the Recorder's Court building in Detroit. Lewis and his aides, initially Martin and Pressman, were assigned the office of the governor's brother George, a Recorder's Court judge, while the GM team of Knudsen, Brown, and Smith occupied one of the jury rooms. Court bailiffs and state police troopers served as ushers and guards. On some occasions during the next few days the two sides met together, but most of the time Murphy, assisted by Conciliator James F. Dewey, carried proposals back and forth between the negotiators. "The governor," Martin declared, "is jumping around like a jack rabbit." On February 6 Wyndham Mortimer replaced Martin in the negotiations. The strain of the day-and-night talks had begun to tell on Martin, who seemed to be losing control of himself, and so Lewis decided that it would be best to remove the UAW president from the bargaining table. The UAW announced that Martin was leaving the negotiations to explain the strike to GM workers across the land. Ed Hall accompanied Martin on the tour to keep an eye on him.[64]

The negotiations began the same day that the Gadola injunction deadline became effective. Murphy was acutely conscious of the difficult position in which he was being placed and of his obligation as the chief executive of Michigan to ensure the enforcement of the court order. He had thus told Brophy the previous night that he did not wish to side with either party to the dispute but that it was his duty to support the judicial powers of the state. A few hours later he had said to Frances Perkins that once the injunction deadline was reached, "I have got to say that I will be obedient to the law or not." It was evident though that the President wanted the conference to get underway and that both Murphy and Roosevelt desired to see the strike settled by negotiation.[65]

Since the peace talks began auspiciously, Murphy had Adjutant General Bersey call Colonel Lewis shortly after noon on February 3 to tell him that "things are going along fine here," that the "whole thing" might be settled that afternoon, and that it would be inadvisable under the circumstances for the sheriff to "stir up things." Murphy, it turned out however, was far too optimistic about what had transpired that day. At his insistence and over the objection of Smith, Knudsen and Lewis had met alone in the morning and had virtually agreed on a settlement. Lewis had emphasized that the crucial issue was representation and that if the UAW were granted the exclusive bargaining rights that it sought, it would pull its men from the occupied plants and then negotiations could begin on its other demands. This had seemed agreeable to the undoctrinaire Knudsen, anxious as ever to get his machines humming again; but, as might have been anticipated, it was altogether unacceptable to Smith—Brown had not yet arrived—who, according to Mortimer, "upset everything."[66]

On February 4 and 5 the UAW and GM set forth their positions on the essential points in dispute and in so doing defined the issues about which the remaining peace talks would center. Retreating from its demand that it be recognized as the exclusive bargaining agency for all GM workers, the union now asked that it be accorded this privilege only in the twenty plants that it claimed to be on strike. The union's other demands were to be considered in a "continuing collective bargaining conference," but pending these negotiations, operations would resume in all plants, and the workers would return to their usual jobs without discrimination by either side against any worker because of his affiliation with or activities in any group.[67]

GM, as was to be expected, stated that it would recognize the union in the struck plants as the bargaining agency for its members only rather than as the exclusive bargaining agency and, contrary to the union's demand, that it would not employ strikers ("former employes," GM called them) who had committed acts of violence or sabotage. GM, however, did attempt to assure the UAW that the corporation would not seek to undermine the union's position in GM plants. It would not interfere with the right of its employees to join the union, nor would it discriminate against, restrain, or coerce employees because of their union membership. Of greater importance, the company promised not "to sponsor, aid or abet" the formation of a rival organization in its plants and to let its employees choose freely the organization to which they wished to belong. Furthermore, Sloan had already agreed that during the life of its contract with the UAW GM would make no more favorable agreement with any other organization and also that GM was willing to give any guarantee required by the state of Michigan or the federal government of its good faith in observing the terms of such an agreement. The degree of recognition GM was willing to concede the union accorded with the terms the CIO had accepted in the glass settlements of January, but the UAW contended that the glass companies in the preceding few years had not, in fact, dealt with other groups whereas GM had, and so it was mistrustful of the auto company's promises in this regard.[68]

Although the GM proposals granted the UAW recognition and would have left it in a reasonably secure position at least in the struck plants, they fell short of exclusive representation. GM, which had neither the legal right nor the desire to request an election under the NLRA, agreed on February 5 to the conduct of a poll among employees in the struck plants under the auspices of the governor of Michigan not less than sixty days after work was resumed, but it is apparent that the purpose of the election would have been to determine the *proportion* of the company's employees the UAW would be permitted to represent rather than to grant it exclusive representation rights should it win a majority.[69]

President Roosevelt, who contrary to what Frances Perkins has written, continued to involve himself in the strike talks from behind the scenes, called Murphy during the evening of February 4 to suggest that he tell the two parties for the President that the public welfare demanded that they come to terms. The next day, the day he sent Congress his plan to reorganize the Supreme Court, the President, possibly after word had been relayed to him from Detroit regarding the minimum terms the union negotiators believed they could accept, phoned once again and expressed his belief that the deadlock could be broken if GM would agree to bargain on national issues with the UAW alone. Roosevelt, perhaps misled by information reaching him into underestimating the importance that the UAW attached to exclusive representation, thought that the two sides were "awfully close" and that there was "a real chance to bridge the gap" between them, and he offered to say this to both Knudsen and Lewis.[70]

After speaking with both sides, Murphy discovered that the President's proposal would not break the stalemate,[71] and he concluded that the hope for a settlement lay in a formula that would accord the union the degree of recognition and the status in the struck plants that GM had already indicated it was willing to concede but that deferred a decision on the question of exclusive representation for six months, at which time it would be resolved by collective bargaining, the examination of union membership cards, or a board appointed by the President. Since Roosevelt had indicated his willingness to speak to Lewis and Knudsen, Murphy asked Perkins that afternoon to request the President to express to the two men his approval of this peace formula. Roosevelt could tell Lewis, the governor advised, that the proposed plan would effectively give the UAW exclusive representation and that he would therefore be yielding nothing in accepting it.[72] Murphy was probably assuming that the UAW would win a majority during the six-month period and that GM would then feel compelled to accord it exclusive representation rights. He was no doubt also assuming that the fate of the NLRA would in the meantime have been resolved by the United States Supreme Court.

On the basis of her conversation with Murphy, the secretary of labor prepared a memorandum for the President to use in speaking to Knudsen and Lewis, and, as Murphy had suggested, she advised Roosevelt to inform the CIO leader that the plan would, in effect, give him the exclusive representation that he was seeking for the UAW. The Perkins memorandum, however, provided for a truce period of only four months and did not specify how the issue of representation was to be resolved at the end of this period. The next day, February 6, Roosevelt spoke to Knudsen and Lewis on the phone, presumably following the memorandum that the secretary of labor had prepared for him. It is likely that Lewis on this occasion made it plain to the President that he would insist on a grant of exclusive representation at once rather than on a vague assurance that the union would gain this status at some future date.[73]

On the same day, but we do not know whether it was before or after the President spoke to Knudsen, GM handed Murphy a confidential letter setting forth its latest alternative to the union's demand for exclusive representation. The UAW, GM asserted, insisted that it must have exclusive representation because GM would otherwise proceed to bargain with other groups in an effort to undermine the union's position. The company had already said that it had no intention of doing this, and, as evidence of its good faith, it would now agree with the governor for a period of ninety days after the basic agreement went into effect not to bargain with any other organization in the struck plants regarding matters of general corporation policy without first submitting the facts to Murphy and gaining his sanction for the procedure.

The new GM plan, a variant of the idea proposed to Murphy by the President on February 5, would have left the UAW, for all practical purposes, as the sole bargaining agency in the struck plants for three months but would have permitted GM to avoid any statement to that effect in the proposed agreement and did not commit it to adopt any particular plan of representation once the truce period had expired. Lewis, however, was unwilling to accept the new GM proposal since it did not grant the UAW exclusive bargaining rights in so many words. He indicated that he would accept a ninety-day agreement only if it specifically granted exclusive representation to the UAW. Murphy supported Lewis in this demand, but GM would not agree to it. The conference was once again thrown into deadlock and seemed on the verge of collapse.[74]

Opposition to granting the UAW exclusive bargaining rights was also expressed on February 6 by the AFL. Erroneously believing that the President was exercising a "powerful influence" on the negotiations in support of the UAW's demand for exclusive representation, the presidents of the Building Trades and Metal Trades Departments and of several of the affiliated craft unions requested William Green on the morning of February 6 to arrange a conference with Roosevelt for himself and the presidents of the two departments so as to explain to the President what was "their only interest in any adjustment." Green told them that he had already seen Roosevelt twice on this subject and that the Chief Executive had assured him that "he was absolutely in agreement" with the AFL on this point, that his only desire was to have the strike settled, and that he was not interfering in the negotiations, which was less than the whole truth.

The craft union leaders insisted, however, that another effort be made to impress upon the President the AFL point of view concerning representation, but Green was able to arrange only a phone conversation with Roosevelt, who gave assurances that his position remained unchanged. At Frey's insistence, the AFL leaders then decided to send a wire to Murphy on the subject of representation and to dispatch a copy of the telegram to the President. Green also put in a call to Murphy and "in a rather long and very clear and definite conversation" urged the governor not to "yield to force and wrong." The wire that arrived soon thereafter stated that the grant of exclusive representation to the UAW would be "unjust and unwarranted" and would constitute a "direct injury" to the trade-union movement represented by the AFL.[75]

Murphy, who told Green that the Federation's views had "not gone unconsidered," decided to show the AFL wire to Lewis in order, no doubt, to impress upon him the obstacles that stood in the path of a GM grant of exclusive representation to the UAW. Lewis then put on one of the prima-donna performances for which he was becoming famous. He got up from the conference table, Pressman trailing behind him, and walked toward his hat and coat. When Murphy asked him where he was going, Lewis replied that if the AFL were the party that should properly be at the conference, he and his associates would leave, and the governor could send for the Federation's representatives and then GM and the AFL could settle the strike. Lewis also suggested that Murphy might invite Haile Selassie to the conference and GM could negotiate with him since he spoke for as many workers in the GM plants as Green did. This relieved some of the tension in a tense day of negotiations, but the intervention of the AFL undoubtedly reinforced GM's determination not to yield on the issue of exclusive representation.[76]

The negotiations deadlock remained unbroken on February 7 despite the usual round-the-clock conferences. Sometime during the next day Murphy suggested to Perkins that the President might ask Lewis to accept the GM proposal of February 6, and it is possible that the President did so.[77] That evening, however, the governor had a "grand talk" with Lewis, and the CIO chieftain, who Murphy claimed characterized the governor as " 'the most persuasive man' " he had ever met, agreed to accept the GM proposal of February 6 if the truce period were extended to six months, even though the proposal did not specifically concede the principle of exclusive representation. Murphy undoubtedly had pointed out to the union leader that he had already gained much in the dispute because of the "sympathetic government" in both Washington and Lansing and that since GM would simply not grant exclusive representation in so many words, he should content himself with the concession of the substance of the UAW's principal demand in the strike. Lewis' acceptance of the six-month plan convinced Murphy that the United Mine Workers president was the biggest man among the negotiators.[78]

Regarding the new peace formula as "the best way out yet," Murphy told Assistant Secretary of Labor McGrady that "we ought to crowd it through." The governor explained that the proposal took the "heat" off Washington and placed the responsibility on him as the court of last resort, and he therefore felt justified, no doubt, in asking for administration support in persuading GM to accept the plan. Since the GM negotiators in Detroit were apparently unwilling to make the concession on their own, Murphy requested Perkins that night to speak to Sloan or, better still, to have the President do so. It is possible that Murphy said at the time that if Roosevelt did not want to involve himself personally, the President's secretary, Marvin McIntyre, should "insist on it at the request of the president" since Knudsen had stated, "if the president told them they would do it."

McIntyre called Knudsen shortly after Murphy had spoken to the secretary of labor, but the GM official was either unwilling or unable to agree to the longer truce period.[79] When McIntyre called Murphy just after the Roosevelt aide's conversation with Knudsen, the Governor said: "The Boss has to get in touch with Sloane [sic] or the Duponts—tell them this is okay. This strike," Murphy warned, "has got to go through tonight or we are done."[80] The "Boss" did not himself pursue the course of action Murphy had recommended, but the administration did come to the governor's assistance within the next thirty-six hours.

The prolonged negotiations of February 8 terminated after midnight without a settlement having been reached and with the conference near a breakup. Reporters who had caught glimpses of the proceedings saw the conferees put on their hats and coats and start for the door on more than one occasion. Seeking to explain their positions, GM and Lewis that day issued their first public statements since the negotiations had been renewed on February 3, and the GM statement made it appear as though the conference were temporarily at an end. Murphy, looking haggard and weary, had not given up hope however. "If we all keep our heads," he declared, "it won't result in a fatality."[81]

The strike talks resumed on February 9 despite the pessimism expressed on the previous day, but when they failed to result in any progress whatsoever,[82] a discouraged Murphy decided that the time had come for him to take a step that he had been contemplating for several days: he would have to clarify to Lewis the obligations of the governor of Michigan with regard to the enforcement of the law. Murphy, as we have seen, had at no time been indifferent to the issues of legality and law enforcement raised by the strike, but it was only when the sit-down strikers decided to ignore the Gadola injunction that the responsibility to act was clearly thrust upon the governor. He had told Frances Perkins on February 2, it will be recalled, that he would have to indicate whether he would be obedient to the law when the injunction deadline expired the next day, but he had discouraged any forcible action against the strikers on February 3 because he had anticipated a quick settlement of the dispute and because the strikers, in any event, had not yet been legally cited as being in contempt of court.

Murphy had hoped that GM might be satisfied with the "moral effect" of the injunction and had sought, successfully he believed, to persuade the company through Smith to delay seeking a writ of attachment, but company lawyers went into Gadola's court on the morning of February 5 and, on the basis of an affidavit sworn to by the plant manager of Fisher Body Nos. 1 and 2 that the injunction had been violated, secured a writ commanding the sheriff "to attach the bodies" of all the sit-downers in the No. 1 and 2 plants, their "confederates" who were picketing, and UAW local and international officers for failure to comply with the February 2 injunction.[83]

Murphy learned shortly before noon on February 5 that the writ had been issued, and soon thereafter he received a wire from Wolcott asking whether the governor would authorize the use of the National Guard to execute the writ or whether it would be necessary for the sheriff to swear in deputies to enforce the order. Murphy, believing that Wolcott's wire had probably been dictated at GM's suggestion by Prosecutor Joseph—Murphy later said that Joseph "looked with awe upon Judge Gadola's intellectual grandeur"—thought it quite "improper" for GM, about whose behavior he had been suspicious at several points in the strike, to have sought the writ while the strike conference was in session. He told Perkins that afternoon that GM had made a "serious mistake" and that it seemed as though the company were trying to "embarrass" him and put him "in a bad position."

It was Murphy's purpose, however, to be "obedient to the court," and he decided that same day to prepare a law-and-order letter to Lewis and Martin; but he was not inclined to accept either of the alternatives posed to him by Wolcott as the means of enforcing the writ. He was not prepared as yet to use the Guard for this purpose, and he certainly had no intention of permitting the sheriff to move on the plant with a motley array of deputies.[84] Instead, the governor authorized the Guard, if it deemed the action necessary, to place a cordon guard around Fisher Body No. 1 to make it impossible for the sheriff or "a mob of deputies" to attack the plant. In the end, however, this proved to be unnecessary since Murphy sent word to Wolcott through Colonel Lewis to delay the enforcement of the writ for the time being, and Wolcott, a loyal Democrat who had no desire to oppose Murphy and who wished to avoid bloodshed and the possible imposition of martial law in Flint, agreed to take no action on the writ unless advised to do so by the governor.[85]

Murphy counseled delay in the enforcement of the court order in good measure because he believed that peace terms would be agreed upon in a few days, that his principal objective should be to obtain a settlement, and that the enforcement of the writ would destroy the chances for a peaceful conclusion of the strike. "I am not a representative for . . . GM or for the labor group but for the people," Murphy told Perkins, "and the public interest requires peace." The mere issuance of the writ, as a matter of fact, nearly broke up the conference on February 5 as Lewis remonstrated that GM was seeking the arrest of one of the union conferees, President Martin.[86]

Murphy was also influenced in his decision to delay the enforcement of the writ of attachment by his overwhelming desire, apparent throughout the strike, to avoid the shedding of blood, which he feared would result from an effort to implement the court order. Strictly speaking, the writ of attachment did not order the ejection of the sit-downers but rather their arrest and transportation to Gadola's court to answer the contempt charge, but since Murphy assumed that the strikers would resist arrest, he was convinced that the enforcement of the order would lead to violence and bloodshed. "You can't put those men out by force without killing them," he told Congressman

Andrew Transue, whose district included Flint, on February 8. "I am not going to do it," he reportedly said to a friend. "I'm not going down in history as 'Bloody Murphy!' If I sent those soldiers right in on the men there'd be no telling how many would be killed. It would be inconsistent with everything I have ever stood for in my whole political life." Like the American Civil Liberties Union, Murphy regarded the sit-down strike as illegal, but he did not believe that the enforcement of the law against the tactic justified the taking of human life.[87]

Murphy may also have had some reservations about the ability of the National Guard to subdue the sit-downers in the face of the expected resistance. The plants were large and well defended, and the militia was made up of youngsters without previous experience in riot duty and with little stomach for an assignment that might have involved the shooting of fellow citizens. Even a GM official who was extremely bitter about Murphy's refusal to use the Guard to evacuate the occupied Flint plants thought the Guardsmen "too young and untrained" for the job. Walter Eisenberg later studied fourteen successful efforts during the period February-May, 1937, to eject sit-downers from the plants they occupied and found that in each instance not more than one hundred strikers, and usually far fewer than that, had been involved and that the occupied buildings or areas had been small in size or were closely grouped.[88] These conditions did not obtain in Flint, certainly not with regard to Fisher No. 1.

Although some writers pictured the National Guard as spoiling for a fight with the strikers,[89] the military staff in Flint, impressed with the difficulty of apprehending and taking to court the several thousand persons inside and outside the plants against whom the court order was directed, was "quite unanimous" in advising Murphy to delay the use of the military in enforcing the writ. "I have never believed," Judge Advocate General Samuel D. Pepper later wrote, "that the State should be a party to unnecessary violence in such matters." It was his understanding that a sheriff in making arrests in a civil process or a contempt proceeding could not take a human life and that even resistance to a sheriff in such circumstances was only a misdemeanor and did not justify the killing of the resistors. Those who thought that the writ could have been executed without bloodshed, Pepper thought, showed "little perception or knowledge of the situation," and he was consequently reluctant to have the military used to support the sheriff in making the arrests.[90]

Disinclined to undertake a direct assault on the plants, the Guard devised an alternative strategy to secure the evacuation of the sit-downers should that prove necessary. On February 1, the day of the hearing on the Gadola injunction, Colonel Lewis, Pepper, and Bersey had conferred with Murphy in Detroit, and "Certain studies were directed to be immediately made and decisions arrived at." Although the records do not tell us more than this about the conference, it can be presumed that it was decided at that time that, in view of the injunction proceedings, the Guard should devise some plan for the possible eviction of the sit-in strikers.

Responsibility for formulating the plan was assigned to the assistant chief of staff, Lieutenant Colonel John H. Steck. Steck considered three possible lines of action for the Guard to follow: the first involved the forcible eviction of the strikers from both Importance #1 (Chevrolet No. 4 and Fisher Body No. 2) and Importance #2 (Fisher Body No. 1); the second called for containing Importance #1 and ejecting the occupants of Importance #2; and the third provided for containing Importance #1 and isolating Importance #2 by a cordon guard and then, if desired, securing the ouster of the strikers by denying them the necessities of life. Steck recommended the third option as "the best tactical solution" because, although it would take time, it could be accomplished without casualties whereas a direct assault on either or both of the plants would not only be difficult to accomplish but would result in casualties that should not be countenanced. Steck considered the possibility of using gas to dislodge the strikers, but he learned from Adjutant General Bersey that only four hundred gas masks were available, which Steck thought was "just enough to get us into trouble," and he doubted that "there was 'gas' enough in the state to gas one end of the Fisher #1."[91] Apparently agreeing with Steck's reasoning, Colonel Lewis endorsed his subordinate's recommendations.[92]

Although the evidence is conflicting on the point,[93] the likelihood is that Murphy and the National Guard leadership were correct in their estimate that the sit-downers would have resisted a forcible effort to eject them. Roy Reuther, Travis, Mortimer, Joe Devitt, and others, although recognizing the probable futility of resistance, have all agreed on this point. There may be some doubt about how the sit-downers in Chevrolet No. 4 would have reacted considering the state of their morale,[94] but certainly the strikers in Fisher No. 1, the plant that would have been the most difficult to assault, were preparing to defend themselves and to carry their resistance, if necessary, to the roof of the plant. The day the writ of attachment was issued they took over the basement of the North Unit, which gave them the wiring and plumbing blueprints of the factory. They plugged up the ventilators in the plant to protect against the introduction of nauseating gas and placed a picket shanty over the manhole just outside the plant, giving them control of the only point at which the supply of city water for the strikers could have been shut off. According to one reporter, the strikers stored gas in the shanty so that they could ignite a wall of flame if the company or the police tried to seize the plant. He did not expect a fight, Bud Simons wrote his wife, but "if it comes I will be here to do my duty as a warrior of the working class. If anything happens it will be for the best cause on earth."[95]

Had the National Guard surrounded Fisher Body No. 1 as it already had Chevrolet No. 4 and Fisher No. 2 and then cut off food to all three plants, the strikers would have been forced to evacuate in relatively short order. There were no significant reserves of food in Chevrolet No. 4 and Fisher No. 2, and the food stored in the No. 1 plant could have sustained the strikers there for only a week or so.[96] Also, if one is to judge from what occurred in the Chevrolet No. 4 plant, the isolation of the No. 1 plant, even if food had not immediately been cut off, would have brought a sharp reduction in striker morale and made the strikers more likely to surrender the plant quickly once food was denied them. The evacuation of the plants would not in itself, of course, have ended the strike, but the advantage in the dispute would certainly have passed to GM.

It is perfectly apparent that Murphy had initially assumed that the enforcement of the writ of attachment meant the ejection of the sit-in strikers by force and the strong probability of bloodshed. He had, to be sure, denied food briefly to the occupants of Chevrolet No. 4, but only because outsiders had helped to seize the plant. It may be that Murphy, who clearly wished to avoid being cast in the role of a strikebreaker, had privately and publicly equated enforcement of the writ with bloodshed because he could then justify to himself and others his reluctance to order the Guard to evict the strikers. It would undoubtedly have been more difficult to explain a refusal to adopt the strategy of a food blockade since it was a course of action less likely to lead to violence, but even doctrinaire supporters of law and order were not advocating this method of procedure, and there is nothing in the record to suggest that Murphy even considered the possibility before February 8. That he had not done so probably indicates where his sympathies lay in the strike, but Murphy would have indignantly rejected any such explanation of his behavior.

As many Americans saw it, public officials had the responsibility of enforcing the law immediately and regardless of the cost; otherwise the government would be one of men rather than of law. This, however, was not Murphy's view. The " 'faithful execution' " of the law required of him, he later told a Senate subcommittee, included "wise administration of the law," not only its "literal instantaneous application at any cost." He was faced as he saw it with "a difficult, practical question" and not simply with a problem of law enforcement, and he was therefore justified, he contended, in exercising some discretion with regard to the manner in which he responded to the court order.[97] For six days, to be sure, the writ of attachment remained in abeyance, and Murphy, in effect, ranged the power of the state on the side of the strikers, but in the meantime the strike was settled without the loss of a single life.

Murphy's delay in enforcing the writ of attachment was not without precedent, and even Gadola conceded at the time that the sheriff possessed "the authority to wait indefinitely before serving it." Commenting in 1938 on the delay, Wolcott agreed that there was "no hurry about it especially when such great issues were at stake." Sheriffs in Michigan and elsewhere, after all, regularly delayed the execution of writs of attachment issued after property had been foreclosed or requiring them to take action to satisfy judgments against merchants. "If the Governor is to be accused of obstructing justice," a member of the Michigan Parole Board wrote Murphy's brother George, "then every sheriff and public officer might be accused of the same thing."[98]

As an administrator Murphy could be quite evasive when it came to making hard decisions, and no doubt he found it difficult to face up to the decision regarding the enforcement of the court order, but there is nevertheless some truth to his observation that the easiest thing for him to have done would have been to let events take their course and permit the sheriff to enforce the injunction. "Some people ought to get it in their heads," he declared on February 8 with regard to the course that he was pursuing, "that this isn't the weak thing to do; it is the strong thing. . . ."[99]

Although he had decided on February 5 to prepare a law-and-order letter addressed to the principal union negotiators, Murphy continued to hope that an early settlement of the strike would make this action unnecessary. As the deadlock continued, however, the governor concluded that he could not delay much longer. Dewey advised him to discuss the matter with the President before making any statement, and Murphy did this on February 7. He told Roosevelt that he hoped to keep the conference going but that he had to make it clear that it was his responsibility as governor to "uphold the existing laws of the state." The President, who was obviously anxious for Murphy to continue his efforts to settle the strike, agreed with the Governor. " 'You are absolutely right,' " Roosevelt said, " 'you are justified in doing that—go right ahead with it.' "[100]

Sit-Down

The next day, February 8, National Guard officials submitted to Murphy their proposed plan of action should he decide to secure the enforcement of the court order. The military believed that the execution of its mission required a formal declaration of martial law, but Murphy vetoed the proposal. Had the governor given his approval, the Special Duty Company of the Guard, whose formation had been authorized on February 5, would have rounded up the leadership of the UAW and the Flint Alliance and would have urged the apprehension of "agitators," Communists, and union organizers in the city, the impounding of union records, the seizure of the union's sound cars, a ban on union meetings, the blocking of the highways leading to Flint, and the taking over of the Pengelly Building. One can well understand why Murphy, although he had considered the possibility on occasion, shied away from a declaration of martial law.[101]

When he spoke to Transue on the evening of February 8, Murphy, after being informed that there was no support whatsoever in Congress for "this sit-down business," told the Congressman, "alright [sic], Andy, I'll do something on it tonight."[102] The letter to Lewis and Martin was completed that evening, but Murphy decided not to use it when Lewis agreed to accept the GM proposal of February 6 if it were extended to six months. Since the deadlock, however, remained unbroken the next day, Murphy concluded that he could wait no longer.

During the afternoon of February 9 Bersey called Murphy and advised him that the "[i]nvestment [of Importance#2] can be made without unduly weakening our position," that it might strengthen the position of the Guard "in the event of orders to be enforced," and that it might have a "moral effect" on union people considered to be "somewhat hostile."[103] That night Murphy took Lewis aside (Martin was no longer in Detroit) and, with Dewey the only other person present, read him the letter that had been prepared the previous day.[104] The governor informed Lewis that he wished to make clear to him in writing, as he had "already done verbally on several occasions," his position as chief executive of Michigan. It was still his hope that the strike could be settled by negotiation, but since the parties had thus far been unable to reach an agreement, "the time has come for all concerned to comply fully with the decision and order of the Court and take necessary steps to restore possession of the occupied plants to their rightful owners." It was his duty "to demand and require" obedience to the laws and court orders, and he would be true to that obligation. Murphy did not state how he intended to enforce the law but simply that, although he would "exhaust every means" to obtain peaceful compliance, he would have to be faithful to his oath of office.[105]

The nature and significance of the Murphy letter to Lewis have been misrepresented by both the Murphy and the Lewis camps. Murphy himself later referred to "that order" as "the turning point" in the strike. He had told Lewis, he said, that if a settlement were not immediately reached he would read the letter to the conferees the next morning and also make it public, with the result that terms were agreed upon a little more than twenty-four hours later. Carl Muller, a Detroit newspaperman close to Murphy, claimed that Murphy on this occasion "grabbed Lewis by the coat collar, and in no uncertain terms told him the men would get out of the plants 'or else.'" George Murphy stated in an interview that Lewis told brother Frank after the letter had been read, "Governor—you win." Lewis took to his bed the next day, allegedly suffering from the grippe, but some of those who attached great significance to the letter claimed Lewis "was not sick. He was knocked out by Murphy's ultimatum."[106]

The fact of the matter, though, is that Lewis did not alter his position in the slightest as the result of the February 9 confrontation with Murphy. The CIO leader had insisted on a six-month truce before the letter was read to him, and he continued to insist on a six-month truce after the letter had been presented. It was GM, not Lewis, that yielded the next day. As for Lewis' illness, it is safe to presume that it was genuine; as a former coal miner he was particularly prone to respiratory ailments,[107] a not uncommon form of illness in any event during a damp February in Detroit.

The Lewis version of what occurred on the evening of February 9 is more dramatic than the Murphy version. As Lewis told the story at the UAW convention in 1940 and, with greater embellishments, to Saul Alinsky, presumably in the same year, after the letter had been read to him by the governor, the CIO leader expressed wonder that Murphy should advise obedience to the law when he had supported the Irish rebellion against England, his father had been imprisoned for Fenian activity, and his grandfather had allegedly been hanged by the British as a revolutionary. As for the warning in the letter, Lewis told the UAW delegates that he had said to Murphy, "'I do not doubt your ability to call out your soldiers and shoot the members of our union out of those plants, but let me say that when you issue that order I shall leave this conference and I shall enter one of those plants with my own people. (Applause.) . . . And the militia will have the pleasure of shooting me out of the plants with you [them?].' The order was not executed." As Alinsky tells the story, Lewis made an even more impassioned reply to Murphy than is presented in the UAW convention version, and then the governor, "white and shaking, seized the order from Lewis's hand and tore out of the room."[108]

The Lewis-Alinsky account of what Lewis said at the February 9 confrontation with Murphy may be sheer retrospective fiction,[109] but it it correct insofar as it indicates that Lewis did not yield to an alleged Murphy ultimatum delivered that night. The Lewis version, however, like most other treatments of the episode, is based on the presumption that Murphy was delivering a veiled threat to the United Mine Workers president to use troops to eject the strikers forcibly from the Flint plants,[110] but Murphy was careful to avoid saying anything of this sort. It is almost certain, as a matter of fact, that he had no intention whatsoever of directing the Guard to eject the strikers by force of arms. The probability is that, following the advice of his military staff, he intended merely to place a cordon guard around Importance #2 and then, if the negotiations broke down and if the isolation of the strikers failed to discourage them, to deny the necessities of life to them and thus to compel their surrender. The only other means of securing the evacuation of the sit-downers that Murphy seemed to be considering was to capitalize on his immense prestige with the strikers by making a personal visit to the plants to ask the men to leave because the law required that they do so.[111] There is, at all events, no basis in fact for the assumption that Lewis' rhetoric and threats caused Murphy to abandon plans that he would otherwise have implemented to shoot the strikers out of the plants.

Allegedly because he did not want to "jeopardize" the consummation of the settlement that he believed imminent by "disturbing" either party represented at the negotiations, Murphy did not make his letter to Lewis known to Knudsen, Brown, and Smith the next day; the contents of the document, as it turned out, were not revealed until January 13, 1939, when Murphy submitted a copy of the letter to a subcommittee of the Senate Committee on the Judiciary that was considering his nomination to be attorney general of the United States. Murphy claimed that he had remained silent about the matter for so long because he had not wished to lessen his "usefulness" as a mediator of labor disputes while serving as governor. Walter Lippmann, who contended that Murphy was right not to have used force when a settlement was so near but wrong to have concealed the letter since as governor he should have left no doubt where he stood on the issue of law and order, thought that Murphy had chosen to remain quiet partly because he regarded it as "politically expedient" to appear as an "unyielding partisan of labor."[112]

There is some truth in both what Murphy and Lippmann said

about the matter, but it may be that Murphy had remained silent about the letter for so long because it had not been a major factor in determining the outcome of the strike but was rather a document for the record, a document that at some later time could be cited as evidence of Murphy's belief in the sanctity of the law. Had Murphy just after the strike used the letter to support a claim that he had caused Lewis to capitulate, he knew that he would be running the risk of instant and unanswerable repudiation.

The successful conclusion of the Detroit strike talks on February 10–11 was endangered by the irascible Flint Chevrolet plant manager, Arnold Lenz, who came within an ace of committing a rash act that might have prolonged the dispute. The Flint Chevrolet management, ever since the seizure of Chevrolet No. 4, had been playing games with the plant's utility services to the increasing annoyance and discomfort of the strikers. The sit-downers, who had previously threatened to build bonfires in the plant unless the heat were turned up, retaliated on February 9 by opening the windows and the skylight of the plant and, having found the control valve, shutting off the heat. Since this action threatened to freeze the pipes in the plant, Lenz, humiliated by the loss of the factory, decided that he had an excuse to drive the strikers from the building. Speaking the next day to a National Guard lieutenant, Lenz and Chris Addison, a Chevrolet personnel official, complained that the National Guard, the sheriff, and the Flint police had prevented GM from recapturing its property but that Chevrolet was "in a position to do something about it now and were [sic] going to do something."

Lenz assembled a force of 330 plant police during the afternoon of February 10 with the intent of ejecting the No. 4 sit-downers. There were fears in Flint that some "untoward incident" might precipitate an explosion,[113] and Lenz's contemplated foray into Chevrolet No. 4 was just the sort of action that might have confirmed these fears had not the National Guard and Knudsen saved the situation. Continuing to play the role of peacemaker in Flint, the Guard quietly warned the UAW of what was impending, and Travis and Roy Reuther thereupon went into the plant with a military escort and persuaded the sit-downers to close the windows and skylight and restore the heat. As a precautionary tactic, the Guard moved troops into the rear of the plant, presumably to resist any effort by Lenz to dislodge the strikers. Before acting, however, Lenz sought permission from Detroit, and Knudsen, opposed to violence in the strike and not wishing to place GM in the position of being the cause for the disruption of the negotiations, instructed his plant manager to demobilize.[114] The last crisis in the strike had been successfully surmounted.

The negotiations that finally brought the strike to an end after more than fifty hours of discussion since February 3 began at 10:45 A.M. on February 10 and continued until 2:35 A.M. on February 11. Since Lewis was confined to his bed in the Statler Hotel, the strike talks were moved from the Recorder's Court to the hotel. Murphy now carried messages from the presidential suite, where the GM negotiators were placed, to Lewis' room four flights below just as he had maneuvered between a Recorder's Court jury room and brother George's office in the preceding days.[115]

The concluding talks centered about three matters, the reemployment of strikers guilty of violence, the number of plants to be covered by the agreement, and, of greatest importance, the length of the truce period. GM sought almost to the end to retain the right to exclude strikers who had committed acts of sabotage and violence,[116] but the union insisted on the nondiscriminatory reemployment of all strikers regardless of their behavior in the strike, and the UAW's view prevailed.

GM contended that Kansas City Chevrolet, Oakland Fisher Body and Chevrolet, and Guide Lamp had been shut down because of a shortage of materials rather than because of strikes and should therefore be excluded from the agreement.[117] The UAW was not inclined to go to the barricades to include the first three of these plants in the agreement, and it is possible that Lewis and Pressman were willing to yield on Guide Lamp as well, even though the GM case with regard to the plant was very weak. When Lewis, however, put the matter of Guide Lamp to Travis, the Flint strike leader argued for the inclusion of the plant. "We've got 'em by the 'balls,'" Travis told Lewis, "squeeze a little."[118] In the end, Guide Lamp was included among the seventeen plants to which the agreement applied.

The crucial issue in the final strike talks was the length of the period during which the UAW would enjoy a privileged position in the struck plants. Murphy on February 8, it will be recalled, had asked for the assistance of the White House in securing GM's consent to a truce period of six months, and that assistance was provided. Not only had McIntyre spoken to Knudsen shortly after Murphy had made his request, but on February 9 Secretary of Commerce Daniel Roper had "a very nice conversation" with Donaldson Brown; and that same day or the next morning, at Roper's request and in response to Perkins' desire that the aid of an "outstanding" business leader who knew Brown should also be enlisted, S. Clay Williams, the chairman of the board of the R. J. Reynolds Tobacco Company and the one-time head of the National Industrial Recovery Board, talked with Sloan and Brown. Brown, curiously, explained to Roper that

GM was less interested in the length of the "experiment" than in "the phraseology relating to a definition of the words 'exclusive bargaining agents' in such an experiment." He was seemingly unaware that Lewis by this time had decided that the substance of the GM concession was more important than its form and no longer was insisting on the grant of exclusive bargaining rights in so many words. Roper, on the basis of what he had been told and the similar information given Williams, concluded that the matter was "on the way to a successful consummation."[119]

It was probably more than the inclusion of satisfactory "phraseology" in the final agreement, however, that caused GM to retreat on the question of the length of the truce period. The corporation's automotive production was approaching zero—GM produced only 151 cars in the United States during the first ten days of February—and it must have appeared to the GM negotiators, who were unaware of Murphy's letter to Lewis, that despite Gadola's writ of attachment the sit-downers were simply not going to be dislodged from the corporation's plants in the near future and that its automotive production, at a time when the outlook for profits was encouraging, would not be resumed until an agreement with the UAW was reached. GM was also, undoubtedly, responding to the pressure being exerted from the White House through McIntyre, Roper, Williams, and, in a sense, Murphy. When Knudsen later reported that "the Government ... practically ordered" the settlement of the strike, it may well have been the President to whom he was referring. Stephen DuBrul had reminded his superiors in the corporation at the very beginning of the strike that "there has been an election," and GM, apparently, had not completely forgotten.[120]

The precise language of the settlement was finally agreed to by Lewis and Smith in Lewis' hotel room, with the United Mine Workers president in bed and Murphy and Dewey sitting on the bed. "Now I can sleep for awhile," Lewis remarked. " 'Well, Mr. Lewis,' " the CIO head reported Smith as having said, " 'you beat us, but I'm not going to forget it. I just want to tell you that one of these days we'll come back and give you the kind of a whipping that you and your people will never forget.' " A weary Murphy then announced to reporters that the strike had been settled. His manner was "restrained," but the sparkle in his eyes showed that he appreciated "the fullness of the occasion."

The signing ceremony itself was held just before noon on February 11 in the Recorder's Court, where Murphy was cheered when he arrived and Judge George Murphy adjourned the case that he was hearing. The governor declared that he hoped the peace would be "a lasting one" and would lead to "a mutual atmosphere of good faith" between employer and employee, improved working conditions, and a "better understanding." The agreement was then taken to Lewis' hotel room, where the CIO head signed with a pen that had been given Murphy by the president of the Philippines, Manuel Quezon. The other two signers for the UAW were Mortimer and Pressman, which means that two of the signatures on the historic document were those of CIO representatives and not of UAW members or officers. Homer Martin was in Chicago when the agreement was concluded and vainly tried to return to Detroit for the signing ceremony. " 'They can't do that!' " he reportedly said about the conclusion of the agreement in his absence, but they did.[121]

GM by the terms of the February 11 agreement recognized the UAW as the collective-bargaining agency for employees of the corporation who were members of the union. It recognized and promised not to interfere with the right of its employees to be union members and agreed that there would be no "discrimination, interference, restraint, or coercion" by GM or its "agents" against company employees because of their union membership. The company agreed to begin bargaining with the UAW on February 16 regarding the union demands of January 4, 1937. The union promised to terminate its strike and to evacuate the plants occupied by the strikers, and the corporation in turn agreed to resume production as quickly as possible. All idle employees were to return to their "usual work" when called, and the corporation was not to discriminate against any of them because of their "former affiliation with, or activities in," the UAW or the strike.

The UAW committed itself not to strike or interfere with production pending the negotiation of an agreement, and during the life of that agreement all efforts to achieve the settlement of a grievance or enforce a demand were to be exhausted before there would be a strike or an interference with production. The UAW, accepting a principle laid down in the President's automobile labor settlement of March 25, 1934, but not included in the NLRA, promised not to coerce employees nor to solicit for membership on company premises, but this did not preclude "individual discussion." After its plants had been evacuated and the strike had ended, GM agreed that it would consent to the dismissal of the injunction proceedings in Flint and Cleveland and, subject to court approval, to discontinue all contempt proceedings that it had instituted.[122]

Even more important to the UAW than the terms of the agreement was a supplementary letter that Knudsen sent to Murphy in which GM, on condition that the union refrain from "coercion and

Negotiated Peace

intimidation" inside or outside the plants to increase its membership, promised not to "inspire" activities on the part of other groups that might weaken the UAW. For six months after the resumption of work, GM would not "bargain with or enter into agreements with any other union or representative of employes of plants on strike" regarding matters of "general corporate policy" specified in the UAW's January 4 letter unless Murphy sanctioned such action as "justified by law, equity or justice."[123] This meant that, although GM in the general agreement recognized the UAW as the bargaining agency for its members only, in the seventeen plants designated as having been on strike the corporation, in effect, recognized the union as the sole bargaining agency unless Murphy permitted it to bargain with other groups. Presumably, the governor would not sanction such bargaining if he believed that GM had stimulated the organization of the rival group or was using it to undermine the position of the UAW. The UAW, obviously, felt secure in leaving this decision to Murphy.

Shortly before the agreement was concluded, GM announced a five-cent hourly pay increase for its workers effective February 15 in accord, the company declared, with its policy of always maintaining the "highest justifiable wage scale." Since the wage increase was announced on the same day as the agreement ending the strike was signed, UAW members were inclined to accept it as "one of the terms" of the agreement and as another indication of union victory, although GM may actually have been responding to a 10 percent wage increase announced by Chrysler the preceding day.[124] If GM had hoped to persuade its employees that it was a compassionate employer that rewarded its employees because of its benevolence rather than because of union pressure, its sense of timing left a good deal to be desired.

On February 13, as a by-product of the general agreement, Knudsen, responding to a demand made by union negotiators toward the close of the strike talks, sent Martin a letter specifying that GM did not object to the wearing of union insignia by its employees on company property.[125] Knudsen's concession strengthened the nondiscrimination clause of the February 11 agreement and was of particular importance to the UAW since the strike movement had ostensibly begun in Atlanta over this very question.

The sit-down strike had idled 136,000 GM workers across the land at a cost in wages of just under $30 million. GM, as the result of the strike, was estimated to have lost the production of more than 280,000 cars, valued at $175 million. GM's share of new passenger car registrations fell from 43.12 percent in 1936 (44.40 percent in the first quarter) to 34.37 percent in the first quarter of 1937, a decline attributable entirely to the strike, but then rose to 41.08 percent for the second quarter of 1937, after the strike had come to an end. The decline in GM's production during the strike had a reverberating effect on the company's numerous suppliers, its dealers, and the firms that hauled its cars, but the total losses that they sustained are extremely difficult to calculate.[126]

The language of the strike settlement permitted GM to contend that the February 11 agreement was entirely consistent with the principles to which the corporation had proclaimed itself committed from the outset of the strike. There had been no surrender on the vital question of exclusive representation, GM explained, since the corporation could continue to discuss local issues at the plant level with any group and could even discuss "general policy issues" if Murphy concluded that the group was "truly representative" of a body of GM workers and that the corporation was acting in consonance with the terms of the agreement.[127] Several of the journals commenting on the settlement shared GM's view that nothing had really changed, but like GM they failed to appreciate how much the position of the UAW had been strengthened as the result of the strike, how important the "psychological impact" of the settlement would be.[128]

The UAW claimed that it had won a historic victory. "The settlement," Martin declared, "is the greatest advance of any single event in the history of the labor movement." "The greatest strike in American history," the *United Automobile Worker* exulted, "has been victoriously concluded." The agreement, the UAW said, meant that workers no longer had to fear discrimination if they joined the union, and it was the UAW position that fear of discrimination had been the major deterrent to its success in the automobile industry. "Even if we got not one damn thing out of it other than that," a St. Louis Fisher Body worker later asserted, "we at least had a right to open our mouths without fear." "The position of the UAW is no longer underground," John L. Lewis declared.

As the UAW interpreted the agreement, it had gained recognition throughout the GM domain and exclusive representation for all practical purposes in seventeen plants. Recognition "was the most wonderful thing that we could think of that could possibly happen to people," one unionist later observed. What the UAW, like other unions at the time, understood by the term "recognition" had always been rather nebulous, but the union believed, and it had reason to, that it had been accorded a status of legitimacy in GM plants that it had never before enjoyed. It was confident that it would be able to consolidate its position in the seventeen plants during the six-month period because it had no rivals to contend with and because Murphy could be depended upon not to permit GM to weaken the union's position; and what was gained in these plants, the UAW believed, would be extended to other GM plants as well. Finally, the UAW interpreted the outcome of the strike as having "conclusively established" the superiority of the industrial over the craft-union form of organization and as paving the way for similar successes in other mass-production industries.[129]

Since the terms of the agreement did not specifically grant the UAW its major demand, the privilege of exclusive representation, the initial reaction to the settlement of some of the sit-downers was negative. When Bud Simons was awakened in the early morning of February 11 and apprised of the terms, he remarked unhappily, "That won't do for the men to hear. That ain't what we're striking for. They'll never get them guys out of here with those terms." When the agreement was explained to the strikers, however, most of them would appear to have agreed with Red Mundale, who commented, "It's been a tough grind, but I believe the benefits we will receive will be worth the hardships we endured."[130]

The AFL, more interested in prosecuting its conflict with the CIO than in realistically assessing the agreement, interpreted the February 11 terms as a UAW and CIO "surrender in a very large way" since the strikers had not gained exclusive representation. The "'militant minority,'" Frey thought, had been unable to impose its will on "an unwilling majority," and the CIO had failed in its effort to drive the AFL from the auto industry. Privately, though, the AFL leadership was not quite so certain that the UAW had "surrendered." Green, Frey, and Williams wrote to Knudsen on February 12 requesting a conference, in view of the February 11 agreement, to clarify the status of GM employees represented by the unions affiliated with the Metal Trades and Building Trades Departments. Knudsen referred the letter to Murphy, who advised the GM executive that a conference for the purpose indicated was perfectly proper according to the terms of the settlement but that there was to be no collective bargaining regarding matters of general corporate policy without the governor's prior approval.[131] The AFL and GM as well must have wondered after the receipt of Murphy's letter whether the February 11 agreement had really returned employer-employee relations in the corporation to pre-strike conditions.

Much of the comment following the strike centered on the role of Governor Murphy during the crisis. Union and management negotiators lauded his efforts as mediator, and even Alfred P. Sloan, Jr., who, unlike Knudsen, came to dislike Murphy intensely, asserted that

GM, its employees, and the general public were indebted to the governor for his "untiring and conscientious efforts, as well as the fairness with which he has handled a most difficult situation. Only his efforts have made it possible to resume work at this time."[132] The political community from President Roosevelt on down was full of praise for Murphy. The President congratulated the governor for "a high public service nobly performed," and Josephus Daniels wrote Murphy that he had "succeeded in what most people thought was an impossible achievement." Arthur Krock of the New York *Times* thought that Washington opinion was perfectly summed up in a wire that he had received from an unidentified disinterested party stating that "No praise [is] too great for Frank Murphy."[133]

Murphy was hailed as "the master diplomat of industrial conflict" and was showered with compliments for his tenacity, his self-control, his tact, his "quiet firmness," and his "balanced handling" of an extremely difficult situation. Above all, he was acclaimed, even by many of those who deplored the sit-down, for having so discharged his responsibilities that not a single life had been lost in the strike. Even the Flint *Journal* thought it "remarkable" that there had not been "more serious consequences to life and property." "It is Governor Murphy's peculiar glory," the columnist Jay Franklin wrote, "that he sent in the troops and handled them so well that no man lost his life after their arrival, and that one of the bitterest industrial strikes on record passed off without the usual dreary lists of killed and wounded in the conventional struggle between scabs, strikers and their respective imported plug-uglies."[134]

There was, on the other hand, some criticism of Murphy for having failed to enforce the law and to drive the sit-downers from the occupied plants. The governor was informed by some of his correspondents that he had "made a joke of the laws of our state," that he had allowed the "seeds of Communism" to be "nurtured, fertilized and cultivated," and that he was "a Yellow Bellied Cur Dog." It was recognized for the most part, however, that although a price had probably been paid in terms of law and order, the results gained justified the expenditure. Walter Lippmann thought that both Murphy and GM were "wiser" than those who had insisted upon the vindication of property rights. "The essential fact," he wrote, "has been that certain rights of property were impaired and could not be repaired until the human right to be represented had been established."

Arthur Krock cited the views of an "eminent" conservative Democrat who said that he would have defended the rights of property had he been in Murphy's place but that then conditions would have been "permanently worse and the country would not have come out as well as it has through the Governor's tactics." Murphy's "compromise" with law enforcement, the conservative Democrat concluded, was "in the spirit of wise statesmanship at the present time." The author of these remarks was none other than Vice-President John Nance Garner, commonly thought of as an archenemy of the sit-down.[135] At a time when the President was calling for the reorganization of the Supreme Court itself, a delay of a few days in enforcing a court order did not, perhaps, seem like such a horrendous crime after all.

Ed Kemp was correct in his later observation that "in terms of public esteem and prestige," the GM sit-down was "the high point in Frank Murphy's entire career." Spencer Fullerton wrote in the Cleveland *Plain Dealer* that "few persons in American political life face quite as rosy a future at the moment" as Murphy, and *Time* thought it apparent that "the first vehicle to roll off General Motors' revived assembly lines will be a bandwagon labeled 'Frank Murphy for President in 1940.' "[136] Quite contrary to the popular impression of a later time, Murphy gained enormously in stature as the result of his performance in the GM strike, and had not the strike been followed by a rash of sit-downs across the land and especially in Michigan, it is unlikely that he would have been subjected to the serious criticism that was soon to be directed at him and that would plague him for the remainder of his days.

The strike agreement, although permitting GM to save face on the principle of exclusive representation, must be regarded as a victory for the UAW. GM had been compelled to sign its first agreement with a union, and it had for the first time agreed to recognize an international union as a party to the collective-bargaining process.[137] It had accepted the UAW contention that all the demands set forth in the January 4 letter should be discussed at a general conference, that strikers were employees, and that even strikers guilty of acts of violence should be returned to their jobs without discrimination. Although the company had insisted that the sit-down was illegal, it had agreed nevertheless to secure the dismissal of injunctions directed against the strikers. Above all, though, the strike had been for organizational purposes, and in this sense too it had been successful. In seventeen plants, including the strategically significant Cleveland Fisher Body, Flint Fisher Body No. 1, and Chevrolet No. 4 plants, the UAW was, in effect, given six months to become the majority union, free from any concern that the company might foster a rival organization; and the concession GM made in these plants, its recognition of the UAW as the bargaining agency for its members in all GM plants, the promise that the corporation made not to discriminate against union members, and the prestige that the union gained from the settlement and from its apparent defeat of "the most powerful industrial aggregation" in the United States placed the UAW in a favorable position to spread its organization throughout the GM domain.[138]

The strike settlement was a victory not only for the UAW but for the CIO and for unionism in the mass-production industries. "The workers," an organizer in the steel industry reported during the strike, "regard the General Motors sit-down as a test of the C.I.O. . . . They hesitate to stick out their necks. 'Wait till you win the auto strike. Then we'll join.'" Like the steel workers, astute observers had recognized from the outset that the auto strike was the "testing ground" for the CIO and that the future of mass-production unionism lay in the hands of the sit-down strikers. Victory over GM, it was predicted, would lead to the conquest of Ford and Chrysler and of steel, rubber, and the other mass-production industries as well. "Future of C.I.O. Hangs On Auto Strike Result," was the New York *Times* headline for a January 24 story on the strike by its able labor reporter, Louis Stark. When victory had been achieved, the secretary of the Communist party in Michigan correctly observed, "The auto workers have cleared the way to planting the flag of unionism over the great factories of this country."[139]

For the victory that had been achieved in the GM strike, the UAW could give credit to its own leadership and tactics, the CIO, and the state and federal governments.[140] A small group of UAW leaders at the national, local, and plant levels, some of them quite radical in their ideological orientation, had outmaneuvered GM from the beginning of the strike to its end. They hit the corporation at its most vulnerable points and by using the sit-down tactic were able to keep strategic plants closed with a relatively small number of workers and to prevent GM from applying the overwhelming force that it could have mustered to defeat an outside strike.

In Flint, the center of the strike from the outset, the leadership of men like Travis and Roy Reuther was nothing short of brilliant. It was they and a handful of others who were responsible for the daring strategy that resulted in the seizure of Chevrolet No. 4, the use of the sound car, the mobilization of women in the Auxiliary and the Emergency Brigade, the utilization of outsiders as a strategic reserve, and the staging of mass demonstrations at crucial moments—all of which contributed to the union victory. What happened on the outside, however, would have been unavailing had not a determined core of unionists been able to organize themselves into a community inside Fisher Body Nos. 1 and 2 and later Chevrolet No. 4 and been willing to remain at their posts until GM came to terms despite a police attack, interrupted utility service, and a court injunction. The strikers in Flint were aided and supported by their international union, and the strike effort as a whole benefited, as we have seen, from the CIO's settlement of the glass strike, the organizers and funds supplied by the new committee, and the talents of John L. Lewis.

The favorable political climate in Washington and Lansing was an indispensable element of union success. The La Follette Committee weakened GM's moral position and appeared to lend credence to union charges that the corporation was engaging in unfair labor practices and was infringing on the civil liberties of its employees. The President and the secretary of labor refused to condemn the sit-down and supported Murphy's efforts to secure a negotiated settlement while delaying the enforcement of a court order. The key decisions insofar as public authorities involved themselves in the strike were, however, made in Michigan by Governor Murphy rather than by Washington officials.[141] It was Murphy who sent the National Guard into Flint not to break the strike but to preserve the public peace and, in effect, to protect the strikers from possible attack; it was Murphy who delayed the enforcement of a court order that could have broken the strike; it was Murphy who insisted that the strike be settled around the conference table and who kept the strike talks going day and night; and it was Murphy who threw his own support to, and gained Washington backing for, the six-month truce plan that was the key to the consummation of the February 11 agreement. Had Michigan's governor been someone like M. Clifford Townsend rather than Frank Murphy, the strike would almost certainly have had a different outcome, and the coming to power of the UAW and the CIO would, at the very least, have been delayed. Murphy's contribution to the outcome of the dispute is a striking example of the truism that history is not the product of inexorable forces alone and that if man is not entirely the master of his fate he nevertheless helps to shape his own destiny.

The union's celebration of its victory in Flint during the late afternoon and evening of February 11 was described by a reporter as "unique in the annals of labor demonstrations." Shortly after 3:00 P.M. Travis, Mortimer, and other union officials entered the vast No. 1 plant and met with the strike committee and then with the strike community as a whole. The strike agreement was read to the men and was discussed for about an hour. There was some grumbling about the terms, but the agreement was in the end unanimously approved. Roy Reuther told the men that they were not leaving the factory because of "a sheriff holding a paper," and Martin declaimed, "The world pays you tribute."

As the moment for departure neared, a dozen or so strikers appeared on the roof of the plant and lowered a sign reading,

"Victory Is Ours." Several hundred automobiles, decked with bunting, pulled up at the plant, and thousands of spectators streamed into the area. The strikers marched out to deafening cheers at 5:42 P.M. About four hundred men left the plant, some of them, anxious to share the glory of the occasion, having entered the factory that day. Most of the strikers carried American flags, nearly all of them carried bundles. A parade line of more than eight hundred persons then formed that included the sit-downers and the ladies of the Women's Auxiliary and the Emergency Brigade. A flag bearer, two drummers, and a drum major headed up the parade, and they were followed by bearers carrying a first-aid stretcher on which an effigy of Boysen had been placed. They paraded down Saginaw Street and Third Avenue toward the area of Chevrolet No. 4 and Fisher Body No. 2 "with a beautiful disregard of red or green lights or traffic."

After the ceremonies at the No. 1 plant, Travis proceeded to Chevrolet No. 4 and to the "dim and ghostly" interior of Fisher Body No. 2, where again he received unanimous approval of the strike agreement. The National Guard relaxed its blockade of the area and allowed the crowd to descend to the valley in which the plants were located. Between two and three hundred sit-down strikers from Chevrolet No. 4 and then about 125 from the No. 2 plant emerged to the accompaniment of honking horns, shouts of joy, and the singing of the inevitable "Solidarity." The parade from Fisher Body No. 1 arrived at the crest of the hill north of the plants, and a half-hour meeting followed addressed by Travis, Mundale, Kermit Johnson, Krzycki, and Brophy, the latter telling the throng that they were celebrating "the coming of industrial democracy to the men in these great plants." Paraders from Chevrolet No. 4 and Fisher Body No. 2 then merged forces with the No. 1 group, and they marched through the downtown district toward the Pengelly Building. They halted on Saginaw Street at the Flint River and slid the effigy of Boysen into the murky waters below, with the quondam Baptist minister Homer Martin proclaiming the last rites.

The crowd that gathered at the Pengelly Building overtaxed the capacity of its two-thousand seat auditorium. The overflow thousands remained outside the building and were addressed by union leaders and organizers who had already spoken to the audience inside. The celebration continued into the night, reminding observers of Mardi Gras, Armistice Day, or community reaction to victory in the World Series. "These people," Rose Pesotta said, "sang and joked and laughed and cried, deliriously joyful. . . . victory . . . meant a freedom they had never known before. No longer would they be afraid to join unions."[142]

Aftermath
XI

I

In view of the nature of social and political controls in Anderson and the lack, as compared to Michigan, of any significant restraining influence exercised by state authority, it is not altogether surprising that the UAW local's celebration of its strike victory led to renewed discord and violence and to the dispatch of the Indiana National Guard to the troubled city. The Anderson UAW, in a possibly justified but nevertheless provocative action, had scheduled a "public trial" of Mayor Harry Baldwin and Chief of Police Joseph Carney for the evening of February 11 on the charge that they had failed to disperse the anti-union mobs on January 25 and 28. The conclusion of the strike transformed the affair into a projected victory meeting at which the terms of the February 11 agreement were to be explained to the assembled unionists.

The meeting was held in the Crystal Theater, a closed and condemned piece of property that was made available to the UAW by a Democratic state legislator after the union had failed to secure the use of any of the usual meeting places in the city.[1] About a thousand unionists and sympathizers assembled inside the theater, while outside, after the meeting had been underway for about thirty minutes, an anti-union crowd estimated at anywhere from two hundred to fifteen hundred persons gathered. The throng outside was composed mainly of Guide Lamp personnel and included some minor GM supervisory officials, but the most reliable evidence indicates that the latter did not play a particularly active part in the proceedings.[2] The angry mob, demanding that Victor Reuther and other outside union organizers be run out of town, pelted the building with rocks and rotten eggs, but the union allegation that shots were also being fired seems incorrect.[3] The police, who had been asked for protection by Reuther, were present in force, but they made no serious effort to disperse the mob although they did prevent the anti-unionists from entering the building.

Police Chief Carney, who the UAW claimed had told the vigilantes, " 'I'm with you boys,' " went into the theater and advised the persons in charge of the meeting that the crowd could be quieted if Reuther and the other non-Anderson organizers left the city. Carney urged that the meeting be adjourned and promised the organizers safe conduct out of town. Reuther put Carney's proposal to a vote of the audience, which decided unanimously that the union leaders should not leave and that the entire group should remain in the theater until all could depart together. The unionists requested the police to use tear gas and fire hoses to disperse the crowd outside, but the police refused for fear, the mayor said, that such action would have "further infuriated" the mob. The beleaguered unionists then called for the use of state troops and police from the surrounding communities to provide the protection the Anderson police were failing to provide and also for the deputization by the governor of three hundred unionists but all to no avail. By about 4:00 or 5:00 A.M. the mob outside had thinned sufficiently to permit the union to send the women and children home under UAW guard, but Reuther and forty others, undoubtedly to dramatize the union's plight, remained in the building until about 8:30. "I can assure you," Reuther recalled many years later, "I aged ten years that night. I can still hear the whimpering of frightened women and children."[4]

When Reuther left the theater, he went directly to Indianapolis to complain to Governor M. Clifford Townsend about the "reign of terror" in Anderson and to request the state to protect the lives and civil liberties of the city's unionists. Townsend promised to consider the dispatch of state police troopers to Anderson, but he took no immediate action.[5] The events of the next few hours, however, finally persuaded the governor that the time had come for the state of Indiana to take command in Anderson.

The Anderson UAW not only appealed to state authorities for protection but also called for union reinforcements from Michigan. While the unionists were under siege in the Crystal Theater, Bob Travis interrupted a victory dance in the Pengelly Building, called forty to fifty trusted unionists together, and told them that the boys in Anderson needed their help. So often aided in the preceding few weeks by UAW members from outside their city, the Flint unionists piled into cars in the early hours of February 12 and left for Anderson. When they arrived in the nearby town of Alexandria, they were met by Anderson unionists who supplied them with pieces of gas pipe and clubs, and they later proceeded to union headquarters in Anderson.[6]

During the course of the afternoon of February 12 Cecil Dunn, an Anderson UAW member whose brother had been assaulted outside the Crystal Theater the previous night, went with some companions to the Gold Band Tavern, a decrepit establishment near the Guide Lamp plant that was alleged to have been an anti-union hangout, to seek his brother's reputed assailant. Precisely what happened in the tavern after Dunn's arrival is unclear, but he apparently became involved in fisticuffs with someone in the tavern and was beaten up, after which Emory Shipley, the owner of the establishment, covered Dunn and two of his friends with a rifle and ordered them from the building.[7]

Soon thereafter an unidentified person who looked like the victim of a recent physical assault[8]—the UAW later concluded that it had probably been led into a trap—rushed into union headquarters and shouted "hysterically" that unionists were being manhandled at the Gold Band Tavern. Two or three carloads of Anderson and Flint unionists then sped to the tavern presumably to rescue their comrades. The stories of what occurred after they arrived on the scene are "vague" at best. Shipley claimed that 150 men surrounded the building, threw stones and fired shots at the establishment, and then "swarmed" into the barroom. In self-defense, he asserted, he fired his shotgun at the unionists, first from inside the tavern and then from the street, and drove them from the area. The regional director of the NLRB, however, reported that the unionists did not have firearms and that there was no evidence inside the tavern of shots having been fired into the building from the outside. It strains credulity, moreover, to believe that Shipley could singlehandedly have driven off an armed mob of 150 men. The UAW alleged that only a small handful of unionists had driven to the tavern, that Shipley began shooting at them as soon as they got out of their cars, and that only then did they begin throwing rocks at the building. At all events, ten unionists were wounded by gunfire, two of them quite seriously.[9]

Mayor Baldwin, learning from the Flint police that a large caravan of cars was proceeding from Flint to Anderson and alarmed further by the events at the Gold Band Tavern and by reports that armed men were appearing on the streets of Anderson, advised Governor Townsend that local authorities could no longer maintain peace and order in the city without outside assistance. The regional director of the NLRB thought it interesting that city officials who had previously given their "passive support or sympathy" to anti-union demonstrations and had not turned to the state for assistance had appealed to the governor for troops following "the first flare up" by the UAW.[10]

Governor Townsend, who had fended off union requests for protection in Anderson, responded quickly to Mayor Baldwin's plea for help. He dispatched seven hundred National Guardsmen to the city on February 13 and placed Madison County, of which Anderson was the seat, under martial law. All crowds and pickets were ordered to disperse at once and all assemblages were prohibited. Only the military and the police were permitted to carry arms, and only persons authorized by the military were to be allowed to enter or leave the district. The state police imposed a virtual blockade at the Madison

County line and late on February 13 intercepted at Alexandria and escorted from the area three to four dozen car loads of out-of-state unionists, including some of the heroes of the Flint strike, who were rushing to Anderson in answer to Victor Reuther's plea for help. The unionists innocently claimed that they were on their way to Anderson for a UAW parade, but the state police found clubs and baseball bats, although no firearms, in their possession.[11]

The UAW in Anderson complained bitterly about the restrictions imposed upon its activities while martial law prevailed in the city. "It's a mess here," Reuther told Travis on the phone on February 13; "the Governor won't give a damn thing." Reuther's remarks illuminated for Travis one of the major reasons for the difference between Flint and Anderson as strike cities. "That God damn Governor," he replied to Reuther, "I guess we will have to move Michigan to Indiana or make Murphy president."

The UAW also complained that twenty unionists and sympathizers, thirteen of them from Flint and including the unionists wounded at the Gold Band Tavern, were being held incommunicado by the Guard after their arrest following the tavern affray but that Shipley had not even been arrested. "Anderson situation desperate," an American Civil Liberties Union representative wired Roger Baldwin. "Militia ruthlessly suppresses democratic prerogatives." Baldwin was advised, however, that the UAW was itself guilty of violence, and Charles B. Salyer, the Anderson attorney who had previously worked closely with the UAW, complained to the La Follette Committee about the union's readiness to take the law into its own hands. "Violence and murder are in the air," Mary Heaton Vorse reported from Anderson on February 16.[12]

The news coming out of Anderson from union and pro-union sources was, however, overly pessimistic. The twenty military prisoners were turned over to civil authorities on February 18, and the next day nineteen of them were indicted by a Madison County grand jury on a "rout and riot" charge, and sixteen of them were additionally charged with malicious trespass. A hearing was set for March 10, but in the meantime life returned to something approaching normal in Anderson, and in the end the accused were not brought to trial. The prisoners were released on bail after they had been indicted, and the military relaxed its restrictions on union activities. On February 23 martial law was terminated in Anderson, and the remnant of the Guard that had remained in the city was withdrawn.[13]

The shape of things to come in employer-employee relations in the automobile industry appeared to be as evident in Anderson as elsewhere in the nation in the weeks that followed the close of the GM strike. Delco-Remy and Guide Lamp resumed operations without incident on February 15 after GM had announced the abolition of the incentive pay system in the plants to which the local UAW had objected. The vigilantes in Anderson, allegedly because the governor had "put the bee" on city officials, were "driven undercover," and the union carried on its organizing drive without molestation. Victor Reuther reported to Homer Martin at the end of March that negotiations with the local GM management were "progressing very well" and that "the sentiment of the workers" was "rapidly changing." The UAW had apparently become "a force" to be reckoned with in a city that only a short time before had been a bastion of the open shop. "The men and women who fought on the picket line; who withstood the terror of vigilantes; who braved cold weather; who kept their faith under trying conditions; these people," the union newspaper triumphantly asserted at the end of the strike, "changed the conditions in the shops." The union leadership, however, was excessively optimistic about the trend of industrial relations in Anderson. Although there were some encouraging signs from the union point of view in the few weeks after the close of the strike, the UAW would be unable to establish itself securely in Guide Lamp and Delco-Remy until many more months had passed.[14]

II

In Flint the conclusion of the GM strike left the city with two labor disputes still unresolved, the sit-down strike that had begun on December 30 at the Standard Cotton Products Company, which manufactured upholstery material for Fisher Body, and the outside strike of the Flint Trolley Coach Company employees. The former dispute was settled on February 16, with the largely "forgotten" workers receiving a substantial wage increase; and the eighty-seven-day bus strike came to an end on March 4 after negotiations involving the UAW as the representative of the workers, federal conciliators, and Frank Murphy.[15]

The echoes of the GM strike continued to be heard in Flint after February 11. GM had agreed to consent to the dismissal of the injunction suits against the union, and the company sought in good faith to implement this part of the strike agreement, but Judge Gadola had other ideas about the matter. When approached by GM counsel on the subject, he took the position that the injunction itself was "out of commission" since the UAW had evacuated company property but that he would not dismiss the writ of attachment until Martin and fourteen other UAW officials and strike leaders had apologized to the court for their "contemptuous action," which was in no way affected by the February 11 settlement. When Martin testified before the Dies Committee on December 1, 1938, he noted that the writ remained in effect and that the court still had not received the apology it desired; and there the matter rested.[16]

The charges of engaging in unlawful assembly and malicious destruction of property brought against Victor and Roy Reuther, Kraus, Travis, and three others after the Battle of the Running Bulls were pending when the strike ended. After the charges had been dismissed against all the defendants but Victor Reuther, the union generalissimo of the January 11 encounter, the UAW insisted that Joseph, a GM stockholder, should not prosecute the case and Gadola, because of his involvement in the injunction suit, should not preside at the trial. Attorney General Raymond W. Starr obliged the union by helping to make the necessary arrangements with Gadola for the appointment of a special prosecutor and the assignment of the case to a different Circuit Court judge, but in the end the charges against Reuther were dismissed on a technicality.[17]

City Manager Barringer was the principal city official to feel the backlash of the union victory in the GM strike and the altered structure of power in Flint. On February 15 the city commission restored to Barringer the extraordinary powers it had temporarily vested in the mayor on February 8, but eight days later the commission, by a five to three vote, dismissed Barringer from his post. The criticism of the city manager centered on his provocative mobilization of the civilian police reserve during the strike, but the three Green Slate commissioners had actually been seeking Barringer's scalp since their election in November, 1936. Barringer's successor, W. G. Findlater, was, interestingly enough, considered to be pro-CIO. In an action of considerable interest to the UAW, he sought to demote Chief of Police Wills to the position of supervisor of traffic safety, only to be balked by the city's Civil Service Commission. Findlater then fired Wills, but the Civil Service Commission restored him to his post.[18]

Concerned lest there be trouble in the city before all GM units had resumed normal production, the National Guard demobilized in Flint on a gradual basis, not completing the process until February 20. As one truckload of Guardsmen left the city, they spontaneously began singing "Solidarity Forever," the song that they had so often heard sung during their tour of duty in Flint. This brought an

Aftermath

319

inquiry to Michigan's adjutant general from Major General Albert H. Blanding, the chief of the National Guard Bureau. Bersey replied that a "partial investigation" revealed that there was nothing to the story, but his research left something to be desired.[19]

The behavior of the Guard in Flint elicited a great deal of praise from responsible officials. Murphy said that he had "never seen a military situation handled better," an observation that although intended as a compliment of the Guard might also have been construed as a favorable reflection upon its commander-in-chief. Both Wolcott and Bradshaw commented glowingly on the "conduct, courtesy and efficiency" of the Guard, and Bradshaw thought it remarkable that so many Guardsmen could have been deployed in the city for so long a time and yet have behaved so admirably and in such a disciplined manner. Colonel Lewis concluded that the tour of duty had "demonstrated that effective use can be made of troops at such times without loss of life or distruction [sic] to property, and the troops to remain in [the] good graces of the community."[20]

Lewis' judgment was accurate and to the point. Not only had Guard leaders restrained their own men from untoward acts, but, as the assistant chief of staff pointed out, they had tried to make all parties in Flint realize that "personal and group differences of opinion should be subordinated" so that nothing would occur in Flint that might "jeopardize the success" of the negotiations the governor was conducting in an effort to settle the strike.[21] The Guard had played an important part in arranging the January 26 truce that preceded the resumption of work in some of GM's Flint plants and the midnight truce of February 3 that lessened the threat of vigilante action against the strikers; it had helped to defeat Arnold Lenz's effort to recapture the Chevrolet No. 4 plant on February 10; and it had, if anything, strengthened Murphy's resolve not to order an assault upon the occupied plants to enforce the Gadola injunction. At least part of the credit for the peaceful outcome of the Flint strike must be accorded the Michigan National Guard.

Guard officials and particularly Judge Advocate General Samuel D. Pepper thought that there were lessons to be learned by the Guard from its Flint tour of duty. Pepper recommended changes in the legislation pertaining to the Guard designed to protect the soldiers against the kind of financial problems that they had experienced at the outset of their Flint service, and his proposals were accepted by the Michigan legislature. Pepper was particularly concerned about the lack of training of officers and men for the type of riot duty to which they had been assigned in Flint. The problem, as he expressed it, was "to tone down the whole military machine to the level of the peace officer's conception of enforcing the laws, after the machine has been trained in the methods and acts of actual warfare."

Pepper thought that each state should have a military organization trained in advance to deal with domestic disturbances, as distinguished from its role in national defense, so that when troops were employed to aid civil authorities in local law enforcement, "proper and legal restraints" could be enforced to avoid unnecessary bloodshed and the use of "wholly unnecessary force" against mobs, individuals, and property. Bersey, however, feared that if Guardsmen were given the same kind of training that peace officers received, the public might conclude that the Guard was being prepared for use against the citizens of the state. He advised Governor Murphy in August, 1937, that some training in dealing with civil disturbances was already being provided by the Guard and that division commanders were free to increase such training if they deemed this proper.[22] Thirty years later the adequacy of the National Guard's training for dealing with domestic disturbances became a live issue once again in Michigan and elsewhere in the nation although the focus of concern now was on racially motivated civil disorder rather than on labor strife.

As work resumed in the various GM plants—all of the company's motor-vehicle factories were in operation by February 18—Homer Martin announced, "We are in a reconstruction period following the war, and it requires cooperation and patience on the part of all." A few weeks later Martin commented, "Some of the General Motors plant managers haven't realized that the civil war is over," a true enough observation but one that applied with equal force to many of Martin's own followers. The heritage of strife between the UAW and GM, the union's view that the corporation had sought to throttle it by resort to unfair labor practices and the corporation's belief that Communists and "outside agitators," aided and abetted by leftish politicians, had employed the illegal sit-down strike to force concessions from the company, created an atmosphere of animosity and resentment in GM plants that was hardly conducive to the establishment of harmonious employer-employee relations. Ten years after the sit-down strike "the scars of the early conflict were [still] plainly visible in spite of a decade of collective bargaining."[23]

GM remained as unwilling after the strike as before the dispute to concede that the solution of its industrial-relations problems involved the establishment of outside unionism in its plants. It thus advised the Special Conference Committee that the leaders of the sit-down had been unionists for only a brief period and that the corporation had erred in " 'not watching such individuals who are aggressive and have initiative' " and in failing to provide them with

" 'special training and inducements to keep them satisfied.' " GM told its supervisory personnel that the strike had been precipitated by " 'foreign elements' from outside the Corporation" who, despite the "great progress ... in practically all phases of employee relations," had taken advantage of "the active dissatisfactions of relatively small numbers." The way to prevent a recurrence of trouble, GM concluded, was not to welcome the advent of unionism in its plants but rather to strengthen the "inside situation" so that it would become "an effective seal" against the intrusion of " 'destructive external factors.' "[24] As a possible first step to strengthen the "inside situation," GM replaced Evan J. Parker as the plant manager of Fisher Body Nos. 1 and 2. Ironically, Parker, who was now deemed guilty of having allowed a strike to develop in his plants, had originally received his assignment as a consequence of the 1930 strike in Fisher Body No. 1.[25]

UAW members, as unfamiliar as GM with the conduct of stable employer-employee relations and assuming that victory in the strike would produce some radical change in the structure of status and power in GM plants, were reluctant to accept the customary discipline exercised by management, and they "ran wild in many plants for months." Union committeemen aggressively pressed the grievances of union members upon oftentimes unyielding foremen, and as one UAW member later conceded, "every time a dispute came up the fellows would have a tendency to sit down and just stop working."[26]

To be sure, reasonably harmonious relations between union and management prevailed in some GM automobile plants following the strike, but in many of the corporation's factories the UAW complained bitterly of discrimination against union members and of efforts by foremen to intimidate workers. The UAW was particularly critical of management behavior in the Flint Chevrolet complex where, in addition to the usual grievances, the union charged that its old antagonist, Arnold Lenz, had armed about one thousand nonunion workers with specially manufactured clubs and was marching them through the plant so as to intimidate union and potential union members. Knudsen conceded that the men had been armed, but he insisted that their only purpose was "to guard against riot" and that the extra pay they were receiving, about which the union had also complained, was for work outside regular shift hours. Harold Cranefield, a La Follette Committee investigator, accepted the union's charges of intimidation and recommended that Senator La Follette should ask Murphy "to crack down on Knudsen with particular reference to [the] Flint Chevrolet plant."[27]

The first post-settlement strike in the GM complex took place in St. Louis. When the Chevrolet plant in that city reopened on February 16, the foremen, according to the report of an NLRB attorney,

Sit-Down

looked on while nonunion assailants, including a confessed murderer, beat up UAW members. The use of physical force against unionists, coupled with the usual allegations of discrimination, led to a sit-down on February 18 that was settled in a matter of hours and led to the complete organization of the Chevrolet plant.[28]

The St. Louis strike was followed eight days later by a strike at Janesville Fisher Body. When work had resumed in Janesville following the February 11 settlement, the union men wore their UAW buttons to work, and so the "loyal" workers of the Alliance decided to do the same. In contravention of management rules, a UAW member in Fisher Body booed an Alliance button-wearer and was promptly dismissed. Unionists in the dismissed worker's department thereupon refused to work until their comrade would be restored to his job, and this led to a shutdown of the entire Fisher Body unit and of Chevrolet as well. The somewhat ridiculous but nevertheless revealing " 'battle of the buttons' " was settled to the union's satisfaction on March 1, and the plant reopened the next day.[29]

There were very brief sit-downs at the Cleveland Fisher Body plant on March 4 and the Buick plant the next day,[30] and then on Saturday night March 6 the smoldering trouble at the Flint Chevrolet plant culminated in a sit-down in the No. 4 and No. 8 units that quickly idled sixty-five hundred workers. The strikers barred the gates of the two plants to all but union members, scores of workers went home to pick up a supply of clothing in preparation for a prolonged stay in the plants, and Emergency Brigade members quickly appeared outside Chevrolet. The UAW agreed to evacuate the plants after three hours, however, on the condition that the affected establishments should remain closed for the rest of the night and that there be a conference between the union and the management when Chevrolet reopened on Monday.

The resumption of work on the morning of March 8 brought discord, however, rather than concord. Without waiting for the projected conference to resume, five hundred workers in Chevrolet No. 4 sat down once again, allegedly because the company had refused a union request to discharge or at least transfer a nonunionist in the plant, an action that idled about sixty-four hundred workers in four Chevrolet units. Some sixty-eight hundred Fisher Body No. 1 workers were also thrown out of work later the same day as the result of a sit-down in the plant by about seven hundred workers in two departments who were seeking an immediate wage increase. After a day of idleness, a temporary armistice was arranged, the sit-downers evacuated the two plants, and work resumed the next day.

Travis wrote Henry Kraus that "everything" was "lovely" following the two Chevrolet sit-downs, but what had happened in Flint was indicative of the chaotic state of industrial relations in GM following the February 11 settlement. It would appear that the strikes in both Chevrolet and Fisher Body had been illegally called by shop stewards who had not bothered to consult with union organizers. Flint plant managers, bewildered by what was going on in the shops, complained with at least some justification that they simply did not know what the UAW wanted.[31]

The sit-downs and slowdowns in GM plants had their repercussions on the negotiations between corporation and union representatives that began in Detroit on February 16 in accordance with the terms of the February 11 settlement. As the talks drew to a close, Vice-President Charles E. Wilson, the principal GM negotiator, complained about the eighteen sit-downs that had occurred in GM plants in the previous twenty days. "We don't like it," he told reporters, and he expressed concern as to whether the UAW could be expected to observe the new contract in view of its alleged failure to have abided by the February 11 terms. Ed Hall retorted for the union that it was the company that had been responsible for the post-settlement strikes, but the UAW at the same time denied that it had called the strikes, which was probably correct, and it gave assurances that work stoppages would cease.[32]

The principal feature of the new GM-UAW contract, to which the negotiators agreed on March 12,[33] was the elaborate grievance procedure that it instituted for all of GM's motor-vehicle plants. The agreement provided for the establishment of shop committees in each of the GM plants, consisting of from five to nine employees. Grievances of individual workers or groups of workers were to be taken up initially with the appropriate foreman and, if not satisfactorily adjusted, could then be referred by stages that involved the participation of the shop committee for eventual joint review by the president of the UAW, the appropriate GM vice-president, and such additional representatives as the two parties desired. If a grievance could not be resolved at even this level, the two parties, by mutual agreement, could refer it to an impartial umpire.

The grievance procedure accorded the UAW effective recognition in all of GM's automotive plants, not just in the seventeen plants where it temporarily enjoyed a somewhat special position. It was in this sense a distinct gain for the union, but it fell considerably short of what the UAW had been seeking in the negotiations. The union had failed to gain recognition of its prized system of shop stewards, and it was altogether dissatisfied with the nine-man limitation imposed on the shop committees, which contrasted sharply with the

UAW practice of having one shop steward for every twenty-five workers. The inadequacy of a shop committee of at most nine members in plants with thousands of workers was rather obvious, and it led to difficulties in many places.[34]

The UAW was unsuccessful in its efforts to have seniority determined on the basis of service alone, as it had requested in its January 4 demands, but it did secure some alteration in the old ALB rules that GM was at the time following. The management continued to have the right to prepare a separate list of employees—the equivalent of the Class D workers under the ALB rules—who in its judgment should be retained or reemployed, regardless of other seniority provisions, so as "to facilitate tooling or rearrangement of the plant, the taking of inventory and the starting of production or similar situations"; but in making up the list management was henceforth to give "reasonable consideration" to length of service, and the members of the shop committees were to be included on the list, a provision that the UAW hoped would persuade able men to seek positions on these committees.[35]

Length of service was otherwise to determine the order of layoff and rehiring except that if in its judgment production in a particular plant was to be reduced substantially for an extended period of time and would thus create "a social problem" in the community, the management could modify the rule "in a manner satisfactory to the employes" so as to give preference to workers with dependents. Since the UAW had consistently opposed the preference in layoff and rehiring given to employees with dependents under the ALB rules, the new provision, although it did not entirely eliminate dependency as a factor in calculating job tenure rights, was for the union a step in the right direction. The UAW also realized one of its seniority objectives in the agreement's provision that during extended periods of reduced production, temporary employees, defined as workers with less than six months of employment, were to be laid off and the work week was to be reduced before employees with seniority were laid off.

The UAW failed, in the main, to secure its demands with regard to wages, hours, and the timing of operations. It had pressed for the abolition of incentive pay systems throughout GM, but the agreement left the matter of wage payment plans to be settled by local plant managers in accordance with the wishes of the employees involved, GM stating that it had no preference regarding such plans. The UAW had also sought a national minimum wage for GM workers, but the agreement accepted the GM position that wage rates had to be determined by local plant managements in consonance with local conditions. It was provided, however, that when wage complaints could not be settled by local plant managers or where minimum wage rates became a matter of dispute, they could be dealt with according to the grievance procedure, which meant that they could ultimately be referred to the highest levels of the union and the corporation. With regard to hours, the agreement confirmed the existing corporation policy—the forty-hour week, the eight-hour day, and time-and-a-half for overtime—rather than meeting the UAW's demand for the thirty-hour week, the six-hour day, and the usual overtime provision.

In its January 4 demands the UAW had called for the mutual determination by the union and the management of the speed of production, an issue of crucial importance for the union. Again, however, the UAW fell short of its goal. The March 12 agreement stated that time studies were to be made "on the basis of fairness and equity consistent with quality of workmanship, efficiency of operations and the reasonable working capacities of normal operators" and that the local management was to have "full authority" to determine these matters. If, however, an employee or group of employees was dissatisfied with the timing for a job and the foreman could not adjust the complaint, the job was to be restudied and an adjustment was to be made if the timing was found to be unfair. This gave the union a voice, but not really an equal voice, in the determination of production standards. The UAW's January 4 demand for the reinstatement of employees who had been discharged "unjustly" was resolved by referring the matter to the established grievance procedure and by providing that employees who were reinstated following a discharge were to be returned to work of a similar type and at the same rate of pay, which accorded with union principles.

GM, understandably intent on putting a stop to the wave of wildcat strikes it was experiencing, secured a clause in the agreement providing that there were to be no work stoppages because of employee grievances until every effort had been made to adjust the complaints through the grievance procedure and the UAW international officers had given their approval. The conditions stipulated before a strike could occur implied a degree of discipline in the union that did not exist at that time. The agreement was to continue in force until terminated by either party or altered by the consent of both. Either party could cancel the agreement by giving sixty-day notice to the other, but no notice to terminate or modify the agreement could be given prior to June 11, 1937, which meant the continuation of the contract at least until August 11, 1937, the last day of the company's six-month commitment to Murphy and the UAW.

When the contract terms were agreed upon, Wyndham Mortimer, who along with Hall and Brophy had conducted the negotiations for the UAW, conceded that the agreement left "much to be desired" from the union point of view, but he thought that its terms could be "conscientiously" recommended to the delegates from the GM locals, who had to approve the contract before it could go into effect. Two hundred union representatives considered the document for thirteen hours on March 13 before giving it their assent. There were complaints about the provisions regarding hours and wages, the degree of recognition, and the failure to incorporate the steward system. Hall, however, advised the delegates that "'we can't expect to get everything at once,'" and Mortimer, appealing for support and indicating his impatience with the lack of discipline in the union, reportedly remarked, "'We've been pretty liberal with you fellows. We've sanctioned all of your strikes even though we didn't know a thing about them beforehand.'"[36]

Knudsen insisted that the agreement did not depart "very much" from the corporation's unilaterally proclaimed statement of its collective-bargaining policy of August, 1934, but simply spelled out that policy in "greater detail" in so far as "procedure" was concerned.[37] This was the same line that GM took with its supervisory personnel, whom it told that events of the "recent stress period" had demonstrated the soundness of "the basic principles and underlying philosophy" of the corporation's policy regarding collective bargaining. Consistent with its long-standing preference for dealing with individuals rather than organizations, GM stressed to its foremen and executives that it was their responsibility to correct and eliminate "sources of irritation or complaint within the organization" so that it would be unnecessary to invoke the grievance procedure. Refusing to acknowledge that the issue of power was also involved, GM continued to insist that most problems in the plant were the result of individual difficulties and that their early detection would tend to eliminate the need for the formal bargaining procedure altogether.

GM was to discover, however, that its analysis of employer-employee relations was far too simplistic and that its advice to its foremen was a counsel of perfection to which it proved impossible for them to adhere. It was in the area of the recognition of the union, an issue of power, and in the changes wrought with regard to such matters as seniority and the timing of operations, not just in questions of detail, that the agreements of February 11 and March 12 most conspicuously departed from GM's August, 1934, statement. GM would now have to train its supervisory staff not just to be alert to the problems of individuals, crucial as that matter was, but also in the procedures for dealing with labor organizations, and the corporation would find it necessary to augment its industrial-relations staff in both Detroit and in the divisions.[38]

The UAW realized when the GM sit-down strike came to an end that it was faced with "the greatest opportunity" in its history to enlist the unorganized automobile workers and that it must in the next six months overwhelm GM's anti-union defenses. The union lowered its initiation fee for a trial period, substantially increased its organizing staff, and aggressively pushed an organizing campaign. The results obtained in a short span of time were remarkable. The dues-paying membership, a rock-bottom indication of union strength, soared from about eighty-eight thousand in February to 166,000 in March, 254,000 in April, and close to 400,000 by the middle of October.[39] Although there is a tendency in the literature to assign a major role to the NLRA in explaining the momentous labor gains of the 1930's, it is noteworthy that the initial breakthrough in the automobile industry came before the constitutionality of the statute was upheld by the United States Supreme Court.

The GM strike itself was undoubtedly the major factor in the UAW's rapid emergence as one of the largest labor organizations in the United States. Not only did the strike lessen the fear of the workers that they would suffer discrimination if they identified with the UAW, but it provided the necessary ingredient for the building of a union, the element of success—the UAW could now tell the auto workers that it was an organization that had "fought and won" for its members and that would continue to fight for them. The effect, as Mortimer recalled, was "like a huge reservoir bursting." It "seemed to open the flood gates of organization." Workers in the mass now joined the union. "There was no type," Norman Bully remembered, "the young fellows, the older men, everyone seemed equally to desire the union, to want the union, and support the union." Organizing was "no problem," one of the UAW's Detroit organizers recalled. "I did not have to go out and seek members, they were seeking me."[40]

The appeal of the UAW in GM plants following the strike was strengthened and given substance by the day-to-day victories the union was achieving—the pay raises that were won in various plants, the acceleration of the shift to hourly rates, the retiming of jobs, the reinstatement of discharged workers, the preparation of seniority lists available to union representatives, and the hundreds of minor grievances that were adjusted. The sit-downs and quickie strikes in the plants may have been called without proper authorization, but when the settlements effected by union organizers resulted in the adjustment of the grievances of individual workers or groups of employees, the union enhanced its appeal to the workers. These strikes, Roy Reuther later declared, were "the greatest organizers."[41]

The effect on the employees of the changes taking place in shop conditions was noted early in March by a Fisher Body No. 1 worker who had opposed the strike and the UAW but who revised his opinion about both after returning to work. "The inhuman high speed," he wrote, "is *no more*. We now have a voice, and have slowed up the speed of the line. And [we] are now treated as human beings, and not as part of the machinery. The high pressure is taken off. . . . It proves clearly that united we stand, divided or alone we fall."[42]

The GM sit-down was followed on March 8 by another sit-down directed at the second largest producer in the automobile industry at that time, Chrysler Corporation. The Chrysler UAW leadership had dispatched representatives to Flint during the GM strike to study the tactics the strikers were employing, and it sought to apply what it had learned in its own strike. "Of course," one of the Chrysler strike leaders recalled, "we had the experience of the General Motors boys. . . . I mean it was a little easier for us than it was for the . . . boys in Flint."[43]

Chrysler secured an injunction against the strikers, and this time Murphy made it unmistakably clear that he would use force, if necessary, to clear the plants. He was, however, able to persuade both sides to accept the kind of truce that he had pressed for unsuccessfully during the GM strike: the union evacuation of the Chrysler plants in return for a company promise that it would make no effort to resume production while strike talks were underway and the stationing of state police around the plants to guarantee the observance of the agreement. As in the GM sit-down, the Chrysler strikers were seeking recognition for the UAW as the exclusive bargaining agency for the company's workers; but in the settlement agreed to on April 6 they received recognition of the union for its members only, although the company promised neither to assist nor to bargain with any other group for the purpose of "undermining" the UAW, and Walter Chrysler may have given private assurances to the union that went beyond this concession.[44] In the succeeding days and weeks, the UAW, in some instances as the result of strikes, secured agreements from Hudson, Reo, Packard, Studebaker, and numerous parts producers. By the summer of 1937 only Ford among important producers in the automobile industry had been able to stem the union advance.[45]

The UAW, however, was an organization beset with serious internal problems and divisions. Two rival groups contended for control of the union: the so-called Progressive Caucus, led by Homer Martin and Richard Frankensteen and including some Lovestoneites,[46] and the so-called Unity Caucus, in which Communist and Socialist elements were conspicuously present. Martin complained that the numerous sit-down strikes called after March 12—their number had reached 170 by the middle of June—were intended to promote factional ends, but he was unable to curb the strikes partly because the international lacked adequate authority, partly because he did not wish to appear to be surrendering to the demands of the automobile manufacturers.

The problems of the UAW were compounded in the fall of 1937 when economic recession added to the difficulties the faction-torn organization was experiencing. The return of good times improved organizational prospects but did nothing to restore internal harmony. The dispute between the Martin and anti-Martin factions degenerated into almost open warfare in 1938 and 1939, culminating in April, 1939, when Martin, whose influence and prestige were rapidly waning, led a rump of the union into the AFL. When NLRB elections were held in GM's plants on April 17, 1940, the UAW-CIO registered a majority in forty-eight of the plants with 120,000 workers, the UAW-AFL in only five plants with fifty-six hundred workers.

In subsequent contract negotiations with GM the UAW-CIO finally realized a long-cherished goal by gaining recognition as the sole bargaining agency in the plants where it had won a majority of the vote. By the time the Japanese attacked Pearl Harbor, the UAW-CIO was paying a per capita tax on a membership of 649,000, and in another six months it was to subdue the last anti-union stronghold in the industry, the Ford Motor Company. What the organization had accomplished in the few short years since the international union had been established represented, as Walter Galenson has observed, "one of the most impressive achievements in the history of American labor."[47]

The GM sit-down strike not only stimulated the rapid growth of unionism in the automobile industry but in the mass-production industries in general, thus demonstrating to a degree the validity of Joseph Shister's theory that union growth in one sector of the economy may be "a necessary condition for growth in another relevant sector." The effects of the strike, the CIO's organ noted on March 1, "continue to spread over the labor waters like waves and ripples in the wake of a boat that is forging ahead." As if to demonstrate the accuracy of this figure of speech, there came the startling news the next day that the great United States Steel Corporation, long a stronghold of the open shop, had come to terms with the Steel Workers' Organizing Committee without a strike. Although other factors were clearly involved, the management of the company, observing what had occurred in the GM sit-down, had undoubtedly concluded that a prolonged and costly steel strike was pointless if United States Steel in the end would have to make concessions analogous to those GM had been compelled to make. As John L. Lewis privately observed just after the steel settlement had been consummated, the GM strike had had "a sweeping effect on steel" and had broken "the united financial front" that had opposed the CIO.

The capitulation of United States Steel, another CIO victory achieved before the NLRA was declared constitutional, further enhanced the prestige of the Lewis organization and increased its appeal to the unorganized. Soon the CIO included within its ranks workers in the oil fields, metal mines, and logging camps and in the textile, shoe and leather, electrical, radio, maritime, and furniture industries, street-car operators, government employees, and even newspaper reporters. "Around mammoth modern mills and at bleak old factories, on ships and on piers, at offices and in public gathering-places, men and women roared, 'C.I.O.! C.I.O.!' ... Labor was on the march as it had never been before in the history of the Republic." By the time of its first national convention in October, 1937, the CIO had thirty-two national affiliates and a claimed membership of four million. The Lewis organization almost certainly exaggerated the number of its adherents, but this does not detract from the remarkable character of its achievements during the first ten months of 1937.[48]

The GM strike not only stimulated the growth of the CIO, but it also exacerbated the tensions between the Lewis group and the AFL and made a reconciliation between them even more difficult to achieve. The Federation's efforts in the strike to counter the UAW's demand for exclusive representation were bitterly resented by the industrial union forces. Lewis described Green's call to Murphy on February 6 as "treason to the labor movement" and "an act of moral turpitude," and Van A. Bittner of the CIO wired Green just after his intervention in the Detroit negotiations that the AFL Executive Council included "men who face this battle between the automobile workers and General Motors with only one thought in mind—to drive the automobile workers back to work so that it might be said that the Committee for Industrial Organization is a failure." When the strike was over, Martin denounced Green as "the modern Judas Iscariot of the labor movement," and the Policy Committee of the United Mine Workers (UMW) condemned both Green and Frey for "their gratuitous, insulting, anti-union, strike-breaking statements" regarding the February 11 settlement and authorized the union's international officers to expel the AFL president from the UMW.[49]

Quite apart from its momentous significance for the organization

Aftermath

331

of the unorganized and its effect on the rivalry of the AFL and the CIO, the GM strike, as a spectacular and successful example of the sit-down, greatly increased the popularity of the tactic. Whereas only forty-eight of 2712 strikes in 1936, affecting less than eigthy-eight thousand workers, had been of the sit-down variety, 477 of the 4740 strikes in 1937 were sit-downs that lasted at least one day, and they affected approximately 400,000 workers, about one-third of whom actually remained inside the plants. The sit-downs involved every conceivable type of worker—kitchen and laundry workers in the Israel-Zion Hospital in Brooklyn, pencil makers, janitors, dog catchers, newspaper pressmen, sailors, tobacco workers, Woolworth girls, rug weavers, hotel and restaurant employees, pie bakers, watchmakers, garbage collectors, Western Union messengers, opticians, and lumbermen. The largest number of sit-downs occurred in the textile industry, where there were eighty such strikes in 1937, as compared to forty-five in the automobile industry.[50]

There were twenty-five sit-down strikes in January, 1937, affecting 74,479 workers, and forty-seven in February affecting 31,236 workers. The sit-down movement reached its all-time high in March when 170 such strikes involved 167,210 workers. Detroit was at the center of the sit-down strike storm in that month, and the tactic had become so ubiquitous that a Detroit *News* reporter remarked, "Sitting down has replaced baseball as a national pastime, and sitter-downers clutter up the landscape in every direction." *Time* thought that Detroiters were "getting an idea of what a revolution feels like," and some of the city's inhabitants undoubtedly agreed, but the shrewd Detroit newsman W. K. Kelsey was closer to the truth when he commented, "Those strikers have no more idea of 'revolution' than pussy-cats." April, 1937, the month of the Jones and Laughlin decision upholding the NLRA, saw a decline in the number of sit-downs to fifty-eight, affecting 33,339 workers, and during the remainder of the year the tactic fell into increasing disfavor among the workers. There were only four sit-downs in December, and they affected a mere 357 workers.[51]

Of the 477 sit-downs in 1937, 279 were called by CIO affiliates and one hundred by AFL affiliates. The CIO did not formally and officially sanction the sit-down as a strike tactic, but neither would it condemn the device, and it recognized that it might be a useful weapon to utilize against employers who refused to bargain. Speaking for the AFL at the end of March, 1937, William Green specifically disavowed the sit-down and denounced it as illegal, but AFL affiliates did not necessarily feel themselves constrained by this pronouncement.[52]

The sit-down strike was primarily utilized by workers seeking to gain recognition from recalcitrant employers: slightly more than half of the sit-down strikes in 1937 were for this purpose as compared to the 29.4 percent of the strikes directed at securing improved wages and hours. "Substantial gains" were achieved by the strikers in 50.8 percent of the 1937 sit-downs, compromises were worked out in 30.6 percent of the strikes, and little or no gain resulted from 14 percent of the strikes. Although the sit-down, "a weapon of minorities," occurred in areas of the economy where unions were weak, the victory record for strikes of this type was somewhat in excess of the 46.4 percent victory figure for all strikes in 1937, which underscores the effectiveness of the technique and the major reason for its use.[53]

The sit-down strike, as already noted, enjoyed somewhat greater public support in January and February, 1937, than one might have anticipated, but when the sit-down reached epidemic proportions in March, it fell into increasing disrepute. In a Gallup poll published on March 21, 67 percent of the respondents thought that legislation should be passed declaring the sit-down illegal, and 65 percent in another poll published on July 4 thought that state and local governments should use force to eject sit-downers. The tactic was especially unpopular with farmers, inhabitants of small towns, and Republicans, less unpopular with city voters, young voters, and Democrats, and favored by people on relief.[54]

Despite the increasing unpopularity of the sit-down and the widespread willingness to see force used to eject sit-downers, there was very substantial opposition to the use of force if it meant bloodshed, a major deterrent, it will be recalled, in Murphy's consideration of the problem. A poll published in *Fortune* in July, 1937, revealed that only 20.1 percent of the respondents believed that sit-downs should be halted even at the cost of bloodshed. Even among "executives" only a minority of 32.9 percent were prepared to see blood spilled if this were required to drive sit-downers from the plants that they occupied.[55]

It is not at all surprising that the wave of sit-down strikes, occurring at a time when the President was pressing his controversial plan to reorganize the Supreme Court, aroused fears among many Americans that the very foundations of the Republic were being undermined. "Armed insurrection—defiance of law, order and duly elected authority—is spreading like wildfire," a group of Boston civic leaders wired the Senate late in March. "It is rapidly growing beyond control. . . . If minority groups can seize premises illegally, hold indefinitely, refuse admittance to owners or managers, resist by violence and threaten bloodshed all attempts to dislodge them, and intimidate properly constituted authority to the point of impotence, then freedom and liberty are at an end, government becomes a mockery, superseded by anarchy, mob rule and ruthless dictatorship."[56]

The sit-down strike had few supporters in Congress, but only a handful of congressmen spoke out against it while the GM strike was underway. The most vociferous Congressional critic of the sit-down from the very outset was Representative Clare Hoffman, a Republican from Allegan, Michigan, who, as Stephen K. Bailey has pointed out, reflected "the provincialism and bigotry of undiluted Anglo-Saxon stock; the rugged individualism of the small-independent farmers."[57] While the GM strike was on, Hoffman charged that a union minority was defying the law but was being backed by Governor Murphy, and he criticized the silence of the President on the subject. On January 29 Hoffman introduced a resolution requesting the secretary of labor to answer a series of loaded questions designed to place both the strikers and the Department of Labor in an unfavorable light. William L. Connery, the chairman of the House Committee on Labor, informed the House on February 3 that his committee unanimously opposed the sit-down but, echoing the objections of Frances Perkins, that it was equally unanimous in reporting the resolution unfavorably since it would make the secretary of labor a "partisan," would "muddy the waters," and would interfere with Department of Labor efforts to compose the dispute. The resolution was then tabled.[58]

Four days after the GM strike was settled, the La Follette Committee began its GM hearings. The purpose of the hearings, the historian of the committee has contended, was "to counter unfavorable public reaction to the sit-down strike" and to influence the negotiations then underway between the corporation and the UAW. During its week-long hearings the committee provided the UAW with a "national forum" to air its grievances against GM; and by exposing the corporation's labor practices and particularly its use of espionage, the committee helped to place the strike in perspective and to demonstrate that wrong was not all on one side.[59] When Hoffman rose in the House shortly after the GM hearings had been concluded to complain once again that Murphy had disregarded his oath of office in the GM strike, Frank Hook of Michigan retorted that Murphy, even though he had "held up the service of a few legal papers," was to be congratulated for his conduct during the strike, a remark that brought applause from the assembled congressmen.[60]

When the sit-down strike reached epidemic proportions in March, an increasing number of members of Congress began to direct their fire at the tactic. Senator Hiram Johnson of California on March 17 characterized the sit-down as "the most ominous thing in our national economic life today," and two days later Senator Allen J. Ellender of Louisiana expressed the view that the tactic was "abhorrent" and "un-American." In the House, Dewey Short of Missouri was soon to charge that Michigan, which had once been a "State of law and order," had become a "State of anarchy," and he explained that he would not have found it necessary to make this criticism had Murphy possessed "a bone instead of a rubber band for a spine." The debate in Congress was not entirely one-sided, however. A few members of the House defended the sit-down as legal, and Senator Robert F. Wagner of New York and others contended that GM's protests about the illegality of the device were compromised by its own defiance of the NLRA, for which the La Follette Committee hearings had provided chapter and verse.[61]

On April 1, as Senator Arthur H. Vandenberg of Michigan reported it, there was "a great explosion . . . on the Floor of the Senate over sit-down strikes." While the Senate was discussing the Guffey-Vinson coal bill, Senator James F. Byrnes of South Carolina, probably hoping to frustrate a CIO invasion of his state's textile mills and possibly to force President Roosevelt to go on record against the sit-down, offered an amendment to the bill's declaration of public policy that in effect prohibited sit-down strikes in the coal industry.

Senator Vandenberg then rose to say that the moment "this formula of violence" appeared in a community "the desperate result" was that "all the lawlessness, all the hoodlumism, all the syndicalism, and all the communism there is in the area rushes for the point to pour oil on the conflagration." Vandenberg criticized Roosevelt's long silence on the sit-down and insisted that both Congress and the executive branch had a "moral responsibility" to condemn the tactic. When the Michigan senator finished his address, Vice-President Garner, who was apparently no longer of the same opinion as he had been at the conclusion of the GM strike, rushed over to Vandenberg and declared, " 'I want to congratulate you; it was about time somebody said that!' "[62]

The Byrnes amendment was attacked by administration supporters partly because it singled out coal miners for special attention—Senator Matthew M. Neely of the coal state of West Virginia remarked that the amendment was as out of place in the coal bill as "a blacksnake would be at a ladies' lawn party"—which prompted Byrnes on April 3 to withdraw it in favor of a resolution introduced by Senator Key Pittman of Nevada declaring it to be the sense of the Senate that the sit-down was "illegal and contrary to sound public policy." The Pittman resolution was defeated that day by a 36-48 vote. Senator Joseph Robinson of Arkansas then collaborated with Pittman in devising a concurrent resolution that condemned the sit-down in the manner of the Pittman resolution but also declared it to be contrary to public policy for an employer to resort to labor espionage, deny the right of collective bargaining to his employees, foster company unions, or engage in any other unfair labor practices as defined in the NLRA. The resolution in this form was approved by the Senate on April 7 by an overwhelming 75-3 vote. Since it was a concurrent resolution, it was without legal force and did not require the signature of the President. It enabled the Senate to express its opinion on the sit-down without at the same time placing all the blame on labor and without in any way embarrassing the administration.[63]

In the House of Representatives, Martin Dies of Texas, anxious to strike at the aliens and radicals who he believed dominated the CIO, had introduced a resolution on March 23 calling for the appointment of a select committee of the House to investigate the sit-down tactic. The resolution emerged from the House Committee on Rules on April 2, the day after the Byrnes amendment had been introduced, but the administration marshalled its forces against the measure, and it went down to defeat on April 8 by a vote of 150 to 236.[64] It was, however, only a temporary setback for Dies, who in the fall of the next year would have his investigation after all. This time, however, his primary target would be Governor Murphy rather than the CIO.

The subject of industrial relations bulked large in the speeches and statements of Murphy in the weeks and months that followed the GM strike. He defended the right of the workers to engage in collective bargaining and to have a voice in determining the conditions under which they labor, and he explained the sit-down and labor excesses as a reaction to a long history of "repression" by employers and government and to management's use of illegal and improper tactics to thwart organization. At the same time he stressed that personal liberties would be of little value unless property rights were protected and the integrity of the courts preserved. The recurrent theme in Murphy's numerous remarks on the labor problem—he was obviously rationalizing his behavior in the GM strike—was the need to settle the differences between labor and management by pacific means rather than by force and violence. His own restraint in the use of force, he insisted, had *"strengthened rather than weakened government and the law."* Had he used force to empty the plants, the state's government would have come to be regarded as "a horrible, oppressive thing which coldly ignored human values and demanded human life as the price of its own ruthless supremacy."

As the embodiment of the public interest, government, in Murphy's view, had to play a large role in the sphere of industrial relations. It should, above all, attempt to remove the causes for industrial conflict and to provide the necessary machinery to facilitate the composition of labor disputes. The industrial-relations bill that the Murphy administration drafted for the consideration of the Michigan legislature but which did not pass was designed to restrain the precipitate resort by labor and management to the strike or lockout and to provide for mediation and arbitration of industrial disputes. One section of the measure, reflecting Murphy's experience in the sit-down strikes, provided that whenever in a strike or lockout local police authorities were unable to maintain order or to protect the owners or operators of the property or those dealing with them in the peaceful exercise of their rights, the governor could place the establishment in the charge of the commissioner of the state police pending further efforts at mediation; and during this period the property was to remain closed or was to be permitted to operate under regulations consistent with the interests of the public and the parties affected.[65]

As the sit-down strike fever spread, Murphy increasingly stressed that "public order must be preserved and public authority must be respected," and, as Adolph Germer recorded in his diary after a conference with the governor during the Chrysler sit-down, "He deplored the sit-down strikes—taking 'possession' of other people's property." He told a law-and-order conference that he had convoked in Detroit on March 17 that public officials and the majority of the people were "gravely disturbed" by the large number of labor disputes and "a disposition in some quarters to ignore the law and violate the security and freedom of individuals and corporations in the exercise of their personal and property rights." He wished it to be known that "we have means to enforce respect for public authority and we propose to use them with proper vigor if need be."[66]

Murphy's conduct in the GM sit-down, which at the time the strike was concluded had seemed like a major political asset for the governor, turned into a political liability when that momentous dispute was followed not by industrial peace but by a rash of sit-down strikes in Michigan and elsewhere. Increasingly, the strikes were blamed on Murphy's failure to have enforced the law in Flint, and the governor's protestations that the sit-downs were not due to the GM strike but to "underlying reasons" and that his use of force in Flint would have led to even more severe labor troubles and possibly to civil war failed to still the criticism. The publisher of the Adrian (Michigan) *Daily Telegram* contended that Flint had been the "first acid test" as to whether the law would be enforced in Michigan and that Murphy's failure of the test "started and kept alive the reign of lawlessness" in the state.[67]

Murphy's conduct during the sit-down strikes, particularly during the GM strike, became a major political issue in Michigan. Meeting in their state convention on February 5 while the Flint strike was still on, Michigan Republicans deplored the "lawlessness" in Flint and attributed it to derelictions on Murphy's part. Frank D. Fitzgerald, whom Murphy had defeated in 1936 and who was again to be the Republican gubernatorial nominee in 1938, declared at the same time, "I never expected to see the courts of Michigan absolutely ignored and laughed at."[68]

The Republicans were aided and abetted in their exploitation of the sit-down strike issue by the House Special Committee on Un-American Activities, the Dies Committee, which on October 18, 1938, while the Michigan gubernatorial campaign was in full swing, began hearings on the interconnections between Communism and the sit-down strikes. For four days a parade of witnesses, none of them friendly to Murphy,[69] stressed the Communist role in the strikes in testimony that was sometimes factually correct but sometimes was not. Murphy was brought under direct attack particularly by Gadola, who charged that the governor had prevented Wolcott from enforcing the law, and Barringer, who referred to Murphy's "treasonable action."[70]

Murphy was anxious to appear before the Dies Committee to rebut what he considered inaccurate and "misleading testimony," but it was decided in the end that the challenge to the committee should come from the President and not the governor. When Roosevelt was asked about the matter at his October 25 press conference, he submitted a written reply in which he stated that he was "disturbed not because of the absurdly false charges made by a coterie of disgruntled Republican officeholders [Gadola and Barringer] against a profoundly religious, able and law-abiding Governor but because a Congressional Committee charged with the responsibility of investigating un-American activities should have permitted itself to be used in a flagrantly unfair and un-American attempt to influence an election." The President then proceeded to defend Murphy's conduct in the strike.[71]

Undeterred, Dies read into the record of the hearings a rebuttal to the President. Roosevelt, he said, was "wholly misinformed" and was relying on "prejudiced sources." The evidence presented before the Dies Committee would be acceptable in any court, and if Roosevelt doubted this, the two of them, Dies brazenly suggested, could each appoint an attorney, the two lawyers could then choose a third man, and the three-man committee could study the matter and report to the nation on the accuracy of the testimony. Dies said that it was his duty "to conduct a fearless investigation, regardless of political expediency," and that it would have been wrong for him to have shielded Murphy just because he was a Democrat and a "strong friend" of Roosevelt.[72]

In a radio address as the day of the election neared, Murphy declared that if the Communists had started the strike, it was certainly without his knowledge. The problem for him had been "not to find out who started the fire but to put it out with as little delay and as little damage as possible."[73] Murphy lost the election by 93,493 votes, and many party leaders thought that the sit-downs had been a major cause for his defeat.[74] Murphy himself saw the strikes as a factor in his loss and bitterly wrote in a letter at a later time, "They practically drove me out of Michigan because my beliefs and sympathies supposedly authored the conflicts." In a more sober and probably more nearly correct analysis, however, Murphy attributed his defeat primarily to the recession of 1937–38. Actually, Murphy had run well in Republican Michigan in an off-year election: he had received 47 percent of the vote as compared to 45.8 percent for the Democrats in 1934 and 42 percent in 1930. He had received 51 percent of the vote in 1936, but he had run about 125,000 votes behind Roosevelt in the state.[75]

III

The GM strike, as some writers have recognized, was really "more than a strike." It was not only the "most critical labor conflict" of the 1930's and perhaps in all of American history, but it was also a part, the most dramatic and important part, of a vast labor upheaval that *Fortune* described as "one of the greatest mass movements in our history."[76] The successful outcome of the strike helped to determine that the decision-making power in large segments of American industry where the voice of labor had been little more than a whisper, if that, would henceforth have to be shared in some measure with the unions in these industries, and the trade-union movement as a whole would enjoy a higher status in American life than it ever had before.

The sit-down strike phase of the labor upheaval of the 1930's, of which the GM strike serves as the best example, was the equivalent in some ways of the civil-rights upheaval that began with the Montgomery bus boycott of 1955–56.[77] In his analysis of the civil-rights movement, Arthur I. Waskow has coined the phrase "creative disorder" to describe the pursuit of change by disorderly but non-violent means such as sit-ins. Insofar as the politics of disorder seeks change, he has argued, "it is generally invented by people who are 'outside' a particular system of political order, and want to bring change about so that they can enter. In doing so, they tend to use new techniques that make sense to themselves out of their own experience, but that look disorderly to people who are thinking and acting inside the system."

The technique of disorder, Waskow contends, is apt to be tolerated or even encouraged to the extent that the "outside" group using it is pursuing ends deemed legitimate. When the state refuses to use its power against the perpetrators of disorder and prevents the use of violence against them, it in effect legitimizes disorder. In the instance of the civil-rights trespassers, Congress and the Department of Justice, quite apart from any belief in the worthiness of the goals sought by the civil-rights movement, tolerated non-violent disorder because the imposition of order might have led to violence.[78]

The GM sit-down had many of the characteristics Waskow associates with the concept of creative disorder—the Congress of Racial Equality, as a matter of fact, "apparently derived" the sit-in technique from the sit-down strikes in the automobile industry.[79] The sit-down strikers, like the civil-rights trespassers, were seeking change by "disorderly" but non-violent means. They were employing a technique that certainly made "sense" to workers familiar with the technology of automobile production; and, like the civil-rights demonstrators, they were "outsiders" insofar as representation in the automobile industry was concerned and were seeking entry into the "system."

Since the sit-downers were pursuing objectives sanctioned by law but denied them by their employer, their unconventional behavior was tolerated by large sections of the public. Governor Murphy, sympathetic with the goals of the strikers and seeking above all to avoid the outbreak of major violence that might have resulted from a no-nonsense law-and-order approach, refused to employ the power of the state to dislodge the sit-downers and forestalled the use of force against them by others, thus ensuring that some non-violent way out of the struggle would have to be found. Murphy and others apparently assumed that the sit-down strike would some day be accepted among the authorized methods of industrial warfare, just as the outside strike and, to a lesser degree, picketing had gained legitimacy by that time after having previously been considered illegal, but this turned out to be an incorrect judgment.

In other respects, also, the sit-down strike movement of the 1930's, and especially the GM strike, anticipated the civil-rights movement of the 1950's and 1960's. College students involved themselves in both movements, and songs—"We Shall Not Be Moved" was sung in Flint in 1937 and in the South in the early 1960's—were used as a morale builder by both UAW and civil-rights organizers. The UAW-CIO drive for recognition was a challenge to the conservative AFL leadership of the labor movement and brought new labor leaders to the fore nationally and locally—"Leaders are popping up everywhere," Travis said about Flint a month after the GM strike"[80]—just as the later civil-rights movement was, in some degree, a revolt against the conservatism of the established and dominant Negro organizations and led to the emergence of new leadership elements in local communities and in the nation as a whole. The UAW addressed its appeal to the mass of the semiskilled and unskilled workers in the automobile plants and not just to an elite of the skilled in the same way that the new civil-rights organizations a generation later sought to bestir the mass of the Negroes and not just "the talented tenth" to join in their protests.[81]

Finally, the GM strike was the beginning of a brief period in the history of the American labor movement when workers saw themselves, or at least were so seen by liberal reformers, as seeking not just to better their own condition but also to better the nation, a moment when group interest and the national interest seemed to merge, when the union was not just another organization but was "a social and moral force."[82] In this sense, too, the labor upheaval of the 1930's suggests the civil-rights movement of the 1950's and 1960's at its height.

Although there were obvious dissimilarities, echoes of the sit-down strikes of the 1930's were heard in 1968 and 1969 when college students, conscious of the tactics of civil disobedience practiced by the civil-rights movement for more than a decade, occupied college and university buildings in an effort to wrest concessions from administrative authorities. University administrators, like the public officials confronted with factory sit-downs in the 1930's, like Governor Murphy, had to decide whether to tolerate the trespass upon university property, to secure the abandonment of the tactic by denying food and utility service to the trespassers, to seek court injunctions against the sit-ins, or to eject the offending students by the use of force. Like GM and other companies in the 1930's some university authorities hesitated to employ force to dislodge the strikers lest it result in damage to university property and win support for the sit-downers from those who opposed or were indifferent to their behavior.

The sit-ins at Columbia University and elsewhere were conducted by a minority of militants who by their action sometimes prevented the majority of students from attending classes, just as the GM sit-downers forestalled the majority of the corporation's employees from going to their jobs. The student sit-downers, like the factory sit-downers, commonly wished to share in the decision-making that affected their lives, but their cry for "participatory democracy," "student power," or "black power" lacked the concreteness of labor's demand for collective bargaining and union power. Like the automotive sit-downers, student sit-downers were disposed to argue that the ends that they were seeking justified the means that they employed, especially since less disorderly tactics had allegedly proved unavailing; and just as the GM strikers insisted that the corporation withdraw the injunction directed against the trespass upon its property, so the student strikers demanded amnesty for their behavior. The most radical of the student leaders in 1968 and 1969 hoped to "radicalize" the campus just as the far left in the UAW in 1937 desired, in vain, to radicalize the union.

The sit-downers, at least at Columbia University, fashioned a community inside the buildings that they occupied that resembled in some ways the sit-in communities of the GM strikers. Like the visitors to the Flint plants in 1937, a visitor admitted to one of the Columbia buildings in the spring of 1968 was impressed with the discipline that prevailed, the resourcefulness of the students in formulating rules "for living together in an isolated society," the effort to maintain cleanliness, and the endless round of meetings (more to be expected, no doubt, of students than of automobile workers). The student strikers, it was later reported, derived "feelings of community, drama, meaning" from their experience just as their labor counterparts did in the 1930's. That the student revolt would lead to the kind of fundamental change in the relationship of students to university administrators and faculty that the sit-down strikes of the 1930's produced in the relationship between labor and management in the giant factories of the country seemed possible as the academic year 1968–69 drew to a turbulent close.[83]

The GM sit-down strike of 1936–37 was, all in all, the most significant American labor conflict in the twentieth century. When the UAW victory in the strike was followed by the capitulation of the United States Steel Corporation to the Steel Workers' Organizing Committee, the *Financial Observer* remarked that "an era of labor-management relations" had come to an end and "a new era" had begun. "Seldom," the journal asserted, "does a single happening appear so clearly to draw the line that closes off the reign of old ideas."[84] The comment of the *Financial Observer* was made with reference to the steel settlement, but it applies with even greater force to the GM sit-down.

Notes

Chapter 1

1. Flint *Journal,* Jan. 3, 1937.
2. Earlier in the strike, the sit-downers in the plant had lifted food into the plant through the windows. New York *Times,* Jan. 4, 1937; E. C. Johnston to Oscar G. Olander, Jan. 5, 1937, Frank Murphy Papers, Michigan Historical Collections, Ann Arbor, Michigan.
3. "The Flint Affair," undated, Sen. 78A-F9, Box 124, Record Group 46, National Archives and Records Service, Washington, D.C. (hereafter cited as La Follette Committee Papers); Flint *Journal,* Jan. 12, 1937; Henry Kraus, *The Many and the Few: A Chronicle of the Dynamic Auto Workers* (Los Angeles, 1947), pp. 125-27; Interview with Robert C. Travis, Dec. 10, 1964, pp. 18-19 (transcripts of all interviews cited are located in the Michigan Historical Collections).
4. The evidence is conflicting with regard to almost every aspect of the battle. The accounts of the affair vary, for example, with regard to such matters as the time when the city police arrived on the scene, whether the strikers were actually able to hoist food into the plant by rope, the number of strikers who descended to the main gate to request that food be allowed to enter the plant, the number of pickets outside the plant, the number of police who first appeared before the plant and how many of them were armed with gas equipment, whether the police forced their way into the plant momentarily during the first attack, the number of times the police charged the plant, the time span of the battle, the location of the spectators, the number who were injured, and whom Governor Murphy saw in Flint and the order in which he saw them. I have consulted the following sources, among others, in attempting to reconstruct the events of the battle: "Flint Affair," La Follette Committee Papers, Box 124; "Statement of the Fight," undated, *ibid.*; Harold Cranefield to Robert Wohlforth, Feb. 10, 1937, *ibid.*; Affidavit of Genora Johnson, Jan. 26, 1937, Box 126, *ibid.*; statements by Travis and Reuther, Subcommittee of Senate Committee on Education and Labor, *Violations of Free Speech and the Rights of Labor, Hearings Pursuant to S. Res. 266,* 75 Cong., 1 Sess. (Washington, 1937), Part 7, pp. 2329-30, 2537-40 (hereafter cited as *La Follette Hearings*); Johnston to Olander, Jan. 12, 1937, Case File #5977, Michigan State Police Records, Lansing, Michigan; Detroit *News,* Jan. 12-13, 1937; New York *Times,* Jan. 12-13, 1937; Flint *Journal,* Jan. 12-13, 1937; Flint *Auto Worker,* Jan. 12, 1937; Kraus, *Many and Few,* pp. 125-45; and Albert Maltz, "'Bodies by Fisher': An Eyewitness Account . . . ," *New Masses,* XXII (Jan. 26, 1937), 25-26. I have relied particularly on the detailed account in Cranefield to Wohlforth, Feb. 10, 1937, which was based on a mass interview with 50 strikers assembled in the refectory of the plant on January 14, and on "Flint Affair," which was also based on the testimony of eyewitnesses and participants.
5. Cranefield to Wohlforth, Feb. 10, 1937, La Follette Committee Papers, Box 124; "Statement of Fight," *ibid.*; "Flint Affair," *ibid.*; *News-Week,*

IX (Jan. 23, 1937), 10. See also Paul Gallico, "Sit-Down Strike," *Cosmopolitan*, CIV (Apr. 1938), [164].
6. *Cf.* "Statement of Fight," La Follette Committee Papers, Box 124; "Flint Affair," *ibid.*; and Maltz, " 'Bodies by Fisher,' " p. 25.
7. *La Follette Hearings*, Part 7, p. 2538.
8. "Flint Affair," La Follette Committee Papers, Box 124; Kraus, *Many and Few*, p. 129.
9. Reuther, an eyewitness, claimed that the police actually forced their way into the plant briefly, but this is not substantiated in other accounts. *La Follette Hearings*, Part 7, p. 2539.
10. *Cf. ibid.*; Kraus, *Many and Few*, p. 134; and "Flint Affair," La Follette Committee Papers, Box 124. The Flint *Journal*, Jan. 12, 1937, whose account of the battle is quite inaccurate at many points, implies that the strikers also used firearms, but this allegation is almost certainly inaccurate. See "Flint Affair."
11. My account of the number injured is based on Detroit *News*, Jan. 12, 1937.
12. "Statement of Fight," La Follette Committee Papers, Box 124.
13. "Flint Affair," *ibid.*; Detroit *News*, Jan. 12, 1937; Oral History Interview of Ted LaDuke, Aug. 5, 1960, p. 19.
14. Minutes of Fisher Body No. 1 Mass Meeting, Jan. 14, 1937, Harry Van Nocker Notebook, Henry Kraus Papers, Box 9, Labor History Archives, Wayne State University, Detroit, Michigan.
15. *La Follette Hearings*, Part 7, p. 2539; Maltz, " 'Bodies by Fisher,' " p. 25; Flint *Journal*, Jan. 12, Feb. 25, 1937; Detroit *News*, Jan. 12, 1937; Cranefield to Wohlforth, Feb. 10, 1937, La Follette Committee Papers, Box 124; House Special Committee on Un-American Activities, *Investigation of Un-American Propaganda Activities in the United States, Hearings Pursuant to H.Res. 282*, 75 Cong., 3 Sess. (Washington, 1938), II, 1645 (hereafter cited as *Dies Hearings*); Kraus, *Many and Few*, pp. 136–38; Adolph Germer Diary, Jan. 11, 1937, Adolph Germer Papers, State Historical Society of Wisconsin, Madison.
16. Johnson Affidavit, Jan. 26, 1937, La Follette Committee Papers, Box 126; Flint *Auto Worker*, Jan. 12, 1937.
17. Detroit *News*, Jan. 12, 1937; Kraus, *Many and Few*, p. 141.
18. "An interested observer" [Jan. 12, 1937], Van Nocker Notebook, Kraus Papers, Box 9.
19. Johnson Affidavit, Jan. 26, 1937, La Follette Committee Papers, Box 126.
20. Evan J. Parker was the plant manager of both Fisher Body No. 1 and No. 2.
21. There is a copy of the song in the Bud Simons Papers, Labor History Archives.
22. Typed notes, Jan. 11, 1937, Murphy Papers; Murphy to Virginia Donaldson, Jan. 26, 1937, *ibid.*; Winston Wessels, "Importance #1: The Michigan National Guard and the 1937 Flint Sit-Down Strike" (MS, 1963), p. 1, in my possession; Detroit *News*, Jan. 12, 1937.
23. Detroit *News*, Jan. 12, 1937; *Dies Hearings*, II, 1686–87; Bradshaw and Wolcott to Murphy, Jan. 12, 1937, Murphy Papers; "E. Kemp narrative" [Jan. 13, 1939], *ibid.*; Germer Diary, Jan. 12, 1937, Germer Papers. Barringer complained to the Dies Committee that Murphy had spoken to Victor and Roy Reuther and other labor leaders before speaking to

Notes to pages 10 to 16

345

city officials. Newspaper accounts do not include the Reuthers among those who spoke to Murphy, but Roy recalled having talked to the governor in the Durant Hotel that night. Travis and Germer definitely spoke to Murphy after he had conversed with city officials. *Dies Hearings,* II, 1686; Interview with Roy Reuther, July 12, 1966, pp. 31–32; Germer Diary, Jan. 12, 1937, Germer Papers.

24. Detroit *News,* Jan. 12–13, 1937; Hill to Murphy, Jan. 12, 1937, Bersey to Murphy, Jan. 12, 1937, Murphy Papers; typed notes, Jan. 12, 1937, *ibid.*; [Detroit *Free Press,* Jan. 13, 1937], Murphy Scrapbooks, *ibid.*
25. UAW Release [Jan. 12, 1937], Kraus Papers, Box 9; Flint *Journal,* Jan. 12, 1937; New York *Times,* Jan. 13, 1937.
26. Flint *Journal,* Jan. 13, 1937; Western Union Press Message, Jan. 13, 1937, Edward Levinson Papers, Box 4, Labor History Archives.
27. R. Reuther interview, pp. 29–30.
28. H. D. Cullen to Charles Kramer, Jan. 26, 1937, La Follette Committee Papers, Box 5.
29. Johnston to Olander, State Police File #5977.
30. *Business Week,* Jan. 16, 1937, p. 13.
31. Detroit *News,* Jan. 13, 14, 1937. Wills's account as to the time the police were sent to Fisher No. 2 was supported by a Flint *Journal* reporter who was on duty at police headquarters from 6:00 P.M. on January 11 to 7:00 A.M. on January 12, but union representatives had detected police in the area *before* 6:00 P.M. Flint *Journal,* Jan. 13, 1937; Cranefield to Wohlforth, Feb. 10, 1937, La Follette Committee Papers, Box 124.
32. *La Follette Hearings,* Part 7, p. 2606.
33. *Dies Hearings,* II, 1684–86. See also Kraus, *Many and Few,* pp. 126–27.
34. Johnston to Olander, Jan. 12, 1937, State Police File #5977; Kraus, *Many and Few,* p. 141.

Chapter II

1. Flint *Journal,* July 9, 1936 (Progress Edition).
2. *Ibid.*; *ibid.,* Nov. 22, 1954 (Souvenir Edition); *ibid.,* Sept. 4, 1955 (Centennial Edition); "General Motors I," *Fortune,* XVIII (Dec. 1938), 158; Carl Crow, *The City of Flint Grows Up* (New York, 1945), pp. 21–22, 29–34; Arthur Pound, *The Turning Wheel: The Story of General Motors through Twenty-Five Years, 1908–1933* (Garden City, New York, 1934), pp. 78–79; John B. Rae, "The Fabulous Billy Durant," *Business History Review,* XXXII (Autumn, 1958), 255–57.
3. Pound, *Turning Wheel,* p. 86.
4. Crow, *Flint,* pp. 39–44; John B. Rae, *American Automobile Manufacturers: The First Forty Years* (Philadelphia, 1959), pp. 18–19; Pound, *Turning Wheel,* pp. 68–72; Flint *Journal,* July 9, 1936.
5. Crow, *Flint,* pp. 44–60; Rae, *Automobile Manufacturers,* p. 19; Pound, *Turning Wheel,* pp. 73–90; Flint *Journal,* July 9, 1936.
6. Flint *Journal,* Nov. 22, 1954.
7. Crow, *Flint,* pp. 73–77; Rae, *Automobile Manufacturers,* p. 87; Pound, *Turning Wheel,* pp. 113–21; Flint *Journal,* Nov. 22, 1954; Alfred P. Sloan, Jr., *My Years with General Motors* (Edited by John McDonald with Catharine Stevens; Garden City, New York, 1964), p. 4. For the

history of Oldsmobile, Cadillac, and Oakland, see Rae, *Automobile Manufacturers*, pp. 30–32, 34–35; and Pound, *Turning Wheel*, pp. 34–36, 41–67, 92–97, 101–110.
8. Pound, *Turning Wheel*, pp. 86, 124–30; Rae, *Automobile Manufacturers*, pp. 88–89.
9. Rae, *Automobile Manufacturers*, pp. 89–92; Pound, *Turning Wheel*, pp. 131–42.
10. Flint *Journal*, July 9, 1936, Nov. 22, 1954; Rae, *Automobile Manufacturers*, pp. 110–12; Pound, *Turning Wheel*, pp. 143–61; Sloan, Jr., *My Years with GM*, pp. 10–11.
11. Pound, *Turning Wheel*, pp. 163–66, 170; Rae, *Automobile Manufacturers*, pp. 111–12.
12. Sloan, Jr., *My Years with GM*, pp. 17–18, 24–25; New York *Times*, Feb. 18, 1966; "Alfred P. Sloan Jr.: Chairman," *Fortune*, XVII (Apr. 1938), 74, 114n.
13. Rae, *Automobile Manufacturers*, p. 137; Pound, *Turning Wheel*, pp. 176–77, 179–83.
14. Pound, *Turning Wheel*, pp. 288–95; Flint *Journal*, Nov. 22, 1954; [Frank Rodolf], "An Industrial History of Flint" (MS, Flint *Journal*, 1949), pp. 491–92.
15. Rae, *Automobile Manufacturers*, pp. 136, 138–40; John B. Rae, *The American Automobile* (Chicago, 1965), pp. 83–84; Pound, *Turning Wheel*, pp. 187–88, 192–93, 341–42; Sloan, Jr., *My Years with GM*, pp. 25–26, 31, 45–46, 54–55, 431, 433; Alfred D. Chandler, Jr., *Strategy and Structure: Chapters in the History of the Industrial Enterprise* (Cambridge, Mass., 1962), pp. 130–61; "General Motors I," p. 41.
16. Ford shut down from May 31, 1927, when production of the Model T was discontinued, until late 1928, when the Model A was introduced. In 1910 GM accounted for 21.7 percent of the new car output as compared to Ford's 17.7 percent. Simon N. Whitney, *Antitrust Policies: American Experience in Twenty Industries* (New York, 1958), I, 468.
17. Rae, *Automobile Manufacturers*, pp. 157–58; Pound, *Turning Wheel*, p. 231; Flint *Journal*, Nov. 22, 1954; Matthew Josephson, "Profiles," *New Yorker*, XVII (Mar. 8, 1941), 22–26, 28.
18. GM earned approximately $68.5 million before income taxes on the accessories and parts portion of its business, a rate of return of 87.13 percent. Federal Trade Commission (FTC), *Report on Motor Vehicle Industry*, 76 Cong., 1 Sess., House Doc. 468 (Washington, 1939), p. 493.
19. *Ibid.*, pp. 431, 491; Whitney, *Antitrust Policies*, I, 468; GM, *Twentieth Annual Report of General Motors Corporation, Year Ended December 31, 1928*, p. 39 (GM annual reports will hereafter be cited as *Report*).
20. GM, *Reports, 1929*, p. 12; *1928*, pp. 36, 39; *1932*, pp. 32, 35; FTC, *Report on Motor Vehicle Industry*, pp. 431, 491; Whitney, *Antitrust Policies*, I, 468; *Ward's 1939 Automotive Year Book*, p. 36.
21. GM, *Reports, 1932*, pp. 32, 35; *1936*, pp. 13, 45; FTC, *Report on Motor Vehicle Industry*, pp. 431, 491. GM's profits before income taxes on its parts and accessories group rose from $10,398,858 in 1932 to $61,465,982 in 1936, and the rate of return on this group increased from 16.33 percent to 70.16 percent during the same period. *Ibid.*, p. 493.
22. "General Motors I," pp. 41, 140; GM, *Reports, 1936*, pp. 6–9, 11, 13,

27-28, 45-46, 50; *1937*, pp. 44-45; "Why Did the Auto Workers Strike?" *Social Action*, III (Feb. 15, 1937), 4; Sloan, Jr., *The Worker in General Motors* (n.p., Dec. 31, 1937), pp. 15-16; Bureau of the Census, *Historical Statistics of the United States, Colonial Times to 1957* (Washington, 1960), pp. 92, 95; *Ward's 1939 Automotive Year Book*, pp. 36, 46.

23. GM, Executive Training Program, Section G-5, Management Principles ... [1937], Session 1, p. 1, General Motors Institute, Flint, Michigan (all of the GM training manuals cited are located in the GM Institute).

24. GM, Labor Relations Diary, Section 1, pp. 1, 7, 16, GM Building, Detroit, Michigan; Sloan, Jr., *My Years with GM*, p. 405; untitled manuscript [July 1934], Henry Kraus Papers, Box 2, Labor History Archives, Wayne State University, Detroit, Michigan; William Ellison Chalmers, "Labor in the Automobile Industry: A Study of Personnel Policies, Workers Attitudes, and Attempts at Unionism" (Ph.D. thesis, University of Wisconsin, 1932), p. 175.

25. Pound, *Turning Wheel*, pp. 177-78; GM, *Report, 1928*, p. 19; Subcommittee of the Senate Committee on Education and Labor, *Violations of Free Speech and the Rights of Labor, Hearings Pursuant to S. Res. 266*, 76 Cong., 1 Sess. (Washington, 1939), Part 45, pp. 16777-17078 (hereafter cited as *La Follette Hearings*); Robert Ozanne, *A Century of Labor-Management Relations at McCormick and International Harvester* (Madison, 1967), pp. 157-60.

26. Pound, *Turning Wheel*, pp. 178, 395-97; GM, *Report, 1936*, pp. 41-42; [Rodolf], "Industrial History," p. 503.

27. Pound, *Turning Wheel*, p. 413; GM, *Reports, 1919*, pp. 13-14; *1920*, p. 9; *1929*, p. 23.

28. Pound, *Turning Wheel*, pp. 402-6; GM, *Reports, 1919*, p. 14; *1924*, p. 23; *1925*, p. 12; *1928*, p. 21; *1932*, p. 15; *1933*, p. 22; *1936*, pp. 9, 43-44.

29. Pound, *Turning Wheel*, pp. 406-7; GM, *Report, 1926*, p. 13. The maximum number of employees to take advantage of the plan in any one year was 3,633, in 1925. *Ibid., 1929*, p. 39.

30. Pound, *Turning Wheel*, pp. 407-8; GM, *Reports, 1926*, p. 11; *1928*, p. 22; *1936*, p. 44; FTC, *Report on Motor Vehicle Industry*, p. 547.

31. [Rodolf], "Industrial History," pp. 508-16; Robert William Dunn, *Labor and Automobiles* (New York, 1929), p. 152; Flint *Journal*, Nov. 22, 1954. See the list of IMA officers in *I.M.A. News*, Jan. 28, 1937.

32. Hartley W. Barclay, "We Sat Down with the Strikers and General Motors," *Mill and Factory*, XX (Feb. 1937), 51; [Rodolf], "Industrial History," p. 516; *Michigan: A Guide to the Wolverine State* (New York, 1941), p. 302. The issues of the *I.M.A. News* indicate the scope of IMA activities.

33. Barclay, "We Sat Down," pp. 47, 51.

34. GM, *Report, 1931*, pp. 13-14.

35. [Rodolf], "Industrial History," p. 504; GM, *Reports, 1932*, pp. 15, 20; *1933*, p. 36; GM, Labor Relations Diary, Section 1, p. 8; "Why Did the Auto Workers Strike?" p. 12.

36. See the testimony of Flint GM workers in Hearing on Regularizing Employment and Otherwise Improving the Conditions of Labor in the Automobile Industry, Dec. 17-18, 1934, pp. 15-16, 24-25, 31-32, 86, 259, 331-32, 346-47, 382-83, 447-48, 450, 498-99, 516-17, 606, Records of

the National Recovery Administration, Box 7265, Record Group 9, National Archives and Records Service, Washington, D.C. (hereafter cited as NRA).
37. New York *Times*, Nov. 9, Dec. 3, 1936; GM, *Report, 1936*, p. 8.
38. Sidney Fine, *The Automobile under the Blue Eagle* (Ann Arbor, 1963), pp. 351–54, 357–58, 411–12; GM, *Report, 1935*, pp. 15–16, 31.
39. The GM Institute developed out of a night school originally established in Flint by the Industrial Fellowship League. At the time of the sitdown strike, the Institute conducted a foremanship training program for more than 5000 GM foremen and also directed a combined work-study program for young men selected by the manufacturing divisions and company dealers. Flint *Journal*, Nov. 22, 1954; Barclay, "We Sat Down," p. 51.
40. Fisher Body Corporation, Department Management [June 29, 1932], unpaginated, GM Institute; GM, Executive Training Program, Section G-2, Employer-Employe Relations, 1934, Session 1, p. 3; Chalmers, "Labor in Automobile Industry," pp. 70–71, 172. Employment had been centralized in GM plants, but the powers of foremen with regard to hiring and firing remained considerable.
41. Sloan, Jr., *My Years with GM*, pp. 392, 405; "General Motors IV: A Unit of Society," *Fortune*, XIX (Mar. 1939), 146; *La Follette Hearings*, 75 Cong., 1 Sess. (Washington, 1937), Part 6, pp. 1886, 1906–7.
42. Fine, *Automobile under Blue Eagle*, pp. 33–34, 46, 53–56, 65, 67–68.
43. GM, *Report, 1933*, pp. 16–17; New York *Times*, Apr. 27, 1934.
44. Lane, *The Regulation of Businessmen* (New Haven, 1954), pp. 34–35; Robert Dubin, "Constructive Aspects of Industrial Conflict," in Arthur Kornhauser *et al.*, eds., *Industrial Conflict* (New York, 1954), p. 42.
45. Fine, *Automobile under Blue Eagle*, pp. 190–91, 217–19.
46. NRA Release No. 3827 [3817], Mar. 15, 1934, Case 209, Records of the National Labor Board, Drawer 35, Record Group 25, National Archives and Records Service, Washington, D.C. (hereafter cited as NLB).
47. Fine, *Automobile under Blue Eagle*, pp. 213–27. For the ALB seniority rules, see *ibid.*, pp. 251–52.
48. Donaldson Brown to Lammot du Pont, Mar. 29, 1934, GM, Labor Relations Diary, Appendix Documents to Accompany Section 1, Doc. 23 (unless otherwise indicated, all appendix documents hereafter cited accompany Section 1).
49. For a detailed account of the strike, see Sidney Fine, "The Tool and Die Makers Strike of 1933," *Michigan History*, XLII (Sept. 1958), 297–323.
50. Fine, *Automobile under Blue Eagle*, pp. 261–66; ALB, Stenographic Report of Hearing, In the Matter of Fisher Body Corporation, May 1, 1934, pp. 8–9, 13, Michigan Historical Collections, Ann Arbor, Michigan.
51. ALB, Fisher Body Hearing, May 1, 1934, pp. 81–82, 84.
52. Fine, *Automobile under Blue Eagle*, p. 267.
53. GM, *Report, 1934*, p. 11; GM, Executive Training Program, Section G-2, Employer-Employe Relations, 1934, Session 1, p. 4.
54. GM, *Report, 1934*, p. 11; Sloan, Jr., to All Employes . . . , Oct. 12, 1934, Joe Brown Collection, Labor History Archives.
55. *Automotive Industries*, LXXI (Sept. 15, 1934), 322–24, 333.

Notes to pages 35 to 43

349

56. *Michigan Manufacturer and Financial Record*, LIV (Oct. 27, 1934), 8; New York *Times*, Oct. 16, 1934.
57. *La Follette Hearings*, Part 6, p. 2035.
58. Fine, *Automobile under Blue Eagle*, p. 289.
59. *Ibid.*, pp. 151, 188–89, 212–13, 268–70, 272.
60. *Ibid.*, pp. 244–50; GM, Labor Relations Diary, Section 1, pp. 42–43, 45.
61. Fine, *Automobile under Blue Eagle*, pp. 189, 213, 215, 232, 326.
62. Senate Committee on Education and Labor, *Violations of Free Speech and Rights of Labor*, 75 Cong., 2 Sess., *Senate Report No. 46* (Washington, 1937), Part 3, pp. 9, 23–25 (hereafter cited as *La Follette Report*); *La Follette Report No. 6*, 76 Cong., 1 Sess. (Washington, 1939), Part 6, p. 144.
63. For evidence that Delco-Remy, at least, had resorted to espionage before 1933, see *Decisions and Orders of the National Labor Relations Board*, XIV (Washington, 1940), 126–27.
64. *La Follette Hearings*, Part 6, p. 2043.
65. *Ibid.*, p. 1879; *La Follette Report No. 46*, Part 3, pp. 23, 46–47.
66. *La Follette Report No. 46*, Part 3, pp. 16, 24, 27–28; *La Follette Hearings*, Part 6, pp. 1905–11, 1928; F. F. Corcoran to M. K. Hovey [1936], Kraus Papers, Box 9. Other than "sketchy financial records," the latter item was the only document pertaining to its espionage activities that remained in GM's files.
67. *La Follette Report No. 46*, Part 3, pp. 61–67.
68. *Ibid.*, pp. 71–73; *La Follette Hearings*, Part 5, pp. 1511–15, 1521–22, 1690–92; Part 6, pp. 1914, 1970–73, 1992, 2066–67.
69. The committee used the word "hooked" to describe the person who was deceived into betraying his friends and was then converted into a professional labor spy.
70. Charles Kramer, "Arthur J. [sic] Dubuc," Sen 78A–F9, Box 127, Record Group 46, National Archives and Records Service (hereafter cited as La Follette Committee Papers); notes on Dubuc's activities, Dec. 19, 24, 30, 1936, and undated, *ibid.*; *La Follette Hearings*, Part 6, pp. 2138–59, 2160, 2162–63, 2222–26; *La Follette Report No. 46*, Part 3, p. 16.
71. *La Follette Hearings*, Part 6, p. 2123; *La Follette Report No. 46*, Part 3, p. 29.
72. *La Follette Report No. 46*, Part 3, pp. 70–71. The UAW paid-up membership for the automobile industry as a whole did not exceed 32,000 at any time in 1934. Fine, *Automobile under Blue Eagle*, p. 220.
73. Anderson testified that he had been "prevailing upon the Fisher Body and the Chevrolet boys to discontinue the service for some months." *La Follette Hearings*, Part 6, p. 1898.
74. *Ibid.*, pp. 1897–1901, 1922–26; *La Follette Report No. 46*, Part 3, pp. 15–16; GM, Labor Relations Diary, Appendix Documents to Accompany Section 2, Doc. 82.
75. GM, Labor Relations Diary, Section 1, pp. 20–21; *Decisions and Orders of NLRB*, XIV, 121; Norman Beasley, *Knudsen* (New York, 1947), p. 153.
76. GM, Labor Relations Diary, Section 1, pp. 21–23; *ibid.*, Appendix Doc. 8.
77. Fine, *Automobile under Blue Eagle*, p. 156; GM, Labor Relations Diary, Section 1, p. 22.

78. There are copies of several of the GM employee-association plans in Case 209, NLB Drawer 35; ALB Drawer 4006 (the ALB Records are part of the NRA Records); and the Brown Collection.
79. ALB, Fisher Body Hearing, May 2, 1934, pp. 50–51; Beasley, *Knudsen*, p. 153.
80. *Decisions and Orders of NLRB*, XIV, 160.
81. *La Follette Hearings*, 76 Cong., 1 Sess. (Washington, 1939), Part 45, p. 16958. For a description of the changes made, see Fine, *Automobile under Blue Eagle*, pp. 284–85.
82. Fine, *Automobile under Blue Eagle*, p. 285.
83. GM, Labor Relations Diary, Section 1, pp. 21, 27, 29; Final Report of the Automobile Labor Board . . . [Aug. 1935], Appendix B; Fine, *Automobile under Blue Eagle*, pp. 315–17.
84. GM, Labor Relations Diary, Section 1, pp. 29–30; *ibid.*, Appendix Doc. 15; Fine, *Automobile under Blue Eagle*, pp. 159–61; *New York Times*, July 29, 1934; *La Follette Hearings*, Part 45, p. 16911.
85. Fine, *Automobile under Blue Eagle*, p. 162.
86. For details of the ALB plan, see *ibid.*, pp. 315–16.
87. Under the ALB plan, unlike the company-union plans, the voter could select whomever he pleased as his representative.
88. GM, Labor Relations Diary, Appendix Doc. 41. For the ALB rules, see Fine, *Automobile under Blue Eagle*, pp. 333–34.
89. For the AFL criticism of the ALB plan, see Fine, *Automobile under Blue Eagle*, pp. 319–20.
90. The Toledo Chevrolet strike is treated in detail in *ibid.*, pp. 387–401, and in Sidney Fine, "The Toledo Chevrolet Strike of 1935," *Ohio Historical Quarterly*, LXVII (Oct. 1958), 326–56.
91. Thomas J. Williams to Hugh Kerwin, Apr. 27, 1935, File 182–370, Records of the Conciliation Service, Record Group 280, National Archives and Records Service; GM, Labor Relations Diary, Appendix Doc. 49; Fine, *Automobile under Blue Eagle*, p. 402.
92. GM, Labor Relations Diary, Section 1, p. 64; *La Follette Hearings*, Part 45, p. 17035.
93. For the best treatment of the enactment of the NLRA, see Irving Bernstein, *The New Deal Collective Bargaining Policy* (Berkeley, 1950), pp. 84–128.
94. *New York Times*, Apr. 10, 1935; *Detroit News*, May 27, 1935. On the opposition of GM and the other automobile manufacturers to Wagner's 1934 bill, see Fine, *Automobile under Blue Eagle*, pp. 217, 227.
95. GM, Executive Training Program, Section G-3, Personnel Problems, 1935, Session 1, pp. 2, 3; UAW Release, Jan. 28, 1937, Box 4, Edward Levinson Papers, Labor History Archives.
96. Fine, *Automobile under Blue Eagle*, pp. 329, 334–35, 343; GM, Labor Relations Diary, Section 1, p. 27; Hartley W. Barclay to Harry W. Anderson, Jan. 20, 1937, and attached memorandum, Murphy Papers.
97. Affidavit of James H. Mangold [Jan. 28, 1937], Kraus Papers, Box 9; Report of Chevrolet Works Council Meeting, Jan. 28, 1937, *ibid.*; *La Follette Hearings*, Part 6, pp. 2111–14, 2122, 2130–31; Robert J. Thurlow Affidavit, Jan. 9, 1937, La Follette Committee Papers, Box 126.
98. [Paul Garrett], "The Focal Point of Public Relations" [1936], pp. 2, 4, 17–18, 21, 25–47, 70, 74, Automotive History Collection, Detroit Public Library.

Chapter III

1. Sidney Fine, *The Automobile under the Blue Eagle* (Ann Arbor, 1963), pp. 12–13, 434–35. For the composition of the population in Detroit and Flint, see Chapter IV.
2. *Ibid.*, p. 13; State Emergency Welfare Relief Commission (EWRC), *Social-Economic Occupational Classification of Workers in Selected Industries, Michigan Census of Population and Unemployment, Employment and Unemployment Statistics*, First Series, No. Four (Lansing, 1937), pp. 12–15 (all State EWRC publications hereafter cited are from this series); State EWRC, *Industrial Classification of Unemployed and Gainfully Employed Workers, No. Three* (Lansing, 1936), p. 17. For a detailed analysis of jobs in the industry, see United States Employment Service, *Job Specifications for the Automobile Industry, June 1935*, 3 vols. (Washington, 1935).
3. Robert Blauner, *Alienation and Freedom: The Factory Worker and His Industry* (Chicago, 1964), pp. 90–91; W. H. McPherson and Anthony Lucheck, "Automobiles," in Twentieth Century Fund, *How Collective Bargaining Works* (New York, 1942), p. 576.
4. Russell B. Porter, "The Assembly Lines Hum," New York *Times*, Feb. 28, 1937.
5. Blauner, *Alienation and Freedom*, pp. 5–6, 98–108, 121, 199–208.
6. William Ellison Chalmers, "Labor in the Automobile Industry: A Study of Personnel Policies, Workers Attitudes, and Attempts at Unionism" (Ph.D. thesis, University of Wisconsin, 1932), pp. 89, 91; [L. G. Lenhardt], "It Can Happen Here," Mar. 9, 1937, Blair Moody Papers, Michigan Historical Collections, Ann Arbor, Michigan; Flint *Auto Worker*, Jan. 28, 1937.
7. Hartley W. Barclay to Harry W. Anderson, Jan. 20, 1937, and attached memorandum, Frank Murphy Papers, Michigan Historical Collections; Detroit *News*, Feb. 21, 1937; Chalmers, "Labor in Automobile Industry," pp. 153–60; Eli Chinoy, *Automobile Workers and the American Dream* (Garden City, New York, 1955), p. 70; Harry Weiss, "What Caused the G.M. Strike?" *New Masses*, XXII (Feb. 23, 1937), 11.
8. Porter, "Speed, Speed . . . ," New York *Times*, Jan. 31, 1937; *News-Week*, IX (Feb. 20, 1937), 14–15; Department of Research and Education, Federal Council of the Churches of Christ, *Information Service*, Feb. 6, 1937, unpaginated.
9. Hearing on Regularizing Employment and Otherwise Improving the Conditions of Labor in the Automobile Industry, Flint, Dec. 17–18, 1934, pp. 54, 93, 109–10, 132, 143, 274–75, 300–301, 452, Records of the National Recovery Administration, Box 7265, Record Group 9, National Archives and Records Service, Washington, D.C. (hereafter cited as Henderson Hearing; NRA Records hereafter cited as NRA).
10. Ed Hall to Henry Kraus, Nov. 5, 1936, Henry Kraus Papers, Box 7, Labor History Archives, Wayne State University, Detroit, Michigan; Flint *Auto Worker*, Nov. 1936; "Why Did the Auto Workers Strike?" *Social Action*, III (Feb. 15, 1937), 11; *Information Service*, Feb. 6, 1937; demands of various departments [Jan. 19, 1937], Records of UAW Local 121, State Historical Society of Wisconsin, Madison; Oral History Interview of Jack Palmer, July 23, 1960, p. 9, Michigan Historical Collections (transcripts of all interviews cited are located in the Michigan

Historical Collections); New York *Times*, Feb. 1, 1937; Porter, "Assembly Lines Hum," *ibid.*, Feb. 28, 1937. See also Interview with Joe Devitt, July 14, 1966, pp. 3–4; and Interview with Roy Reuther, July 12, 1966, pp. 20–21.

11. Porter, "Assembly Lines Hum"; Herbert Harris, *American Labor* (New Haven, 1939), 271n.
12. Richard, "On the Assembly Line," *Atlantic Monthly*, CLIX (Apr. 1937), 425, 428; Germer to Henry–, July 22, 1936, Adolph Germer Papers, State Historical Society of Wisconsin.
13. Porter, "Assembly Lines Hum"; Detroit *News*, Feb. 21, 1937; Barclay memorandum, Murphy Papers.
14. Bureau of Labor Statistics, *Productivity and Unit Labor Cost in Selected Manufacturing Industries, 1919–1940* (Washington, 1942), pp. 1, 66; Analysis and Comments on 'Preliminary Report by Research and Planning Division, NRA . . . ,' Feb. 23, 1935, Oscar P. Pearson Papers (privately held).
15. Detroit *News*, Feb. 21, 1937; Ward Lindsay to Robert La Follette, Jan. 10, 1937, Sen 78A–F9, Box 123, Record Group 46, National Archives and Records Service (hereafter cited as La Follette Committee Papers); Palmer interview, pp. 8, 12; Porter, "Assembly Lines Hum." See also Harris, *American Labor*, pp. 268–69; Saul Alinsky, *John L. Lewis* (New York, 1949), p. 94; Richard, "On the Assembly Line," p. 427; and Flint *Auto Worker*, Oct. 1936. Motivation theory today recognizes that the specific demands of workers may "veil unverbalized strivings for self-respect and dignity." Arthur Kornhauser, "Human Motivations Underlying Industrial Conflict," in Kornhauser *et al.*, eds., *Industrial Conflict* (New York, 1954), p. 64.
16. Albert Kramer to Roosevelt, Jan. 12, 1937, File 182-2067, Records of the Conciliation Service, Record Group 280, National Archives and Records Service (hereafter Conciliation Service Files will be cited as CS); Henderson Hearing, p. 611.
17. Chalmers, "Labor in Automobile Industry," p. 144; Automobile Manufacturers Association (AMA), Analysis of Factory Employee Age as Related to Industry Growth, Aug. 1935, NRA Box 661; State EWRC, *Age and Industry of Gainful Workers, No. 9* (Lansing, 1937), p. 12; Barclay, "We Sat Down with the Strikers and General Motors," *Mill and Factory*, XX (Feb. 1937), 12; Robert S. Lynd and Helen Merrell Lynd, *Middletown* (New York, 1929), p. 35.
18. Chalmers, "Labor in Automobile Industry," p. 143; "Instability of Employment in the Automobile Industry," *Monthly Labor Review*, XXVIII (Feb. 1929), 20, 23; Herman Byer and John Anker, "A Review of Factory Labor Turn-Over, 1930 to 1936," *ibid.*, XLV (July 1937), 157–58; *Twenty-Eighth Annual Report of General Motors Corporation Year Ended December 31, 1936*, p. 28 (GM annual reports will hereafter be cited as *Report*); "Why Did the Auto Workers Strike?" p. 12. In 1934 the total layoff rate in all manufacturing was 36.26, as compared to 90.41 in the automobile and body industry and 92.64 in the automobile parts industry. The total separation rates were 49.17, 117.30, and 117.01 respectively. I am not at liberty to reveal the source of my instability figures for GM.
19. Clayton W. Fountain, *Union Guy* (New York, 1949), pp. 41–42; *United Automobile Worker*, Nov. 1936; "Why Did the Auto Workers Strike?"

Notes to pages 61 to 67

353

p. 13; demands of departments [Jan. 19, 1937], Records of UAW Local 121; Reuther interview, pp. 2, 23–24.
20. Henderson Hearing, p. 580; *Business Week*, Dec. 5, 1936, p. 19; *ibid.*, Jan. 16, 1937, p. 13; GM, *Report, 1936*, p. 28; Porter, "Speed, Speed . . . ." Steady workers in AMA plants earned an average of $1618 (above the GM figure) during the period September, 1935–August, 1936, and all hourly workers averaged $1270 during the same period. AMA, *Automobile Facts and Figures, 1937*, p. 49.
21. Margaret Loomis Stecker, *Intercity Differences in Costs of Living in March 1935, 59 Cities*, Works Progress Administration, Division of Social Research, *Research Monograph XII* (Washington, 1937), p. 10; Barclay, "We Sat Down," pp. 55–56; Bureau of the Census, *Historical Statistics of the United States, Colonial Times to 1957* (Washington, 1960), p. 95. See Chapter IV for the condition of housing in Flint.
22. Fine, *Automobile under Blue Eagle*, p. 126; Barclay memorandum, Murphy Papers; Barclay, "We Sat Down," p. 58; "Why Did the Auto Workers Strike?" p. 10; Oral History Interview of William Genske, July 23, 1960, p. 2.
23. Barclay memorandum, Murphy Papers; Barclay, "We Sat Down," pp. 42–43.
24. Hartman and Newcomb, eds., *Industrial Conflict: A Psychological Interpretation* (New York, 1939), p. 103.
25. Jack Skeels, "Early Carriage and Auto Unions: The Impact of Industrialization and Rival Unionism," *Industrial and Labor Relations Review*, XVII (July 1964), 566–83; Fine, *Automobile under Blue Eagle*, pp. 22–23; "Automobile Workers Today . . ." (MS, [1934]), p. 49, Kraus Papers, Box 1.
26. Fine, *Automobile under Blue Eagle*, pp. 24–25. Somewhat higher membership figures are given in Phil Raymond, Report on Automobile Industry [1929], Kraus Papers, Box 1.
27. Fine, *Automobile under Blue Eagle*, p. 25; Chalmers, "Labor in Automobile Industry," p. 269.
28. Fine, *Automobile under Blue Eagle*, pp. 178–81.
29. Chalmers, "Labor in Automobile Industry," pp. 205–9, 227–28; "Record of Struggles," Kraus Papers, Box 1.
30. For an account of the strike, see Chalmers, "Labor in Automobile Industry," pp. 211–25; "Automobile Workers Today . . . ," Kraus Papers, Box 1; untitled MS on labor problems in the auto industry, July 1934 [1930?], *ibid.*, Box 2; Robert L. Cruden, "Flint Strikes Fire," *Labor Defender*, Aug. 1930, p. 165; Flint *Journal*, July 2–12, 18–19, 1930; New York *Times*, July 4, 6, 1930; House Special Committee to Investigate Communist Activities in the United States, *Investigation of Communist Propaganda, Hearings Pursuant to H. Res. 220*, 71 Cong., 2 Sess., Part IV, I (Washington, 1930), 5–13, 17–18.
31. Palmer interview, pp. 1–2, 5. See also Oral History Interview of Everett Francis, July 6, 1962, pp. 5–6.
32. Fine, *Automobile under Blue Eagle*, pp. 21–24.
33. *Ibid.*, pp. 38–39, 300–301.
34. *Ibid.*, pp. 39, 143, 442.
35. The account of the reasons for the AFL's failure in the automobile industry is taken from *ibid.*, pp. 142–49, 403–4, 466.

36. Irving Bernstein, *The Lean Years: A History of the American Worker, 1920–1933* (Boston, 1960), p. 97.
37. Adolph Germer Diary, July 13, 1936, Germer Papers.
38. Fine, *Automobile under Blue Eagle*, pp. 193–94.
39. Green to George Addes, July 16, 1935, CIO Historical File, Reel 1, AFL-CIO Archives, Washington, D.C.
40. Fine, *Automobile under Blue Eagle*, pp. 42, 299, 339–41, 407.
41. *Ibid.*, pp. 214–15.
42. *Ibid.*, pp. 214, 220, 230; Mr. Dewey's memorandum . . . [Mar. 1934], CS 176–1339.
43. Oral History Interview of Leonard Woodcock, Apr. 30, 1963, p. 6; Minzey to Dillon, Nov. 17, 1934, Automobile Labor Board (ALB) Drawer 3990 (the ALB records are part of the NRA Records); Fine, *Automobile under Blue Eagle*, p. 518. See also Palmer interview, pp. 5–6, and Henderson Hearing, p. 536.
44. Fine, *Automobile under Blue Eagle*, pp. 262–66; W. Ellison Chalmers, "Collective Bargaining in the Automobile Industry" (MS, [1935]), VII, 35–36, Littauer Industrial Relations Library, Harvard University, Cambridge, Mass.; Edward A. Wieck, "The Automobile Workers under the NRA" (MS, Aug. 1935), pp. 105–6, in possession of Mrs. Edward A. Wieck.
45. The Fisher Body No. 1 local went on strike on May 10, 1934, because of dissatisfaction with production standards and piece rates. The strike agreement did not alter the status of the union in the plant, but the union leadership felt that a victory had been won since the company union was to be excluded from the negotiations with management provided for by the agreement. Fine, *Automobile under Blue Eagle*, pp. 273–74.
46. On this point, see Fine, *Automobile under Blue Eagle*, pp. 368–73.
47. *Ibid.*, pp. 382–84.
48. *Ibid.*, pp. 384–87. The paid-up membership figures are given in Minutes of the Meeting of the Executive Council, AFL, Jan. 29–Feb. 14, 1935, p. 60.
49. For detailed accounts of the strike, see Sidney Fine, "The Toledo Chevrolet Strike of 1935," *Ohio Historical Quarterly*, XLVII (Oct. 1958), 326–56; and Fine, *Automobile under Blue Eagle*, pp. 388–401.
50. Fine, *Automobile under Blue Eagle*, pp. 518–19.
51. *Ibid.*, pp. 401–2.
52. *Ibid.*, pp. 293–98, 304–5.
53. See *ibid.*, pp. 301–3.
54. *Ibid.*, pp. 386–87; *United Automobile Worker*, May 1936.
55. *United Automobile Worker*, May 1936; Oral History Interview of Ed Hall, Oct. 26, 1959, p. 1; Oral History Interview of Carl Haessler, Nov. 27, 1959–Oct. 24, 1960, p. 7; Henry Kraus, *The Many and the Few: A Chronicle of the Dynamic Auto Workers* (Los Angeles, 1947), p. 29.
56. *United Automobile Worker*, May 1936; *Time*, XXIX (Jan. 18, 1937), 17–18; *Literary Digest*, CXXIII (Jan. 16, 1937), 6; *Michigan Christian Advocate*, LXIV (Jan. 14, 1937), 7; Fine, *Automobile under Blue Eagle*, p. 425; Jack Skeels, "The Development of Political Stability within the United Auto Workers" (Ph.D. thesis, University of Wisconsin, 1957), pp. 32–33; Irving Howe and B. J. Widick, *The UAW and Walter Reuther* (New York, 1949), p. 52; Benjamin Stolberg, *The Story of the CIO* (New

Notes to pages 79 to 84

355

York, 1938), pp. 161–62; Germer Diary, June 17, Sept. 25, Oct. 4, Nov. 10, 1936, Germer Papers; Germer to Philip Murray, Nov. 30, 1936, *ibid.*; Hall interview, p. 10; John Brophy, "The Struggle for an Auto Union" (undated MS), p. 10, John Brophy Papers, Catholic University, Washington, D. C.; Personality Sketch of Mr. Homer Martin, undated, Mary Heaton Vorse Papers, Labor History Archives.

57. *United Automobile Worker*, May 1936; *Daily Worker*, Jan. 21, 1937; Oral History Interview of Wyndham Mortimer, June 20, 1960, p. 1; Haessler interview, p. 4; Federated Press Central Bureau Sheet, Jan. 19, 1937, Kraus Papers, Box 9; Flint *Weekly Review*, Nov. 27, 1936; Stolberg, *Story of CIO*, p. 164; House Special Committee on Un-American Activities, *Investigation of Un-American Propaganda Activities in the United States, Hearings Pursuant to H. Res. 282*, 76 Cong., 1 Sess. (Washington, 1939), IX, 5456.

58. Fine, *Automobile under Blue Eagle*, pp. 303–4, 306; Minutes of Toledo Progressives Meeting of June 8–9, 1935, Kraus Papers, Box 5.

59. Fine, *Automobile under Blue Eagle*, pp. 304, 306.

60. *Ibid.*, p. 305.

61. On this point, see David Brody, "The Emergence of Mass-Production Unionism," in John Braeman *et al.*, eds., *Change and Continuity in Twentieth-Century America* (Harper Colophon Books; New York, 1966), pp. 230–31, 236–37.

62. Fine, *Automobile under Blue Eagle*, pp. 403–4; AFL Executive Council Minutes, Jan. 29–Feb. 14, 1935, pp. 58, 60–62, 67–69, 208, 221–22.

63. Fine, *Automobile under Blue Eagle*, pp. 404, 406.

64. "The Need of a Progressive Program in the United Automobile Workers Union" [June 1935], Kraus Papers, Box 5; "Statement of the Progressive Delegates to the Convention of the United Automobile Workers Union" [Aug. 1935], *ibid.*, Box 4.

65. *Proceedings of the First Constitutional Convention of the International Union, United Automobile Workers of America, 1935* (Detroit, n.d.), *passim*; AFL Executive Council Minutes, Oct. 5 . . . , 1935, pp. 20, 23, 35, 48–49; Fine, *Automobile under Blue Eagle*, pp. 416–19, 525; *United Auto Worker*, Sept. 1935.

66. Fine, *Automobile under Blue Eagle*, pp. 419–21; Mortimer interview, p. 18; AFL Executive Council Minutes, Oct. 5 . . . , 1935, pp. 23–24, 109.

67. AFL Executive Council Minutes, Jan. 15–29, 1936, pp. 201, 207; Fine, *Automobile under Blue Eagle*, pp. 421–22.

68. Fine, *Automobile under Blue Eagle*, pp. 402–3, 418–19, 422; AFL Executive Council Minutes, Oct. 5 . . . , 1935, p. 48; Report of F. J. Dillon . . . , Apr. 27, 1936, Kraus Papers, Box 6.

69. For accounts of the Motor Products strike, see Harry Dahlheimer, *A History of the Mechanics Educational Society of America in Detroit from Its Inception in 1933 through 1937* (Detroit, 1951), pp. 30–36; CS 182–928; Summary of Motor Products Strike, Kraus Papers, Box 4; "History of the Motor Products Strike . . . ," Apr. 18, 1936, *ibid.*; Oral History Interview of Richard Frankensteen, Oct. 10, 1959–Dec. 7, 1961, pp. 20–22; Fine, *Automobile under Blue Eagle*, pp. 422–23; and Matthew Smith to Sidney Hillman, undated, Sidney Hillman Papers, Amalgamated Clothing Workers, New York, New York.

70. Brophy Memorandum, Nov. 15, 1935, Hillman Papers; The Reminiscences of John Brophy, 1957, p. 568, Oral History Research Office, Columbia

University, New York, New York; Smith and Frankensteen to Lewis, Nov. 29, 1935, Kraus Papers, Box 4; Germer to Brophy, Jan. 9, 1936, Germer Papers; Fine, *Automobile under Blue Eagle*, p. 423. Germer, on December 8, 1935, reported the Detroit strength of the three organizations as between 13,000 and 16,000. Germer to Brophy, Dec. 8, 1935, Germer Papers.

71. Martin to Harry F. Marlett, Nov. 19, 1935, Martin to William E. Dowell, Nov. 20, 1935, Homer Martin Papers, Labor History Archives; Elmer Davis *et al.* to Dear Sir and Brother, Nov. 27, 1935, Kraus Papers, Box 5; "Summary of Conference on Auto Situation," Nov. 26, 1935, enclosed with Brophy to Germer, Nov. 27, 1935, Germer Papers; Notes on meeting of Nov. 26, 1935, Katherine Pollak Ellickson CIO Collection, Franklin D. Roosevelt Library, Hyde Park, New York; Brophy Memorandum to Members of CIO on Auto Workers Situation, Nov. 27, 1935, Hillman Papers; Brophy Reminiscences, pp. 571–72; *United Auto Worker*, Dec. 1935; Fine, *Automobile under Blue Eagle*, p. 424.

72. Germer Diary, Nov. 26, 1935, Germer Papers; *United Auto Worker*, Dec. 1935; New York *Times*, May 28, 1966; John Brophy, *A Miner's Life* (Edited and supplemented by John O. P. Hall; Madison, 1964), pp. 102, 259.

73. Germer Diary, Dec. 6, 7, 1935, Feb. 16, 1936, Germer Papers; Germer to Lewis, Dec. 8, 1935, Germer to Brophy, Dec. 8, 1935, Feb. 14, 18, 1936, *ibid.*; AFL Executive Council Minutes, Jan. 15–29, 1936, pp. 160–61.

74. Report by Director for Meeting of Dec. 9, 1935, Hillman Papers; CIO Minutes, Dec. 9, 1935, *ibid.*; CIO Minutes (a more detailed set), Dec. 9, 1935, Ellickson Collection; CIO Release, Dec. 10, 1935, Germer Papers; Brophy to Germer, Dec. 12, 20, 1935, *ibid.*; *United Auto Worker*, Dec. 1935.

75. Germer to Brophy, Jan. 2, 3, 7, 9, 1936, CIO File (notes on this file in possession of Irving Bernstein); Report of Director, Jan. 9, 1936, Hillman Papers; AFL Executive Council Minutes, Jan. 15–29, 1936, p. 161; Dahlheimer, *History of MESA*, pp. 34–35.

76. CIO Release, Dec. 10, 1935, Germer Papers; Brophy to Germer, Dec. 12, 20, 1935, Brophy to Green, Jan. 13, 1936, *ibid.*; *United Auto Worker*, Dec. 1935, Feb. 1936; CIO Release, Jan. 20, 1936, Kraus Papers, Box 5; New York *Times*, Jan. 19, 1936.

77. AFL Executive Council Minutes, Jan. 15–29, 1936, p. 164; *ibid.*, May 5–20, 1936, p. 189; New York *Times*, Jan. 28, 1936; Harry F. Marlett to Frank Morrison, Pattern Makers File, UAW-CIO Archives; Germer Diary, Jan. 28, 1936, Germer Papers; Germer to Brophy, Jan. 28, 1936, Alan Strachan to Germer, Feb. 1, 1935 [1936], *ibid.* Dillon told Germer that he too was opposed to the Executive Council decision, but he nevertheless moved to put it into effect. See Germer to Brophy, Feb. 18, 1936, CIO File.

78. *United Auto Worker*, Feb. 1936; New York *Times*, Jan. 28, 1936; [Martin *et al.*] to Dear Sirs and Brothers, undated, Kraus Papers, Box 4; Michael Manning to Green, Feb. 19, 1936, Clyde W. Cook to Members of the General Council, Feb. 21, 1936, *ibid.*, Box 3; AFL Executive Council Minutes, May 5–20, 1936, p. 193; Germer to Brophy, Feb. 14, 15, 1936, Germer Papers.

79. Fine, *Automobile under Blue Eagle*, pp. 424–25; Germer to Brophy, Feb. 18, 1936, Germer Papers; *United Auto Worker*, Mar. 1936.

80. AFL Executive Council Minutes, May 5–20, 1936, p. 193; Germer Diary,

Feb. 10, 20, 23, Apr. 16, 1936, Germer Papers; Germer to Brophy, Feb. 11, 1936, *ibid.*; Germer to Brophy, Feb. 11, 16, 20, 1936, Germer to Lewis, Feb. 24, 1936, CIO File; Mortimer to Martin, Feb. 25, 1936, Martin Papers; Fine, *Automobile under Blue Eagle*, p. 425.
81. *United Auto Worker*, Mar., Apr. 1936; (Toledo) *Union Leader*, Mar. 20, 1936; *New Militant*, May 9, 1936.
82. Jack Skeels, "The Background of UAW Factionalism," *Labor History*, II (Spring 1961), 171; Germer Diary, Jan. 21, Feb. 9, 18, 21, Apr. 9, 23–24, 1936, Germer Papers; Mortimer to Germer, Apr. 15, 1936, Germer to Mortimer, Apr. 21, 1936, *ibid.*; Germer to Brophy, Mar. 31, Apr. 11, 15, 1936, CIO File; Fine, *Automobile under Blue Eagle*, p. 419; *United Auto Worker*, Apr. 1936; Martin to Dowell, Mar. 18, 1936, Martin Papers; William Weinstone, "Advancing against Reaction in the Center of the Motor Industry," *Communist*, XV (Aug. 1936), 749–50.
83. Dillon Report, Apr. 27, 1936, p. 44, Kraus Papers, Box 4; "Roll Call" [Apr. 1936], *ibid.*; AFL Executive Council Minutes, May 5–20, 1936, p. 280; Germer to Brophy, Apr. 15, 1936, CIO File. Each delegate at the convention represented a maximum of 100 paid-up members. In Detroit, in some instances, a single individual, possibly a Communist or a Dillonite, illegally paid a per capita tax on seven members so as to be able to hold a charter and to have a local to represent. Germer Diary, Apr. 14, 1936, Germer Papers; Germer to Brophy, Apr. 15, 1936, CIO File.
84. Haessler interview, p. 4; *United Automobile Worker*, May 1936; George Douglas Blackwood, "The United Automobile Workers of America, 1935–51" (Ph.D. thesis, University of Chicago, 1951), p. 52.
85. *United Automobile Worker*, July 7, 1936; *Proceedings of the Second Convention of the International Union, United Automobile Workers of America . . . , Apr. 27–May 2, 1936* (n.p., n.d.), pp. 96–98, 137–44; Dahlheimer, *History of MESA*, pp. 36–37; Blackwood, "United Automobile Workers," p. 357. The UAW claimed that the merger with the independents added 25,000 members to the organization, but the New York *Times* reported that those closest to the "actual situation" in the plants placed the number at not more than 5000. UAW Release, Aug. 28, 1936, Kraus Papers, Box 6; New York *Times*, June 26, 1936.
86. *Proceedings of Second Convention, UAW*, pp. 124–25 *et passim*; Blackwood, "United Automobile Workers," pp. 355–56; Brophy to Germer, Apr. 13, 1936, Germer Papers; Germer Diary, Apr. 30, May 2, 1936, *ibid.*; Joe Brown to Edward A. Wieck, Edward A. Wieck Papers, Box 10, Labor History Archives; Walter Galenson, *The CIO Challenge to the AFL: A History of the American Labor Movement, 1935–1941* (Cambridge, Mass., 1960), p. 131.
87. Germer Diary, Apr. 27, 1936, Germer Papers; *Proceedings of Second Convention, UAW*, p. 13; *United Auto Worker*, Jan., Apr. 1936; *United Automobile Worker*, May 1936; Martin to Jack Swift, Apr. 3, 1936, Martin Papers; Rose Pesotta, *Bread upon the Waters* (Edited by John Nicholas Beffel; New York, 1944), pp. 228, 233; Galenson, *CIO Challenge to AFL*, p. 131; Krzycki to Hillman, Apr. 29, 1936, Hillman Papers; AFL Executive Council Minutes, May 5–20, 1936, p. 195.
88. *Proceedings of Second Convention, UAW*, pp. 217–18, 239, 243.
89. Interview with Robert C. Travis, Dec. 10, 1964, pp. 1, 59; Henry Kraus to William E. Siefke, Mar. 18, 1936, Kraus Papers, Box 6; "Lets [*sic*] Face Facts," undated MS in *ibid.*; Haessler interview, pp. 14–15; Palmer

interview, p. 11; R. Reuther interview, p. 15; Oral History Interview of Ted LaDuke, Aug. 5, 1960, p. 16; Kraus, *Many and Few*, pp. 31-32; Blackwood, "United Automobile Workers," p. 57.
90. Germer Diary, Apr. 28, 1936, Germer Papers; *Proceedings of Second Convention, UAW*, pp. 157-58.
91. *United Automobile Worker*, July 7, 1936; New York *Times*, July 3, Aug. 4, 1936; UAW Release, Aug. 28, 1936, Kraus Papers, Box 6; CIO Minutes, July 2, 1936, Hillman Papers; Report of Director for CIO Meeting, Nov. 7 and 8, 1936, *ibid.*
92. Germer Diary, July 24, Sept. 1, Nov. 13, 16, Dec. 5, 1936, Germer Papers; Martin to Mortimer, Mar. 24, 1936, Martin Papers; *Daily Worker*, Nov. 24, Dec. 4, 1936.
93. Germer Diary, Oct. 4, 8, Nov. 30, 1936, Germer Papers.
94. *Ibid.*, July 1, Nov. 28, 30, 1936.
95. *Ibid.*, June 17, Sept. 25, Nov. 8, 10, 30, 1936; Germer to Murray, Nov. 30, 1936, Germer to Brophy, Nov. 30, 1936, Germer Papers.
96. *United Automobile Worker*, July 7, Aug., Oct. 1936; Germer to Brophy, June 23, 1936, Germer to Henry—, July 22, 1936, Martin to Officers and Members, July 23, 1936, Germer Papers.
97. *United Automobile Worker*, Aug. 1936; *Flint Weekly Review*, Sept. 18, 1936; Martin to Officers and Members, Sept. 16, 1936, Delmond Garst to Hugh Thompson, Sept. 17, 1936, Hugh Thompson Papers, Labor History Archives.
98. Edward Levinson, *Labor on the March* (University Books; New York, 1956), pp. 147-48; *United Automobile Worker*, Oct. 1936; Kenneth Cole to Travis, Oct. 22, 1936, Kraus Papers, Box 8. The details of the agreement are given in *United Automobile Worker*, Oct. 1936.
99. George Wolfskill, *The Revolt of the Conservatives: A History of the American Liberty League* (Boston, 1962), pp. 25-26, 59, 63, 207; Sloan, Jr., to GM Employees, Oct. 15, 1936, Kraus Papers, Box 8; Martin to Officers and Members, Nov. 10, 1936, *ibid.*, Box 7; UAW leaflet [Nov. 1936], Brown Collection; Notes on CIO Meeting, Nov. 7 and 8, 1936, Ellickson Collection; *Daily Worker*, Nov. 14, 1936.
100. Germer to Brophy, Oct. 18, 1936, CIO File; Brophy, "Struggle for Auto Union," pp. 1-2, Brophy Papers; Meeting of General Officers, Nov. 9, 1936, Kraus Papers, Box 6; Martin to Officers and Members, Nov. 10, 1936, *ibid.*; Martin to Murray, Sept. 30, 1936, Martin to Brophy, Oct. 1, 1936, Auto Workers File, AFL-CIO Archives; *United Automobile Worker*, Nov. 1936.
101. *United Automobile Worker*, Nov. 1936; *Union News Service*, Nov. 16, 1936; *Daily Worker*, Nov. 17, 1936.
102. Although the CIO aided with organizers and advice, nearly all of the $4800 donated to the UAW in December for its strike fund and its organization fund came from UAW locals. Donations from December 1, 1936 to December 31, 1936, Incl., Kraus Papers, Box 7.
103. *Business Week*, Dec. 5, 1936, pp. 16, 19; Charles Kramer to Robert Wohlforth, Sept. 14, 1936, La Follette Committee Papers, Box 125; Jerold S. Auerbach, *Labor and Liberty: The La Follette Committee and the New Deal* (Indianapolis, 1966), pp. 109-10; New York *Times*, Dec. 20, 1936; *United Automobile Worker*, Nov. 1936; *Automotive Industries*, LXXV (Dec. 5, 1936), 765; *ibid.*, Dec. 12, 1936, p. 812; "Settlement of

Strikes in the Glass Industry," *Monthly Labor Review*, XLIV (Mar. 1937), 670–71.
104. GEB to Officers and Members, Dec. 1, 1936, Kraus Papers, Box 6; UAW Release, Dec. 29, 1936, *ibid.*; *United Automobile Worker*, Nov., Dec. 1936; Addes to Germer, Dec. 19, 1936, Germer Papers.
105. UAW-CIO Per Capita Tax Report [1937], Kraus Papers, Box 11; *Report of George Addes . . . , April 1, 1936 to June 30, 1937*, pp. 3–4, *ibid.*, Box 12.
106. Boris Stein, "Production, Employment, and Pay Rolls in 1936," Bureau of Labor Statistics, *Labor Information Bulletin*, IV (Mar. 1937), 6; Oral History Interview of Paul E. Miley, July 24, 1961, p. 18; Sumner H. Slichter, "Labor Faces the Future," *Christian Science Monitor* (Weekly Magazine Section), Mar. 3, 1937, p. 3. On the limitations of union membership figures, see William Paschell, "Limitations of Union Membership Data," *Monthly Labor Review*, LXXVIII (Nov. 1955), 1265–69.
107. Milton Derber, "Growth and Expansion," in Milton Derber and Edwin Young, eds., *Labor and the New Deal* (Madison, 1957), pp. 7–9; Irving Bernstein, "The Growth of American Unions," *American Economic Review*, XLIV (June 1954), 303.

Chapter IV

1. Carl Crow, *The City of Flint Grows Up* (New York, 1955), pp. 1–6, 9–14, 20, 37; Flint *Journal*, July 9, 1936 (Progress Edition), Sept. 4, 1955 (Centennial Edition).
2. Crow, *Flint*, pp. 17–18, 21–24; Flint *Journal*, July 9, 1936, Sept. 4, 1955.
3. Crow, *Flint*, pp. 24–38; Flint *Journal*, July 9, 1936.
4. Crow, *Flint*, pp. 44–70; Flint *Journal*, July 9, 1936.
5. Clarence H. Young and William A. Quinn, *Foundation for Living: The Story of Charles Stewart Mott* (New York, 1963), p. 1; Crow, *Flint*, p. 73. See Chapter II.
6. Flint *Journal*, July 9, 1936; Arthur Pound, *The Turning Wheel: The Story of General Motors through Twenty-Five Years, 1908–1933* (New York, 1934), p. 89; [Frank Rodolf], "An Industrial History of Flint" (MS, Flint *Journal*, 1949), pp. 244–46, 427–28, 498–500, 503–4; A. C. Findlay, "The Population of Flint, Michigan" [1937], in Flint Institute of Research and Planning, Compiled Studies [1936–38], pp. 1–2.
7. Carl E. Buck, "Genesee County's Health Facilities and Needs" (Mar. 1936), in Compiled Studies, pp. 1–2; William H. Chafe, "The Good Years: The Great Depression in Flint" (MS, 1967), pp. 2–3, 10–11, copy in my possession; Genesee County Welfare Relief Commission (WRC), Bi-Annual Report covering the period November 1, 1933 to June 30, 1935, no page given.
8. Findlay, "Population of Flint," p. 2; Chafe, "Good Years," p. 5; Pierce F. Lewis, "Politics in the Geography of Flint" (Ph.D. thesis, University of Michigan, 1958), p. 25.
9. Bureau of the Census, *Fifteenth Census of the United States: 1930, Population*, III, Part 1 (Washington, 1932), 1147, 1158; IV (Washington, 1933), 803, 806; Bureau of the Census, *Sixteenth Census of the United States: 1940, Population*, II, Part 3 (Washington, 1943), 892, 894, 899,

901; Lewis, "Politics in Flint," p. 24. There are slight differences in the figures given in the 1930 and 1940 censuses for the components of the Flint population in 1930. I have relied on the 1940 figures.
10. Erdmann D. Beynon, "Characteristics of the Relief Case Load in Genesee County, Michigan" (Flint, 1940), pp. 11, 29, 47–48; Beynon, "The Southern White Laborer Migrates to Michigan," *American Sociological Review*, III (June 1938), 334–40; [Rodolf], "Industrial History," p. 428; Findlay, "Population of Michigan," pp. 3–4. My estimate of the proportion of whites born in Flint as of 1930 is derived from Findlay's figures for 1934 indicating that 36,503 of the city's 144,429 inhabitants were Flint natives.
11. Findlay, "Population in Flint," pp. 1, 3, 9; Beynon, "Characteristics of Relief Case Load," pp. 11, 48; Beynon, "Southern White Laborers," p. 337; New York *Times*, Jan. 22, 1937.
12. Chafe, "Good Years," pp. 4–8, 13, 28; Flint *Journal* [Nov. 29, 1932]; Genesee County WRC, Bi-Annual Report; Beynon, "Characteristics of Relief Case Load," p. 3.
13. State EWRC, *Industrial Classification of Unemployed and Gainfully Employed Workers* (Lansing, 1936), *Michigan Census of Population and Unemployment, Employment and Unemployment Statistics*, First Series, *No. Three* (Lansing, Dec. 1936), p. 17 (all State EWRC publications hereafter cited are from this series). The EWRC may have underestimated the number of automobile workers in Flint. According to GM, the company's total employment in the city on January 1, 1935, was 30,261. Thomas L. Pond to author, Nov. 18, 1966.
14. State EWRC, *Duration of Unemployment of Workers Seeking Reemployment, No. Five* (Lansing, Mar. 1937), p. 19; State EWRC, *Total Income during 1934 of Gainful Workers, No. Six* (Lansing, Mar. 1937), pp. 17, 20.
15. New York *Times*, Jan. 22, 1937; William Haber and Paul L. Stanchfield, *Unemployment and Relief in Michigan* (Lansing, 1935), Table 3; Haber and Stanchfield, *Unemployment, Relief and Economic Security* (Lansing, 1936), p. 302; George F. Granger and Lawrence R. Klein, *Emergency Relief in Michigan, 1933–1939* (Lansing, 1939), pp. 65, 124, 138; Beynon, "Characteristics of Relief Case Load," p. 30; Margaret Pakney to author, Nov. 9, 1966.
16. Flint Public Welfare Board, Second Annual Report for the Period May 1, 1934 to June 30, 1935 (n.p., n.d.), unpaginated.
17. 375 homes were built in 1930, 131 in 1931, 29 in 1934, 81 in 1935, and 307 in 1936. A. C. Findlay, "The Housing Situation in Flint" (Feb. 1938), in Compiled Studies, p. 26.
18. *Ibid.*, pp. 9, 15–17; Russell B. Porter, "Speed, Speed . . . ," New York *Times*, Jan. 31, 1937; Henry Kraus, *The Many and the Few: A Chronicle of the Dynamic Auto Workers* (Los Angeles, 1947), p. 6; Wyndham Mortimer to Fellow Workers, Aug. 12, 1936, Henry Kraus Papers, Box 8, Labor History Archives, Wayne State University, Detroit, Michigan. The central heating figures are based on Bureau of the Census, *Sixteenth Census of the United States: 1940, Housing. Characteristics by Type of Structure* (Washington, 1945), p. 179.
19. Brody, *Nobody Starves* (London, 1932), p. 128; Lewis, "Politics in Flint," pp. 20, 24; Paul Gallico, "Sit-Down Strike," *Cosmopolitan*, CIV (Apr.

Notes to pages 106 to 110

361

1938), [156, 158]; Interview with Roy Reuther, July 12, 1966, p. 2 (transcripts of all interviews cited, unless otherwise indicated, are located in the Michigan Historical Collections, Ann Arbor, Michigan).
20. Young and Quinn, *Foundation for Living*, pp. 45–51; Flint *Journal*, July 9, Nov. 4, 1936; Lewis, "Politics in Flint," pp. 27, 29, 46, 70.
21. Frank M. Landers, *Local Government in Genesee County* (Ann Arbor, 1941), pp. 21, 23; [Rodolf], "Industrial History," pp. 461–62; Flint *Journal* [July 8, 1934], Feb. 25, 1937; Interview with Colin J. MacDonald, May 15, 1967 (untranscribed). Barringer lost his position briefly in the fall of 1932 when a rival bloc gained temporary control of the commission.
22. R. M. Atkins to William H. Phelps, Feb. 23, 1937, William H. Phelps Papers, Michigan Historical Collections; Brody, *Nobody Starves*, pp. 137–38.
23. *Michigan: A Guide to the Wolverine State* (New York, 1941), p. 297; New York *Times*, Jan. 14, 22, 1937; [Paul Garrett], "The Focal Point of Public Relations" [1936], p. 74, Automotive History Collection, Detroit Public Library.
24. Porter, "Speed, Speed . . . ," New York *Times*, Jan. 31, 1937; *United Automobile Worker*, Nov. 1936; Travis to Germer, Oct. 28, 1936, Kraus Papers, Box 8; Adolph Germer Diary, July 2, Aug. 3, 1936, Germer Papers, State Historical Society of Wisconsin, Madison.
25. Harold F. Sylvester, "City Management: The Flint Experiment, 1930–1937" (Ph.D. thesis, Johns Hopkins University, 1938), pp. 127–28; [Rodolf], "Industrial History," p. 461; Detroit *News*, Feb. 9, 24, 1937; Travis to Germer, Oct. 28, 1936, Kraus Papers, Box 8; New York *Times*, Feb. 9, 1937.
26. Senate Subcommittee on Education and Labor, *Violations of Free Speech and Rights of Labor*, 76 Cong., 1 Sess., *Report No. 6* (Washington, 1939), Part 3, pp. 47, 137, 213; GM, Labor Relations Diary, Appendix Documents to Accompany Section 1, Doc. 51, GM Building, Detroit.
27. Germer Diary, June 6, 1936, Germer Papers; Kraus, *Many and Few*, p. 28; Mortimer to Travis, Oct. 22, 1936, Kraus Papers, Box 8.
28. Kraus, *Many and Few*, pp. 16–17, 25; Germer Diary, Sept. 25, 1936, Germer Papers; *Report of Wyndham Mortimer . . .* , Aug. 23, 1937, pp. 4–5; Mortimer to International Executive Officers, Sept. 27, 1936, Homer Martin Papers, Box 1, Labor History Archives; *United Automobile Worker*, July 7, Nov. 1936; Flint *Weekly Review*, July 10, 1936; *Daily Worker*, Nov. 24, 1936. On the Black Legion, see Forrest Davis, "Labor Spies and the Black Legion," *New Republic*, LXXXVII (June 17, 1936), 169–71; Paul W. Ward, "Who's Behind the Black Legion?" *Nation*, CXLII (June 10, 1936), 731; and New York *Times*, June 4, Oct. 4, 1936.
29. *Mortimer Report*, pp. 4–5; Kraus, *Many and Few*, pp. 18–20; Mortimer to International Executive Officers, Sept. 27, 1936, Martin Papers, Box 1; Flint *Weekly Review*, July 17, Aug. 14, 1936; *United Automobile Worker*, Aug., Sept. 1936; *Daily Worker*, Nov. 24, 1936; Mortimer to Fellow Workers, Aug. 12, 1936, Kraus Papers, Box 8; Oral History Interview of Wyndham Mortimer, June 20, 1960, pp. 28–29, 32–33. The initiation and reinstatement fees were reduced from $3 to $1, and the reinstatement fee was counted as dues for the first month of membership.
30. *United Automobile Worker*, Sept. 1936. Mortimer puts the number of

recipients of the letter at 2000, Kraus at more than 7000. Mortimer Report, p. 5; Kraus, *Many and Few*, p. 20. The letters were reprinted in the Flint *Weekly Review*, the organ of the Flint Federation of Labor.
31. Flint *Weekly Review*, July 10, 17, 24, 31, Aug. 7, 14, 21, 28, Sept. 4, 11, 18, 25, Oct. 2, 9, 16, 23, 1936; Mortimer to Fellow Workers, Aug. 12, 1936, Kraus Papers, Box 8; Flint *Auto Worker*, Nov. 1936.
32. See, especially, Kraus, *Many and Few*, pp. 15–26.
33. The total reinstatement fees and dues for the period July 25–September 11, 1936, amounted to $293 and the total initiation fees to $7. Local 156 Financial Secretary Report, July 25–Sept. 11, 1936, Kraus Papers, Box 8. See also *Daily Worker*, Nov. 24, 1936.
34. *Mortimer Report*, p. 5; Oral History Interview of Tom Klasey, Sept. 10, 1960, pp. 17–19; Oral History Interview of Ted LaDuke, Aug. 5, 1960, p. 15; Germer Diary, Sept. 27, 29, Oct. 4–5, 8, 1936, Germer Papers; Kraus, *Many and Few*, pp. 28–30; Meeting of General Officers, Sept. 21, 28, 1936, Kraus Papers, Box 6.
35. Mortimer to International Executive Officers, Sept. 27, 1936, Martin Papers, Box 1; *Mortimer Report*, p. 5.
36. Interview with Robert C. Travis, Dec. 10, 1964, pp. 1–2; Germer Diary, Oct. 2, 1936, Germer Papers; Pieper to Travis, Oct. 10, 1936, Kraus Papers, Box 8.
37. Irving Howe and B. J. Widick, *The UAW and Walter Reuther* (New York, 1949), pp. 187–94; Murray Kempton, *Part of Our Time* (New York, 1955), pp. 264–79; Anderson *Auto Worker*, Mar. 11, 1937; Oral History Interview of Victor Reuther, Mar. 7, 1963, pp. 1–8; Walter and Roy Reuther to Victor Reuther, Nov. 28, 1936, Victor Reuther Papers, Labor History Archives; Detroit *News*, Jan. 12, 1937; James O. Morris, *Conflict within the AFL: A Study of Craft Versus Industrial Unionism, 1901–1933* (Ithaca, 1958), pp. 90–96, 111–20, 124–25; R. Reuther interview, pp. 1, 15–16; Meeting of General Officers, Nov. 27, 1936, Kraus Papers, Box 6; Merlin D. Bishop to Thomas Linton, June 10, 1957, Merlin D. Bishop Papers, Labor History Archives.
38. Travis to Pieper, Oct. 19, 1936, Travis to Germer, Oct. 28, 1936, Kraus Papers, Box 8; Travis interview, pp. 3–4, 6; Oral History Interview of Bud Simons, Sept. 16, 1960, pp. 22–23; George Douglas Blackwood, "The United Automobile Workers of America, 1935–51" (Ph.D. thesis, University of Chicago, 1951), pp. 57–58.
39. Travis to Germer, Oct. 28, 1936, Kraus Papers, Box 8; *Mortimer Report*, p. 5.
40. Flint *Journal*, Jan. 5, 1937; Travis to Allen, Oct. 7, 1936, Travis to Germer, Oct. 28, 1936, Kraus Papers, Box 8; Flint *Auto Worker*, Nov. 1936.
41. Jerold S. Auerbach, *Labor and Liberty: The La Follette Committee and the New Deal* (Indianapolis, 1966), pp. 85, 166–69; Earl Latham, *The Communist Controversy in Washington: From the New Deal to McCarthy* (Cambridge, Mass., 1966), pp. 109–10, 121.
42. "General Motors–Flint," Nov. 6–7, 1936 (two items), Sen 78A-F9, Box 124, Record Group 46, National Archives and Records Service, Washington, D.C. (hereafter cited as La Follette Committee Papers); Travis to Kramer, Nov. 11, 1936, *ibid.*; Kramer to Robert Wohlforth, Nov. 8, 1936, *ibid.*, Box 4.
43. Flint *Auto Worker*, Dec. 30, 1936; Kraus, *Many and Few*, pp. 61–69;

Kramer to Wohlforth, Dec. 11, 1936, La Follette Committee Papers, Box 4.
44. Travis to Kenneth Cole, Oct. 21, 1936, Travis to Mortimer, Oct. 22, 1936, Kraus Papers, Box 8.
45. Mortimer to Fellow Workers, Nov. 10, 1936, *ibid*.
46. Simons interview, pp. 1–15; Kraus, *Many and Few*, pp. 32–38; *Daily Worker*, Dec. 13, 1936, Jan. 11, 1937.
47. Travis to Kraus, Oct. 30, 1936, Kraus Papers, Box 7; Flint *Auto Worker*, Nov. 1936; Kraus, *Many and Few*, p. 42.
48. I have followed the account of the November 13 strike in *United Automobile Worker*, Nov. 1936. There is a somewhat different version in Kraus, *Many and Few*, pp. 47–54. See also Interview with Joe Devitt, July 14, 1966, pp. 8–9; and Blackwood, "United Automobile Workers," pp. 57–58.
49. *Daily Worker*, Nov. 20, 1936; *United Automobile Worker*, Nov. 1936; Germer to John Brophy, Nov. 30, 1936, Germer Papers.
50. Flint *Auto Worker*, Dec. 15, 1936.
51. For the trolley strike, see Flint *Auto Worker*, Dec. 15, 1936; *United Automobile Worker*, Dec. 1936; *Automotive Industries*, LXXV (Dec. 19, 1936), 844; Detroit *News*, Dec. 8–10, 13–16, 1936; and File 182-2002, Records of the Conciliation Service, Record Group 280, National Archives and Records Service.
52. *Flint City Commission Proceedings*, V (Apr. 6, 1936–July 2, 1937), 2035–37, 2053, 2061; *Daily Worker*, Nov. 23, 1936; Flint *Auto Worker*, Dec. 15, 1936; *United Automobile Worker*, Dec. 1936; Detroit *News*, Dec. 10, 13, 1936.
53. *United Automobile Worker*, Dec. 1936; UAW-CIO Per Capita Tax Report [1937], Kraus Papers, Box 11; Germer to Brophy, Nov. 30, 1936, Germer Papers; [L. G. Lenhardt], "It Can Happen Here," Mar. 9, 1937, Blair Moody Papers, Michigan Historical Collections; Oral History Interview of William Genske, July 23, 1960, pp. 3–4; Flint *Auto Worker*, Dec. 30, 1936.
54. MacDonald interview; Brody, *Nobody Starves*, p. 159; Jay Green to author, June 13, 1967; New York *Times*, Jan. 31, 1937.
55. See Chapter II.
56. Roy Reuther Affidavit [Dec. 1936?], La Follette Committee Papers, Box 126; Kramer to John Abt and Wohlforth [Dec. 1936], *ibid.*, Box 5; Subcommittee of the Senate Committee on Education and Labor, *Violations of Free Speech and Rights of Labor, Hearings Pursuant to S. Res. 266*, 75 Cong., 1 Sess. (Washington, 1937), Part 7, 2320–22; Kraus, *Many and Few*, pp. 57–60. Kraus has Lenz directing his "vinegar" remark at Travis, a Kraus hero; Kempton (*Part of Our Time*, p. 263) sees Reuther as the object of the remark and misdates the event. The Reuther affidavit makes it clear that the remark was directed at both Travis and himself.

Chapter v

1. Union representatives at the time of the GM strike used the term "stay-in" strike to describe the type of extended work stoppage in which the

auto workers were engaged and "sit-down" to describe the quickie that did not extend beyond a single shift. The *Monthly Labor Review* distinguished three additional types of sit-downs: a work stoppage by a group of workers that led to a general walkout; a brief sit-down that ended when the employer expelled the workers and closed the plant; and a refusal to work by employees who came to their job at the regular hour and then left the plant after each shift. Flint *Journal*, Jan. 3, 1937; "Review of Strikes in 1936," *Monthly Labor Review*, XLIV (May 1937), 1233-34.

2. For the advantages of the sit-down strike, see Joel Seidman, *"Sit-Down"* (New York, 1937), pp. 3, 19-20; Louis Adamic, "Sitdown," *Nation*, CXLIII (Dec. 5, 1936), 653-54; Adamic, "Sitdown: II," *ibid.* (Dec. 12, 1936), 704; Adamic, *My America, 1928-1938* (New York, 1938), p. 415; Leo Wolman, in *Independent*, Jan. 15, 1937, Edward A. Wieck Papers, Box 5, Labor History Archives, Wayne State University, Detroit, Michigan; *Daily Worker*, Dec. 6, 15, 30, 1936; William Weinstone, *The Great Sit-Down Strike* (New York, 1937), pp. 29-32; Sumner H. Slichter, "Labor Faces the Future," *Christian Science Monitor* (Weekly Magazine Section), Mar. 3, 1937, p. 3; Solomon Diamond, "The Psychology of the Sit-Down," *New Masses*, XXIII (May 4, 1937), 15-16; Melvin J. Vincent, "The Sit-Down Strike," *Sociology and Social Research*, XXI (July-Aug. 1937), 527-28; and Herbert Harris, *American Labor* (New Haven, 1939), pp. 288-90.

3. Murphy address, Oct. 21, 1938, pp. 2-3, Frank Murphy Papers, Michigan Historical Collections, Ann Arbor, Michigan.

4. For the history of the sit-down before 1936, see Fred Thompson, *The I.W.W. Its First Fifty Years (1905-1955)* (Chicago, 1955), pp. 7-8, 28, 166, 168; "The Sit-Down Strike . . . ," *Congressional Digest*, XVI (May 1937), 135-36; Seidman, *"Sit-Down,"* pp. 5-8; Adamic, "Sitdown: II," p. 702; Edward Levinson, "Labor on the March," *Harper's Magazine*, CXXIV (May 1937), 643; Fred Thompson to Wieck, Feb. 23, 1937, Wieck Papers, Box 9; and Wieck, "Sit-Down Strikes, 1933-1937: A Chronological Compilation" (MS, 1937), pp. 23-26, *ibid.*, Box 5. On the Italian "occupation strikes," see Maurice F. Neufeld, *Italy: . . . The Italian Labor Movement . . . 1800 to 1960* (Ithaca, 1961), pp. 373-74, 378-81; and Daniel L. Horowitz, *The Italian Labor Movement* (Cambridge, Mass., 1963), pp. 143-53.

5. "Review of Strikes in 1936," p. 1234.

6. For the details of the strike and its background, see Walter Galenson, *The CIO Challenge to the AFL: A History of the American Labor Movement, 1935-1941* (Cambridge, Mass., 1960), pp. 266-72; Harold Selig Roberts, *The Rubber Workers* (New York, 1944), pp. 93-151; Ruth McKenney, *Industrial Valley* (New York, 1939); Rose Pesotta, *Bread upon the Waters* (Edited by John Nicholas Beffel; New York, 1944), pp. 195-227; Akron *Beacon Journal*, Feb. 14-15, 17-19, 1936; "The Goodyear Tire and Rubber Co. Strike," *Monthly Labor Review*, XLII (May 1936), 1288-93; Sherman Dalrymple to John Brophy, Feb. 20, 1936, Adolph Germer to Brophy, Mar. 5, 18, Apr. 6, 1936, CIO file (notes on this file are in the possession of Irving Bernstein); and Report of Director for CIO, Nov. 7 and 8, 1936, Sidney Hillman Papers, Amalgamated Clothing Workers, New York, New York. The Akron *Beacon Journal* contains the most reliable account of the actual beginnings of the strike.

7. See *Automotive Industries*, LXXIV (Feb. 8, 1936), 172; and *ibid.*, LXXVI

Notes to pages 125 to 129

365

    (Mar. 6, 1937), 381, 407. *Automotive Industries* described the Firestone strike as "The first modern sitdown strike."
8. Detroit District Council to Germer, Mar. 6, 1936, Germer to Brophy, Mar. 12, 25, 1936, Adolph Germer Papers, State Historical Society of Wisconsin, Madison; *United Auto Worker*, Mar. 1936.
9. Pesotta, *Bread upon the Waters*, p. 227; *United Auto Worker*, Apr. 1936; Oral History Interview of Merlin D. Bishop, Mar. 29, 1963, p. 39, Michigan Historical Collections (transcripts of all interviews cited are located in the Michigan Historical Collections).
10. For the background, course, and aftermath of the French sit-down strikes, see Henry W. Ehrmann, *French Labor from Popular Front to Liberation* (New York, 1947), pp. 3, 20, 25–26, 38–45, 50–51, 284–85; Val R. Lorwin, *The French Labor Movement* (Cambridge, Mass., 1954), pp. 72–77; Salomon Schwarz, "Les Occupations d'Usines en France de Mai et Juin 1936," *International Review for Social History*, II (1937), 50–104; J. Bouissounouse, "Paris Sets a Strike Style," *Survey Graphic*, XXV (Sept. 1936), 516–19; and Joel Colton, *Léon Blum* (New York, 1966), pp. 134–41, 145–59, 164–65, 414–15. Colton corrects the standard treatments of the strike at several points.
11. The employers committed themselves to conclude collective-bargaining agreements with their workers, to recognize the right of their workers to join unions without suffering discrimination, and to grant a 7–15 percent wage increase. Provision was made in the Matignon Agreement for the selection of shop stewards in the plants. Ehrmann, *French Labor*, pp. 42, 284–85.
12. The French government, after first talking of applying the Wagner Act principle of exclusive representation, officially interpreted the law so as to permit plural union representation in a given bargaining unit or area. Lorwin, *French Labor Movement*, p. 76.
13. *United Automobile Worker*, July 7, 1936; *Daily Worker*, Dec. 2, 1936; Interview with Robert C. Travis, Dec. 10, 1964, p. 15. *Cf.* Edward Levinson, *Labor on the March* (University Books; New York, 1956), pp. 169–70.
14. Norman Beasley, *Knudsen* (New York, 1947), pp. 165–66; Alfred P. Sloan, Jr., *My Years with General Motors* (Edited by John McDonald with Catharine Stevens; Garden City, New York, 1964), pp. 362, 368; Richard D. Lunt, "The High Ministry of Government: The Political Career of Frank Murphy" (Ph.D. thesis, University of New Mexico, 1962), pp. 247–48. Beasley attributes the French warning to Panhard, Lunt to Renault.
15. The NLRB had ordered a representation election in the plant, but the management had secured an injunction to stave off the vote.
16. For the details of the strike, see Detroit *News*, Nov. 18–26, 1936; New York *Times*, Nov. 18–26, 1936; and File 182-1928, Records of the Conciliation Service, Record Group 280, National Archives and Records Service, Washington, D.C. (Conciliation Service files will hereafter be cited as CS).
17. There is a copy of the agreement in the Homer Martin Papers, Box 2, Labor History Archives.
18. The local had a paid-up membership of about 3000 at the end of 1936. UAW-CIO Per Capita Tax Report [1937], Henry Kraus Papers, Box 11, Labor History Archives. See also *Socialist Call*, Dec. 5, 1936.
19. UAW Release, Nov. 24, 1936, Kraus Papers, Box 6; Edward C. McDonald

and Robert C. Fox to Hugh L. Kerwin, Nov. 26, 1936, CS 182-1928; Edwin H. Cassels to Frances Perkins, Nov. 28, 1936, Perkins File, Records of the Department of Labor, Record Group 174, National Archives and Records Service; Detroit *News*, Nov. 19, 1936.
20. Adolph Germer Diary, Nov. 18–25, 1936, Germer Papers; Germer to Philip Murray, Nov. 30, 1936, *ibid*.
21. Detroit *News*, Nov. 28–Dec. 6, 1936; CS 182-1976; "What We Strike For . . . ," undated, Kraus Papers, Box 7; E. J. Kulas to Perkins, Dec. 4, 1936, *ibid*.; UAW Releases, Dec. 2, 8, 1936, Records of UAW Local No. 121 (Janesville Chevrolet), State Historical Society of Wisconsin; *United Automobile Worker*, Dec. 10, 1936; Germer Diary, Dec. 3–5, 1936, Germer Papers; Germer to Brophy, Dec. 5, 1936, CIO File.
22. *United Automobile Worker*, Dec. 10, 1936; UAW Releases, Dec. 2, 8, 1936, Records of Local No. 121; Detroit *News*, Nov. 28–29, 1936; "What We Strike For . . . ," Kraus Papers, Box 7; *Daily Worker*, Dec. 23, 1936.
23. House Special Committee on Un-American Activities, *Investigation of Un-American Propaganda Activities in the United States, Hearings Pursuant to H. Res. 282*, 75 Cong., 3 Sess. (Washington, 1938), I, 125; II, 1290, 1347, 1493–94, 1561; Oral History Interview of Nat Ganley, Apr. 16, 1960, pp. 1, 8, 10; *Daily Worker*, Dec. 1–2, 4–7, 1936. The handbill is in the Kraus Papers, Box 7.
24. Detroit *News*, Dec. 8, 10–12, 17–18, 20, 24, 28–30, 1936.
25. *Ibid*., Dec. 20, 1936.
26. The minimum wage had been 65 cents for men and 58 cents for women.
27. For the details of the Kelsey-Hayes strike, see Detroit *News*, Dec. 11–24, 1936; CS 182-2026; *Workers Age*, Jan. 2, 1937; *United Automobile Worker*, Dec. 1936; Merlin D. Bishop, "The Kelsey-Hayes Sit-In Strike" [Dec. 1936], Michigan Historical Collections; and Oral History Interview of Richard Frankensteen, Oct. 10, 1959–Dec. 7, 1961, pp. 32–36.
28. *Iron Age*, Dec. 31, 1936, p. 40; Oral History Interview of Victor Reuther, Mar. 7, 1963, pp. 10–11.
29. Bishop, "Kelsey-Hayes Sit-In Strike"; Bishop interview, pp. 1–4, 13–22; V. Reuther interview, pp. 8, 12.
30. Frank Winn to Kraus, Dec. 15, 1936, Kraus Papers, Box 6; *Iron Age*, Dec. 31, 1936, p. 41.
31. Oral History Interview of Frank Manfred, June 26, 1960, p. 26.
32. *Socialist Call*, Dec. 12, 1936; *Workers Age*, Jan. 2, 1937; *Daily Worker*, Dec. 21, 1936.
33. See Germer to Brophy, May 4, 1936, CIO File; *Business Week*, Jan. 9, 1937, p. 14; Henry Kraus, *The Many and the Few: A Chronicle of the Dynamic Auto Workers* (Los Angeles, 1947), p. 79; and Interview with Wyndham Mortimer, Dec. 9, 1964, p. 33.
34. Statement of Mr. Martin . . . , Sept. 11, 1936, Joe Brown Collection, Labor History Archives; Sidney Fine, *The Automobile under the Blue Eagle* (Ann Arbor, 1963), pp. 386–87.
35. Report of Committee Elected by Fisher Body Employees . . . , Oct. 30, 1936, Kraus Papers, Box 7; list of demands, Nov. 6, 1936, *ibid*.; Pieper to GM Advisory Committee, Nov. 7, 1936, *ibid*.; Weekly News Bulletin #13, Nov. 9, 1936, *ibid*.; *United Automobile Worker*, Nov. 1936.
36. Flint *Auto Worker*, Nov. 1936 (Nos. 2 and 3); Travis to Pieper, Nov. 9,

1936, E. P. Geiger to General Officers and Executive Board, UAW, Dec. 16, 1936, Kraus Papers, Box 8. The Toledo Chevrolet local had previously authorized its executive shop committee to support any or all GM locals and had stated that Martin could call it out on strike at any time. Kansas City said that it was ready to act at the request of the international. St. Louis indicated that it would strike in support of "a national issue."

37. Pieper to GM Advisory Committee, Nov. 25, 1936, Kraus Papers, Box 7; W. P. Allen, Atlanta, Ga., Nov. 23, 1936, *ibid.*; P. W. Chappell to Kerwin, Dec. 13, 14, 1936, CS 176-2211. The strike demands included straight seniority, a 25 percent reduction in the speed of the line, and exclusive representation. "Demands of Local Union No. 34 . . . ," Kraus Papers, Box 7. GM insisted that Chevrolet had been closed because of the lack of bodies. Detroit *News*, Jan. 3, 1937.
38. Pieper to GM Advisory Committee, Nov. 25, 1936, Kraus Papers, Box 7.
39. Oral History Interview of Wyndham Mortimer, June 20, 1960, pp. 33-34; Oral History Interview of Carl Haessler, Nov. 27, 1959-Oct. 24, 1960, p. 10; Interview with Roy Reuther, July 12, 1966, p. 25.
40. Germer Diary, Dec. 3, 11, 19, 21, 1936, Germer Papers; Germer to Brophy, Nov. 30, 1936, *ibid.*; Pieper to GM Advisory Committee, Nov. 25, 1936, Kraus Papers, Box 7; Chappell to Kerwin, Dec. 13, 1936, CS 176-2211; *Daily Worker*, Nov. 20, 1936; New York *Times*, Nov. 20, 1936.
41. Martin to Travis, Nov. 21, 1936, Kraus Papers, Box 6; Kraus, *Many and Few*, pp. 71-72; Germer Diary, Nov. 22, 1936, Germer Papers. Frank Winn informed Walter Galenson in 1958 that Martin had directed him (Winn) to prepare a telegram instructing GM locals to strike. When Winn protested, Martin allegedly said that his purpose was to "'scare'" GM and he would call off the strikes before the deadline. Winn claims that John L. Lewis himself had to persuade Martin to abandon his plan. Galenson, *CIO Challenge to AFL*, pp. 152-53. It is possible that Winn is actually referring to the November 21 "stand by" wire.
42. The president of the UAW could approve a strike in an emergency, pending GEB approval, but Martin had not *officially* sanctioned the strike, and it would be difficult to place the Atlanta strike in the emergency category. *Constitution of the . . . United Automobile Workers . . . Completed Sept. 1, 1936*, pp. 24-25.
43. Germer to Brophy, Nov. 30, 1936, Germer Papers; Germer Diary, Dec. 23, 1936, *ibid.*
44. Travis to Joseph Ditzel, Nov. 24, 1936, Kraus Papers, Box 8; Germer Diary, Nov. 22, 28-29, Dec. 1, 4, 1936, Germer Papers; Germer to John L. Lewis, Nov. 30, 1936, Germer to Philip Murray, Nov. 30, 1936, *ibid.*
45. Germer to Brophy, Nov. 30, 1936, Germer to Lewis, Nov. 30, 1936, Germer to Murray, Nov. 30, 1936, Germer Papers; Germer Diary, Nov. 22, Dec. 1, 1936, *ibid.*
46. Germer Diary, Nov. 28, 30, 1936, *ibid.*; Germer to Brophy, Nov. 30, 1936, Germer to Lewis, Nov. 30, 1936, *ibid.*; Germer to Brophy, Dec. 5, 1936, CIO File; Kraus, *Many and Few*, pp. 73-74; GEB Minutes, Dec. 1-2, 5, 1936, Kraus Papers, Box 7.
47. GEB Minutes, Nov. 30, Dec. 4, 1936, Kraus Papers, Box 7; Hall to Anderson, Nov. 30, 1936, *ibid.*; Germer Diary, Dec. 5, 9, 12, 14, 16, 18, 21, 23, 1936, Germer Papers; Germer to Brophy, Dec. 16, 23, 1936, CIO

Notes to pages 138 to 142

File; Germer Affidavit, Jan. 11, 1937, Sen 78A-F9, Box 121, Record Group 46, National Archives and Records Service; Chappell to Kerwin, Dec. 13, 16, 18, 1936, CS 176-2211. Germer found it difficult to persuade Martin to come to Atlanta or to remain there when he did come. Germer Diary, Dec. 12, 14, 16, 1936, Germer Papers.
48. Detroit *News*, Dec. 17, 24, 1936, Jan. 1, 1937; *Automotive Industries*, LXXV (Dec. 19, 1936), 837; *Iron Age*, Dec. 31, 1936, p. 43.
49. Louis Rall, "The Kansas City Strike," undated, Kraus Papers, Box 10; Knudsen to Martin, Dec. 31, 1936, GM, Labor Relations Diary, Appendix Documents to Accompany Section 1, Doc. 64, GM Building, Detroit; Kraus, *Many and Few*, pp. 74–75; Flint *Auto Worker*, Jan. 5, 1937; *United Automobile Worker*, Dec. 1936; Detroit *News*, Dec. 18, 20, 24, 1936; *Daily Worker*, Dec. 21, 1936.
50. Detroit *News*, Dec. 19, 1936.
51. Brophy to Germer, Dec. 19, 1936, Germer Papers; *Proceedings of the Fifth Annual Convention of the . . . United Automobile Workers . . . 1940* (n.p., n.d.), p. 104.
52. Kraus, *Many and Few*, pp. 75–76; New York *Times*, Dec. 19, 1936; Brophy to Germer, Dec. 19, 1936, Addes to Germer, Dec. 19, 1936, Germer Papers; Detroit *News*, Dec. 18, 1936.
53. *United Automobile Worker*, Dec. 1936; Adamic, "Sitdown: II," p. 704; Detroit *News*, Dec. 22, 1936.
54. Martin to Knudsen, Dec. 21, 1936 (wire and letter), GM, Labor Relations Diary, Appendix Doc. 62.
55. Detroit *News*, Dec. 23–24, 1936; New York *Times*, Dec. 23–25, 1936; Martin to Sloan, Jr., and Knudsen, Dec. 24, 1936, GM, Labor Relations Diary, Appendix Doc. 63, Knudsen to Martin, Dec. 31, 1936, *ibid.*, Appendix Doc. 64.
56. For local bargaining at the Fleetwood plant, see Oral History Interview of John W. Anderson, Feb. 17–May 21, 1960, pp. 45–46.
57. On these points, see New York *Times*, Dec. 30, 1936; Flint *Journal*, Jan. 1, 1937; Hartley W. Barclay to H. W. Anderson, Jan. 20, 1937, and attached memorandum, Murphy Papers; Barclay, "We Sat Down with the Strikers and General Motors," *Mill and Factory*, XX (Feb. 1937), 37–38; *Business Week*, Jan. 30, 1937, p. 15; Oral History Interview of William Genske, July 23, 1960, pp. 3–4; J. B. [Joe Brown], "Why Auto Body Workers Are [More] Militant Than Other Production Workers," undated, Brown Collection; William Ellison Chalmers, "Labor in the Automobile Industry: A Study of Personnel Policies, Workers Attitudes, and Attempts at Unionism" (Ph.D. thesis, University of Wisconsin, 1932), pp. 227–28; and Kraus, *Many and Few*, p. 56.
58. Anderson interview, p. 46; Travis interview, p. 16.
59. Cleveland *Plain Dealer*, Dec. 29, 1936; Stanley and Smoyer, Petition for Temporary Restraining Order, Injunction and Equitable Relief [Feb. 1, 1937], Kraus Papers, Box 10.
60. *United Automobile Worker*, Aug., Oct., Nov. 1936; Louis F. Spisak to Kraus, Sept. 16, 1936, Kraus Papers, Box 7; "Local 45 of Fisher Body . . . ," undated, *ibid.*; "Elmer Davis . . . Nov. 30, 1936," *ibid.*; Steve Jenso to Dear Sir and Brother, Oct. 30, 1936, Brown Collection; *Daily Worker*, Nov. 29, 1936.
61. The per capita dues paid for December indicate a membership of about 800, but 1974 new members were initiated in that month, most of them,

Notes to pages 142 to 146

369

in all probability, toward the end of the month. UAW-CIO Per Capita Tax Report [1937], Kraus Papers, Box 11.
62. Paul Miley speech, undated, Kraus Papers, Box 10; Petition for Injunction [Feb. 1, 1937], *ibid.*; Travis interview, p. 13; Cleveland *Plain Dealer*, Dec. 28-29, 1936, Feb. 10, 1937; New York *Times*, Dec. 29, 1936; Oral History Interview of Paul E. Miley, July 24, 1961, pp. 19-20; Oral History Interview of Bert Foster, July 26, 1961, pp. 9-10.
63. Charles K. Beckman, one of the sit-down leaders, still contends, "It was just a spontaneous movement on the part of the workers." Oral History Interview of Charles K. Beckman, July 25, 1961, p. 7. *Cf.* Foster interview, p. 9.
64. Miley alleges that Mortimer had also been urging a Cleveland strike at this time (Miley interview, p. 22), but Mortimer's recollections do not seem to confirm this. Mortimer interview, June 20, 1960, pp. 34-35; Mortimer interview, Dec. 9, 1964, p. 1.
65. Germer Diary, Dec. 31, 1936, Germer Papers; Miley interview, pp. 18-22.
66. Kraus, *Many and Few*, pp. 78-79, 82-85; Mortimer interview, June 20, 1960, pp. 27, 34-35.
67. In the December 9, 1964, interview (p. 3), Mortimer said that he called Travis from Cleveland to ask him to tie up Flint, but it is hard to believe that the two men had not discussed the matter before Mortimer left Flint for Cleveland.
68. Cleveland *Plain Dealer*, Dec. 29, 1936; New York *Times*, Dec. 29, 1936; *Daily Worker*, Dec. 30, 1936.
69. Cleveland *Plain Dealer*, Dec. 29-31, 1936; *Daily Worker*, Jan. 1, 1937; New York *Times*, Dec. 29-30, 1936.
70. Cleveland *Plain Dealer*, Jan. 1, 1937; Mortimer interview, Dec. 9, 1964, pp. 2-3. Miley says that the strikers evacuated the plant because the leaders were on the inside and the membership on the outside. Miley interview, p. 21.
71. See, for example, New York *Times*, Dec. 30, 1936; and *Daily Worker*, Dec. 30, 1936.
72. Detroit *News*, Dec. 29, 1936; New York *Times*, Dec. 30, 1936; Flint *Journal*, Jan. 1, 1937.
73. Detroit *News*, Dec. 30, 1936, Jan. 3, 1937; Flint *Journal*, Jan. 1, 3, 1937; Flint *Auto Worker*, Jan. 5, 1937; Oral History Interview of Clayton Johnson, June 1, 1961, pp. 3-4. The Standard Cotton Products Co. of Flint, which manufactured upholstery material for Fisher Body, was also closed by a sit-down on December 30. New York *Times*, Dec. 31, 1936.
74. The fullest account is in Kraus, *Many and Few*, pp. 86-90. See also Flint *Auto Worker*, Jan. 5, 1937; Flint *Journal*, Jan. 1, 1937; Detroit *News*, Dec. 31, 1936; R. Reuther interview, pp. 14-15, 24-25; and Interview with Joe Devitt, July 14, 1966, pp. 9-11. The UAW constitution required a two-thirds vote of the membership by secret ballot as a precondition for a strike. *Constitution . . . 1936*, pp. 24-25. For the "Fisher Strike," see Kraus Papers, Box 9.
75. R. Reuther interview, pp. 14-15.
76. Oral History Interview of Bud Simons, Sept. 6, 1960, pp. 28-30; Flint *Journal*, Jan. 1, 1937.
77. Minutes of Conference for the Protection of Civil Rights, Jan. 17, 1937, Civil Rights Congress of Michigan Papers, Box 1, Labor History

Notes to pages 146 to 150

Archives; Travis interview, pp. 13–15. For other indications of the relationship of the glass strike to the Flint sit-down, see Weinstone, *Great Sit-Down Strike*, p. 21; and Kraus, *Many and Few*, pp. 80–81.
78. Travis interview, pp. 13–14; Mortimer interview, June 20, 1960, p. 36; Anderson interview, p. 46.
79. Germer Diary, Dec. 31, 1936, Germer Papers.
80. New York *Times*, Jan. 26, 1937; *United Automobile Worker*, Feb. 25, 1937.
81. See, for example, *Time*, XXIX (Jan. 11, 1937), 16; *Business Week*, Jan. 9, 1937, p. 13; New York *Times*, Jan. 1, 1937; Benjamin Stolberg, "The C.I.O. Moves On," *Nation*, CXLIV (Feb. 20, 1937), 203–4; [L. G. Lenhardt], "It Can Happen Here," Mar. 9, 1937, Blair Moody Papers, Michigan Historical Collections; Irving Howe and B. J. Widick, *The UAW and Walter Reuther* (New York, 1949), p. 55; Sidney Lens, *Left, Right and Center: Conflicting Forces in American Labor* (Hinsdale, Ill., 1949), pp. 306–7; Saul Alinsky, *John L. Lewis* (New York, 1949), p. 87; and James A. Wechsler, *Labor Baron: A Portrait of John L. Lewis* (New York, 1944), p. 61.
82. Frank N. Trager, "Autos: The Battle for Industrial Unionism," Jan. 11, 1937, MS in Norman Thomas Papers, New York Public Library.
83. CIO Minutes, Dec. 9, 1935, Katherine Pollak Ellickson CIO Collection, Franklin D. Roosevelt Library, Hyde Park, New York.
84. *Time*, XXII (Jan. 11, 1937), 16.
85. Bishop interview, p. 40. On this point, see New York *Times*, Jan. 1, 1937; Slichter, "Labor Faces Future," p. 3; Edward Levinson, "Detroit Digs In," *Nation*, CXLIV (Jan. 16, 1937), 64–65; Stolberg, "C.I.O. Moves On," p. 203; Lens, *Left, Right and Center*, p. 308; Galenson, *CIO Challenge to AFL*, p. 135; Weinstone, *Great Sit-Down*, p. 21; Mortimer interview, June 20, 1960, pp. 34–36; Oral History Interview of George Addes, June 25, 1960, pp. 15–16; and R. Reuther interview, p. 14.
86. New York *Times*, Jan. 10, 1937; Germer Diary, Dec. 31, 1936, Germer Papers. On the autonomous tendencies within the UAW, see Chapter III and Jack William Skeels, "The Development of Political Stability within the United Auto Workers Union" (Ph.D. thesis, University of Wisconsin, 1957), pp. 7–9, 14.
87. Mortimer interview, June 20, 1960, p. 35.
88. For Murphy's career, see Richard D. Lunt, *The High Ministry of Government: The Political Career of Frank Murphy* (Detroit, 1965); and J. Woodford Howard, *Mr. Justice Murphy* (Princeton, 1968).
89. Detroit *News*, Nov. 4, 1936; Detroit *Times*, Mar. 25, 1923; Carl Muller, in Washington *Star*, Jan. 8, 1939.
90. F. Murphy to George Murphy, July 7, 1934, George Murphy Papers, Michigan Historical Collections; Murphy to Mrs. J. F. Murphy, Dec. 31, 1918, John F. Murphy Papers, *ibid.*
91. See, for example, Detroit *Labor News*, Nov. 28, 1930. Murphy enjoyed a long and warm friendship with Roger Baldwin, Morris L. Ernst, and Arthur Garfield Hays of the American Civil Liberties Union.
92. Detroit *Labor News*, Mar. 29, 1929.
93. Edward G. Kemp, "Frank Murphy as Government Administrator," Mar. 6, 1951, Edward G. Kemp Papers, Michigan Historical Collections; "(Capital Punishment Debate)," Jan. 31, 1927, F. Murphy Papers.
94. F. Murphy to G. Murphy, Dec. 7, 1943, G. Murphy Papers; Addresses

Made at . . . the Ascension of the Bench by . . . Frank Murphy, Jan. 2, 1924, F. Murphy Papers.
95. Murphy to Mrs. J. F. Murphy, Mar. 5, 1918, J. F. Murphy Papers; [Manila *Tribune*, Aug. 2, 1933], Murphy Scrapbooks, F. Murphy Papers; Detroit *Free Press*, Jan. 2, 1927; Detroit *Labor News*, May 16, 23, July 11, 18, Aug. 29, 1930; Lunt, *Murphy*, pp. 30–37, 58–60; Joseph R. Hayden, "The Philippine Policy of the United States" (MS, Institute of Pacific Relations, 1939), p. 25, Joseph R. Hayden Papers, Box 7, Michigan Historical Collections.
96. Cited in William L. Stidger, *The Human Side of Greatness* (New York, 1940), p. 20; Murphy, "Politics and the Laborer" (MS [1911]), pp. 1–2, F. Murphy Papers.
97. Murphy, "A Mayor's Interpretation of the Encyclical of Leo XIII, Forty Years After" [Nov. 20, 1932], pp. 1–2, 5, 9–11, Mayor's Office Records, Burton Historical Collection, Detroit, Michigan; Detroit *News*, Feb. 6, 1933; "Interview" [1937], F. Murphy Papers, Box 143.
98. J. Weldon Jones to author, Jan. 29, 1966.
99. Murphy to William L. Stidger, Apr. 5, 1937, F. Murphy Papers; Detroit *Labor News*, Feb. 16, 23, Mar. 23, 1923, Mar. 27, 1925, Dec. 6, 1929.
100. Address before Detroit Federation of Labor, Apr. [15], 1929, F. Murphy Papers.
101. Draft of address to DFL [Apr. 6, 1932], Mayor's Office Records; Detroit *News*, Sept. 8, 26, 1931; Detroit *Labor News*, Apr. 8, 1932.
102. [Manila *Tribune*, July 13, 1933], Murphy Scrapbooks; Murphy to John Wasilewski, Feb. 9, 1933, Murphy to N. Robinson, Feb. 2, 1933, Mayor's Office Records; Detroit *News*, Jan. 28, Feb. 4, 23, 1933. For an account of the Briggs strike, see Fine, *Automobile under Blue Eagle*, pp. 27–29.
103. Murphy to Brian McCluskey, Feb. 3, 1933, Murphy to West Side Branch, Polish Chamber of Labor, Feb. 7, 1933, Murphy to Polish-American Political Club . . . , Feb. 27, 1933, Briggs Strike Defence [sic] Committee to Murphy and James K. Watkins, Feb. 6, 1933, Watkins to Murphy, Feb. 7, 1933, Mayor's Office Records; Detroit *News*, Feb. 6–7, 1933.
104. Murphy to L. W. Wickson, Mar. 23, 1933, Murphy to McCluskey, Feb. 3, 1933, Mayor's Office Records; Detroit *News*, Jan. 27, Feb. 6, 12, 1933.
105. Twenty-Fifth Annual Report of the Bureau of Labor for the Fiscal Year Ending Dec. 31, 1933, Philippine Manuscript Reports, Vol. 1769, pp. 46–47, Bureau of Insular Affairs Records, Record Group 350, National Archives and Records Service; Annual Report of the Department of Labor, 1934, Philippine Manuscript Reports, Vol. 1789, pp. 1, 3–4, *ibid.*; Annual Report of the Governor General of the Philippine Islands, 1933, Philippine Manuscript Reports, Vol. 1767, pp. 8–10, *ibid.*; [Manila *Bulletin*, Dec. 11, 1933], Norman Hill Scrapbooks, Michigan Historical Collections; Murphy to Frank Martel, Nov. 9, 1933, F. Murphy Papers.
106. [*Philippines Herald*, Sept. 11, 18, 1934], [Manila *Bulletin*, Sept. 11, 13, 18, 1934], clippings in F. Murphy Papers; Memorandum Order, Sept. 14, 1934, *ibid.*; C. E. Piatt to Secretary of Interior, Sept. 20, 1934, Teofilo Sison to Murphy, Sept. 20, 1934, *ibid.*; American Civil Liberties Union to Murphy, Sept. 30, 1934, Murphy to Baldwin, Oct. 2, 1934, Baldwin to Murphy, Nov. 6, 1934, *ibid.*
107. Detroit *Labor News*, Sept. 11, Dec. 25, 1936; Murphy to Green, Nov. 7, 1936, F. Murphy Papers; Detroit *News*, Oct. 21, 1936.

108. Hayden, Stone and Co. to Murphy, Oct. 3, 5, 1936, Eleanor Bumgardner to Kemp [Dec. 31, 1936?], F. Murphy Papers; copy of Murphy's 1936 income tax return, *ibid.*; J. E. Swan to Margaret [Marguerite] Teahan, Dec. 29, 1937, Feb. 16, 1939, Marguerite Murphy Papers, Michigan Historical Collections; New York *Times*, Jan. 1, 1937. It might appear from the Swan letter to Mrs. Teahan of December 29, 1937, that the GM stock had been transferred to Mrs. Teahan sometime before January 18, 1937, but it is clear from the February 16, 1939, letter that Murphy did not transfer his brokerage account to his sister's name until February 11, 1937, and that, in any event, the transfer was purely nominal. Since the stock was held in the name of the broker, GM was probably unaware of Murphy's investment in the corporation.

109. Porter, "Governor Murphy's Star in the Ascendant," New York *Times*, Feb. 21, 1937; Joseph H. Creighton, "Frank Murphy—Off the Record," Part Two (MS [Aug. 1938]), pp. 28–29, F. Murphy Papers.

Chapter VI

1. The Henry Kraus Papers in the Labor History Archives, Wayne State University, Detroit, Michigan, contain the minutes of many of the strikers' meetings within Fisher Body No. 1. In addition, some of the outsiders who were permitted to enter the occupied plants recorded their impressions of the life of the sit-down strikers. For the sit-down community in the Guide Lamp plant, see Claude E. Hoffman, *Sit-Down in Anderson: UAW Local 663, Anderson, Indiana* (Detroit, 1968) pp. 38–41.
2. Oral History Interview of Bud Simons, Sept. 6, 1960, pp. 30–31, 35 (transcripts of all interviews cited are located in the Michigan Historical Collections, Ann Arbor, Michigan); Detroit *News*, Dec. 31, 1936; Minutes of Fisher Body No. 1 Board Meeting, Jan. 4, 1937, Minutes of Fisher Body No. 1 Strike Committee, Jan. 12, 21, 1937, Minutes of Fisher Body No. 1, Mass Meeting, Jan. 27, 1937, Harry Van Nocker Notebooks, Kraus Papers, Box 9. All minutes cited refer to meetings in the No. 1 plant and are included in these two notebooks.
3. Official Strike Bulletin No. 7, Joe Brown Collection, Labor History Archives. See also *Daily Worker*, Jan. 16, 1937; and Bruce Bliven, "Sitting Down in Flint," *New Republic*, LXXXIX (Jan. 27, 1937), 377.
4. Barclay, "We Sat Down with the Strikers and General Motors," *Mill and Factory*, XX (Feb. 1937), 37. See also Detroit *News*, Jan. 14, 1937; Russell B. Porter, "The Broad Challenge of the Sit-Down," New York *Times*, Apr. 4, 1937; and George A. Krogstad, "A Brief Resume of My Trip Through the Strike Area in Flint . . . ," Feb. 9, 1937, attached to Krogstad to Frank Murphy, Feb. 11, 1937, Frank Murphy Papers, Michigan Historical Collections.
5. *Daily Worker*, Jan. 16, 1937.
6. Walker, "Work Methods, Working Conditions, and Morale," in Arthur Kornhauser *et al.*, eds., *Industrial Conflict* (New York, 1954), p. 353.
7. Melvin J. Vincent, "The Sit-Down Strike," *Sociology and Social Research*, XXI (July-Aug. 1937), 527–28; Henry Kraus, *The Many and the Few*:

Notes to pages 158 to 161

373

A Chronicle of the Dynamic Auto Workers (Los Angeles, 1947), p. 93; Herbert Harris, *American Labor* (New Haven, 1939), p. 289; Oral History Interview of Joe Devitt, July 14, 1966, p. 20; Saul Alinsky, *John L. Lewis* (New York, 1949), p. 90; Solomon Diamond, "The Psychology of the Sit-Down," *New Masses*, XXIII (May 4, 1937), 16. See also *United Automobile Worker*, Feb. 25, 1937.

8. Paul Gallico, "Sit-Down Strike," *Cosmopolitan,* CIV (Apr. 1938), [159]; Devitt interview, pp. 11-12; Simons interview, pp. 41-43; Minutes of Executive Board, Jan. 4, 1937; *Daily Worker*, Jan. 11, 17, 1937; Simons Notebook, Bud Simons Papers, Labor History Archives.
9. See the Van Nocker Notebooks, Kraus Papers, Box 9.
10. Minutes of Mass Meeting, Jan. 13, 1937; Anderson *Auto Workers Daily News*, Jan. 14, 1937.
11. There is some conflict in the evidence concerning the length of the shifts in the No. 1 plant. *Cf.* Minutes of Meeting [Jan. 1, 1937]; Flint *Journal*, Jan. 11, 1937; New York *Times*, Feb. 1, 1937; and Kraus, *Many and Few*, p. 93.
12. Minutes of Meeting [Jan. 1, 1937]; Minutes of Strike Committee, Jan. 20, 1937 (and notes by Kraus thereon); Simons interview, pp. 35-37; Devitt interview, pp. 13-15, 22-23; *Daily Worker*, Jan. 16, 17, 1937; *Union News Service*, Jan. 25, 1937; Kraus, *Many and Few*, p. 95.
13. Louis Rall, "The Kansas City Strike," undated, Kraus Papers, Box 10; Edward Levinson, *Labor on the March* (University Books; New York, 1956), p. 178; Simons interview, pp. 43-45.
14. Minutes of Meeting [Jan. 18, 1937?]; Minutes of Strike Committee, Jan. 19, 21-22, 24, 1937 (and Kraus notes on latter); Minutes of Council, Jan. 23, 1937 (and Kraus notes thereon).
15. Mundale to Travis, undated, Kraus Papers, Box 9.
16. *Workers Age*, Feb. 20, 1937.
17. Minutes of Strike Committee, Jan. 19, 1937; Minutes of Mass Meeting, Jan. 27, 1937. Devitt, who was one of the two men assigned to establish the court, could not recall many years later that he had been given this duty and did not believe that the court had played a particularly important role in the plant. Devitt interview, pp. 19-20.
18. Court Members and Regulations [Jan. 28, 1937], Case File #5977, Michigan State Police Records, Lansing, Michigan; *Socialist Call*, Feb. 13, 1937; *Workers Age*, Feb. 20, 1937; Levinson, *Labor on March*, p. 177; Joel Seidman, *"Sit-Down"* (New York, 1937), p. 26; Barclay to Harry W. Anderson, Jan. 20, 1937, and attached memorandum, Murphy Papers; Minutes of Mass Meetings, Jan. 4, 12, [20], 1937; *Daily Worker*, Jan. 16, 1937; *Union News Service*, Jan. 25, 1937; Bliven, "Sitting Down in Flint," p. 377; Devitt interview, p. 21; Kraus, *Many and Few*, p. 96. The minutes of the Strike Committee, Jan. 21, 1937, state simply that those who failed to perform their duties were to be exposed.
19. Flint *Auto Worker*, Jan. 31, 1937; Levinson, "Labor on the March," *Harper's Magazine*, CLXXIV (May 1937), 645.
20. *Michigan Christian Advocate*, LXIV (Jan. 28, 1937), 6; *Daily Worker*, Jan. 11, 16, 1937; Minutes of Strike Committee, Jan. 5, 1937; Minutes of Council, Jan. 10, 1937; Simons interview, p. 45; Bliven, "Sitting Down in Flint," p. 377; *Socialist Call*, Feb. 13, 1937; Detroit *News*, Feb. 8, 1937; New York *Times*, Jan. 31, Feb. 8, 1937; Gallico, "Sit-Down Strike," p. [157].

21. New York *Times*, Jan. 5, 1937; Rose Pesotta, *Bread upon the Waters* (Edited by John Nicholas Beffel; New York, 1944), p. 238; Kraus, *Many and Few*, pp. 93–94; Official Strike Bulletin No. 15, Feb. 11, 1937, Kraus Papers, Box 9.
22. Flint *Auto Worker*, Jan. 12, 1937; Kraus, *Many and Few*, pp. 101–2.
23. Official Strike Bulletin No. 5, Feb. 11, 1937, Kraus Papers, Box 9; "Jan. 29, 1937," *ibid.*; Kraus, *Many and Few*, pp. 101–2; Flint *Journal*, Feb. 7, 1937; Powers Hapgood to Mary Hapgood, Jan. 18, 1937, Powers Hapgood Papers, Lilly Library, Bloomington, Indiana; Minutes of Strike Committee, Jan. 25, 1937 (and Kraus notes thereon); New York *Times*, Feb. 1, 1937.
24. Gallico, "Sit-Down Strike," p. [159]; Seidman, *"Sit-Down,"* p. 24; *Union News Service*, Jan. 25, 1937; Kraus, *Many and Few*, pp. 94–95; Simons and Van Nocker to Walter Reuther, Feb. 5, 1937, Simons AVO Notebook, Simons Papers.
25. Minutes of Meeting, Jan. 2, 1937; Minutes of Strike Committee, Jan. 14, 1937; Minutes of Mass Meetings, Jan. 14, 25, 1937; *Socialist Call*, Feb. 13, 1937; Krogstad, "Brief Resume," Murphy Papers; Simons interview, p. 46; Devitt interview, p. 13; Anderson *Auto Workers Daily News*, Jan. 9, 1937; Kraus, *Many and Few*, p. 103.
26. Minutes of Strike Committee, Jan. 23, 1937 (and Kraus notes thereon); *United Automobile Worker*, Feb. 25, 1937; Seidman, *"Sit-Down,"* p. 27; "Jan. 29, 1937," Kraus Papers, Box 9; *Searchlight*, Feb. 2, 1962; *Union News Service*, Feb. 1, 1937; Flint *Auto Worker*, Feb. 2, 1937.
27. Local 156 Release, Feb. 9, 1937, Brown Collection; Flint *Auto Worker*, Feb. 10, 1937; *United Automobile Worker*, Feb. 25, 1937.
28. *Union News Service*, Jan. 25, 1937; *United Automobile Worker*, Feb. 25, 1937; Anderson *Auto Workers Daily News*, Jan. 9, 1937; Rall, "Kansas City Strike," Kraus Papers, Box 10; Minutes of Strike Committee, Feb. 8, 1937, *ibid.*, Box 9; Official Strike Bulletin No. 3, Jan. 21, 1937, *ibid.*; *Daily Worker*, Jan. 11, 16, 1937.
29. Oral History Interview of Merlin D. Bishop, Mar. 29, 1963, p. 43.
30. There are copies of these and other strikers' verses in the Kraus Papers, Box 9.
31. *Ibid.*
32. Minutes of Strike Committee, Jan. 19, 1937 (and Kraus notes thereon); *Daily Worker*, Jan. 17, 1937; Flint *Auto Worker*, Feb. 2, 1937; *United Automobile Worker*, Feb. 25, 1937; Mary Heaton Vorse, "The Emergency Brigade at Flint," *New Republic*, XC (Feb. 17, 1937), 39.
33. See, for example, the account by "An interested observer" [Jan. 12, 1937], Van Nocker Notebook, Kraus Papers, Box 9; *Daily Worker*, Jan. 16, 1937; and Bishop, in *United Automobile Worker*, Feb. 25, 1937.
34. Flint *Journal*, Feb. 7, 1937; P. Hapgood to M. Hapgood [Jan. 13, 1937], Hapgood Papers.
35. New York *Times*, Feb. 1, 1937; William Weinstone, "The Great Auto Strike," *Communist*, XVI (Mar. 1937), 219; G-2 Report, Jan. 23, 1937, Records of the Michigan Military Establishment Relating to the Flint Sit-Down Strike, 1937, microfilm copy in Michigan Historical Collections (hereafter cited as National Guard Records); Simons *et al.* to Pete Kennedy, Feb. [5], 1937, Simons AVO Notebook, Simons Papers; Devitt interview, p. 33.

Notes to pages 165 to 169

375

36. Devitt interview, p. 33; New York *Times*, Jan. 13, Feb. 1, 1937; Adolph Germer Diary, Jan. 30, 1937, Adolph Germer Papers, State Historical Society of Wisconsin, Madison; Barclay memorandum, Murphy Papers; Bliven, "Sitting Down in Flint," p. 377. National Guard reports, otherwise unsubstantiated, indicated that the men were armed with rifles. See, for example, G-2 Report, Jan. 19, 1937, National Guard Records.
37. Kraus, *Many and Few*, p. 94; Krogstad, "Brief Resume," Murphy Papers; Barclay memorandum, *ibid*. See also Bliven, "Sitting Down in Flint," p. 377; *Michigan Christian Advocate*, LXIV (Jan. 28, 1937), 6; and O. H. Walburn to Robert Wohlforth, Feb. 3, 1937, Sen 78A-F9, Box 124, Record Group 46, National Archives and Records Service, Washington, D.C. (hereafter cited as La Follette Committee Papers).
38. Barclay memorandum, Murphy Papers; Krogstad, "Brief Resume," *ibid*.; Walburn to Wohlforth, Feb. 3, 1937, La Follette Committee Papers, Box 124; Oral History Interview of John W. Anderson, Feb. 17, May 21, 1960, p. 48. See also Bliven, "Sitting Down in Flint," p. 377; E. C. Johnston to Oscar G. Olander, Jan. 13, 1937, State Police File #5977; *Michigan Christian Advocate*, LXIV (Jan. 28, 1937), 6; and "Observations of an Unofficial Committee of Methodist Ministers," undated, Flint Public Library.
39. Minutes of Strike Committee, Jan. 15, 20, 1937; Simons interview, pp. 36–37.
40. Flint *Journal*, Feb. 12, 1937; New York *Times*, Feb. 13, 1937. *Automotive Industries* (LXXVII, 4) reported on July 3, 1937, that an insurance adjuster had guessed that the damage done to auto plants in Michigan during *all* the auto strikes of the preceding few months was about $200,000.
41. Flint *Journal*, Feb. 14, 1937.
42. Audrey to Clarence [Feb. 1937], Bess to Erwin [Feb. 1937], Kraus Papers, Box 9. There are copies of a few dozen letters to and from Chevrolet No. 4 strikers in the Kraus Papers. In citing these letters, I have preserved the original spelling and punctuation.
43. Simons interview, pp. 48–49; Interview with Wyndham Mortimer, Dec. 9, 1964, p. 30; P. Hapgood to M. Hapgood [Feb. 10, 1937], Hapgood Papers.
44. Edwin Chapman to Dear Liz and All, Feb. 3, 1937, —— to Mrs. Jean Wilson, Feb. 3, 1937, Kraus Papers, Box 9.
45. G-2 Journal, Jan. 17, 1937, National Guard Records; G-2 Report, Feb. 2, 1937, *ibid*.; Simons interview, p. 47. See also Devitt interview, p. 17; and Oral History Interview of Arthur Case, Aug. 4, 1960, p. 6.
46. G-2 Journal, Jan. 26, 1937, National Guard Records; Johnston to Olander, Jan. 5, 1937, State Police File #5977.
47. On this point, see Devitt interview, pp. 17–18. *Cf*. Oral History Interview of Clayton Johnson, June 1, 1961, p. 9.
48. Minutes of Strike Committee, Jan. 5, 12, 1937; Minutes of Council, Jan. 10, 23, 1937; Mundale to Travis, undated, Mundale to ——, undated, Kraus Papers, Box 9 (I have preserved the original spelling and punctuation); New York *Times*, Jan. 6, 1937; Gallico, "Sit-Down Strike," pp. [157, 160]; Harold Mulbar to Olander, undated, State Police File #5977.
49. Oral History Interview of Norman Bully, Oct. 12, 1961, pp. 4–5; Case

interview, p. 6; Oral History Interview of Frank Manfred, June 26, 1960, p. 31; Simons interview, p. 47.
50. Minutes of Mass Meeting, Jan. 13, 1937; Minutes of Special Meeting, Jan. 18, 1937.
51. Minutes of Special Meeting, Jan. 18, 1937; Lewis to Stay-In Strikers, Jan. 22, 1937, Simons Papers (I have inserted the commas); "Hello, Boys of Fisher Two!" Kraus Papers, Box 9; Flint *Journal*, Jan. 11, 1937.
52. For evidence of concern about the welfare problem, see, for example, Minutes of Strike Committee, Jan. 21–22, 1937.
53. —— to Dear husband and dady [sic], Feb. 10, 1937, Kraus Papers, Box 9. See also Johnson interview, p. 8.
54. Manfred interview, p. 26; Anderson *Auto Workers Daily News*, Jan. 9, 1937; Tony Klimes to Emma [Feb. 1937], Art Lowell to Vic et al. [Feb. 1937], Kraus Papers, Box 9; Gallico, "Sit-Down Strike," p. [159]. See also Detroit *News*, Jan. 15, 1937; *Daily Worker*, Jan. 16, 1937; and Devitt interview, p. 20.
55. G-2 Report, Jan. 17, 1937, National Guard Records; Estimate of the Situation, Feb. [Jan.], 22, 1937, *ibid.*; Mulbar to L. A. Lyon, Jan. 28, 1937, State Police File #5977; Barclay memorandum, Murphy Papers; New York *Times*, Feb. 1, 1937.
56. Interview with Roy Reuther, July 12, 1966, p. 44; Devitt interview, p. 15. "Those fellows down at No. 1 are a lot more radical than we are," a No. 2 sit-downer told a reporter. New York *Times*, Jan. 31, 1937.
57. Minutes of Strike Committee, Jan. 4 [?], 20, 1937.
58. Minutes of Strike Committee, Jan. 23, 1937; New York *Times*, Feb. 1, 9, 1937.
59. Minutes of Mass Meeting, Jan. 14, 1937.
60. See Chapter X.
61. New York *Times*, Feb. 8, 1937; G-2 Journal, Feb. 2, 1937, National Guard Records; —— to Joe and Kids [Feb. 1937], Kermit Johnson to Mr. Spalding [Feb. 1937], Jim to Gertrude [Feb. 1937], Sam [?] to Lorene et al. [Feb. 6, 1937], Simons et al. to Travis, Feb. 7, 1937, Kraus Papers, Box 9; Roscoe Van Zandt Notes, Feb. 6, 1937, *ibid.*; Flint *Auto Worker*, Dec. 30, 1936; Kraus, *Many and Few*, pp. 253–54.
62. Pesotta, *Bread upon the Waters*, pp. 248, 250. See the Chevrolet No. 4 letters in Kraus Papers, Box 9.
63. Pesotta, *Bread upon the Waters*, p. 247; Kraus, *Many and Few*, pp. 254–55; Local 156 Releases, Feb. 6, 7, 1937, Kraus Papers, Box 9; Nellie to Husband [Feb. 1937], Audrey to Clarence [Feb. 1937], *ibid.*; Van Zandt Notes, Feb. 6, 1937, *ibid.*; G-2 Journal, Feb. 5, 1937, National Guard Records; 63d Brigade S-3 Periodic Report, Feb. 6, 1937, *ibid.*; Krogstad, "Brief Resume," Murphy Papers; P. Hapgood to M. Hapgood, Feb. 6, 1937, P. Hapgood to Mother and Father [Feb. 12, 1937], Hapgood Papers.
64. Marie McNeese to Cecil [Feb. 1937], Bess and Kiddies to Erwin [Feb. 6, 1937], Billie to Red [Feb. 1937], Jim to Gertrude [Feb. 1937], Gus to Mother and Dormin, Feb. 6, 1937, Lawrence to Mother and Dad, Feb. 5, 1937, Quincey to Ma [Feb. 1937], —— to Honey [Feb. 1937], Kraus Papers, Box 9; Local 156 Release, Feb. 7, 1937, *ibid.*; Pesotta, *Bread upon the Waters*, pp. 249–50.
65. See, for example, Pesotta, *Bread upon the Waters*, p. 248; and G-2 Journal, Feb. 2, 1937, National Guard Records.

66. Johnson to Travis [Feb. 1937], Harold to Mable [Feb. 1937], Kraus Papers, Box 9. See also [Jay Chapman] to Nellie and Virginia, Feb. 3, 1937, —— to Mrs. Jean Wilson [Feb. 1937], Earnest Post to Margarett [Feb. 1937], Tony Klimes to Emma [Feb. 1937], Art Lowell to Vic *et al.* [Feb. 1937], *ibid.*
67. On this point, see Oral History Interview of Everett Francis, July 6, 1962, p. 35; Devitt interview, p. 31; Louis Stark, "Sit-Down," *Survey Graphic*, XXVI (June 1937), 320; and Seidman, "Sit-Down," p. 4. For the Italian "occupation strikes," see Chapter V.
68. New York *Times*, Feb. 1, 1937.
69. Lipset, *The First New Nation: The United States in Historical and Comparative Perspective* (New York, 1963), pp. 173–76.
70. Notes prepared for Pontiac auto workers [Jan. 1937], Kraus Papers, Box 10; Anderson *Auto Workers Daily News*, Jan. 9, 1937; Flint *Auto Worker*, Jan. 12, 1937; UAW Release, Jan. 20, 1937, Edward Levinson Papers, Box 4, Labor History Archives.
71. Pontiac notes [Jan. 1937], Kraus Papers, Box 10; New York *Times*, Feb. 1, 1937; Seidman, "Sit-Down," p. 30; Stark, "Sit-Down," p. 320; Flint *Auto Worker*, Jan. 12, 1937. See also UAW Release, Jan. 20, 1937, Levinson Papers, Box 4; and Maurice Sugar speech, Apr. 14, 1937, Kraus Papers, Box 11.
72. See Green, "The Case for the Sit-Down Strike," *New Republic*, XC (Mar. 24, 1937), 199–201.
73. Chase S. Osborn to Franklin D. Roosevelt, Mar. 3, 1937, President's Personal File 2680, Franklin D. Roosevelt Library, Hyde Park, New York; Rabbi Barnett R. Brickner, "Strikes," Feb. 14, 1937, Kraus Papers, Box 9; Robert Morss Lovett, "A G.M. Stockholder Visits Flint," *Nation*, CXLIV (Jan. 30, 1937), 124.
74. UAW Release, Jan. 19, 1937, Levinson Papers, Box 4; Flint *Journal*, Feb. 2, 1937; *Union News Service*, Apr. 12, 1937; Oral History Interview of Richard Frankensteen, Oct. 10, 1959–Dec. 7, 1961, pp. 36–37.
75. Flint *Journal*, Jan. 25, 1937; *Information Service*, Feb. 6, 1937.
76. *National Labor Relations Board* v. *Fansteel Metallurgical Corporation*, 306 U.S. 240, 252.
77. "Is the Sit-Down Unfair?" *New Republic*, XC (Feb. 17, 1937), 33; Arthur G. Hays to Lucille Milner, Jan. 8, 1937, Roger N. Baldwin to Members of Committee on Civil Rights in the Automobile Industry, Jan. 30, 1937, Baldwin to Ed F. Alexander, Feb. 26, 1937, American Civil Liberties Union Archives, Reel 152, Vols. 1046, 1047, New York Public Library.
78. Merlin Wiley, "Was the Sit-Down Strike a Crime in Michigan?" *Michigan State Bar Journal*, XIX (Feb. 1940), 66, 68–69, 85; William L. Brunner to McCrea [Mar. 1937], Samuel D. Pepper Papers (privately held).
79. Detroit *News*, Dec. 20, 1936; Charles C. Spangenberg, "Legal Status of Sit-Down Strike—Legal and Equitable Remedies," *Michigan Law Review*, XXXV (June 1937), 1339, 1342, 1349.
80. Detroit *News*, Jan. 3, 1937; Act. No. 168, *Public and Local Acts of the Legislature of the State of Michigan . . . 1935* (Lansing, 1935), p. 266; Opinion of Judge Paul V. Gadola—General Motors Case, Feb. 2, 1937, Kraus Papers, Box 9; Flint *Journal*, Feb. 12, 1937.
81. New York *Times*, Jan. 1, 1937.

Notes to pages 179 to 186

Chapter VII

1. SMD, "The Problem of Union Agreements," Dec. 31, 1936, GM, Labor Relations Diary, Appendix Documents to Accompany Section 1, Doc. 74-A, GM Building, Detroit, Michigan.
2. New York *Times*, Jan. 1, 1937.
3. *Ibid.*, Jan. 3, 1937; Detroit *News*, Jan. 3, 1937. Knudsen made it clear on January 2 that he was willing to negotiate concerning plants that had been evacuated. *Ibid.* For a critique of GM's collective-bargaining policy, see Walter Lippmann, in Detroit *Free Press*, Jan. 7, 1937.
4. New York *Times*, Jan. 2, 1937; Martin to Sloan, Jr., and Knudsen, Jan. 4, 1937, Henry Kraus Papers, Box 9, Labor History Archives, Wayne State University, Detroit, Michigan.
5. Detroit *News*, Jan. 3, 1937.
6. UAW Releases, Jan. 7, 16, 1937, Edward Levinson Papers, Box 4, Labor History Archives.
7. Detroit *News*, Jan. 3, 1937; Flint *Journal*, Jan. 6, 1937; New York *Times*, Jan. 24, 1937; UAW Release, Jan. 16, 1937, Levinson Papers, Box 4; Department of Research and Education, Federal Council of the Churches of Christ, *Information Service*, Feb. 6, 1937.
8. See Chapter III.
9. Sloan, Jr., to All Employes . . . , Jan. 5, 1937, Kraus Papers, Box 9.
10. UAW Release, Jan. 6, 1937, Kraus Papers, Box 9; New York *Times*, Jan. 6, 1937; *Decisions and Orders of the National Labor Relations Board*, XIV (Washington, 1940), 134; Howard C. Reed to Frank Winn, Jan. 6, 1937, Kraus Papers, Box 10.
11. Minutes of the Meeting of the Executive Council, AFL, Feb. 10, 1937, pp. 43, 45–47, 49–51, 55–56; copy of telegram from Frey, received Jan. 9, 1937, GM, Labor Relations Diary, Appendix Doc. 73; New York *Times*, Jan. 8, 10, 1937; Cleveland *Plain Dealer*, Jan. 8, 10, 1937; Detroit *News*, Jan. 8–9, 1937; Flint *Journal*, Jan. 10, 1937.
12. Anderson to Metal Trades Department, Jan. 9, 1937, GM, Labor Relations Diary, Appendix Doc. 73; AFL Executive Council Minutes, Feb. 10, 1937, pp. 44–45.
13. AFL Executive Council Minutes, Feb. 10, 1937, pp. 48–49. Italics supplied.
14. See Chapter X.
15. William Green to George A. Strain, Feb. 10, 1937, Auto Workers File, 1935–37, AFL-CIO Archives, Washington, D.C.; Detroit *News*, Jan. 6, 8, 1937; Flint *Journal*, Jan. 9, 1937; Cleveland *Plain Dealer*, Jan. 7, 12, 21, 1937; New York *Times*, Jan. 8, 10, 22, 1937; AFL Executive Council Minutes, Feb. 10, 1937, p. 42; Frey to Rev. Peter E. Dietz, Jan. 16, 1936 [1937], Frey to James Oneal, Jan. 22, 1937, John P. Frey Papers, Box 6, Library of Congress, Washington, D.C. Daniel J. Tobin, the president of the Teamsters, declared in his organization's journal that he hoped that the UAW would win the strike. Detroit *Labor News*, Feb. 12, 1937.
16. Frey to W. A. Appleton, Feb. 16, 1937, Frey Papers, Box 1.
17. Flint *Journal*, Jan. 5, 9, 14, 1937; Cleveland *Plain Dealer*, Jan. 8, 1937; Ternstedt Employees' Association to Fellow Worker, Jan. 7, 1937, Cleveland Employees Committee to Our Fellow Workers, undated, To Chevrolet Motor Co., Atlanta Division, Jan. 8, 1937, [Flint] Fisher Body Volunteers to Fellow Employe, Jan. 12, 1937, Kraus Papers, Box 9;

Notes to pages 186 to 188

379

GM Release, Jan. 21, 1937, *ibid.*; GM Release, Jan. 31, 1937, Levinson Papers, Box 4.

18. A Resolution to . . . Frank Murphy . . . , Jan. 28, 1937, Frank Murphy Papers, Michigan Historical Collections, Ann Arbor, Michigan; Mrs. Leo Sullivan to Murphy, Jan. 12, 1937, George Gilbert to Murphy, Jan. 25, 1937, and enclosed wire to Lewis, various letters in Boxes 41–43, *ibid.*; Walden Wilkens to Roosevelt, Jan. 13, 1937, and similar letters, File 182-2067, Records of the Conciliation Service, Record Group 280, National Archives and Records Service, Washington, D.C. (hereafter Conciliation Service Files will be cited as CS); Detroit *News*, Jan. 9–11, 1937; Flint *Journal*, Jan. 8, 1937; [Detroit *Free Press*, Jan. 15, 1937], Murphy Scrapbooks, Murphy Papers.

19. UAW Release, Jan. 21, 1937, Levinson Papers, Box 4; Flint *Auto Worker*, Jan. 12, 15, 24, 1937; Subcommittee of Senate Committee on Education and Labor, *Violations of Free Speech and Rights of Labor, Hearings Pursuant to S. Res. 266*, 75 Cong., 1 Sess. (Washington, 1937), Part 6, pp. 2115–17, 2133, 2135; Part 7, pp. 2326–27 (hereafter cited as *La Follette Hearings*); Cleveland *Plain Dealer*, Jan. 10, Feb. 9, 1937; Stanley and Smoyer, Petition for Temporary Restraining Order, Injunction and Equitable Relief [Feb. 1, 1937], Kraus Papers, Box 10; Eugene L. Stauder to Martin, Jan. 8, 1937, *ibid.*, Box 9; *Information Service*, Feb. 6, 1937; Detroit *News*, Jan. 7, 1937; Clayton W. Fountain, *Union Guy* (New York, 1949), pp. 52–55.

20. *Information Service*, Feb. 6, 1937; Mary Scott to Roosevelt, Jan. 7, 1937, CS 182-2067.

21. Crawford to Roosevelt, Jan. 14, 1937, Official File 407-B, Franklin D. Roosevelt Library, Hyde Park, New York; Dwight W. Chapman, "Industrial Conflict in Detroit," in George W. Hartmann and Theodore Newcomb, eds., *Industrial Conflict: A Psychological Interpretation* (New York, 1939), pp. 47–48; Lynd and Lynd, *Middletown in Transition* (New York, 1937), 73n; Alice Pollock to Murphy, Jan. 20, 1937, Murphy Papers; New York *Times*, Jan. 14, 1937. The Flint Chevrolet personnel manager estimated that 90 percent of the Flint workers were uncommitted to either side. G-2 Report, Jan. 26, 1937, Records of the Michigan Military Establishment Relating to the Flint Sit-Down Strike, 1937, microfilm copy in Michigan Historical Collections.

22. Flint *Journal*, Jan. 7, 1937, [Sept. 15, 1957], [Feb. 21, 1961]; Detroit *News*, Jan. 10, 1937; Edward Levinson, "Detroit Digs In," *Nation*, CXLIV (Jan. 16, 1937), 65; Interview with Roy Reuther, July 12, 1966, p. 28, Michigan Historical Collections (transcripts of all interviews cited, unless otherwise noted, are located in the Michigan Historical Collections).

23. Flint *Journal*, Jan. 7, 1937; *I.M.A. News*, Jan. 8, 1937; H. D. Cullen to Robert Wohlforth, Jan. 22, 1937, Sen. 78A-F9, Box 122, Record Group 46, National Archives and Records Service (hereafter cited as La Follette Committee Papers).

24. Flint *Journal*, Jan. 8, 11–12, 1937; Detroit *News*, Jan. 18, 1937; Boysen to Robert La Follette, Jan. 16, 1937, La Follette Committee Papers, Box 124. Saul Alinsky claims that Boysen sued GM after the strike to recover the funds that he had spent on the Alliance. *John L. Lewis* (New York, 1949), p. 119.

25. E. C. Johnston to Oscar G. Olander, Jan. 11, 1937, Case File #5977, Michigan State Police Records, Lansing, Michigan; Boysen to Murphy,

Jan. 14, 1937, Murphy Papers. Johnston observed that Alliance pledges might have been coming in by mail. Boysen was willing to submit his records for investigation. William Eaton to Lawrence A. Lyon, Jan. 23, 1937, State Police File #5977. The UAW opposed a poll of Alliance members on the grounds that it was a coerced membership. Martin to Murphy, Jan. 25, 1937, Murphy Papers.
26. Henry Kraus, *The Many and the Few: A Chronicle of the Dynamic Auto Workers* (Los Angeles, 1947), pp. 119–20; R. Reuther interview, p. 42; "A concurrent resolution . . ." [Jan. 1937], Kraus Papers, Box 9; Flint *Auto Worker*, Jan. 12, 1937; *United Automobile Worker*, Jan. 19, 1937.
27. Interview with Robert C. Travis, Dec. 10, 1964, pp. 29–30. See also R. Reuther interview, p. 28.
28. Johnston to Olander, Jan. 9, 1937, State Police File #5977.
29. Similar committees were established in such places as Saginaw, Anderson, and Janesville. For Boysen's post-1937 career, see Flint *Journal* [Sept. 15, 1957].
30. Kraus sees Barringer as the evil genius behind the Alliance and identifies Boysen as a friend of Barringer. *Many and Few*, pp. 114–16.
31. Player to Murphy, July 11, 1938, Murphy Papers; Flint *Journal*, Jan. 7, 1937; Eaton to Lyon, Jan. 19, 1937, State Police File #5977.
32. Johnston to Olander, Jan. 9, 10, 1937, State Police File #5977; *Information Service*, Feb. 6, 1937; George W. Shinn to Roosevelt, Jan. 11, 1937, CS 182-2067; Ward Lindsay to La Follette, Jan. 10, 1937, La Follette Committee Papers, Box 123.
33. Kraus, *Many and Few*, pp. 118–19.
34. *I.M.A. News*, Jan. 7–8, 14, 21, 30, Feb. 10, 1937; "General Motors Meets the Enemy," *Nation*, CXLIV (Jan. 9, 1937), 33.
35. New York *Times*, Jan. 3, 31, 1937; *I.M.A. News*, Jan. 7, 1937; "General Motors Meets the Enemy," p. 33.
36. GM Releases, Jan. 26, 27, 1937, Levinson Papers, Box 4.
37. GM Releases, Jan. 23, 24, 29, 1937, *ibid.*; *I.M.A. News*, Jan. 28, 30, 1937; New York *Times*, Jan. 30–31, 1937.
38. *I.M.A. News*, Jan. 21, 28, 1937; GM Release, Jan. 23, 1937, Levinson Papers, Box 4; *Business Week*, Feb. 6, 1937, p. 15; The Reminiscences of Nicholas Kelley, 1957, pp. 372–73, Oral History Research Office, Columbia University, New York, New York; *Steel*, C (Jan. 18, 1937), 29.
39. [L. G. Lenhardt], "It Can Happen Here," Mar. 9, 1937, Blair Moody Papers, Michigan Historical Collections; Public Relations Planning Committee, Minutes of Meeting . . . , Sept. 25, 1945, and attached documents. Copies of the latter material were generously made available to me by Professor David L. Lewis.
40. For the legal remedies available to GM, see Dean Dinwoody, in New York *Times*, Jan. 17, 1937.
41. The full text of the injunction is in the Flint *Journal*, Jan. 3, 1937.
42. *Ibid.*; Detroit *News*, Jan. 7, 1937; Minutes of Conference for the Protection of Civil Rights, Jan. 17, 1937, Civil Rights Congress of Michigan Papers, Box 1, Labor History Archives.
43. See, for example, Lucille Milner to Gardner Jackson, Jan. 6, 1937, American Civil Liberties Union Archives, Reel 152, Vol. 1047, New York Public Library.

44. New York *Times*, Jan. 3, 1937; Detroit *News*, Jan. 3, 5, 1937; Flint *Journal*, Jan. 3–5, 1937; Minutes of Meeting Held in Flint . . . , May 19, 1938, Murphy Papers; Interview with Martin S. Hayden *et al.*, Oct. 6, 1964, pp. 42–44.
45. Adolph Germer Diary, Jan. 3, 1937, Adolph Germer Papers, State Historical Society of Wisconsin, Madison. Pressman has generally been given credit for having suggested that Black might be a GM stockholder, but I have preferred to rely on Germer's contemporary account. See Kraus, *Many and Few*, p. 113; and Interview with Lee Pressman, Nov. 12, 1964, p. 12.
46. Flint *Journal*, Jan. 3, 1937; New York *Times*, Jan. 3, 6, 1937; Germer Dairy, Jan. 5, 1937, Germer Papers; *The Compiled Laws of the State of Michigan, 1929* (Lansing, 1930), III, 4936; Martin to Speaker of House of Representatives, Jan. 6, 1937, Kraus Papers, Box 9; Statement of Mr. Martin [Jan. 1937], Joe Brown Collection, Labor History Archives.
47. Detroit *News*, Jan. 7, 1937; Flint *Journal*, Jan. 7–8, 1937; Black to H. W. Arant, Feb. 8, 1937, Roy E. Brownell to Arant, Feb. 3, 1937, Edward D. Black Papers, Michigan Historical Collections.
48. Brownell to Arant, Feb. 3, 1937, Black Papers; Flint *Journal*, Jan. 7, 1937; Kraus, *Many and Few*, p. 114; The Reminiscences of Lee Pressman, 1958, p. 58, Oral History Research Office.
49. *La Follette Hearings*, Part 6, pp. 1761–68, 2017–20, 2093; Part 7, pp. 2327–28, 2606; *Decisions and Orders of NLRB*, XIV, 135–36; Senate Committee on Education and Labor, *Violations of Free Speech and Rights of Labor*, 75 Cong., 2 Sess., *Report No. 46* (Washington, 1937), Part 3, p. 16; *ibid.*, 76 Cong., 1 Sess., *Report No. 6* (Washington, 1939), Part 3, p. 199; Cullen to Wohlforth, Jan. 27, 1937, La Follette Committee Papers, Box 124; Oral History Interview of Bud Simons, Sept. 6, 1960, pp. 36–37.
50. *La Follette Hearings*, Part 6, pp. 1761–68, 2151–52, 2154, 2161–62; Oral History Interview of Harold D. Cranefield, May 17, 1963, p. 20; Cullen to Wohlforth, Jan. 31, 1937, La Follette Committee Papers, Box 122; O. H. Walburn to Wohlforth [Feb. 6, 1937], *ibid.*, Box 124; Dubuc file, *ibid.*, Box 127; Lawrence Barker file, *ibid.* For an espionage report dated Jan. 14, 1937, that was discovered in the Chevrolet No. 4 plant, see Kraus Papers, Box 9.
51. Cullen to Wohlforth, Jan. 31, 1937, La Follette Committee Papers, Box 122; *La Follette Hearings*, Part 6, pp. 1899–1901.
52. See Chapter X.
53. Western Union Press Message, Jan. 13, 1937, Levinson Papers, Box 4; Flint *Journal*, Jan. 13, 1937.
54. See Chapters VIII and XI.
55. Flint *Journal*, Jan. 8, 1937; New York *Times*, Jan. 8, 1937; Johnston to Olander, Jan. 7, 9, 20, 1937, State Police File #5977; Cranefield to Wohlforth, Feb. 10, 1937, La Follette Committee Papers, Box 124; LaDuke Affidavit, Jan. 6 [?], 1937, *ibid.*, Box 126; C. C. Probert, "Sit Down" [1939], Kraus Papers, Box 9; Minutes, Jan. 17, 1937, Civil Rights Congress of Michigan Papers, Box 1.
56. Francis J. Michel Affidavit, Jan. 14, 1937, Kraus Papers, Box 9; Cullen to Wohlforth, Jan. 21, 1937, La Follette Committee Papers, Box 124; *La Follette Hearings*, Part 7, p. 2520 (Exhibit 700); Powers Hapgood to

Mary Hapgood [Jan. 18, 1937], Jan. 19 [1937], Jan. 22, 1937, Powers Hapgood Papers, Lilly Library, Bloomington, Indiana.
57. P. Hapgood to M. Hapgood, Jan. 27, 28 [1937], Hapgood Papers; *La Follette Hearings*, Part 7, pp. 2305–12, 2520–28; Detroit *News*, Jan. 28, 1937; Robert R. Rissman to Wohlforth, Jan. 29, 1937, Cullen to Wohlforth, Jan. 29, 1937, La Follette Committee Papers, Box 122; Flint *Auto Worker*, Jan. 28, 1937. There are conflicting accounts as to just where the cab was sideswiped and whether it was escorted or unescorted at the time. I have relied primarily on Ditzel's testimony before the La Follette Committee and the affidavit that he submitted.
58. Flint *Auto Worker*, Jan. 28, 1937.
59. "General Motors IV: A Unit of Society," *Fortune*, XIX (Mar. 1939), 148.

Chapter VIII

1. Flint *Auto Worker*, Jan. 5, 1937; Adolph Germer Diary, Jan. 2, 1937, Adolph Germer Papers, State Historical Society of Wisconsin, Madison; Flint *Journal*, Jan. 24, 1937; Detroit *News*, Jan. 4, 1937.
2. Interview with Roy Reuther, July 12, 1966, p. 13 (transcripts of all interviews cited are located in the Michigan Historical Collections, Ann Arbor, Michigan).
3. Henry Kraus, *The Many and the Few: A Chronicle of the Dynamic Auto Workers* (Los Angeles, 1947), p. 100; Oral History Interview of William Genske, July 23, 1960, pp. 6–7; Oral History Interview of Joseph Ditzel, Sept. 25, 1960, p. 13; Frank N. Trager, "Autos: The Battle for Industrial Unionism," Jan. 11, 1937, MS in Norman Thomas Papers, New York Public Library; Mary Heaton Vorse, *Labor's New Millions* (New York, 1938), pp. 67–69.
4. Lists of strike assignments, Henry Kraus Papers, Box 9, Labor History Archives, Wayne State University, Detroit, Michigan; [Strike Notes of Lou Scott], *ibid.*
5. H. D. Cullen to Robert Wohlforth, Jan. 23, 1937, Sen 78A-F9, Box 124, Record Group 46, National Archives and Records Service, Washington, D.C. (hereafter cited as La Follette Committee Papers); Cullen to Charles Kramer, Jan. 26, 1937, *ibid.*, Box 5; Interview with Robert C. Travis, Dec. 10, 1964, pp. 29–31; R. Reuther interview, p. 7; Oral History Interview of John W. Anderson, Feb. 17, May 21, 1960, p. 50; State Police Daily Log, Jan. 20, 1937, Case File #5977, Michigan State Police Records, Lansing, Michigan; G-2 Journal, Jan. 20, 1937, Records of the Michigan Military Establishment Relating to the Flint Sit-Down Strike, 1937, microfilm copy in Michigan Historical Collections (hereafter cited as National Guard Records); G-2 Report, Jan. 17, 1937, *ibid.*
6. *United Automobile Worker*, Jan. 22, 1937; Flint *Auto Worker*, Jan. 24, 1937; *Socialist Call*, Feb. 13, 1937; Kraus, *Many and Few*, pp. 237–41.
7. Flint *Auto Worker*, Jan. 26, 1937.
8. *Socialist Call*, Feb. 13, 1937; Detroit *News*, Jan. 20, 1937; *Daily Worker*, Jan. 27, 1937; Flint *Auto Worker*, Jan. 24, 1937; Kraus, *Many and Few*, pp. 234–35; New York *Times*, Feb. 2, 1937.
9. *United Automobile Worker*, Feb. 25, 1937; *Daily Worker*, Feb. 14, 1937; Mrs. Violet Baggett, undated MS, Kraus Papers, Box 9; Eva Stone, "When Auto Women Advance," *Women's Auxiliary Number Ten, Offi-*

cial Monthly Magazine, Apr. [1937], *ibid.*, Box 10; "For Women Only" [Feb. 6, 1937], Joe Brown Collection, Labor History Archives; Mary Heaton Vorse, "What the Women Did in Flint," *Woman Today*, Mar. 1937, pp. 3, 29.

10. Kraus, *Many and Few*, pp. 247-48; Flint *Auto Worker*, Jan. 26, 1937; "Company Formations," Kraus Papers, Box 9; UAW Release, Feb. 1, 1937, *ibid.*; Local 156 Release, Feb. 8, 1937, *ibid.*
11. Minutes of Fisher Body No. 1 Strike Committee, Jan. 19, 21, 1937, Harry Van Nocker Notebook, Kraus Papers, Box 9; *Daily Worker*, Jan. 27, 1937; Kraus, *Many and Few*, p. 172.
12. New York *Times*, Jan. 10, 1937; R. Reuther interview, pp. 41-42; Minutes of Cleveland Fisher Body Strike Committee, Jan. 25, 1937, Kraus Papers, Box 10; Oral History Interview of Norman Bully, Oct. 12, 1961, p. 5.
13. Flint *Journal*, Jan. 4, 1937; Detroit *News*, Jan. 11, 1937; [Detroit *Times*, Jan. 11, 1937], Frank Murphy Scrapbooks, Frank Murphy Papers, Michigan Historical Collections.
14. Flint *Auto Worker*, Jan. 26, 1937; Detroit *News*, Jan. 20, 1937.
15. See *United Automobile Worker*, Nov. 1936, and Flint *Auto Worker*, Dec. 1936.
16. The number of persons working for the county relief administration grew from about 60 on January 1 to 137 on January 24. Flint *Journal*, Jan. 25, 1937.
17. Detroit *News*, Jan. 16, 1937; Flint *Journal*, Jan. 17, 1937; Kraus, *Many and Few*, pp. 171-72; Haber to Murphy, Jan. 16, 1937, Murphy Papers; George F. Granger and Lawrence R. Klein, *Emergency Relief in Michigan, 1933-1939* (Lansing, 1939), p. 172.
18. Minutes of Fisher Body No. 1 Strike Committee, Jan. 21-22, 1937, Van Nocker Notebook, Kraus Papers, Box 9; Cogwill to Charles Killinger, Jan. 22, 1937, *ibid.*; "Relief in the Sit-Down Strike," *Survey*, LXXIII (Mar. 1937), 69-70; Flint *Auto Worker*, Jan. 26, 1937. For Cleveland and relief, see Cleveland *Plain Dealer*, Jan. 15, 20, 1937; and Minutes of Cleveland Fisher Body Strike Committee, Jan. 20, 1937, Kraus Papers, Box 10.
19. Granger and Klein, *Emergency Relief*, pp. 126, 134, 138; Detroit *News*, Feb. 12, Mar. 12, 1937; Flint *Journal*, Feb. 9, 11, 1937. In March 44,629 persons (11,360 cases) received relief under all programs, but in April the number fell to 10,610 (3006 cases). The state, at the time, was paying about 60 percent of the county's relief costs, but it contributed an additional $250,000 to help defray the relief costs occasioned by the strike. The county relief administration distributed $160,000 in relief in January and $297,000 in February. Granger and Klein, *Emergency Relief*, pp. 134, 138; Flint *Journal*, Mar. 8, 1937.
20. "Relief in the Sit-Down Strike," p. 70.
21. Kraus, *Many and Few*, p. 168n; Donations from January 1, 1937 to February 9, 1937, Kraus Papers, Box 9; Hillman to Martin, Feb. 5, 1937, JSP to Martin, Feb. 10, 20, 1937, Martin to Hillman, Feb. 8, 10, 1937, Sidney Hillman Papers, Amalgamated Clothing Workers, New York, New York; Anderson *Auto Workers Daily News*, Feb. 11, 1937.
22. New York *Times*, Jan. 7, Feb. 1, 1937; Oral History Interview of Len DeCaux, Mar. 11, 18, 1961, pp. 18-19, 20-21; Oral History Interview of Carl Haessler, Nov. 27, 1959-Oct. 24, 1960, pp. 1-2, 11-13.
23. Interview with Ralph Segalman, May 2, 1967 (untranscribed); Rose

Pesotta, *Bread upon the Waters* (Edited by John Nicholas Beffel; New York, 1944), pp. 237–38; Vorse, *Labor's New Millions*, p. 68.

24. UAW Releases, Jan. 19, 20, 1937, Edward Levinson Papers, Box 4, Labor History Archives; Detroit *News*, Jan. 21, 1937; Minutes of CIO Meeting, July 2, 1936, Katherine Pollak Ellickson CIO Collection, Franklin D. Roosevelt Library, Hyde Park, New York.

25. Flint *Journal*, Jan. 30, 1937; Flint *Auto Worker*, Jan. 31, 1937; "An Appeal to the Citizens of Flint," undated, Flint Public Library. It is not clear if this is the "Citizens Forum" that Haessler claims was "maneuvered behind the scenes" by the union but was "fronted by a bourgeois committee." Haessler interview, p. 13.

26. UAW Release, Feb. 1, 1937, Kraus Papers, Box 9; Local 156 Release, Feb. 1, 1937, *ibid*.

27. UAW Release, Jan. 8, 1937, Levinson Papers, Box 4; Cleveland *Plain Dealer*, Jan. 11, 1937; *Michigan Christian Advocate*, LXIV (Feb. 11, 1937), 6.

28. UAW Releases, Jan. 16, 20, 1937, Levinson Papers, Box 4; notes prepared for Pontiac workers, undated, Kraus Papers, Box 10; Detroit *News*, Jan. 24, 1937; Flint *Auto Worker*, Jan. 24, 28, 31, 1937.

29. New York *Times*, Jan. 7, 1937; Detroit *News*, Jan. 23, 1937.

30. New York *Times*, Jan. 17, 21, 1937; Detroit *News*, Jan. 22, 1937; *Union News Service*, Jan. 11, 1937; UAW-CIO Per Capita Tax Report [1937], Kraus Papers, Box 11. The latter report does not include an initiation fee figure for January for Local 156. The local paid a per capita tax for the month on about 4500 members.

31. Bully interview, pp. 4–5; Oral History Interview of Arthur Case, Aug. 4, 1960, pp. 6–7.

32. *United Automobile Worker*, Jan. 19, Feb. 25, 1937; Oral History Interview of Frank Manfred, June 26, 1960, p. 31; Ditzel interview, p. 12; Travis to Ellsworth Kramer, Mar. 9, 1937, Kraus Papers, Box 10; B. D. Snyder to Martin, Jan. 23, 1937, *ibid.*, Box 9; *Socialist Call*, Feb. 6, 1937; New York *Times*, Jan. 13, 1937.

33. Kraus, *Many and Few*, p. 173; Travis interview, pp. 58–59; Oral History Interview of Victor Reuther, Mar. 7, 1963, p. 13; Hartley W. Barclay, "We Sat Down with the Strikers and General Motors," *Mill and Factory*, XX (Feb. 1937), 36; Saul Alinsky, *John L. Lewis* (New York, 1949), p. 87; Johnston to Olander, Jan. 8, 1937, State Police File #5977.

34. Johnston to Olander, Jan. 9, 1937, State Police File #5977; Travis interview, pp. 16–17; Genske interview, pp. 5–6; R. Reuther interview, p. 45.

35. Libby-Owens-Ford, which supplied GM with glass, had received an order from Chrysler at the end of November, 1936. *Automotive Industries*, LXXV (Dec. 5, 1936), 765.

36. New York *Times*, Jan. 21, 1937; Detroit *News*, Jan. 16, 21–22, 28, 1937; [L. G. Lenhardt], "It Can Happen Here," Mar. 9, 1937, Blair Moody Papers, Michigan Historical Collections; UAW Release, Jan. 31, 1937, Kraus Papers, Box 9. GM's share of new passenger car registrations fell from 44.40 percent in 1936 to 34.37 percent in the first quarter of 1937 despite a vastly increased output in March, 1937, as compared to March, 1936. *Ward's 1939 Automotive Year Book*, pp. 36–37; New York *Times*, May 9, 1937. GM produced 59,604 passenger cars in the United States in January, which was about 7000 units above the UAW estimate. Maurice Wyss to author, Aug. 30, 1967.

37. New York *Times*, Jan. 5, Feb. 12, 1937.
38. New York *Times*, Jan. 6, 1937; L. C. Walhood to Publicity Department, UAW, Jan. 7, 1937, Kraus Papers, Box 10; undated MS accounts of strike in *ibid.*; Traxler, "I Went through a Strike," *Public Management*, XIX (Apr. 1937), 99–100; Oral History Interview of Louis Adkins, Aug. 16, 1961, pp. 10-12.
39. Detroit *News*, Jan. 8, 12, 26–28, 1937; Germer Diary, Jan. 26–27, 1937, Germer Papers; *United Automobile Worker*, Feb. 25, 1937; Anderson interview, pp. 47–50. On January 19 more than 2000 UAW members and sympathizers picketed the Briggs Meldrum plant in Detroit because of the allegedly discriminatory dismissal of 350 unionists. The pickets were tear gassed by the Detroit police, who were warned by Richard Frankensteen, "If you don't want another Flint riot, you'd better not try to break up the line." The next day the Briggs personnel director, after consulting with Ford's Harry Bennett, agreed to rehire the 350, and the plant was reopened. Detroit *News*, Jan. 19–20, 1937; *United Automobile Worker*, Jan. 22, 1937.
40. GM claimed that five workers had been ejected when they attempted to start a sit-down, but the UAW version was that the unionists had attempted to stage a walkout and had been clubbed by city police and company guards. New York *Times*, Jan. 12, 1937; Flint *Journal*, Jan. 11, 1937. See also Pontiac notes, Kraus Papers, Box 10.
41. New York *Times*, Jan. 14, 1937; Garst to Gary ——, Jan. 13, 1937, Kraus Papers, Box 11.
42. New York *Times*, Jan. 26, 1937; *United Automobile Worker*, Feb. 25, 1937; Knudsen to Murphy, Feb. 11, 1937, Kraus Papers, Box 9.
43. New York *Times*, Jan. 24, Feb. 2, 1937; Detroit *News*, Feb. 6, 1937.
44. H. W. Denton to Travis, Jan. 12, 1937, Kraus Papers, Box 9.
45. "Kansas City Strike," undated, *ibid.*, Box 10; Executive Board to Frank Winn [Feb. 1, 1937], *ibid.*; *United Automobile Worker*, Feb. 25, 1937.
46. Minutes of Cleveland Fisher Body Strike Committee, Jan. 1, 3, 5–6, 13–14, 20, Kraus Papers, Box 10; Stanley and Smoyer, Petition for Temporary Restraining Order, Injunction and Equitable Relief [Feb. 1, 1937], *ibid.*; Cleveland *Plain Dealer*, Jan. 5, 14–15, 20, Feb. 8, 1937.
47. Employee's Bargaining Committee to Fellow Worker, undated, Philip G. Phillips to Wohlforth, Feb. 2, 1937, La Follette Committee Papers, Box 123; Black to Dear Sir, Feb. 3, Black to La Follette, Feb. 4, 1937, *ibid.*, Box 121.
48. According to the 1940 census, 39,610 of the city's 41,572 inhabitants were native-born whites. Bureau of the Census, *Sixteenth Census of the United States: 1940, Population*, II (Washington, 1943), Part 2, p. 786.
49. For differing figures of employment at the two plants, see *Decisions and Orders of the National Labor Relations Board*, XIV (Washington, 1940), 119; and Writers Program of the Works Projects Administration, *Indiana: A Guide to the Hoosier State* (New York, 1941), pp. 329–30.
50. [Paul Garrett], "The Focal Point of Public Relations" [1936], p. 17, Automotive History Collection, Detroit Public Library; [Salyer] Memorandum, Feb. 8, 1937, La Follette Committee Papers, Box 125.
51. Detroit *News*, Jan. 3, 6, 1937; New York *Times*, Jan. 4, 7, 1937; *Decisions and Orders of NLRB*, XIV, 133, 135; Anderson *Auto Workers Daily News*, Jan. 6, 1937; Claude E. Hoffman, *Sit-Down in Anderson: UAW Local 663, Anderson, Indiana* (Detroit, 1968), p. 40.

Notes to pages 213 to 218

52. Articles of Association of Citizens League for Industrial Security, La Follette Committee Papers, Box 125; [Salyer] Memorandum, Feb. 8, 1937, *ibid.*; *Decisions and Orders of NLRB*, XIV, 132–34; New York *Times*, Jan. 10, 1937; Anderson *Auto Workers Daily News*, Jan. 11, 1937; Anderson *Daily Bulletin*, Jan. 9, 1937; "Yours the Gang Who Mean Business" to Thompson, Jan. 10, 1937, Hugh Thompson Papers, Labor History Archives; Oral History Interview of Hugh Thompson, Mar. 28, 1963, pp. 21–22. The NLRB found no evidence that GM had "encouraged or assisted" the League.
53. *Decisions and Orders of NLRB*, XIV, 135–36.
54. Robert H. Cowdrill to Wohlforth, Feb. 8, 1937, La Follette Committee Papers, Box 122.
55. My account of the events of January 25 is based on *Decisions and Orders of NLRB*, XIV, 136–37; Ira Latimer (Executive Secretary, Chicago Civil Liberties Committee), Report on Civil Liberties Investigation of Anderson, Indiana, American Civil Liberties Union Archives, Reel 151, Vol. 1041, New York Public Library; Thompson Affidavit, Jan. 29, 1937, Kraus Papers, Box 10; Thompson interview, pp. 22–23; Detroit *News*, Jan. 26, 1937; Flint *Journal*, Jan. 26, 1937; Affidavits of Arnold Chapman and Richard Greenwalt, undated, and of Lucille Stevens, Feb. 1, 1937, La Follette Committee Papers, Box 125; and "Anderson," undated MS, *ibid.* See also Hoffman, *Sit-Down in Anderson*, pp. 47–50.
56. *Decisions and Orders of NLRB*, XIV, 137; Latimer Report, Feb. 19, 1937, ACLU Archives, Reel 151, Vol. 1041; Cowdrill and G. Watson to Wohlforth, Jan. 29, 1937, Cowdrill to Wohlforth, Feb. 8, 1937, La Follette Committee Papers, Box 122; [Salyer] Memorandum, Feb. 8, 1937, *ibid.*, Box 125.
57. V. Reuther interview, pp. 17–19.
58. *Decisions and Orders of NLRB*, XIV, 138–42, 155–57; Cowdrill and Watson to Wohlforth, Jan. 29, 1937, La Follette Committee Papers, Box 122; "Anderson," *ibid.*, Box 125, and undated affidavits in *ibid.*
59. Hall Affidavit, Jan. 29, 1937, Kraus Papers, Box 10; Latimer Report, Feb. 19, 1937, ACLU Archives, Reel 151, Vol. 1041; Memorandum, Jan. 29, 1937, *ibid.*; Detroit *News*, Jan. 28–30, 1937; Hoffman, *Sit-Down in Anderson*, p. 53.
60. *Decisions and Orders of NLRB*, XIV, 143–45; Latimer Report, Feb. 19, 1937, ACLU Archives, Reel 151, Vol. 1041; "Anderson," La Follette Committee Papers, Box 125.
61. Detroit *News*, Jan. 29, 1937; Roland Affidavit, Feb. 6, 1937, La Follette Committee Papers, Box 125; MS of V. Reuther speech, intended for delivery Jan. 28, 1937, Victor Reuther Papers, Labor History Archives.
62. New York *Times*, Jan. 29, 31, Feb 1, 1937; Detroit *News*, Jan. 31, 1937; Anderson *Auto Workers Daily News*, Feb. 5, 10–11, 1937; V. Reuther interview, p. 19; affidavits in La Follette Committee Papers, Box 125.
63. Anderson *Auto Workers Daily News*, Feb. 10, 1937.
64. Riesman, "The Suburban Dislocation," in Philip Olson, ed., *America as a Mass Society* (Glencoe, Ill., 1963), p. 291.
65. New York *Times*, Jan. 2, 1937; Detroit *News*, Jan. 4, 1937; Flint *Journal*, Jan. 19, 1937; Trager, "Autos," Jan. 11, 1937, Thomas Papers.
66. Flint *Journal*, Jan. 19, 25, 1937; New York *Times*, Jan. 20, 1937; Travis interview, pp. 51–52; Haessler interview, p. 17. See also Pesotta, *Bread upon the Waters*, pp. 245–46.

Notes to pages 218 to 221

387

67. This is the thesis that informs Jerold S. Auerbach, *Labor and Liberty: The La Follette Committee and the New Deal* (Indianapolis, 1966).
68. Some ACLU members would have liked the organization to take this position. See, for example, Mary Van Kleeck Memorandum to Board of Directors, Jan. 11, 1937, ACLU Archives, Reel 152, Vol. 1047. Miss Van Kleeck saw the sit-down as a species of peaceful picketing.
69. Arthur G. Hays to Lucille Milner, Jan. 8, 1937, and enclosed memorandum of same date, *ibid.*, Vol. 1046; Hays, Morris Ernst, and Roger N. Baldwin to Murphy, Jan. 30, 1937, Baldwin to Ed F. Alexander, Feb. 26, 1937, Baldwin to Edward D. Tittman, Feb. 24, 1937, Baldwin to Committee on Civil Rights in Automobile Industry, Jan. 30, 1937, Milner to Gardner Jackson, Jan. 6, 1937, *ibid.*, Vol. 1047; ACLU Releases, Jan. 8, 15, 1937, *ibid.*; Hays *et al.* to Townsend, Jan. 29, 1937, *ibid.*, Reel 151, Vol. 1041; Latimer Report, *ibid.*; Detroit *News*, Jan. 9, 1937; New York *Times*, Jan. 17, 1937.
70. The activities of the Conference during the strike are detailed in *Civil Rights Guardian* [Feb. 1937], Brown Collection. See also "Important Call for Emergency Conference" [Jan. 13, 1937], *ibid.*; and Minutes of Conference for the Protection of Civil Rights, Jan. 17, 1937, Civil Rights Congress of Michigan Papers, Box 1, Labor History Archives.
71. Minutes of Fisher Body No. 1 Strike Committee, Jan. 22, 1937, Van Nocker Notebook, Kraus Papers, Box 9; *Civil Rights Guardian*, Brown Collection.
72. Ryan *et al.* to Murphy, Jan. 8, 1937, Murphy Papers; Auerbach, *Labor and Liberty*, p. 31; Department of Research and Education, Federal Council of the Churches of Christ, *Information Service*, Feb. 6, 1937; Local 156 Release, Feb. 8, 1937, Kraus Papers, Box 9.
73. *Michigan Christian Advocate*, LXIV (Jan. 14, 1937), 7; *ibid.* (Jan. 28, 1937), 6. The brief report of the three clergymen is contained in "An Appeal to the Citizens of Flint."
74. Vorse, *Labor's New Millions*, p. 68; Flint *Journal*, Feb. 9, 1937; Travis interview, p. 54; Segalman interview; Mary Heaton Vorse, "The Emergency Brigade at Flint," *New Republic*, XC (Feb. 17, 1937), 39.
75. Thomas to Martin, Jan. 4, 1937, Thomas to John Monarch *et al.*, Jan. 15, 1937, Trager to Thomas, Jan. 12, 1937, Thomas Papers; Trager, "Autos," Jan. 11, 1937, *ibid.*; *Daily Worker*, Jan. 16, 1937; Donations from January 1, 1937 to February 9, 1937, Kraus Papers, Box 9; William Weinstone, "The Great Auto Strike," *Communist*, XVI (Mar. 1937), 225–26.
76. See Irving Howe and B. J. Widick, *The UAW and Walter Reuther* (New York, 1949), pp. 51–52; Philip Taft, "Ideologies and Industrial Conflict," in Arthur Kornhauser *et al.*, eds., *Industrial Conflict* (New York, 1954), pp. 262–63; and Frank A. Warren, III, *Liberals and Communism: The "Red Decade" Revisited* (Bloomington, 1966), p. 120.
77. Loewe to Thomas, Jan. 7, 1937, Thomas Papers; Trager report [Jan. 25, 1937], *ibid.*; *Socialist Call*, Feb. 6, 1937; Oral History Interview of Larry Davidow, July 14, 1960, p. 10; Ditzel to Germer, Apr. 8, 1936, Germer Papers; Gordon Carroll, "Revolution in Michigan," *American Mercury*, XL (Apr. 1937), 393.
78. Weinstone, *The Great Sit-Down Strike* (New York, 1937), p. 37; House Special Committee on Un-American Activities, *Investigation of Un-American Propaganda Activities in the United States*, 75 Cong., 3 Sess.

Notes to pages 222 to 224

(Washington, D.C., 1938), II, 1454, 1494–96, 1551, 1554, 1649, 1689; III, 2020 (hereafter cited as *Dies Hearings*); Davidow interview, pp. 22–23; Interview with Mortimer, Dec. 9, 1964, p. 27.
79. Haessler interview, p. 14; Haessler to author, Apr. 5, 1967; Max M. Kampelman, *The Communist Party vs. the C.I.O.* (New York, 1957), pp. 67–69; R. Reuther interview, pp. 15–19; Travis interview, p. 59; George Douglas Blackwood, "The United Automobile Workers of America, 1935–51" (Ph.D. thesis, University of Chicago, 1951), 84n. See also Oral History Interview of Jack Palmer, July 23, 1960, p. 11; Benjamin Stolberg, *The Story of the CIO* (New York, 1938), p. 164; and Clayton W. Fountain, *Union Guy* (New York, 1946), p. 68.
80. *Communist*, XIV (Feb. 1935), 108. See also Murray Kempton, *Part of Our Time* (New York, 1955), pp. 284–85.
81. DeCaux interview, pp. 29–30; House Un-American Activities Committee, *Hearings regarding Communism in the United States Government*, 81 Cong., 2 Sess. (Washington, 1950), Part 2, pp. 2844–2901; Earl Latham, *The Communist Controversy in Washington: From the New Deal to McCarthy* (Cambridge, Mass., 1966), pp. 107–9, 118–19.
82. A. B. Magil, "Detroit's Labor Candidate," *New Masses*, XIV (Mar. 19, 1935), 14–15; *Labor Defender*, Nov. 1928, p. 256, Aug. 1935, pp. 14, 23; *New Force*, I (Jan. 1932), 10–12, (Mar.–Apr. 1932), 10–13, (May 1932), 10–11; Detroit *Saturday Night*, Feb. 6, 1937; Daniel Aaron, *Writers on the Left* (New York, 1961), p. 224; Detroit *News*, Oct. 7, 1932, Jan. 7, 16, 1933, June 30, 1939; *Michigan Worker*, Nov. 6, 1932; *Soviet Russia Today*, Jan. 1933, p. 18, May 1933, pp. 4–5, 11–12, Apr. 1934, p. 21; Davidow interview, pp. 26–28; The People vs Raymond Tessmer, No. 8890, 1939, Recorder's Court for the City of Detroit, copy of transcript in my possession. The prosecution charged that Sugar had been libelously accused of advocating criminal syndicalism as defined by the laws of Michigan. Most of the evidence presented at the trial related to a period before the sit-down strike.
83. Latham, *Communist Controversy*, pp. 109–10, 121; Auerbach, *Labor and Liberty*, pp. 85, 110, 167–68; Travis interview, pp. 10–12; Travis to Kramer, Nov. 11, 1936, La Follette Committee Papers, Box 124; Germer Diary, Jan. 11, 1937, Germer Papers; Detroit *News*, Jan. 14, 1937.
84. R. Reuther interview, p. 20; Ross, "The Natural History of the Strike," in Kornhauser et al., eds., *Industrial Conflict*, pp. 29–30.
85. The UAW did apparently file a complaint with the NLRB alleging intimidation of unionists for failure to sign nonunion petitions. Detroit *News*, Jan. 8, 12, 1937. The NLRB found in August, 1939, that GM and Delco-Remy had been guilty of engaging in unfair labor practices at the Delco-Remy plants during the course of the strike, although Delco-Remy had not been struck. *Decisions and Orders of NLRB*, XIV, 113–68. For the proposed legislative investigation, see "A concurrent resolution . . . ," undated, Kraus Papers, Box 9.
86. Cullen to Wohlforth, Jan. 21, 1937, Kramer to Travis, Feb. 1, 1937, La Follette Committee Papers, Box 124; Auerbach, *Labor and Liberty*, pp. 85, 111–12; Flint *Journal*, Jan. 5, 1937.
87. Frank H. Bowen to Kraus, Jan. 19, 1937, Kraus Papers, Box 9; affidavits in La Follette Committee Papers, Box 126; Cranefield to Wohlforth, Jan. 20, 1937, Cullen to Wohlforth, Jan. 27, 28, 1937, *ibid.*, Box 122;

Cranefield to Wohlforth, Feb. 10, 1937, Cullen to Wohlforth, Jan. 22, 23, 1937, Wohlforth to Cullen, Jan. 26, 1937, *ibid.*, Box 124; Cullen to Wohlforth, Jan. 20, 1937, *ibid.*, Box 125; Cullen to Kramer, Jan. 26, 1937, *ibid.*, Box 5; New York *Times*, Jan. 26, 1937; Detroit *News*, Jan. 26, Feb. 10, 1937; Auerbach, *Labor and Liberty*, pp. 111–12; Alinsky, *Lewis*, p. 109.

88. New York *Times,* Feb. 4, 1937. See also *ibid.*, Jan. 14, 1937; Detroit *News*, Jan. 29, 1937; Flint *Journal*, Feb. 10, 1937; and Interview with Joe Devitt, July 14, 1966, pp. 27–28.
89. Flint *Journal*, Jan. 22, Feb. 10, 14, 1937; New York *Times*, Jan. 10, 19, 21, 1937; Detroit *News*, Feb. 10, 1937.
90. Weldon A. Lampshire to Gernsley F. Gorton, Mar. 8, 1937, William H. Phelps Papers, Michigan Historical Collections; Gallico, "Sit-Down Strike," *Cosmopolitan*, CIV (Apr. 1938), [170]; Howard H. Jackson to H. Lynn Pierson, Apr. 8, 1937, President's Personal File 403, Franklin D. Roosevelt Library, Hyde Park, New York; Paul Jones, in [Akron *Times-Press*], Jan. 22, 1937, Kraus Papers, Box 9; Cullen to Wohlforth, Jan. 21, 1937, O. H. Walburn to Wohlforth, Feb. 2, 1937, La Follette Committee Papers, Box 124; G-2 Report, Feb. 9, 1937, National Guard Records; R. Reuther interview, pp. 6–7, 40–41.
91. *Automotive Industries*, LXXVI (Jan. 16, 1937), 73; R. Reuther interview, p. 40; Cullen to Wohlforth, Jan. 31, 1937, La Follette Committee Papers, Box 122; G-2 Report, Feb. 7, 1937, National Guard Records.
92. For the depth of the union's suspicions, see Kraus to Winn, May 28, 1937, Kraus Papers, Box 10; and Kraus, *Many and Few*, p. 173. Cf. Travis interview, pp. 10–13.
93. *Dies Hearings*, II, 1683–91; Walburn to Wohlforth, Feb. 5, 1937, La Follette Committee Papers, Box 124; R. M. Atkins to William H. Phelps, Feb. 23, 1937, Phelps Papers.
94. The commission on January 18 voted to allow the UAW to solicit contributions for two weeks. Flint *Journal,* Jan. 19, 1937. See Chapters X, XI.
95. *Punch Press*, Feb. 10, 1937, Kraus Papers, Box 9; Johnston to Olander, Jan. 8, 1937, State Police File #5977; Flint *Journal*, Jan. 8, 1937; New York *Times*, Jan. 8, 1937; Kraus, *Many and Few*, pp. 123–24; Flint *Auto Worker*, Jan. 12, 1937; *Dies Hearings*, II, 1643, 1684–86. There are slight differences in the available accounts of the events of January 7. I have relied in the main on the report of a state police trooper who witnessed the scene.
96. Kraus, *Many and Few*, pp. 107–8; Germer Diary, Jan. 3, 1937, Germer Papers; Travis interview, pp. 48–49; Devitt interview, pp. 31–32.
97. Minutes of Fisher Body No. 1 Council, Jan. 28, 1937, Van Nocker Notebook, Kraus Papers, Box 9; comment on form sent out by Gorton, Mar. 4, 1937, Phelps Papers.
98. Board of Education Resolution, Feb. 9, 1937, Kraus Papers, Box 9; "Statement of Flint Federation of Teachers," undated, Flint Public Library; "Teachers View a Sit-Down," *American Teacher*, XXI (Jan.–Feb. 1937), 19; *I.M.A. News*, Jan. 30, 1937; Kraus, *Many and Few*, pp. 170–71; Data on Cases of Dismissed Teachers of Flint Federation of Teachers, Arthur Elder-Detroit Federation of Teacher Papers, Box 13, Labor History Archives; Elder to Martin, Aug. 20, 1937, *ibid.* For subsequent developments in this case, see Box 13, *ibid.*

99. Cranefield to Wohlforth, Feb. 10, 1937, La Follette Committee Papers, Box 124; Cullen to Wohlforth, Jan. 31, 1937, *ibid.*, Box 122.
100. There is a copy of one of these forms in Kraus Papers, Box 9.
101. Flint *Journal*, Jan. 11–12, 1937; L. G. Newman to Gorton, Mar. 8, 1937, Phelps Papers; *Business Week*, Jan. 16, 1937, p. 46; Kraus, *Many and Few*, p. 171; Flint Chamber of Commerce to Roosevelt, Jan. 12, 1937, File 182-2067, Records of the Conciliation Service, Record Group 280, National Archives and Records Service (Conciliation Service files will hereafter be cited as CS). There are many anti-strike wires from Flint middle-class organizations in *ibid*.
102. Minutes of Fisher Body No. 1 Strike Committee, Feb. 8, 1937, Kraus Papers, Box 9; R. Reuther interview, p. 39; Oral History Interview of Clayton Johnson, June 1, 1961, p. 9; Kraus, *Many and Few*, p. 171; Travis interview, p. 17.
103. R. Reuther interview, pp. 40–41; Estimate of the Situation, Feb. [Jan.] 22, 1937, National Guard Records; Mulbar to Lyon, Jan. 23, 1937, State Police File #5977; Nellie to Husband [Feb. 1937], Audrey to Clarence [Feb. 1937], Kraus Papers, Box 9. There are numerous letters from workers expressing their strike sentiments in Murphy Papers, Boxes 41 and 42, and CS 182-2067.
104. Of Flint's 46,092 church members in 1936, 6027 identified with the Methodist Episcopal church. The Presbyterians, with 2825 members, ranked second among the Protestant denominations. There were 17,604 Roman Catholics in the city. Bureau of the Census, *Religious Bodies: 1936* (Washington, 1941), I, 70–71.
105. William H. Phelps and John E. Marvin to Gorton, Feb. 19, 1937, Gorton to Dear Friends, Mar. 4, 1937, Phelps Papers. The results of the poll are in *ibid*.
106. Atkins to Phelps, Feb. 23, 1937, Lampshire to Gorton, Mar. 8, 1937, Jack R. Forshee to Editors, Feb. 5, 1937, H. A. Troxel to Phelps, Feb. 15, 1937, Floyd E. Harris to Gorton, Mar. 5, 1937, J. George Carey to Editor, Feb. 12, 1937, Phelps Papers. On the opinion of Flint clergymen concerning the strike, see William H. Chafe, "The Good Years: The Great Depression in Flint" (MS, 1967), pp. 16–17n, copy in my possession.
107. Detroit *News*, Jan. 31, 1937.
108. Local 156 Release, Feb. 1, 1937, Kraus Papers, Box 9. John Tibby, a Gallup associate, thought that the poll revealed "surprisingly strong sentiment" in favor of the UAW. Flint *Auto Worker*, Feb. 10, 1937.
109. Detroit *News*, Feb. 7, 1937; *Business Week*, Feb. 13, 1937, p. 15.
110. For this and other views critical of the strike, see David Lawrence, in Flint *Journal*, Jan. 3, 15, 1937; editorials in New York *Times*, Jan. 2, 4, 19, 1937; views of New York Board of Trade and National Civic Federation, in *ibid*., Feb. 11, 1937; views of the Most Rev. Michael J. Gallagher, in Flint *Journal*, Jan. 11, 1937; *Literary Digest*, CXXIII (Jan. 16, 1937), 6–7; *Ward's Automotive Reports* Release, Jan. 9, 1937, Kraus Papers, Box 9; Barclay, "We Sat Down," pp. 33, 35; *American Machinist*, LXXXI (Jan. 13, 1937), 32a; Murphy Papers, Boxes 41 and 42; and CS 182-2067.

Notes to pages 232 to 235

391

Chapter IX

1. The Reminiscences of Lee Pressman, 1958, pp. 69–70, Oral History Research Office, Columbia University, New York, New York; Matthew Josephson, "Profiles," *New Yorker*, XVII (Mar. 8, 1941), 31–32; Alfred P. Sloan, Jr., *My Years with General Motors* (Edited by John McDonald with Catharine Stevens; Garden City, New York, 1964), pp. 117–18; Donaldson Brown, *Some Reminiscences of an Industrialist* (n.p., [1957]), pp. 95–96; Frank Murphy to George Murphy, May 19, 1947, Frank Murphy Papers, Michigan Historical Collections, Ann Arbor, Michigan; Adolph Germer Diary, Jan. 7, 1937, Adolph Germer Papers, State Historical Society of Wisconsin, Madison.
2. Oral History Interview of Len DeCaux, Mar. 11, 18, 1961, pp. 19–20, 24–28 (transcripts of all interviews cited, unless otherwise noted, are located in the Michigan Historical Collections); Brophy, "The Struggle for an Auto Union" (undated MS), pp. 10–11, John Brophy Papers, Catholic University, Washington, D.C.
3. Interview with Wyndham Mortimer, Dec. 9, 1964, p. 16; DeCaux interview, pp. 28–30; Brophy, "Struggle for an Auto Union," p. 21.
4. Perkins, *The Roosevelt I Knew* (New York, 1946), pp. 321–22; Roosevelt to Samuel I. Rosenman, Nov. 13, 1940, President's Personal File 64 (hereafter cited as PPF), Franklin D. Roosevelt Library, Hyde Park, New York; Bascom N. Timmons, *Garner of Texas* (New York, 1948), pp. 215–16.
5. Detroit *News*, Jan. 31, Feb. 9, 1937; "Mr. Lewis and the Auto Strike," *New Republic*, LXXXIX (Feb. 3, 1937), 398; Minutes of the Meeting of the Executive Council, AFL, Feb. 10, 1937, p. 60.
6. New York *Post*, Jan. 16, 1937, Murphy Scrapbooks, Murphy Papers; Russell B. Porter, "Governor Murphy's Star in the Ascendant," New York *Times*, Feb. 21, 1937; *ibid.*, Feb. 12, 1937; Mortimer interview, p. 35; Interview with Lee Pressman, Nov. 12, 1964, pp. 20–21; Interview with Irene Murphy, July 30, 1964, p. 35. Cf. *Business Week*, Jan. 9, 1937, p. 13.
7. [Manila *Daily Tribune*, July 13, 1933], Murphy Scrapbooks; Flint *Journal*, Jan. 19, 1937; Detroit *News*, Jan. 4, Feb. 11, 1937; New York *Times*, Feb. 12, 1937; Porter, "Murphy's Star"; *Liberty*, Feb. 25, 1939, p. 7; Interview with Norman H. Hill, Aug. 21, 1963, p. 22; Murphy to Joseph R. Hayden, Apr. 8, 1937, Murphy to Stuart H. Perry, June 1, 1938, Murphy Papers.
8. Murphy to Lewis and Martin, Feb. 8, 1937, Murphy Papers; Interview with Roy Reuther, July 12, 1966, p. 33; Mortimer interview, p. 7; Henry Kraus, *The Many and the Few: A Chronicle of the Dynamic Auto Workers* (Los Angeles, 1947), p. 268; Detroit *News*, Jan. 12–13, 1937. Cf. Murphy to Octave P. Beauvais, July 7, 1937, Murphy Papers.
9. *Pipp's Weekly*, Nov. 12, 1921; Outline of Lecture [1920's], Murphy Papers; Porter, "Murphy's Star"; Carl Muller, "Frank Murphy, Ornament of the Bar," *Detroit Lawyer*, XVII (Sept. 1949), 181–82; New York *Times*, Jan. 14, 1937; Murphy to James Bryant, Sept. 28, 1937, Murphy to P. H. Calahan, May 25, 1937, Murphy Papers; "First Quarterly Accounting," July 10, 1937, *ibid.*; Oral History Interview of Stanley Brahms,

Nov. 23, 1959, p. 35; Local 156 Release, Feb. 8, 1937, Joe Brown Collection, Labor History Archives, Wayne State University, Detroit, Michigan.
10. Kemp, "Frank Murphy as Government Administrator," 1951, Edward G. Kemp Papers, Michigan Historical Collections; Flint *Journal*, Jan. 4, 1937; Kemp Memoranda to Murphy, Jan. 27, 1937, Murphy to Hayden, Apr. 8, 1937, Murphy to Mark Sullivan, Jan. 4, 1939, Murphy Papers.
11. Murphy to Atkins, Jan. 9, 1937, Murphy to Warren E. Kelley, Apr. 2, 1937, Murphy to George O. Hackett, June 18, 1937, Murphy Papers; "First Quarterly Accounting," July 10, 1937, *ibid.*; New York *Times*, Jan. 29, Feb. 12, 1937; [*Catholic Worker*, Oct. 1937], Murphy Scrapbooks; Cleveland *Plain Dealer* [Feb. 12, 1937], *ibid.*
12. Norman Beasley, *Knudsen* (New York, 1947), pp. 168–69; Murphy to Mark Sullivan, Jan. 4, 1939, Murphy Papers; [Charlotte *Republican-Tribune*, Apr. 16, 1937], clipping in *ibid.*; speech by John Lovett, Apr. 1937, p. 6, *ibid.*; Joseph H. Creighton Memorandum to Murphy, May 11, 1938, *ibid.*; speech by Murphy, Oct. 21, 1938, *ibid.*; Hill interview, pp. 22–23; New York *Times*, Jan. 30, Feb. 9, 1937. There are several extant versions of Fisher's statement to Murphy regarding bloodshed.
13. Murphy to Albert H. Dale, Feb. 25, 1937, Murphy to B. E. Hutchinson, June 24, 1937, Murphy Papers; Perkins, *Roosevelt I Knew*, p. 323.
14. Jerold S. Auerbach, *Labor and Liberty: The La Follette Committee and the New Deal* (Indianapolis, 1966), *passim*; Murphy to Virginia Donaldson, Jan. 26, 1937, Murphy Papers; Arthur G. Hays, Morris L. Ernst, and Roger N. Baldwin to Murphy, Jan. 30, 1937, Baldwin to Committee on Civil Rights in the Automobile Industry, Jan. 30, 1937, American Civil Liberties Union Archives, Reel 152, Vol. 1047, New York Public Library.
15. J. Weldon Jones to author, Jan. 29, 1966; Hayden to Frank Parker, Jan. 21, 1937, Joseph R. Hayden Papers, Box 16, Michigan Historical Collections; Hayden to Murphy, Feb. 26, 1937, Murphy Papers.
16. New York *Times*, Jan. 3–5, 1937; Detroit *News*, Jan. 4, 8, 1937; Germer Diary, Jan. 4, 1937, Germer Papers.
17. Detroit *News*, Jan. 5–9, 1937; New York *Times*, Jan. 5–9, 12, 1937; "Following information from James F. Dewey to Hugh L. Kerwin," Jan. 7, 1937, File 182-2067-A, Records of the Conciliation Service, Record Group 280, National Archives and Records Service, Washington, D.C. (henceforth Conciliation Service files will be designated as CS); Germer Diary, Jan. 6–8, 1937, Germer Papers; draft of agreement, Jan. 7, 1937, Murphy Papers; Knudsen to Murphy, Jan. 8, 1937, *ibid.* Murphy placed the word "general" after each of the UAW's proposals on his copy of the union's January demands.
18. Germer Diary, Jan. 6–7, 1937, Germer Papers; "Following information from Dewey to Kerwin," Jan. 7, 1937, CS 182-2067-A; New York *Times*, Jan. 8–10, 1937. See the ink and pencil insertions on the January 7 draft of an agreement in the Murphy Papers.
19. New York *Times*, Jan. 7–10, 1937; "Following information from Dewey to Kerwin," Jan. 7, 12, 1937, CS 182-2067-A; "Following information received from J. M. O'Connor," Jan. 9, 1937, *ibid.*; Murphy notes, Jan. 8, 1937, Murphy Papers; Detroit *News*, Jan. 10, 1937; GM Release, Jan.

Notes to pages 239 to 243

393

9, 1937, Edward Levinson Papers, Box 4, Labor History Archives; Germer Diary, Jan. 7-9, 1937, Germer Papers.
20. Germer Diary, Jan. 7-9, 1937, Germer Papers.
21. See New York *Times*, Jan. 10-11, 1937.
22. Detroit *News*, Jan. 12, 1937. Italics supplied.
23. *Ibid.*, Jan. 13, 1937.
24. See, for example, *Detroit Saturday Night*, Jan. 16, 1937.
25. Typed notes, Jan. 12, 1937, Murphy Papers; [Detroit *Free Press*, Jan. 13, 1937], Murphy Scrapbooks; Detroit *News*, Jan. 13, 1937; New York *Times*, Jan. 14, 1937.
26. New York *Times*, Jan. 13, 1937; Detroit *News*, Jan. 13-14, 1937; Germer Diary, Jan. 12, 1937, Germer Papers; Flint *Journal*, Jan. 14, 1937.
27. Hill to Murphy, Jan. 12, 1937, Murphy Papers; Detroit *News*, Jan. 13, 17, 21, 1937; New York *Times*, Jan. 14, 1937. Judge Gadola later claimed that Joseph was threatened with removal from office if he served the warrants. Flint *Journal* [Oct. 27, 1938].
28. Detroit *News*, Jan. 13-16, 21, 1937; Flint *Journal*, Jan. 13, 16-17, 1937; Germer Diary, Jan. 15-16, 1937, Germer Papers. The Flint *Auto Worker* of January 24 claimed that the strikers had been subjected to "incredible cruelty" by the police.
29. Olander to Murphy, Jan. [4], 1937, Murphy Papers; Harold Mulbar to Olander [Feb. 1937], Mulbar to Lawrence A. Lyon, Jan. 16, 22, 1937, Case File #5977, Michigan State Police Records, Lansing, Michigan.
30. Flint *Journal*, Jan. 13, 1937; G-1 Reports, Jan. 13, 30, 1937, Records of the Michigan Military Establishment Relating to the Flint Sit-Down Strike, 1937, microfilm copy in Michigan Historical Collections (hereafter cited as National Guard Records); New York *Times*, Jan. 14, 1937; O. H. Walburn to Robert Wohlforth, Feb. 3, 1937, Sen 78A-F9, Box 124, Record Group 46, National Archives and Records Service (hereafter cited as La Follette Committee Papers).
31. Howard H. Jackson to H. Lynn Pierson, Apr. 8, 1937, enclosed with Pierson to Marvin McIntyre, Apr. 8, 1937, PPF 403, Roosevelt Library; Kraus, *Many and Few*, p. 141; Detroit *News*, Jan. 14, 1937; New York *Times*, Jan. 13, 1937.
32. Winston Wessels, "Importance #1: The Michigan National Guard and the 1937 Flint Sit-Down Strike" (MS, 1963), p. 19, in my possession; New York *Times*, Jan. 14, 1937; *Daily Worker*, Jan. 20, 1937; G-2 Journal, Feb. 1, 1937, National Guard Records; Flint *Auto Worker*, Jan. 15, 1937; Interview with Robert C. Travis, Dec. 10, 1964, pp. 26-28; R. Reuther interview, pp. 42-43.
33. Frank Martel to Murphy, Apr. 28, 1936, Murphy Papers; *Civil Rights Guardian* (1937), Brown Collection; Wessels, "Importance #1," p. 10; Interview with Joseph H. Lewis, Mar. 14, 1968 (untranscribed). Colonel Thomas Colladay of Flint was also senior to Lewis, but Murphy passed him over because of his associations with GM. *Ibid.*
34. Interview with Philip C. Pack, Sept. 9, 1965, pp. 3, 13-14 (first draft of transcript); Wessels, "Importance #1," pp. 73-74; Raymond W. Starr to Murphy, Oct. 18, 1939, Murphy Papers; Press information, undated, State Police File #5977.
35. Bersey to Commanding Officer, Jan. 12, 1937, National Guard Records.

36. Michigan National Guard Bulletin No. 1, Jan. 19, 1937, *ibid.*; *Detroit News*, Feb. 3, 1937.
37. Flint *Journal*, Jan. 13, 21, 24, 1937; Michigan National Guard Bulletin No. 2, Jan. 20, 1937, National Guard Records; John H. Steck to Lewis, Feb. 20, 1937, *ibid.*; Field Report on Sanitation and Medical Service, Feb. 17, 1937, *ibid.*; Michigan National Guard Bulletin No. 9, Jan. 30, 1937, Samuel D. Pepper Papers, privately held; H. D. Cullen to Wohlforth, Jan. 31, 1937, La Follette Committee Papers, Box 122.
38. Report of Lester W. Pringle, Feb. 27, 1937, National Guard Records; Field Report on Sanitation and Medical Service, Feb. 17, 1937, *ibid.*
39. Flint *Journal*, Jan. 21, 24, 1937; Final Report, Chaplain's Section (William P. Schulte), undated, National Guard Records; Leroy Pearson to Adjutant General, Jan. 21, 1937, Pepper to Lewis, Feb. 20, 1937, *ibid.*; Report of F. C. Standiford for Feb. 1–20, 1937, *ibid.*; *Detroit News*, Feb. 10, 1937; Pepper to Bersey, Feb. 24, 1937, Pepper Papers.
40. Steck to Lewis, Feb. 20, 1937, Lewis to Murphy, June 18, 1937, National Guard Records; Plan of Action of Sixty-Third Brigade, Jan. 17, 1937, *ibid.*; Flint *Journal*, Jan. 24, 1937.
41. John I. Croshaw to Commanding Officer, undated, National Guard Records; G-2 Report, Jan. 28, 1937, *ibid.*; G-2 Journal, *passim*; Michigan National Guard Bulletin No. 3, Jan. 31, 1937, *ibid.*; Flint *Journal*, Jan. 24, 1937.
42. [Pepper] Memorandum [Feb. 1937], Pepper Papers; Field Order No. 1, Jan. 13, 1937, National Guard Records; Conference Notes, Jan. 15, 1937, *ibid.*; Bersey Conference with Murphy, Jan. 19, 1937, *ibid.*
43. Pepper to Lewis, Feb. 20, 1937, National Guard Records; James P. Stewart and Joseph Zwerdling memorandum to [John H.] Brennan, Jan. 27, 1937, Murphy Papers.
44. Western Union Press Message, Jan. 13, 1937, Levinson Papers, Box 4; *New York Times*, Jan. 13, Feb. 3, 1937; *Detroit News*, Jan. 13, 1937; Kraus, *Many and Few*, pp. 146–47, 154–56; Travis and Minzey to Fellow Strikers [Jan. 12, 1937], Henry Kraus Papers, Box 9, Labor History Archives; Oral History Interview of Jack Palmer, July 23, 1960, p. 13.
45. Murphy to Knudsen and Martin, Jan. 12, 1937, Martin to Murphy, Jan. 13, 1937, Knudsen to Murphy, Jan. 13, 1937, Murphy Papers; typed Murphy notes, Jan. 12, 1937, and Murphy notes, Jan. 13, 1937, at end of this document, *ibid.*; Western Union Press Release, Jan. 13, 1937, Levinson Papers, Box 4; *New York Times*, Jan. 13–14, 1937.
46. Murphy speech, Jan. 14, 1937, Murphy Papers; Murphy notes, Jan. 14, 15, 1937, *ibid.*; Germer Diary, Jan. 14, 1937, Germer Papers; *New York Times*, Jan. 15, 1937.
47. Murphy notes, Jan. 14, 1937, Murphy Papers; "Notes," Jan. 14, 1937, *ibid.*
48. Draft of GM proposal, Jan. 14, 1937, *ibid.*; Minutes of Fisher Body No. 1 Strike Committee, Jan. 15, 1937, Harry Van Nocker Notebook, Kraus Papers, Box 9.
49. Brophy, "Struggle for Auto Union," pp. 11–12, Brophy Papers; Brophy, *A Miner's Life* (Edited and supplemented by John O. P. Hall; Madison, Wisconsin, 1964), pp. 269–70; M. Camilla Mullay, "John Brophy: Militant Labor Leader and Reformer: The CIO Years" (Ph.D. thesis, Catholic University, 1966), p. 80.

Notes to pages 249 to 253

395

50. The small Toledo sit-down was apparently ignored by the negotiators.
51. The Fisher Body No. 1 strike committee was told that there was a separate agreement providing for union inspection of any shipments out of the struck plants for the export trade. Minutes of Fisher Body No. 1 Strike Committee, Jan. 15, 1937, Van Nocker Notebook, Kraus Papers, Box 9.
52. Detroit *News*, Jan. 15, 1937; New York *Times*, Jan. 16, 1937; Knudsen, Brown, and Smith to Murphy, Jan. 15, 1937, Murphy Papers.
53. On this point, see Minutes of Fisher Body No. 1 Strike Committee, Jan. 15, 1937, Van Nocker Notebook, Kraus Papers, Box 9.
54. See Detroit *News*, Jan. 14, 1937; and "Notes," Jan. 14, 1937, Murphy Papers.
55. GM Release, Jan. 15, 1937, Levinson Papers, Box 4; New York *Times*, Jan. 16, 1937; Detroit *News*, Jan. 16, 1937.
56. Martin to Board Members *et al.*, Jan. 15, 1937, Levinson Papers, Box 4; Martin, Hall, and Addes to Sit-In Strikers, Jan. 15, 1937, Kraus Papers, Box 9; New York *Times*, Jan. 16, 1937.
57. Detroit *News*, Jan. 15, 1937; Kraus, *Many and Few*, pp. 157–58; Mulbar to Lyon, Jan. 15, 1937, State Police File #5977; Travis interview, p. 26; Interview with Joe Devitt, July 14, 1966, p. 23; Minutes of Fisher Body No. 1 Mass Meetings, Jan. 15–16, 1937, Minutes of Fisher Body No. 1 Council Meeting, Jan. 15, 1937, Minutes of Fisher Body No. 1 Strike Committee [Jan. 15, 1937] and Jan. 15, 1937, Van Nocker Notebook, Kraus Papers, Box 9; Powers Hapgood to Mother and Father [Jan. 15, 1937], Powers Hapgood Papers, Lilly Library, Bloomington, Indiana.
58. Flint *Journal*, Jan. 16, 17, 1937; Hutchinson to Murphy, Jan. 16, 1937, Murphy Papers; Detroit *News*, Jan. 16, 1937; Battle Creek *Enquirer and Evening News*, Jan. 17, 1937, Murphy Scrapbooks.
59. New York *Times*, Jan. 17, 1937; Detroit *News*, Jan. 17, 1937; UAW Releases, Jan. 17, 18, 1937, Levinson Papers, Box 4; GM Release, Jan. 18, 1937, *ibid*.
60. UAW Releases, Jan. 17, 18, 1937, Levinson Papers, Box 4; GM Release, Jan. 18, 1937, *ibid*.; Claude E. Hoffman, *Sit-Down in Anderson: UAW Local 663, Anderson, Indiana* (Detroit, 1968), p. 44.
61. Johnston to Olander, Jan. 17, 1937, State Police File #5977; Minutes of Fisher Body No. 1 Mass Meetings, Jan. 15, 17, 1937, Van Nocker Notebook, Kraus Papers, Box 9; Flint *Journal*, Jan. 18, 1937; Kraus, *Many and Few*, pp. 161, 165.
62. New York *Times*, Jan. 17, 1937; Flint *Journal*, Jan. 17, 1937.
63. Other organizations of loyal employees had previously demanded representation in any conference GM might hold with the UAW. Detroit *News*, Jan. 11, 1937; Daniel M. Robins to Murphy, Jan. 12, 1937, Murphy Papers.
64. New York *Times*, Jan. 18, 1937; GM Release, Jan. 17, 1937, Levinson Papers, Box 4.
65. For the varying versions of this episode, see New York *Times*, Jan. 19, 24, 1937 (statements by Martin); Brophy, *Miner's Life*, p. 270; *Daily Worker*, Jan. 19, 1937; Kraus, *Many and Few*, pp. 161–64; and Mortimer interview, pp. 6–7. Mr. Lawrence supplied me with an account of the affair in a letter of May 1, 1967.
66. Brophy, "Struggle for Auto Union," pp. 12–13; Brophy, *Miner's Life*, p. 270; New York *Times*, Jan. 16, 18, 1937; Kraus, *Many and Few*, pp.

162–63; AFL Executive Council Minutes, Feb. 10, 1937, p. 57.
67. UAW Release, Jan. 17, 1937, Levinson Papers, Box 4; Germer Diary, Jan. 17, 1937, Germer Papers.
68. New York *Times*, Jan. 18–19, 1937; Detroit *News*, Jan. 18, 1937; Flint *Journal*, Jan. 18, 1937; Kraus, *Many and Few*, pp. 164–65; UAW Release, Jan. 17, 1937, Levinson Papers, Box 4; GM Release, Jan. 18, 1937, *ibid*. The UAW rewarded Lawrence for his part in the affair by permitting him to phone the news that the plants would not be evacuated one hour before the union issued a general release to that effect. Lawrence to author, May 1, 1967.
69. New York *Times*, Jan. 24, 1937.
70. *Ibid.*, Jan. 19, 1937; Flint *Journal*, Jan. 19, 1937.
71. Perkins Memorandum to the President, Jan. 19, 1937, President's Secretary's File (hereafter cited as PSF), Department of Labor File, Roosevelt Library.
72. New York *Times*, Jan. 20, 1937.
73. *Ibid.*, Jan. 20–22, 1937; Perkins Memorandum, Jan. 19, 1937, PSF, Department of Labor File, Roosevelt Library; "General Motors Situation," undated, CS 182-2067-A; Murphy to Grace Smith Gribble, Jan. 25, 1937, Murphy Papers; Flint *Journal*, Jan. 21, 1937; Detroit *News*, Jan. 22, 1937.
74. Detroit *News*, Jan. 23–24, 1937; New York *Times*, Jan. 24, 30, 1937.
75. Brophy, "Struggle for Auto Union," p. 14; New York *Times*, Jan. 22, 1937; Detroit *News*, Jan. 22, 1937; "General Motors Situation," undated, CS 182-2067-A.
76. *The Secret Diary of Harold L. Ickes*, II (New York, 1954), p. 58; Press Conference No. 338, pp. 99–100, Roosevelt Library; New York *Times*, Jan. 23, 1937; AFL Executive Council Minutes, Feb. 10, 1937, pp. 60–61; Paul W. Ward, "Did John L. Lewis Blunder?" *Nation*, CXLIV (Jan. 30, 1937), 119–20. G-2 of the National Guard reported that the morale of the sit-downers in Fisher Body Nos. 1 and 2 had sagged when they learned that Sloan had refused to meet with Lewis but had gone up when they heard of Lewis' reply. Estimate of the Situation, Feb. [Jan.] 22, 1937, National Guard Records.
77. New York *Times*, Jan. 23, 1937; Detroit *News*, Jan. 23, 1937.
78. Detroit *News*, Jan. 24, 1937; New York *Times*, Jan. 26, 1937; Brophy, "Struggle for Auto Union," p. 15, Brophy Papers; Perkins to Martin, Jan. 23, 1937, Kraus Papers, Box 9; GM Release, Jan. 25, 1937, Levinson Papers, Box 4.
79. Press Conference No. 339, pp. 106–7; New York *Times*, Jan. 27, 1937; Detroit *News*, Jan. 27, 1937; Flint *Journal*, Jan. 27, 1937.
80. GM Release, Jan. 27, 1937, Levinson Papers, Box 4; New York *Times*, Jan. 28, 1937.
81. Flint *Journal*, Jan. 28, 1937.
82. New York *Times*, Jan. 30–31, 1937; Detroit *News*, Jan. 30–31, 1937; GM Release [Jan. 30, 1937], Levinson Papers, Box 4.
83. New York *Times*, Jan. 31, 1937.
84. *Ibid.*; Minutes of Cleveland Fisher Body Strike Committee, Jan. 27, 1937, Kraus Papers, Box 10.
85. On this point, see [L. G. Lenhardt], "It Can Happen Here," Mar. 9, 1937, Blair Moody Papers, Michigan Historical Collections.
86. This was the opinion of Lawrence Fisher, judging from what he told

Richard D. Lunt. Lunt, "The High Ministry of Government: The Political Career of Frank Murphy" (Ph.D. thesis, University of New Mexico, 1962), p. 217.
87. Flint *Journal*, Jan. 26, 1937.
88. New York *Times*, Jan. 19, 23, 1937; Flint *Journal*, Jan. 20, 1937; H. H. Curtice to All Buick Employes, Jan. 20, 1937, Kraus Papers, Box 9; Cullen to Wohlforth, Jan. 21, 1937, La Follette Committee Papers, Box 124.
89. GM Releases, Jan. 22, 23, 1937, Levinson Papers, Box 4; Detroit *News*, Jan. 25, 1937; Flint *Journal*, Jan. 25, 1937.
90. Flint Alliance Bulletin, Jan. 25, 1937, Kraus Papers, Box 9; New York *Times*, Jan. 26, 1937; UAW Release, Jan. 25, 1937, Levinson Papers, Box 4; Pepper to Lewis, Feb. 20, 1937, National Guard Records; G-2 Journal, Jan. 25, 1937, *ibid.*; Cullen to Wohlforth, Jan. 25, 1937, La Follette Committee Papers, Box 122.
91. Reuther interview, pp. 7–8; Cullen to Wohlforth, Jan. 26, 1937, Travis to La Follette, Jan. 26, 1937, La Follette Committee Papers, Box 124; Cullen to Wohlforth, Jan. 27, 31, 1937, *ibid.*, Box 122; Flint *Journal*, Jan. 27, 1937; New York *Times*, Jan. 26–27, 1937; Mortimer interview, pp. 9–10. *Cf.* Kraus, *Many and Few*, pp. 182–83.
92. New York *Times*, Jan. 27, 1937; Pepper to Lewis, Feb. 20, 1937, National Guard Records; Mr. Germer's conversation with Mr. Lewis [Jan. 26, 1937], Germer Papers; Germer Diary, Jan. 26, 1937, *ibid.*
93. This is the estimate of Russell B. Porter, who said that about 2500 people were turned away. If the crowd was as large as Porter indicated, it exceeded the seating capacity of the IMA Auditorium, where the meeting was held. The UAW insisted that only 6000 were present, and it claimed that 2000 of this number were union members. New York *Times*, Jan. 27–28, 1937.
94. Cullen to Wohlforth, Jan. 27, 1937, La Follette Committee Papers, Box 122; New York *Times*, Jan. 27, 1937; Detroit *News*, Jan. 27, 1937; Flint *Journal*, Jan. 27, 1937; Notes on Flint Alliance Meeting, Jan. 26, 1937, Kraus Papers, Box 9; *I.M.A. News*, Jan. 28, 1937.
95. New York *Times*, Jan. 28, 1937; "Flint Alliance Meeting, Jan. 25 [26]," 1937, Kraus Papers, Box 9; Flint *Auto Worker*, Jan. 28, 1937; Cullen to Wohlforth, Jan. 27, 31, 1937, La Follette Committee Papers, Box 122.
96. New York *Times*, Jan. 28, 1937; GM Release, Jan. 27, 1937, Levinson Papers, Box 4; G-3 Reports, Jan. 26–27, 1937, National Guard Records.
97. There is a copy of the resolution in the Murphy Papers.
98. Flint *Journal*, Jan. 29, 1937.
99. New York *Times*, Jan. 27, 29, 1937; Flint *Journal*, Jan. 28, 1937.
100. A Resolution to . . . Murphy . . . , Jan. 28, 1937, Murphy Papers; Detroit *News*, Jan. 29–30, 1937; New York *Times*, Jan. 30, 1937; Flint *Journal*, Jan. 29, 1937.
101. P. Hapgood to Mary Hapgood, Jan. 28 [1937], [Jan. 31, 1937], Hapgood Papers; Detroit *News*, Jan. 29, 1937; UAW Release, Jan. 29, 1937, Kraus Papers, Box 9; Kraus, *Many and Few*, pp. 185–86, 189.
102. Germer Diary, Jan. 26, 30–31, 1937, Germer Papers; Germer's Conversation with Lewis [Jan. 26, 1937], *ibid.*; New York *Times*, Jan. 28, Feb. 1, 1937; Detroit *News*, Feb. 1, 1937; Eleanor M. Bumgardner to the Haydens, Jan. 31, 1937, Hayden Papers, Box 20.

Chapter x

1. Adolph Germer Diary, Jan. 31, 1937, Adolph Germer Papers, State Historical Society of Wisconsin, Madison; Local 156 Release, Feb. 1, 1937, Henry Kraus Papers, Box 9, Labor History Archives, Wayne State University, Detroit, Michigan; UAW Release, Feb. 2, 1937, *ibid.*; Joe Brown interview with George Edwards, Jan. 14, 1938, Joe Brown Collection, *ibid.*; John Brophy, "The Struggle for an Auto Union" (undated MS), p. 16, John Brophy Papers, Catholic University, Washington, D.C.; Interview with Wyndham Mortimer, Dec. 9, 1964, p. 10 (transcripts of all interviews cited, unless otherwise noted, are located in the Michigan Historical Collections, Ann Arbor, Michigan); *New York Times*, Feb. 2, 1937; William Weinstone, "The Great Auto Strike," *Communist*, XVI (Mar. 1937), 217–18; Henry Kraus, *The Many and the Few: A Chronicle of the Dynamic Auto Workers* (Los Angeles, 1947), pp. 189–90; *United Automobile Worker*, Feb. 25, 1937; *Socialist Call*, Feb. 13, 1937; Gallico, "Sit-Down Strike," *Cosmopolitan*, CIV (Apr. 1938), [176].
2. See Chapter VI.
3. Louis G. Seaton to H. W. Anderson, Feb. 2, 1937, GM, Labor Relations Diary, Appendix Documents to Accompany Section 1, Doc. 71-A, GM Building, Detroit, Michigan; *Socialist Call*, Feb. 13, 1937; "The Industrial War," *Fortune*, XVI (Nov. 1937), 164.
4. Kempton, *Part of Our Time* (New York, 1955), p. 284.
5. George Douglas Blackwood ("The United Automobile Workers of America, 1935–51" [Ph.D. thesis, University of Chicago, 1951], p. 73n), Irving Howe and B. J. Widick (*The UAW and Walter Reuther* [New York, 1949], p. 58), and Kempton (*Part of Our Time*, pp. 285–86) give the principal credit to Reuther. Brophy ("Struggle for Auto Union," p. 17) and Edward Levinson (*Labor on the March* [University Books; New York, 1956], p. 161) give Travis and Powers Hapgood the major credit (Levinson also includes Kermit Johnson). Mortimer (Interview, p. 11) and Kraus (*Many and Few*, pp. 189–92) assign the key role to Travis.
6. Interview with Robert C. Travis, Dec. 10, 1964, pp. 37–39. There is a diagram of the Chevrolet plant layout, in Reuther's hand, in the Labor History Archives.
7. Interview with Roy Reuther, July 12, 1966, pp. 13, 34–35; Kermit Johnson, in *Searchlight*, Feb. 2, 1962; Powers Hapgood to Mother and Father [Feb. 12, 1937], Powers Hapgood Papers, Lilly Library, Bloomington, Indiana.
8. The three Chevrolet plants formed a more or less equilateral triangle, each one being about 300 yards from the other two.
9. The company said that the unionists involved had been dismissed for illegally wearing union buttons in the plant, soliciting for the union on the premises, and fighting with nonunionists. Local 156 Release, Feb. 1, 1937, Kraus Papers, Box 9; *New York Times*, Feb. 2, 1937; *Detroit News*, Feb. 2, 1937.
10. Flint *Auto Worker*, Jan. 28, 31, 1937; UAW Release, Feb. 1, 1937, Kraus Papers, Box 9; Kraus, *Many and Few*, pp. 193–99; Travis interview, pp. 35–40; *Detroit Free Press*, May 29, 1966 (interview with R. Reuther); R. Reuther to author, Aug. 29, 1967; Oral History Interview of Merlin D. Bishop, pp. 22–23; Oral History Interview of Ted LaDuke, Aug. 5, 1960, p. 20; *Socialist Call*, Feb. 13, 1937.

Notes to pages 269 to 272

399

11. Local 156 Release, Feb. 1, 1937, Kraus Papers, Box 9; Kraus, *Many and Few*, p. 199; New York *Times*, Feb. 2, 1937; Flint *Auto Worker*, Feb. 2, 1937; Flint *Journal*, Feb. 1, 1937; G-2 Journal, Jan. 30–31, Feb. 1, 1937, Records of the Michigan Military Establishment Relating to the Flint Sit-Down Strike, 1937, microfilm copy in Michigan Historical Collections. National Guard intelligence on January 30 guessed that there might be a sit-down in Chevrolet No. 4 on February 1.
12. My account of the Chevrolet No. 9 battle is based on the following: *Socialist Call*, Feb. 13, 1937; A. Bosschem and James S. Valentine to Lawrence A. Lyon, Feb. 1, 1937, Case File #5977, Michigan State Police Records, Lansing, Michigan; Seaton to Anderson, Feb. 2, 1937, GM Appendix Doc. 71-A; Subcommittee of the Senate Committee on Education and Labor, *Violations of Free Speech and Rights of Labor, Hearings Pursuant to S. Res. 266*, 75 Cong., 1 Sess. (Washington, 1937), Part 6, pp. 2119–20; Part 7, p. 2541; Travis interview, pp. 42–43; LaDuke interview, pp. 20–22; New York *Times*, Feb. 2, 1937; Detroit *News*, Feb. 2–3, 1937; Flint *Journal*, Feb. 1–2, 1937; UAW Release, Feb. 2, 1937, Kraus Papers, Box 9; P. Hapgood to M. Hapgood, Feb. 2 [1937], P. Hapgood to Mother and Father [Feb. 12, 1937], Hapgood Papers; and Kraus, *Many and Few*, pp. 200–203, 209–11. There are discrepancies in these accounts regarding the exact time the fighting started in the plant and the exact time the Emergency Brigade and the strike sympathizers arrived outside the plant, the number of unionists involved in the fighting inside the plant, and the role played by the city police and sheriff's deputies.
13. The account of the seizure of Chevrolet No. 4 is based on *Socialist Call*, Feb. 13, 1937; Johnson, in *Searchlight*, Feb. 2, 1962; Bosschem and Valentine to Lyon, Feb. 1, 1937, State Police File #5977; New York *Times*, Feb. 2, 1937; Detroit *News*, Feb. 3, 1937; Seaton to Anderson, Feb. 2, 1937, GM Appendix Doc. 71-A; UAW Release, Feb. 2, 1937, Kraus Papers, Box 9; Detroit *Free Press*, May 29, 1966; Levinson, *Labor on March*, p. 163; Bishop interview, pp. 23–24; and Kraus, *Many and Few*, pp. 211–19.
14. Flint *Journal*, Feb. 1–2, 1937; Detroit *News*, Feb. 2, 1937; New York *Times*, Feb. 2, 1937; *Socialist Call*, Feb. 13, 1937; Mary Heaton Vorse, *Labor's New Millions* (New York, 1938), p. 77.
15. Edwin Chapman to Dear Liz and all, Feb. 3, 1937, Kraus Papers, Box 9.
16. Detroit *News*, Feb. 2, 1937.
17. See Strike Chronology, Feb. 1, 1937, Frank Murphy Papers, Michigan Historical Collections. This invaluable document, which covers the period February 1–8, contains a detailed and yet incomplete record of strike events, and particularly strike negotiations, as seen through Murphy's eyes.
18. State Police Daily Log, Feb. 1, 1937, State Police File #5977; Strike Chronology, Feb. 1, 1937, Murphy Papers; G-3 Report for Feb. 1, 1937, National Guard Records; G-2 Journal, Feb. 1, 1937, *ibid.*; Pepper to Lewis, Feb. 20, 1937, *ibid.*; Wolcott to Murphy (letter and wire), Feb. 1, 1937, Bradshaw to Murphy, Feb. 1, 1937, Murphy Executive Order to Bersey, Feb. 1, 1937, Wolcott to Murphy, Aug. 17, 1938, Murphy Papers.
19. Strike Chronology, Feb. 1, 1937, Murphy Papers; John H. Steck to Lewis, Feb. 20, 1937, National Guard Records; G-3 Report for Feb. 1, 1937, *ibid.*; 63rd Brigade S-3 Report, Feb. 2, 1937, *ibid.*; 63rd Brigade Field

Order No. 1, Feb. 2, 1937, *ibid.*; G-1 Reports, Feb. 1–7, 1937, *ibid.*; O. H. Walburn to Robert Wohlforth, Feb. 3, 1937, Sen 78A-F9, Box 124, Record Group 46, National Archives and Records Service, Washington, D.C. (hereafter cited as La Follette Committee Papers); New York *Times*, Feb. 2–3, 1937; Detroit *News*, Feb. 2, 1937; Flint *Journal*, Feb. 3, 1937.

20. Bishop interview, pp. 24–26; Detroit *News*, Feb. 2–3, 1937; Flint *Journal*, Feb. 2, 1937; New York *Times*, Feb. 3, 1937; Kraus, *Many and Few*, pp. 220–22; G-2 Journal, Feb. 2, 1937, National Guard Records; Strike Chronology, Feb. 2, 1937, Murphy Papers; Seaton to Anderson, Feb. 2, 1937, GM Appendix Doc. 71-A.
21. Strike Chronology, Feb. 2, 1937, Murphy Papers; Detroit *News*, Feb. 2, 1937; New York *Times*, Feb. 2, 1937.
22. Strike Chronology, Feb. 2, 1937, Murphy Papers; *Daily Worker*, Feb. 3, 1937; R. Reuther interview, p. 38.
23. Brophy, "Struggle for Auto Union," pp. 18–19, Brophy Papers; Brophy Diary, Feb. 2, 1937, *ibid.*; Kraus, *Many and Few*, pp. 222–26; Strike Chronology, Feb. 2, 1937, Murphy Papers; Local 156 Release, Feb. 2, 1937, Kraus Papers, Box 9; UAW Release, Feb. 2, 1937, *ibid.*; G-3 Report for Feb. 2, 1937, National Guard Records; Official Strike Bulletin No. 10, Brown Collection; P. Hapgood to M. Hapgood, Feb. 2 [1937], P. Hapgood to Mother and Father [Feb. 12, 1937], Hapgood Papers.
24. Murphy's reference was to the February 1, 1937, issue of the *New Center News*, a publication that circulated in the area of the GM and Fisher Buildings in Detroit and which had asked, "Why not impeach Governor Murphy?" It had offered to circulate the necessary petitions if the answer was affirmative. Plans to circulate petitions were announced in the February 8 issue. *New Center News*, Feb. 1, 1937, Murphy Papers; Detroit *News*, Feb. 8, 1937.
25. Strike Chronology, Feb. 2, 1937, Murphy Papers; Official Strike Bulletin No. 10, Brown Collection; New York *Times*, Feb. 3, 1937.
26. George A. Krogstad, "A Brief Resume of My Trip through the Strike Area . . . ," Feb. 9, 1937, attached to Krogstad to Murphy, Feb. 11, 1937, Murphy Papers.
27. Regulation No. 2 issued by the Guard on February 10 (National Guard Records) permitted strikers in the blockaded plants a single visitor from their immediate family between 2:00 and 3:00 P.M. on Tuesdays, Thursdays, and Saturdays.
28. Opinion of Judge Paul V. Gadola, Feb. 2, 1937, Kraus Papers, Box 9; Sugar to Murphy, Oct. 25, 1938, Murphy to Sugar, Nov. 2, 1938, Murphy Papers; House Special Committee on Un-American Activities, *Investigation of Un-American Propaganda Activities in the United States, Hearings Pursuant to H. Res. 282*, 75 Cong., 3 Sess. (Washington, 1938), II, 1675–76, 1679; IV, 2677–78 (hereafter cited as *Dies Hearings*); Detroit *News*, Dec. 2, 1938; New York *Times*, Feb. 7, 1937. Sugar contended that he told Gadola only what Murphy had authorized him to say, but Gadola's recollection was that Sugar and Lee Pressman, after talking to Murphy, claimed that the governor desired a delay. Gadola said that he believed that Murphy was improperly interfering with court processes.
29. Strike Chronology, Feb. 1, 1937, Murphy Papers; Flint *Journal*, Feb. 1–2, 1937; Detroit *News*, Feb. 2, 1937.
30. Flint *Journal*, Feb. 1–3, 1937; Detroit *News*, Feb. 2, 1937.

31. Gadola opinion, Feb. 2, 1937, Kraus Papers, Box 9; New York *Times*, Feb. 3, 1937; Flint *Journal*, Feb. 3, 1937. A GM attorney did speak to Gadola on February 6 regarding an injunction covering Chevrolet No. 4, and it was reported that GM would request such an injunction if the Detroit strike talks should fail. New York *Times*, Feb. 7, 1937.
32. On this point, see Walter Eisenberg, "Government Policy in Sitdown Strikes" (Ph.D. thesis, Columbia University, 1959), p. 156.
33. Petition for Temporary Restraining Order, Injunction and Equitable Relief [Feb. 1, 1937], Kraus Papers, Box 10; New York *Times*, Feb. 2, 1937.
34. See Chapter VI.
35. Committee on Civil Rights in Automobile Industry to Pressman, Feb. 3, 1937, American Civil Liberties Union Archives, Reel 152, Vol. 1047, New York Public Library.
36. Federated Press Release, Feb. 10, 1937, Kraus Papers, Box 9; Interview with Lee Pressman, Nov. 12, 1964, p. 14; *Daily Worker*, Feb. 8, 1937.
37. H. L. McClintock, "Injunctions against Sit-Down Strikes," *Iowa Law Review*, XXIII (Jan. 1938), 152–53, 157–59, 162–63.
38. Eisenberg, "Government Policy in Sitdown Strikes," pp. 50–51, 156; Detroit *News*, Feb. 3, 1937; *Dies Hearings*, II, 1677; Flint *Journal*, Feb. 3, 1937.
39. G-3 Report for Feb. 2, 1937, National Guard Records; Detroit *News*, Feb. 3, 1937; Flint *Journal*, Feb. 3, 1937; New York *Times*, Feb. 3, 1937. Lewis many years later could not recall that he had given Gadola any assurances regarding the enforcement of the injunction. Interview with Lewis, Mar. 14, 1968 (untranscribed).
40. *Cf.* Mortimer interview, Dec. 9, 1964, p. 29; and Interview with Larry S. Davidow, May 12, 1967, p. 2 (first draft of transcript).
41. Flint *Journal*, Feb. 3, 1937; Kraus, *Many and Few*, pp. 232–33; Fisher No. 1 Sit-In Employes to Murphy, Feb. 3, 1937, Stay In Strikers of the Fisher Body Plant No. 2 to Murphy, Feb. 3, 1937, Murphy Papers.
42. Brophy Papers.
43. See Davidow interview, p. 3; Pressman interview, p. 16; Mortimer interview, p. 29; and Travis interview, pp. 32–33.
44. There is a copy of the unissued press release in the Murphy Papers.
45. Detroit *Times*, Feb. 4, 1937, Brown Scrapbooks, Brown Collection; Strike Chronology, Feb. 2, 1937, Murphy Papers; G-2 Journal, Feb. 1, 1937, National Guard Records; Mortimer interview, pp. 31–32; Kraus, *Many and Few*, p. 234.
46. Levinson, *Labor on March*, p. 165; Kraus, *Many and Few*, pp. 234–35; G-2 Journal, Feb. 3, 1937, National Guard Records; New York *Times*, Feb. 4, 1937; Local 156 Release, Feb. 1, 1937, Kraus Papers, Box 9; "A Dance in Front of Fisher #1," undated, *ibid*.; Walburn to Wohlforth, Feb. 3, 1937, La Follette Committee Papers, Box 124; Vorse, "What the Women Did in Flint," *Woman Today*, Mar. 1937, pp. 3, 29; Flint *Auto Worker*, Feb. 6, 1937.
47. A "huge crowd" but no pickets gathered on the hills overlooking the blockaded Fisher Body No. 2 plant as the zero hour for obedience to the injunction approached. Detroit *News*, Feb. 4, 1937. There are wide discrepancies in the estimates of the size of the crowd in front of Fisher Body No. 1.

48. My account of the demonstration is based on Brophy, "Struggle for Auto Union," pp. 20–21, Brophy Papers; Walburn to Wohlforth, Feb. 3, 1937, La Follette Committee Papers, Box 124; H. A. Hudgins to Editors, *Michigan Christian Advocate*, Feb. 24, 1937, William H. Phelps Papers, Michigan Historical Collections; W. S. Needham and Purlett Hinckley to Lyon, Feb. 3, 1937, State Police File #5977; G-2 Journal, Feb. 3, 1937, National Guard Records; Vorse, "What the Women Did," p. 29; Detroit *Times*, Feb. 4, 1937, Brown Scrapbooks; Detroit *News*, Feb. 4, 1937; New York *Times*, Feb. 4, 1937; Flint *Journal*, Feb. 4, 1937; and Kraus, *Many and Few*, pp. 235–37.
49. State Police Daily Log, Feb. 3, 1937, State Police File #5977; Germer Diary, Feb. 3, 1937, Germer Papers; Detroit *News*, Feb. 4, 1937; Detroit *Times*, Feb. 4, 1937, Brown Scrapbooks.
50. Hudgins to Editors, Feb. 24, 1937, Phelps Papers; Brophy, "Struggle for Auto Union," pp. 20–21, Brophy Papers; Flint *Auto Worker*, Feb. 6, 1937.
51. New York *Times*, Feb. 4, 1937; Detroit *Times*, Feb. 4, 1937, Brown Scrapbooks; State Police Daily Log, Feb. 3, 1937, State Police File #5977; Harold Mulbar to Oscar G. Olander, n.d., *ibid.*; *Dies Hearings*, II, 1687–88; Detroit *News*, Feb. 4, 1937; Flint *Journal*, Feb. 4, 1937; *Flint City Commission Proceedings*, V (Feb. 6, 1937), 2109; Interview with Colin J. MacDonald, May 15, 1967 (untranscribed).
52. State Police Daily Log, Feb. 3, 1937, State Police File #5977; Flint *Journal*, Feb. 4, 1937; Local 156 Release, Feb. 6, 1937, Kraus Papers, Box 9; Flint *Auto Worker*, Feb. 6, 1937; MacDonald interview; Flint *Journal*, Feb. 5, 1937; Detroit *News*, Feb. 4, 1937; Strike Chronology, Feb. 3, 1937, Murphy Papers; *Dies Hearings*, II, 1690–91. The Pinkerton official was in Flint to pay Dubuc. Walburn to Wohlforth [Feb. 6, 1937], La Follette Committee Papers, Box 124.
53. Detroit *News*, Feb. 4, 1937; Mulbar to Olander, n.d., State Police File #5977; Detroit *Times*, Feb. 4, 1937, Brown Scrapbooks; [William J. Cronin], *Sit-Down*, June 27, 1939, pp. 16–17, 19; Kraus, *Many and Few*, p. 252.
54. Flint *Journal*, Feb. 4, 1937; *Dies Hearings*, II, 1689; Vern C. Snell to Lyon, Feb. 4, 1937, State Police File #5977; [Detroit *Legal Record*], Apr. 8, 1937; MacDonald interview; Phone call from . . . [Wolcott], Oct. 23, 1938, Murphy Papers; Detroit *News*, Feb. 4, 1937.
55. Detroit *News*, Feb. 4, 1937; New York *Times*, Feb. 4, 1937; undated text of agreement, National Guard Records; Detroit *Times*, Feb. 4, 1937, Brown Scrapbooks; Flint *Journal*, Feb. 4, 1937; Mulbar to Olander, n.d., State Police File #5977.
56. Wills's reference was to a battle between United Mine Workers members and strikebreakers in Herrin, Illinois, in 1922, that had resulted in the death of 19 strikebreakers and 2 strikers. Selig Perlman and Philip Taft, *History of Labor in the United States, 1896–1932* (New York, 1935), pp. 483–84. Wills had apparently forgotten who had come off second best in the encounter.
57. Detroit *News*, Feb. 4–5, 7, 1937; Walburn to Wohlforth, Feb. 5, 1937, La Follette Committee Papers, Box 124; State Police Daily Log, Feb. 4, 1937, State Police File #5977; Needham and Hinckley to Lyon, Feb. 4, 1937, *ibid.*; G-2 Journal, Feb. 4, 1937, National Guard Records; Flint

Journal, Feb. 4–5, 1937; UAW Release, Feb. 4, 1937, Kraus Papers, Box 9; Local 156 Releases, Feb. 4, 5, 1937, Brown Collection.
58. "A Dance in Front of Fisher #1," undated, Kraus Papers, Box 9; Detroit *News*, Feb. 5, 1937.
59. Report by UAW . . . , Feb. 8, 1937, Kraus Papers, Box 9; Kraus, *Many and Few*, pp. 244–45; Flint *Journal* [July 8, 1934], Feb. 7, 1937, [Oct. 1, 1951]; *Flint City Commission Proceedings*, V (Feb. 6, 1937), 2109; New York *Times*, Feb. 7, 1937; Detroit *News*, Feb. 7, 1937.
60. *Flint City Commission Proceedings*, V (Feb. 8, 1937), 2113; Walburn to Wohlforth, Feb. 9, 1937, La Follette Committee Papers, Box 124; New York *Times*, Feb. 9–10, 1937; Detroit *News*, Feb. 10, 1937; Flint *Journal*, Feb. 11, 1937; *Dies Hearings*, II, 1687; P. Hapgood to M. Hapgood [Feb. 10, 1937], Hapgood Papers.
61. Travis interview, pp. 45–46; Pressman interview, pp. 15–16; draft of answers prepared by Brophy for an interview, June 12, 1961, Brophy Papers; Saul Alinsky, *John L. Lewis* (New York, 1949), pp. 128–30; Kraus, *Many and Few*, pp. 227–28; *Proceedings of the Fifth Annual Convention of the International Union, United Automobile Workers of America, 1940* (n.p., n.d.), p. 104; Matthew Josephson, *Sidney Hillman* (Garden City, New York, 1952), p. 410; New York *Times*, Feb. 3, 1937. The nature of Lewis' conversation with Roosevelt is not entirely clear.
62. Strike Chronology, Feb. 2, 1937, Murphy Papers; Donaldson Brown, *Some Reminiscences of an Industrialist* (n.p., [1957]), pp. 95–98; Alfred P. Sloan, Jr., *My Years with General Motors* (Edited by John McDonald with Catharine Stevens; Garden City, New York, 1964), p. 393. *Cf.* Norman Beasley, *Knudsen* (New York, 1947), p. 172.
63. Strike Chronology, Feb. 2, 1937, Murphy Papers; Murphy to Knudsen, Feb. 2, 1937, Knudsen to Murphy, Feb. 2, 1937, *ibid*.
64. Flint *Journal*, Feb. 9, 1937; Detroit *News*, Feb. 6, 11, 1937; Alinsky, *Lewis*, pp. 136–37; Walter Galenson, *The CIO Challenge to the AFL: A History of the American Labor Movement, 1935–1941* (Cambridge, Mass., 1960), p. 153; Kraus, *Many and Few*, pp. 264–65; *Iron Age*, CXXXIX (Feb. 25, 1937), 57; UAW Release, Feb. 9, 1937, Kraus Papers, Box 9; Oral History Interview of Ed Hall, Oct. 26, 1959, pp. 25–26; Pressman interview, p. 21; Mortimer interview, pp. 12–13.
65. Strike Chronology, Feb. 2, 1937, Murphy Papers.
66. *Ibid.*, Feb. 3, 1937; Germer Diary, Feb. 3–4, 1937, Germer Papers; New York *Times*, Feb. 4, 1937; GM Statement, Feb. 8, 1937, Brown Collection; Alinsky, *Lewis*, p. 130.
67. Proposals of UAW, Feb. 4, 1937, Murphy Papers.
68. Typed sheet, Feb. 4, 1937, *ibid.*; GM to Murphy, Feb. 5, 1937, *ibid.*; Proposal for General Motors-Lewis Agreement [Feb. 5, 1937], President's Secretary's File (hereafter PSF), Department of Labor File, Franklin D. Roosevelt Library, Hyde Park, New York; New York *Times*, Feb. 10, 1937.
69. GM to Murphy, Feb. 5, 1937, Murphy Papers; GM Statement, Feb. 8, 1937, Brown Collection.
70. Strike Chronology, Feb. 4–5, 1937, Murphy Papers. The Sidney Hillman Papers, Amalgamated Clothing Workers, New York, New York, contain an undated, unidentified statement of the union's minimum demands that may have reached the President on February 4 or 5.

71. It is possible that GM was willing to accept the proposal for a two-month period. Strike Chronology, Feb. 5, 1937, Murphy Papers.
72. *Ibid.*
73. Memorandum for the President, Feb. 5, 1937, PSF, Department of Labor File, Roosevelt Library; Memorandum for the President's Conversation with John Lewis and with Knudsen and Brown [Feb. 5, 1937], *ibid.* The latter contains Perkins' handwritten note, "get exclusive agreement for 2 months." The New York *Times* of February 7 claimed that the President's intervention kept GM from quitting the conference.
74. GM to Murphy, Feb. 6, 1937, Murphy Papers; Murphy Statement, Feb. 6, 1937, *ibid.*; Perkins Memorandum for the President, Feb. 8, 1937, Official File (hereafter OF) 407-B, Roosevelt Library; New York *Times*, Feb. 7, 1937.
75. Minutes of the Meeting of the Executive Council of the AFL, Feb. 10, 1937, pp. 51–55; Strike Chronology, Feb. 6, 1937, Murphy Papers; Green, J. W. Williams, and Frey to Murphy, Feb. 6, 1937, *ibid.*
76. Strike Chronology, Feb. 6, 1937, Murphy Papers; Joseph H. Creighton Memorandum to Murphy, May 11, 1938, *ibid.*; New York *Times*, Feb. 9, 14, 1937; Pressman interview, pp. 22–24; Oral History Interview of Mortimer, June 20, 1960, p. 39; Alinsky, *Lewis*, pp. 138–39; Perkins Memorandum for the President, Feb. 8, 1937, OF 407-B, Roosevelt Library.
77. Perkins Memorandum for the President, Feb. 8, 1937, OF 407-B, Roosevelt Library; Detroit *News*, Feb. 9, 1937; Alinsky, *Lewis*, pp. 133–34; The Reminiscences of Lee Pressman, 1958, p. 73, Oral History Research Office, Columbia University, New York, New York; Mortimer interview, June 20, 1960, pp. 41–42.
78. Strike Chronology, Feb. 8, 1937, Murphy Papers.
79. Knudsen's biographer claims that Knudsen told McGrady that he would accept such terms as the President specified but that McIntyre replied that Roosevelt did not wish to do this. Beasley, *Knudsen*, p. 169.
80. Strike Chronology, Feb. 8, 1937, and pencil notes [Feb. 8, 1937?] attached to copy of same, Murphy Papers.
81. Detroit *News*, Feb. 9, 1937; GM Statement, Feb. 8, 1937, Brown Collection; Lewis Press Conference, Feb. 8, 1937, Kraus Papers, Box 9; New York *Times*, Feb. 9–10, 1937; Alinsky, *Lewis*, p. 138.
82. See GM to Murphy, Feb. 9, 1937, Murphy Papers.
83. New York *Times*, Feb. 3, 1937; Subcommittee of the Senate Committee on the Judiciary, *Nomination of Frank Murphy*, 76 Cong., 1 Sess. (Washington, 1939), pp. 9–10; Detroit *News*, Feb. 5, 1937; Richard D. Lunt, "The High Ministry of Government: The Political Career of Frank Murphy" (Ph.D. thesis, University of New Mexico, 1962), p. 225; E. J. Parker Affidavit, Feb. 4, 1937, National Guard Records; Gadola Court Order, Feb. 5, 1937, *ibid.*
84. The deputies Wolcott had in mind were Legionnaires, GM plant police, members of the state's Sheriffs Association, and members of the special police reserve. Flint *Journal*, Feb. 5, 1937; New York *Times*, Feb. 6, 1937.
85. Strike Chronology, Feb. 5, 1937, Murphy Papers; Minutes of a Meeting Held in Flint, May 19, 1938, *ibid.*; Wolcott to Murphy, Aug. 17, 1938,

Notes to pages 293 to 295

405

Murphy to Norman H. Hill, Jan. 23, 1939, *ibid.*; Statement by Thomas Wolcott, Oct. 21, 1938, *ibid.*; *Nomination of Murphy*, p. 10; *Detroit News*, Feb. 6–7, 1938; *New York Times*, Feb. 7, 1937. In a further effort to avoid trouble in Flint, the State Liquor Control Commission on February 5 forbade the sale of beer, wine, and liquor in Genesee County. Flint *Journal*, Feb. 5, 1937.

86. Strike Chronology, Feb. 5, 1937, Murphy Papers; typed sheet, Oct. 22, 1938, *ibid.*; Murphy to John Nance Garner, Dec. 28, 1938, *ibid.*; *Nomination of Murphy*, pp. 3–4, 10; *New York Times*, Feb. 6, 1937.
87. Strike Chronology, Feb. 8, 1937, Murphy Papers; Murphy to Florence H. Mann, July 17, 1937, Murphy to Josiah W. Bailey, Jan. 19, 1939, *ibid.*; Interview with Mrs. Fielding H. Yost, Oct. 28, 1963, p. 6; Roger N. Baldwin to Edward D. Tittman, Feb. 24, 1937, ACLU Archives, Reel 152, Vol. 1047; Roger N. Baldwin and Clarence B. Randall, *Civil Liberties and Industrial Conflict* (Cambridge, Mass., 1938), pp. 36–38.
88. Interview with Martin Hayden *et al.*, Oct. 6, 1964, p. 45; Walburn to Wohlforth, Feb. 3, 1937, La Follette Committee Papers, Box 124; [L. G. Lenhardt], "It Can Happen Here," Mar. 9, 1937, Blair Moody Papers, Michigan Historical Collections; Eisenberg, "Government Policy in Sit-down Strikes," p. 61; Charles R. Walker, "Flint Faces Civil War," *Nation*, CXLIV (Feb. 13, 1937), 175. There were at that time at least 125 men in Fisher Body No. 2, 200–300 in Chevrolet No. 4, and several hundred in Fisher Body No. 1. The number in the latter plant could easily have been augmented from the outside since it was not under blockade. *New York Times*, Feb. 12, 1937.
89. See, for example, Herbert Harris, *American Labor* (New Haven, 1939), p. 300; James L. Wechsler, *Labor Baron: A Portrait of John L. Lewis* (New York, 1944), p. 63; Howe and Widick, *UAW and Walter Reuther*, p. 61; and Levinson, *Labor on March*, p. 163.
90. Copy of clipping from Port Huron, Michigan, newspaper, Mar. 18, 1937, Murphy Papers; Pepper to Raymond W. Starr, Mar. 22, 1937, Pepper to Murphy, Dec. 23, 1938, Pepper to Kemp, Jan. 12, 1939, *ibid.*
91. Pepper to Lewis, Feb. 20, 1937, Steck to Lewis, Feb. 5, 1937, Steck Memorandum to Lewis, undated, National Guard Records; Steck to Pepper, Mar. 11, 1937, Samuel D. Pepper Papers, privately held. The Guard did provide for the armoring of three two-and-a-half ton trucks on which 37-millimeter gas guns could be mounted to fire gas into Chevrolet No. 4 through the unbarricaded windows more than eight feet above ground. 63rd Brigade S-3 Report for Feb. 4, 1937, National Guard Records; Harry T. Hanover to Lewis, Mar. 1, 1937, *ibid.*; G-4 Report, Feb. 9, 1937, *ibid.* For efforts of the Guard to increase its supply of gas and gas equipment, see Bersey Report to Murphy, Jan. 19, 1937, Leroy Pearson to Bersey, Jan. 20, 1937, and Hanover to Lewis, Mar. 1, 1937, *ibid.*
92. There is an "O.K.L." written on the plan recommended by Steck.
93. National Guard intelligence made different estimates of the situation from day to day. See G-2 Reports, Feb. 1–2, 1937, and G-2 Journal, Feb. 5, 7, National Guard Records.
94. The Guard chaplain, after visiting the plant on February 5, concluded that the sit-downers would "come out damn quick" if the Guard moved on the plant. One striker wrote his wife that the men had been ordered

Notes to pages 296 to 299

"to go out peaceful" if the Guard attacked. G-2 Journal, Feb. 5, 1937, *ibid.*; —— to Mrs. Jean Wilson, Feb. 3, 1937, Kraus Papers, Box 9. See Chapter VI.
95. R. Reuther interview, p. 28; Travis interview, pp. 32–33; Mortimer interview, Dec. 9, 1964, pp. 8–9; Oral History Interview of Everett Francis, July 6, 1962, p. 35; Interview with Joe Devitt, July 14, 1966, p. 26; Bud Simons and Jay Green to Homer Corven and Earl Aldred, Feb. 5, 1937, Simons *et al.* to Pete Kennedy, Feb. 5, 1937, Simons to Hazel Simons [Feb. 3, 1937?], Simons Papers, Labor History Archives; Kraus, *Many and Few*, pp. 252–53; G-2 Report, Feb. 6, 1937, National Guard Records; New York *Times*, Feb. 6, 1937; Edward Levinson, "Labor on the March," *Harper's Magazine*, CLXXIV (May 1937), 645.
96. Minutes of Fisher Body No. 1 Strike Committee, Jan. 25, 1937, and Kraus notes on same, Harry Van Nocker Notebook, Kraus Papers, Box 9; Devitt interview, p. 27. *Cf.* Travis interview, pp. 40–41.
97. New York *Times*, Feb. 12, 1937; Murphy to Stuart H. Perry, June 1, 1938, Josiah W. Bailey to Murphy, Jan. 30, 1939, Murphy Papers; *Nomination of Murphy*, pp. 3–4.
98. Detroit *News*, Feb. 8, 1937; Statement by Wolcott, Oct. 21, 1938, Murphy Papers; John H. Eliasohn to George Murphy, Oct. 24, 1938, *ibid.*
99. Detroit *News*, Feb. 9, 1937. He later told Dorothy Day, "Machine guns are always the last refuge of the undisciplined, impotent official in time of crisis." [*Catholic Worker*, Oct. 1937], Murphy Scrapbooks.
100. Strike Chronology, Feb. 7, 1937, Murphy Papers.
101. 63rd Brigade S-3 Report for Feb. 6–7, 1937, National Guard Records; Pepper to Lewis, Feb. 20, 1937, *ibid.*; Report of F. C. Standiford, undated, *ibid.*; Standiford, Recommendations in the Event of Martial Law, undated, *ibid.*; Pepper to Kemp, Jan. 12, 1939, Murphy Papers; Strike Chronology, Feb. 5, 1937, *ibid.*; Murphy note to Kemp on N.M. Lacy to Murphy, Jan. 27, 1937, *ibid.*
102. Strike Chronology, Feb. 8, 1937, Murphy Papers.
103. Record of Phone Conversation with Murphy, Feb. 9, 1937, National Guard Records.
104. The original of the letter and the several copies of it in the Murphy Papers bear the date February 9 rather than February 8. When the letter was typed, probably on February 8, the space for the day of the month was left blank, and the "9" was later added, presumably to make the date of the letter conform to the date of its presentation to Lewis. When a copy of the letter was first publicly revealed on January 13, 1939 (see below), it bore the date February 8 and the notation that it had been read and delivered at 9:15 P.M. on February 9.
105. Murphy to Lewis and Martin, Feb. 8, 1937, Murphy Papers.
106. Pencil notes by Murphy, Aug. 1938 folder, *ibid.*; *Nomination of Murphy*, p. 10; Carl Muller, "Frank Murphy, Ornament of the Bar," *Detroit Lawyer*, XVII (Sept. 1949), 183; Interview of George Murphy, Mar. 28, 1957, p. 4; Blair Moody, in Detroit *News*, Jan. 15, 1939; [Lenhardt], "It Can Happen Here," Mar. 9, 1937, Moody Papers. See also Kemp, "Frank Murphy as Government Administrator," 1951, Edward G. Kemp Papers, Michigan Historical Collections; and Arthur Krock to P. H. Calahan, May 3, 1937, Murphy Papers.
107. Pressman interview, Nov. 12, 1964, p. 32.

Notes to pages 300 to 305

407

108. Alinsky, *Lewis,* pp. 144–46; UAW, *Proceedings, 1940,* p. 105. Alinsky has Lewis reading the letter, but it was actually read to him. Pressman recalls Lewis' references to Murphy's ancestry and the Irish question, but Pressman was not present when Murphy read the letter to Lewis. Pressman interview, Nov. 12, 1964, pp. 26–28.
109. The only other person present, Dewey, "confirmed in full" Murphy's version of what transpired. Detroit *News,* Jan. 16, 1939.
110. See, for example, Kraus, *Many and Few,* pp. 275–76; Flint *Journal,* Feb. 10, 1937; and Lunt, "High Ministry," p. 229. *Cf.* Porter, in New York *Times,* Feb. 8, 10, 1937.
111. New York *Times,* Feb. 9, Mar. 16, 1937; Kraus, *Many and Few,* p. 275.
112. Murphy to Guy H. Jenkins, Jan. 28, 1939, Murphy Papers; New York *Times,* Jan. 6, 1939; Kemp, "Murphy," Kemp Papers; Detroit *News,* Jan. 15, 1939; Lippmann, in [Washington *Post,* Jan. 17, 1939], Murphy Scrapbooks.
113. See, for example, G-2 Report, Feb. 10, 1937, National Guard Records.
114. My account of the utility problem in Chevrolet No. 4 and of Lenz's abortive effort to recapture the plant is based on 63rd Brigade, S-3 Report, Feb. 11, 1937, *ibid.*; G-2 Reports, Feb. 10–11, 1937, *ibid.*; G-2 Journal, Feb. 10, 1937, *ibid.*; State Police Daily Log, Feb. 10, 1937, State Police File #5977; Walburn to Wohlforth [Feb. 10, 1937], La Follette Committee Papers, Box 124; P. Hapgood to M. Hapgood, Feb. 6, 1937, [Feb. 7, 9, 10, 1937], Hapgood Papers; GM Release [Feb. 10, 1937], Kraus Papers, Box 9; Local 156 Release, Feb. 10, 1937, *ibid.*; New York *Times,* Feb. 8, 11, 1937; and Kraus, *Many and Few,* p. 254.
115. Detroit *News,* Feb. 10–11, 1937.
116. See the draft of a strike agreement dated Feb. 10, 1937, Murphy Papers.
117. See the list of plants in Knudsen to Murphy, Feb. 10, 1937, *ibid.*
118. Travis interview, p. 45; Kraus, *Many and Few,* pp. 280–81.
119. Roper Memorandum for McIntyre, Feb. 10, 1937, OF 407-B, Roosevelt Library.
120. Maurice Wyss to author, Aug. 30, 1967; Detroit *News,* Oct. 29, 1937; DuBrul, "The Problem of Union Agreements," Dec. 31, 1936, GM Appendix Doc. 74-A.
121. Detroit *News,* Feb. 11, 1937; Alinsky, *Lewis,* p. 146; New York *Times,* Feb. 12, 1937; Kraus, *Many and Few,* p. 285. The agreement was signed by Knudsen, Brown, and Smith for GM, Lewis, Mortimer, and Pressman for the UAW, and Murphy and Dewey.
122. The original of the agreement is in the Murphy Papers.
123. Knudsen to Murphy, Feb. 11, 1937, *ibid.* The 17 plants to which this letter applied were Fisher Body and Chevrolet in Atlanta, Janesville, Norwood, and St. Louis, Fisher Body in Cleveland and Kansas City, Chevrolet in Toledo, Fisher Body Nos. 1 and 2 and Chevrolet No. 4 in Flint, Cadillac and Fleetwood in Detroit, and Guide Lamp in Anderson. Knudsen to Murphy, Feb. 11, 1937, *ibid.*
124. GM Release, Feb. 11, 1937, Edward Levinson Papers, Box 4, Labor History Archives; Flint *Journal,* Feb. 11, 1937; Detroit *News,* Feb. 10, 1937; UAW Release, Feb. 10, 1937, Murphy Papers; Anderson *Auto Workers Daily News,* Feb. 13, 1937; Levinson, *Labor on March,* pp. 167–68; Brophy, "Struggle for Auto Union," p. 23, Brophy Papers.
125. Knudsen to Martin [Feb. 13, 1937], Levinson Papers, Box 4; Martin

Press Interview, Feb. 13, 1937, *ibid.* Cf. Kraus, *Many and Few*, pp. 278–79, and Beasley, *Knudsen*, p. 173, on this question.
126. Detroit *News*, Feb. 11, 1937; New York *Times*, Feb. 12, 1937; George E. Sokolsky, "Strikes Cost Us Plenty," reprinted in Egbert Ray Nichols and James W. Logan, compilers, *Arbitration and the National Labor Relations Board, Reference Shelf* (New York, 1937), XI, No. 7, 215–18; *Ward's 1939 Automotive Year Book*, pp. 36–37.
127. GM Releases, Feb. 11, 1937, Kraus Papers, Box 9; Alfred P. Sloan, Jr., *The Story of the General Motors Strike* (New York, 1937), p. 11.
128. Detroit *News*, Feb. 12, 1937; New York *Times*, Feb. 12, 1937; *Iron Age*, Feb. 18, 1937, pp. 58–59. Cf. Wechsler, *Labor Baron*, pp. 65–66.
129. Detroit *News*, Feb. 12, 1937; *United Automobile Worker*, Feb. 13, 1937; New York *Times*, Feb. 12, 14, 1937; Oral History Interview of Walter Schilling *et al.*, Aug. 26, 1961, p. 26; Statement by John L. Lewis, Feb. 11, 1937, Kraus Papers, Box 9; UAW Release, Feb. 11, 1937, Brophy Papers; Brophy, "Struggle for Auto Union," p. 23, *ibid.*; UAW Release, Feb. 16, 1937, Levinson Papers, Box 4; Oral History Interview of Norman Bully, Oct. 12, 1961, p. 6; Oral History Interview of Clayton Johnson, June 1, 1961, p. 14; Travis interview, p. 49.
130. *Literary Digest*, CXXIII (Feb. 20, 1937), 36; G-2 Journal, Feb. 11, 1937, National Guard Records; Detroit *News*, Feb. 11, 1937.
131. AFL Release, Feb. 11, 1937, Levinson Papers, Box 4; Frey, "The Automobile Strike Settlement" [Feb. 16, 1937], John P. Frey Papers, Box 6, Library of Congress, Washington, D.C.; Frey to W. A. Appleton, Feb. 16, 1937, *ibid.*, Box 1; Green, Williams, and Frey to Knudsen, Feb. 12, 1937, Knudsen to Murphy, Feb. 17, 1937, Murphy to Knudsen, Feb. 18, 1937, Murphy Papers.
132. GM Releases, Feb. 11, 1937, Levinson Papers, Box 4; Lewis Statement, Feb. 11, 1937, Kraus Papers, Box 9; New York *Times*, Feb. 12, 1937; Sloan to Margery Abrahams, Feb. 7, 1939, Murphy to Lawrence P. Fisher, Mar. 20, 1939, Murphy Papers.
133. Roosevelt to Murphy, Feb. 11, 1937, Daniels to Murphy, Feb. 12, 1937, Murphy Papers; New York *Times*, Feb. 12, 1937.
134. Perkins to Murphy, Feb. 11, 1937, Felix Frankfurter to Murphy, Feb. 12, 1937, Daniels to Murphy, Feb. 12, 1937, Newton D. Baker to Murphy, Feb. 12, 1937, John M. Carmody to Murphy, Feb. 15, 1937, Murphy Papers; New York *Times*, Feb. 12, 1937; Flint *Journal*, Feb. 12, 1937; Detroit *News*, Feb. 12, 1937; Franklin column in unidentified newspaper [Feb. 18, 1937], Murphy Papers; miscellaneous clippings for post-strike period in Murphy Scrapbooks.
135. White E. Gibson to Murphy, Feb. 12, 1937, Mitchell E. Foster to Murphy, Feb. 23, 1937, Frank Gaines to Murphy, Feb. 25, 1937, Krock to Murphy, Feb. 12, 1937, Murphy Papers; Phil S. Hanna, in Flint *Journal*, Feb. 17, 1937; *Commercial and Financial Chronicle*, CXLIV (Feb. 20, 1937), 1164; George E. Sokolsky, "The Law and Labor," *Atlantic Monthly*, CLIX (Apr. 1937), 433–34; New York *Times*, Feb. 12, 1937.
136. Kemp, "Murphy," Kemp Papers; [Cleveland *Plain Dealer*], Feb. 16, 1937, Murphy Scrapbooks; *Time*, XXIX (Feb. 22, 1937), 14. See also Russell B. Porter, "Governor Murphy's Star in the Ascendant," New York *Times*, Feb. 21, 1937.

137. On this point, see GM, Labor Relations Diary, Section 1, pp. 80–81.
138. See, for example, *Socialist Call*, Feb. 20, 1937; *United Automobile Worker*, Feb. 13, 1937; Brophy, "Struggle for Auto Union," p. 23, Brophy Papers; and "After the Motors Strike," *Christian Century*, LIV (Feb. 24, 1937), 240.
139. Robert R. R. Brooks, *As Steel Goes* (New Haven, 1940), p. 120; Frank N. Trager, "Autos: The Battle for Industrial Unionism," Jan. 11, 1937, MS in Norman Thomas Papers, New York Public Library; New York *Times*, Jan. 10, 24, 31, 1937; Levinson, "Detroit Digs In," *Nation*, CXLIV (Jan. 16, 1937), 64; Detroit *News*, Feb. 8, 1937; *New Republic*, XC (Feb. 24, 1937), 60–61; *Daily Worker*, Feb. 12, 1937.
140. On these points, see draft of Brophy answers, Brophy Papers; William Weinstone, *The Great Sit-Down Strike* (New York, 1937), pp. 8–15; *Daily Worker*, Feb. 27, 1937; Kraus, *Many and Few*, p. 268; Hall interview, p. 25; Oral History Interview of Carl Haessler, Nov. 27, 1959–Oct. 24, 1960, p. 17; Pressman interview, Nov. 12, 1964, p. 43; and Oral History Interview of Larry S. Davidow, July 14, 1960, p. 17.
141. In his autobiography, Martin Dies claims that when Murphy was on the Supreme Court he told Dies, "'I am ashamed of my role in the sit-down strikes, but I was under terrific pressure from the President and many of my political friends, and I let them pressure me against my better instincts.'" Dies, *Martin Dies' Story* (New York, 1963), p. 124. The President and Perkins, the evidence indicates, did not urge Murphy to evict the strikers, but there is no reason to think that this is why Murphy failed to enforce the injunction. In a letter to *Liberty Magazine*, published in the February 25, 1939, issue, p. 7, Murphy repudiated the contention that his strike policy had been "dictated by Washington. ... My policy," he wrote, "was dictated to me by no one."
142. My account of the victory celebration is based on Flint *Journal*, Feb. 12, 1937; Detroit *News*, Feb. 12, 1937; New York *Times*, Feb. 12, 1937; Joe Brown to Edward A. Wieck, Feb. 13, 1937, Edward A. Wieck Papers, Box 10, Labor History Archives; unsigned wire to Kraus, Feb. 12, 1937, Kraus Papers; Oral History Interview of Bud Simons, Sept. 6, 1960, pp. 49–50; Kraus, *Many and Few*, pp. 286–93; and Pesotta, *Bread upon the Waters* (Edited by John Nicholas Beffel; New York, 1944), p. 252. For the victory celebration in Cleveland, see Cleveland *Plain Dealer*, Feb. 14, 1937.

Chapter XI

1. Mayor Baldwin claimed that the owner had refused the use of the theater but that someone had picked the locks of the building. Affidavit of Harry R. Baldwin, Feb. 13, 1937, Sen 78A-F9, Box 125, Record Group 46, National Archives and Records Service, Washington, D.C. (hereafter cited as La Follette Committee Papers). *Cf.* UAW Release, Feb. 16, 1937, Edward Levinson Papers, Box 4, Labor History Archives, Wayne State University, Detroit, Michigan; and Oral History Interview of Victor Reuther, Mar. 7, 1963, p. 20 (transcripts of all interviews cited are located in the Michigan Historical Collections, Ann Arbor, Michi-

gan); and Claude E. Hoffman, *Sit-Down in Anderson: UAW Local 663, Anderson, Indiana* (Detroit, 1968), pp. 60–61.
2. Robert H. Cowdrill to Robert Wohlforth, Feb. 14, 1937, La Follette Committee Papers, Box 126.
3. *Ibid.*
4. The account of the February 11 meeting is based on the following: Charles B. Salyer to V. Reuther, Feb. 11, 1937, Victor Reuther Papers, Labor History Archives; Resolution Passed at Victory Meeting, Feb. 11, 1937, Cecil C. Roeder Papers, Box 2, *ibid.*; Ira Latimer, Report of Civil Liberties Investigation of Anderson . . . , Feb. 19, 1937, American Civil Liberties Union Archives, Reel 151, Vol. 1041, New York Public Library; G. Watson Memorandum [Feb. 1937], La Follette Committee Papers, Box 122; "Anderson," undated, *ibid.*, Box 125; Victor Reuther Affidavit, Feb. 15, 1937, *ibid.*; Cowdrill to Wohlforth, Feb. 14, 1937, *ibid.*, Box 126; Anderson *Auto Workers Daily News*, Feb. 13, 1937; and V. Reuther interview, pp. 20–23.
5. Anderson *Auto Workers Daily News*, Feb. 13, 1937; V. Reuther interview, p. 23.
6. Cowdrill to Wohlforth, Feb. 14, 1937, La Follette Committee Papers, Box 126; Andrew Nichols Affidavit, with Cowdrill to Wohlforth, Feb. 18, 1937, *ibid.*, Box 125; typescripts [Feb. 15, 18, 1937], Mary Heaton Vorse Papers, Labor History Archives.
7. Watson Memorandum [Feb. 1937], La Follette Committee Papers, Box 122; Cecil Dunn Affidavit, with Cowdrill to Wohlforth, Feb. 18, 1937, *ibid.*, Box 125; Chester Hiday Affidavit, Feb. 14, 1937, *ibid.*; Statement of Shipley to Cowdrill, Feb. 15, 1937, *ibid.*; "Anderson," *ibid.*
8. According to one source ("Anderson," *ibid.*, Box 125), the person was none other than Dunn, but this seems incorrect.
9. Statement of Shipley to Cowdrill, Feb. 15, 1937, and Cowdrill comment concerning same, *ibid.*; Cowdrill to Wohlforth, Feb. 14, 1937, *ibid.*, Box 126; "Anderson," *ibid.*, Box 125; Latimer Report, Feb. 19, 1937, ACLU Archives, Reel 151, Vol. 1041; UAW Release, Feb. 16, 1937, Levinson Papers, Box 4; New York *Times*, Feb. 14, 1937; Hoffman, *Sit-Down in Anderson*, pp. 62–63.
10. Cowdrill to Wohlforth, Feb. 14, 1937, La Follette Committee Papers, Box 126; Anderson *Daily Bulletin*, Feb. 15, 1937, in *ibid.*
11. Cowdrill to Wohlforth, Feb. 14, 1937, *ibid.*; Anderson *Daily Bulletin*, Feb. 15, 1937, in *ibid.*; Anderson *Sunday Herald*, Feb. 14, 1937, Indianapolis *Star*, Feb. 14, 1937, and Anderson *Daily Bulletin*, Feb. 13, 1937, in *ibid.*, Box 125; Townsend Proclamation, Feb. 13, 1937, Roeder Papers, Box 2; V. Reuther interview, p. 24; New York *Times*, Feb. 14, 1937.
12. New York *Times*, Feb. 15, 1937; UAW Release, Feb. 16, 1937, Levinson Papers, Box 4; James S. Valentine and A. Bosschem to Lawrence A. Lyon, Feb. 13, 1937, Case File #5977, Michigan State Police Records, Lansing, Michigan; Indianapolis *News*, Feb. 16, 1937, in La Follette Committee Papers, Box 126; Cowdrill to Wohlforth, Feb. 17, 1937, *ibid.*, Box 124; Charles B. Salyer to Wohlforth, Feb. 18, 1937, *ibid.*, Box 126; Anderson *Auto Workers Daily News*, Feb. 19, 1937; George F. Delaplane to Roger N. Baldwin, Feb. 17, 1937, ACLU Archives, Reel 151, Vol. 1041; Vorse to Carl Haessler, Feb. 16, 1937, Henry Kraus Papers, Box 11, Labor History Archives.

13. New York *Times*, Feb. 19–21, 24, 1937; Indiana National Guard Order No. 55, Feb. 22, 1937, Roeder Papers, Box 1; Milton Siegel to Harry A. Poth, Jr., Feb. 24, 1937, Heaton Vorse to Poth, Apr. 14, 1937, ACLU Archives, Reel 151, Vol. 1041.
14. New York *Times*, Feb. 16, 19, 1937; Anderson *Auto Workers Daily News*, Feb. 13, 17, 1937; Heaton Vorse to Poth, Apr. 14, 1937, ACLU Archives, Reel 151, Vol. 1041; V. Reuther to Martin, Mar. 31, 1937, V. Reuther Papers; V. Reuther interview, pp. 24–25. For the history of the UAW in Anderson after the GM strike, see Hoffman, *Sit-Down in Anderson*, pp. 68–117.
15. Detroit *News*, Feb. 14, 1937; Flint *Journal*, Feb. 17, Mar. 5, 1937; File 182-2002, Records of the Conciliation Service, Record Group 280, National Archives and Records Service (hereafter Conciliation Service Files will be referred to as CS).
16. Detroit *News*, Feb. 17, 1937; Flint *Journal*, Feb. 17, 23, 1937; House Special Committee on Un-American Activities, *Investigation of Un-American Propaganda Activities in the United States, Hearings Pursuant to H. Res. 282*, 75 Cong., 3 Sess. (Washington, 1938), IV, 2678 (hereafter cited as *Dies Hearings*).
17. Flint *Journal*, Feb. 25–26, 1937; Detroit *News*, Feb. 26, June 2, 1937; Starr to Edward G. Kemp, May 17, 1937, Martin to Starr, June 1, 1937, Frank Murphy Papers, Michigan Historical Collections.
18. Detroit *News*, Feb. 16, 1937; Flint *Journal*, Feb. 24, 1937; Harold F. Sylvester, "City Management: The Flint Experiment, 1930–1937" (Ph.D. thesis, Johns Hopkins University, 1938), pp. 131–35.
19. John S. Bersey to Murphy, Feb. 19, 1937, John H. Steck to Joseph H. Lewis, Feb. 11, 20, 1937, Blanding to Bersey, Feb. 24, 1937, Bersey to Blanding, Mar. 4, 1937, Records of the Michigan Military Establishment Relating to the Flint Sit-Down Strike, 1937, microfilm copy in Michigan Historical Collections (hereafter cited as National Guard Records); G-1 Reports, Feb. 11–20, 1937, *ibid*. Blanding cited a clipping said to have been from the *Daily Worker*; the story was confirmed by the New York *Times*, Feb. 17, 1937.
20. Detroit *News*, Feb. 11, 1937; Bradshaw to Lewis, Feb. 19, 1937, Wolcott to Lewis, Feb. 19, 1937, Lewis to Murphy, June 18, 1937, National Guard Records. Knudsen informed Lewis at the end of the strike that he had no complaints about the Guard's behavior in Flint. Interview with Lewis, Mar. 14, 1968 (untranscribed).
21. Steck to Lewis, Feb. 20, 1937, National Guard Records.
22. Pepper to Lewis, Feb. 22, 1937, *ibid*.; Bersey to Murphy, Aug. 12, 1937, Murphy Papers.
23. Flint *Journal*, Feb. 18, Mar. 8, 1937; New York *Times*, Feb. 15, 1937; Frederick H. Harbison and Robert Dubin, *Patterns of Union-Management Relations* (Chicago, 1947), p. 21.
24. GM Executive Training Program, Section G-5, Management Principles in Department Supervision, Organization, and Personnel [Jan. or Feb. 1937], Session 1, pp. 1-2, Session 2, pp. 3-4, General Motors Institute, Flint, Michigan; Robert Ozanne, *A Century of Labor-Management Relations at McCormick and International Harvester* (Madison, 1967), p. 153.

25. [Frank Rodolf], "An Industrial History of Flint" (MS, Flint *Journal*, 1949), p. 494.
26. Harbison and Dubin, *Patterns*, p. 23; Oral History Interview of William Genske, July 23, 1960, p. 9.
27. Flint *Journal*, Feb. 18, 1937; New York *Times*, Feb. 19, 1937; Cranefield to Wohlforth, Feb. 16, 17, 1937, Wyndham Mortimer to Robert M. La Follette, Jr., Feb. 22, 1937, La Follette Committee Papers, Box 124; Information from E. C. McDonald, Feb. 18, 1937, CS 182-2002.
28. David C. Shaw to Wohlforth, Feb. 25, 1937, La Follette Committee Papers, Box 123; Flint *Journal*, Feb. 19, 1937. There was another sit-down in St. Louis on March 11. New York *Times*, Mar. 12, 1937.
29. New York *Times*, Feb. 27, Mar. 2, 1937; Flint *Journal*, Mar. 1, 1937; Henry Traxler, "I Went through a Strike," *Public Management*, XIX (Apr. 1937), 100–102.
30. Edward A. Wieck, "Sit-Down Strikes 1933–1937: A Chronological Compilation" (MS, 1937), pp. 55, 57, Edward A. Wieck Papers, Box 5, Labor History Archives.
31. New York *Times*, Mar. 7, 9, 1937; Flint *Journal*, Mar. 7–10, 1937; Travis to Kraus [Mar. 1937], Kraus Papers, Box 10.
32. Flint *Journal*, Mar. 11–12, 1937.
33. There is a copy of the agreement in the Murphy Papers. The negotiations can be followed in the Flint *Journal*, especially Feb. 20, 26, Mar. 3, 5, 10, 1937.
34. *United Automobile Worker*, Mar. 20, 1937; Oral History Interview of John W. Anderson, Feb. 17, May 21, 1960, pp. 55–56; Walter Galenson, *The CIO Challenge to the AFL: A History of the American Labor Movement, 1935–1941* (Cambridge, Mass., 1960), p. 148; *Business Week*, Apr. 10, 1937, p. 17.
35. *United Automobile Worker*, Mar. 20, 1937.
36. Flint *Journal*, Mar. 12, 14, 1937; Sidney Lens, *Left, Right and Center: Conflicting Forces in American Labor* (Hinsdale, Ill., 1949), pp. 309–10.
37. Flint *Journal*, Mar. 12, 1937.
38. GM Executive Training Program, Section G-6, Labor Policies and Procedures [1937], Session 1, pp. 1, 3–4, Session 2, p. 4, GM Institute; Harbison and Dubin, *Patterns*, pp. 23–25. GM, on March 25, 1937, issued a revision of its August, 1934, statement to incorporate the changes resulting from the February 11 and March 12 agreements. There is a copy of the revision (*General Motors Labor Policies and Procedures*) in the Kraus Papers, Box 16.
39. *United Automobile Worker*, Feb. 25, Mar. 20, 1937; Anderson *Auto Workers Daily News*, Feb. 17, 1937; Detroit *News*, Mar. 7, 1937; UAW GEB Minutes, Mar. 15–16, 1937, Kraus Papers, Box 7; Report of . . . George F. Addes to the GEB . . . , Sept. 13, 1937, *ibid.*, Box 11; Report of John Brophy to CIO Meeting, Oct. 11, 1937, John Brophy Papers, Catholic University, Washington, D.C.
40. Anderson *Auto Workers Daily News*, Feb. 13, 1937; Oral History Interview of Wyndham Mortimer, June 20, 1960, pp. 43–44; Oral History Interview of Norman Bully, Oct. 12, 1961, pp. 5–6; Oral History Interview of Joseph Pagano, May 23, 1960, p. 15.
41. UAW Release, Feb. 16, 1937, Levinson Papers, Box 4; Flint *Auto Worker*, Mar. 26, 1937; Genske interview, pp. 8–9; Anderson interview,

pp. 57–58; William H. McPherson and Anthony Lucheck, "Automobiles," Twentieth Century Fund, *How Collective Bargaining Works* (New York, 1942), p. 612; Oral History Interview of Roy Reuther, July 12, 1966, pp. 10–12.
42. Alfred H. Lockhart to Gernsley F. Gorton, Mar. 7, 1937, William H. Phelps Papers, Michigan Historical Collections.
43. Oral History Interview of Harry Ross, July 10, 1961, p. 20; Oral History Interview of Richard Harris, Nov. 16, 1959, p. 22; Oral History Interview of Nick Digaetano, Apr. 29, May 7, 1959, pp. 56–57.
44. On the Chrysler strike, see Doris McLaughlin, "The Chrysler Strike of 1937" (MS, 1963), in my possession; and Galenson, *CIO Challenge to AFL*, pp. 148–49.
45. Galenson, *CIO Challenge to AFL*, pp. 149–50.
46. The Lovestoneites were followers of Jay Lovestone, who had been expelled from the leadership of the Communist party in 1929 for "right wing deviationism." A few of them had established close relations with Martin. See Irving Howe and B. J. Widick, *The UAW and Walter Reuther* (New York, 1949), p. 71.
47. For an account of the fortunes of the UAW following the GM sit-down, see Galenson, *CIO Challenge to AFL*, pp. 148–92.
48. Shister, "The Logic of Union Growth," *Journal of Political Economy*, LXI (Oct. 1953), 422; *Union News Service*, Mar. 1, 1937; *New York Times*, Feb. 14, 1937; *Daily Worker*, Feb. 13, 1937; *Workers Age*, Mar. 13, 1937; Minutes of CIO Meeting, Mar. 9, 1937, Katherine Pollak Ellickson CIO File, Franklin D. Roosevelt Library, Hyde Park, New York; Galenson, *CIO Challenge to AFL*, pp. 31–32, 93, *et passim*; Edward Levinson, *Labor on the March* (University Books; New York, 1956), pp. 236–78.
49. *United Automobile Worker*, May 15, 1937; Bittner to Green, Feb. 9, 1937, Sidney Hillman Papers, Amalgamated Clothing Workers, New York, New York; *New York Times*, Feb. 13, 16, 1937.
50. "Review of Strikes in 1936," *Monthly Labor Review*, XLIV (May 1937), 1234; "Number of Sit-Down Strikes in 1937," *ibid.*, XLVII (Aug. 1938), 360, 362; Levinson, *Labor on March*, pp. 173–74; *Detroit News*, Mar. 14, 1937.
51. "Number of Sit-Down Strikes in 1937," p. 361; *Dies Hearings*, II, 1611–14; *Detroit News*, Mar. 14, 19, 1937; *Time*, XXIX (Mar. 29, 1937), 11–13; Carol A. Westenhoefer, "Non-Automotive Sit-Down Strikes in Detroit" (MS, 1964), in my possession. See also Mary Heaton Vorse, "Detroit Has the Jitters," *New Republic*, XC (Apr. 7, 1937), 256–58.
52. "Number of Sit-Down Strikes in 1937," p. 361; Galenson, *CIO Challenge to AFL*, p. 145; Levinson, *Labor on March*, pp. 169, 179–80.
53. "Number of Sit-Down Strikes in 1937," pp. 361–62; Sumner H. Slichter, "Labor Faces the Future," *Christian Science Monitor* (Weekly Magazine Section), Mar. 3, 1937.
54. *Detroit News*, Mar. 21, 1937; Hadley Cantril, ed., *Public Opinion, 1935–1946* (Princeton, 1951), p. 816. 73 percent of the farmers, 71 percent of the small-town voters, and 80 percent of the Republicans wanted to see laws passed against the sit-downs (March 21 poll). 74 percent of the farmers thought that force should be used to eject sit-downers (July 4 poll). 65 percent of the city voters, 62 percent of the young voters and

the Democrats, and 47 percent of the reliefers favored laws proscribing the sit-down (March 21 poll). 62 percent of city people, 64 percent of the young voters, and 43 percent of the people on relief thought that the state should use force against sit-downers (July 4 poll). *Ibid.* Cantril incorrectly assigns a July 4 date to the first of the two polls.
55. *Ibid.*, p. 817. Seven governors specifically condemned the sit-down strike tactic in 1937, and four states in that year enacted statutes directed against it. Ten states had enacted laws against the sit-down by the end of 1947. Walter L. Eisenberg, "Government Policy in Sitdown Strikes" (Ph.D. thesis, Columbia University, 1959), pp. 76–79, 131–47.
56. New York *Times*, Mar. 27, 1937.
57. Stephen K. Bailey, *Congress Makes a Law: The Story behind the Employment Act of 1946* (New York, 1950), pp. 199–200.
58. *Congressional Record*, 75 Cong., 1 Sess., pp. 245–47, 324–26, 601, 818–19, 826–27.
59. Jerold S. Auerbach, *Labor and Liberty: The La Follette Committee and the New Deal* (Indianapolis, 1966), pp. 112–15.
60. *Cong. Record*, 75 Cong., 1 Sess., pp. 1623, 1632.
61. *Ibid.*, pp. 2337, 2472, 2476–78, 2521–22, 2642, 2794, 2921–30, 2943, 3038, 3041–43; J. Joseph Hutmacher, *Senator Robert F. Wagner and the Rise of Urban Liberalism* (New York, 1968), pp. 232–33.
62. Vandenberg to Frank Knox, Apr. 2, 1937, Arthur H. Vandenberg Papers, William L. Clements Library, Ann Arbor, Michigan; Vandenberg Scrapbooks, Apr. 2, 1937 entry, *ibid.*; James T. Patterson, *Congressional Conservatism and the New Deal* (Lexington, Ky., 1967), pp. 136–37; *Cong. Record*, 75 Cong., 1 Sess., pp. 3017, 3022–24.
63. *Cong. Record*, 75 Cong., 1 Sess., pp. 3017–25, 3061–88, 3121–36, 3232–48; Patterson, *Congressional Conservatism*, pp. 136–38.
64. Patterson, *Congressional Conservatism*, pp. 167–68; *Cong. Record*, 75 Cong., 1 Sess., pp. 2665, 3113–14, 3301. See also Martin Dies, *Martin Dies' Story* (New York, 1963), pp. 140–41.
65. New York *Times*, Feb. 14, 1937; Georges Schreiber, "Roosevelt's Successor? . . . ," *Common Sense*, VI (June 1937), 9; Murphy, "The Shaping of Labor Policy," *Survey Graphic*, XXVI (Aug. 1937), 411; Murphy, "Industrial Peace," *Christian Front*, II (Nov. 1937), 156–58; *Selected Addresses of Frank Murphy . . . January 1, 1937, to September 30, 1938* (Lansing, 1938), pp. 8–9, 13–14, 20–25, 47–50; State of Michigan, Legislature of 1937–38, Regular Session, House Bills, House Bill No. 571, University of Michigan Law Library, Ann Arbor, Michigan.
66. Murphy statement [Mar. 13, 1937], Murphy Papers; Statement by Governor Murphy, Mar. 17, 1937, *ibid.*; Germer Diary, Mar. 12, 1937, Adolph Germer Papers, State Historical Society of Wisconsin, Madison.
67. New York *Times*, Mar. 21, 26, 1937; [Adrian *Daily Telegram*], Apr. 20, 1938, clipping in Murphy Papers; Stuart H. Perry to Murphy, May 18, 1938, *ibid.* See also Dr. Carl D. Brooks to Murphy, July 19, 1937, Clare E. Hoffman to Murphy, Nov. 26, 1937, *ibid.*; and *Time*, XXIX (Mar. 29, 1937), 12.
68. Detroit *News*, Feb. 6, 1937.
69. Homer Martin was to have testified on October 21, but he begged off and did not testify until December 1, 1938. *Dies Hearings*, II, 1639; IV, 2675–2727.

Notes to pages 337 to 341

70. *Dies Hearings*, II, 1423, 1454, 1494–96, 1551, 1554, 1649, 1679–80, 1687–89; Detroit *News*, Oct. 12, 1938.
71. Murphy to Dies, Oct. 23, 1938 (probably not sent), Murphy Papers; New York *Times*, Oct. 26, 1938; Detroit *News*, Jan. 15, 1939; August Raymond Ogden, *The Dies Committee . . . 1938–1943* (Washington, 1943), pp. 79–81; Walter Goodman, *The Committee* (New York, 1968), pp. 49–51.
72. *Dies Hearings*, III, 2019–20.
73. Murphy address, Nov. 2, 1938, Murphy Papers.
74. See the numerous post-mortem letters in Official File 300, Box 105, Franklin D. Roosevelt Library, Hyde Park, New York.
75. Murphy to James A. Farley, Nov. 23, 1938, Dec. 7, 1938, Murphy to Mrs. James Crowley, Nov. 29, 1939, Murphy Papers; John P. White, *Michigan Votes: Election Statistics, 1928–1956* (Ann Arbor, 1958), pp. 17, 31, 39–40, 47. In Genesee County, the principal scene of the GM strike, Murphy's percentage of the vote fell from 59.9 in 1936 to 49.3 in 1938, but in Wayne County, where there had been an epidemic of sit-downs, the Murphy vote fell only from 59.3 to 58.1 percent. *Ibid.*, pp. 40, 47.
76. Levinson, *Labor on March*, p. 149; Galenson, *CIO Challenge to AFL*, p. 134; "The Industrial War," *Fortune*, XVI (Nov. 1937), 105, 107.
77. On this point, see Arthur M. Schlesinger, Jr., *A Thousand Days: John F. Kennedy in the White House* (Boston, 1965), p. 966.
78. Waskow, *From Race Riot to Sit-In, 1919 and the 1960s* (Anchor Books; New York, 1966), pp. 204, 228–30, 278–79, 284, 297–98.
79. August Meier and Elliott M. Rudwick, *From Plantation to Ghetto: An Interpretive History of American Negroes* (New York, 1966), p. 223.
80. Travis to Kraus [Mar. 1937], Kraus Papers, Box 10.
81. On the leadership and the rank-and-file of the civil-rights movement, see Louis E. Lomax, *The Negro Revolt* (Signet Book; New York, 1963), *passim*.
82. John Brooks, *The Great Leap: The Past Twenty-Five Years in America* (New York, 1966), p. 157.
83. For the Columbia sit-in of 1968 in particular, see New York *Times*, May 4, 24, June 10, 1968; *Barron's*, May 20, 1968, p. 1+; and *New York Review of Books*, XVI (July 11, 1968), 41–42.
84. *Financial Observer*, I (Mar. 9, 1937), 3.

Bibliographical Note

No attempt has been made in the pages that follow to list all the works that have already been mentioned in the footnotes. Comment has been reserved for unpublished and published materials that were of particular value and interest for this study.

Manuscript Sources

The Henry Kraus Papers are the most important of several manuscript collections pertaining to the GM strike in the Labor History Archives, Wayne State University, Detroit, Michigan. The collection contains invaluable information on the UAW before, during, and after the GM strike and on the strike itself both inside and outside the plants in Flint, Anderson, and elsewhere. It is the most important manuscript source for the UAW in Flint during the strike era and for the Mortimer-Travis wing of the organization. The Bud Simons Papers contain several items pertaining to the Flint sit-down not found in the Kraus Papers. There is material relating to the strike in Anderson in the Victor Reuther Papers, the Cecil C. Roeder Papers, the Hugh Thompson Papers, and the Opel Young Papers. The Mary Heaton Vorse Papers, a disappointing collection, include a few items on the Anderson strike as well as some personality sketches of UAW principals. The Civil Rights Congress of Michigan Papers contain the minutes of the January 17, 1937, meeting of the Conference for the Protection of Civil Rights, which was addressed by several strike leaders.

There are copies of the press releases issued by GM and the UAW during the strike in the Edward Levinson Papers. The Homer Martin Papers are especially valuable for the history of the UAW before the strike, but there is, unfortunately, a gap in the correspondence for the period October, 1936–May, 1937. There are a few relevant items in the Edward A. Wieck Papers but nothing of consequence in the Carl Haessler or Fred C. Pieper Papers. There is a considerable variety of unpublished and published material pertaining to the sit-down in the Joe Brown Collection, located like all the above in the Labor History Archives. Both the Brown Collection and the Kraus Papers include nearly complete sets of *Punch Press*, the bulletin of the Flint strikers.

The Frank Murphy Papers, in the Michigan Historical Collections, Ann Arbor, Michigan, are the single most valuable source for Governor Murphy's role in the strike and for the strike negotiations as a whole. The Murphy Papers also contain a large number of letters to the governor indicative of citizen reaction to the strike. The Records of the Michigan Military Establishment Relating to the Flint Sit-Down Strike, 1937, a microfilm copy of which is in the Michigan Historical Collections, are not only indispensable for an understanding of the role of the National Guard in the strike but also include considerable information on striker and company activity in Flint. The reaction to the strike of members of the Methodist Episcopal church in Michigan in general and in Flint in particular is revealed in the William H. Phelps Papers. The Edward D. Black Papers contain a few items relative to Judge

Black and his ill-fated injunction. The Blair Moody Papers, also in the Michigan Historical Collections, include a highly interesting analysis of strike events by L. G. Lenhardt, Detroit's commissioner of the Department of Public Works.

There is a brief account of the strike in General Motors, Labor Relations Diary, Section 1, and some pertinent documents among the Appendix Documents to Accompany Section 1, located in the General Motors Building in Detroit. The Mayor's Office Records in the Burton Historical Collection of the Detroit Public Library include material on Murphy's policy during the 1933 Briggs strike and on other aspects of his mayoralty not found in the Murphy Papers in Ann Arbor. The Samuel D. Pepper Papers, in the custody of Winston Wessels, supplement the National Guard Records for the strike period. The role of the state police in the strike and the reports of its investigators on strike events in Flint are contained in Case File #5977, Michigan State Police Records, Lansing, Michigan, which I examined on microfilm. There are a few unique strike items in the Flint Public Library.

The CIO's relations with the UAW from the late fall of 1935 to the end of the strike are revealed in the Adolph Germer Papers, in the State Historical Society of Wisconsin, Madison. The correspondence in the Germer Papers is spotty, but the Germer Diary, which contains daily entries for the entire period, is an exceedingly valuable source, particularly for the background of the strike. The State Historical Society also possesses the records for the strike period of the Janesville Chevrolet local of the UAW, which I examined on microfilm. The Powers Hapgood Papers, in the Lilly Library, Indiana University, Bloomington, Indiana, contain several interesting letters about the strike written by Hapgood during his service in Flint.

There are a few sit-down items, particularly relating to the strike negotiations, in the Official File, the President's Personal File, and the President's Secretary's File in the Franklin D. Roosevelt Library, Hyde Park, New York. The Katherine Pollak Ellickson CIO Collection, available on microfilm at the Roosevelt Library, consists of the working files for the period November 15, 1935–December, 1937, of the assistant to John Brophy and includes the most complete set of CIO minutes available for the first eighteen months of the organization's history. The civil-liberties issues raised by the GM sit-down are reflected in the American Civil Liberties Union Archives, a microfilm copy of which is located in the New York Public Library. The Norman Thomas Papers, also in the New York Public Library, illuminate the Socialist interest in the strike and contain an interesting analysis of the dispute by Frank N. Trager, the Socialist party's National Labor and Organization Secretary.

The La Follette Committee Papers (Sen 78A-F9), in Record Group 46, National Archives and Records Service, Washington, D.C., are a mine of information on GM labor practices, especially in Flint and Anderson, and make crystal clear the links between committee investigators and the UAW both before and during the strike. The Records of the Conciliation Service (Record Group 280), also in the National Archives, contain files on the sit-downs preceding the GM strike and on the GM strike itself and also include hundreds of telegrams and letters to President Roosevelt from interested citizens indicating their reaction to the GM sit-down. When peace terms were arranged, Conciliator James F. Dewey promised to write "a full and complete statement" regarding the GM strike upon his return to Washington, but if he composed such an account, it has disappeared from the files.

The most interesting among several items relevant to the GM strike in the John Brophy Papers, in the Catholic University, Washington, D.C., is an account of the dispute and its background composed by Brophy as a chapter of a book on which he was working. The John P. Frey Papers, in the Library of Congress, Washington, D.C., document Frey's opposition to the UAW's demand that it be accepted as the exclusive bargaining agency for GM workers. The William Green Letterbooks, the Auto Workers File, and the CIO National Unions File, all available on film in the AFL-CIO Archives in Washington, D.C., contain only scattered items pertaining to the strike. The minutes of the meetings of the Executive Council of the AFL, which I examined on film, are the best source for the Federation's intervention in the strike. The report made by Frey at the February 10 session of the Executive Council is of special significance in this regard.

The Sidney Hillman Papers, in the New York office of the Amalgamated Clothing Workers, contain several items bearing on the relationship of the CIO to the UAW and the GM strike, including the minutes of CIO meetings in 1935 and 1936. There is a collection of CIO Papers in the Catholic University, and the main body of CIO Papers is in the Labor History Archives of Wayne State University, but I could not locate the principal CIO files for the strike period, once housed in the AFL-CIO Building. Professor Irving Bernstein, however, permitted me to examine his notes on this file, which serves as a valuable supplement to the Germer Papers.

Interviews

About one-third of the 127 oral history interviews resulting from the UAW Oral History Project of the Institute of Labor and Industrial Relations of the University of Michigan and Wayne State University, transcripts of which are located in both the Michigan Historical Collections and the Labor History Archives, contain information pertinent to the GM sit-down. The interviews with Bud Simons, Wyndham Mortimer, Paul Miley, Norman Bully, Victor Reuther, and Merlin D. Bishop are of special interest. The Reminiscences of Lee Pressman, John Brophy, and Nicholas Kelley, all located in the Oral History Research Office of Columbia University, include information on various aspects of the strike. In addition to the above, I interviewed Robert Travis, Roy Reuther, Joe Devitt, Dr. Ralph Segalman, Wyndham Mortimer, Lee Pressman, Larry Davidow, Norman H. Hill, Mrs. Fielding H. Yost, Martin Hayden, Irene Murphy, Joseph H. Lewis, Philip C. Pack, and Colin MacDonald. Frances Perkins, Roy Reuther, Jay J. Green, Carl Haessler, Fred C. Pieper, William H. Lawrence, Maurice Wyss and Thomas L. Pond of the public relations staff of GM, and Margaret Pakney of the Flint Chamber of Commerce responded by letter to my questions concerning the strike.

Periodicals and Newspapers

The UAW version of the background of the strike and of strike events can be gleaned from the files of the Flint *Auto Worker*, the *United Auto Worker* (Cleveland, 1935–36), the *United Automobile Worker,* the Anderson *Auto Workers Daily News*, the *Union News Service* (the CIO's organ), and the Flint

Weekly Review (the organ of the Flint Federation of Labor). The *I.M.A. News* faithfully mirrored the GM position in the strike. The intense Communist interest in the strike is evidenced in the extensive coverage the strike received in the *Daily Worker*, which had excellent contacts with some of the strike leaders. The *New Masses* featured several articles on the strike, and William Z. Foster and William Weinstone commented on the sit-down in the *Communist*. The Lovestoneite journal, *Workers Age*, and the organ of the Socialist party, the *Socialist Call*, contain several important articles on the strike and its background.

As one of the major news events of the era, the GM sit-down was the subject of a good deal of attention in the periodicals of the time. *Business Week, Iron Age, Automotive Industries, Nation, New Republic, Christian Century, Literary Digest, Time, News-Week, Atlantic Monthly*, and *Harper's* all have noteworthy material on the strike. In addition to the numerous articles in these periodicals, a variety of pieces in other journals are important for one or another aspect of the strike. Statistical information concerning the sit-downs is contained in "Review of Strikes in 1936," *Monthly Labor Review*, XLIV (May 1937), 1221-35, and "Number of Sit-Down Strikes in 1937," *Monthly Labor Review*, XLVII (August 1938), 360-62. Working conditions in GM plants and the attitudes of GM workers are explored in Hartley W. Barclay, "We Sat Down with the Strikers and General Motors," *Mill and Factory*, XX (February 1937), 33-60; "Why Did the Auto Workers Strike?" *Social Action*, II (February 15, 1937), 3-22; and Department of Research and Education, Federal Council of the Churches of Christ, *Information Service*, February 6, 1937. The first of these articles is an expanded version of a memorandum that Barclay prepared for GM's Harry W. Anderson, a copy of which is in the Murphy Papers.

The relief problem in Flint is considered in "Relief in the Sit-Down Strike," *Survey*, LXXIII (March 1937). Erdmann D. Beynon provides data on the Southern laborer in Flint in "The Southern White Laborer Migrates to Michigan," *American Sociological Review*, III (June 1938), 333-43. The "sociology" of the sit-down is explored in Melvin J. Vincent, "The Sit-Down Strike," *Sociology and Social Research*, XXI (July-August 1937), 524-33. Henry Traxler, the Janesville city manager, comments on the Janesville strike in "I Went through a Strike," *Public Management*, XIX (April 1937), 99-103.

The New York *Times* is the most valuable newspaper source for the GM sit-down. Russell B. Porter, who was on the scene in Flint, and Louis Stark, who covered the negotiations, both contributed many excellent articles on the strike. There is a wealth of information on the dispute in both the Detroit *News* and the Flint *Journal*. The former was reasonably objective in its treatment of strike news, but the Flint *Journal* tended to see strike events through GM's eyes. A large number of additional newspapers are represented in the clippings on the strike included in Vol. XII of the Frank Murphy Scrapbooks in the Michigan Historical Collections.

Published and Unpublished Government Documents

The Flint Fisher Body No. 1 strike of 1930 is the subject of testimony in House Special Committee to Investigate Communist Activities in the United States, *Investigation of Communist Propaganda, Hearings Pursuant to H.*

Res. 220, 71 Cong., 2 Sess. (Washington, 1930), Part IV, Volume I. The Communist role in the sit-down strikes in Michigan is exaggerated in House Special Committee on Un-American Activities, *Investigation of Un-American Propaganda Activities in the United States, Hearings Pursuant to H. Res. 282,* 75 Cong., 3 Sess. (Washington, 1938), 4 vols. The testimony of John Barringer and Judge Paul V. Gadola in the hearings helps to explain the part that they played in the Flint strike. GM's labor practices and particularly its use of espionage are explored in Subcommittee of the Senate Committee on Education and Labor, *Violations of Free Speech and Rights of Labor, Hearings Pursuant to S. Res. 266,* 75 Cong., 1 Sess., Parts 5–7 (Washington, 1937), 76 Cong., 1 Sess., Part 45 (Washington, 1939); Senate Committee on Education and Labor, *Violations of Free Speech and Rights of Labor,* 75 Cong., 2 Sess., *Report No. 46,* Part 3 (Washington, 1937); and, to a much lesser extent, in Senate Committee on Education and Labor, *Violations of Free Speech and Rights of Labor,* 76 Cong., 1 Sess., *Senate Report No. 6,* Part 3 (Washington, 1939). GM profit figures and an account of the growth of the corporation are included in Federal Trade Commission, *Report on Motor Vehicle Industry,* 76 Cong., 1 Sess., *House Doc. No. 468* (Washington, 1939).

The Automobile Manufacturers Association presented its version of the sit-down strikes in Senate Committee on Education and Labor, *National Labor Relations Act and Proposed Amendments, Hearings on S.1000 . . . ,* 76 Cong., 1 Sess. (Washington, 1939), Part 13, pp. 2445–87 (reprinted by the AMA in pamphlet form with the title *Sit-Down*). Murphy defended his role in the strike in Subcommittee of the Senate Committee on the Judiciary, *Nomination of Frank Murphy,* 76 Cong., 1 Sess. (Washington, 1939). Aspects of the strike in Anderson are dealt with in *Decisions and Orders of the National Labor Relations Board,* XIV (Washington, 1940), 113–68.

The relief and welfare problem in Flint and Genesee County as the result of the depression and the GM sit-down is set forth in the three Annual Reports of the Flint Public Welfare Board for the period May 1, 1933–June 30, 1936; the Bi-Annual Report and the Second Annual Report (Neighbors on Relief) of the Genesee County Welfare Relief Commission, covering the period November 1, 1933–June 30, 1936; and in the following three reports of the State Emergency Welfare Relief Commission: William Haber and Paul L. Stanchfield, *Unemployment and Relief in Michigan* (Lansing, 1935); Haber and Stanchfield, *Unemployment, Relief and Economic Security* (Lansing, 1936); and George F. Granger and Lawrence R. Klein, *Emergency Relief in Michigan, 1933–1939* (Lansing, 1939).

There is a great deal of valuable statistical information on Flint's labor force in general and its automobile workers in particular in State Emergency Welfare Relief Commission, *Michigan Census of Population and Unemployment, Employment and Unemployment Statistics,* First Series, Numbers 1–9 (Lansing, 1936–37). The decisions taken by the Flint City Commission during the strike period but not the substance of its debates can be followed in *Flint City Commission Proceedings,* V (April 6, 1936–July 2, 1937).

Miscellaneous Unpublished Sources

GM explained its industrial-relations policy to its supervisory personnel before, during, and after the strike in the materials prepared for its executive training program, copies of which are available in the General Motors Institute in Flint. [Paul Garrett], "The Focal Point of Public Relations" [1936], a copy of which is located in the Automotive History Collection of the Detroit Public Library, explains how GM's public relations could be made to serve the corporation's industrial-relations goals.

Industrial relations in the automobile industry before the sit-down are the subject of two first-rate studies by William Ellison Chalmers, "Labor in the Automobile Industry: A Study of Personnel Policies, Workers Attitudes, and Attempts at Unionism" (Ph.D. thesis, University of Wisconsin, 1932), and "Collective Bargaining in the Automobile Industry" [1935], a copy of which is in the Littauer Industrial Relations Library of Harvard University. George Douglas Blackwood, "The United Automobile Workers of America, 1935–51" (Ph.D. thesis, University of Chicago, 1951), includes a chapter on the sit-down strike; and Jack William Skeels, "The Development of Political Stability within the United Auto Workers Union" (Ph.D. thesis, University of Wisconsin, 1957), is concerned with the problem of factionalism in the UAW. The reaction of the various branches of the federal, state, and local governments to the sit-down strikes is described in Walter L. Eisenberg, "Government Policy in Sitdown Strikes" (Ph.D. thesis, Columbia University, 1959). There is a brief account of John Brophy's role in the GM strike in M. Camilla Mullay, "John Brophy: Labor Leader and Reformer: The CIO Years" (Ph.D. thesis, Catholic University, 1966).

There are valuable studies of the composition of Flint's population and of the city's housing and health problems in the 1930's in Flint Institute of Research and Planning, Compiled Studies [1936–1938]. Erdmann D. Beynon, "Characteristics of the Relief Case Load in Genesee County, Michigan" (Flint, 1940), provides important demographic data not elsewhere available. William H. Chafe, "The Good Years: The Great Depression in Flint" (MS, 1967), copy in my possession, stresses the innovative effects of the depression in Flint. The history of GM in Flint is traced in [Frank Rodolf], "An Industrial History of Flint" (MS, Flint *Journal*, 1949), an interesting but undocumented study. Pierce F. Lewis, "Geography in the Politics of Flint" (Ph.D. thesis, University of Michigan, 1958), relates voting behavior to residential patterns; and Harold F. Sylvester, "City Management: The Flint Experiment, 1930–1937" (Ph.D. thesis, Johns Hopkins University, 1938), focuses on the turbulent early history of the city-manager plan in Flint. Winston Wessels, "Importance #1: The Michigan National Guard and the 1937 Flint Sit-Down Strike" (MS, 1963), in my possession, evaluates the role of the National Guard in Flint.

Miscellaneous Published Sources

The most valuable and most detailed published account of the strike is Henry Kraus, *The Many and the Few: A Chronicle of the Dynamic Auto Workers* (Los Angeles, 1947). Kraus, a participant in the strike as editor of the Flint *Auto Worker*, recaptures the atmosphere of the sit-down in Flint, but his predilections have unduly colored some of his judgments, and his recounting of strike events is not always accurate. The book is undocumented, although, as the Kraus Papers indicate, the author did a considerable amount of research on some aspects of the strike. *The Many and the Few* is at its best in dealing with the ebb and flow of the battle in Flint, at its weakest in dealing with strike negotiations.

Bibliographical Note

Thomas A. Karman, "The Flint Sit-Down Strike," *Michigan History*, XLVI (June 1962), 97–125; (September 1962), 223–50, is a superficial account of the strike in Flint based almost entirely on the Flint *Journal* and the Grand Rapids *Press*. Paul Gallico's novelette, "Sit-Down Strike," *Cosmopolitan*, CIV (April 1938), [155–80], although a work of fiction, contains some shrewd insights into the Flint sit-down based on the author's own observations in the city during the strike. William Weinstone, *The Great Sit-Down Strike* (New York, 1937), is an analysis of the strike by the Michigan secretary of the Communist party, who was in touch with events in Flint. Joel Seidman's *"Sit-Down"* (New York, 1937), published for the Educational Department of the UAW, has a brief account of the Flint strike and of the history of the sit-down tactic.

There are two lively chapters on the sit-down era in Edward Levinson, *Labor on the March* (University Books; New York, 1956), written from a UAW and CIO point of view. Walter Galenson has a fine chapter on the UAW from 1935 to 1941 in *The CIO Challenge to the AFL: A History of the American Labor Movement, 1935–1941* (Cambridge, Mass., 1960), but his account of the GM strike is unexceptional. There is a sympathetic chapter on the UAW in the 1930's in Herbert Harris, *American Labor* (New Haven, 1939), an evaluation of some of the strike leaders in Benjamin Stolberg, *The Story of the CIO* (New York, 1938), and some brief comments on the strike in Sidney Lens, *Left, Right and Center: Conflicting Forces in American Labor* (Hinsdale, Ill., 1949). David Brody's chapter, "The Emergence of Mass-Production Unionism," in John Braeman *et al.*, eds., *Change and Continuity in Twentieth-Century America* (Harper Colophon Books; New York, 1966), helps to explain the unionization of the automobile and other mass-production industries in the 1930's. Sidney Fine, *The Automobile under the Blue Eagle* (Ann Arbor, 1963), is concerned with industrial relations in the automobile industry from 1933 to 1935.

The Italian occupation strikes of 1919–1920 are described and analyzed in Daniel L. Horowitz, *The Italian Labor Movement* (Cambridge, Mass., 1963), and Maurice F. Neufeld, *Italy . . . The Italian Labor Movement in Its Political, Social, and Economic Setting from 1800 to 1960* (Ithaca, 1961). Salomon Schwarz, "Les Occupations d'Usines en France de Mai et Juin 1936," *International Review for Social History*, II (1937), 50–104; Henry W. Ehrmann, *French Labor from Popular Front to Liberation* (New York, 1947); Val R. Lorwin, *The French Labor Movement* (Cambridge, Mass., 1954); and Joel Colton, *Léon Blum* (New York, 1966), are basic for an understanding of the course of the sit-down strikes in France in 1936. The Goodyear strike of 1936 is treated in Ruth McKenney, *Industrial Valley* (New York, 1939), and Harold Selig Roberts, *The Rubber Workers* (New York, 1944), but neither account is entirely satisfactory.

Some of the participants in the GM sit-down strike published descriptions of the affair. Rose Pesotta, *Bread upon the Waters* (Edited by John Nicholas Beffel; New York, 1944), includes a chapter on the Goodyear strike and another on the Flint sit-down, written by a CIO organizer who took part in both strikes. The writer Mary Heaton Vorse recorded her impressions of what she saw in Flint in *Labor's New Millions* (New York, 1938). Some of John Brophy's recollections of the strike are included in *A Miner's Life* (Edited and supplemented by John O. P. Hall, Madison, 1966). In a *Report* (August 23, 1937) to the second annual convention of the UAW,

Wyndham Mortimer provided an account of his organizing efforts in Flint and of the origins of the strike in Cleveland and Flint; and John L. Lewis reported briefly on his part in the strike in *Proceedings of the Fifth Annual Convention of the International Union, United Automobile Workers of America, 1940* (n.p., n.d.). Claude E. Hoffman, who was one of the sit-downers in the Guide Lamp plant, provides an account of the strike in Anderson in *Sit-Down in Anderson: UAW Local 663, Anderson, Indiana* (Detroit, 1968).

Donaldson Brown comments briefly on the strike negotiations in *Some Reminiscences of an Industrialist* (n.p., 1957). There is a good deal of information on the history and policies of GM but very little on the sit-down in Alfred P. Sloan, Jr., *My Years with General Motors* (Edited by John McDonald with Catharine Stevens; Garden City, New York, 1964). *The Story of the General Motors Strike* (New York, 1937), is Sloan's report on the strike to GM's stockholders. Sloan is treated in an interesting and sympathetic manner in "Alfred P. Sloan Jr.: Chairman," *Fortune*, XVII (April 1938), 73–77+. Frances Perkins in *The Roosevelt I Knew* (Harper Colophon Books; New York, 1964), comments briefly on President Roosevelt's and her own part in the strike negotiations.

In his biography *John L. Lewis* (New York, 1939), Saul Alinsky describes Lewis' role in the strike, primarily on the basis of interviews with the CIO leader and Pressman, but the account is a mixture of fact and fiction. There is a far briefer and less dramatic version of Lewis and the sit-down in James Wechsler, *Labor Baron: A Portrait of John L. Lewis* (New York, 1944). Murray Kempton's *Part of Our Time* (New York, 1955), has an interesting chapter on the Reuther brothers, and there is a brief treatment of the sit-down in Irving Howe and B. J. Widick, *The UAW and Walter Reuther* (New York, 1949).

Norman Beasley's *Knudsen* (New York, 1947), is an undocumented biography that must be used with great caution. There is an interesting "profile" of Knudsen, written by Matthew Josephson in the *New Yorker*, XVII (March 8, 1941), 22–26+; (March 15, 1941), 26–30+; (March 22, 1941), 24–28+. Josephson also deals with Sidney Hillman's behind-the-scenes part in the strike in *Sidney Hillman* (Garden City, New York, 1952). J. Woodford Howard, Jr.'s article "Frank Murphy and the Sit-Down Strikes of 1937," *Labor History*, I (Spring, 1960), 103–40, deals sympathetically with the key public official involved in the GM and the later sit-downs in Michigan. Howard's thoughtful biography of Murphy, *Mr. Justice Murphy: A Political Biography* (Princeton, 1968), contains an account of the strike that is marred by several factual errors and incorrectly concludes that John L. Lewis and Murphy were referring to different meetings in their clashing versions of the famous confrontation between the two men on February 9, 1937. There is a thinly researched chapter on the GM strike in Richard D. Lunt's biography of Murphy to 1940, *The High Ministry of Government: The Political Career of Frank Murphy* (Detroit, 1965). Sidney Fine, "The General Motors Sit-Down Strike: A Re-examination," *American Historical Review*, LXX (April 1965), 691–713, which focuses on the strike negotiations, was the first treatment of the strike based, among other sources, on the Murphy Papers.

The best general histories of the automobile industry are John B. Rae, *American Automobile Manufacturers: The First Forty Years* (Philadelphia,

Bibliographical Note

1959), and the same author's *The American Automobile* (Chicago, 1965). The standard but somewhat superficial history of GM before the New Deal is Arthur Pound, *The Turning Wheel: The Story of General Motors through Twenty-Five Years, 1908–1933* (Garden City, New York, 1934). There is an interesting and revealing analysis of the corporation in a four-part series in *Fortune*: "General Motors I," XVIII (December 1938), 41–47+; "General Motors II: Chevrolet," XIX (January 1939), 37–46+; "General Motors III: Sales," XIX (February 1939), 71–78+; "General Motors IV: A Unit of Society," XIX (March 1939), 45–52+. There is considerable information on GM and its divisions in the Flint *Journal*, July 9, 1936 (Progress Edition), November 22, 1954 (Souvenir Edition), and September 4, 1955 (Centennial Edition). The *Annual Reports* of the corporation are valuable for the statistics that they contain and for information on GM's program of welfare capitalism in the 1920's and 1930's. The best account of Sloan's plan of organization for GM is contained in Alfred M. Chandler, Jr., *Strategy and Structure: Chapters in the History of the Industrial Enterprise* (Cambridge, Mass., 1962). Frederick H. Harbison and Robert Dubin, *Patterns of Union-Management Relations* (Chicago, 1947), indicates the long-range effects of the sit-down on the "pattern" of GM-UAW relations. The activities of the Special Conference Committee are briefly considered in Robert Ozanne, *A Century of Labor-Management Relations at McCormick and International Harvester* (Madison, 1967).

There is, lamentably, no adequate published or unpublished history of Flint. Carl Crow's *The City of Flint Grows Up* (New York, 1945), is primarily concerned with the Buick Division, which financed the book's publication. Aspects of the history of the city are described superficially in the three special issues of the Flint *Journal* noted above. Flint ("Micmac") at the outset of the depression of 1929 and following is the setting for the major portion of Catharine Brody's novel, *Nobody Starves* (London, 1932), which includes some observations on the life of the auto worker in a company town.

William H. McPherson, *Labor Relations in the Automobile Industry* (Washington, 1940), and McPherson and Anthony Lucheck, "Automobiles," in Twentieth Century Fund, *How Collective Bargaining Works* (New York, 1942), are mainly concerned with collective-bargaining issues in the automobile industry but also provide some information on the structure of the industry and the development of automobile unionism. Robert Blauner, *Alienation and Freedom: The Factory Worker and His Industry* (Chicago, 1964), is concerned, inter alia, with the alienation of the assembly-line worker in the automobile industry. Clayton W. Fountain, *Union Guy* (New York, 1946), includes comments on working conditions in the automobile industry in the 1930's by a one-time GM worker. Several of the chapters in Arthur Kornhauser *et al.*, eds., *Industrial Conflict* (New York, 1954), and George W. Hartmann and Theodore Newcomb, eds., *Industrial Conflict: A Psychological Interpretation* (New York, 1939), provide perspectives for the evaluation of the GM strike. The results of public-opinion polls on the sit-down strikes are summarized in Hadley Cantril, ed., *Public Opinion, 1935–1946* (Princeton, 1951). The concept of "creative disorder" is developed in Arthur I. Waskow, *From Race Riot to Sit-In, 1919 and the 1960's* (Anchor Books; New York, 1966).

The La Follette Committee's support of the UAW before, during, and after the strike is revealed in Jerold S. Auerbach's excellent study, *Labor and Liberty: The La Follette Committee and the New Deal* (Indianapolis, 1966). There is some material on the Dies Committee's investigation of the sit-down in August Raymond Ogden's *The Dies Committee: A Study of the Special House Committee for the Investigation of Un-American Activities, 1938–1943* (Washington, 1943), and in Walter Goodman, *The Committee* (New York, 1968); and Dies himself reports an alleged confession of error by Murphy in *Martin Dies' Story* (New York, 1963). The Congressional reaction to the sit-down is considered in the context of growing conservative opposition to the New Deal in James T. Patterson, *Congressional Conservatism and the New Deal: The Growth of the Conservative Coalition in Congress, 1933–1939* (Lexington, 1967). Bascom N. Timmons, in *Garner of Texas* (New York, 1948), notes Garner's opposition to the sit-down tactic but seems unaware of the vice-president's initial approval of Murphy's role in the GM strike.

Index

(The superior figures indicate notes on the pages specified.)

AC Spark Plug Division, 101, 107, 119, 245, 259; unionism in, 73
Adamic, Louis, 139
Adams, Edgar T., 1
Addes, George, 90, 94, 140, 194, 250
Addison, Chris, 301
Adrian *Daily Telegram*, 337
Alexandria (Indiana), 214, 215, 216, 314
Alinsky, Saul, 299–300, 379[24], 407[108]
Allen, Ben, 114
Aluminum Co. of America: sit-down in, 130–31
Amalgamated Association of Street Electric Railway and Motor Coach Employees of America, 117
Amalgamated Clothing Workers, 91, 204, 217–18
American Bar Association, 194–95
American Civil Liberties Union, 236; and Murphy, 149, 154, 218, 370[91]; on legality of sit-down, 176, 294, 387[68]; on Black and Gadola injunctions, 193, 218; and aid to UAW, 218; and Anderson, 218, 316
American Federation of Labor, 30, 35, 39, 43, 49, 64, 84, 89, 99, 110, 113, 147, 152–53, 220, 233; GM view of, 29; and collective bargaining, 31; and discrimination, 36; and company unions, 45, 47, 52; boycott of ALB elections by, 45, 48; on representation, 48, 183, 184, 185, 289–90, 307, 330; and efforts to organize automobile industry, 63–64, 66–72; and jurisdiction of UAW, 63–64, 68–69, 77, 79, 80–81, 81–82, 85–86, 87; and March, 1934, strike movement, 72–73; and April, 1934, strike, 73–74; and 1935 strike movement, 74–75; and Toledo Chevrolet strike of 1935, 75–76; and an auto international union, 77, 79–81; 1934 convention of, 80; progressive criticism of, 81; and UAW constitutional convention, 81–82; 1935 convention of, 82, 87; and Motor Products strike, 83–84; and UAW South Bend convention, 91; intervention of in GM strike, 183–85, 238, 289–90, 330, 378[15]; Metal Trades Department of, 183–84, 185, 290, 307; Building Trades Department of, 183–84, 185, 290, 307; and February 11 settlement, 307; and CIO, 307, 330–31, 340; and sit-down strikes, 331
American Federationist, 76
American Legion, 201–2, 282, 404[84]
American Liberty League, 91, 95–96, 246
American Newspaper Guild, 163, 172
American Workers party, 75
Anderson, Harry W., 28, 62; and espionage, 42, 196, 349[73]; and Atlanta strike, 137; and Frey, 184
Anderson, John, 90, 94, 130
Anderson (Indiana), 56, 58–59, 95, 146, 148, 186, 218, 219, 262; unionism in, 98, 313; violence in, 196, 213–14, 258, 261, 266, 313; GM influence in, 211–12, 214, 216; reaction in to strike, 212–13; and Citizens League for Industrial Security, 212; strike victory celebration in, 313–14, 409[1]; and Gold Band Tavern affair, 314–15, 316; martial law in, 315–16; industrial relations in after strike, 316–17
Associated Automobile Workers of America, 71–72; merger of with UAW, 90
Atkins, R. M., 229, 236
Atlanta Chevrolet, 75, 135
Atlanta Fisher Body, 75, 77, 134
Atlanta Fisher Body and Chevrolet strike, 138, 140, 144, 210–11, 305, 367[37, 42], 407[123]; background of,

427

Atlanta Fisher Body and
Chevrolet strike *(Cont.)*
134; beginning and spread of, 134–36; and UAW efforts to settle, 137–38
Atwood, J. B., and Co., 100
Auto Vim and Power Co., 15
Auto Workers Union, 64–65, 116, 222; and Fisher Body No. 1 strike (1930), 65, 66
Automobile Labor Board, 31, 35, 37; and April, 1934, strike, 32; and representation, 33, 50, 181; seniority rules of, 31, 34, 50, 60, 182, 183, 324; and discrimination, 36; elections of, 45, 47, 48, 49, 350[87]; bargaining agencies of, 47, 51–52, 72, 262
Automobile Manufacturers Association, 27–28, 54, 353[20]
Automotive Industrial Workers' Association, 71–72; and Motor Products strike, 83, 84; and merger with UAW, 84, 86, 90
Automotive Industries, 225

Bailey, Stephen K., 333
Baldwin, Harry, 215, 216, 409[1]; and Guide Lamp evacuation, 251; and post-strike events in Anderson, 313, 315
Baldwin, Roger, 154, 316, 370[91]
Barclay, Hartley W.: on Flint auto workers, 61; on GM wage payment methods, 62; on hours in GM, 62, 182; on Fisher Body No. 2 sit-down, 156, 166, 171
Barringer, John, 108; and Battle of the Running Bulls, 9, 12, 13, 344–45[23]; career of, 106–7, 361[21]; and UAW, 118, 226; and violence of January 7, 227; and demonstration of February 3, 281; and civilian police reserve, 281–84, 318; dismissal of, 318; criticism of Murphy by, 337
Battle Creek *Enquirer and Evening News*, 250–51
Battle of the Running Bulls, 1–13, 167, 169, 172, 186, 188, 196, 201, 207, 210, 224, 226, 227, 231, 234, 237, 239, 242, 246, 284, 318, 343, 344–45
Bay City (Michigan): violence in, 197–98
Beckman, Charles K., 369[63]
Begole, Fox and Co., 100, 101
Bendix Products Corporation: unionism in, 67; 1936 sit-down strike in, 97, 128–29, 132–33, 365[15, 18]; company union in, 128–29
Bennett, Harry, 385[39]
Bersey, John S., 9, 10, 243, 271, 272, 286, 295, 298, 319, 320
Bishop, Merlin, 95, 147, 221, 227; and Kelsey-Hayes sit-down, 132; and singing, 163; and education in Flint sit-downs, 165; and plan to seize Chevrolet No. 4, 269, 270; arrest of, 272
Bittner, Van A., 330
Black, Edward D., 106, 240; injunction of, 193–95, 198, 218, 219, 235, 236, 263, 276, 277, 381[45]
Black, John D., 211
Black, William H., 211
Black Legion, 109
Blackwood, George Douglas, 398[5]
Blanding Albert H., 319, 409[19]
Blauner, Robert, 55
Blum, Léon: and French sit-downs, 126–27
Bohn Aluminum and Brass Corporation: sit-down in, 131, 208
Bowles, Charles, 152
Boysen, George E., 187–88, 189, 224, 240, 312, 379[24]; and January 15 truce, 252–54 *passim*; and resumption of work at Flint Chevrolet, 260–63 *passim*; and civilian police reserve, 282
Bradshaw, Harold, 226; and Battle of the Running Bulls, 9–10; career of, 108; UAW opposition to, 118; and resumption of work at Flint Chevrolet, 260, 261; and seizure of Chevrolet No. 4, 271; and demonstration of February 3, 281; and civilian police reserve, 281, 282–83, 284; emergency powers of, 284; on Michigan National Guard, 319
Brickner, Barnett R., 219

Index

429

Briggs Manufacturing Co., 129; 1933 strike in, 112, 153, 154, 203; 1937 strike in, 207, 385[39]
Briscoe, Benjamin, 15, 16
Briscoe, Frank, 15
Brody, Catherine, 106, 107
Brookwood Labor College, 95, 113, 132, 162, 163, 205
Brophy, John, 125, 126, 139, 194, 237, 239, 279, 286, 398[5]; and UAW organizing campaign of 1935–36, 84, 85, 86, 96–97, 139; and aid to UAW in strike, 217, 218; and strike negotiations, 232, 247–49; and January 15 truce, 249, 253; on Sloan, 256; and seizure of Chevrolet No. 4, 267, 272–73; and demonstration of February 3, 281; and victory celebration, 312; and March 12 contract, 325–26
Browder, Earl, 222
Brown, Donaldson, 178; and strike negotiations, 231, 232, 247–48, 255, 257, 286, 287, 300, 302–3, 407[121]; and Sloan, 231–32
Buick, David Dunbar, 14–16
Buick Division, 17, 18, 21, 25, 31, 73, 101, 107, 108, 112, 140, 143, 144, 187, 188, 189, 190, 245, 259, 261, 262, 284; history of, 14–16; company union in, 43; and speed-up, 56, 57; unionism in, 72, 119, 169; and Toledo Chevrolet strike of 1935, 75–76; post-settlement sit-down in, 322
Buick News, 108
Bully, Norman, 169, 202, 327
Burke, F. L., 213
Burton, Harold, 143
Business Week, 12, 230
Byrnes, James F., 334

Cadillac Division, 16, 18, 21, 146, 210
Cadillac strike, 146, 201, 242, 407[123]; kangaroo court in, 159; and Flint strike, 207; origin of, 209; violence in, 210; and January 15 truce, 249; and evacuation of plant, 251, 252
Carney, Joseph, 212, 216, 313
Carney, William, 130, 221, 241

Carriage, Wagon and Automobile Workers' International Union, 63–64, 66
Carriage and Wagon Workers' International Union, 63
Catholic Worker, 235
Central Conference of American Rabbis, 219
Chambers, Whittaker, 114
Champion, Albert, 101
Chaplin, Charles, 56
Chevrolet, Louis, 17
Chevrolet Division, 21, 37, 38, 58, 67, 73, 101, 140, 141, 144, 186, 226, 261; origin of, 17; and Knudsen, 20; espionage in, 38, 42, 349[73]; company unions in, 44; and wages, 61; plant police of, 266, 267. *See also* General Motors Corporation and individual Chevrolet plants
Chevrolet Gear and Axle plant, 46, 60, 186, 263
Chevrolet No. 4 sit-down strike, 57, 146, 147, 201, 209, 210, 229, 231, 232, 310, 407[123]; sense of community in, 157; and feeding of strikers, 161, 296, 272–73; sleeping arrangements in, 162; recreation and entertainment in, 162, 163–64; sanitary and safety arrangements in, 166; morale in, 168, 171, 172–74, 295; and utility service, 172–73, 301; and Emergency Brigade, 201; and plan to seize plant, 266–68, 398[5]; and seizure of plant, 269–71, 273, 285, 310; and cordon guard, 271–74, 296, 400[27]; and outsiders, 273; and Gadola injunction, 276, 400[31]; and Lenz plan to recapture plant, 301, 319; and evacuation of plant, 312; and number of strikers, 312, 405[88]; espionage in, 381[50]
Chrysler, Walter, 108, 155, 191, 209, 328
Chrysler Corporation, 71, 72, 90, 95, 129, 133, 139, 155, 207, 250, 305, 310; glass supply of, 97, 209; unionism in, 130; and GM strike, 191–92, 209; sit-down strike in, 255, 328, 336

Citroen, 126
Civil-rights movement: and sit-down strikes, 338–40
Civil Works Administration, 104
Cleveland: automobile unionism in, 79, 81, 84–85, 91, 98; and Cleveland Auto Council, 79, 85, 87, 124, 143
Cleveland Federation of Labor, 185
Cleveland Fisher Body, 69, 261, 309; importance of to GM, 32, 73, 141; April, 1934, strike in, 32, 53, 73–74, 98, 141, 142; unionism in, 33, 75; company union in, 43, 45; and 1935 strike movement, 74; post-settlement sit-down in, 322
Cleveland Fisher Body strike (1936–37), 146, 183, 202, 247, 259, 407[123]; origin of, 141–43, 147, 368–69[61, 63, 64]; and evacuation of plant, 144, 369[70]; AFL intervention in, 183–84; and loyalty movement, 186; and relief, 203, 211; and picketing of plant, 211; injunction against, 276–77, 304
Cleveland *Plain Dealer*, 144, 309
Cogwill, Ella Lee, 203, 204
Colladay, Thomas, 9, 245, 271, 393[23]
Collective bargaining, 47, 48, 165, 174, 176, 232, 247, 250, 288, 335; and GM, 28, 30–31, 32–33, 33–35, 48–49, 50, 51, 53, 76, 140, 178, 179, 183, 237, 239, 248, 252, 253–54, 255, 326, 412[38]; and AFL, 31; and President's settlement, 31; and UAW, 97, 140, 144, 180–81, 183, 199, 248, 287; and Knudsen, 138–39, 144, 179–80, 231, 254, 378[3]; and Lewis, 139, 140; and Martin, 140; and January 15 truce, 249–50; and Flint Alliance, 252, 254; and February 11 settlement, 304–5, 307, 309; and March 12 contract, 323–24, 325; and Murphy, 335. *See also* Representation
Collins, William, 66, 70–71, 77, 110; on craft unionism, 68; and use of strike, 69–70; and March, 1934, strike movement, 72; and April, 1934, strike, 73–74

Columbia University: and student sit-in, 340–41
Committee for Industrial Organization, 9, 67, 72, 82, 88, 91, 96, 99, 103, 110, 185, 191, 194, 206, 220, 221, 222, 230, 233, 256, 263, 267, 285, 291, 299, 303, 307, 311, 318, 334, 335; and UAW organizing campaign of 1935–36, 84–87, 93, 96–97, 358[102]; and Martin, 84–85, 93, 94, 96, 137, 217; and South Bend convention, 91; and sit-down strikes, 123, 139, 331; and Goodyear strike, 123, 124, 125; and Bendix strike, 128, 129; and Kelsey-Hayes and Midland strikes, 132; and origins of GM strike, 137, 139, 146–47, 148; role of in GM strike, 169–70, 199, 204, 205, 208–10, 217–18, 240, 248, 254, 287, 304, 311; and Gadola injunction, 278; effect of GM strike on, 310, 329–30; and AFL, 307, 330–31, 340. *See also* Lewis, John L.
Communism and Communists, 40, 81, 194, 334; and AWU, 64–65, 116, 222; and UAW, 64–65, 79, 82, 89, 90, 91, 93–94, 109–10, 111, 220, 357[83]; and Fisher Body No. 1 strike of 1930, 65, 66; and Toledo Chevrolet strike of 1935, 76; and auto international, 79–80, 220, 222; and Harold Ware group, 114, 222; and Italian sit-downs, 123; and French sit-downs, 127; role of in GM strike, 127, 130, 190–91, 220, 221–23, 226, 229, 262, 263, 284, 298, 320, 337, 338; and Midland strike, 130; and Unity Caucus, 329
Communist League of America, 75
Confédération Générale de la Production Française, 126
Confédération Générale du Travail, 125
Conference for the Protection of Civil Rights, 218–19, 220, 236
Congress of Racial Equality, 339
Connery, William L., 333
Contemporary Theater (Detroit), 162
Cook, Ray, 161

Corporations Auxiliary Co., 38, 41, 115, 224
Cranefield, Harold, 223, 224, 321
Crapo, Henry H., 14, 100
Crawford, Fred L., 187
"Creative disorder": in civil-rights movement and sit-down strikes, 339–40
Cronk, Ed, 268, 269–70
Cudner, Arthur, 189
Cullen, H. D., 198, 223, 224; and Flint Alliance, 260, 261, 262
Curtice, Harlow, 189
Cuyahoga County Relief Administration, 203
C V S Manufacturing Co., 187

Daily Worker, 117, 130, 133, 162, 220
Daniels, Josephus, 308
Davey, Martin, 124
Davidow, Larry, 194, 221, 237
Davis, Elmer, 141, 142
Dayton Engineering Laboratories, 17
DeCaux, Len, 205
Delco-Remy Division, 211–12, 317, 349[63]; company union in, 42, 45; and NLRB, 183, 213, 214, 388[85]; shutdown of, 212; conditions in after reopening, 213, 214, 215. *See also* Anderson and Guide Lamp strike
Detroit, 7, 9, 14, 18, 61, 66, 77, 79, 81, 83, 84, 85, 91, 94, 100, 104, 114, 136, 152, 153, 154, 155, 169, 187, 192, 205, 207, 209, 210, 213, 217, 243, 253, 262, 263, 264, 270, 279, 281, 285, 288, 298, 299, 304, 323, 327, 330, 385[39]; automobile unionism in, 39, 64, 67, 68, 69, 88, 90, 124; automobile workers of, 54, 70, 102–3; Employers' Association of, 68; union membership in, 71–72, 75, 85, 89–90, 95, 98; sit-down strikes in, 129–32, 161, 209–10, 333, 336; Recorder's Court of, 148, 150, 151, 152, 222, 286, 302, 303; Free Employment Bureau of, 153
Detroit and Wayne County Federation of Labor, 9, 87, 185; and Murphy, 152, 155

Detroit Athletic Club, 161
Detroit Federation of Musicians, 251
Detroit Gear plant, 90
Detroit *Labor News*, 154
Detroit *News*, 7, 250, 283, 331
Detroit *Times*, 5
Devitt, Joe, 116, 295; and Fisher Body No. 1 sit-down, 158, 171–72, 373[17]
Dewey, James F., 237, 254, 286, 297, 298, 303, 407[21]
Dies, Martin, 221; and sit-down strikes, 335; and Murphy, 335, 337–38, 409[141]; and Roosevelt, 337–38
Dies Committee, 79, 221, 318; investigation of sit-down strikes by, 337–38, 344–45[23], 414[69]; and Roosevelt, 337–38
Dillon, Francis, 39, 66, 73, 110, 220; and collective bargaining with GM, 35, 76; and use of the strike, 69–70; and Toledo Chevrolet strike of 1935, 75–76; and UAW constitutional convention, 81, 82–83; and GEB, 83; and chartering of Toledo locals, 83; and Motor Products strike, 83–84, 88; and Martin and Hall, 84, 87–88; and Germer, 85–86, 356[77]; and South Bend convention, 89, 90
Ditzel, Joseph B., 197–98, 221, 264
Dodge Brothers Corporation, 72, 129; seniority in, 95, 96; unionism in, 130, 210
Dort, J. Dallas, 14, 101
Dubinsky, David, 82
DuBrul, Stephen M., 178–79, 259, 303
Dubuc, Arthur G., 39–41, 195
Dunckel-Baldwin Act, 177, 277
Dunn, Cecil, 314–15
Du Pont, Pierre S., 19, 20
Du Pont, T. Coleman, 231
Du Pont Co., 19, 133, 206, 230, 291
Durant, William Crapo, 14, 15, 16–17, 19, 101
Durant-Dort Carriage Co., 14, 101
Durant Motors, 18

Edward, Stanley, 170
Eisenberg, Walter, 294
Ellender, Allen J., 334
Emergency Peace Campaign, 113

Ernst, Morris L., 370[91]
Espionage, 70, 335; and GM, 36, 37–42, 97, 109, 113, 114–15, 195–96, 217, 224, 333, 349[63, 66, 73], 381[50]
Evanoff, Michael, 226

Fansteel Metallurgical Corporation, 176
Farm Equipment Workers Union, 222
Faye, Eugene, 165, 206
Federal Bureau of Investigation, 216
Federal Council of the Churches of Christ, 56, 178, 187, 219
Federal Emergency Relief Administration, 104, 113
Federal Theater Project, 163
Federal Trade Commission, 20
Federated Press, 205
Federation of Flat Glass Workers, 97, 138, 199
Federoff, Anthony, 197–98
Fiat, 174
Financial Observer, 341
Findlater, W. G., 318
Firestone Tire and Rubber Co., 123
Fisher, Alfred J., 8
Fisher, Charles T., 18, 44
Fisher, Edward F., 18
Fisher, Fred J., 18
Fisher, Lawrence P., 18, 155, 236, 285, 396–97[86]
Fisher, William A., 18
Fisher Body Division, 20, 43, 62, 64, 67, 119, 134, 140, 141, 155, 170, 175, 177, 317, 369[73]; plant police of, 1–3, 3–4, 7, 11, 12, 240, 343[4]; origin of, 18–19; and April, 1934, strike, 32–33, 48, 73–74; and espionage, 38, 42, 349[73]; and company unionism, 44; strikes in before 1933, 65. *See also* General Motors Corporation and individual Fisher Body plants
Fisher Body No. 1, 73, 107, 113, 144, 193, 245, 255, 261, 295, 309, 321, 328; establishment of, 18–19, 101, 102; unionism in, 31, 115, 116, 117, 118–19; company union in, 45; and speed-up, 56; methods of wage payment in, 62; 1930 strike in, 65–66, 108, 141, 321; and March, 1934, strike movement, 72–73; importance of to GM, 73, 143; November, 1936, sit-down in, 97, 116–17, 118, 119; post-settlement sit-down in, 322, 323; May, 1934, strike in, 354[45]
Fisher Body No. 1 sit-down strike (1936–37), 156, 221, 227, 266, 268, 284–85, 293, 294, 310, 407[123]; and Battle of the Running Bulls, 1, 7, 12, 172; and number of strikers, 1, 168–69, 312, 405[88]; and defense preparations, 7, 165, 264, 295–96; origins of, 144–46, 147–48, 221, 238, 369[67]; and songs, 145; organization of, 156; administrative structure in, 157–58; police patrol in, 158; committees in, 158–59; and contact with outside, 159–60; kangaroo court in, 159, 160, 373[17]; punishable offenses in, 159–60; and visitors, 160–61, 219; and food, 161, 296; sleeping arrangements in, 161–62; recreation and entertainment in, 162, 163; sanitary arrangements in, 166; and damage to plant, 166–67, 375[40]; morale in, 170, 171–72, 396[76]; left-wingers in, 171–72, 222; and Black injunction, 193; espionage in, 195; and Conference for the Protection of Civil Rights, 219; and January 15 truce, 249, 250, 252, 253, 395[51]; sense of community in, 250; and Gadola injunction, 275–76, 277, 278; outsiders in, 279; and demonstration of February 3, 279–81, 283, 401[47]; and dancing outside, 283; and writ of attachment, **292, 293**; and evacuation of plant, 311–12
Fisher Body No. 2, 107, 144, 193, 245, 255, 261, 266, 272, 295, 321; location of, 1; output of, 1; employment in, 1; establishment of, 18, 101, 102; unionism in, 31, 117, 118–19; and superannuation, 52; company union in, 43, 45; and speed-up, 56, 57; method of wage payment in, 62; and March, 1934, strike movement, 72–73; manual labor in, 141

Index

433

Fisher Body No. 2 sit-down strike (1936–37), 57, 156, 174, 200, 260, 266, 310, 407[123]; and Battle of the Running Bulls, 1–13 *passim*, 227, 240; and food, 1, 3, 161, 296, 343[4]; and number of strikers, 12, 167, 168–69, 312, 405[88]; origins of, 144, 147; organization of, 156; and contact with outside, 159; sanitary and safety arrangements in, 166; morale in, 171, 396[76]; and Black injunction, 193; espionage in, 195; and January 15 truce, 249, 250, 252, 253; and defense plans, 264; and cordoning of plant, 274, 296; and Gadola injunction, 275–76, 278; and writ of attachment, 292; and evacuation of plant, 312; and demonstration of February 3, 401[47]

Fitzgerald, Frank, 137, 149, 337

Fleetwood strike, 146, 407[123]; and plant safety, 166; origin of, 209–10; and Flint strike, 207; and January 15 truce, 249; and evacuation of plant, 251

Flint, 1, 3, 5, 8, 10, 13, 28, 79, 91, 99, 113, 125, 142, 143, 144, 162, 169, 172, 180, 186, 189, 191, 192, 193, 198, 209, 223, 224, 235, 236, 263, 264, 265, 285, 293, 294, 337, 340, 341; police of, 1–13 *passim*, 65–66, 108, 114, 141, 159, 172, 192, 194, 196, 198, 226, 239, 242, 245, 269, 270, 278, 280, 284, 343[4], 344[9], 345[31], 398[12]; influence of GM in, 5, 11–12, 107–8, 136–37, 189, 195, 199–201, 219, 224, 226–28, 240, 273; opinion in about strike, 12, 187, 188, 190, 202, 225–26, 228–30, 280, 379[21]; lumber industry in, 14, 100; carriage industry in, 14, 25, 100–101; automobile industry in, 15, 17, 18–19, 23, 100, 101–2; 107; housing in, 23, 61, 102, 105–6, 110; and IMA, 25; espionage in, 38, 39–42, 109, 114–15, 195–96, 224; automobile unionism in, 39, 74, 108–9; UAW membership in, 41–42, 71, 72–73, 75, 85, 89, 98, 111, 117, 118, 119, 136, 188, 202, 207, 246, 266, 362[33], 384[30]; automobile workers in, 54, 56, 57, 58, 59, 61, 78, 102–5, 107, 118–19, 360[13]; and UAW organizing efforts in 1936, 95, 106, 107–8, 108–20, 132, 361–62[29], 362[30]; early history of, 100; population of, 101, 102–4, 105, 110; health conditions in, 102; Southern whites in, 103–4; and relief, 104–5, 202–4, 383[16, 19]; politics of, 106, 284, 318; city government of, 106–7; and city commission, 106, 108, 118, 226, 281, 283–84, 318, 389[94]; Civic League of, 107, 284; Methodist Episcopal church in, 107, 219, 229, 390[104]; Manufacturers' Association of, 108; bus strike in, 117–18, 317; pre-strike negotiations in, 144; strike organization in, 159, 165, 169, 170–71, 172, 173, 196, 204–5, 266, 278, 310; violence of January 7 in, 196–97, 226–27; Union War Veterans of, 201–2, 242–43; cost of strike in, 204; UAW strike publicity in, 204–7; and students, 205; free-speech forum in, 205–6; and presence of outsiders, 207–8; and use of automobile in strike in, 208; effect of strike on, 224–25, 259–60; Board of Education in, 227–28; Federation of Teachers in, 229; Chamber of Commerce of, 228, 244; arrest of strikers in, 241, 318, 393[28]; role of Michigan State Police in, 241–42; role of Michigan National Guard in, 242–46, 319; and January 15 truce, 250; and resumption of work at Chevrolet, 260–62; decline of striker morale in, 266; tension in, 274, 301; turmoil of February 3 in, 279–83, 401[47]; union celebration of strike victory in, 311–12; and Anderson, 314, 315–16; and Standard Cotton Products Co. strike, 317, 369[73]; post-strike events in, 317–19; Civil Service Commission of, 318, post-strike GM-UAW relations in, 321, 322–23; and Chrysler sit-down, 328; church membership in, 390[104]; ban of liquor in, 404–5[86]

Flint Alliance, 208, 217, 228, 238, 258, 298, 379–80[24, 25]; origin of, 187–88, 189–90; as a citizens' alliance, 188; support of, 188; and UAW, 188–89, 190, 200; and coercion, 190, 224; and January 15 truce, 252–54; on representation, 252; and collective bargaining, 252, 254; and resumption of work at Chevrolet, 260–62, 263, 397[93]; and Murphy, 263, 264; and civilian police reserve, 281, 282, 284

Flint *Auto Worker*, 114, 115, 130, 169, 175, 198, 204, 206, 242, 393[28]

Flint Automobile Co.: and Flint Roadster, 101

Flint Chevrolet, 19, 66, 72–73, 101, 102, 107, 108, 112, 119, 195, 245, 271, 272, 275, 301; No. 2, 1, 5; company union in, 43, 45; espionage in, 38, 39, 115; No. 10, 41; ALB bargaining agency in, 52, 283; and speed-up, 56, 57, 59; and superannuation, 59; method of wage payment in, 62; No. 4, 172, 266, 267, 295, 309, 322, 379[21], 398[8]; No. 9, 196–97, 267, 268, 269, 398[12]; resumption of work at, 260–62; No. 5, 266; No. 6, 268, 269–70; discrimination in, 268, 398[9]; plant police of, 269, 270, 301; post-strike labor relations in, 321; post-strike sit-downs in, 322–23; No. 8, 322

Flint Federation of Labor, 185

Flint *Journal*, 166, 228, 240, 242, 244, 250, 282; and Battle of the Running Bulls, 5, 344[10], 345[31]; and GM, 107–8; and Flint Alliance, 188, 189–90; and Murphy, 309

Flint Trolley Coach Co., 117–18, 161, 317

Flint Vehicle Factories Mutual Benefit Association, 25

Flint Vehicle Workers Club, 25

Flint Wagon Works, 15, 101

Ford, Henry, 29

Ford Motor Co., 16, 20, 21, 38, 71, 112, 124, 133, 208, 310, 328, 329, 346[16]; and Knudsen, 20; and Midland strike, 129, 130, 207; and Kelsey-Hayes strike, 131, 207; and GM strike, 192, 209; and Briggs strike (1937), 207, 385[39]

Fortune, 14, 21, 28, 198, 332, 338

Foy, Byron C., 155

Frankensteen, Richard, 86, 87, 95, 98, 328, 385[39]

Franklin, Jay, 308

Frey, John, 330; intervention of in strike, 183–85, 290; and February 11 settlement, 307

Friends of the Soviet Union, 222

Frigidaire Division, 18

Fullerton, Spencer, 309

Gadola, Paul V., 106, 195, 263, 292, 318, 393[27]; injunction of, 218, 236, 266, 269, 274–78, 286, 292, 295, 304, 317–18, 319, 400[28], 401[31, 39]; and Murphy, 275, 337, 400[28]; and writ of attachment, 292, 293, 297, 303, 318

Galenson, Walter, 329, 367[41]

Gallico, Paul, 161, 171, 225, 266

Gallup Poll, 229–30, 332

Ganley, Nat, 130

Garner, John Nance, 308–9, 334

Garst, Delmond, 95, 210

Gazan, Max, 161

Gealer, Maxie, 162

General Electric Co., 122

General Motors Acceptance Corporation, 18

General Motors Corporation, 78, 91, 92, 93, 99, 100, 115, 124, 155, 168, 170, 174, 175, 199, 206, 215, 236, 243, 263, 279, 299, 310, 311, 313, 317, 328, 330, 331, 393[33]; and Battle of the Running Bulls, 1, 10–12, 13, 196, 210, 239, 240, 343[4]; influence of in Flint, 5, 11–12, 107–8, 136–37, 189, 195, 219, 224, 226–28, 240, 273; history of to 1929, 14–20, 101–2, 346[16, 18]; and Sloan plan of organization, 19; employment in, 20, 21, 22, 104–5, 107, 360[13]; share of market of, 20, 21, 22, 305–6, 346[16], 384[36]; effect of depression on, 20–21, 26; progress of, 1933–36, 21; condition of in 1936, 21–

Index

435

22, 346[21]; executive training program of, 22, 28, 46, 348[39]; and labor relations before 1933, 22–23, 28; and introduction of welfare capitalism, 23; bonus plan of, 23; Employes Savings and Investment Plan of, 23–24, 26, 27, 191; housing program of, 23, 26, 27, 102, 106; stock subscription plan of, 24, 347[29]; group insurance plan of, 24–25, 27, 191; and IMA, 25; recreational programs in, 25–26; and Appreciation Fund bonus, 27, 225; regularization of employment by, 27–28; and collective bargaining, 28, 30–31, 32–33, 33–35, 48–49, 50, 51, 53, 76, 140, 178, 179, 183, 237, 239, 248, 252, 253–54, 326, 412[38]; department of industrial relations in, 28, 34, 38; foremen in, 28, 33, 43, 46, 51, 52, 55, 56, 58, 60, 173, 184, 186, 190, 196, 197, 213, 321, 323, 324, 326, 348[39, 40]; and NLRA and NLRB, 29, 50–51, 99, 176, 178, 180, 181–82, 217, 234, 275, 288, 329, 334, 388[85]; on unionism, 29, 35, 50–51, 119–20, 320–21; and representation, 30, 34, 35, 48–49, 51, 53, 178, 219, 249, 252, 254, 287, 289, 290, 291, 303; and President's settlement, 31–32; view of Roosevelt of, 32; and April, 1934, strike, 32–33, 73–74; on seniority and job tenure, 34, 50, 182, 324; and discrimination, 36, 37, 140, 142, 249, 268, 287, 304, 309–10, 321, 322, 398[9]; and company unions, 36, 42–47, 51–52, 134; and espionage, 36, 37–42, 97, 109, 113, 114–15, 195–96, 217, 224, 333, 349[63, 66, 73], 381[50]; and compliance with labor-board decisions, 37; union membership in, 41–42, 63, 71, 72–73, 75, 85, 89–90, 98, 108–9, 111, 117, 118–19, 136, 185, 188, 207, 211, 246, 266, 362[33], 368–69[61], 384[30]; and ALB bargaining agencies, 47–48, 51–52; and Toledo Chevrolet strike of 1935, 48–49, 75–76, 92, 145; effect of NIRA on, 49–50; and public opinion in plant cities, 52–53, 107; on speed-up, 58; and 1935 strike movement, 74–75; glass supply of, 97, 138, 145; and Flint bus strike, 118; and French sit-downs, 128; and Bendix, 128; UAW plans for strike of, 133–39 *passim*; and Atlanta Fisher Body and Chevrolet strike, 134–35, 137–38; and pre-strike negotiations with UAW, 139–40, 179–80; and origins of Fisher Body No. 1 and No. 2 sit-downs, 144–46; on Oakland shutdown, 146; and Chevrolet No. 4 sit-down, 172–73, 272, 301; view of sit-down of, 177, 191, 275, 309, 320; DuBrul strategy advice to, 178–79; and 1936 election, 178–79, 246, 303; negotiations of with Frey, 183–85; and loyalty movement, 185–87, 206, 209, 211, 217, 224, 395[63]; and Flint Alliance, 188, 189–90, 252–54, 379[24]; strike publicity of, 190, 191–92, 206; and back-to-work movement, 191, 249, 257, 260, 266, 319, 397[93]; public relations of in strike, 192, 259; and Black injunction, 193, 194–95, 198, 235, 263; plant police of, 195, 242, 404[84]; and use of violence, 196–98, 213–14, 215, 216, 218, 235–36, 301, 340, 382[57]; effect of strike on, 209, 210, 225, 303, 305–6, 384[36]; and abortive Pontiac sit-down, 210, 385[40]; influence in Anderson of, 211–12, 214, 216; and UAW strike tactics, 216–17, 367[41]; opinion of during strike, 228–30; and strike negotiations to January 15, 231–32, 247–48; and January 15 truce, 248–49; and breakdown of January 15 truce, 251–54; 395[51]; and strike negotiations, January 19–31, 254–59 *passim*, 264–65; and Gadola injunction, 263, 271, 275, 276, 278, 304, 317–18, 401[31]; Murphy criticism of, 264, 265, 274, 293, 400[24]; and injunction against Cleveland Fisher Body strike, 276–77, 304; and writ of attachment, 280, 292; and civilian police reserve, 282;

General Motors Corporation (*Cont.*) and strike negotiations, February 2–11, 285–92, 298, 302–3, 404[71, 73, 79]; and Michigan National Guard, 294, 409[20]; and February 11 settlement, 304–5, 306–7, 307–8, 309–10, 323, 325, 326; analysis of strike by, 320–21; and post-strike labor relations, 320–21; post-settlement strikes in, 321–23, 327–28; and March 12 contract, 323–25, 326–27. *See also* General Motors workers and individual divisions and plants

General Motors Institute, 28, 348[39]

General Motors workers, 63, 100, 118–19, 202, 250, 286; number of, 20, 21, 22; hours of, 22, 62, 180, 182, 325; wages of, 22, 27, 61, 119, 179, 180–81, 182, 191, 206, 305, 324–25, 327; reaction to welfare capitalism of, 26–27; irregular employment of, 27–28, 60, 61, 102, 206, 352[18], 354[20]; and discrimination, 31, 36, 249, 327; and seniority and job tenure, 31, 50, 60–61, 111, 140, 179, 181, 324, 326, 327; and company unions, 43, 45, 47; and ALB bargaining agencies, 52; geographical origin of, 54, 102; ethnicity of, 54; skill of, 54; nature of job of, 54–55; and the speed-up, 55–59, 111, 140, 179, 181, 325, 326, 327, 328; superannuation of, 59, 111; lack of union experience of, 63; and methods of wage payment, 61–62, 140, 179, 180, 181, 182, 317, 324, 327; and 1936 election, 96; composition of in Flint, 102–4; and relief, 104–5, 204; employment and unemployment among in Flint, 104–5; reaction of to grooving-in period, 140; and working conditions in body plants, 140–41; and exclusive representation, 182; loyalty movement among, 185–87, 263; and Flint Alliance, 188, 190; effect of strike on, 225, 259–60, 305; reaction to strike of, 228–29, 262, 379[21]. *See also* General Motors Corporation

Genesee County, 1, 5, 66, 108, 198, 219, 224, 236, 240, 269; relief in, 105, 204, 383[16, 19]; politics of, 106; bar association of, 194; circuit court of, 193, 195, 266; Emergency Relief Commission of, 202–3, 383[16, 19]; ban on liquor in, 404–5[85]

Germer, Adolph, 56–57, 107, 136, 142, 148, 221, 222, 237, 238–39, 261; and Battle of the Running Bulls, 9, 10, 344–45[23]; career of, 85; and auto organizing campaign, 1935–36, 85–86, 193; and Dillon, 85–86, 356[77]; and Martin-Dillon dispute, 88; and South Bend convention, 90–91, 92; and Martin, 94, 129, 137; on 1936 election, 96; and Mortimer, 111–12; and Goodyear strike, 124, 125; and Bendix strike, 128, 129; GM strike strategy of, 133, 136–37, 139, 143; and Atlanta strike, 138; and Black injunction, 194, 381[45]; and aid to UAW in strike, 217, 218; on Knudsen, 232; on John Doe warrants, 240; on Joseph, 240; and January 15 truce, 250, 253; and strike negotiations, 264, 265; and plan to seize Chevrolet No. 4, 267

Goodrich Rubber Co., 123

Goodyear Tire and Rubber Co.: 1936 strike in, 123–25, 130, 170, 201, 204, 208; company union in, 124

Gordon Baking Co.: sit-down strike in, 130, 131, 174

Gorman, Michael, 189, 282

Gorton, Gernsley F., 229

Graham-Paige Motors Corporation, 207

Green, Leon, 175

Green, William, 39, 154, 233, 330; and organization of the automobile industry, 66, 67, 68, 69; and April, 1934, strike, 73–74; and 1935 strike movement, 74–75; and an auto international, 77, 81, 82; and jurisdiction of UAW, 80; and UAW constitutional convention, 81, 82, 89; and Dillon-Martin dispute, 88; and South Bend convention, 91; and Lewis-Roosevelt exchange, 256;

Index

intervention in GM strike of, 290, 330; and Roosevelt, 290; and February 11 settlement, 307; on sit-down strike, 331
Greene, Nathan, 277
Guffey-Vinson Bill, 334
Guide Lamp Division, 211, 313, 314, 317; and speed-up, 56
Guide Lamp strike, 146, 147–48, 210, 212, 407[123]; morale in, 171; end of sit-down in, 213, 251, 252; and violence of January 25, 213; and picketing, 216; and January 15 truce, 249; and February 11 settlement, 302

Haber, William, 203, 204
Haessler, Carl, 205, 222, 384[25]
Hale, Merle C., 28, 38, 39, 43
Hall, Ed, 82, 86, 87, 90, 142, 194, 237, 286; described, 77–78; and Dillon, 87; and South Bend convention, 91; and Anderson, 95, 214–15; strike strategy of, 136, 137, 139; and Atlanta strike, 137–38; and January 15 truce, 250; and March 12 contract, 323, 325–26
Hapgood, Powers, 221, 264; and Fisher Body No. 1 sit-down, 167, 170; and Saginaw and Bay City, 198; and aid to UAW in strike, 217, 218; and January 15 truce, 250; and plan to seize Chevrolet No. 4, 267, 269, 273, 398[5]
Hardy, A. B. C., 101
Hartmann, George, 62–63
Hayes Body Co., 116
Hays, Arthur Garfield, 370[91]
Haywood, Allan, 137, 148
Herbst, Josephine, 163
Herrin massacre, 283, 402[56]
Hillman, Sidney, 86, 91, 204, 257, 285
Hoffman, Clare, 333
Hook, Frank, 333
Hormel Packing Co., 123
Howard, Charles, 91
Howe, Irving, 78, 398[5]
Hudson Motor Car Co., 72, 90, 328; unionism in, 31, 72
Hughes, Edwin H., 4

Hutcheson, William, 82
Hutchinson, B. E., 155, 250
Hyatt Roller Bearing Co., 17
Hynes, William J., 197–98

Ickes, Harold L., 256
I.M.A. News, 25, 190–91, 262
Importance #1, 245, 272, 295
Importance #2, 245, 295, 298, 300
Importance #3, 245
Indiana National Guard, 213, 216, 313, 315, 316
Indiana State Police, 212, 213, 314, 315–16
Industrial Fellowship League, 25, 348[39]
Industrial Mutual Association, 25, 27, 244
Industrial Workers of the World, 122
International Association of Machinists, 68
International Labor Defense, 222
International Ladies' Garment Workers' Union, 91, 204, 217–18
Iron Age, 132
Israel-Zion Hospital, 331

Jackson Brewery Co., 122
Janesville Chevrolet, 209; and speed-up, 56; unionism in, 134; post-settlement strike in, 322
Janesville Chevrolet and Fisher Body strike, 146, 209, 407[123]
Janesville Fisher Body, 209; post-settlement strike in, 322
Janesville (Wisconsin), 76, 209; GM housing in, 23; Alliance in, 209, 322
Johnson, Genora, 221; and Battle of the Running Bulls, 6–7; and speed-up, 57; and Women's Emergency Brigade, 200–201; and seizure of Chevrolet No. 4, 270
Johnson, Hiram, 334
Johnson, Kermit, 57, 201, 221, 312; and Chevrolet No. 4 sit-down, 173, 267, 270, 398[5]
Joseph, Joseph R., 224, 292–93; and John Doe warrants, 240–41, 393[27]; and arrest of Flint strike leaders,

Joseph, Joseph R. (*Cont.*)
241, 318; and resumption of work at Chevrolet, 260–61
Justice, Department of, 339

Kampelman, Max, 222
Kansas City Chevrolet, 78, 138, 302, 366–67[36]; and April, 1934, strike, 32, 36, 73; unionism in, 134
Kansas City Fisher Body, 138, 366–67[36]; and April, 1934, strike, 32, 36, 73; unionism in, 134
Kansas City Fisher Body (and Chevrolet) strike (1936–37), 140, 143, 144, 302, 407[123]; origin of, 138; entertainment in, 161; spread of, 210
Keim (John R.) Mills, 20
Kelsey, W. K., 331
Kelsey-Hayes Wheel Co.: strike in, 97, 131–33, 207; unionism in, 169, 207–8, 210
Kemp, Edward G., 148, 235, 248, 271, 279, 309
Kempton, Murray, 267, 363[56], 398[5]
Kennedy, Pete, 158, 221
Knights of Labor, 79
Knudsen, William, 180, 206; and Battle of the Running Bulls, 11; biography of, 19–20; and April, 1934, strike, 32–33; and company unions, 42, 44; and Toledo Chevrolet strike of 1935, 48, 49, 76; on NLRA, 51; and French sit-downs, 128, 365[14]; and collective bargaining, 138–39, 144, 179–80, 231, 254, 378[3]; and pre-strike negotiations, 139–40; view of sit-down of, 177, 179–80; and Frey, 184; and use of violence, 196, 216, 236, 246; on Murphy, 223; and representation, 231, 238, 252, 287; and strike negotiations, 231, 232, 238, 247–49, 255, 257, 265, 285–86, 286–87, 288, 289, 291, 300, 302–3, 404[79], 407[121]; and January 15 truce, 249, 254; and Flint Alliance, 252–54; and back-to-work movement, 260; and civilian police reserve, 282; and Lenz plan to recapture Chevrolet No. 4, 301; and February 11 letter to Murphy, 304–5; and union insignia, 305; and February 11 settlement, 307; on arming nonunion men, 321; and March 12 contract, 326; and Michigan National Guard, 409[20]
Kramer, Charles, 114–15, 222
Kraus, Dorothy, 130, 161, 163
Kraus, Henry, 115, 136, 145, 161, 166, 190, 204, 273, 322, 363[56], 398[5]; and Flint *Auto Worker*, 114, 115; and Black injunction, 195; and organization of union veterans, 201; on Wolcott, 227; arrest of, 241, 318; and plan to seize Chevrolet No. 4, 267, 268; and Gadola injunction, 279
Krock, Arthur, 308
Krogstad, George A., 166
Krzycki, Leo, 91, 93, 128, 217, 312

Labor, Department of, 48, 216, 258, 333
LaDuke, Ted, 197
La Follette, Robert M., Jr., 42, 59, 190, 211, 222, 321
La Follette Civil Liberties Committee, 166, 186, 198, 200, 225, 226, 228, 244, 260, 280, 282, 321, 334; and Battle of the Running Bulls, 3, 11, 224; and espionage, 37–42, 97, 195–96, 224, 333, 349[66, 69]; and Anderson, 216, 316; and aid to UAW, 222, 223–24, 311, 333; and Flint Alliance, 260; and post-strike hearings, 333
Lambert, Homer, 212
Landon, Alfred M., 95–96, 230
Lane, Robert E., 29
Lane v. *Au Sable*, 275, 276
Lansing Fisher Body, 195
Lawrence, William H., 252–53, 396[68]
Lee, Higginson and Co., 16
Leland, Henry D., 15
Lenz, Arnold, 363[56]; and Chevrolet bargaining agency, 52; and unionism, 119–20; and plan to recapture Chevrolet No. 4, 268, 301, 319; and arming of workers, 321
Leo XIII, 151
Levinson, Edward, 160, 398[5]

Index

439

Lewis, John L., 84, 85, 94, 110, 137, 155, 170, 172, 178, 186, 190, 229, 230, 242, 262, 283, 367[41]; and auto international union, 80; and auto organizing campaign of 1935-36, 82, 84, 85, 86-87; on 1936 election, 96; strike strategy of, 139; and collective bargaining, 139, 140; and origins of GM strike, 146-47; role of in strike, 170, 217, 232-33, 247, 248, 253, 311; and glass strikes, 208-9; and strike negotiations, 237, 238, 254-59 *passim*, 264, 265, 285-92, 298, 302-3, 304, 396[76], 407[121]; and Battle of the Running Bulls, 246; and Roosevelt, 256-57, 259, 285; and Sloan, 257; and representation, 286-87, 290-91, 293, 303; and Murphy's law-and-order letter, 293, 297-301, 303, 406[104], 407[108]; on February 11 settlement, 306; on U.S. Steel agreement, 330; on AFL intervention in strike, 330. *See also* Committee for Industrial Organization

Lewis, Joseph H., 245, 261, 271, 286, 393[33], 409[20]; career of, 243; instructions of to Guardsmen, 243-44; and jurisdiction over Guard, 245-46; and cordoning of Importance #1, 272, 273; and Gadola injunction, 277, 401[39]; and demonstration of February 3, 281; and Flint-UAW peace treaty, 282-83; and writ of attachment, 293; and plan to secure evacuation of Flint plants, 295; appraisal of Guard role by, 319

Libby-Owens-Ford Glass Co., 97, 145; strike in, 138, 209

Lincoln-Zephyr, 129

Lippmann, Walter, 259, 300-301, 308

Lipset, Seymour Martin, 174

Little Motor Car Co., 17

Loewe, Julia, 221

Loisel, Paul, 282

Lovestone, Jay, and Lovestoneites, 328-29, 413[46]

Lynd, Robert and Helen, 187

Lyon, Lawrence, 172

McCabe, Glenn, 138, 139
McCrea, Duncan, 131, 176-77
McGrady, Edward F., 39, 237, 254, 291
McIntyre, Marvin, 291, 302, 404[79]
McKeighan, William H., 284
MacLeish, Archibald, 218
Mangold, James H., 41, 52
Maritain, Jacques, 235
Marshall, Alfred, 37
Martel, Frank, 9, 87, 261
Martin, Homer, 39, 77, 82, 87, 172, 177, 190, 220, 221, 237, 293, 298, 305, 317, 366-67[36]; and Battle of the Running Bulls, 11; biography of, 78; and Dillon and Dillonites, 84, 87-88, 93-94; and CIO, 84-85, 93, 94, 96, 137, 217; elected UAW president, 90; and South Bend convention, 90, 91; and Communists, 93-94; and Mortimer, 93, 94, 109, 111-12; as administrator, 94; on 1936 election, 96; and Goodyear strike, 125; and Bendix strike, 128, 129; GM strike strategy of, 133-34, 135-36, 137, 138, 139, 142, 143, 146, 147-48, 367[41, 42]; and Cleveland Fisher Body strike, 143-44; and pre-strike negotiations, 139-40; and collective bargaining, 140; and UAW strike demands, 180, 181; on Sloan's January 5 letter, 183; on GM strike tactics, 191; on Black injunction, 194; and financing of strike, 204; on use of radio, 205; and UAW strike publicity, 206, 207; and strike negotiations, 232, 247-48, 256, 264, 286, 293; and January 15 truce, 249-50, 253; and Gadola injunction, 263, 278; and February 11 strike settlement, 304, 306; and strike victory celebration, 311, 312; and Gadola writ of attachment, 318; on post-strike relations with GM, 320; and post-strike factionalism, 328-29, 413[46]; on Green, 330; and Dies Committee, 414[69]

Marvin, John E., 219
Matignon Agreement, 126 365[11]

Maxwell-Briscoe, 16
Mayo, John, 197–98
Mayor's Fact-Finding Committee, 153
Mechanics Educational Society of America, 65, 72; and Motor Products strike, 83, 84; and merger with UAW, 84, 86, 90
Meiklejohn, Alexander, 218
Merrill, Russell, 94
Metal Polishers International Union, 68
Michel, F. J., 93–94
Michigan: legality of sit-down in, 176–77, 192; legality of picketing in, 177, 277; legislature of and sit-down strike, 223, 262–63; industrial-relations bill in, 336; State Liquor Control Commission of, 404–5[85]
Michigan, University of, 148, 151; students of and Flint strike, 165, 205, 219
Michigan Christian Advocate, 219, 229
Michigan Manufacturer and Financial Record, 35
Michigan National Guard, 158, 168, 171, 173, 225, 226, 239, 240, 261, 375[36], 396[76], 399[11], 405[91, 93], 406[94]; and Battle of the Running Bulls, 9, 10, 13; and UAW, 13, 200, 242–43; and cordoning of Importance #1, 172, 272–74, 312, 400[27]; and Michigan State Police, 242, 245; and number of Guardsmen in Flint, 242, 272; deployment of in Flint, 242–44; neutrality of in strike, 243–44; plan of to deal with strike disturbance, 245; gathering of intelligence by, 245; jurisdiction over, 245–46, 261, 277; and resumption of work at Chevrolet, 260, 262, 319; and seizure of Chevrolet No. 4, 271; and demonstration of February 3, 281; and civilian police reserve, 282, 319; and writ of attachment, 292, 293, 294; and riot control, 294; plan of to secure evacuation of Flint plants, 294–95, 296, 298, 300; Special Duty Company of, 298; and Lenz plan to recapture Chevrolet No. 4, 301, 319; demobilization of, 318–19, 409[19]; appraisal of role of, 319; and lessons of strike, 319–20; and GM, 409[20]
Michigan State Emergency Welfare Relief Commission, 54, 104, 203, 360[13]
Michigan State Police, 172, 198, 239, 240, 269, 336; and Battle of the Running Bulls, 9, 10, 13; and Fisher Body No. 1 strike (1930), 65–66; and Flint Alliance, 188, 189, 190; and January 7 violence, 197; and Barringer, 226, 227; role of in Flint, 241–42; and Michigan National Guard, 242, 245; and demonstration of February 3, 281
Midland Flash, 130
Midland Steel Products Corporation: 1936 strike in, 97, 129–30, 131, 132–33, 207
Miley, Paul: and Cleveland Fisher Body strike, 142–43, 369[64, 70]
Mill and Factory, 25, 61, 156, 166
Minzey, Delmar, 73, 246
Modern Housing Corporation, 102
Modern Times, 56
Monarch, John, 269, 270
Montgomery (Alabama): bus boycott in, 338
Moore, Walter, 116
Morgan, J. P., 19, 206, 230
Morrison, Frank, 35
Mortimer, Wyndham, 79, 82, 84, 87, 89, 124, 205, 237, 267, 295, 398[5]; biography of, 78–79; and Martin-Dillon dispute, 88; and South Bend convention, 88, 89, 90, 91; and Travis, 91–92, 111–12, 113, 222; and Martin, 93, 94, 109, 111–12; and organizing work in Flint, 95, 109–12, 113–14, 115–16, 117, 119, 120, 221; and Midland strike, 130; GM strike strategy of, 139; and Cleveland Fisher Body strike, 143, 369[64]; and origins of Fisher Body No. 1 strike, 144, 148, 369[67]; on Murphy, 148; on role of Com-

munists, 221; and strike negotiations, 221-22, 232, 247-48, 286, 287, 304, 407[121]; and Cadillac evacuation, 251; and January 15 truce, 253; and Gadola injunction, 279; and demonstration of February 3, 280; and victory celebration, 311; and March 12 contract, 325-26; on post-strike UAW growth, 327
Motor Products Corporation: 1935 strike in, 83-84, 88
Mott, Charles Stewart, 101, 106
Muller, Carl, 299
Mundale, William, 312; and speed-up, 57; and Fisher Body No. 2 sit-down, 159, 169, 171; and February 11 settlement, 307
Mundy, John, 197
Munger, William, 95
Murphy, Frank, 39, 96, 137, 139, 186, 187, 188, 206, 217, 226, 231, 258, 259, 316, 317, 320, 321, 330, 341, 409[141]; and Battle of the Running Bulls, 9-10, 11, 13, 239-40, 343[4], 344-45[23]; on history of sit-down, 122; and Léon Blum, 127; and use of violence, 127, 150, 224, 234, 235-36, 239-40, 241, 247, 264, 279, 293-94, 296, 308, 332, 335-36, 336-37, 339; career of, 148-49; ambition of, 149, 236-37; and public service, 149; and unpopular causes, 149; and civil liberties, 149-50, 218, 236, 277, 370[91]; compassion for weak of, 150-51; views on organized labor of, 151-55, 236; on role of government in strikes, 153, 154, 234, 336; and Briggs strike (1933), 153, 154; and relief for strikers, 153, 154, 202, 203, 224, 383[16, 19]; and Manila cigar strike, 154; friendship of with auto magnates, 155; as GM stockholder, 155, 372[108]; appearance of, 155; AFL intercession with, 185, 290; Knudsen on, 290; aid of to UAW in strike, 224, 311; as a negotiator, 233, 234, 311; on legality of sit-down, 234-35, 239-40, 247, 248, 294, 339; and strike negotiations before January 15, 237-38, 247-48; use of National Guard by, 239, 240-41, 242, 243, 245-46, 254-55, 260, 261, 264, 271, 274, 277, 281, 288, 293, 294, 295, 296, 300, 311, 319, 393[33]; use of state police by, 239, 241, 242; and John Doe warrants, 240-41, 393[27]; and arrest of union leaders, 241; and January 15 truce, 248-49, 250-51, 252, 253, 254; and strike negotiations, January 19-31, 254-55, 264-65; and resumption of work at Chevrolet, 260-61, 262; and Michigan Senate, 262-63; and Flint Alliance, 263-64; and loyalty movement, 264; criticism of GM by, 264, 265, 274, 293, 400[24]; and UAW Saginaw meeting, 264; and law enforcement, 264-65, 286, 292-94, 296-301, 308-9, 311, 328, 330; and seizure of Chevrolet No. 4, 271-74; and Gadola injunction, 274-75, 277, 278-79, 400[28]; and civilian police reserve, 282; and strike negotiations, February 2-11, 285-92, 302-3, 407[121]; law-and-order letter of to Lewis, 293, 297-301, 303, 406[104], 407[108]; and February 11 settlement, 303-5, 306, 307-8, 311; and Chrysler sit-down, 328, 336; and Congress, 333, **334**; and Dies and Dies Committee, 335, 337-38, 409[141]; and post-strike discussion of industrial relations, 335-36; industrial-relations bill of, 336; and appraisal of role in strike of, 336-37; and Gadola, 337, 400[28]; and Barringer, 337; and 1938 election, 338, 415[75]
Murphy, George, 149, 286, 297, 299, 302, 303
Murray, Philip, 96-97
Muste, A. J., 75, 76
Myers, James, 56, 57, 187, 190, 219

Nash Motors Co., 71, 207; unionism in, 90; Racine plant of, 93-94
National Automotive Fibres, Inc.: sit-down strike in, 131

National Catholic Welfare Conference, 219
National Citizens Committee for Civil Rights in the Automobile Industry, 218, 277
National Guard Bureau, 319
National Industrial Recovery Act, 28–29, 30, 31, 32, 35, 36, 48, 60, 65, 66, 98; effect of on GM, 49–50
National Industrial Recovery Board, 302
National Labor Board, 30, 36, 37, 43, 45
National Labor Relations Act, 45, 127–28, 183, 217, 255, 288, 289, 304, 331, 335, 366[12]; and GM, 27, 50–51, 99, 176, 178, 180, 181–82, 217, 234, 275, 288, 334; terms of, 50; and UAW, 181–82; and union growth, 327, 330
National Labor Relations Board, 45, 50, 83, 181–82, 321–22, 365[15]; first NLRB, 30, 37; and GM, 51, 329, 388[85]; and Delco-Remy, 183, 213, 214, 388[85]; and violence in Anderson, 213, 214, 315; and UAW, 223, 388[85]; on strikers as employees, 276
National Labor Relations Board v. Jones and Laughlin, 331
National Recovery Administration, 27, 29, 32, 37, 38, 42, 56, 58, 61, 70, 72, 75, 115, 141
National Textile Workers Union, 130
Neely, Matthew M., 334
Negroes: in auto industry, 102–3, 110; and civil-rights movement, 338–40
New Center News, 400[24]
Newcomb, Theodore W., 63
New Departure Manufacturing Co., 17
New Masses, 157
New Republic, 176
New York Times, 54, 56, 57, 155, 167, 171, 172, 187, 205, 308, 310, 404[73]
Niebuhr, Reinhold, 218
Nobody Starves, 106
Norris-La Guardia Act, 278

North Tarrytown Chevrolet: April, 1934, strike in, 32, 73
North Tarrytown Fisher Body: April, 1934, strike in, 32, 73
Norwood Chevrolet: and Toledo Chevrolet strike of 1935, 75; unionism in, 134
Norwood Fisher Body: and Toledo Chevrolet strike of 1935, 75; unionism in, 134
Norwood Fisher Body and Chevrolet strike (1936–37), 146, 147–48, 211, 407[123]

Oakland Chevrolet: shutdown of, 146, 209, 210, 302
Oakland Fisher Body: shutdown of, 146, 209, 210, 302
Oakland Motor Car Co., 16
Ohio Valley Trades and Labor Assembly, 112
Olander, Oscar G., 9, 241, 245, 261, 271. *See also* Michigan State Police
Olds, Ransom E., 15
Oldsmobile Division, 16, 21, 73, 143; unionism in, 95
O'Rourke, Francis, 197–98

Packard Motor Car Co., 155, 328
Palmer, Jack, 66
Parker, Evan J., 8, 117, 144, 193, 321
Parker, James S., 106
Paterson, W. A., 100, 101
Pathé News, 160
Pattern Makers' League, 87
Pengelly Building, 3, 159, 171, 199, 200, 226, 268, 269, 298, 312, 314
Pepper, Samuel D., 243, 246, 261, 271, 295; on use of violence by National Guard, 294; on National Guard and riot control, 319–20
Perkins, Frances, 287, 292, 293, 311, 333; and Sloan, 183, 258–59; and strike negotiations, 231, 233, 237, 254–59 *passim*, 285, 286, 288, 289, 291, 302, 404[73], 409[141]; and Congress, 258; on legality of sit-down, 258
Perlman Rim Corporation, 17

Index

443

Pesotta, Rose, 91, 173, 217, 312
Peterson, Captain, 3
Philippine Islands, 148, 151, 154, 246
Pickert, Heinrich, 243
Pieper, Fred C., 90, 107, 112; biography of, 77; and Martin, 93–94; strike strategy of, 133–34, 135–36, 137; and Atlanta strike, 134–35, 138
Pinchot, Mrs. Gifford, 206
Pinkerton's National Detective Agency, 38, 39–40, 41, 42, 167, 195–96
Pittman, Key, 334–35
Pittsburgh Plate Glass Co., 97, 209
Pius XI, 151
Player, Cyril, 189
Plymouth Motor Corporation, 129
Pontiac Division, 21, 73, 143; abortive sit-down in, 210, 385[40]
Pontiac Fisher Body, 32
Porter, Russell B., 155, 171, 187, 205, 262, 278, 397[93]
Pound, Arthur, 23
President's settlement (March, 1934), 31–32, 35, 36, 37, 45, 50–51, 72, 73, 109, 118, 178, 233, 304
Pressman, Lee, 114, 222, 237, 285, 407[108]; and Black injunction, 194, 195, 381[45]; and strike negotiations, 222, 232–33, 286, 291, 302, 304, 407[121]; on Knudsen, 231; on Brown, 232; and Gadola injunction, 275, 277, 279, 400[28]
Progressive Caucus, 328
Pugmire, Arthur Lawrence, 39–41
Punch Press, 205, 219

Quezon, Manuel, 304

Rae, John B., 19
Rasbach, Sanford, 262, 263
Reed, John, Clubs, 222
Remy Electric Co., 17
Renault, 126
Reo Motor Car Co., 328
Representation, 37, 180, 232, 248, 288, 289; and GM, 30, 34, 35, 48–49, 51, 53, 178, 182–83, 219, 249, 252, 254, 287, 289, 290, 291, 303; and UAW, 30, 97, 128–29, 131–32, 181–82, 183, 185, 219, 237, 254, 257, 287, 288, 329; and Section 7(a), 30; and President's settlement, 31; and ALB, 33, 45, 50; and AFL, 48, 183, 184, 185, 289–90, 307, 330; and Toledo Chevrolet strike of 1935, 48–49, 176; NLRA on, 50; and Goodyear strike, 124; and French sit-downs, 126, 365[12]; liberal clergymen on, 219; and Knudsen, 231, 238, 252, 287; and Flint Alliance, 252; and Lewis, 255–56, 286–87, 289, 290, 291, 303; and February 11 settlement, 304–5, 306, 307, 309; and Chrysler sit-down, 328; and loyal employees, 395[63]. *See also* Collective bargaining
Rerum Novarum, 151–52
Reuther, Roy, 115, 132, 145, 170, 188, 221, 223, 295, 328, 363[56]; career of, 112–13; and organizing in Flint in 1936, 113, 117–18, 119; and Flint bus strike, 117–18; and Fisher Body No. 1 sit-down, 172; and January 7 violence, 196, 226; as strike leader, 199, 310; on Travis, 222; on opinion in Flint, 225; arrest of, 241, 318; and resumption of work at Chevrolet, 261; and plan to seize Chevrolet No. 4, 267–69, 398[5]; and Chevrolet No. 4 sit-down, 273, 301; and civilian police reserve, 282–83; and strike victory celebration, 311
Reuther, Victor, 170, 221; and Battle of the Running Bulls, 3, 4, 5–6, 344–45[9, 23]; career of, 112–13; and Kelsey-Hayes sit-down, 132; in Anderson, 214, 215, 216, 218, 313–14, 316–17, 318; arrest of, 241, 318
Reuther, Walter, 39, 90, 170, 221; career of, 112–13; and Goodyear strike, 125; and Kelsey-Hayes sit-down, 131–32; and Cadillac and Fleetwood strikes, 209–10, 251; and seizure of Chevrolet No. 4, 270, 273; and demonstration of February 3, 279
Reynolds, R. J., Tobacco Co., 302

Rich, Roscoe, 3
Richard, Gene, 57
Riesman, David, 217
Robinson, Edward G., 40
Robinson, Joseph, 335
Roland, James, 75, 215
Roosevelt, Franklin D., 27, 28, 31, 59, 90, 91, 115–16, 148, 178, 186, 187, 190, 230, 246, 311, 332, 334, 335, 338; GM view of, 32; and NLRA, 50; 1936 election of, 95–96; AFL intercession with, 185, 290; and strike negotiations, 233, 285–86, 287–88, 290, 291, 297, 303, 404[73, 79], 409[141]; view of sit-down of, 233; and John L. Lewis, 256–57, 259, 285; and Sloan, 257–58, 259; praise of Murphy by, 308, 337; criticism of in Congress, 333, 334; and Dies and Dies Committee, 337–38. *See also* President's settlement
Roper, Daniel, 302–3
Roper, Elmo, 55
Ross, Arthur M., 223
Ryan, John A., 219

Saginaw, 49, 264; violence in, 196, 197–98, 219, 266
Saginaw Steering Gear Division, 43
St. Francis, Third Order of, 152
St. Louis Chevrolet, 51; April, 1934, strike in, 32, 36, 73; unionism in, 95, 134, 306, 366–67[36]; post-settlement sit-down in, 321–22
St. Louis Chevrolet and Fisher Body strike (1937), 146, 209, 210, 407[123]
St. Louis Fisher Body, 51; April, 1934, strike in, 32, 36, 73; unionism in, 95, 134, 306, 366–67[36]
Salyer, Charles B., 212, 214, 216
Scafe, Lincoln R., 142, 184, 186
Seaman Body Co., 77, 90
Sears, Roebuck and Co., 225
Section 7(a), 28, 29, 30–31, 35, 37, 42, 45, 66, 98–99; and representation, 30; effect of on GM, 49–50
Securities Act, 24
Segalman, Ralph, 205
Selden patent, 101

Seligman, J. and W., 16
Shears, Joseph, 283–84
Sherwood, William S., 14
Shipley, Emory, 315
Shister, Joseph, 329
Short, Dewey, 334
Simons, Berdine Arlington (Bud): career of, 116, 222; and Fisher Body No. 1 sit-down (November, 1936), 116, 117, 119; and origins of Fisher Body No. 1 sit-down (1936–37), 145–46; and Fisher Body No. 1 sit-down (1936–37), 156, 157–58, 162, 166, 168, 169, 171, 172, 195, 296; on February 11 settlement, 307
Sit-down strikes: and sound car, 3, 5–6, 111, 132, 202, 208, 250, 262, 272, 310; songs in, 4, 8, 158, 163–64, 200, 251, 270, 279, 280, 318, 340; Motor Products strike, 84; Fisher Body No. 1 strike (November, 1936), 116–17, 118, 119; popularity of, 120; types of, 121, 363–64[1]; legality of, 121, 131, 174–77, 179, 192, 229, 234–35, 239–40, 247–48, 257, 258, 259, 262, 275, 294, 309, 320, 339, 387[68]; advantages of, 121–22, 141, 146; history of, 122–23; in Italy, 122–23, 174; number of, 123, 331, 332; and CIO, 123, 139, 331; in rubber companies, 123–24; in France, 125–28, 365[11, 12]; comparison of French and GM sit-downs, 126–28; Bendix strike, 128–29, 132–33, 365[15, 18]; Midland strike, 129–30, 131, 132–33, 207; and feeding of strikers, 130, 132, 202; Gordon Baking Co. strike, 130, 131, 144; ALCOA strike, 130–31; Kelsey-Hayes strike, 131–33, 207; National Automotive Fibres strike, 131; Bohn Brass and Aluminum strike, 131, 208; educational programs in, 132, 165, 219; effect on UAW of, 133; degree of organization of, 156; sense of community in, 157, 341; kangaroo courts in, 159–60; and visitors, 160–61, 165–66; recreation and entertainment

Index

in, 162–64; provisions for sanitation and protection of machinery in, 165–66; fluctuating numbers in, 167–69; use of outsiders in plants, 169, 236; and morale of strikers, 169–74; non-revolutionary character of, 174; defense of by UAW, 174–76, 206, 273; GM view of, 177, 191, 206; post-GM strike spread of, 309, 333–34, 336; Standard Cotton Products Co. strike, 317, 369[73]; Chrysler strike, 328, 336; AFL on, 331; purpose of, 332; victory record of, 332; public opinion on, 332–33, 413–14[54]; and law-and-order issue, 332–33; and Congress, 333–35; and Michigan politics, 337; and civil-rights movement, 338–40; and college sit-ins, 340–41; state action against, 414[55]. *See also* individual GM strikes

Sloan, Alfred P., Jr., 16, 28, 180, 190, 206; biography of, 17–18; and reorganization of GM, 19; and Knudsen, 19, 20; on unionism, 29; and collective bargaining, 33, 35, 255; on NLRA, 51; and 1936 election, 96; response of to UAW strike demands, 182–83; and representation, 182–83; and Brown, 231; and strike negotiations, 254–59 *passim*, 287, 291, 302, 396[76]; on legality of sit-down, 257, 258, 259; and Roosevelt, 257–58, 259; and Lewis, 257; and Perkins, 258–59; on Murphy, 307–8. *See also* General Motors Corporation

Smith, Jacob, 100
Smith, John T.: and Frey, 184; and strike negotiations, 232, 247–49, 255, 286–87, 300, 303, 407[121]
Smith, Matthew, 84, 86, 87
Social Security Act, 24
Socialism and Socialists, 91, 93, 106, 126; role of in strike, 219, 220, 269; and Unity Caucus, 329
"Solidarity Forever," 4, 158, 162, 312, 318

Sparks, C. Nelson, 124
Special Conference Committee, 23, 28, 320
Spisak, Louis, 74, 142, 143
Standard Cotton Products Co.: sit-down strike in, 317, 369[73]
Starr, Raymond W., 235, 318
Steck, John H., 295
Steel, 192
Steel Workers' Organizing Committee, 96, 329, 341
Stolberg, Benjamin, 79
Strike Marches On, 162–63
Studebaker Corporation, 71, 90, 94, 116, 204, 207, 328; unionism in, 204
Sugar, Maurice, 222, 388[82]; and "Sit-Down!" 164; and abortive Anderson visit, 214–15; and arrest of union leaders, 241; and January 15 truce, 250; and Gadola injunction, 274–75, 279, 400[28]

Teahan, Marguerite, 372[108]
Ternstedt Division, 112
Thomas, Elbert D., 41
Thomas, Norman, 220, 221
Thompson, Dorothy, 176
Thompson, Hugh, 212–13, 214
Time, 147, 309, 331
Tobin, Daniel J., 378[15]
Toledo: UAW in, 85, 88, 169, 279; and Toledo parts local, 88, 90, 208
Toledo Chevrolet, 90; April, 1935, strike in, 48–49, 53, 75–76, 77, 83, 91, 92, 108, 143, 145, 197–98, 238; unionism in, 88, 91, 115, 134, 169, 208, 366–67[36]
Toledo Chevrolet sit-down strike, 146, 209, 407[123]
Towner, Leslie, 241
Townsend, M. Clifford, 215, 216, 218, 311, 314, 315
Trade Union Unity League, 64, 130
Transue, Andrew, 293–94, 298
Travis, Robert C., 41, 159, 173, 202, 206, 208, 211, 219, 223, 236, 295, 340, 363[56]; and Battle of the Running Bulls, 1, 5, 9, 10, 246, 344–45[23]; career of, 91–93; and Mor-

Travis, Robert C. (*Cont.*)
timer, 91–92, 111–12, 113, 222; and GM Advisory Council, 95; and Flint organizing campaign in 1936, 107, 111–12, 113–20; and planning for GM strike, 134; and Cleveland Fisher Body strike, 142; and origins of Fisher Body No. 1 sit-down, 143, 144–46, 148, 369[67]; and Fisher Body No. 1 sit-down, 167, 169, 172; and Flint Alliance, 189; and Black injunction, 193; and espionage, 195; as strike leader, 199, 222, 310; and CIO, 218; ideological commitments of, 222; on Wolcott, 227; arrest of, 241, 318; and National Guard, 242–43; and January 15 truce, 250, 253; and resumption of work at Chevrolet, 261; and plan to seize Chevrolet No. 4, 267–69, 398[5]; and Chevrolet No. 4 sit-down, 273, 301; and Gadola injunction, 279; and civilian police reserve, 282–83; and Lewis, 285; and February 11 settlement, 302; and strike victory celebration, 311, 312; and Anderson, 314, 316; on post-settlement sit-downs, 322–23

Traxler, Henry: and Janesville strike, 209

Union News Service, 205
United Auto Worker, 114, 124
United Automobile, Aircraft and Vehicle Workers of America, 64
United Automobile Worker, 117, 118, 306
United Automobile Workers—AFL, 329
United Automobile Workers Federal Labor Unions, 31, 36, 39, 53, 78, 79; and representation, 30; and April, 1934, strike, 32–33, 73–74; and discrimination, 36, 37; and espionage, 41; and company unions, 43, 45; and Toledo Chevrolet strike of 1935, 48–49, 75–76; and wages, 61; jurisdiction of, 63, 68–69, 79, 81; and Communism, 64–65; reasons for weakness of, 67–71; National Council of, 67, 69, 74, 75, 77, 78, 79, 82; membership of, 71, 72–73, 75, 349[72]; and AAWA, 72; and March, 1934, strike movement, 72–73; progressives in, 72, 74, 77, 79, 81; and 1935 strike movement, 74–75; and an international union, 77, 79–80; and constitutional convention, 81

United Automobile Workers of America, International Union, 21, 52, 53, 59, 123, 160, 163, 168, 169, 172, 173, 178, 193, 198, 204–7, 298, 301, 310, 340, 341; and Battle of the Running Bulls, 1–13 *passim*, 246; and speed-up, 56; jurisdiction of, 80–81, 81–82, 85–86, 87, 89; constitutional convention of, 81–82, 82–83, 89, 91–92; and Communism, 82, 89, 90, 91, 93–94, 109–10, 111, 130, 220, 221–23, 357[83]; GEB of, 82, 83, 88, 90, 93–94, 94–95, 112, 113, 133, 135, 136, 137–38, 139, 147, 217, 367[42]; membership of, 82, 85, 89, 98, 108–9, 111, 117, 118–19, 122, 133, 139, 141–42, 182, 188, 211, 246, 255, 266, 327, 329, 357[83], 362[33], 365[18], 368–69[61], 384[30]; and chartering of Toledo local, 83, 88; and Motor Products strike, 83–84, 88; and CIO, 84–87, 91–92, 93, 137, 217–18, 304, 311; and merger with independents, 84, 86, 90, 95, 357[85]; progressives in, 88–89, 90–91, 93, 94, 99, 100, 116, 125, 135; South Bend convention of, 88, 89–91, 92–93, 94, 95, 113, 132, 357[83]; GM Advisory Council of, 92, 95, 134, 136, 137; factionalism in, 93–94, 328–29; lack of discipline in, 94, 136, 148; and organizing campaign of 1936, 94–98, 358[102]; and seniority in Dodge plant, 95, 96; 1936 demands of, 97; and collective bargaining, 97, 140, 144, 180–81, 183, 199, 248, 287; and representation, 97, 128–29, 131–32, 181–82, 183, 185, 219, 237–38, 254, 257, 287, 288, 329; and La Follette

Index

447

Civil Liberties Committee, 97, 114–15, 222, 223, 333; and Federation of Flat Glass Workers, 97, 138, 199; organizing efforts in Flint in 1936, 106, 107–8, 108–20, 361–62[29, 30]; West Side local of, 112–13, 131, 209, 210, 276, 279; and Goodyear strike, 124–25; and origins of GM strike, 127, 133–43, 147–48; and French sit-downs, 128; and Bendix strike, 128–29; and Midland strike, 129–30; and URW, 130, 170, 204, 208, 218, 221; and legality of sit-down, 131; and Kelsey-Hayes strike, 131–32; and Detroit sit-downs of 1936, 132–33; effect of sit-downs on, 133; and Atlanta strike, 137–38; and origin of Cleveland Fisher Body strike, 141–43; and origin of Flint sit-downs, 144; constitution of, 145, 147, 367[42], 369[74]; and feeding of Flint strikers, 161; and Flint bus strike, 161, 317; and use of outsiders in strike, 169, 207–8, 270, 273, 279; defense of sit-down by, 174–76, 206, 273; and pre-strike negotiations, 179–80; strike demands of, 180–82, 199, 237, 239, 247, 248, 254, 304, 305, 309, 324, 325; and NLRA, 181–82; and AFL intervention in strike, 185, 378[15]; and GM loyalty movement, 185–87; and Flint Alliance, 188–89, 190, 200, 379–80[25]; public relations of in strike, 192, 384[25]; and Black injunction, 193–94, 240, 381[45]; and violence in Saginaw and Bay City, 197–98, 382[57]; strike organization of, 199–202; and role of women in strike, 200–201, 310; and financing of strike, 204, 217–18; strike publicity of, 206–7; and spreading of strike, 208–10; and abortive Pontiac sit-down, 210, 385[40]; picketing of GM Buildings by, 210; and Anderson, 212–16 *passim*, 218, 313–17; and GM strike tactics, 216–17; support of by civil-liberties groups, 218–19; support of by clergymen, 219, 229; and University of Michigan students, 219, 340; and aid of Socialists, 220, 221, 269; and Murphy, 224, 311; and Barringer, 226; and Flint power structure, 226–28; and Flint *Journal*, 228; opinion of during strike, 228–30; and Gallup polls, 230; and strike negotiations to January 15, 231–32, 237–38, 247–48; and NLRB, 233, 388[85]; and Joseph, 240; and National Guard, 242–43; and truce of January 15, 248–50, 395[51]; and breakdown of January 15 truce, 251–54 *passim*, 396[68]; and back-to-work movement, 260, 261, 262, 397[97]; and Gadola injunction, 263, 274–75, 276, 278–79, 317–18, 400[28]; and Saginaw protest meeting, 264; and strike negotiations, January 19–31, 264–65; and plan to seize Chevrolet No. 4, 267–69; and discrimination, 268, 306, 321, 322; and civilian police reserve, 281–83, 284–85; and strike negotiations, February 2–11, 285–92, 302–3; and writ of attachment, 292; 1940 convention of, 299–300; and February 11 settlement, 304–5, 306–7, 309–10, 323, 325, 326; reasons for strike victory of, 310–11; and post-strike events in Flint, 317–18; and post-strike relations with GM, 320–21; and post-settlement strikes, 321–23, 327–28, 329; and March 12 contract, 323–26; post-strike growth of, 327–28; effect of strike on, 327–28; and Chrysler sit-down, 328; and Briggs strike (1937), 385[39]
United Brewery Workers, 112
United Mine Workers, 79, 85, 147, 197, 217, 285, 291, 299, 300, 303, 330, 402[56]
United Motors Corporation, 17–18
United Press, 253
United Rubber Workers: and Goodyear strike, 123, 124–25; and UAW, 125, 130, 170, 204, 208, 218, 221
United States Congress: and sit-downs, 246, 298, 333–35

United States Employment Service, 54
United States Steel Corporation, 329–30, 341
Unity Caucus, 329

Vandenberg, Arthur H., 334
Veblen, Thorstein, 231
Virtue Rewarded, 162
Vorse, Mary Heaton, 163, 201, 316

Wagner, Robert F., 50, 51, 334
Walker, Charles R., 157
Ware, Harold, 114, 222
Waskow, Arthur I., 338–39
Watson, Morris, 163
Weinstone, William, 130, 221, 222
Wells, Walter N., 90
Western Union, 331
Weston-Mott Co., 101
Weyl, Nathaniel, 114
White Motor Co., 71, 78, 79, 84, 90, 251
Whiting, James H., 15, 101
Widick, B. J., 78, 221, 241, 398[5]
Wilkinson, Ellen J., 206
Williams, J. W., 183–84, 307
Williams, S. Clay, 302, 303
Williamson, Floyd, 188, 253
Wills, James V., 108, 196, 224, 226, 240, 245, 260, 318; and Battle of the Running Bulls, 9, 12, 345[31]; and demonstration of February 3, 280, 281, 283, 402[56]
Willys-Overland Co., 207

Wilson, C. R., Body Co., 18
Wilson, Charles E., 323
Winn, Frank, 205, 367[41]
Wise, Phil, 221
Witt, Lawrence, 188
Wolcott, Thomas, 224, 227, 241, 245, 260, 279, 337; and Battle of the Running Bulls, 5, 9–10; and Black injunction, 193–94; and seizure of Chevrolet No. 4, 271; and Gadola injunction, 276, 278; and demonstration of February 3, 280, 281; and writ of attachment, 292, 293, 297, 404[84]; on Michigan National Guard, 319
Woll, Matthew, 152
Wolman, Leo, 36
Women's Auxiliary, 310; origin of in Flint, 200; effect of, 201; and demonstration of February 3, 279–80; and victory celebration, 312
Women's Emergency Brigade, 310, 322; origin of, 200–201; effect of, 201; and diversionary strike in Chevrolet No. 9, 269, 398[12]; and seizure of Chevrolet No. 4, 270; and demonstration of February 3, 279–80; and victory celebration, 312
Woodcock, Leonard, 73
Woodward, Victor S., 203
Workers Party, 75
Works Progress Administration, 61

Zack, Joseph, 79